PSYCHOANALYSIS
and
CONTEMPORARY SCIENCE

PSYCHOANALYSIS
and
CONTEMPORARY SCIENCE

An Annual of Integrative
and Interdisciplinary Studies
VOLUME II, 1973

volume editor
BENJAMIN B. RUBINSTEIN

Macmillan Publishing Co., Inc.
New York
Collier Macmillan Publishers
London

Library of Congress Catalog Card Number: 72-84741

Macmillan Publishing Co., Inc.

Collier-Macmillan Canada Ltd.

printing number
1 2 3 4 5 6 7 8 9 10

CONTENTS

6   ISSUES IN THE PHILOSOPHY OF PSYCHOANALYSIS

7   DISCUSSION OF MICHAEL SHERWOOD'S "THE LOGIC OF EXPLANATION IN PSYCHOANALYSIS"

8   CRITICISM OF THEORY

ACKNOWLEDGMENTS

The editors wish to thank the following persons and publishers for permission to use certain materials included in this volume.

"Is Psychoanalysis Relevant?," by George S. Klein, Ph.D., is published by permission of Bessie Boris Klein.

In "A Technical Device in Psychoanalysis and Its Implications for a Scientific Psychotherapy," by Donald M. Kaplan, Ph.D., the quotation from "In Memory of Sigmund Freud," by W. H. Auden, is reprinted from *Collected Shorter Poems 1927–1957* by permission of Random House, Inc. Copyright 1940, renewed 1968, by W. H. Auden.

"The Developmental Sciences: A Bibliographic Analysis of a Trend," by Ilse Bry, Ph.D., appeared originally as an editorial in *Mental Health Book Review Index*, Vol. 16, 1971, pp. i–xvi, and is reprinted by permission. Copyright © 1971 by Council on Research in Bibliography, Inc.

In "Language Development in Young Schizophrenic Children," by Theodore Shapiro, M.D., Figures 1–4 are reprinted by permission from T. Shapiro and B. Fish, "A Method to Study Language Deviation as an Aspect of Ego Organization in Young Schizophrenic Children," *Journal of the American Academy of Child Psychiatry*, Vol. 8, 1969, pp. 36–56. Copyright 1969 by the Journal of the American Academy of Child Psychiatry. Figures 5 and 6 are reprinted by permission from T. Shapiro, A. Roberts, and B. Fish, "Imitation and Echoing in Young Schizophrenic Children," *Journal of the American Academy of Child Psychiatry*, Vol. 9, 1970, pp. 548–567. Copyright 1970 by the Journal of the American Academy of Child Psychiatry.

In "Sherwood on the Logic of Explanation in Psychoanalysis," by Morris Eagle, Ph.D., and "On the Logic of Explanation in Psychoanalysis," by Benjamin B. Rubinstein, M.D., the quotations from Michael Sherwood are reprinted from *The Logic of Explanation in Psychoanalysis* by permission of the author and Academic Press, Inc. Copyright 1969 by Academic Press, Inc.

ACKNOWLEDGMENTS

LIST OF CONTRIBUTORS

Ilse Bry, Ph.D., Research Scientist, Research Center for Mental Health, New York University, New York, N. Y.; Adjunct Professor of Library Science, Queens College of the City University of New York; Editor, *Mental Health Book Review Index.*

Morris Eagle, Ph.D., Professor of Psychology, York University, Ontario, Canada.

Edi Franceschini, Research Scientist, Courant Institute of Mathematical Sciences, New York University, New York, N. Y.

Leo Goldberger, Ph.D., Professor of Psychology; Director, Research Center for Mental Health, New York University, New York, N. Y.

Donald M. Kaplan, Ph.D., Psychoanalyst, New York, N. Y.

* George S. Klein, Ph.D., Professor of Psychology; Director, Research Center for Mental Health, New York University, New York, N. Y.

Jane Loevinger, Ph.D., Research Professor of Psychology, Washington University, St. Louis, Mo.

William Gene Miller, Ph.D., Chairman, Department of Psychology, Western Maryland College, Westminster, Md.

Elliot G. Mishler, Ph.D., Harvard Medical School and Massachusetts Mental Health Center, Boston, Mass.

Lois Barclay Murphy, Ph.D., Clinical Professor of Pediatrics (Child Development), George Washington University, Washington, D. C.

Stanley R. Palombo, M.D., Psychoanalyst; Clinical Associate Professor of Psychiatry, Georgetown University, Washington, D. C.

Emanuel Peterfreund, M.D., Assistant Clinical Professor of Psychiatry, Mount Sinai School of Medicine, New York, N. Y.

Benjamin B. Rubinstein, M.D., Psychoanalyst, New York, N. Y.

Eleanor Rutstein, Ph.D., Clinical Psychologist, New York, N. Y.

Theodore Shapiro, M.D., Associate Professor of Psychiatry, Department of Child Psychiatry, New York University School of Medicine, New York, N. Y.

Michael Sherwood, M.D., Department of Psychiatry, Harvard Medical School, Boston, Mass.

Robert K. Shope, Ph.D., Associate Professor, Department of Philosophy, University of Massachusetts, Boston, Mass.

Donald P. Spence, Ph.D., Professor of Psychology, New York University, New York. N. Y.

Leo Stone, M.D., Faculty of the New York Psychoanalytic Institute, New York, N. Y.

McCay Vernon, Ph.D., Professor of Psychology, Western Maryland College, Westminster, Md.; Editor, *American Annals of the Deaf.*

Emmett Wilson, Jr., M.D., Ph.D., Clinical Instructor in Psychiatry, Cornell University Medical College, New York, N. Y.

* Deceased

PREFACE

In preparing this, the second volume of *Psychoanalysis and Contemporary Science,* the editors have adhered to the policy stated in the introduction to the first volume, which is to provide a forum for a variety of approaches to psychoanalysis. As analysts we want to communicate what we have learned in our own field, but we also want to learn from others. Hence the emphasis on interdisciplinary and integrative studies in the subtitle of the Annual. We do not, however, strive to be eclectic, at any rate not in the sense of trying to smooth over differences. If anything, we want differences to be expressed, forcefully and succinctly. In any science and, for that matter, in art and philosophy, premature closure may be detrimental. The one thing we are most afraid of is that our discipline may freeze into a new orthodoxy.

Obviously, we do not want to stress differences for their own sake nor to be different merely to be different. One does not have to be a very acute observer to know that the whole field of psychology and psychoanalysis is in ferment, partly because of the wave of irrationality that, as so often before, is sweeping our civilization, but partly also because in our field the standards of rationality, the sifting of evidence, and the methods of theory construction are extremely difficult to specify, let alone to apply. Because of the existing uncertainties it would be unwise to exclude on an a priori basis any scientific position that is clearly and logically expressed.

This volume is divided into eight sections, each representing a different viewpoint, method, or subdivision of the field. The first paper in the volume, "Is Psychoanalysis Relevant?" by the late George S. Klein, forms a section all by itself. It is a bold statement about the dispensability of theory in psychoanalysis which, the brilliant exposition notwithstanding, is bound to be controversial. The author no doubt has an important point, but it is possible to disagree with his conclusion. It is *in effect,* if not directly, contradicted by most of the other papers in the volume. It should be noted, however, that Klein does not argue in favor of irrationality but rather for a humanistic approach to man, to whose basic humanness, he feels, our current scientific approaches have tended to make us blind.

The second section of the volume includes two papers the essential thrust of which is clinical psychoanalytic. Leo Stone presents a detailed study of resistance to the psychoanalytic process which is in the best psychoanalytic tradition, and Donald M. Kaplan develops an interesting idea about the technique of clinical psychoanalysis as a device for observing mental activity in its resistance to an interposing set of circumstances.

The focus of the third section is on development. Jane Loevinger presents the main phases of ego development in the form of an outline for a course, and

Lois B. Murphy shows how psychoanalysis and nonanalytic studies of child development have enriched one another. McCay Vernon and William G. Miller report highly interesting observations on the apparently unimpaired intellectual development of congenitally deaf children. The authors use these observations to emphasize the significance of nonverbal communication, generally as well as in psychotherapy. In a thorough bibliographic study, Ilse Bry demonstrates how interest in development has grown over the years. This study will also serve as a valuable guide to the pertinent literature.

Section four includes three clinical experimental studies. Eleanor Rutstein and Leo Goldberger find significant differences in the responses to aggressive stimuli of suicidal and nonsuicidal psychiatric patients. This finding is—justifiably—regarded as evidence in support of the psychoanalytic hypothesis that aggression and suicide are closely connected. Theodore Shapiro demonstrates a serious language disturbance in schizophrenic children which, he believes, casts doubt on the validity of historical constructions in the analysis of both children and adults who have suffered from this affliction. By imaginative use of a computer procedure for doing content analysis, Donald P. Spence shows how it is possible to trace the development of a specific category (derivatives of pregnancy) through five contiguous hours in the psychoanalysis of a young woman, and indicates how certain thoughts are likely to have been formed without, however, having reached unequivocal conscious expression. These studies all indicate that experimental approaches to clinical problems, if sufficiently informed psychoanalytically, hold great promise for the further development of psychoanalysis as a science.

In the fifth section we shift from experiment to the construction of theory. Stanley Palombo outlines what is essentially a computer model of free association. Emanuel Peterfreund and Edi Franceschini then present a sophisticated, carefully worked out information-processing model of a number of clinically significant mental processes. The usefulness of the model is demonstrated on clinical examples.

The sixth section is concerned with certain issues in the philosophy of psychoanalysis. Morris Eagle refutes the claim that a patient's avowal at some point in the analysis is a necessary condition for assigning any degree of probability to the hypothesis that a particular mental event was unconsciously present at an earlier date. Robert K. Shope, in an analysis of Freud's uses of the word "meaning," concludes that Freud did not use this word to exclude the notion of causal relationships. In direct contradiction to Klein's contention that theory is dispensable, Emmett Wilson argues forcefully in favor of the indispensability for psychoanalysis as a science of high-level theoretical concepts. Peterfreund and Franceschini's paper especially, and others as well, may be regarded as an illustration of the philosophical point Wilson is making. The disparity in outlook expressed in the papers by Klein and Wilson exemplifies the diversity of ideas the editors want the Annual to reflect.

The philosophical discussion continues in section seven, in which Morris Eagle, Benjamin B. Rubinstein, and Michael Sherwood discuss the latter's important book, *The Logic of Explanation in Psychoanalysis.* One of the main themes of this philosophically highly sophisticated work—namely, that psychoanalysis is a science like other sciences—is emphasized in the discussion, which thus adds its weight to the similar themes underlying not only the papers by Eagle, Shope, and Wilson but also the experimental and theoretical papers in earlier sections.

In the last section of the volume, Elliot G. Mishler presents a critical evaluation of the work of the British psychiatrist-analyst R. D. Laing. Laing, it seems, shares Klein's disenchantment with psychological—including psychoanalytic—theory but, unlike Klein, he comes out squarely in favor of the irrational. However, even Laing uses his irrationality for a rational end, namely, for attempts at curing seemingly hopeless psychotic patients. It seems fair to say that Mishler's presentation has contributed substantially to our understanding of this very controversial author.

1

NEW PERSPECTIVES ON PSYCHOANALYSIS

IS PSYCHOANALYSIS RELEVANT? [1]

George S. Klein, Ph.D.

Some psychologists, especially critics of psychoanalysis, will regard a concern with the continuing identity of the psychoanalytic body of thought as a reversion to schoolism. Aren't schools of psychology an anachronism in our maturing science of psychology? Aren't ambitious images of the "whole man" out of date? Besides, haven't the major principles of psychoanalysis been absorbed into the mainstream of American psychology? And aren't psychology and psychoanalysis both better off for the fact that psychoanalysis has gone the way of all schools?

Granted the many signs of absorption. Even in behavioristic psychology, defense, displacement, conflict, and drive are common coin. Within psychoanalysis itself as a profession the eclectic spirit has been so insistent that it is hard to trace the common thread among the diverse groups who pre-empt the label "psychoanalyst." And perhaps the most dramatic evidence of absorption is the change in commonsense psychology. Consider how much of yesterday's psychoanalytic jargon is today's lingo of everyday life. Even the young, among whom formal psychoanalytic theory finds little favor, would be tongue-tied without it.

But is there cause for satisfaction with this state of "absorbed psychoanalysis"? Does it speak for a maturing science of psychology which has separated wheat from chaff and arrived at a superior integration?

There are plenty of indications that the absorption has not actually been integrative, but rather a process that subtly obscures the stronger features of psychoanalysis; in effect it denies them by deflecting attention from their investigative possibilities, giving a net result, as Lindzey (1967) put it, that is perhaps "a more palatable but less powerful set of ideas." It is striking, for example, that

[1] Presented in a briefer version at a meeting of Psychologists Interested in Psychoanalysis, annual convention of the American Psychological Association, September, 1970. Preparation of this paper was aided by United States Public Health Service Research Career Award No. K6-MH-19728 from the National Institute of Mental Health.

3

the theory of infantile sensuality has never really been investigated systematically, either experimentally or naturalistically. The emphasis on infantile sexuality has become instead a generalized emphasis on infantile experience, important, but not *quite* the same thing. Far from a good reason for interment, therefore, "absorption" of the allegedly best parts of psychoanalysis calls instead for a fresh affirmation, for an articulate rediscovery of the center of psychoanalysis.

A perhaps more important justification for a revitalized appreciation of root psychoanalytic principles has to do with their relevance to the troubled cultural climate and to psychology itself as a science. Addressing itself to this context is a vital responsibility of psychoanalysis.

It is customary to describe our age in metaphors of explosiveness: Political revolution, family disintegration, population explosion, mind-blowing, generation gaps, are the order of the day. Certainly there is going on something akin to the Industrial Revolution of two centuries ago, which was called a revolution because it created a new environment—a new average expectable environment, and with it a revolution in aspirations and social values.

We don't have the words or the concepts of social change to characterize the present "revolution." But it doesn't take much probing to notice that among the major signs of its psychological impact are an impressive heightening of self-consciousness, a sensibility and savoring of what it means to be "myself." Never was the "self" more "in," or sideburns longer. The modern appetite is for pluralistic selfhood, in the insistence among the young on an ever more prolonged moratorium on commitment, of resistance to every structure, form, convention, and practice that edges us to singleness of view or option, or that forces us to accept this or that single role as the whole truth of our being. There is a longing to live one's life rather than to be lived by it, preferably for an indefinite young manhood, defined by psychological rather than biophysical time. There is a striving to feel time itself on different terms from those hitherto customary—an urge to shed linear time, before and after, cause and effect, historical understanding of events, even in our personal lives. There is a distaste for those views such as psychoanalysis that speak of hierarchical meanings, of experiences that point to meanings beyond them, of in-between experiences and consequent experiences linked in historical configuration, for to do so is to be insufficiently alive to the *Moment;* it is the Moment that we must savor, live into, and inhabit without thought of antecedent and consequent.

There is ethical aspiration in the rejection of past structures, as Erikson reminds us (1969), in the heightened sensibility to selfhood, the wariness of alienating commitment. But surely it must catch our concern in psychoanalysis that the distrust with which the intervention of intellect beween self and experience is regarded has ominous aspects to be reckoned with, that abandonment of ethical positions, however justified, is invariably accompanied by regressions, hopefully only experimental. In this Babel of chaotic admixtures of the fresh and novel, the empty, the ugly, and the pathetic, by what perspective to man's nature are we to preserve the power to compare, and to choose?

Here the central strength of psychoanalysis as an orientation to psychical reality could not be more relevant. Freud's discovery of unconscious motivating and symbol-inducing processes was a discovery not merely of a new range of facts but a guide to self-knowledge. For voyagers into the inner reality that we live by he held out the warning that the occasions on which we to a greater or lesser degree misrepresent to ourselves what we are trying to do, and why, are much more common than we prefer to think, that we have an unconscious stake in disavowing self-knowledge even when we are pointedly striving for truth. The cornerstone discovery of Freud's method was, of course, resistance and repression—the breeding devices of self-delusion.

As a perspective to the social structure of Freud's own time, psychoanalysis brought to cultural historians the shocking insight that a European society which harbored the illusion that it was most enlightened tended to produce psychic cripples as a result of maimed instincts, that the individual life paid a psychical price for a secure adaptation and position in that society. Psychoanalysis thus opened the door to a search for the requirements of developmental integrity and the conditions that undermine it, a search which has certainly contributed to the poignant self-consciousness of this, the first generation that grew up "under Freud." Particularly timely, too, is an important suggestion from psychoanalytic ego psychology, that the craving for pluralistic selfhood may be a peculiarly contemporary transcription of the biologically rooted need to create and preserve coherence, continuity, and integrity of selfhood, and therefore, that the quest for coherent identity is no less now than it was before, despite the avowed emphasis on plurality of selves; that behind the frenetic displays and regressions of self-expression there is a search for integrating values and integrative growth.

And what about our parent field of psychology; what is the climate there which justifies a renewed psychoanalytic identity? Contemporary psychology, particularly the version we find in academic departments, has been characterized by Koch (1961, 1969) as a citadel of "ameaningful thinking." "Ameaning" is not "meaningless" thinking nor is it nonsense; it is an orientation which severs thought and action from the thinking and acting *subject* and treats them as objects—"process"—in their own right, eligible for objective scrutiny on premises drawn from natural science, usually physics. The program of ameaningful science requires scrupulous avoidance of *why* questions—that is, explanation in terms of intentionality or directional tendency, which is considered to be "prescientific" —in favor of *how* explanations in terms of process and mechanism. Hence the popularity of models of mechanism.

Some behaviorists, especially since the "New Look" period of the fifties, began to suspect that maybe there is a psychological *subject* as well as psychological process after all. They talked of plans and "totes," of thinking, and even, well, ego, and these sometimes without quotation marks. Some have even allowed themselves the label "subjective behaviorists." If on balance, however, the first enthusiasms for models, fitted to animal behavior, tended to conclude that basically man is a rat or a monkey, there has not been much edification either from the later sophistications which tried to prove that a rat is basically human. While recognizing the need to dust off the acting person, psychology in the main simply has not been able to give up the image of studying him in a natural-science mold. So the strategy shifts to the engineering discipline: As Koch remarks, we not only get the observational methods of physics, but the answers from physics as well. We have seen a long succession of efforts to prove that man is a telephone exchange, a servomechanism, an analogue computer, a processor of input and output, and the like.

It is instructive to see how our natural-science bent in American psychology has tried to shape "absorbed psychoanalysis." Following Freud's first impact, the study of motives in psychological laboratories soon turned to a focus on motive from the standpoint of mechanism; motives were and are studied in the laboratory very much as "objects." For instance, departing from the clinical meaning of repression as a concept that alerts us to reasons that a patient cannot avow, the mechanism viewpoint attempts to specify a locatable process of repression, permitting detached observation like the functioning of a pancreas.

In short, psychology has been and still is plagued by a phobic retreat from the psychological *subject*. It shies away from what should in fact be the first requirement of a psychology of human action: to find a language adequate to the description of disposition and intentionality as clued by testimony regarding the subject's own vantage point. It is precisely because an orientation to *intentionality* is its distinctive mark that clinical psychoanalysis fills a gap in contemporary psychology.

Behavior therapy is a showcase achievement of ameaning psychology because it has successfully sallied forth, with its rejection of person-oriented explanation, into the very sanctuary of the psychotherapist himself—the clinic. Behavior therapy challenges psychoanalysis both in theory and practice. It challenges its orientation to intentionality as a prescientific form of explanation, but even more important, it challenges its very relevance to the objective of bringing about effective changes of behavior. There is a crucial and basic difference here: Whereas for psychoanalysis behavior and experience are critical only for what they imply about what is hidden to view, for behavior therapists it is behavior itself that is the focus of interest. It is, after all, the painful behavior that is to be changed, they say, so why hover over "hidden," unobservable meanings? For the behaviorist clinician the point is to break into the tight chain of antecedent-consequent *behavioral* links of which a "symptom" consists.

When we turn to that growing sector of "humanistic psychology" which has acquired the label "Third Force," we find, curiously, that psychoanalysis is only slightly more popular. In fact, some proponents of the new humanism include psychoanalysis (Freudian) among the hated positivisms. This increasingly popular backlash against American behaviorism includes among its diverse forms an extreme version of existentialist doctrine which advocates exploration of the glow and shade of conscious experience in its every nuance as the royal road to psychological freedom. Translated into an approach to psychotherapy, the goal of therapy is experience known in its own moment-to-moment quality, texture, delight, or misery, rather than as a backdrop for wishes and intentions, conscious or unconscious, aborted and conflicted, or of repetitive iterations of fantasy. It is no accident that this offshoot of existentialism has become an ideological anchorage for many contemporary youth. However, from the psychoanalytic viewpoint, it tends to encourage the delusion that novel experience itself *is* insight and achieved selfhood, not in-between indications which along with action point to directive aims that, while not directly accessible to the subject's experience, have a molding influence upon it. It is this difference of emphasis that makes for a divisive departure from psychoanalysis. In this version, applied existentialism follows a route surprisingly akin to behavior therapy: to manipulate the person via exercises, drugs, and stimuli—tactile, gustatory, or whatever—into dramatically novel sensation and feeling. The *dominant* thrust of existential thinking seems to me eminently consistent with psychoanalysis. But in the zeal for seeing the here and now without gloss, to comprehend the subject in his own terms, to see him as a person rather than as an object, to see structures and situations as they emerge from *his* side and not simply from the observer's side, it may tend to bypass, even reject, interpreted meaning of experience and the question of therapeutic relevance of insight into such meanings (see Edelheit, 1967).

And lastly there is the movement of "social psychiatry," a relatively new venture that has crystallized from the increased responsiveness of clinics and hospitals to community appeals for prevention and rehabilitation. Community psychiatry at the present time is more an anguished response to social ills than a theory; at best it is a developing operational strategy. However, it inclines generally toward principles of etiology derived from social science; it tends to view even psychoses as a societal phenomenon. Actually, community psychiatry is not a declared antagonist of psychoanalysis, but it is clearly disposed to view psychoanalytic therapy as elitist, and generally to take a dim view of the one-to-one therapist-patient duality, doubting its practicality or even its theoretical relevance for understanding the "real" breeding ground of illness—"social systems." It is inclined to favor the idea that therapeutic effectiveness is better achieved through the treatment of families and other social groupings definable as "systems" whose principles are not a simple extension of individual psychology.

Now in drawing attention to the climate of mixed disenchantment and uninterest, coolness, even hostility which once again confronts psychoanalysis, I am definitely not advocating retreat to a Maginot line of psychoanalytic-institute bunkers identified by precepts hardened into dogma, unresponsive to challenge, and paranoidally resistive to change. It is perhaps too easy to take comfort in Freud's belief that it is the fate of psychoanalysis to suffer periodic cultural repression. I have even heard some psychoanalysts say, in a nostalgic backward look at the pioneering days when Freud's intimate coterie was creating a Movement, that they welcome the prospect of becoming once again an elite cultural corps.

But just as psychoanalysis gathered a certain momentum as a reaction to nineteenth-century psychiatry (an intellectual history of psychoanalysis will one day give proper recognition to this fact), so we should not ignore the possibility that further advances in psychoanalysis could be sparked by directly confronting these currents. Again, by responsiveness I don't mean dressing up psychoanalysis in the current fashions of what is "proper" science, or a leap to one of the system-mechanism models of mod psychology. There were those, you remember, who once prescribed for psychoanalysis an emetic purge with an S-R model—and they lost clinical psychoanalytic theory in the bargain; there are those who now trumpet the engineering models, and we can once again be skeptical that they will contribute much to the basic objectives of clinical psychoanalytic explanation.

Rather, I mean the kind of confrontation that is receptive to concepts from received psychology that are consistent with the psychoanalytic aim of understanding intentionality, and that offer genuine, perhaps superior, alternatives on this level of explanation. There is a healthy reminder in such responsiveness that discovery and fresh conception are as possible in a science dedicated to the aim of reading intentionality as in one devoted to brain physiology and the mechanisms of systems, that development of this level of explanation need not have dried up with Freud's death.

At the same time, responsiveness and confrontation should be accompanied by a sense of continuity—a resolve to be wary of sophisticated forms of denial which pose as corrective change. We need to update the clinical theory, but in a fashion that would not leave behind insights of the past nor the empirical base of the original principles. If Freud's conceptual solutions are to be put aside, the phenomena they were meant to capture must at least adequately, and hopefully even more effectively, be provided for in the conceptual modifications.

Perhaps I can illustrate what I mean by a sense of continuity in revision by examining two short summaries of basic psychoanalytic theory offered by Freud. In 1923 and again in 1925, in a few terse sentences he capsuled the substantive center of clinical psychoanalysis. He wrote:

The assumption that there are unconscious mental processes, the recognition of the theory of resistance and repression, the appreciation of the importance of sexuality and of the Oedipus complex—these constitute the principal subject-matter of psycho-analysis and the foundations of its theory. No one who cannot accept them all should count himself a psycho-analyst (1923, p. 247; italics mine).

In a slightly different version he wrote:

The theories of resistance and of repression, of the unconscious, of the aetiological significance of sexual life and of the importance of infantile experiences—these form the principal constituents of the theoretical structure of psycho-analysis (1925, p. 40).

I think it would be a mistake to dismiss these as formulae for detecting heresy. They summarize what Freud considered at that time to be fundamental in clinical *theory*, vital to psychoanalytic clinical explanation, principles interlocked in such a way that adherence to one required, in his opinion, adherence to the others; he regarded them as the distinguishing marks of *psychoanalytic* as compared to other conceptions of intentionality.

But that was 45 years ago, and certainly these cannot be the last words on the vitals of the theory—even perhaps as a fair distillation of the span of Freud's own career as theorist. To assess the adequacy of these principles would seem to be very much in order, if not indeed a sign of progress in psychoanalysis, and to replace them if need be but without losing sight of the empirical base of the earlier principles. For example, in speaking of the etiological significance of sexuality, Freud was able to relate such diverse phenomena as perversions and strong interests. In questioning his theory of psychosexual development—and there is plenty in it to question, especially his assumption of a libidinal energy— our responsibility is to find a viable conception of sexuality that provides for the observations that led Freud to suppose that there are such far-reaching extensions of sexuality; it would include an assessment of his original observations, re- fining them where necessary, and juxtaposing them with others made since Freud's time that are not easily fitted within his earlier framework of "sexual etiology."

Responsiveness could begin, then, with an attempt to define the sinews and bones of clinical psychoanalytic theory, its core principles, those fundaments distinctive of psychoanalysis which separate it from other existing theories. How are these seminal concepts dependent on each other and what concepts lead out from them? Do they require reformulation to accommodate developments in received psychology? And what of these developments *should* it accommodate? What other principles are needed? This sort of articulation has rarely been at- tempted; not even Freud tried it except in the terse summaries cited. The guid- ing consideration of change should be the objectives of psychoanalytic explana- tion, for it is these aims which underlie the substantive principles of clinical psychoanalysis.

But in reaching for this core of the theory we quickly find that our course leads back over not one but two lines of development in psychoanalysis. We must recognize now, some 70 years since *Studies on Hysteria* and some 30 years after Freud's death, that psychoanalytic theory itself has acquired a history in which it is not easy to separate genuine developments in psychoanalytic insight from ideological currents of the cultural context as well as elements of the scientific community's image of what is "real" science. The two lines of development ex- press different conceptions of what psychoanalysis is and ought to be. If not exactly analogous to the Talmud and Kabbala of Judaic tradition, they represent the same kind of uneasy fit, sometimes in open conflict over which should pre- vail in tradition. To get to the core assumptions of clinical psychoanalysis (these fundamentals that are distinctively psychoanalytic) surgery is necessary—a theo- rectomy, so to speak—that separates one from the other so as to free the irre- placeable core concepts of clinical psychoanalytic theory for further exploration, application, and differentiation.

It seems to me that this objective is best served by our first being as clear as possible about the *kind of inquiry* that clinical psychoanalysis is, and the type of explanations of behavior that it sets itself the problem of delivering. The important difference between the two traditions of psychoanalysis is not the energy-discharge model of the one—the so-called "metapsychology"—which is absent in the other. The more profound point of distinction is that they derive from two different philosophies of inquiry and explanation. Each leads to different conceptions of what psychoanalysis is all about, of where efforts at discovery should be directed, how psychoanalytic knowledge should be systematically organized, on what problems and in what settings we should do research, what objectives of explanation should be served in doing research. The tragedy is that the two orientations have often been confounded, creating theoretical and empirical havoc.

It has taken us a long time and the efforts largely of certain philosophers of science to whom we owe a debt of gratitude—particularly Peters (1958) of the English school tracing to Wittgenstein, Ricoeur (1970) in France, and in this country Kohut (1959), Apfelbaum (1965, 1966), Loevinger (1966), Holt (1965, 1968), and others—to become aware of the intricate confoundings of these contrasting orientations within psychoanalysis.

The central objective of psychoanalytic clinical explanation is the *reading of intentionality;* behavior, experience, testimony are studied for meaning in this sense, as jointly exemplifying directive "tensions," avowed, disavowed, repressed, defended. This orientation to explanation generates concepts that reflect a picture of individual development as a problem-solving, meaning-seeking, meaning-organizing venture, involving and resulting from the constant resolution of incompatible aims and tendencies. Applied to the understanding of symptoms, for example, such explanation consists in going back from a symptom not to the workings of a mechanism which is itself actually or potentially observable, but to a life-history context in which the symptom becomes intelligible as exemplifying an aimful solution.

Freud's rather confusing word "overdetermined" expressed this idea. From the clinical standpoint, it amounts to saying that a symptom is positioned in several configurations of meaning that make it intelligible as a solution, that at the time of its onset the symptom was not, so to speak, *externally* determined but represented a strategy of resolution, a compromise among inner tendencies felt to be incompatible.

Having this objective of answering "why" questions—the reasons of behavior—clinical explanation requires us, then, to identify not only the intentionality exemplified by a configuration of experience and behavior, but the history of such guiding directives in a person's life (the "genetic point of view"), to identify the milestones, crisis points, and conflicts in this development ("dynamic point of view"), and to see how certain capacities and functions participate in the logic of his intentional behavior (e.g., attention, intellectual capacities, cognitive style). Explanatory objectives of this type provide the base for the analyst's efforts to bring about behavior change in therapy; "psychoanalytic insight," and hopefully, change, depend on the shared understanding by patient and therapist of the patient's aims, goals, and beliefs.

A distinguishing mark of psychoanalytic explanation is that it aims at specifying the subject's own vantage point. All the explorations and probes as well as concepts of the clinical theory are dedicated to this effort. Having this orientation to inquiry and explanation, the analyst relies upon a perceptual process, still little understood, which Polanyi has called "indwelling" (1958), and Home "cognitive identification" (1966), in which the analyst reconstructs the subject's orientations by dwelling within his patient's experiences and behavior while standing back from them sufficiently to enable him to detect configurations of intention, especially disavowed ones, that the patient is living out in his experiences and movements. The patient's point of view is reconstructed by putting together the patient's avowed experiences of behavior with those that he cannot avow, or resists avowing. It is more a process of seeing pattern or "fit" than detecting causes in the patient's behavior, given his aims, goals, and beliefs as revealed in his behavior and conscious avowals. Questions of validation and rules of evidence are no less critical for this orientation to explanation in terms of meanings perceived by an observer and lived out by a subject. They are in fact a matter of great and neglected importance in psychoanalysis, but pursuit of this topic would get us off the track I have set for myself.

Cognitive identification or indwelling joins with existentialism's emphasis on the exploration of conscious experience. However, the analyst will not rest with the assumption that intentionality is exhausted in what the patient is able to avow consciously; he does not believe that he is abandoning the objective of reading the patient's own vantage point when he looks for directives which even the patient himself cannot admit or has a stake in not admitting. However, any account of such disavowed aims must encompass what the subject *can* experience or insists upon as *the* "real" reasons. For example, to an observer a person may be exhibiting the defensive maneuver of undoing. At the same time, the subject's avowed reasons for behaving as he does may give no hint of acknowledging a defensive intent, and may indeed even contradict this tacit reason. A complete accounting of the intentionality of his behavior, however, is obliged to relate the two by showing how the subject's conscious rationale is consistent with or may actually have been tailored to suit the defensive requirement of veiling certain wishes and the defensive intent itself. Thus, an analyst plunges into phenomenology, but goes beyond it to generalizations that connect accessible and inaccessible levels of experience in hypotheses regarding dispositions and aims. The process does not rest there, of course. Reading the patient's experience with the aim of perceiving intentionality in depth, he must then translate his perception back to the patient's own experience in a way that is meaningful to the patient, so that the patient comes to share in the discovery of the configuration.

The substantive concepts of the clinical theory are meant to aid the analyst's efforts to listen for directive tendencies and their vicissitudes. Although they vary in abstractness, i.e., in reflecting actual conscious experience, all are meant to aid the indwelling process by pointing to something in the mind of the patient which the patient does not experience but is part of his inner reality or psychical *Umwelt*. Such is the status of such concepts as resistance, repression, repetitive unconscious fantasy.

Now none of the clinical concepts nor their underlying explanatory intent have much to do with the "how" of behavior—its causal texture in the sense of mechanisms. For example, the conception of repression is useful and indispensable, but a model of the mechanism of repression is neither crucial to the analyst's clinical explanatory objectives nor directly testable by the kind of evidence the analyst's inquiry produces—unless he takes up the vantage point of the engineer or the physiologist and leaves off being an analyst.

The second side of psychoanalytic metapsychology and theoretical aspiration draws a different bead on explanation. I have dealt with it elsewhere (Klein, 1969), as have others (see, for example, Apfelbaum, 1965, 1966; Holt, 1965, 1967), and I will here confine myself to the contrast with clinical explanation. In this other side of psychoanalytic explanation, the terms of explanation have nothing to do with the subject's own vantage point; it is the person *observed as a physical process* that is the main objective. In pursuing this aim of detailing impersonal cause and mechanism, this strategy of explanation leaves the process of indwelling altogether and instead transposes data to an assumed model of mechanism. When this premise is made operational, the experience of the subject and his aims become "objects" for study. They are no longer aims and intention within reach of the subject's experience, but structural facts of the psyche, "properties" of an object. In psychoanalysis this objective has been served by a model of mechanism and causation in the mold of physical science of half a century ago, but similar objectives are shared by proposals which reject this older model and would replace it with more plausible versions of hardware or software. Translated to these models, experience and aim henceforth become "representations," "bound cathexes," or "structures that can be cathected," or in more modish terms, "memory banks," "templates," "input and output channels," "feedback circuits," and the like.

The different explanatory aims have led to different theoretical constructions, and to different meanings of terms shared by the two contexts of theory. Within the clinical frame of reference, for example, the ego is a high-level abstraction referring to a class of aims or directional configurations of behavior and experience. Within the process-mechanism theory, however, ego is reified as a *system of regulation*. Similarly, both theories have concepts embodying genetic and dynamic viewpoints. In the clinical theory the genetic point of view refers to the fact that aims have a history, not in the sense of trying to specify invariable and unconditional antecedents, but in the sense of specifying an inner logic of development.

The concept of conflict is again differently interpreted from these two points of view. Within the energic or mechanical model, conflict (the dynamic point of view) is imaged as a clash of *forces*. The terms of conflict are conceived as agents that push against each other and against a reactive ego. But the clinical theory need harbor no such notion of the actual mechanism of conflict, although our training is so contaminated by the energy model that it is still hard to see the misplaced concreteness and attributes of positioned force, required by the other frame of reference but irrelevant to the clinical focus.

For the aims of clinical psychoanalytic explanation it is sufficient to assume that conflict is a state specified through a person's experiences and actions which reveal him to be living out an inner conviction that two or more directive tendencies are irreconcilably in opposition. (There may be such an incompatibility in actuality, e.g., weaning involves the irreconcilability of the desire to be at the breast with a desire to be free of it, or the incompatibility may be merely so in the person's *fantasy*, out of, say, guilt about masturbation or fear of castration.) Conflicts have an underlying physiology, of course, perhaps representable in metaphors of hard- and software, or in a physiology of forces, but for the psychoanalytic clinical objective of explaining why a person is pointed toward the world temporally and spatially in the way he is, it is conflict viewed as the subject's way of understanding *his* world—a cognitive configuration—that needs to be understood.

If there exists a crisis in psychoanalysis, one aspect of it is in the question of which course to emphasize in theorizing and research. My point is that it is the clinical orientation to explanation, and the concepts anchored to it, that are the most distinctively psychoanalytic—more relevant to psychotherapy and more applicable to other humanistic endeavors in which reading the directionality of man's behavior is central. This kinship of explanatory focus links clinical psychoanalytic theory more closely to the humanistic disciplines than to natural science. The analyst's job of explaining has much in common with the historian's obligation of narrative construction and with the playwright's responsibility for depicting a logic of motivation. I am skeptical whether conceptions of mechanisms or physiological models, on the other hand, can lead deductively to concepts of intentionality of the sort that serve the aims of clinical explanation. They may win a researcher a Nobel Prize, but I doubt that they will make him a better analyst.

A clinician's interest in conceptual innovation, like that of any scientist, is likely to be guided by tacit criteria of relevance to his explanatory objectives. On this basis he judges "importance." The clinician's attraction will be greater for concepts that seem to issue from applications of the indwelling process in contexts such as therapy (but not only in therapy), where a human subject's engagement with his inner reality of aims and directive tensions can be reconstructed. A clinician is, therefore, less likely to be intrigued by the proposal that the ego is a "stimulation maximizer" than by a concept like "negative identity" which holds out the promise of disclosing to him still another vein of intentionality by which to explain a person's behavior.

This is not to deny the importance of models of mechanism nor the explanatory objective which is satisfied by nothing less than the specification of a system's workings. Explanations in these terms are likely to be, in fact already are, of tremendous assistance in dealing therapeutically with behavior patterns that reflect system disintegration or failure, and where considerations of intentionality are irrelevant. It is still the better part of wisdom to recommend surgery for a brain tumor rather than a psychoanalysis. But it is the clinical side of psychoanalysis that is more likely to give useful guidance in a society which badly needs a viable guide by which to view the reasons men live by, their course, divergence, and miscarriages in an individual's life, as a psychological anchorage for theories of social change.

CORE PRINCIPLES OF THE CLINICAL THEORY

I have paused over the tacit objectives of clinical psychoanalytic explanation. The *substantive core* of the clinical theory, the empirical fruit of this explanatory orientation, consists of certain root propositions about universal basic tendencies. Without these assumptions of human tendency psychoanalysis loses its identity in a rootless empiricism.

It would obviously take a book-length effort to attempt such a specification, and to do justice to such useful efforts in this direction by Apfelbaum, Loevinger, Yankelovich and Barrett (1970), Schafer (1968), and others, and particularly to Erikson's psychohistorical perspective as a comprehensive framework for such an attempt. I must content myself with a brief summary of my own version of certain core principles.

In trying to come to grips with them I find it useful to think of them according to Scriven's (1964) notion of "normic statements," universals which specify lawlike regularities but not of the nature of cause and effect. A normic principle describes a basic mode of change undergone by dispositions and relationships to people and events as they become internalized as inner structures; these principles of transformation are posed as universally true but with no pretense of describing rigorously the antecedents and consequences that would enable one to speak of them as causal laws. They are, however, in my view, basic anchorages of the psychoanalytic way of thinking. Whether they are sufficient, and whether they can themselves be subsumed under others, or need to be supplemented, remains to be explored in fuller discussion. Seven such principles have emerged for me as fundamental.

First, that psychical structure, whether in normal or pathological development, is an outcome of contrarieties—*the resolution of incompatible aims or dispositions.*

For a long time it was the resolution of a particular type of opposition, namely, a conflict between defense and drive, that occupied stage center in the theory. However, major changes have come about in the conception of the polarities that are constantly at play in the organism. A most important one is this addition: Where previously resolution of crisis was taken to mean resolution of conflict, equal emphasis is now given to the *developmental crises* that arise when adaptational modes of one stage are no longer suited to the unfolding requirements of an emerging biological potential, creating an urgency for adaptational change. In psychoanalytic conceptions of normal development, crises and dilemmas are inescapable, indeed, positive conditions of normal growth; neuroses are miscarriages of this process.

Thus Freud's original insight into conflict as a source of motivation is now better regarded as but one expression of a more general principle which holds that psychological growth is a product of continuing efforts to resolve incompatibility, crises, and impasse. Out of such felt or actual incompatibilities emerge structures of action and thought.

Second is a basic principle suggested but not adequately captured by the conception of ego. The necessity of resolving conflict at any cost, and indeed the fact of conflict itself, imply a need for integration at all life stages, a requirement for coherence among dispositions and tendencies. Psychoanalytic theory thus carries with it an assumption, which has been more or less tacit up to now in the theory, of a developing self which is the referent of a sense of coherence, continuity, and integrity at every stage of life. Two components of selfhood must be recognized: a centrifugal assertion of personal autonomy, and a centripetal requirement for being an integrated and needed part of a larger, more encompassing entity or social unit. The reconciliation of this dual requirement as a condition for integrated selfhood itself creates one of the most basic sources of potential conflict. Exploration of the dynamics of this polarity seems to me a neglected area of psychoanalytic theoretical development.

A third key tenet of clinical psychoanalytic theory concerns the formative influence of pleasure experience and anxiety in the development of self-identity and in the structuring of motives. Articulation of this principle requires a thorough disengagement of the conception of pleasure from the bland and contentless form in which the pleasure principle has come to be known in psychoanalytic metapsychology. Doing so requires also that we free the notion of pleasure from the confines of the model of libidinal development which narrows considerations of pleasure to those of sensual experience alone (Klein, 1972).

Pleasure, even sexual, does not reflect something essentially external to the ego impinging on it as a "force" to be controlled, a "stimulus" to be dealt with, something to be disposed of, or to be reacted to. Rather, pleasure and anxiety are to be seen as two great and contrasting states of feeling, generated by contacts with things, events, and people. Both might be said to refer to states of selfhood, complementary to each other: Just as anxiety is informative of estrangement, denoting threat or conflict, pleasure is informative of accord and well-being, of things and objects acquiring values of approachability and desirability. Anxiety and pleasure are motivating in distinctively different ways, the one to minimize experiences of threat, the other to reinstate and to sustain affiliative contact. Further specification of this principle of the structuring importance of pleasure experience must go on to delineate the prototypical conditions or classes of pleasure and the differing roles of these varieties of pleasure in the structuring of motives, relationships, and conflicts.

An accounting of seminal propositions could hardly omit the principle of repression or dissociative splitting on the one hand, and, on the other, what Loevinger (1966) has called the active reversal of passively endured experience— two distinct and equally basic modes of confronting and resolving conflict, impasse, and crisis. From these lead such indispensable concepts concerning inner structure such as defense, introjection and identification, positive and negative identity. The principle that internalization of interpersonal relationships as schemata is accomplished in the form of introjects through repression, and identifications through active reversal, itself deserves separate recognition as a sixth basic principle of the clinical theory.

Lastly, there is the core principle of *regressive repetition,* which proposes that crises are occasions for the activation and enactment of earlier prototypes of conflict, pleasure prototypes, and earlier, proven modes of resolution.

A potential for repetition is implicit in all the core principles. That growth, and even life itself, is in critical ways a repetition is basic to psychoanalytic understanding and knowledge. For example, it is in the nature of pleasure once experienced that it is savored and thereafter sought in its prototypical forms (see, e.g., Klein, 1972), and it is of the nature of a repressed conflict, because it is outside of the orbit of self-determined control, that it remains a potentially pre-emptive, though unconscious, basis of action and thought (see, e.g., Kubie, 1954). Such a tendency for regressive repetition is vital for the understanding of transference; transference phenomena are understood as the reliving of past prototypes in their conflictual wish-gratifying and defensive aspects.

Regression has come to be emphasized primarily as a maladaptive retreat rather than as also a setting of reconstructive growth; clinical observations have tended to dwell exclusively on stereotypic, passively experienced reiterations which remain "outside the ego." Consequently even in psychoanalytic writings regression has taken on a somewhat pejorative meaning. But as Loewald (1971) has pointed out:

. . . *this notion is no stranger to psychoanalysis, although "neurotic" repetitions have been stressed more in psychoanalytic writings than repetition as a "normal" phenomenon. . . . The whole conception of psychosexual development, . . . of typical "traumatic" experiences . . . , of prototypical complexes and conflicts and imaginés, in determining the life course of the individual, undoubtedly contains the general notion of repetition, in one form or another, of prototypical events and complexes which took place and shape in the early days of the individual. Of equal importance in psychoanalytic thinking . . . is the concept of repetition as contained in the theory of identification and internalization (p. 64).*

Of course, Kris's (1932–1952) concept of regression in the service of the ego has been a particularly useful formulation of the same point.

Loewald (1960, 1962, 1971) and Erikson (1970) must be singled out for having particularly drawn attention to phenomena of *normative* progression via regressive repetition. Such regressions seem to occur within a context of a relatively intact sense of personal causation (that is, of *willing changes* rather than of being compelled) and sense of future. Regression in this context is a form of experimental maneuvering toward the development of new ethical positions, ground rules, and values, which involves creatively repeating, in the present, prototypically crucial conflicts of the past and early levels of organized life experience; these are lived out within a sense of present realities and an experienced need for arriving at a new level of coherent selfhood. Passive, essentially duplicative reproduction of prototypes Loewald contrasts with this active, re-constitutive form of regression which he calls "re-creative repetition," and which Erikson terms "re-enactment." Loewald (1971) notes, for example:

The dissolution (not repression) of the oedipal conflict, to the extent to which it succeeds, in its aspects of mourning and internalization of abandoned object-relations, with the erection of the superego as a new differentiation in the ego, is a prime example of re-creative repetition in the psychic field—in contrast to passive reproduction in the psychic field represented by the perpetuation of oedipal fantasies or pathological introjections (p. 60).

This expanded view of regression has extended the understanding of trans-ference as involving both passive and active forms of regressive repetition (Loe-wald, 1971). Through his studies of Luther and, more recently, of patterns of dissent in the young, Erikson (1958, 1970) has shown how different forms of regressive retreat from abandoned ethical positions may actually reflect the gropings of self-articulation toward more viable standards of accepted self-co-herence and identity.

Needless to say, all of these principles allow plenty of latitude for further delineation; changes and additions to them are undoubtedly in order. I cite them to illustrate the point that elaborations and modifications of such principles, pointed to the aims of clinical explanation, are more characteristically the mark of progress in psychoanalysis than are so-called interface concepts with natural-science disciplines.

DOES "CLASSICAL PSYCHOANALYTIC" THERAPY HAVE A FUTURE?

My remarks have dealt almost exclusively with matters of theory and with an eye to the relevance of psychoanalytic method to theory, considered apart from the treatment situation from which the theory has evolved. Is such a separation possible? And what about the relevance of the therapeutic setting of "classical psychoanalysis"? I would like to touch briefly on an issue that is bound to affect its future.

This has to do with the persistent and unresolved dilemma of whether the long-term leisurely one-to-one classical format of analytic therapy, which has been so tremendously productive of insights into human tendency and person-ality, is also the most effective setting for *behavior change* and *therapeutic relief.* We really don't know to what extent the interventions, probes, and observations that have yielded such a vast store of explanatory insight have yielded the same gains in therapeutic effectiveness. Psychoanalysis has always had faith in the con-junction of these two aims; we still do not know if this faith is justified. Much as analysts would like to think so, the measure of the power of psychoanalytic theory has surely not been its achievements as a therapy in its "classical" mold. Even the basic assumption of psychoanalytic therapy that it is the shared insights by therapist and patient that produce therapeutic change is by no means solidly established. Freud chose not to tamper with the observational context of "classical psychoanalysis," possibly because of the incomparable investigative opportunity it offered; he looked with distrust on all attempts to manipulate the psychoanalytic situation for purposes of therapeutic advantage alone.

It is with this problem in mind that the challenges from behavior therapy, other humanistic therapies, and socially minded psychiatry must be faced. We hear much from these quarters about the "outdatedness" of psychoanalysis as a therapy, its eliteness and impracticality, even callousness in the face of pressing issues of social change and misery, and the uncertain outcomes of the one-to-one therapeutic context. From such considerations of *therapeutic* economy and effectiveness, it has not been uncommon for critics to imply, if not actually to proclaim, that therefore the substantive psychoanalytic principles themselves on understanding directionality in behavior and the methods and guidelines of its probes into such directionality, are inadequate at best or downright wrong.

If the classical psychoanalytic treatment situation is founded on dubious grounds of practicality and shaky evidence of therapeutic success, how to justify it? I believe we ought to retain the classical psychoanalytic treatment setting, but we must justify its retention mainly as an indispensable resource for the study in depth of personality and pathology, without leaning upon claims of superior therapeutic effectiveness. There is no sensible basis for denying the impracticality of classical analysis, whatever its virtues as therapy, as a routine recommendation for psychotherapy—even for those who can pay 50 dollars an hour, five hours a week. I believe, however, that there are plenty of grounds for claiming that as a training experience in self-understanding the classical psychoanalytic procedure is unparalleled for anyone aspiring to a career as therapist. Furthermore, as a context for the continued study of man the analytic situation, with its unique therapeutic pact, is surely one of the most extraordinary contexts of human observation ever invented, whose potential for generating further insights about directionality is far from exhausted. It used to be thought that the psychological laboratory would be the testing ground of insights gained in the consulting room. This is in my opinion a failed hope, and I think we are beginning to realize that the analytic *situation* is itself a kind of "laboratory," not, to be sure, for manipulative experiment of the standard kind, but for controlled naturalistic observation that is difficult to match in other observational contexts.

Thus, other therapies may be quicker and even more effective in getting a person through life's tasks and the relief of symptoms. Yet it would be a sad loss if the objective of understanding human intentionality and in depth could not avail itself of the intensive, long-term probe of an individual life which is made possible by the classical context of the psychoanalytic treatment situation. This setting has been a lifeline for the development of psychoanalytic theory; the theory that has emerged from it has in turn been a nourishing artery for the humanistic disciplines. A way of resolving the dilemma, therefore, is to look upon the future of classical psychoanalytic therapy as a limited and restricted enterprise, justified mainly for its importance in the *training of therapists* and as a *research context;* its justification would be primarily educative and investigative. Support for it, therefore, must be sought not in the usual fashion of a patient paying his doctor for services rendered, but from public and private foundations—resources dedicated to investigative and educative goals of scholarship.

If these are the ultimately important rewards for the psychoanalyst-researcher, he owes it to the patient (and his own conscience) to have a rationally confident belief that, for the patients he engages in such a long-term commitment, there is a better than fair chance of therapeutic benefit as well. It seems to me vitally important, therefore, for the psychoanalytic community to initiate efforts, involving the coordinated resources of psychoanalytic institutes over the United States, to see what kinds of people are especially likely to profit from the "classical" procedure and analytic setting—not compared with other therapies, but simply by the yardstick of criteria of success in psychoanalysis. The routine recommendation of analysis for nonpsychotic applicants who are able to afford it may have been justified earlier, when "classical psychoanalysis" was the only psychotherapy; in the present, when alternatives are available, even psychoanalytically oriented ones, it is irresponsible.

It is worthwhile to ask, in closing, what favors the psychoanalytic perspective to personality in this period when, as never before, other competing orientations have thrown a cold glare of disapproval upon its gaps, dilemmas, imperfections, and rigidities. Why psychoanalysis still? Other humanistic orientations have emerged, and the names Rogers, Maslow, Fromm, Heidegger, have gained popularity as "correctives" to the alleged sins of psychoanalysis. Let me affirm at least my own credo. The persisting strength of the line of tradition leading out from Freud is not only as a conceptual structure but as an orientation to self-truth guided by considerations of the human inclination for self-delusion. This general orientation has opened us to a many-faceted inner world of directional aims, conscious and unconscious, dissonant and convergent, which behavior and experience exemplify. This is the saving perspective provided by psychoanalysis which Schafer (1970) calls a "tragic view of man" as against the romantic view which typifies other humanistic ideologies.

In highlighting the dialectic of contrariety which is both stimulus to progress and context of failure, the psychoanalytic viewpoint keys us to the inescapability of conflict, the ineradicable fantasies of early years, the unshakable ambivalences in human relationships, the terrible power of fixation, repression, regression, and repetition; it also tells us that these are the soil not only of hate, ill health, and failure, but the conditions of love, health, and achievement.

The essence of this outlook, and why calling it the *tragic outlook* is so apt, is that it captures the paradox that one's identity is shaped by the very distorting components one is trying to revise; the *patient* experiences it in his gradual realization that he himself has been the unconscious saboteur of his work and love, owing to guilt, and anxiety, and compulsively re-enacted early themes.

For the *analyst,* the tragic perspective is the foundation and safeguard of his objectivity; it accounts for the special quality of his indwelling in the patient's experience and behavior. The indwelling of the analyst is *not* an intimacy of feeling of the kind that describes friendships, but awareness of the emotional and changing atmosphere of his relationships with his patient; as Schafer points out, it is an empathy nurtured and enlarged by the analysis of resistance and crisis and the working through of regressive yearnings.

The sense of the tragic in our humanness which psychoanalysis gives us is not an invitation to pessimism and despair. Pessimism and cynicism are products of a traumatized romanticism. Applied as a therapeutic perspective, the psychoanalytic probe is a goad to shed apathy and accept responsibility for one's one and only life, but with a strengthened sense of reality and with less frequent recourse to the anodynes of self-delusion. Its objective is an intensified sense of options and responsibility—not happiness, not adjustment, not a delusional psychedelic high, but a sense of self-rule and a rationale for it, and an anchoring within a sense of linear, irreversible time and future.

The vitality of this perspective to man and its orientation to explanation are well worth the continued commitment of the psychoanalytic psychologist to the future of psychoanalysis. They augur well, I think, for a distinctive psychoanalytic identity in a science of psychology.

REFERENCES

Apfelbaum, B. (1965). Ego Psychology, Psychic Energy, and the Hazards of Quantitative Explanation in Psycho-Analytic Theory. *International Journal of Psycho-Analysis,* 46:168–181.

——— (1966). On Ego Psychology: A Critique of the Structural Approach to Psycho-Analytic Theory. *International Journal of Psycho-Analysis,* 47:451–475.

Edelheit, H. (1967). Binswanger and Freud. *Psychoanalytic Quarterly,* 36:85–90.

Erikson, E. H. (1958). *Young Man Luther.* New York: Norton.

——— (1969). *Gandhi's Truth.* New York: Norton.

——— (1970). Reflections on the Dissent of Contemporary Youth. *International Journal of Psychol-Analysis,* 51:11–22.

Freud, S. (1923). Two Encyclopaedia Articles. (A) Psycho-Analysis. *Standard Edition,* 18:235–254. London: Hogarth Press, 1955.

——— (1925). An Autobiographical Study. *Standard Edition,* 20:7–70. London: Hogarth Press, 1959.

Holt, R. R. (1965). A Review of Some of Freud's Biological Assumptions and Their Influence on His Theories. In: *Psychoanalysis and Current Biological Thought,* ed. N. S. Greenfield and W. C. Lewis. Madison: University of Wisconsin Press, pp. 93–124.

——— (1967). Beyond Vitalism and Mechanism: Freud's Concept of Psychic Energy. In: *Science and Psychoanalysis,* ed. J. H. Masserman, 11:1–41. New York: Grune and Stratton.

——— (1968). Sigmund Freud. In: *International Encyclopedia of the Social Sciences,* 6:1–12. New York: Macmillan and Free Press.

Home, H. J. (1966). The Concept of Mind. *International Journal of Psycho-Analysis,* 47:42–49.

Klein, G. S. (1969). The Ego in Psychoanalysis: A Concept in Search of Identity. *Psychoanalytic Review,* 56:511–525.

———— (1972). The Vital Pleasures. *Psychoanalysis and Contemporary Science,* 1:181–205. New York: Macmillan.

Koch, S. (1961). The Allures of Ameaning in Modern Psychology: An Inquiry into the Rift between Psychology and the Humanities. La Jolla, Cal.: Western Behavioral Sciences Institute Report No. 5. Also in: *Science and Human Affairs,* ed. R. Farson. Palo Alto, Cal.: Science and Behavior Books, 1965.

———— (1969). Psychology Cannot Be a Coherent Science. In: *Readings for an Introduction to Psychology,* ed. R. A. King. New York: McGraw-Hill, 1971.

Kohut, H. (1959). Introspection, Empathy, and Psychoanalysis: An Examination of the Relationship between Mode of Observation and Theory. *Journal of the American Psychoanalytic Association,* 7:459–483.

Kris, E. (1932–1952). *Psychoanalytic Explorations in Art.* New York: International Universities Press, 1952.

Kubie, L. S. (1954). The Fundamental Nature of the Distinction between Normality and Neurosis. *Psychoanalytic Quarterly,* 23:167–204.

Lindzey, G. (1967). Some Remarks concerning Incest, the Incest Taboo, and Psychoanalytic Theory. *American Psychologist,* 22:1051–1059.

Loevinger, J. (1966). Three Principles for a Psychoanalytic Psychology. *Journal of Abnormal Psychology,* 71:432–443.

Loewald, H. (1960). On the Therapeutic Action of Psycho-Analysis. *International Journal of Psycho-Analysis,* 41:1–18.

———— (1962). The Superego and the Ego Ideal. II. Superego and Time. *International Journal of Psycho-Analysis,* 43:264–268.

———— (1971). Some Considerations on Repetition and Repetition Compulsion. *International Journal of Psycho-Analysis,* 52:59–66.

Peters, R. S. (1958). *The Concept of Motivation.* New York: Humanities Press.

Polanyi, M. (1958). *Personal Knowledge: Towards a Post-Critical Philosophy.* London: Oxford University Press.

Ricoeur, P. (1970). *Freud and Philosophy: An Essay on Interpretation.* New Haven: Yale University Press.

Schafer, R. (1968). *Aspects of Internalization.* New York: International Universities Press.

———— (1970). The Psychoanalytic Vision of Reality. *International Journal of Psycho-Analysis,* 51:279–297.

Scriven, M. (1964). Truisms as the Grounds for Historical Explanations. In: *Theories of History,* ed. P. Gardiner. New York: Free Press, pp. 443–475.

Yankelovich, D., and Barrett, W. (1970). *Ego and Instinct.* New York: Random House.

2

CLINICAL PSYCHOANALYSIS

A TECHNICAL DEVICE
IN PSYCHOANALYSIS AND ITS IMPLICATIONS
FOR A SCIENTIFIC PSYCHOTHERAPY

Donald M. Kaplan, Ph.D.

1.

Scientific observation often involves the strategy of obstructing the activity of a phenomenon with a technical device whose activations then reveal something about the phenomenon being studied. When an anemometer, for example, is positioned in the wind, the velocity of the wind can be determined by the velocity of the anemometer's revolving cups. Similarly, when photographic plates are situated in the path of nuclear particles, the streaks imparted to the plates by the activated particles inform the physicist's conception of a whole array of imperceptible entities. The invention of technical devices that will interact informatively with otherwise only grossly identified phenomena is no small part of the praxis we call science.

Freud's psychoanalytic method, as I shall soon describe, is yet another instance of the strategy exemplified by the anemometer and the photographic plate. The technique of clinical psychoanalysis can be regarded as a device for observing mental activity in its resistance to an interposing set of circumstances, which is structured and maintained by the therapist. Freud's method, to be sure, can be regarded in other ways—as a purely hermeneutic venture, for example, belonging to the humanities, as Ricoeur (1970) regards it. And I mention this at the outset to preclude the inference that in viewing psychoanalysis as a species of scientific instrumentation I am claiming for this point of view some ultimate validity that eclipses other conceptions of psychoanalysis. But I must hasten to admit my conviction that psychoanalysis is an embodiment of a scientific procedure before it is anything more, and that a point of view that neglects to take this into account cannot retain a compelling interest for anyone in whose professional life psychoanalysis has achieved a serious priority. At any rate, it is this sense of psychoanalysis as a scientific methodology that I shall be returning to shortly.

But Freud's technical construction involves more than a pursuit of a theory of mind. It is also a psychotherapeutic procedure. In combining a psychological methodology and a clinical activity, Freud's technical construction acquires a precedence in the history of psychotherapy. Though I intend to emphasize the nonclinical aspects of Freud's technical device, I shall, further on, recall something of the historical intersection of psychoanalysis and psychotherapy and then compare the persisting characteristics of psychoanalytic psychotherapy with certain other conceptions of psychotherapeutic activity prevailing at this present social moment. Among these issues we might glimpse how a conscientiously scientific procedure actually advances the humanistic values which it often is reputed to subvert.

2.

The instrumentation of a scientific inquiry is shaped to a large extent by the experimentalist's provisional notions about the phenomenon being investigated. Often—and this has become a formality in physics and molecular biology—the experimentalist is furnished provisional notions by a theoretician. The instrument the experimentalist then goes on to design has the purpose of confirming, refining, or refuting the theoretician's informed guesses. In a study on "The Scientific Style of Breuer and Freud in the Origins of Psychoanalysis," Schlessinger and his collaborators (1967) suggest that Breuer's relationship to Freud was that of theoretician to experimentalist. They summarize a part of their investigations into the method of *Studies on Hysteria* as follows:

[Freud's] hypothesis formation through deductive logic was clearly labeled and sparingly employed. He used deduction to validate his theories by making clinical predictions which could then be tested in the consulting room. Breuer, on the other hand, presented some data of observation but mostly theory (indeed, the "Theoretical" chapter was his sole responsibility). We could not demonstrate a clear and consistent connection between his theoretical constructs and the clinical evidence presented. . . . This appeared in sharp contrast to Freud's contributions in the work which demonstrated systematic methods of scientific thinking (p. 404).

The technical device in psychoanalysis which I want to describe Freud began to construct in connection with the provisional notions about symptom formation that originated in his collaboration with Breuer. This early theory of symptom formation was a preliminary stage of the more general theory of mind that was to emerge in *The Interpretation of Dreams* (1900). Freud himself conceded to Breuer the greater share in this early stage of the theory, notably the aspect of the theory having to do with the "restricted capacity for association," which Breuer regarded as primary to a "secondary and acquired splitting of consciousness" such as was seen in certain hysterical states (Freud, 1894, p. 46). The technical activity that originated in the proposal of a "restricted capacity for association" Breuer and Freud described in the first chapter of *Studies on Hysteria* (1893–1895). Written in 1892, this chapter reported a method of hypnosis and suggestion for bringing about an "associative correction" of dissociated (warded-off) "reminiscences."

Over the next several years Breuer and Freud were to part company intellectually. Near the outset of the last chapter of *Studies on Hysteria* Freud reported that "fresh points of view have forced themselves on my mind. . . . For this reason the considerations which follow stand principally under my own name" (1893–1895, pp. 255–256). Freud is referring here to an enlarged conception of symptom formation and a technical procedure commensurate with this conception and going beyond suggestion and hypnosis.

When the concept of a symptom loses its strictly morbid denotation and goes on to connote virtually any manifest psychological event, e.g., a dream, fantasy, affect state, a lapse in recall, a doubt, a parapraxis, then a theory of symptom formation is on its way to becoming a general theory of mind. And a clinical technique addressed to symptoms so conceived is on its way to becoming an investigatory method of a general psychology. This conceptual drift was already evident in Freud's thinking around the time he produced *Studies on Hysteria*, the last chapter of which purports to be on psychotherapy but is in fact a treatise on an experimental psychological method. The experimental character of Freud's psychotherapeutic method was, indeed, paramount. For Freud insisted that once the therapeutic situation was set in motion, it took on a life of its own, independent of both the doctor and the patient. Investigator and subject deferred to method and mind. "I make it a rule," Freud noted in passing, "during the analysis to keep my estimate of the reminiscence that comes up independent of the patient's acknowledgement of it. I shall never be tired of repeating that we are bound to accept whatever our procedure brings to light. If there is anything in it that is not genuine or correct, the context will later on tell us to reject it" (Breuer and Freud, 1893–1895, pp. 299–300). This willing suspension of disbelief was what protected the researcher in Freud against the temptations of pragmatic healing on the one hand and hyperbolic theorizing on the other.

A précis of Freud's enlarging theory of symptom formation will suffice to account for his experimental method, which, in its essentials, has not changed over the ensuing decades, despite an appearance to the contrary due to an improved facility with the method. Since a set of essential principles is what we are after, rather than the practicalities of the method, we need not enter the realms of concern which the application of the method subsequently staked out. We can restrict ourselves to Freud's clinical theory at the time he produced *Studies on Hysteria*. I have in mind a paper from 1894 called "The Neuro-Psychoses of Defence." An abstract of this paper could go as follows:

Affects acquire meaning by their association with ideas. Ideas acquire felt significance by their association with affects. The psychological unity of affect and idea can be observed in the subjective sense of familiarity and purpose—the sense of "compatibility with the ego"—that accompanies thinking, fantasizing, wishing, striving. An affect and an idea are susceptible to detachment from one another, to splitting or dissociation. This occurs when the ideational and affective unity of a psychological event leads to a subjective experience of incompatibility with the ego, to a sense of unfamiliarity. (Freud is using the term ego, at this point, to mean roughly the sense of self.) The distortion of an event by a dissociation of idea and affect is an attempt to regulate the traumatic quality of that event. The dissociated ideas and affects go on to form new but also subjectively alien unities of ideas and affects. These new unities are symptoms, but they are less painful manifestly than the trauma that remains latent by virtue of symptom formation. Thus a detached affect may become associated with an otherwise subjectively insignificant idea, imbuing that idea with an unaccountable emotional force. Such a vicissitude is observed in obsessional symptoms where previously trivial ideas acquire a compelling affect-laden quality, while the original idea from which the affect has been detached remains conscious but devoid of felt significance.[1]

In other words, symptoms, though consciously discrete experiences, are actually continuous with nonsymptomatic psychological processes. The painful interruption of the sense of psychological integrity by the return in the symptom of something unsuccessfully repressed serves to regulate the potentially felt importance of fantasies, wishes, strivings, etc., entertained at other moments in the patient's life. Freud added that the return of the repressed in the symptom is subjectively an undecipherable symbol of the original wish whose "incompatibility" was the trauma now repeated in the symptom. The psychic economics of the process have to do with the possibility that a partial expression of a trauma-laden wish can repress a fuller expression of the wish. In terms of the ego, this means that a part of the self can be sacrificed to manifest conflict for the sake of the rest. Finally, the process of symptom formation and the regulatory advantage it possesses are beyond the patient's conscious awareness.

We might note incidentally that in this brief paper Freud used this general theory of symptom formation to account for obsessions, compulsions, phobias, conversions (a term that was first coined in this paper), and psychotic phenomena. This theoretical scheme, which rests on the principles of conservation of psychological events and the displaceability of affect, is still, at this late date, a quite plausible one.

What kind of clinical situation might be structured to investigate more fully this preliminary scheme of symptom formation? Again, I want to stress that in psychoanalytic psychology the theory of symptom formation is the nucleus of a general psychology. Hence the clinical situation tailored to a scheme of

---

[1] The principal concept here is defense and its failure. The concept has been an abiding one, though, as I noted, other realms of defensive activity have been discovered. In *The Interpretation of Dreams*, for example, Freud went on to speak of affect transformations serving defense, as occurs in the transformation of anal pleasure into disgust (1900, p. 604). "Reaction formation" as an instance of defense comes up again in connection with the "supervalent ideas" of Freud's patient Dora (Freud, 1905). Internalization as an instance of defense Freud amplified in a study of its failure in depressive reactions (1917). And so on.

symptom formation becomes a psychological method for constructing a theory of mind.

Referring to Freud's clinical motives, we could also ask what must a technique accomplish if it is to deal with an impairment to perception and apperception as we have conceived such an impairment from Freud's ideas of the failure of defense? That the dissociated affect and idea must be reassociated is obvious. But Freud's experience with the limitations of hypnosis and suggestion in achieving a lasting reintegration of dissociated ideas and affects led him to the realization that a technique appropriate to his theory had to accomplish at least two additional related tasks. The technique must come to terms with the patient's unwitting motives for retaining the very symptom he consciously complains about. To provide the wherewithal to a patient to gain a conviction that a symptom has a cherished aspect, that its removal is also a deprivation, is as much derived from Freud's psychological theory as the task of reintegrating ideas and affects. Indeed, the actual labor that accrues to this task of revealing the investment in the symptom is what sets the technique on a course very different from the cathartic, suggestive, and recreational possibilities to which the therapist-patient relationship is susceptible.

Then, in addition to the tasks of reassociation and of overcoming unconscious commitments to the symptom, the technique must allow the patient to express apparently trivial thoughts as well as those he experiences as important. For Freud's theory of symptom formation has it that the formation of a symptom deprives certain experiences of felt significance while creating other experiences of new, though apparently "pointless," significance.

The mechanics of the technique addressed to these tasks are well-known. The patient is invited to give a verbal report of all affects and ideas that arise in the presence of the therapist, whose function during such utterances is to listen. Moreover, the patient's reports of what is occurring to him at the moment should not be ruled by considerations of meaning or sense. Nor should he defer to the fact that he is being listened to. The point of departure in this assignment is the symptom, but thereafter one thing should lead to the next. Thus far two operations are set in motion: Affects and ideas may arise in arbitrary combinations, and trivialities become possible topics for report, this by virtue of the listener's declared interest in them.

The accomplishment of the remaining task—the revelation of the symptom's unknown regulatory purpose—is the hallmark of the technique, its most ingenious feature. It is what I had in mind when I suggested at the outset that psychoanalytic technique could be regarded as a device inserted obstructionally into the field of a phenomenon.

Let us look into the chapter on psychotherapy in Studies on Hysteria. Read as a narrative of the development of psychoanalytic technique, this chapter reveals a remarkable scientific cunning. Empirically, Freud discovered that the task assigned to the patient, which I have just described, could not be executed by him, though there was no immediately apparent reason why not. The patient was motivated by suffering; the task was clear and simple enough. Yet no patient could bring it off. There was always a hitch in the patient's performance: His self-perception went blank, a thought was skipped over, a selectiveness arose and prevailed, embarrassment triumphed, impatience intruded, interest slackened. Freud was appalled. Now and again in this chapter he expressed his exasperation. A lesser man would have abandoned the whole enterprise.

But Freud went on to discern in his own exertions to enforce the fundamental rule upon the patient that the inevitable breaches of the rule were, themselves, lawful. Shrewdly he incorporated into the technique itself the patient's failure to follow the rule of free disclosure. He began to anticipate the patient's failure, finally to conclude that to a greater or lesser degree all free association was determined and therefore from the observer's point of view not free, regardless of how free it seemed to the subject. Moreover, the presence of the observer proved to be one of the several constant factors that determined the drift and quality of the patient's self-reports. The revelation of this state of affairs to a patient could convince the patient that his functioning was dominated by forces which the patient was hitherto unaware of. To put it another way: If you want to convince a subject that he is at the mercy of forces he is unaware of, assign him a task which he has no conscious reason to believe he cannot fulfill and, more, which he has every reason to want to fulfill. Then at his first failure he will be in a position to recognize an obstacle within himself that he could not have predicted. The actual practice of the method involves many complications. But these complications belong to another discussion about the practicalities of the method.

For the present discussion I want to convey an idea of what sort of technical situation we have here essentially. Specifically, I want to conceive of the situation as an articulation of two phases: an activation of a psychological task ("free association") and a resistance ("being listened to"). In the encounter of the task with the obstruction, the patient's actual performance is subject to controlled scrutiny. Here is where the patient's mental activity manifests properties otherwise imperceptible. And here we can drop our emphasis upon the psychotherapeutic characteristics of the clinical situation and take up its experimental characteristics, though these categories are really artificial and serve merely to identify the purpose of the procedure—therapy or research. Also, before long, we shall want to say something about the properties of mind to which this experimental situation is addressed.

As for the experimental situation, I am stressing the relationship between the performance of an assigned, specific task and the presence of a *critical* observer. I emphasize "critical" because while the observer may not be judgmental about the content of the subject's performance, he does judge the quality of its execution. Hence the analyst is not a mere presence but an audience.

Conceiving of the psychoanalytic situation in this way, we place it for the moment into an existing realm of experimental psychology, which goes by the name of "social facilitation" and which, in fact, studies the effects upon performance of the presence of others. Though this experimental realm, exemplified by the work of Thibaut and Kelley (1959), Zajonc (1965), Cottrell (1968), has not included much of psychoanalytic psychology, its concerns are strikingly similar to the concerns of the psychoanalytic situation. Zajonc, for example, summarizes a principal experimental paradigm from the vast literature on social facilitation as involving "the observation of behavior when it occurs in the presence of passive spectators" (1965, p. 269). Cottrell (1968) adds that the effects upon performance of a passive (not coacting) spectator are especially manifest and clear when the spectator has a stake in the quality of the performance, as is the case when the spectator has actually assigned the performance. These effects can be generalized. In the presence of a critical spectator there is notable drive arousal in the subject. "We also know from extensive research literature that arousal, activation or drive all have as a consequence the enhancement of dominant responses" (Zajonc, 1965, p. 273). An important corollary here is that dominant responses that fail to lead to mastery of tasks are enhanced in the presence of a spectator, so that the presence of a spectator can actually worsen performance and reveal precisely those dominant responses that lead to failure (Zajonc, 1965, p. 270).

These findings are one way of accounting for why Freud's patients invariably had difficulties in executing the free-association task. The patient's task is to produce nondominant responses (as in play, rehearsal, practice, and other preliminaries to learning), but the presence of the analyst evokes dominant responses in him. A comparison of the patient's dominant responses with his efforts to produce nondominant responses is one which the technique offers to an investigation of mental states and activities. Freud's inventiveness consisted in his decision that the subject's assigned task was quite all right, and though the presence of the analyst himself was a principal source of the patient's difficulties in the execution of the task, this was also quite all right. For the interesting thing was not the free associations in themselves but the resistance that revealed the stress between a fictitious spontaneity and an actual response dominance (which Freud sometimes called a repetition compulsion, an effort to master the anxieties of drive arousal).

Here we leave the realm of social facilitation. For Freud went into certain other matters that concern the patient's dominant responses. He took the position that when you structure this investigaion as one which consists of spectator and performer, and the performer, rather than performing, instead interacts with the spectator (e.g., by selectiveness of free association in deference to fantasies about the spectator), this interaction embodies the performer's specific confusion of his personal existence and the present shared situation with the analyst. Transference is Freud's term for the unsolicited dominant responses of the patient who strives for interaction with the analyst at the expense of free association. (From a clinical point of view, note that in psychoanalytic therapy interaction is a resistance.) Two principal characteristics of the transference are its unsolicited appearance and the priority it gains over the patient's current, conscious efforts in the psychoanalytic situation. Transference describes how the current situation loses its identity to a misperception the patient unwittingly brings to it. Toward the end of the chapter on psychotherapy in *Studies on*

Hysteria, Freud observed that the transference is an obstacle to free association that we can "reckon on meeting in every comparatively serious analysis" (p. 301); ". . . in these transferences onto the figure of the physician it was a question of a compulsion and an illusion which melted away with the conclusion of the analysis" (p. 304).

Summarizing this experimental state of affairs, we might say that the activation of the patient's mental processes in the psychoanalytic situation enables the analyst to study the patient's capacity to retain contact with an actual external situation (via free association) against the claims of the patient's personal, internal inclinations toward misperception (via the transference). Psychoanalysis can be said to be a study of the complex, fluctuating relationship between perception and apperception.

The properties of mind elicited by the psychoanalytic situation are memory, affect, consciousness, and action (see Freud, 1900, Chapter 7). It would not be difficult to transpose Freud's theory of symptom formation into a dynamic organization of these properties. But the leading concern of psychoanalytic psychology involves more than an account of the dynamic relationship among these functions of mind. Fundamentally, the question pursued in the psychoanalytic situation is how these functions safeguard or impair reality testing, which has come to be defined in the psychoanalytic literature as the capacity to develop and maintain a distinction between what is external (perception) and what is internal (apperception) (e.g., Freud, 1911). (Freud's discussion of jealousy and paranoia [1922] is a classic explanation of the fate of reality testing due to a defective relationship between perception and apperception.) Thus psychoanalysis can be said to be a psychology of one aspect of adaptation, namely, reality testing and its extraordinary vulnerabilities in the human being. Psychoanalysis is a clinical psychology only insofar as the vulnerabilities of reality testing to emotional distortion are regarded as symptoms, but we have already noted how general a concept symptom is in psychoanalysis.

One last observation in this section on the specific experimental method of psychoanalysis, that is, the clinical situation. Clearly, the instrumentation is purely procedural, and the procedure is maintained by the analyst. Ideally, the analyst's training in and experience with the method prepare him to safeguard the procedure in as fixed a way as an anemometer is fixed in its interaction with the wind. But obviously ideals are one thing and actualities another. This fact has led many experimentalists to deplore the psychoanalytic method, as if the inevitable discrepancy between the ideal and the actuality signifies that the findings of the method must be completely disreputable. The implication is that if you have a physical instrument (hardware as against software, hence "hard" science as against "soft" science) you have, to that extent, guaranteed an objectivity not possible in its absence. Compelling as this assumption often seems, it is simply not true, and I struggle mightily at the moment against the temptation to digress at length onto this path and into the philosophy and history of science. Suffice it to say that only a fanatic would equate a discrepancy and a catastrophe, and that fanaticism is inconsistent with scientific-mindedness. In a paper called

"Biology and the Nature of Science," Simpson (1963) deals with this charge against procedural instrumentation, and it may be well to quote him briefly:

To say that we cannot learn anything materially factual about a situation if we ourselves are in it is utter and nonsensical negation of the very meaning of learning. The essential in objectivity is not the pretense of eliminating ourselves from a situation in which we are objectively present. It is that the situation should not be interpreted in terms of ourselves but that our roles should be interpreted realistically in terms of the situation (p. 85).

3.

I should like to go on to a final set of issues having to do with the psychoanalytic method as a psychotherapy. Though I began my description of the method with its psychotherapeutic origins in Freud's clinical concerns, I went on to regard the method as a research procedure leading to a particular concept of mind. But the method is also a psychotherapy, which always embodies a version of human existence. Thus the method possesses historical and cultural meaning. As a therapy the method has been called into question, both in its striving for objectivity and in its narrow scope of interest. This amounts to a charge against the method's scientific veracity; for the charge suggests that the psychoanalytic method no longer apprehends a currently significant aspect of mind. To be sure, all scientifically constructed versions of nature are limited by the methods employed and concerns pursued. But when is an expectable limitation to be regarded as a terminal state of a theory and its method? To use Kuhn's terminology (1970), is the psychoanalytic paradigm in a state of crisis? This is a question, as Kuhn argues, which cannot be decided empirically but rather by the current importance of the problems which the paradigm involves. In turning to these issues, I shall be saying something about yet another characteristic of the method, its enduring cultural vitality, its relevance to an enduring aspect of the existence of the subject it studies.

Historically, the psychoanalytic method can be said to have been the first scientific psychotherapy, in the sense that its procedures embraced a complex theory of symptom formation in a highly determined and rational manner. I shall bring in a current definition of psychotherapy momentarily. When we carry this definition back to the 1890s and even some years after, we discover that psychotherapy, as its practice has come to be envisioned in many various quarters, virtually did not exist before Freud's technical invention, unless we want to enlarge the definition of psychotherapy preposterously by regarding the omnipresence of psychological variables in human affairs as synonymous with the omnipresence of psychotherapeutic activity, that is, by regarding loose analogies as firm congruencies as is sometimes done in, say, comparisons of shamanism and psychotherapy.

A definition of psychotherapy is not as difficult to come by as might be thought at first blush. Consulting a range of texts of differing conceptual persuasions, one finds a surprising degree of agreement about the defining elements of psychotherapy. Wolberg (1967) and Hinsie and Campbell (1970), for example, include in their definitions of psychotherapy the idea of a trained and deliberate activity that engages psychological processes in the patient with a view toward ameliorative change in the psychology of the patient. Zilboorg (1941) and Ellenberger (1970), in their historical inquiries into the development of contemporary varieties of psychotherapeutic procedures, are in search of the complex body of knowledge of matters psychological that finally furnished a rationale for the activity of the psychotherapist with the patient. Both Zilboorg and Ellenberger assume that the variety of procedures called psychotherapy came into existence with a deliberateness that grew with the emergence of a body of psychological knowledge. In virtually all definitions of psychotherapy there is an emphasis upon a trained faculty and a minimization of pragmatism. Needless to say, definitions do not go on to indicate how the defined activity is actually conducted or how it achieves its defined goals. That is where agreement about psychotherapy begins to diminish.

Now the definition of psychotherapy of Meltzoff and Kornreich (1970) is one that represents a good consensus, and I should like to present their definition. I might note that their text, *Research in Psychotherapy*, from which I am about to quote, is in no way partial to psychoanalysis as a psychotherapy. Their definition is as follows:

Psychotherapy is taken to mean the informed and planful application of technique derived from established psychological principles by persons qualified through training and experience to understand these principles and to apply these techniques with the intention of assisting individuals to modify such personal characteristics as feelings, values, attitudes and behaviors which are judged by the therapist to be maladaptive or maladjustive (p. 4).

There are provisos here worth stressing. For one, this definition discounts the psychological benefits incidental to the exercise of certain roles, such as teaching, which may enhance adaptation and adjustment very powerfully but only incidentally. Psychotherapy is an intentional undertaking. The patient must be aware that psychotherapy is what he is getting or hoping to get. The intentionality of the psychotherapeutic activity is also connoted in Meltzoff and Kornreich's phrase "persons qualified through training."

I should like to stress another implication. The definition before us contains the phrase "techniques derived from established psychological principles." Thus the psychotherapist possesses some theory or other of mind that accounts for the personal characteristics deemed "maladaptive or maladjustive" in his patient. His would-be psychotherapeutic deeds are in accord with a theory of symptom formation. He wants to be more methodical than pragmatic.

A reading of psychiatric history makes it abundantly clear that before Freud's method no such activity as we have just defined actually existed. Even the historically celebrated activity of Freud's collaborator Josef Breuer is a case in point. While it was true that Breuer's famous patient Anna O. enjoyed notable remissions of her complaints in connection with Breuer's professional care, I submit that whatever Breuer had been doing does not quality as psychotherapy according to the definition we have just examined. At the time he treated Anna O., Breuer had neither a *psycho*therapeutic intention nor a theory of symptom formation. What Breuer did was not quite "informed and planful," and his treatment of Anna O. ended as fortuitously as it had begun. Breuer was a well-meaning and resourceful physician. But Freud's letters to Wilhelm Fliess (Freud, 1887–1902) contain the story of Breuer's confusions and reservations about Freud's theoretical and technical formulations in the mid-nineties.

It is true that elsewhere during this period the idea of psychotherapy had a certain impendingness livelier than what it had for Breuer. Zilboorg (1941) tells us that in 1890 a Dr. Felkin published a book called *Hypnosis or Psychotherapeutics,* which was one of the earliest uses of the term psychotherapy. Ellenberger (1970) has found that the term psychotherapy was used by some of Bernheim's disciples and that a Frederik van Eeden published a paper called "The Theory of Psycho-Therapeutics" in an 1895 number of *The Medical Magazine;* van Eeden expressed a hope for a more humane and nontyrannical procedure than described by, say, Felkin, whose psychotherapeutic method was coercive and abusive. Liébault and Charcot were, of course, other exponents of nonphysical procedures for mental patients.

Also true, around this time the description of mental states and symptoms was relatively sophisticated. Classification became something quite substantial, notably in the work of Kraepelin (1903), who was onto the problem of differential outcome in mental disease. There was also a growing sense, an accumulating lore, in the medical profession that mental symptoms have something to do with the patient's larger existence. Freud himself recalled in subsequent autobiographical works (1914b, 1925) how common it was in the 1890s for a doctor to relate the exacerbation of a hysterical symptom to the patient's sexual behavior.

But withal there was no *psychological theory* of symptom formation. The psychiatrist was truly a neuropsychiatrist, and nonorganic activities with mental patients were expedients incidental to the doctor's central therapeutic hopes and visions.

"The Psychotherapy of Hysteria" is the title of Freud's concluding chapter to *Studies on Hysteria*—yet another early use of the term psychotherapy. A reading of that chapter in its historical context lays to rest any question as to whether psychotherapy emerged or was emerging independent of Freud in those years. For there was nothing even remotely equivalent to that chapter on psychotherapy in all the annals of psychiatry and psychology. Its originality is awesome. It was the first specification of a psychotherapeutic technique that fulfilled the definition of psychotherapy which we have examined above. In that chapter Freud gave us an "informed and planful application of techniques derived from established psychological principles." Moreover, his method assigned to the patient the responsibility of an intentional undertaking; the patient was given a large share of the knowledge of the technique. In that chapter Freud even considered the question of the therapist's qualifications, which exceeded the physician's fundamental professional qualifications and called for a certain temperament, personal honesty, and a high degree of psychological-mindedness. (From this point it is a short step to the whole idea of selection and training.)

Within 15 years after outlining the technique in *Studies on Hysteria*, Freud unfolded its myriad procedural details in a series of papers on technique (Freud, 1912a, 1912b, 1913, 1914a). These papers contain a rationale for all sorts of practical contingencies, e.g., how to handle fees, why not to treat friends and colleagues, how many appointments a week the patient should be given, when to take up this business of the patient's transferring feelings and ideas onto the therapist and when not to take it up, why to discourage the patient from discussing the treatment outside of sessions, when the treatment should begin. All this kept pace with the progressive enlargement of the theory of mind in which the major outlines of the procedure originated. This entire enterprise was unique.

Into the bargain, Freud left a legacy not only to psychology but to psychotherapy—I was about to say *modern* psychotherapy, but that would have been redundant, for there is no other kind. Today, whatever our methods, Freudian or not, one large debt we owe to psychoanalysis is for its having demonstrated the possibility of a technique based on a theory of symptom formation, the possibility of a method to madness. Whether the methodological and theoretical unities we apply clinically belong to comparative or conditioning or learning or social psychology or to nonpsychoanalytic varieties of clinical psychology, the actuality of "an informed and planful application of techniques derived from established psychological principles" was first achieved by Freud. Indeed, much of Freud's early clinical experience has become the universal experience of almost all mental-health professionals of whatever persuasion. Is it not, for example, a general expectation on the professional's side that the patient's earnest effort to obtain help is hobbled by his compulsion to repeat in the professional situation what has gotten him into difficulty elsewhere in his life? All clinicians nowadays are prepared to deal with the discrepancy between a patient's avowed good intentions to carry out whatever task we assign and his unwitting inability to do so. Far from disqualifying the patient, such discrepancies will soon become the subject of the therapy itself. Shades of the free-association rule and the inevitable transference resistance! Here we should remember that in Freud's day mental patients, even mildly neurotic ones, were regarded as pests to be put off with reassurance and avoided as much as possible; the exasperation they aroused in their doctors was not turned to professional account. The present pervasive climate of clinical expectation and therapeutic possibility makes us heirs to Freud, willingly or not. "To us he is no more a person / Now but a whole climate of opinion," was how Auden put it.

During the past decade there has been an exodus from this climate by a notable number of practitioners of psychotherapy, who have been declaring that the lives of Western persons have been so transformed by social processes that certain modes of psychological comprehension and technique that originated earlier in the century no longer reach any essence of contemporary existence. I do not mean that a large number of practitioners has given up practicing psychoanalytic therapy—a large number never has practiced it. I mean that certain familiar conditions of psychotherapy deriving directly and indirectly from the scientific ethos of the psychoanalytic situation have been abandoned. I am thinking, for example, of the condition of divided and noninterchangeable roles for therapist and patient, this in the belief that the attainment of objectivity in human affairs is both desirable and feasible. Related to this is the idea that the patient's interactional impulses toward the therapist will result in counsel for the patient only if such impulses occur in a context of abstinence on the therapist's part. Also, the clinical activity takes place in one prevailing set of circumstances. And so on. The contravention of all this by the professional movement I have been alluding to has come to exceed even what was available for Wallerstein (1966) to report on in the mid-sixties in his detailed review of "The Current State of Psychotherapy: Theory, Practice, Research." In the therapies that Wallerstein reported it was still possible to distinguish the therapist from the patient and to appreciate (if not approve of) how interaction was employed as a measure of process. Nor was the psychotherapeutic situation subject to capricious alterations. At the present moment, however, there is a vast psychotherapeutic activity representing a radical alternative to psychoanalytically informed versions of psychotherapy, an activity in which the helper and helped appear to exchange roles, in which interaction is something solicited and pursued for its own sake, in which the setting and circumstances of the clinical transaction are subject to change, indeed are short-lived. And so on.

Except for its present extensiveness, the alternative to the psychoanalytic situation being represented here is not exactly new. From its very inception, the clinical technique of psychoanalysis has been criticized for its ambitious exactitude. This has often led to the complaint, for example, that analytic methods violate "production norms." (Riesman [1954], however, has referred to Freud approvingly as a "rate buster," who conferred upon the individual patient, otherwise shunted aside, the dignity of prolonged and undivided attention.) Another complaint, the one more at issue in the movement we are noting, is that the psychoanalytic therapist, maintaining an objectivity toward experience, inhibits experiences that would otherwise arise in the clinical situation. What accrues to the strict maintenance of the analytic role is not worth what the role deprives the analyst of as a reciprocating, experiencing participant in the clinical situation. The pursuit of objectivity curtails interaction. But then, from our examination of the psychoanalytic method, this charge about objectivity is one that the psychoanalyst would not deny. And doubtless the contemporary movement making this charge succeeds in what it strives for, a reclamation of subjective experience from the regulation of cognition of that experience. The question is whether such success is more authentically modern than the fuller reflection of the psychoanalytic method.[2]

---

[2] Lionel Trilling (1971) pursues this question along nonclinical lines in one of his Charles Eliot Norton Lectures called "Authenticity and the Modern Unconscious."

Interestingly, there was a brief period in the development of the psychoanalytic method when Freud himself attempted a nonreflective solution to the problems he had set himself. I have in mind his fleeting interest in cathartic experience before *Studies on Hysteria*. Freud had the idea at this early stage that symptoms represented an inhibition of affect which the patient could release under the sponsorship of the doctor's authority. In this scheme, the evocation of experience had a priority over any meaning the symptom had for the patient. I would characterize this solution as romantic, in the sense of an imbalance between apperception and the cognition of apperception, with the weight heavily on the former. Had Freud continued along these lines he would have produced not a dynamic methodological system but, at best, an interesting "anatomy," a compendium of experiences and the ills which their inhibition gives rise to. (Wilhelm Reich might be said to have succeeded in something like this.) Such an anatomy would have had little to do with the life of mind which the late nineteenth century was preparing for the twentieth century.

Nourished by Darwin, Marx, Nietzsche, Freud, a paramount feature of twentieth-century intellection has been, and continues to be, epistemology. By epistemology I mean here the demystification of the sources of knowledge and the validation of the means of demystification. What was lost in faith (mystification) was replaced by the Nietzschean assertion, "Things are not what they seem to be," an assertion implying that what is manifest must be met by an interpretive response. Surely our age is an age of skepticism and criticism; we are also concerned with the validation of the means by which knowledge is acquired, namely, technique (this is true even in our most representative and influential art—think of James Joyce, Stravinsky, Jackson Pollock); and science, of course, is an extraordinary enterprise in our age. But Trilling assures us that there is no malice in the interpretive response Nietzsche prescribes. "It has for its purpose not 'reduction' but comprehension, such grasp upon a man's thought as may be had through the perception of its unarticulated and even unconscious intention. It is a mode of critical investigation whose propriety and efficiency Freud himself of course confirms" (1971, p. 45).

Under the impact of epistemology, psychology, which is the source of psychotherapy, runs the risk of losing the very subject matter of psychology itself. Indeed, in the late nineteenth century and long thereafter, the best psychology became temporarily a species of "psychophysics," neurophysiology, endocrinology, and so on. Passion, fear, guilt, sensuality, suffering—the specifically human experiences—went neglected, as William James (1890) complained at that very time. Nor was this wholly unfortunate. For the way was prepared for a replacement of the purely psychological variables but in a manner consistent with an epistemological spirit.

We know from many sources—Shakow and Rapaport (1964), for example—that Freud was committed to the "Helmholtz Program," and this commitment guaranteed that, when he restored the psyche to psychology, he would do so with the firm fastenings of a scientific method that would enable a constant interpretation of the specifically human experiences he had recalled to psychology. (Ernest Jones [1955] tells us that William James, after hearing Freud lecture at

Clark University in 1909, proclaimed that "the future of psychology belongs to your work," meaning to psychoanalysis.) The strategy of admitting psychological processes into a theory of symptom formation and the fervor with which Freud held to a method rescued his work from a sterile scientism on the one hand, and a romantic phenomenalism on the other. The emphasis in Freud's canon on method is a corrective against the subject matter running away with itself, what Kohut (1971) calls "cognitive infantilism," "a sentimentalizing regression to subjectivity" (p. 301). The subject matter, on its side, is a corrective against "a mechanistic and lifeless conception of psychological reality" (p. 301). The employment in the psychoanalytic situation of both a method and a content but neither for its own sake leads to what I have called above a "full reflection." When Freud abandoned his cathartic efforts and achieved this technology of apperception, as I have described it earlier, he advanced from a *fin de siècle* romanticism into a twentieth-century scientific psychology.

The alternative at this social moment in the so-called "encounter movement," for which claims of greater modernity are made, ratifies human existence at its manifest level, in the sense that experience itself, unreflected upon and uninterpreted, is the ultimate verification of existence. The literature of this movement is purely a phenomenology of experience. The verification of existence is thus limited to an Ego/Cogito equation: "I am what I am capable of feeling." This is the Cartesian apodictic which Ricoeur (1970) calls "as feeble as it is peremptory, as sterile as it is irrefutable." His objection to the sterility of such phenomenology is precisely that it fails to engage the present century's concern with replacing meaning where faith has been lost. In the clinical situation, the opportunity to engage this concern exists only insofar as a concept of transference exists, a methodological rule that the unsolicited interactions of the patient must be reacted to with an interpretive response. Ricoeur writes: "Freud stresses the fact that the 'handling' of the transference is where the technical character of psychoanalysis is evidenced in its highest degree. This too is where the philosopher schooled in phenomenology realizes his exclusion from an experiential understanding of what occurs in the analytic relationship. Ultimately, this is where analytic praxis differs from all its conceivable phenomenological equivalents" (p. 414). The point is that radical alternatives to psychoanalytic therapy at this moment are convenient only in their evasions of what remains philosophically crucial to our times.

But if not modern, what then are these alternatives? Surely they are not reactionary in the sense that cruelty toward mental patients or attempts at exorcism are reactionary. Perhaps what they might best be called is simulations of the modern. As such their relation to science and to the intellectual strivings of the age is like the relation of propaganda to knowledge. One of the quarrels with psychoanalysis is over its nonaccommodation of immediacy, impact, simultaneity, and sensation. But any therapy that emphasizes these modes is consistent with the most prevalent current processes of socialization (Bell, 1965), and as such is a medium of social propaganda. Such activity is the very symptom it purports to cure.

The relationship of psychoanalysis to society has always been uneasy. A cultural activity ultimately, psychoanalysis has been wary of the social environment in which it functions, as all culture seems to be toward society in our age. Psychoanalysis in its truest identity has never been fashionable. Yet the record of nearly eight decades of psychoanalytic research is replete not only with what psychoanalysis finds enduring in the mind but with the changes in the possibilities of human adventure and misadventure. The psychoanalytic literature of the past decade, for example, belongs with the very best documentation of the period. Nor are there any signs that this quality will give out, even as we approach the century ahead.

REFERENCES

Bell, D. (1965). The Disjunction of Culture and Social Structure. *Daedalus,* Winter, pp. 208–222.

Breuer, J., and Freud, S. (1893–1895). Studies on Hysteria. *Standard Edition,* 2. London: Hogarth Press, 1955.

Cottrell, N. B. (1968). Performance in the Presence of Other Human Beings: Mere Presence, Audience and Affiliation Effects. In: *Social Facilitation and Imitative Behavior,* ed. E. C. Simmel, R. A. Hoppe, and G. A. Milton. Boston: Allyn and Bacon, pp. 91–110.

Ellenberger, H. F. (1970). *The Discovery of the Unconscious.* New York: Basic Books.

Freud, S. (1887–1902). *The Origins of Psychoanalysis: Letters to Wilhelm Fliess, Drafts and Notes, 1887–1902.* New York: Basic Books, 1954.

——— (1894). The Neuro-Psychoses of Defence. *Standard Edition,* 3:45–61. London: Hogarth Press, 1962.

——— (1900). The Interpretation of Dreams. *Standard Edition,* 4 & 5. London: Hogarth Press, 1953.

——— (1905). Fragment of an Analysis of a Case of Hysteria. *Standard Edition,* 7:7–122. London: Hogarth Press, 1953.

——— (1911). Formulations on the Two Principles of Mental Functioning. *Standard Edition,* 12:218–226. London: Hogarth Press, 1958.

——— (1912a). The Dynamics of the Transference. *Standard Edition,* 12:99–108. London: Hogarth Press, 1958.

——— (1912b). Recommendations to Physicians Practising Psycho-Analysis. *Standard Edition,* 12:111–120. London: Hogarth Press, 1958.

——— (1913). On Beginning the Treatment (Further Recommendations on the Technique of Psycho-Analysis I). *Standard Edition,* 12:123–144. London: Hogarth Press, 1958.

——— (1914a). Remembering, Repeating and Working-Through (Further Recommendations on the Technique of Psycho-Analysis II). *Standard Edition,* 12:147–156. London: Hogarth Press, 1958.

——— (1914b). On the History of the Psycho-Analytic Movement. *Standard Edition,* 14:7–66. London: Hogarth Press, 1957.

——— (1917). Mourning and Melancholia. *Standard Edition,* 14:243–258. London: Hogarth Press, 1957.

——— (1922). Some Neurotic Mechanisms in Jealousy, Paranoia and Homosexuality. *Standard Edition,* 18:223–232. London: Hogarth Press, 1955.

——— (1925). An Autobiographical Study. *Standard Edition,* 20:7–74. London: Hogarth Press, 1959.

Hinsie, L. E., and Campbell, R. J. (1970). *Psychiatric Dictionary,* 4th ed. New York: Oxford University Press.

James, W. (1890). *The Principles of Psychology.* New York: Dover, 1950.

Jones, E. (1955). *The Life and Work of Sigmund Freud,* Vol. 2. New York: Basic Books.

Kraepelin, E. (1903). *Lehrbuch der Psychiatrie,* 7th ed. Leipzig: Barth.

Kohut, H. (1971). *The Analysis of the Self.* New York: International Universities Press.

Kuhn, T. S. (1970). *The Structure of Scientific Revolutions,* 2nd ed. Chicago: University of Chicago Press.

Meltzoff, J., and Kornreich, M. (1970). *Research in Psychotherapy.* New York: Atherton.

Ricoeur, P. (1970). *Freud and Philosophy.* New Haven: Yale University Press.

Riesman, D. (1954). The Themes of Heroism and Weakness in the Structure of Freud's Thought. In: *Individualism Reconsidered.* New York: Anchor Books, pp. 246–275.

Schlessinger, N., Gedo, J. E., Miller, J., Pollock, G. H., Sabshin, M., and Sadow, L. (1967). The Scientific Style of Breuer and Freud in the Origins of Psychoanalysis. *Journal of the American Psychoanalytic Association,* 15:404–422.

Shakow, D., and Rapaport, D. (1964). The Influence of Freud on American Psychology. *Psychological Issues,* Monograph 13. New York: International Universities Press.

Simpson, G. G. (1963). Biology and the Nature of Science. *Science,* 139:81–88.

Thibaut, J. W., and Kelley, H. H. (1959). *The Social Psychology of Groups.* New York: Wiley.

Trilling, L. (1971). Authenticity and the Modern Unconscious. *Commentary,* September, pp. 39–50.

Wallerstein, R. S. (1966). The Current State of Psychotherapy: Theory, Practice, Research. *Journal of the American Psychoanalytic Association,* 14:183–225.

Wolberg, L. R. (1967). *The Technique of Psychotherapy.* New York: Grune and Stratton.

Zajonc, R. B. (1965). Social Facilitation. *Science,* 149:269–274.

Zilboorg, G. (1941). *A History of Medical Psychology.* New York: Norton.

ON RESISTANCE TO THE
PSYCHOANALYTIC PROCESS
Some Thoughts on Its Nature and Motivations [1]

Leo Stone, M.D.

It is important to mention at the outset that, whereas resistance is, in certain fundamental references, an operational equivalent of defense, its scope is really far larger and far more complicated. It utilizes an array of mechanisms which sometimes defy classification in the way that fundamental genetically determined defenses, derived from important and common developmental trends, can be classified. From falling asleep to brilliant argument, there is a limitless and mobile spectrum of devices with which the patient may protect the current integrations of his personality, including his system of permanent defenses. In fact, resistances of a surface, conscious type, related to individual character and to educational and cultural background, often present themselves at the patient's first confrontation with an unique and often puzzling treatment method. While some of these phenomena are continuous with deeper resistances, others must be met at their own level. These considerations are obviously very important. However, I must leave them for now to the much-neglected faculty of informed and reflective common sense, and move on to the less readily accessible and explicable dynamisms, which inevitably supervene in analytic work, even if these initial surface resistances have been largely or wholly mastered. Nor shall I attempt to discuss the specific influence of the immediate cultural climate, especially the general attitudes of many young people (A. Freud, 1968) toward the psychoanalytic process and its goals.

When Freud gave up the use of hypnosis for several reasons, beginning with the personal difficulty in inducing the hypnotic state and culminating in his ultimate and adequate reason—that it bypassed the essential lever of lasting

[1] This paper, in its essential content, was presented as the John B. Turner Lecture of the Psychoanalytic Clinic for Training and Research, Columbia University, April 29, 1970. It was also presented before the Baltimore–District of Columbia Society for Psychoanalysis, November 21, 1970, and before the Atlanta Psychoanalytic Group, January 7, 1972.

therapeutic change, the confrontation with the repressing forces themselves—
he turned to the method of waking discourse with the patient, in which insistence, with a sense of infallibility, accompanied by head pressure and release,
were the essential tools for the overcoming of resistances (Breuer and Freud,
1893–1895). While various forms of resistance (general sense) had been observed
before (for example, inability to be hypnotized, total and willful rejection of
hypnosis, selective refusal to discuss certain topics under hypnosis, adverse reactions to testing for trance), it was the effectiveness of insistence in inducing the
patient to fill memory gaps, or to accept the physician's constructions, which led
Freud to a first—and enduring—formulation: since effort—psychic work—by the
physician was required, it was evident that a psychical force, a resistance which
was opposed to the pathogenic ideas becoming conscious (or being remembered), had to be overcome. This was thought to be the same psychic force which
had initiated the symptom formation by preventing the original pathogenic idea
from achieving adequate affective discharge, establishing adequate associations
—in short, from remaining or becoming conscious. The motive for invoking such
a force would be the abolition (or avoidance) of some form of psychical distress or pain, such as shame, self-reproach, fear of harm, or equivalent cause for
rejecting or wishing to forget the experience. Such defensive effort was attributed
to the constellation of ideas already present, later clearly the ego, and especially
the character. It was thought important to show the patient that his resistance was
the same as the original "repulsion" which had initiated pathogenesis. The step
thereafter was short to the essentially equivalent, and permanent, concept of
defense, at first repression. What I have said is, I believe, a brief but essentially
sound amalgam of quotation, paraphrase, and condensation (Breuer and Freud,
1893–1895). While Freud gave tremendous weight to the effectiveness of the hand
pressure manoeuvre, he saw it essentially as a mode of distracting the patient's
will and conscious attention and thus facilitating the emergence of latent ideas
(or images). From a present-day point of view, one cannot but think of the powerful transferences excited by an infallible parental figure in a procedure only one
step removed from the relative abdication of will and consciousness involved in
hypnosis, and that this quasi-archaic qualitative pattern of relationship was actually more important, in the sense of effectiveness or failure, than the exchanges
of psychic energy postulated by Freud. In this sense, the "laying on of hands,"
granted its effect on attention, was probably even more significant in inducing
transference regression than in the role which the great discoverer assigned to it.

    What is of the first importance, however, is the establishment of a viable
scientific and working concept of resistance to the therapeutic process as a
manifestation of a reactivated intrapsychic conflict in a new interpersonal context. This in its essentials persists to this day in psychoanalytic work, in the concept of ego resistances.

    Pari passu with this development, less explicitly formulated but often de-
scribed or implied, was a more nearly total rejecting or hostile or unruly attitude
of the patient, sometimes evoking spontaneous antagonistic reactions in the
physician. In occasional direct references in the early work and in the choice

of figurative phraseology for years thereafter, Freud recognizes this "balky child" type of struggle against the doctor's efforts. One need only recall Elizabeth von R., who would tell Freud that she was not better "with a sly look of satisfaction" at his discomfiture (Breuer and Freud, 1893–1895, pp. 144–145). When deep hypnosis failed with her, Freud "was glad enough that on this occasion, she refrained from triumphantly protesting: 'I'm not asleep, you know; I can't be hypnotized' " (p. 145). I mention this category of resistance phenomenon because it represents a type of ego-syntonic struggle with the physician which remains potentially important in the course of any analysis, when the patient is motivated by what we call (in shorthand) the negative transference, regardless of its particular nuances of motivation. This is, of course, a manifestly different phenomenon from the earnest effortful struggles of the cooperative patient whose associations fail him, or who forgets his dream, or who comes at the wrong hour, to his extreme humiliation. Yet there is an important dynamic relationship between the two sets of phenomena, on which I shall touch again later on.

Even in the period of experimentation with techniques strikingly different from those now employed, Freud made the analysis of resistances the central obligation of analytic work, and proceeded from primitive beginnings, with rapidly increasing sophistication, both technical and psychopathologic, to concepts which remain valid to this day: that conscious knowledge transmitted to the patient may have no, or an adverse, effect in the mobilization of what is similar or identical in the unconscious; [2] that the repressing forces, the resistances, are more like infiltrates than discrete foreign body capsules in their relation to preconscious associative systems; that the physician must begin with the surface and proceed centripetally; that hysterical symptoms are more often serial and multiple than mononuclear; that resistances participate in all productions and must be dealt with at every step of analytic work; and other matters of equal significance (Breuer and Freud, 1893–1895).

While Freud always maintained the central concept of resistance stated before, and bequeathed it (reinforced later by the structural theory) to the generations of analysts who have followed him, as the years went on he elaborated the general scope of resistance far beyond the basic concept of intrapsychic defense, recognizing that a great variety and range of mechanisms could impede psychoanalysis as a recognizable process or, beyond this, nullify or reverse expected therapeutic responses, or extend indefinitely the patient's dependence on the analyst. When extended beyond its direct equation with the anticathexes of defense, the variety of sources—not to speak of manifestations—of resistance multiplied rapidly. To mention only a few which were recognized very early: secondary gain of illness (Freud, 1905); "external" resistances, for example, the hostility of the patient's family to the treatment (Freud, 1917a, pp. 458–461); persistence of illness, with detachment, superciliousness, and mechanical compliance, as a weapon for frustrating the analyst, as in the case of the homosexual

---

[2] This principle, however, always remained subject to some reservation. See Freud (1920b, p. 152), for example, or the Outline (Freud, 1940a, p. 160).

girl (Freud, 1920b); gratification from the dependent aspects of the transference (Freud, 1918); sense of security in the symptom as a primary mode of conflict solution (Freud, 1910a, p. 49); and most crucially, the complicated, subtly evolving concept of the "transference-resistance" in its oscillating pluralistic sense (for example, Breuer and Freud, 1893–1895; Freud, 1912a, 1917a). In his last writings, conspicuously in "Analysis Terminable and Interminable" (1937), Freud, in considering several possible factors in human personality which might obstruct or render ineffectual the successful termination of the analytic procedure, offered a variety of psychodynamic considerations which could be fundamental in the extended or broadened concept of resistance: the question of the constitutional strength of instincts and their relation to ego strength; the problem of the accessibility of latent conflicts when undisturbed by the patient's life situation; (briefly but pointedly) the impingement of the analyst's personality on the analytic situation and process; the existence of certain qualities of the libidinal cathexes—especially undue adhesiveness or excessive mobility; rigid character structure; the existence of certain sex-linked "bedrock" conflicts which Freud regarded as biologically determined (insoluble penis envy in the female, and the male's persisting conflict with his passivity). Finally and most formidably, there was the cluster of dynamisms and phenomena which Freud, beginning with *Beyond the Pleasure Principle* (1920a) and *The Ego and the Id* (1923), attributed consistently and with deepening conviction to the operation of a death instinct. I refer to the "unconscious sense of guilt" and need for punishment, the repetition compulsion, the negative therapeutic reaction, and the more general operations of the need to suffer or to die or to seek outer or inner destruction. In an earlier presentation (Stone, 1971) I have examined critically the theories of primary masochism and the death instinct in their relation to aggression. In the course of this paper I hope to offer, incidental to other comments, some simpler and somewhat more proximal, although similarly general, explanations of the deeper strata of resistance to the analytic process, and their synergistic sources, than the effects of primary masochism. I do this not because I believe it an imperative to be "optimistic" (Freud, incidentally, with justice rejected the imputation of "pessimism" in this connection), but because, in my view, it may more closely tally with the clinical facts and because it may be clinically more useful. It remains an inexorable truth that the resistances inherent in the nature of certain cases, or certain limitations implicit in the nature of psychoanalytic work, are at times invincibly formidable, and cannot be disestablished by a theoretical position any more than they can be thus created.

The varied clinical manifestations of resistance are dealt with extensively throughout Freud's own writings, in many individual papers of other analysts, and also in comprehensive works on analytic technique, for example, those of Fenichel (1941), Glover (1955), and more recently Greenson (1967). I shall therefore make only selective and occasional references to their kaleidoscopic variety.

When free association and interpretation displaced hypnosis and derivative primitive techniques, psychoanalysis, as we now construe it, came into being. To the extent that free association was the patient's active participation, it was in this sphere that his "resistance" to the new technique was most clearly recognized as such. Cessation, slowing, circumlocution, lack of informative or relevant content, emotional detachment, obsessional doubt or circumstantiality, became established as relatively obvious impediments to the early (no longer exclusive but still radically important) topographic goal: to convert unconscious ideas, largely via the interpretation of preconscious derivatives, into conscious ideas. Only with time and increasing sophistication did it become evident that fluency, even vividness of associative content, indeed tendentious "relevancy" itself could, like overcompliant acceptance of interpretations, conceal and implement resistances which were the more formidable because expressed in such "good behavior."

One may define resistance (and in so doing include a rather liberal and augmenting paraphrase of Freud's own most pithy definition [*The Interpretation of Dreams*, 1900, p. 517]) as anything of essentially intrapsychic significance in the patient which impedes or interrupts the progress of psychoanalytic work or interferes with its basic purposes and goals. In specifying "in the patient" I do not underestimate the possibly decisive importance of the analyst's resistances; rather, I separate the "counterresistance" as a different matter, in a practical sense, requiring separate study. One may concur in general with Glover's statement (1955, p. 57) that "However we may approach the mental apparatus there is no part of its function which cannot serve the purposes of mental defence and hence give rise during the analysis to the phenomena of resistance." One may also concur with his formulation that the most successful resistances (in contrast with those employing manifest expressions) are silent (p. 54), but demur to the paradoxical sequel: ". . . and it might be said that the sign of their existence is our unawareness of them." For the absence of important material is in itself a sign; and it is necessary to become aware of such absence, if possible.

Freud, in his technical papers and in numerous other writings, despite his reluctance in this direction did lay down the general and essential technical principles and precepts for analytic practice. We must note, however, that the clear and useful technical precepts are largely in what I would regard as the "tactical sphere," i.e., they deal with the manifest process phenomena of ego resistances. Other resistances, those largely subsumed in the "silent" group (for example, delays or failure of expectable symptomatic change, omission of decisive conflict material from free association or [more often] from the transference neurosis, inability to accept termination of the analysis, and allied matters), I would think of as in the "strategic sphere," relating to the depths of the patient's psychopathology and personality structure, and to his total reactions to the psychoanalytic situation, process, and the person of the analyst. My use of the terms "strategic" and "tactical," I should note, differs from their use by others, for example, Kaiser (1934). While I do not presume to offer simple precepts for the ready liquidation of the massive silent resistances, I would hope to contribute something, however slight, to understanding them better and thus, potentially, to their better management. Some of these considerations, for example, iatrogenic regression, I have dealt with in other contexts (1961, 1966). In the "strategic" sphere of resistance, so often manifested by total or relative "absence," it is the informed surmise regarding the existence of the silent territory, by way of ongoing reconstructive activity, which is the first and essential "activity" of the analyst. Beyond this lie the subtle potentialities of the shaping and selection of inter-pretive direction and emphasis, and the tactful indication of tendentious distor-tion or absence.

Because of a possible variety of factors, beginning with the strange mag-netism which the verbal statement of unconscious content exerts on analysts and patients alike (in itself a frequent resistance or counterresistance), the priority of the analysis of resistance over the analysis of content, as discretely separate, did not readily come to full flower. This may well have been owing to the diffi-culties of dealing with more complicated resistances, or of developing an ade-quate methodology in this sphere—or even to the fact that a well-timed and tactful reference to content (or its general nature) sometimes seems the only way of mobilizing (reflexively) and thus exposing the corresponding resistance for interpretation and "working through," an echo of Freud's early, never fully relinquished biphasic process (1940a, p. 160).

Since this is not a technical paper, I must omit an extended discussion of the evolution of views on methods of resistance analysis, even though such views are inevitably related to our immediate subject matter. I have in mind approaches that range from the strict systematic analysis of character resistances of Wilhelm Reich (1933), or the absolute exclusion of content interpretation of Kaiser (1934), to the special efforts toward dramatization of the transference of Ferenczi and Rank (1925), or Ferenczi's own experiments with active techniques of deprivation and (on the other hand) the gratification of regressed transfer-ence wishes in adults (for example, 1919, 1920, 1930, 1931, 1932). Developments in ego psychology (for example Anna Freud's classic contribution on the mech-anisms of defense [1936]) brought the variety and importance of defense mech-anisms securely into the foreground of analytic work, and the subsequent more widely accepted priority of defense analysis has indeed rectified a great deal of the original (and not entirely inexplicable) "cultural lag" in this fundamentally important, if not exclusive, sphere of resistance analysis. Concomitant with a more widespread functional acceptance of the essentiality and priority (in prin-ciple) of resistance analysis over content interpretation, there is in general a more flexible view of the technical implementation of the essential precepts, permitting interpretive mobility, in accordance with intuition or judgment, be-tween the psychic structures, somewhat in accordance with Anna Freud's (1936) principle of "equidistance." Resistances may sometimes be dealt with other than by discrete specification of them, apart from the intrinsic conceptual diffi-culty in the latter intellectual process, i.e., the specifying of a resistance without indicating that against which it is directed (Waelder, 1960). There is also a gen-eral broadening of the scope of interpretive method. Witness, for example, Loewenstein's "reconstruction upward" (1951), and my own differently derived but somewhat allied conception, the "integrative interpretation" (1951), which recognize that resistance may indeed be directed "upward," or against the integration of experience, rather than against the explicitly and exclusively infantile or against the past. Similar considerations are also reflected in Hartmann's "principle of multiple appeal" (1951).

It is noteworthy that, while the emphasis on resistance in Freud's early clinical presentations is in general proportionate to his theoretical statements, the methods of dealing with the concealed and more formidable resistances are not very clear, except in certain very active interventions, such as the magical intestinal prognosis in the "Wolf Man" (1918), or the "time limit" in the same case, or the principle that at a certain point patients should confront phobic symptoms directly (1910b, p. 145), or the suggestion of transfer to a woman analyst, in the case of the homosexual girl (1920b). In these manoeuvres and attitudes there is (1) an explicit recognition that interpretation, the prime working instrument of analysis, may not seldom reach an impasse in relation to powerful "strategic" resistances; and (2) an implicit recognition that elements in the personal relationship of the analytic situation, specifically the transference, may subvert the most skillful analytic work by producing massive although "silent" resistances to ultimate goals, and that in some instances, where energic elements are formidable, they may indeed have to be dealt with directly and holistically, in the patient's living and actual situation.

Freud's own interest in active techniques (see above) stimulated Ferenczi to extreme developments in this sphere (1919, 1920), later combined with his oppositely oriented methods of indulgence (1930). As time went on, noninterpretive methods, especially those involving gratification of transference wishes, whether libidinal or masochistic, were set aside with increasing severity, in recognition of their contravention of the indispensability of the undistorted transference and the unique importance of transference analysis in analytic work. The same has been largely true of tendentious, selective instinctual frustrations (Ferenczi, 1919, 1920). However, there is no doubt that the use of interpretive alternatives (sometimes suggestions for the deliberate control of obstinate resistance phenomena in this sphere) has been sharpened by—to some degree colored by—the earlier experiments in prohibition, whose transference implications were not fully apparent at the time of their introduction. The type of active intervention introduced by Freud (the time limit, the confrontation of symptoms), confined in actuality to the sphere of the demonstrably clinical relationship, has retained a certain optional place in our work, although the potential transference meaning and impact of such interventions, with corresponding variations or limitations of effectiveness, are increasingly understood and considered. The broad general principle of abstinence in the psychoanalytic situation, stated by Freud in its sharpest epitome in 1919, remains a basic and indispensable context of psychoanalytic technique. The nuances of application remain open to, in fact require, continuing study (Stone, 1961, 1966).

In addition to important developments in ego psychology and characterology (for conspicuous examples: A. Freud, 1936; Kris, 1956; Hartmann, 1951; Loewenstein, 1951; Waelder, 1930), the principal factor in deepening, broadening, and complicating the conceptual problem of resistance, and thus modifying the strict layerlike sequential approach (Reich, 1933) to the analysis of resistance and content respectively, even in principle, has been the progressive emergence of transference analysis as the central and decisive task of analytic work. For, to state it oversuccinctly, and thus to risk some inaccuracy, the transference is far more than the most difficult implementation of resistances and (at the same time) an indispensable element in the therapeutic effort. Given the mature capacity for working alliance, it is the central dynamism of the patient's participation in the analytic process, and at the same time the proximal or remote source of all significant resistances, except those manifest phenomena originating in the conscious personal or cultural attitudes and experiences of the adult patient, or those deriving from the inevitable cohesive-conservative forces in the patient's personality, for which we must still summon briefly the Goethe-Freud "witch," metapsychology (Freud, 1937, p. 225n.). Later on I shall comment further on the relationship between transference and resistance.

In relation to the "tactical," i.e., process, resistances, a general view of what is immediate and confronting, for example, the threatened emergence of ego-dystonic sexual or aggressive material, may be adequate. However, in order to gain access to what I have called the "strategic" sphere of resistance, one must have a tentative working formulation of the total psychic situation in mind, including an informed surmise regarding large and essential unconscious trends. Such suggested procedure is, I know, open to discussion on more than one score; and it does involve one immediately in some of the basic epistemological problems of psychoanalysis. Unfortunately, we cannot become involved in this fascinating sphere of dialectic in the course of a brief paper on a large subject. In his early work Freud relied enthusiastically on his own capacity to fill primary gaps in the patient's memory through informed inferences from the available data, and then, with an aura of infallibility, actively persuaded the patient to accept these constructions. However, with the further elaboration of psychoanalysis as process, in the sense of the increasing importance of free association, of the analyst's relative passivity, and other characteristics of the process as we now know it, there have inevitably been some important modifications of the attitudes reflected in such procedures. While, as far as I know, Freud never revised or repudiated his view that the resistances are operative in every step of the analytic work, I know that there exists in many minds a paradoxical mystique, to the effect that the patient's free associations as such, unimpeded (and uninterpreted), could ultimately provide the whole and meaningful story of his neurosis, in the sense of direct information. This is, of course, manifestly at variance with Freud's basic assumptions about the role of resistance, and the germane roles of defense and conflict in the origin of illness.

In any case, among Freud's "Recommendations" (1912b, p. 114) is his advice against attempting to reconstruct the essentials of a case while the case is in progress. Such a reconstruction, he assumes, would be undertaken for scientific reasons. The caution, however, rests on both scientific and therapeutic grounds, on the assumption that the analyst's receptiveness to new data, and also his capacity for evenly suspended attention, would be impaired by such an effort. It is true, of course, that rigid preoccupation with an intellectual formulation can impair these capacities. But it is also true that the "formulation" or structuring of a case can and largely does proceed preconsciously, in some references even unconsciously, and usually quite spontaneously. One must assume at the very least that some such process enters into the analyst's first perception of a "resistance." I do not believe that Freud would have demurred to the utilization of such a process. In any case, its utilization, whatever the form, is in my view a necessity; and, at times, it requires and should have the hypercathexis of conscious and concentrated reflection. One may, of course, assign the more purposive intellectual processes to periods outside of hours, and thus better preserve the other equally important response to the dual intellectual demand of psychoanalytic technique. The "voice of the intellect," however, should not be deprived of this essential place in analytic work. It goes without saying that it must never be allowed to foreclose mobile intuitive perceptiveness or openness to unexpected data. Nor must ongoing formulations in the mind of the analyst be allowed to cramp the spontaneity of the patient's associations. They should remain "in the analyst's head." To epitomize the technical situation: Strategic considerations require varying degrees of reflective thought, possibly outside of hours. Except for the perspectives and critiques they silently lend to understanding, they should not influence the natural and spontaneous, often intuitive, responses of the trained analyst to the endlessly variable nuances of his patient's "tactics." In relation to any category of clinical psychoanalytic problem, it is the structure of the transference neurosis, and its unfolding, with the adumbrative material in characterology, symptom formation, personal and clinical history, and the clues from specific data of the psychoanalytic process, taken as an ensemble, which provide the most reliable basis for general tentative reconstruction and thus for the understanding of resistances. While we must marshal our entire body of data, theory, and technology to see the transference neurosis as an epitome of the patient's emotional life, our comprehension of it is nonetheless based essentially on something which is right before us. Again: The total ensemble is essential; the objectively observable phenomena of the transference neurosis are of crucial and central valence.

In the background data, the large outlines of life history are uniquely important because they do represent, or at least strikingly suggest, the patient's gross strategies of survival and growth, of avoidance and affirmation; and one may reasonably infer that they will be invoked again in the confrontation with the analyst, in his pluralistic significance. Allow me a few oversimplified and fragmentary illustrations. Chosen occupational commitments with children and the mood in which they are carried out, with the general character of manifest sexual adaptation, can certainly contribute to rational surmise about whether neurotic childlessness is based predominantly on disturbances of the Oedipus complex, or on an original inability to achieve an adequate psychic separation from parent representations, or on the vicissitudes of extreme sibling rivalry. It must surely illuminate illness and analytic process if one knows that a patient lives, by choice, the breadth of an ocean removed from parents and siblings with whom there has been no evident quarrel, when this is not a crucial matter of occupational opportunity or equivalently important reality. Certainly a male patient's gross psychosexual biography helps us to understand which "side" of the incestuous transference is more likely to be surfacing in his first paroxysm of heterosexual "acting out." While it is true that dreams, parapraxes, and other traditionally dependable psychoanalytic material may dramatically reveal the ego-dystonic directions of impulse and fantasy life, and also the specific nature of opposing forces, it is only the composite historical and current picture which reveals the prevailing or alternative defenses, the large-scale economic patterns, and the preferred or relatively stable, i.e., most strongly overdetermined, trends of conflict solution.

Tactical problems of resistance were earliest observed largely in disturbances of free association, which, in frequent tacit assumption, would, or in principle could, lead without assistance to the ultimate genetic truth. This truth was construed to be the awareness of hitherto repressed memory (or the acceptance of convincing and germane constructions). As time went on, in Freud's own writing, terms of conative import appeared—such as "tendency" or, more vividly, "impulse." But the critical etiological and (reciprocally) therapeutic importance of memory has, of course, never really lost its importance. What has changed is its significance, a matter which I have discussed elsewhere (Stone, 1966). For, while the recovery of traumatic memories, with abreaction, is still dramatic in its therapeutic effect, for example in war neuroses or equivalent civilian experiences, and occasionally in isolated sexual experiences of childhood or adolescence, neuroses of isolated traumatic origin are actually rare in current psychoanalytic experience. Traumata are usually multiple, repetitive, often serving to crystallize, dramatize, and fix (sometimes even "cover") more chronic disturbances, such as distortions or pathological pressures in the instinct life, against the background of larger problems of basic object relationships. Actually, Freud was already becoming aware of the complex structure of neuroses when he wrote his general discussion for the *Studies on Hysteria* (Breuer and Freud, 1893–1895). Thus, to put it all too briefly, when hitherto structuralized impulses or general reaction tendencies can truly be accepted in terms of memory, i.e., as matters of the past, other than in a tentative explanatory sense, much of the analytic work with the dynamics of the transference neurosis has necessarily been accomplished. One does not readily give up a love or a hatred, personal or national, only because one learns that it is based on a crushing defeat of the remote past.

The manifest communicative phenomena of resistance remain very important, just as the common cold remains important in clinical medicine. It will never cease to be important to be able to tell a patient that he is avoiding the emergence of sexual fantasies, or that his blank silence covers latent thoughts about the analyst, or (somewhat more sophisticated) that glib and enthusiastic erotic fantasies about the analyst conceal and include a wish to humiliate or degrade him. However, we can be better prepared, even for these problems, on the basis of ongoing holistic reconstruction. Certainly we shall be better prepared for the formidable resistances of patients who apparently do "tell all," or even "feel all," in a most convincing fashion and in all sincerity, yet may finish apparently thorough analyses without having touched certain nuclear conflicts of their lives and characters, or (more often) having failed to make effective contact with them in the transference neurosis, with a sense of affective reality. I do not, in this comment, refer to the instances described by Freud (1937) where such conflicts remain dormant because current life does not impinge on them, but rather to those in which the "acting out" in life, or the solution in severe symptoms, is desperately elected by the personality in apparently paradoxical preference to the subjective vicissitudes of the transference neurosis (Stone, 1966, pp. 31–32n.).

Having worked backward, or perhaps in circular fashion, I may at this point state a brief tentative formulation of the respective natures of the two general groups of resistance phenomena. These are, I believe, ultimately and fundamentally related, and exist in varying degree in all analyses. However, one or the other is usually of preponderant importance; and they are, in a practical and prognostic sense, quite different: (a) Those manifested largely in discernible impediments of the psychoanalytic process in its immediate operational sense. These are usual in the neuroses, in persons who have achieved relatively satisfactory separation of the "self" from the primary object, but whose lives are disturbed by the residues of instinctual and other intrapsychic conflicts in relation to the unconscious representations of early objects, and thus to transference objects. (b) Those which may be similarly manifested at times, but may indeed be relatively or even exaggeratedly free of them, where the essential avoidance is of the genuine and effective biphasic involvement in the transference neurosis, with regard to fundamental and critical conflicts, and thus of the potential relinquishment of symptomatic solutions and the ultimate satisfactory separation from the analyst. Here, among other phenomena, there may be large-scale hiatuses in (biographically indicated) analytic material in the usual experiential sense; or there may be a striking absence of available and appropriate cues of connection with the transference; or failure of significant reaction to the pointing out of fleeting but vivid cues. In some instances, this complex of phenomena may repeat an original disturbance in "separation and individuation," to use Mahler's terminology (1965). Or other severe disturbances in early object relationships, or related pregenital (especially oral) conflicts, can have given rise to tenacious narcissistic avoidance of transference involvement, or to façade involvement, or to the alternative of inveterate regressed and ambivalent dependency. Dependable and largely affirmative secondary identifications have usually not been achieved originally; and this phenomenon, related to basic disturbances of separation, contributes importantly to the variously manifested fears of the transference.

Certainly, the phenomena of the two groups may overlap. There may indeed be deceptively benign "epineurosis" in the more severe group. In the troublesome phenomenon of "acting out," for example, one may deal with a relatively transitory resistance to an emergent transference fragment, in some instances due to delay of effective interpretation; or one may be confronted by a deep-seated, variably structuralized, and sometimes even ego-syntonic, "refusal" to accept the verbal mode of communication with an unresponsive transference parent in dealing with exigent and disturbing affects and impulses.

SOME REMARKS ON THE RELEVANCE OF STRUCTURAL AND TOPOGRAPHIC CONCEPTS

Whereas the ego and the Cs.-Pcs. (as a system) were once thought of as practically coextensive in their struggle with unruly instinctual strivings, the more refined observations of phenomena have clarified their essentially different natures and references (Freud, 1923; Arlow and Brenner, 1964). Conflict as such is now considered to exist largely between the psychic structures or elements within them. "Conscious," "preconscious," and "unconscious" are viewed principally as qualities, conditions, or states of certain psychic processes. However, it is possible that such undoubted advances have given structural concepts and their role in conflict and process a dominant position in psychoanalytic thought which tends to overshadow topographical considerations to a disadvantageous degree. For example, the merit of the psychoanalytic goal of ego change—let us say the abandonment or relative abandonment of a pathological defense, or the extension of ego control over certain elements in the id, or a revised relationship with the superego—cannot be questioned. However, the process of making all of the psychic components of such processes conscious is of the first importance; furthermore, the fact of persisting availability to consciousness, i.e., the preconscious state, is probably an important functional element in the relative permanence of ego change. It would seem that the topographic consideration is indispensable to the pursuit of the goal epitomized in Freud's aphorism: "Where id was, there ego shall be" (Freud, 1933, p. 80). The reason is, at least in part, quite clear. With consciousness comes access to the voluntary nervous system, thus the capacity for action, and thus the mobilization of special dangers inherent in certain gratifications, or the seeking for them.

Germane to this simple nuclear fact is the fact that the conscious wish in itself involves responsibility, and thus guilt of a more pervasive type than that involved in unconscious mechanisms. Everyday morality, religion, the law, give crucial significance to this distinction, which is still importantly related to the distinction between a person's "It" and his "I." However, this "I" would be more exactly the "self" rather than an objectively conceived structure, the ego. The person struggles, even consciously, to maintain freedom from the manifest subjective guilt that comes with full consciousness. "It's only a dream, after all!" However, in view of the subterranean but all-too-real life of the unconscious, where the wish is more thoroughly at one with its magical powers, he can rarely exculpate himself fully by this device—i.e., free himself from endogenous suffering—as society does exculpate him in the everyday sense. In the sense that speech, even in the psychoanalytic situation, is closer to action than is thought, that it is, indeed, the patient's only psychoanalytic "action," it is fraught with even greater guilt—or anxiety—than its precursor, conscious thought. Thus resistance does indeed have a special function in the relationship between the *Ucs.* and *Pcs.-Cs.* systems, and the process of change between them, even though this be anterior or precursive to the more radical process of lasting structural change. It is to avoid these subjective dangers in the transference—or anterior to the awareness of transference—from the patient's own superego, the original (now internalized) punitive parent. That the emergence may lead to new solutions is known to the analyst and (presumably and tentatively) to the adult portions of the patient's ego, but not necessarily to the intimidated child in the patient, a child who has, furthermore, never quite given up his ancient and original goals. Unless one views the ego resistance directed against the specific idea becoming conscious exclusively as an inborn tendency of ego function, one must look for its further meaning in a larger functional concept of resistance as a dynamism.

We must note the pathological instances of relative failure of structure formation, or reversible pathological regressions of structures, as in psychoses, exceeding those normally occurring in sleep, not to speak of the massive transitory revisions which may occur under the stresses of group dynamics (for example, riots, revolutions, wars, or regressive ideologies). One may therefore assume that, granted the primary constitutional endowment, the development of structures is in good part a sustained dynamic response to powerful dynamic elements in the human situation: to the prolonged biological helplessness of the human infant, and to the indispensable and germane environmental influences of kinship and the human family (Fries, 1946). Related to these factors are the evolution of the instinct life in practically exclusive relation to parents and siblings, before either executive capacities in this sphere or their acceptance by the adult environment are established (not to speak of the permanent barriers to incest and murder), and the complexly related (primary and secondary) struggles against separation. The mental capacity for permanent representations and the processes of identification—indeed internalization in general—facilitate (and in turn are perhaps to some degree derived from) structure formation. Certainly the earliest ego functions themselves include identification with the caretaking mother (Freud, 1923; Hartmann, Kris, and Loewenstein, 1946; Hendrick, 1951).

The original tendency of the infant organism is to react as a whole. The striving of the adult organism is to do the same. However, it can do so, or rather preserve the subjective illusion of doing so, only with the aid of an elaborate unconscious system, various compromise formations (ranging from dreams to well-marked symptoms or pathological character traits), and, paradoxically, through the operations of the underlying tripartite structural system. These structures and dynamisms respond, in their cooperation and conflict, to the need for a consistent sense of self, for a consistent sense of identity, which can at the same time permit survival, growth, and the likelihood of certain basic gratifications in external reality. The "principle of multiple function" formulated by Waelder (1930) is, in effect, a statement of the tendency to react as a total "self," in terms of already-established divisions within the mind. There is no need to postulate a basic and intrinsic antagonism between structures as such. The superego which can torture, even murder (or command the murder of), the self in melancholia can contribute to the calm of a "quiet conscience" in the healthy person, and facilitate his social adaptation. The ego which defends itself vigorously against persisting incestuous or destructive fantasies and impulses (lest the person himself be castrated or destroyed) facilitates and implements acceptable aggressive or sexual impulses. It is indeed indispensable for the external conveyance of "drive" in the human. As Hartmann has emphasized (1948), it replaces, with its myriad perceptive, adaptive, and conative capacities, the relative stereotypy of instinctual response in other animals. If the human infant is confronted with the special stimulations and frustrations, as well as the "privileges," attendant on its prolonged physical helplessness, and then the psychological extensions of the same state in the protective and hierarchical structure of the human family, the adult lives in a further modified elaboration of the same general milieu in one form or another, in the extended human community, especially his tribe or nation.

The earlier passing reference to sleep and the corresponding changes in the structures reminds us of certain quasi resemblances of elements in the psychoanalytic situation to those in sleep (see Lewin, 1954, 1955). In our present context we should note that, in the light of the latent transference, the obligatory character of free association tends, like the hypnotic command, to reduce energies invested in defense, or at least permits their reduction. Also, the inhibition of motor activity (although voluntarily assumed), the fact that the psychoanalytic work is in effect confined to "words," while not as "safe" as pure subjective visual imagery, does tend in itself to reduce the ordinary ego and superego resistances, as compared with their defense correlates in "everyday life." It may also give substance to another radically different form of resistance, which has been mentioned in the literature (Kaiser, 1934) but has not stimulated sufficient concern and thought, i.e., the separation of the analytic work from the processes and demands of everyday life and the consequent heightening of its regressive attraction for certain persons.

Both the restraints and conveniences of human social organization intensify the potential discreteness of structural development. However, as Waelder has emphasized (1960, p. 84), Freud himself was not at all inclined to the conceptual sharpness of demarcation which has sometimes been expressed. Apart from the question of interstructural "shading," the relatively direct connection between the presumed instinctual reservoir in the id and the severe aggressive activities of the superego in certain persons appears to outweigh, in its archaic power, the role of identification with actual parents in superego formation. An allied theoretical conception, less accessible empirically, would be the assumption that the energies of defense derive, at least in good part, from aggression (Hartmann, 1950, pp. 131ff.). In both instances, often clearly demonstrable with regard to the superego, the incipient aggressive responses evoked by parents would have been turned against the self or its instinctual strivings, in the interest of improved object relationships and adaptations.

In intense conflict, the antagonistic aspects of these groups of functions (i.e., the structures) do become conspicuous, and in extreme instances can overshadow the essential integrative tendency. Where such conflict arises in the infantile period, or in very early childhood, when both executive and adaptive capacities are few or nonexistent, the invocation of ego defenses leads to a species of structuralization of the conflict itself, due in part to sequestration and banishment from consciousness. It is certainly rendered largely inaccessible, by these mechanisms, to the direct modifications and influences of maturation, education, favorable experience, and allied phenomena. The development of neurotic symptoms or ego-syntonic character distortions permits the relative reestablishment of a consistent sense of self, of integrated voluntary behavior, in relative safety from attack or deprivation by parents or their intrapsychic representations. The adjective "relative" is important; for with the unconscious gratification afforded by symptoms, punishment is also sustained, thereby permitting the gratification. However, the investment of psychic representations, sometimes embodied in the subject's own person, rather than original objects, and above all the sequestration of the entire process from consciousness, permit the "relative safety" of which I have spoken. A crude parallel would be the self-reproaches, anxiety, or guilt connected with masturbation, with repressed incestuous fantasies, compared with the punishment envisaged for actual incest and parricide (see Freud, 1908, and Arlow, 1953). In more severe illnesses, such as melancholia, where the demands, reproaches, and latent violence toward the internalized primal mother are the issue, in intense and primitive energic terms, the penalty for the patient may indeed be his death.

The process of punishment, of course, includes the internalized image of the early parental disciplinarian, the superego, which, with the rarest of exceptions, remains an integral and indispensable part of human personality, an especially eloquent testimony to the irredentist struggle against separation as well as a unique mode of dealing with it. In this immediate context of our discussion, the emergence of ego-dystonic material is "resisted" by the infantile "experiencing" portion of the ego, in the relative materialization of speech (one of Freud's earliest conceptions of "transference": from unconscious [imagery] to preconscious [words] [1900, p. 562]), because of fear of superego punishment, anterior to the investment of the analyst with the superego functions. It is also resisted, to some degree by the entire ego, as disruptive to the conscious integrated sense of self and, secondarily, its narcissistic overevaluation as such. With this, in a more functional and objective sense yet related to the subjective sense of self, there is a "struggle" to maintain, against disorganizing intrusion, the economies of interstructural balance, i.e., the character, developed in accordance with the "principle of multiple function" (Waelder, 1930).

If we think of the long-term aspects of the psychoanalytic situation, expressed in structural concepts, in relation to the assumption (for me, the conviction) that the earliest relations with objects decisively influence both the qualitative and economic characteristics of psychic structures (evolving from the "givens" of constitution), we must assume the powerful impact of the transference on the activities of all three. Insofar as this impact permeates all details of process it is, of course, a critical and complicated influence in the general pattern of resistances. For while the patient's ego reacts to the analyst always, to varying degree, in terms of the perceived and immediate realities, these reactions also receive impetus from the sphere of regressed genetically early experience in object relationships. To the patient's id, the analyst is primarily an object—for love, aggression, and any of their nuances. In relation to the superego, he is a parental surrogate, eminently suitable for investment as an alternate, with potential punitive, disciplinary, or allied more temperate functions. Each plays its respective role in facilitating or impeding the psychoanalytic process, as traditionally recognized; and each is susceptible to modification by the mood and structure of the psychoanalytic situation and by its interpretive interventions. A priori, and probably in actual statistical incidence, the superego, the initiator of the sense of guilt, would seem readiest for such change. However, for reasons mentioned before (the relation to the patient's own reservoir of destructive aggression; later subsumed in Freud's more forbidding views of the negative therapeutic reaction [1920a, 1923]), this is not always achieved so readily as we would hope, or even expect, in the light of the identificatory aspects of superego origin. However, that prolonged "working through" does sometimes produce such modifications in ego or superego, when despair has almost supervened, impedes the ready acceptance of rigid etiological views of such phenomena, for example the role of the death instinct (see above). In general, we may say that the degree of structural plasticity and its responsiveness to involvement and analysis in the transference neurosis is one of the important elements in both the limitations and potentialities of genuine change occasioned by the psychoanalytic process.

THE RELATIONSHIP OF RESISTANCE TO TRANSFERENCE

Several decades ago Freud (1925, pp. 40–41) pointed out that everything said in the analytic situation must have some relation to the situation in which it is said. This is, of course, consistent not only with reflective common sense but also with the theory of transference, and the current view of the central position of the transference neurosis in analytic work. Furthermore, despite his earliest view of the "false connection" as pure resistance (Breuer and Freud, 1893–1895) and the continuing high estimation of this aspect of transference, Freud early established the (nonconflictual) positive transference as the analyst's chief ally against resistances. Thereafter he never stinted in his appreciation of the primitive driving power of the transference and its indispensable function of conferring a vivid and living sense of reality on the analytic process (Freud, 1912a, for example). In my own view, elaborated in past communications, the transference is indeed the central dynamism of the entire psychoanalytic situation; and the transference neurosis certainly provides the one framework which gives essential and accessible configuration to the potentially panpsychic scope of free association (Stone, 1961, 1966). In this frame of reference the irredentist drive to reunion with the primal mother, as opposed to the benign processes of maturation and separation, underlies neurotic conflict in its broadest sense, and is the basis of what I have called the "primordial transference" whose striving is toward renewed physical approximation or merger. Speech, which is the veritable stuff of psychoanalysis, serves as the chief "bridge" of mastery for the progressive somatic separations of earliest childhood. The "mature transference," in continuum, alternative and contrast, is that series and complex of attitudes, contingent on maturation and benign predisposing elements of early object relationships (conspicuously, the wish to be understood, to learn, and to be taught), which enable increasing somatic separation in a continuing affirmative context of object relationship, as later reflected in the psychoanalytic situation. In this interplay, speech—our essential working tool—plays an oscillating, curiously intermediate role, ranging from the threat of regression in the direction of its primitive oral substrate to its ultimately purely communicative-referential function, linked with insight (Stone, 1961, 1966).

In general, however, the origin of the "transference" as we usually perceive it clinically, and as the term is traditionally employed, is in the primordial transference. Be it essentially the classical triadic incestuous complex, or an oral drive toward incorporation, or toward permanent nursing dependency, or a sadomasochistic anal striving toward a parent, it will be re-experienced in the analytic situation, in good part in regressive response to its deprivations (Macalpine, 1950), and give rise to the central, and ultimately the most formidable, manifest resistance, the transference-resistance.

The "transference-resistance," while sometimes used in varying references, meant originally the resistance to effective insight into the genetic origins and prototypes of the transference, expressed in the very fact of its emergence (originally, the "false connection" described by Freud [Breuer and Freud, 1893–1895, especially pp. 302–303]). Thereafter, as the transference became established in its own autochthonous validity, the same resistance could be viewed as an obstruction to genetic understanding of the transference, and thus putatively to its dissolution. I say "putatively" because empirical experience has not often shown that simple awareness of such origins is adequate for the dissolution of the transference.[3] Rather, such dissolution (using this word in a relative and pragmatic sense) is contingent on much germane analytic work, on analysis of the dynamics of the attitude as represented in the transference neurosis, on working through, and on complicated and gradual responsive emotional processes in the patient (Stone, 1966). Nevertheless, this genuine genetic insight is indispensable for the demarcation of the transference from the real relationship, and for the intellectual incentive toward its dissolution within the framework of the therapeutic alliance.

Before going further, we should comment on the intimately related (although apparently opposite) "resistance to the awareness of transference." While there are patients whose confrontation with the analyst is characterized

---

[3] This experience began to assert itself quite early: See Freud (Breuer and Freud, 1893–1895, p. 303): "Strangely enough, the patient is deceived afresh every time this is repeated."

by the immediate emergence of intense (even stormy) transference reactions, most patients experience these emergent attitudes as essentially ego dystonic, except in the sense of the attenuated derivatives which enter into (or vitiate) the therapeutic alliance, or in the sense of chronic characterological reactions which would appear in other parallel situations, however superficial and approximate the parallels might be.

The clinical actualities of emergent transference require analysis in its usual technical sense, including the prior analysis of defense. Transference may appear in dreams long before it is emotionally manifest; in parapraxes, in symptomatic reactions, in acting out within the analytic situation, or—most formidably—in acting out in the patient's essential life situation. Except in cases of dangerous acting out, or very intense anxiety or equivalent symptoms, which can constitute emergencies, the technical approach involves the same patient centripetal address to the surface that is prescribed for analysis in general. However, in this connection, I would suggest a modification of the classical precept that one does not interpret the transference until it becomes a manifest resistance. At that point, the interpretation is obligatory. The resistance to awareness should be interpreted, and its content brought to awareness, as soon as the analyst believes that the libidinal or aggressive investment of the analyst's person is economically a sufficient reality to be influencing the dynamics of the analytic situation and/or the patient's everyday life situation.

It is useful to strip the matter of nuances, reservations, and exceptions, for the purpose of clarity in an essential direction. The avoidance of awareness of transference derives from all of the hazards that accompany consciousness: accessibility of the voluntary nervous system, hence heightened "temptation" to action; heightened conflict in relation to the sanctions and satisfactions of impulse materialization; the multiple subjective dangers of communication of "I-you" impulses and wishes, or germane fears, to an object invested with parental authority; the heightened sense of responsibility (thus guilt) connected with the same complex; and, very far from least, the fear of direct humiliating disappointment—the narcissistic wound of rejection or, perhaps worst of all, *no* affective response at all from the analyst. In "acting out," sometimes so destructive in the patient's life situation, amid a great range of important determinants, this need for response, the avoidance of this particular helplessness of impact, plays an important part. There is also the exceeedingly important fact that the transference conflicts remaining outside awareness retain their unique access to autoplastic symptomatic expression, in compact and narcissistically omnipotent, if painful, solution, without the direct challenge and confrontation with alternative (and essentially "hopeless") solutions.

Why, then, if such fears weigh heavily against the analytic effort and the ultimate therapeutic advantages of awareness, does the patient cling tenaciously to his view of the analyst and the system of wishes connected with this view, once it has become established in his consciousness? In the earliest view, where the cognitive elements in analysis were heavily preponderant, not only in technique but in the understanding of process, such clinging to transference attitudes was thought to be, as our traditional term implies, a resistance to recall (or reconstruction) as such, since the latter was indeed the essential goal of the analytic effort and was thought to be, in itself, the essential therapeutic mechanism. But why is the patient not willing, like the historian Lecky's dinner partner, to "let bygones be bygones"? Unless one accepts this aversion to recall or reconstruction, a preference for "present pain," as a primary built-in aversion, in itself an unexplained fact of "human nature," one must look further. In my view, the situation is more nearly the reverse. The patient rejects these elements of "insight" because they vitiate or diminish both the affective and cognitive significance of this central object relationship, which is a current materialization of crucial unconscious wish and fantasy, hitherto warded off. If it is to be given up, why was it pried out of its secure nest in the unconscious? Such resolution is always felt, at least incidentally, as an attack on the patient's narcissism, and on his secure sense of self, secondarily re-established. Moreover, to the extent that there is a genuine translation of the subjectively experienced somatic drive elements into verbal and ideational terms related to past objects, there is an inevitable step toward separation from the current object which parallels the original and corresponding developmental movement.

An essential dynamic difference from the past lies in the different somatic and psychological context in which the renewed struggle is fought. Old desires, old hatreds, old irredentist urges toward mastery, have been reawakened in a mature and resourceful adult, in certain spheres still helpless subjectively, but no longer literally and objectively, a fact of which he is also aware. It was pointed out by Freud (1910a, p. 53) that this great quantitative discrepancy between infant conflict and adult resources makes possible and facilitates therapeutic change, through insight. In many important respects, this remains true. However, the remorseless dialectic of psychoanalysis again asserts itself. Truly effective insight requires validating emotional experience, which is only rarely achieved through recollection alone. The affective realities of the transference neurosis are necessary (sometimes inevitable!); and with this experience comes the renewal of the ancient struggle, in which, with varying degrees of depth, the maturity and resources of the analysand often play a role at variance with his capacity for understanding.[4] This is true not only of the subjective quality and experience of his strivings but of the resources which support his resistances, in either phase of the transference involvement. Whether the wish be to seduce, to cling, to defeat and humiliate, to spite, or to win love, mature resources of mind—sometimes of body!—may be invoked to implement this purpose, including what in some instances may be an uncanny intuitiveness regarding the analyst's personal traits, especially his vulnerabilities.

The persistence of old desires for gratification and the urge to consummate them, or indeed the urge to restore and maintain an original relationship with an omnipotent (and omniscient) parent, are intelligible to everyday modes of

---

[4] See Freud's quotation from Diderot, which is indirectly, but nonetheless pointedly, relevant to this idea (Freud, 1917a, pp. 337–338).

thought. That the transference, like the neurosis itself, may also entail guilt, anxiety, frustration, disappointment, and narcissistic hurt is another matter. If it gives
so much trouble, why does it reappear? The latter-day explanation of Freud involved the complex general theory of primary masochism, and the repetition
compulsion. One cannot, in a brief discussion, enter into disputation which has
already occasioned voluminous writing. In ultimate condensation, the operational
view to which I adhere is that all painful elements may be understood as: (1)
accompanying the renewed unregenerate drive for gratification of hitherto
warded-off wishes, whether libidinal or aggressive, based on the presentation of
an actual object who bears significant functional "resemblances" to the indispensable parent of early childhood, in a climate and structure of instinctual
abstinence; and/or (2) based on the latent alternative urge to understand, assimilate, perhaps alter parental response, or otherwise to master poignantly painful situations as they were actually experienced in a state of relative helplessness
in the past. Both may be viewed as independent of adult motivations, although
the power of the first may at times importantly subserve such motivations, and
the second may often be phenomenologically congruent with them. Implicit in
both, in contrast with the experiential plasticities and varieties of mature ego development, is the persistent and continuous theme of adhesion to the psychic
representation of the decisive original parent figure or a perceptually variant
substitute. Inasmuch as I have stated my conviction that the fractional but profoundly important struggle against original separation from the primal mother,
with its potential phase specifications, as opposed to the powerful urges toward
independent development, provides the underlying basis for developmental, and
later neurotic, conflict, I must observe that these conflicting tendencies, in the
sense of the profundity which I assign to them, provide a certain parallel to the
Thanatos-Eros struggle which assumed a decisive role in Freud's final contributions. In a recent study of aggression (Stone, 1971), I have examined Freud's
views on this subject. While—in seeming paradox—I find the existence of a
profound "alternative" impulse to die at least conceptually tenable and susceptible to clinical inferential support, it is my conviction, from both observation and
inference, that aggression as such is an essentially instrumental phenomenon (or
cluster of phenomena) capable of serving self-preservative and sexual impulses
alike, and that it is thus, in its original forms, pitted against a postulated latent
impulse to die, as it is against external threats to life. These urges and instru-
mentalities find primal organismic expression and experience in the phenomenon of birth and the immediate neonatal period, the biological prototype of all
subsequent specifications, elaborations, and transmutations of the experience of
separation. At the very outset the "conflict" may find expression in the delay of
breathing or, shortly thereafter, in the disinclination to suck. There is thus an
intertwining of the two conceptions of basic conflict. It may be that time will
validate Freud's latter-day views of the fundaments of human conflict. For the
time being, however, I can only adhere to and present what I believe to be an
empirically more accessible and a heuristically more useful view of the ultimate
human intrapsychic struggle. Thus the originally unmastered or regressively reac-

tivated struggle around separation, revived by developmental conflict, would in this schema represent the "bedrock" of ultimate resistances, although never—at least in theory—utterly and finally insusceptible to influence. If we assume that the vicissitudes of object relationships, initiated by the special relationship of the human infant to his family, are fundamental in the accessible processes of personality (thus, structural) development and thus of neuroses, and that, in "mirror image," the transference and thus the transference-resistance have a comparable strategic position in the psychoanalytic process, can we extend these assumptions into the detailed technical phenomenology of process resistance in its endless variety of expressions? I believe that this extension is altogether valid.

We may first, however, devote a brief detour to certain important phenomena of personality integration. The latter include the relative consistencies of character and identity and, further, the hard-won sense of optimal effectiveness in adaptation and drive gratification, in the light of available modes of spontaneous conflict solution, deriving from what we may call the established "parts" of the personality. The continuing and actual biological unity of the self, the psychological principle of "multiple function," and the postulated role of the libido in maintaining syntheses (Freud, 1920a; Nunberg, 1930) are objectively conceived elements in the tenacity of established personality manifestations. These in themselves pose a conservative obstacle to change. There is indubitably a "sparing of psychic energy" involved in fixed, relatively structuralized modes of reaction. Far from minimal in invoking struggle against incipient or "threatened" change is the inevitable and essentially healthy narcissistic investment in the secondary neurotic "self."

Furthermore, whether or not one thinks of it as "motivation" in its usual sense, one can without extravagance postulate an even more intense cohesiveness at the first signal of that stimulus which contributed to the establishment of the organization and its basic strategies in the first place, i.e., the analyst as transference object. In the subjective sense, the regressive trend of the transference, stimulated by the total structure of the psychoanalytic situation (i.e., the basic rule of free association, and the systematic deprivations of the personal relationship), confronts the patient with one who is perceived ultimately as his first and all-important object, the prototypical source of all gratification, all deprivation, all rejection, all punishment—the object involved in the primordial serial experiences of separation (Stone, 1961). This may seem an exaggeratedly magniloquent way to view a practitioner who sits in an armchair, listens, tries to understand, and then interprets, when he can, toward a therapeutic end. To a large portion of the adult patient's personality, the "observing" portion of his ego, the portion that enters into the therapeutic alliance, that is just what he is and what he should remain. To another portion, largely unchanged from its past, sequestered in the unconscious, but powerfully influential albeit in derivative and indirect ways, he is indeed a formidable object. It is in this field of force that, along with the drive toward better solutions, the range of clinical transferences as we know them is awakened. I have already mentioned that, in a broad sense, the entire effort to translate the patient's view of drives for reunion and contact, whether libidinal or aggressive, into genuine language, insight, and voluntary control (or appropriate conative implementation elsewhere) is "resisted," as it was originally, as an expression (or at least precursor) of separation, thus repeating aspects of the original developmental conflict. It is, however, also true that the later and clinically more accessible vicissitudes of childhood create more accessible resistances, within the postulated metapsychological context created by the infant-mother relationship just described. I refer to those patients in whom the phenomena of general bodily unity or approximation have been largely renounced, not only as physical *faits accompli,* in perceptual and linguistic fact, but in terms of deployment of cathexis among other essential intrapsychic representations. Such changes remain subject to regression, or to the primary investment of certain phase strivings, conspicuously the Oedipus complex, in excessive libidinal or aggressive cathexis. Such strivings, paradigmatically the incest complex, are in themselves the narrowed, potentially adaptive, maturational expressions of the basic conflict aroused by separation. If the analyst is, to this infantile portion of the patient's personality, an indispensable parent because cognition is, in this reference, subordinate to drive, it follows that the analyst becomes the central object in the complicated infant system of desires, needs, and fears which have hitherto been incorporated in symptoms and character distortions. The patient must, furthermore, tell these "secrets" to the very object of a complex of disturbing impulses. This is a new vicissitude, not usually encountered in childhood, indeed guarded against, even within the patient's own personality, by the very existence of the unconscious. Ordinarily he does not even have to "tell himself" about them, in the sense that he is to a considerable degree identified with his parents, originally in his ego, then, in a punitive or disciplinary sense, in his superego. To be sure, the adult "observing" portion of his personality, except where matters of adult guilt, embarrassment, or shame interfere, usually cooperates with the analyst. It can at least try to maintain the flow of derivative associations, which provide the analyst with material for informed inferences. The tolerant and accepting attitude of the analyst, tested by all of the patient's rational and intuitive capacities, even more decisively his interpretative activity, which suggests to the unredeemed child in the patient that he "knows (or at least surmises) already," gradually overcome the patient's fear of his own warded-off material, and finally the fear of its frank expression.

There are, then, three broad aspects of the relationship between resistance and transference. Assuming technical adequacy, the proportional importance of each one will vary with the individual patient, especially with the depth of psychopathology. First, the resistance to awareness of the transference, and its subjective elaboration in the transference neurosis. Second, the resistance to the dynamic and genetic reductions of the transference neurosis, and ultimately the transference attachment itself, once established in awareness. Third, the transference presentation of the analyst to the "experiencing" portion of the patient's ego, as id object and as externalized superego simultaneously, in juxtaposition to the therapeutic alliance between the analyst in his real function and the rational "observing" portion of the patient's ego. These phenomena give intelligible dynamic meaning to resistances ordinarily observed in the cognitive-communicative aspects of the analytic process. These are the process or "tactical" resistances, largely deriving from the ego under the pressure or threat of the superego.

In this connection, a word about "working through." Sometimes, as Freud (1914) mentioned, there is yielding of the structure only when a peak manifestation of resistance has apparently been achieved. The patient appears to require time, repetition, and a sort of increasing familiarity with the forces involved, for real change to occur. Also, Freud originally thought of the energy transactions as having some relation to the phenomenon of abreaction in the earlier methods. One is indeed impressed with the insistent recurrence of transference affects, conspicuously irrational anger in essentially rational patients, as though the structuralized tendency from which they derive can give way only on the basis of repetitive re-enactment and gradual reduction of affect. Insofar as circumscribed symptom formations, or equivalent forms of neurotic suffering (and gratification), play an ongoing and inevitable economic role in the psychoanalytic situation and process, apart from usually having been the basis for its initiation, one might assume that they bear an important relationship to working through. Even when extinguished for shorter or longer periods under the influence of the transference, their continued latent existence (or potentiality) is opposed to the vicissitudes of the current transference neurosis, or its gradual relinquishment via working through. This is true whether one thinks of the symptom in the quasi-neurophysiological sense of Breuer's early formulation of pathways of "lowered resistance" (Breuer and Freud, 1893–1895), or in a more empirical sense, as a perennially seductive regressive condensation of impulse, gratification, and punishment. A useful and well-grounded concept, allied to the struggle against separation, is the relationship of working through to the process of mourning (Freud, 1917b). (See also Greenson's [1965] comprehensive paper, with references to several other authors.)

While from the adult point of view the gratifications may be small and the suffering great, the symptom is nevertheless autoplastic, narcissistic in an isolated sense, already structuralized, and subject to no outside interference (except by the analysis!), an expression of localized infantile omnipotent fantasy, however large or small this fantasy kingdom may be. By the same token, in the sense mentioned earlier, with regard to unconscious processes in general, the symptom affords protection from both the challenges and sanctions of the world of reality, and from the temporary disruptive intrusions of new elements into the narcissistically invested conscious personality organization. In working through, there is the biphasic and arduous problem of restoring original or potential object cathexes in the transference neurosis, reducing their pathological intensities or distortions, and then deploying them in relation to the outer world. One may thus think of "working through" as opposed to the renewal of symptom formation, as repeating some of the postulated vicissitudes of one of the earliest conceptions of "transference," the infantile transition from autoerotism to object love (Ferenczi, 1909). In this sense, the clinging to the incestuous object, represented in the clinical transference, would represent an intermediate process.

There is thus a tenacious reluctance to bow to the threat of the "quiet voice" of the intellect which, with the cooperation of the "observing" ego, might seduce the involved portion from its inveterate clinging to the actual transference object or to its autoplastically equivalent symptomatic representations. The postulated two portions of the ego (Freud, 1940b, [with earlier adumbrations]; Sterba, 1934, in different references) are, after all, "of the same blood," to put it mildly, and the urge to reunion in integrated function, the libidinal (synthetic) bond, is indeed strong. This same affinity between ego divisions may, of course, take an opposite and adverse turn, a triumph of the "resistance." I refer to those instances of chronic severe transference regression, where the adult segment of the ego is "pulled down" with the other, and remains recalcitrant to interpretative effort (Freud, 1940a). While this is, of course, often contingent on the depth of manifest or latent illness, it may be facilitated by iatrogenic factors, such as excessive and superfluous deprivations in inappropriate and essentially irrelevant spheres. With these considerations, of whose importance I am increasingly convinced with the passage of time, I have dealt at length in the past (Stone, 1961, 1966).

A WORD ABOUT CERTAIN SPECIAL SOURCES OF RESISTANCE

It is important to mention, even if briefly, that certain special factors, sometimes extrinsic to analysis as such, may indefinitely prolong apparently satisfactory analyses. Real guilt, for example, may not be faced. Emotional distress based on real-life problems may not be confronted and accepted as such. A person of the type described by Freud (1916) as an "exception," who feels himself to have been abused by Fate, even if in other respects not more ill than others may consciously or unconsciously reject the psychoanalytic discipline or the instinctual renunciations derived from its insights. Fixed and unpromising life situations, or organic incapacities, may permit so little current or anticipated gratification that the attractiveness of the regressive, aim-inhibited analytic relationship is strong in comparison to the barrenness of the extra-analytic situation. The last general consideration is, of course, always an essential (if silent) constituent of the psychoanalytic field of force, especially in relation to the dissolution of the transference-resistance (Stone, 1966, p. 34). Or, more accessibly, the "rules of procedure" of analysis itself may be consciously or unconsciously exploited by the patient. He may, in "obedience" to a traditional rule, delay certain decisions to the point of absurdity, invoking the analytic work in support of his neurosis and sometimes in contempt of important obligations in real life. Financial support of the analysis by someone other than the analysand can provide a basis for chronic, concealed "acting out." In general, the analysis itself can, on occasion, become a lever for subtle evasion of the obligations, vicissitudes, and contingent gratifications of everyday life, and thus, paradoxically, become a resistance to its own essential goals and purposes. It may indeed become too much like the dream, to which it bears certain dynamic resemblances (Lewin, 1954, 1955). The analyst's perceptive and tactfully illuminating obligation is no less important in these spheres than in other sectors of his commitment.

A FEW WORDS ABOUT EGO-SYNTONIC RESISTANCES

Where resistance is a sustained conscious rebellion against the authority and methods of the analyst, or a fear or mistrust of him in reality, or appears as another full-blown interpersonal difficulty of the same order (assuming, of course, that there is no basis for such attitudes in reality), we are dealing with a special category of resistance, based on early disorders of object relationships and germane character problems, which may require long-term preanalytic preparatory work, or may, indeed, make actual analytic work impossible. That such phenomena may occur in the usual period of preliminary interpersonal testing, or episodically, with transference crises, in many patients, is well-known; the phenomena remain in the sphere of technical skill and personal resourcefulness, including its emotional components.

In such ego-syntonic "resistances" the patient is, in a subjective sense, really defending himself against a seducer, a deceiver, a cruel or punitive or unloving parent—ultimately and unequivocally, one who will, in the end, certainly put him aside. He fears to tell him his secrets, and he fears even more deeply to become emotionally involved with him. These, and his secondary fears of the objective process components, are not essentially different in a qualitative sense from the unconscious, largely ego-dystonic resistances of the more mature and cooperative patient, who is capable of the twofold (ostensibly "split") ego reaction which is indispensable to analytic work. The critical economic difference lies in the fact that the participation of the more difficult patient's ego in object relationships is controlled by his transferences in a total and unitary sense; sometimes even his autonomous perceptual functions are subordinated to them, in critical references and junctures. Certainly, unless and until the patient's personality undergoes certain necessary preliminary changes—pre-eminently some degree of benign identification with the analyst, which permits a therapeutic alliance, with some distance from and conflict with, his infantile self—the challenge of placing in hazard the personality integrations so painfully established in dealing with the analyst's prototypes in the past cannot even be seriously entertained. It is really in the sphere of intrapsychic conflict that the phenomena which we usually have in mind in speaking of "resistances" come into play, although never entirely unrelated to the primitive and unhappy paradigm to which I have just referred. All human beings have inevitably experienced some degree of deception, desertion, and rejection at the hands of their parents, at least subjectively; fortunately, most have also experienced love, protection, and understanding to a degree which permits or facilitates affirmative development. In the patient more suitable for analysis in the primary sense (with regard to the above referent, not traditional nosological considerations), the analyst is largely and firmly accepted in his actual functions, however tinged this acceptance may be by derivatives of repressed transferences.

One may legitimately ask, in response to this generally gloomy disquisition on one major force in the analytic process: Where is the other side, the will to recovery? the forces which support it? the patient's adult personality? the therapeutic alliance? the upward thrust from the id? and other attitudes and processes of an affirmative dynamic thrust? These are, of course, what makes psychoanalysis a therapy instead of a bitter struggle between patient and analyst. We have been speaking of the resistance, the force which is manifestly inimical to the analytic process, although based on an integral and essential element in human personality. Furthermore, we must note that even this dynamism, apart from its indigenous and integral functional dignity, has, like the skin, muscle, and fascia which oppose the surgeon, its affirmative aspect, even within the scope of psychoanalytic process.

SOME AFFIRMATIVE ASPECTS OF RESISTANCE

Even if we put aside adult and rational "resistances" such as intellectual skepticism and critique, the phenomena of resistance are largely if not exclusively of self-protective, conservative orientation. That their purposes are usually irrational in derivation, and largely ego dystonic, renders them amenable to analytic work. It must be recalled that they exist, in a subjectively purposive sense, to protect the encapsulated unconscious aspects of the personality, and, reciprocally, to protect the adult functioning personality syntheses from the potentially disruptive intrusions and demands of hitherto unconscious content. I mentioned earlier the "blood brotherhood" of the adult "observing" ego and the regression-prone "experiencing ego." Thus the resistance can arise just as importantly, although from subtly variant or even opposite motivation, from the "rational" ego as from its more thoroughly infantile counterpart, i.e., from the dread of its own regression. We all know the deceptively stilted "ultrarealistic" reactions and communications of the ego which doubts its own strength and reliability. If I may be permitted a brief obiter dictum: It is my conviction that this "blood kinship" between the two portions of the ego is an important factor both in the economic limitations of analytic cure in many instances and in its potentiation in others, where the "threat" (based on corresponding vicissitudes of development) is less severe. Unfortunately, analysis cannot actually repeat development, nor can it "imitate" it too closely without serious trouble. Where the economic problem is not too severe for the potentialities of the psychoanalytic situation, there is the opportunity for the two ego sectors to come to terms, in their respective modes, with the id and with the superego, and thus with one another. In this event, the synthetic function of the ego can be restored to its primary place in the personality, as differentiated from the driven need for symptom formation.

In another direction: We are both intuitively and rationally skeptical, sometimes alarmed, about the patient who appears to show no "ordinary" resistances early in the analytic work. We suspect a serious lack of firm organization in his personality. Why does he seem to have no amnesias for early experiences; why does his transference fulminate in ego-syntonic form? We fear that impossible symbiotic fantasies, demands, and impulses will appear—or the psychotic defenses of delusion and hallucination. Such unhappy developments are not, of course, inevitable; but it is, by common agreement, sound practice to be alert to their possibility. There is, to be sure, a disturbing cognitive deficit in a person who wholeheartedly develops prompt, violent, and inappropriate attitudes toward a person whom he hardly knows. But apart from this important observation, we expect a personality to be integrated, to be "stuck together," whether with the libidinal glue of the ego's synthetic function, metapsychologically considered, or on the basis of other functional tendencies such as the economies of structuralization, or from more explicitly narcissistic motivations, or the anxieties and natural guardedness against change which derive from these considerations. The current folk phrases—"coming apart," "falling apart," and, in contrast, "well put together"—are not without their intuitive perceptiveness.

The resistances, insofar as they assume essentially intrapsychic form, i.e., if a viable therapeutic alliance has been established, oppose themselves to the suggestibility deriving from the positive transference (see Freud, 1917a, p. 453). The resistances permit, indeed require, the testing of the analyst, both as to his perceptive and interpretative skill and as to his actual personal reliability, including latent countertransferences. They support—to some degree express—the healthy aspects of the "I'm from Missouri" reaction, as well as its impeding effect. In the same sense, they pace the development of the transference neurosis, according to the personality's intuitively perceived ability to sustain it and to bring it to a more satisfactory resolution than that of the antecedent infantile neurosis. It would seem productive that the affirmative functional aspects of the resistances be appreciated by the analyst, and also their contingency on his general traits and methods beyond the ad hoc accuracy of his interpretations. The same is true of the structure and mood of the psychoanalytic situation, whether in its individual nuances or in its basic elements. To put this last in more blunt terms: The dissolution of resistances is as much an affective as an interpretative-cognitive process. Every interpretation, in fact—in content, mood, and timing—impinges on both spheres in the patient. This was, in effect, recognized even by such a die-hard "resistance analyst" as Kaiser (1934). It was recognized by Freud from the earliest period of his work onward. The positive transference, in its nonconflictual sense, can render a seemingly accusatory or irrelevant interpretation acceptable, at least for serious consideration. There are patients for whom the psychoanalytic situation in its basic essentials is intolerable, and others for whom a changed nuance of mood and method can permit or restore its viability and usefulness (Stone, 1961). The quality of the resistance may announce either one to the analyst.

And now for some concluding remarks, without the expedient of orderly recapitulation. Resistance, whether practically or conceptually considered, is not really identical with defense, although intimately related to it. This fact was emphasized by Jacobson in a recent panel discussion (1968). In the ultimate "showdown" in relation to an established transference, a resistance may be practically coextensive with a major defense, for example in relation to a powerful instinctual impulse. However, anterior to this confrontation, it may strongly interfere with the analyst's first efforts to make the patient aware that a given trait or process *is* indeed a defense. For example, a patient who deals with powerful sadistic impulses by reaction formation, especially if the latter is an integral part of his character and thus of his adult sense of self, will struggle with all his resources against the awareness that his exaggerated pity or solicitude is not exclusively motivated by love or compassion, however tactful the analyst's approach may be. Resistance is a dynamism specifically directed against the psychoanalytic process and its goals. This process, to be sure, seeks to reactivate, reconstruct, or recall many important factors in personal development, as a necessary step toward potential affirmative change, but by way of a specific method and in a special and highly disciplined context. It cannot actually recapitulate development; it is at best neodevelopmental, in a partial and special sense.

The first—and continuing—struggle of the patient is to maintain personality cohesion and narcissistic pleasure in the self, in the specifications mentioned earlier. With this struggle, related to it from the the beginning but conceptually separate, and ultimately of more profound dynamic significance, is the struggle to avoid the awareness of basic infantile conflict in a new and powerfully dynamic interpersonal context. The functional significance of awareness as such, anterior to "working through," and in recent years overshadowed theoretically by the ultimate importance of structural change in therapy, is not to be underestimated in the genesis of process resistances. Implicit in the attainment of all technical aims, and intrinsic in the nature and dynamics of the psychoanalytic situation, is the tendency toward the development of the transference neurosis, which occasions, in varying proportions, a hingelike process of resistance: avoidance of effective involvement in the relationship, and—ultimately—the avoidance of its resolution in separation. In this sense, the analyst is from the beginning experienced as a threat by the infantile aspect of the ego—and in some instances even by the relatively more mature sectors. To hide from him, in this sense, is like the hiding of the hurt and mistrustful child from a deceitful and treacherous parent. Not only may the essential methods of analysis (free association, for traditional example) be the targets of resistance, but also its intermediate and larger goals. The latter resistances, for example the concealed avoidance of important issues, are in the strategic sphere, the resistances of choice in more severe disorders. It is an important fact, however, that resistances originating in the general personality motives and tendencies described earlier, and implemented by any of the adult personality's deficits or resources—from new symptom formation to highly developed autonomous ego functions—may find expression in *any* of the broadly conceived areas of psychoanalytic process and goals.

Whatever form or direction the resistance takes, it interferes actively or by default in the broad, inclusive, and complex operational synthesis of effective analytic work. In a remote but real functional sense, this complex synthesis corresponds to the very organization of personality which "the resistance" seeks to defend. At the heart of this synthesis are, of course, the analytic situation and process as such, with intrinsic dialectic, balance, and integration of past and present, thought and feeling, communication and resistance in free association, transference and reality, the analyst's interventions and the immediate or remote responses to them. Inextricably interrelated with this complex is the patient's

everyday reality: the obligations, gratifications, sufferings, limitations, and potentialities inherent in his life situation and its dramatis personae, including the
roles of these persons in reality and as conscripted participants in the transference
neurosis. These inevitably present the requirements for confrontation with important realities and for dealing with them as such: the exertion of sheer will,
effort, and endurance, where necessary, and the continuing acceptance of legitimate personal responsibilities. The latter considerations, to be sure, also obtain
within the scope of the analysis proper. The chronic passive expectation of ultimate magical intervention by the analyst can disqualify the most richly productive
analytic process.

It is the synthesis and continuum of these briefly sketched and merging
components of psychoanalytic field and process, in its larger sense, against which
the resistances in general are directed. For it is the synthesis which confers ultimate life and meaning on individual components, and facilitates the integrations
of cognitive and emotional experience which are most effective in analytic change.
This synthesis finds its accessible epitome in the analysis of the genetically
determined transference neurosis (and its extra-analytic ramifications) (Stone,
1966). Exterior to specific correlation with certain characteristic defenses, resistances will in general be motivated by the dynamics of transference, personality
cohesion, structural conflict, and other factors which have been described, always in the light (or darkness) of the ubiquitous topographic consideration.
However, the mode and the site of operation of resistances will derive not only
from habitual defensive and characterological tendencies, but from the patient's
autonomous ego functions, even specific gifts or specific lacks, in interaction
with the routine requirements and procedures of psychoanalytic work, the individual qualities of the immediate psychoanalytic situation, and—not seldom
—the personal traits and interests of the analyst, including, of course, his interpretive style, his countertransferences and his counterresistances. Verbal fluency, scholarship, "psychological giftedness," talents as a raconteur, real or
spurious obtuseness, dialectical superiority, and myriad other possible endow-
ments (or lack of them) can be employed by the patient in the maintenance of the
status quo.

An essential problem for the analyst, apart from the demonstrable process
phenomena, is to become aware of what is omitted, hidden, or kept from asserting its genuine proportions. Comparable to the holistic scope of the analytic
process and the analytic view of personality, the patient's involvement in analysis
is in relation to all of his life activities, past and current. We assume that this fact
is reflected in what I have called the "panpsychic scope" of his associations,
shaped to ultimate meaningfulness by his transference neurosis (Stone, 1961, p.
77). However, we can only be truly aware of the gaps and distortions in the
communications of our single informant by keeping in mind not only the chal-
lenging and taxing details of analytic material, but the larger biographical background of the patient, his consistencies (and inconsistencies) of character, his
system of current relationships and activities, his talents and sublimations, and his
modes of symptomatic solution, to which the details of analytic data and process

are always intimately related. For the patient may often, in his larger strategies of resistance, tend to repeat both the exaggerated affirmations and the evasions or concealments which have characterized his life history. If we cannot, as Freud (1937) pointed out, artificially mobilize a transference conflict which is dormant in the patient's life context, we may at times, by tactful interpretive address to its analytic "absence," and in an affective climate which permits the patient to accept a second confrontation, to some degree mobilize a conflict which is indeed active but, because of archaic dread of the transference, moving toward delayed but severe symptomatic solution or unhappy large-scale materialization in the patient's everyday life (Stone, 1966).

REFERENCES

Arlow, J. A. (1953). Masturbation and Symptom Formation. *Journal of the American Psychoanalytic Association,* 1:45–58.

———, and Brenner, C. (1964). *Psychoanalytic Concepts and the Structural Theory.* New York: International Universities Press.

Breuer, J., and Freud, S. (1893–1895). Studies on Hysteria. *Standard Edition,* 2. London: Hogarth Press, 1955.

Fenichel, O. (1941). *Problems of Psychoanalytic Technique.* Albany, N.Y.: The Psychoanalytic Quarterly.

Ferenczi, S. (1909). Introjection and Transference. In: *Sex in Psycho-Analysis and* (with O. Rank) *The Development of Psycho-Analysis.* New York: Dover, 1956, pp. 30–79.

——— (1919). Technical Difficulties in the Analysis of a Case of Hysteria. In: *Further Contributions to the Theory and Technique of Psycho-Analysis.* London: Hogarth Press, 1926, pp. 189–197.

——— (1920). The Further Development of an Active Therapy in Psycho-Analysis. In: *Further Contributions to the Theory and Technique of Psycho-Analysis.* London: Hogarth Press, 1926, pp. 198–216.

——— (1930). The Principle of Relaxation and Neo-catharsis. *International Journal of Psycho-Analysis,* 11:428–443.

——— (1931). Child Analysis in the Analysis of Adults. In: *Final Contributions to the Problems and Methods of Psycho-Analysis.* London: Hogarth Press, 1955, pp. 126–142.

——— (1932). Confusion of Tongues between the Adult and the Child. (The Language of Tenderness and of Passion.) *International Journal of Psycho-Analysis,* 13:225–230, 1949.

———, and Rank, O. (1925). *The Development of Psychoanalysis.* New York and Washington: Nervous and Mental Disease Publishing Co.

Freud, A. (1936). *The Ego and the Mechanisms of Defence.* New York: International Universities Press, 1946.

——— (1968). *Difficulties in the Path of Psychoanalysis: A Confrontation of Past with Present Viewpoints.* New York: International Universities Press, 1969.

Freud, S. (1900). The Interpretation of Dreams. *Standard Edition,* 4 & 5. London: Hogarth Press, 1953.

——— (1905). Fragment of an Analysis of a Case of Hysteria. *Standard Edition,* 7:7–122. London: Hogarth Press, 1953.

——— (1908). Hysterical Phantasies and Their Relation to Bisexuality. *Standard Edition,* 9:155–166. London: Hogarth Press, 1959.

——— (1910a). Five Lectures on Psycho-Analysis. Fifth Lecture. *Standard Edition,* 11:49–55. London: Hogarth Press, 1957.

———— (1910b). The Future Prospects of Psycho-Analytic Therapy. *Standard Edition*, 11:139–151. London: Hogarth Press, 1957.

———— (1912a). The Dynamics of Transference. *Standard Edition*, 12:97–108. London: Hogarth Press, 1958.

———— (1912b). Recommendations to Physicians Practising Psycho-Analysis. *Standard Edition*, 12:109–171. London: Hogarth Press, 1958.

———— (1914). Remembering, Repeating and Working Through. (Further Recommendations on the Technique of Psycho-Analysis II.) *Standard Edition*, 12:145–156. London: Hogarth Press, 1958.

———— (1916). Some Character Types Met with in Psycho-Analytic Work. *Standard Edition*, 14:309–333. London: Hogarth Press, 1957.

———— (1917a). Introductory Lectures on Psycho-Analysis. Part III. *Standard Edition*, 16. London: Hogarth Press, 1963.

———— (1917b). Mourning and Melancholia. *Standard Edition*, 14:237–258. London: Hogarth Press, 1957.

———— (1918). From the History of an Infantile Neurosis. *Standard Edition*, 17:1–122. London: Hogarth Press, 1955.

———— (1919). Lines of Advance in Psycho-Analytic Therapy. *Standard Edition*, 17:157–168. London: Hogarth Press, 1955.

———— (1920a). Beyond the Pleasure Principle. *Standard Edition*, 18:7–64. London: Hogarth Press, 1955.

———— (1920b). The Psychogenesis of a Case of Homosexuality in a Woman. *Standard Edition*, 18:145–172. London: Hogarth Press, 1955.

———— (1923). The Ego and the Id. *Standard Edition*, 19:1–66. London: Hogarth Press, 1961.

———— (1925). An Autobiographical Study. *Standard Edition*, 20:3–74. London: Hogarth Press, 1959.

———— (1933). New Introductory Lectures on Psycho-Analysis. *Standard Edition*, 22:1–182. London: Hogarth Press, 1964.

———— (1937). Analysis Terminable and Interminable. *Standard Edition*, 23:209–253. London: Hogarth Press, 1964.

———— (1940a). An Outline of Psycho-Analysis. *Standard Edition*, 23:141–207. London: Hogarth Press, 1964.

———— (1940b). Splitting of the Ego in the Process of Defence. *Standard Edition*, 23:271–278. London: Hogarth Press, 1964.

Fries, M. E. (1946). The Child's Ego Development and the Training of Adults in His Environment. *The Psychoanalytic Study of the Child*, 2:85–112. New York: International Universities Press.

Glover, E. (1955). *The Technique of Psycho-Analysis*, rev. ed. New York: International Universities Press.

Greenson, R. R. (1965). The Problem of Working Through. In: *Drives, Affects, Behavior*, Vol. 2, ed. M. Schur. New York: International Universities Press, pp. 277–314.

———— (1967). *The Technique and Practice of Psychoanalysis*, Vol. 1. New York: International Universities Press.

Hartmann, H. (1948). Comments on the Psychoanalytic Theory of Instinctual Drives. In: *Essays on Ego Psychology*. New York: International Universities Press, 1964, pp. 69–89.

———— (1950). Comments on the Psychoanalytic Theory of the Ego. In: *Essays on Ego Psychology*. New York: International Universities Press, 1964, pp. 113–141.

———— (1951). Technical Implications of Ego Psychology. In: *Essays on Ego Psychology*. New York: International Universities Press, 1964, pp. 142–154.

————, Kris, E., and Loewenstein, R. M. (1946). Comments on the Formation of Psychic Structure. *The Psychoanalytic Study of the Child*, 2:11–38. New York: International Universities Press.

Hendrick, I. (1951). Early Development of the Ego: Identification in Infancy. *Psychoanalytic Quarterly*, 20:44–61.

Jacobson, E. (1968). In Panel on Narcissistic Resistance. Fall Meeting of the American Psychoanalytic Association, 1968. Chairman: C. Kligerman, Reporter, N. P. Segel. *Journal of the American Psychoanalytic Association*, 17:941–954, 1969.

Kaiser, H. (1934). Probleme der Technik. *Internationale Zeitschrift für Psychoanalyse*, 20:490–522.

Kris, E. (1956). On Some Vicissitudes of Insight in Psycho-Analysis. *International Journal of Psycho-Analysis*, 37:445–455.

Lewin, B. D. (1954). Sleep, Narcissistic Neurosis, and the Analytic Situation. *Psychoanalytic Quarterly*, 23:487–510.

——— (1955). Dream Psychology and the Analytic Situation. *Psychoanalytic Quarterly*, 24:169–199.

Loewenstein, R. M. (1951). The Problem of Interpretation. *Psychoanalytic Quarterly*, 20:1–14.

Macalpine, I. (1950). The Development of Transference. *Psychoanalytic Quarterly*, 19:501–539.

Mahler, M. S. (1965). On the Significance of the Normal Separation-Individuation Phase, with Reference to Research in Symbiotic Child Psychosis. In: *Drives, Affects, Behavior*, Vol. 2, ed. M. Schur. New York: International Universities Press, pp. 161–169.

Nunberg, H. (1930). The Synthetic Function of the Ego. In: *Practice and Theory of Psychoanalysis*. New York: International Universities Press, 1961, pp. 120–136.

Reich, W. (1933). *Character Analysis*. New York: Orgone Institute Press, 1945.

Sterba, R. (1934). The Fate of the Ego in Analytic Therapy. *International Journal of Psycho-Analysis*, 15:117–126.

Stone, L. (1951). Psychoanalysis and Brief Psychotherapy. *Psychoanalytic Quarterly*, 20:215–236.

——— (1961). *The Psychoanalytic Situation, an Examination of Its Development and Essential Nature*. New York: International Universities Press.

——— (1966). The Psychoanalytic Situation and Transference: Postscript to an Earlier Communication. *Journal of the American Psychoanalytic Association*, 15:3–58.

——— (1971). Reflections on the Psychoanalytic Concept of Aggression. *Psychoanalytic Quarterly*, 40:195–244.

Waelder, R. (1930). The Principle of Multiple Function. *Psychoanalytic Quarterly*, 5:45–62, 1936.

——— (1960). *Basic Theory of Psychoanalysis*. New York: International Universities Press.

3

APPROACHES TO THE PROBLEM
OF DEVELOPMENT

EGO DEVELOPMENT
Syllabus for a Course [1]

Jane Loevinger, Ph.D.

The purpose of this article is to present the outline of a seminar on ego development that I have been teaching for several years. Although the subject is old, the way of organizing it is probably new in the college curriculum. It is part of a new approach in developmental psychology which differs both from conventional child psychology and from the exegesis of a particular school of thought, such as psychoanalysis. The course is keyed to the graduate level, but advanced undergraduates are admitted and have done well. So little of what is taught in psychology courses is germane to this field that no particular courses are prerequisite; students from fields other than psychology are at no disadvantage. Few students in the course have previously read anything written by Freud, Piaget, or Sullivan.

To set the tone for a more abstract and conceptual approach than is usual in psychology and particularly in child psychology, students are urged to read Kuhn's *The Structure of Scientific Revolutions* (1970) early in the term. The disanalogies between psychology and the more mathematically exact sciences, about which Kuhn mainly writes, are evident; nonetheless, most students grasp the point that science, including psychology, is a more conceptual and less exclusively empirical undertaking than they had previously been inclined to believe.

BEYOND THE PLEASURE PRINCIPLE

The first topic of the course might be called "beyond the pleasure principle," although Freud's book of that name is not introduced until later. An exercise can be made of either a class discussion or a brief written report before the second class meeting concerning the students' expectations of the course, including a

[1] Preparation of this essay was supported by Research Scientist Award No. K5-MH-657 and by Public Health Service Research Grant No. MH-05115, both from the National Institute of Mental Health.

definition or explication of what they understand by the term ego development and a list of previous reading they have done that seems germane to the topic. This exercise has value for the instructor as well as for the students, since it enables him to key his presentation to the students' level of preparation.

The central question at this point is why a new subject is needed in the area of ego development. What is there that remains to be explained after psychology based on stimulus-response and reinforcement principles has had its say? By way of answer, the biggest thing that anyone learns is how to be the person that he is, and for this kind of learning "learning theory" hardly has words. Motivational psychology cannot entirely pre-empt the field, for the topic is (among other things) the transformation of motives and values. Since other kinds of development are occurring simultaneously, including intellectual and psychosexual development, one cannot simply observe ego development; thus, it is an abstraction.

There are many excellent essays that could be called "beyond the pleasure principle." DeCharms's (1968) *Personal Causation* and Chein's (1972) *The Science of Behavior and the Image of Man* both show that behavior cannot be accounted for adequately in stimulus-response or reinforcement terms. Use of Mill's (1838) essay on Bentham has the advantage of introducing historical perspective. Bentham's "hedonic calculus" took account of precisely what B. F. Skinner today calls "schedules of reinforcement." Mill showed many complexities of human motivation that Bentham had left out of account. Both psychoanalysis and scientific (or scientistic) psychology adopted a version of the hedonic calculus after philosophers had discarded it as naïve.

HISTORY AND DEFINITIONS

Definition of terms and the history of the field are interrelated and constitute the second topic. Going to the card catalogue and looking up the term "ego" is one of the least rewarding approaches: Nineteenth-century philosophical discussions of the transcendental ego are not nutritious, nor is there much sustenance in the many discussions in philosophical psychology of the ego versus the self, the I and the me, the ego as knower and as known. Ego development is something that happens in the real world, and the boundaries of the topic are to be found there, not in an arbitrary definition. Adler's (1956) conception of style of life is an important clue.

Many students believe that the concept of ego came into modern psychology from Freud. They are shocked to hear that he virtually never used the term, on purpose. He intentionally chose terms from common speech rather than terms of Latin origin. The literal English equivalent of the term for which his translators have used "the ego" is "the I." As soon as one is alerted to the sources of the topic in writings in different languages, one starts to look for a concept, not a particular word, in tracing history. What some have called ego development (Ausubel, 1952; Erikson, 1963; Loevinger, 1966a) turns out to be similar to what others have called interpersonal integration (Sullivan, Grant, and Grant, 1957), interpersonal relatability (Isaacs, 1956), character development (Peck and Havighurst, 1960), development of moral ideology (Kohlberg, 1964), and cognitive complexity (Harvey, Hunt, and Schroder, 1961). The sequences traced under those various names are too much alike to be different phenomena, whatever formal definitions the authors may make. Ego development is the only term broad enough to cover all of them. Hence preference for this term is not arbitrary.

In the psychoanalytic literature there are two usages of the term ego development that I eschew. In one usage the ego is a kind of bag of tricks or congeries of functions, with the development of any of the functions labeled as ego development. This usage neglects the organic unity of the ego and its development, which is the subject of the course. A second usage pre-empts the term for that period when the ego is coming into being. Logically this is correct enough, but it leaves one with no distinctive term for the later transformations of the ego. Moreover, at that first stage the development of the ego is inseparable from other strands of development that can be considered separate topics as they pertain to later life, such as psychosexual development and cognitive development and, indeed, adjustment.

The subject of the course could be individual ontology, it could be the history of the conception, or it could be increasing potential for development of mankind. Primary emphasis is on the first two topics, but one of the earliest and best books on the subject, John Dewey and James Tufts's *Ethics* (1908), also includes the third topic. A brief essay by Jaspers (1948) is an accessible source for the topic. Flugel (1945), whose book is required in the final segment of the course, covers some of the historical and anthropological materials also.

Although the subject of ego development has a modern sound, interest in it was probably greatest around the turn of the century, when Baldwin (1897) made contributions that are still valuable. McDougall (1908), Cooley (1902), and especially Mead (1934) also made contributions. The Dewey and Tufts book was probably the most widely used text in ethics for many years after it was written, and ethics was a more popular course then than now. We must assume, therefore, that a far greater percentage of college students was exposed to the rudiments of the topic of ego development half a century ago than at present.

Students like to believe that their instructors are in the vanguard, that they are riding the crest of an irresistible wave of change. I resist being cast in such a role. I maintain that there are alternative views of man, that there always have been (*vide* Mill and Bentham), and that these alternative views are grounded in the very characterological differences that are the content of the course. This is not a matter of scientific immaturity, as Kuhn would have it, but a permanent feature of man's view of himself. Scientific rigor is to be sought for psychology elsewhere than in unanimity of paradigm.

The relation of psychoanalysis to the subject is complex. Freud was familiar with and admired the writings of Mill; still, he was a long time going "beyond the pleasure principle." Early psychoanalysis was explicitly a reaction to the ego psychology of its time. The Clark lectures (Freud, 1910) are valuable to give students a picture of the tenets of psychoanalysis before the introduction of the terms superego and id and the current usage of the term ego in psychoanalysis. Not long after those lectures were delivered, Adler and other analysts in his wake split from Freud over this very issue, Adler maintaining that Freud unduly subordinated the psychology of the ego, Freud maintaining that Adler would give away the hard-won gains of the psychology of the unconscious. Many analysts at the time believed that the two positions could in principle be reconciled, as indeed they now have been in some quarters. Thus psychoanalysis arose in part as a reaction to ego psychology, and ego psychology was given some impetus as a reaction to psychoanalysis. The later development of psychoanalytic ego psychology is itself falsified if all of ego psychology is seen (as some students and analysts do see it) as created by Freud.

Much of what is called superego development is subsumed under the heading of ego development, a classification that some analysts would find acceptable. Freud used the terms superego and ego ideal interchangeably, and referred to them as a differentiated level within the ego. The term ego ideal, like the term his translators render as ego, was taken from the common domain by Freud, for it or a similar term appears in the writings of James, Baldwin, Dewey, McDougall, and no doubt of many others before Freud used it in 1914. The originality of Freud's contribution lies elsewhere, in its theoretical context. (Whether the concept of the superego is necessary in relation to psychopathology is irrelevant here.)

What is new in the contemporary study of ego development and related variables, as compared both to early ego psychology and most psychoanalytic accounts, is a conception that is at once a developmental sequence and a characterology or dimension of individual differences at each age; it must, therefore, be an abstraction (Loevinger, 1966a, 1969).

STAGES

One way to define what is meant by the term ego development is to point to the successive stages. There are two advantages to using my version (Loevinger, 1966a; Loevinger and Wessler, 1970) as the framework for the course (in addition to my familiarity with this version). One advantage is that it has in some respects a more detailed empirical grounding than other systems of stages. The other is that it is not original but rather an amalgam of insights from many sources. Both the empirical base and the process of amalgamation act as protection against turning personal idiosyncrasies into grand theory.

Each of the stages to be described is both a normal developmental period and a point on a dimension of individual differences. Among adults there are representatives of every stage, that is, persons who developed up to that particular stage and then ceased to progress on this continuum. There are as yet no definitive data on the age limits of the several stages among normal children. Armchair accounts are, however, far more optimistic about the speed of ego development than such data as are available will support. Consider, for example, the psychoanalytic formula that the superego is heir to the Oedipus complex. We find, by contrast, an appreciable number of normal children still at the impulsive stage at the age of 10, a number that becomes negligible by the age of 18.

Many accounts of ego development contrast the earliest stage with the highest stage the author can imagine, the latter usually depicted as an amalgam of all virtues. Almost everything significant about ego development is distorted by such an exposition, if not by the author, then by his reader. A lowest and a highest stage are included in the following account but are deliberately understressed and left somewhat vague, in order to represent accurately the open-endedness of the sequence.

The state of the newborn infant may be called presocial or normal-autistic. At first he is more or less oblivious to everything except the gratification of his physical needs, but he quickly develops other capacities, such as "making interesting spectacles last." The next period is that of symbiotic attachment to the mother or mother surrogate. This early stage is the time of the formation of the world of objects and the simultaneous formation of the ego. It comes to an end at approximately the time that language begins; it is therefore not accessible to psychologists who study their subjects through the medium of language. Although my colleagues and I never study this period, its importance for psychopathology requires that it be included in our schema for completeness. The most primitive stage that we study, the impulsive stage, is itself an achievement.

The child at the next, or impulsive, stage is the creature of his impulses. His behavior must be controlled by immediately imposed rewards and punishments. His ability to make demands and to say no to the demands of others not only serves to secure satisfaction of his physical needs; it also affirms for him his sense of self. His relations with others are largely a matter of giving and getting. His view of the world is egocentric and concrete. He is preoccupied with his own physical needs.

The next stage is self-protective. In small children it is usually ritualistic; in older children or adults it may assume an opportunistic cast. While external rewards and punishments remain the chief moral sanction, the person calculates his self-interest rather than simply acting on impulse. However immoral opportunism may seem, it represents the first step toward control of impulses and hence is a necessary forerunner of all morality. Relations with other people at this stage are manipulative and may be exploitive; however, there will often be less dependence than there is in impulsive persons. The person at the self-protective stage is concerned about "getting into trouble." If he does, he is quick to blame others or external circumstances. Work is perceived as onerous, something to be avoided when possible. There may be preoccupation with domination, control, taking advantage, deceiving, and the like. This is the lowest level that can pass for normal in an adult.

Most people at some time during childhood or adolescence take the next step to the conformist stage. The conformist obeys the rules just because they are the rules. Normally the child adheres at first to the rules of the family, later to those of his peer group. If a conformist transgresses, usually disapproval is sanction enough, since he wants above all to be loved, to be approved of, and to belong. The conformist tends to think in terms of stereotypes, clichés, sweeping generalizations, and absolute injunctions. He has a very limited conception of inner life and of individual differences. He is concerned with the externals of life, such as material possessions and good looks. He conceptualizes relations between people in terms of behaviors rather than in terms of enduring dispositions.

Obviously many adults remain permanently at the conformist stage of ego development. Precisely what combination of circumstances enables a person to advance beyond that stage is not yet established. Recent results from longitudinal studies that followed representative samples of children through childhood to maturity suggest that highly successful adjustment in the junior high-school or high-school years may portend remaining at the conformist stage (Block, 1971). This in turn has suggested that the discomfort of not quite making it in the period when popularity, physical prowess, and conformity are the chief standards acts as a spur to a higher level of ego development, at least in some persons.

Our own data suggest a different though compatible hypothesis. Some people seem to begin to move out of the conformist stage as they first come to appreciate that they themselves, and particularly their own feelings, do not always conform to the norms or stereotypes. In one way or another, most adults come to recognize that the world in general and people in particular are not so simple: People, even those of the same age, race, and sex, are not all alike, and most situations offer multiple possibilities. This period of dawning awareness of individuality, of inner life, and of complexity is the level most frequently found in college undergraduates and other late adolescents and adults.

At the next stage, which we call conscientious, the world, both inner and outer, becomes more complex. The person becomes aware of cognitively differentiated feelings in himself and others. Social interaction is seen not merely as behavior but as emotional interaction, as expressive of enduring traits, and as motivated. Individual differences among people are perceived in place of broad stereotypes. In labeling this stage conscientious we do not mean that conscience originates at this time, for the conformist usually has a conscience also. The impulsive person does not recognize rules; the self-protective person knows there are rules but obeys them only to avoid punishment; the conformist obeys the rules because they are the rules. The person at the conscientious stage evaluates and chooses for himself the rules he will obey. Moral progress is not measured by right conduct but by autonomy of conscience.

Distinctive of the person at the conscientious stage, and increasingly characteristic at higher stages, is seeing problems in terms of a longer time perspective and in a broader social context than do people at lower stages. What is wrong for a person at the conscientious stage is not simple violation of rules, like not going to church, but doing something that causes harm or anguish to another person. But to every virtue there corresponds a problem. The conscientious person may be too driven for his own good. Other persons, too, may resent him when he feels excessively responsible for molding the character or behavior or shaping the destiny of people in his charge.

A small proportion of adults and even an occasional adolescent proceed beyond the conscientious stage of ego development. Having recognized the wealth of individual differences in traits and the complexity of choices that situations offer, the person's next step is toleration rather than moral condemnation of those who make choices different from his own. At man's highest estate he learns to cherish human variety as part of what gives life its zest and worth. Where the conformist is ambitious for recognition by others and the conscientious person strives for achievement by his own standards, the person at the next level, which we call autonomous, seeks fulfillment of his own best self.

The title of any stage can be misleading. Conformity begins before the conformist stage, and conscience begins before the conscientious stage. The striving for autonomy is characteristic of healthy ego development from early childhood, even though it is also balanced by contrary yearnings: Every baby demands to "do it by self." Labeling this particular stage as autonomous summarizes two features: The person at this stage is at least partly liberated from his own excesses of conscience, and he respects other people's need for autonomy. (It is also consistent with ego autonomy as a desideratum of psychoanalysis [Holt, 1965].) The crucial question is not whether he can let other people, in particular his own children, have their own way when he knows they will choose correctly, but whether he can grant them the right to choose mistakenly. The parent at the autonomous stage does not have an automatic laissez-faire attitude. He feels responsibility, but that responsibility may at times take the paradoxical form of refraining from influencing his children.

The person at the autonomous stage contrasts inner life with outward appearances and is aware of their interaction. He explains behavior not only in terms of traits but also in terms of the course of the person's development, including the personalities and interpersonal relations experienced in the past.

It is not necessarily true that the higher one's ego level the happier and more serene one is. It is just as true to say that at higher levels one perceives more problems and more complex ones, though one usually also has more resources to cope with them. The problems of lower ego levels do not disappear at higher levels; they are seen in different terms and in a broader perspective. One of the distinctive marks of the autonomous level is awareness of and honest grappling with inner conflict. This is part of what Frenkel-Brunswik (1949) called "tolerance of ambiguity."

There is a theoretical higher stage which we call integrated; however, there are methodological difficulties in arriving at an empirical description of this stage. There is no simple touchstone that tells us who is at this stage, as birth tells us who is at the lowest stage. Everyone tends to project his own aspirations and self-deceptions into his conception of the highest stage, so that the person depicted becomes a paragon of virtues, some of which are probably not germane to ego development, for example, the capacity for mature genital sexuality, and others of which are unrealistic, for example, being kind to everyone. If a highest stage is presented, there is a tendency to think of ego development as a smooth continuum that can be described in terms of its lowest and highest poles; such a description omits the vicissitudes of its course and thus the whole substance of the topic. Statistically, the highest stage is so rare that nothing is lost if, for research purposes, it is combined with the autonomous stage. Despite the statistical rarity of this stage, it is by no means rare for persons hearing or reading descriptions of the stages of ego development to conclude that they are at the integrated stage. Conformists, who are deficient in self-criticism and for whom "good adjustment" is both their ideal and their self-image, are particularly likely so to class themselves.

The demand for some picture of the highest stage can be answered by reference to Jahoda's (1958) summary of literature on positive mental health, which turns out to be essentially the same as the highest ego stage. Perusal of that volume also shows how little of the topic of ego development is invoked by the search for its ideal outcome.

RELATED FORMULATIONS OF STAGES AND TYPES

Much of the course is occupied by setting up relations and correspondences between the sequence described above and other lines of research with which the student can be assumed to be more or less familiar. A major segment of what is here called ego development has been discovered by many persons, who have described it either in terms of a set of developmental stages or in terms of a characterology or dimension of individual differences. Such persons can be found in many disciplines, including psychology, psychiatry, psychoanalysis, philosophy, sociology, literature, and religion. Because different authors have written most sensitively and fully about different stages and aspects, one's views can always be enriched by new versions. There is, however, danger of dazzling the students with too many versions, each with its own vocabulary and its own research or measurement paradigm.

H. S. Sullivan's *The Interpersonal Theory of Psychiatry* (1946–1947) is a kind of watershed for the modern theory of ego development. His account of the stages in the development of the self-system is a forerunner of all the major contemporary conceptions of ego development. He had a clearly hierarchical conception; that is, he showed how arrest of development of the self-system at various of the childhood stages colors the person's approach to all the problems of later life, a topic on which Erikson is less clear. A unique feature of Sullivan's account is his description of the chumship, which occurs during the period that psychoanalysis treats somewhat slightingly as "latency." Ego-developmental aspects of late adolescence and maturity receive richer treatment from Erikson (1963), however. A weakness of Sullivan's account is that each stage is described in age-specific terms; thus, he obscures the fact that the developmental sequence generates a characterology or major dimension of individual differences in adult life.

The Berkeley studies of the authoritarian personality (Adorno, Frenkel-Brunswik, Levinson, and Sanford, 1950) were influential in turning the attention of psychologists to the aspects of character here called ego development; yet the authors explicitly denied that the authoritarian person was in any sense less mature than the nonauthoritarian person. (Those of the authors who are still living probably no longer hold that view.) There is no reference to Piaget in *The Authoritarian Personality,* yet the differences between those high and those low in authoritarianism are remarkably like the differences Piaget (1932) discerned between heteronomous and autonomous morality. Piaget, on the other hand, saw only the developmental sequence, missing the implication of a trait or characterology.

Several psychologists in recent years have proposed developmental characterologies that resemble what I call ego development in all but name and detail. Kohlberg (1964) has used his measure of the moralization of judgment in an extensive research program on normal adolescents, recently broadened to include cross-cultural research and studies of delinquency. C. Sullivan, Grant, and Grant (1957) have as their central conception the growth of capacity for interpersonal relations; their studies have largely centered on delinquency and its treatment. Isaacs's (1956) conception of interpersonal relatability is similar, but his research base lies primarily in psychotherapy. Peck (Peck and Havighurst, 1960) used his typology of character development in the study of normal adolescents. Ausubel (1952), whose data base is not clear, is one of the few to use the term ego development; he stresses the age sequence more than the dimension of individual differences, and his exposition is of value chiefly for its vivid depiction of satellization and desatellization. Perry's (1970) subjects are Harvard students talking about the problems of their college careers; students therefore find his presentation close to home.

The spirit of the course is to glean the best from every author. Some students begin with a legalistic approach, as if establishing that a man made some error therefore discredits him as a witness on all further matters. A legalistic approach can establish differences between authors, but that says nothing. A more sympathetic approach is important at many points, for example, in matching the stage concepts of one author with those of another. One must feel one's way into each stage described by an author to match it with the appropriate stage described by another author. The differences in detail between authors are accounted for neither by lack of data nor by disregard for evidence but by methodological difficulties (Loevinger and Wessler, 1970, Chapter 1).

The conceptions that can be called developmental characterologies have certain characteristics in common: Ego development (or a related variable) is seen as proceeding by qualitatively distinct stages, it generates a typology, and it is therefore an abstraction. The ego is a process; it is structural; it functions holistically; it is social in origin; and it is purposive, that is, meanings are determinative of behavior. The concept of development implied is that of Werner (1940); the process of growth is in the direction of increasing differentiation and hierarchical integration. Each of the above assertions is controversial and can be expanded in a small essay (Loevinger, 1969).

DIFFERENTIAL CONCEPTION

There is constant temptation to assimilate the conception of ego development to some other conception already familiar; this may be intellectual development, psychosexual development, adjustment, or age-specific tasks. Rogers (1959), for example, has given identical definitions of adjustment and maturity. If one listens to small talk in psychological clinics, one often hears "immaturity" as a euphemism for "maladjustment" (Loevinger, 1963). Such confusion is intolerable if adjustment in childhood and in later periods is to be understood, for surely there are some well-adjusted children who are, perforce, immature.

Erikson's (1963) successive crises of the healthy personality, although they enrich the picture of ego development, do not match the sequence of stages postulated here. Neither with respect to psychosexual development nor with respect to the ego crises is Erikson explicit as to how the outcome of one stage or crisis affects the subsequent course. The formal aspects of psychosexual development appear to be logically different from the formal aspects of ego development (Loevinger, 1966b). Psychosexual development is paced by biological maturation; successive stages, involving as they do different organs, are at least partially independent. Successive stages of ego development involve the transmutation of a single "organ," the ego; each stage is built on the previous one. Hence failure to deal with the problems of one stage virtually precludes facing the problems of the next one. By tying his exposition to age-specific tasks, Erikson loses or blurs the abstract and characterological implications; he nowhere explicitly makes the point that the successive stages of ego development generate a dimension of individual differences in adult life. So long as both ego and psychosexual development are described in terms of age-specific tasks, the difference between the two lines of development is bound to be blurred. Only when they are conceptually distinct will it be possible to investigate empirically the relations between them.

The relation of ego development to intellectual development is also complex. One may demand a clear conceptual distinction, as clear as the conceptual distinction between height and weight, without asserting that the traits are independent of each other. Nature does not promise that everyone, regardless of intellectual endowment, will have an equal opportunity to reach the highest ego stages. An attempt to pin a numerical value on the correlation between ego development and intellectual development is bootless. Consider, for comparison, the correlation between mental age and chronological age. If you test an entire grade school you will get one value, no doubt positive. If you test a single classroom, say the sixth grade, you will almost certainly get a negative value. Thus it is meaningless to ask what is the correlation between mental age and chronological age. It is equally meaningless to ask the correlation between ego development and intelligence.

Another approach to the question of the relation of intellectual development to ego development is to ask what is the minimum intellectual requirement for reaching a given ego stage. The writings of Piaget can be used to give approximate age anchorages of different relevant cognitive achievements. For example, the kind of decentration exhibited in understanding the word "brother" as a relation rather than as a category, shown by the ability to state how many brothers the child's brother has, would appear to be a prerequisite for the corresponding affective decentration of the conscientious stage. If you cannot, so to say, sit in your brother's seat long enough to see how many brothers he has, you are unlikely to be able to understand that he has feelings just as you do. Similar speculations can be made about other stages. Generally speaking, far more people have the intellectual prerequisites to reach the higher ego stages than ever do so. This topic is a potential area for research.

FORMAL ASPECTS AND MEASUREMENT

While ego level can be conceptually distinguished from psychosexual level, intellectual level, adjustment, and age-specific problems, it does not follow that measurement of one is uncontaminated by the others. Work on ways of measuring ego development, moral development, or closely related variables is going on in various groups, particularly in that associated with Kohlberg and in my own group. Most investigators have used measures scored intuitively or tests that have not had psychometric details worked through. Only fragmentary information is available in published form about any of these measures, with the exception of our sentence-completion measure of ego development (Loevinger and Wessler, 1970; Loevinger, Wessler, and Redmore, 1970).

On a more theoretical level, formal features of developmental processes can be identified in a way pertinent to problems of measuring ego development (Loevinger, 1966b). Formal features of the stage concept in relation to cognitive development have been expounded by Piaget and Inhelder (Tanner and Inhelder, 1956, 1960). Their conceptions of *equilibré* and of the inner logic of development are often neglected by Americans who take up their ideas. Kohlberg (1964, 1968) has applied the ideas effectively both to moral development and to cognitive development. When one takes account of the dynamics of development per se, it becomes redundant and misleading to account for those developmental features that are intrinsic to the process in terms either of reinforcement or of psychodynamics, or, indeed, of maturation. At this point the question of measurement leads into problems of theory.

THEORY OF STABILITY

If one tries to say what the term *theory* means, it can turn out to be almost the same as what one has just said *ego* means; both can be more or less defined as "frame of reference." Kuhn's (1970) account of the resistance of scientific paradigms to change is more than an analogy with ego stability; psychologically the same processes are involved.

The definitive theory of ego stability is that of Sullivan (1946–1947), well-known before its posthumous publication in 1953. Merleau-Ponty (1942) arrived independently at essentially the same theory. According to Sullivan, the self-system, his term for the ego, arises in large part as a defense against anxiety, which he believed to be the most unpleasant experience a baby can have. As the child grows older, he tends always to construe the world in ways consistent with the current organization of his self-system. Any observations discordant with it cause anxiety; therefore the self-system, by means of selective inattention, screens out such observations. But the observations that are screened out are the very ones that might lead to change in the self-system if they were assimilated. I call this the anxiety-gating theory of ego stability. Anxiety is, so to speak, the gatekeeper. The gating process, admitting perceptions that support the current system and excluding those that disturb the system, insures its stability.

As Kuhn describes it, the maintenance of the stability of scientific paradigms is a similar process. New data are, so far as possible, construed in terms of the received paradigm. When they do not fit, they may be excluded as irrelevant ("unscientific" or "superficial"), or ad hoc amendments may stretch the paradigm to cover the new instances. (Misperception, the favored device of the individual in defense of his ego, is presumably made less likely by the public nature of science.) A scientific revolution, the overthrow of one paradigm and its replacement by a new one, is preceded by widespread anxiety in the scientific community involved.

The theory of the stability of the ego also supplies the theory of its measurement by projective tests. A projective test requires the subject to respond in terms of his own frame of reference. From the subject's free response to several questions one can usually reconstruct enough about his frame of reference to infer his level of ego development. Several projective tests have served in this fashion, including sentence-completion, story-completion, and role-playing tests.

THEORIES OF CHANGE

All of the major contributions to the dynamics of development originated in the writings of Freud. There are, however, some anticipations in earlier writings. Preyer (1881) wrote about the child's "gratification at being a cause." Baldwin's (1897) two major contributions were the dialectic of personal growth and his depiction of the growth of the child's ethical self. The dialectic of personal growth portrays how the child learns to understand himself in terms of others and others in terms of himself. Baldwin describes the child's ethical self as originating in altruistic behavior toward his father and others in authority and aggressive behavior toward younger sibs. These behaviors are not inconsistent, and they are gradually integrated with age.

Mead (1934) followed Baldwin in considering the growth of a sense of self as the central topic of psychology; he was, however, more sophisticated philosophically. His social theory of mind was the direct ancestor of what Sullivan later called the interpersonal theory. Mead rejected Baldwin's moving principle, an instinct of imitation, and called on a more complex mechanism. The child in his play learns to take on the roles of others, first particular others and then the "generalized other." The self arises from the process of symbolization, from representing one's actions and role to oneself as they would be seen by another.

An adequate introduction to psychoanalytic theory requires, at a minimum, a semester of its own, and in the present anti-intraceptive mood of psychology, few students will come so prepared. Inadequate as it must be, a survey of the history of psychoanalytic theory is nonetheless an integral part of the history of ego theory. The version presented in the course is similar to and in part drawn from the writings of Erikson, Holt, and Loewald.

It can be argued that Freud's major contribution was not so much specific concepts, such as the unconscious, or the ego, the superego, and the id—those concepts in particular can all be shown to have come from the common domain—as the introduction of the equivalent of what Kuhn calls a paradigm. This is something more than what psychoanalysts call a model. Freud was the first psychologist to attempt a clear and intimate interrelation of his theory, his therapeutic methods, and his data. Another respect in which Freud was closer to the spirit of modern science than his predecessors or, indeed, than most subsequent psychologists, was his belief in the unity and lawfulness of nature (Lewin, 1931). One often hears this described as a conclusion Freud arrived at after studying dreams, parapraxes, and jokes. On the contrary, it was an assumption that underlay his whole approach to psychology and psychopathology. It seems probable that Freud discovered the Oedipus complex because he was analyzing his own and his patients' dreams at the same time and in the same terms.

Obviously there is a close relation between Freud's assumption of the unity and lawfulness of nature and his first major discovery, the principle of psychic determinism, but they are not identical. The belief in the lawfulness of nature is not distinctively a psychoanalytic idea, nor is it distinctively human in its application. Psychic determinism, that is, the principle that ideas can both cause and remove physical symptoms, is distinctively applicable to humans and is distinctively, though perhaps not exclusively, characteristic of psychoanalysis. Psychology students are usually surprised to learn of the many years of work in neurology, hypnosis, and psychiatry that led Freud to the discovery of psychic determinism.

The foregoing interpretation of psychic determinism, although different from many versions in psychoanalytic writings, is compatible with that of Loewald:

What has been mainly emphasized about psychic determinism is the fact of cause-effect relations between psychic events, the causes being unconscious, the effects frequently being conscious psychic events or processes. But the main impact of psychic determinism resides in its being psychic determinism: the causes are conceived not as purely external or physical and biological, but as potentially personal, unconscious processes having a psychological effect on overt behaviour. And secondly, these causes thus are susceptible to being influenced and modified in their turn by psychological processes. If this were not so, the whole idea that the reactivation of unconscious conflicts and their recreation and working through in analysis could lead to change in present behaviour would fall to the ground (1971, p. 61).

The second major principle discovered by Freud is the principle of the dynamic unconscious, that unconscious experiences or ideas influence behavior in much the same way that conscious ones do, but that the feedback from behavior to its originating idea is limited to conscious sources. Unconscious ideas thus do not suffer extinction under negative reinforcement, to use today's lingo.

Freud's first paradigm, really a protoparadigm, was based on the principles of psychic determinism and the dynamic unconscious. It can be called the trauma paradigm because the chief force in creating neurosis was considered to be trauma. More limited but distinctively psychoanalytic ideas arrived at during this period were that neurosis is the result of inner conflict and that the conflict always has a sexual basis. During this period, time-honored adjunct therapies were dropped, including hypnosis and suggestion, because they had no place in his theory. The resistance of the patient to remembering unpleasant ideas, which began as an observation, became a central concept.

One element of the trauma paradigm was Freud's belief that neurotics had, as children, invariably been subjected to a seduction by an adult. For various reasons, however, he came to believe that that was improbable. The crisis which Freud experienced when he came to doubt this cornerstone of his trauma paradigm is well-known, and it corresponds exactly to the crisis that Kuhn sees as characterizing scientific revolutions, that is, changes of paradigm. In discarding sexual seduction as the origin of neurosis, Freud discovered childhood sexuality, the force of fantasy in childhood, and the Oedipus complex. These discoveries led to a new paradigm, the instinct paradigm. Ultimately the major discoveries of the first period proved to be even more compatible with the instinct paradigm. Much of what was added in the period of the instinct paradigm can be summarized under the heading of "the plasticity of the interpersonal drives" (Loevinger, 1966c).

Ernest Jones (1953) considered Freud's greatest contribution to psychology to be his discovery of the primary and secondary processes, that is, the discovery that the mind has a primitive stage or layer governed entirely by wish rather than by reality. The nature and measurement of the primary process is still an active field of interest (Holt, 1967). Relations of primary-process thought to ego development and to the work of Piaget on children's thought and the work of Lévi-Strauss (1958) on the thought of primitive peoples have not yet been worked out completely. Displacement of affect and condensation of ideas, conspicuous in dreams but also present in symptoms and parapraxes, are related conceptions. Primary process, displacement, and condensation are the solid observational core underlying the disputed cathexis model.

Freud worked closely with Ferenczi during the period of the instinct paradigm. One of the clearest expositions of the drive-derivative view of ego development is found in Ferenczi's essay, "Stages in the Development of the Sense of Reality" (1913). The concept of transference also became clarified in this era (Ferenczi, 1909), though it, like the other major ideas, was anticipated in the previous period. The phenomena of transference are not subjects of additional principles but are, rather, accounted for by all of the psychoanalytic principles, including ones that had not yet been clearly formulated at the time of the instinct paradigm (Loewald, 1960). During this period the primary emphasis of psychoanalysis as a method of research and therapy changed from the recovery of unconscious conflicts to the analysis of resistance and transference.

During World War I Freud wrote a series of essays in which he explored difficulties and anomalies to which his ideas were leading. The outcome was a whole series of new ideas in the 1920s and 1930s, which subsequent psychoanalytic writers have consolidated, in a way that Freud did not, to form a new or ego paradigm. Freud's fourth major principle, and the first principle of the ego paradigm, is that experience is mastered by actively repeating what one has passively undergone. This "repetition compulsion" is what is "beyond the pleasure principle" (Freud, 1920). (This principle was partly anticipated in Preyer's notion of "joy in being a cause," an idea often attributed to Groos.) The importance of the transformation from passive to active can be seen from the integral part it plays in later essays on ego development in relation to impulse control and the development of conscience (Freud, 1923, 1930), the problem of anxiety (Freud, 1926), and such defenses as identification with the aggressor and altruism (A. Freud, 1936). (Obviously I am neglecting those parts of *Beyond the Pleasure Principle* that do not fit my thesis.)

Freud's fifth major principle is that interpersonal relations provide the model and impetus for intrapersonal differentiation, though of course those are not his words. The idea first appeared in "Mourning and Melancholia" (1917), but it is developed more cogently in *The Ego and the Id* (1923) and in *Civilization and Its Discontents* (1930), where it is applied to the resolution of the Oedipus complex, the origin of impulse control, and the development of the superego. Mead also had independently discovered that interpersonal schemas give rise to intrapersonal schemas, but his version is pallid compared with Freud's.

A sixth major principle, concerning the relation of progression and regression, is only implicit in Freud's writings and perhaps has never been formulated with complete generality. Freud's discussion of how the ego ideal is formed to save narcissism is the prototypic discussion (1914). Kris's (1934) discussion of "regression in the service of the ego" is another partial version. All of Freud's major principles—and this is what makes them major principles and Freud a major theorist—span the topics of psychopathology, psychotherapy, and ego development. Thus, grounding of progression on regression is an important aspect of psychoanalysis as therapy (Loewald, 1960).

PSYCHOANALYTIC EGO PSYCHOLOGY AFTER FREUD

Anna Freud's (1936) *The Ego and the Mechanisms of Defence* and Hartmann's (1939) *Ego Psychology and the Problem of Adaptation* both signaled and caused major changes in psychoanalysis. Henceforth the ego was considered as much within the purview of psychoanalysis, both as theory and as therapy, as the instinctual drives had theretofore been. For anyone who comes to contemporary psychoanalytic ego psychology via the classics of psychoanalysis, the importance of these writings and subsequent ones by Hartmann, Kris, and Loewenstein (1945–1962) is evident. Where Freud had stated that the ego is derived from the id under the impact of reality and that the ego ideal is set up in order to save narcissism, Hartmann argued for a differentiation of ego and id out of a common matrix and for conflict-free ego functions. However, the primary terms of Hartmann's exposition remain those of Freud's instinct paradigm, stretched to accommodate observations from ego psychology. New terms were added, such as "conflict-free ego sphere," "ego functions of primary autonomy," and "ego functions of secondary autonomy," but basically ego development was explained in terms of neutralization of drive energies, or countercathexis. The very success of Hartmann, Anna Freud, and others in impressing on psychoanalysis the importance of new observations in ego psychology led other psychoanalysts to propose more radical revisions. Erikson (1946–1959, 1963, 1969) and Loewald (1951, 1960) have both proposed psychoanalytic ego paradigms, absorbing the insights of drive theory and ego theory into a new whole. Although they differ somewhat in their terms of discourse, their paradigms appear to be essentially compatible.

In retrospect, the instinct paradigm was doomed by the very essay that took it to its farthest reach, Freud's (1914) essay on narcissism. To derive the ego ideal, an essential element of conscience, from instinctual drives was a tour de force. But this remarkable theory subtly altered the conception of instinctual drives. A drive that can be satisfied by creating within oneself an ideal can hardly be a tissue need. The range of possible gratifications in a sense defines the drive. Thus Freud's conception of drive was here changing from physiological need to human urge. Jones (1955, pp. 302–303) records that this essay caused the kind of consternation among psychoanalysts that Kuhn mentions as preceding scientific revolutions.

To trace the broadening of psychoanalytic theory into the area of ego development one must include Hendrick's (1942) paper on the instinct of mastery and White's (1960) paper differentiating ego from psychosexual development. One of George Klein's (1969) last papers exemplifies some of the reasoning that supports the psychoanalytic ego paradigm. Klein's topic is the psychoanalytic theory of sexuality. Surely if drive theory applies anywhere, it must apply to sexuality. Yet even there, Klein shows—indeed, particularly there—the clinical facts are poorly represented in the drive theory of sexuality, that is, in terms of tension reduction. Precisely the same clinical facts—infantile sexuality, use of sexual behavior to express other needs, use of other body parts to express sexual desires, sublimation, and so on—gave rise to the psychoanalytic clinical theory of sexuality, which is what the drive theory is meant to explain. Klein emphasized the distinctive poignancy of sensual pleasure, which cannot be reduced to tension reduction and hence has no place in drive theory. In order to encompass the clinical observations, one must think of sexual behavior not in terms of tensions seeking discharge but as patterns of actions with conscious and unconscious purposes, evidently an ego-theory version of sexuality. One must distinguish drives from drive theory; Klein did not at all minimize the importance of sex as a motive. On the contrary, as Klein pointed out, it was Rapaport, who remained a proponent of drive theory, who discounted somewhat the distinctive importance of sexuality as a motive (Klein, 1969, pp. 163–164).

The conflict between the instinct or drive paradigm and the ego paradigm is still an active one in psychoanalysis, though proponents of both acknowledge the importance of ego development. Among the valuable more recent contributions are those of Rapaport (1958, 1959, 1960) and Hartmann, Kris, and Loewenstein (1945–1962) on the one hand, and White's (1963) monograph on ego and reality, Holt's (1965) paper on ego autonomy, and Schafer's (1968) book on internalization on the other. These works are, however, too difficult for students without further background in the psychoanalytic literature. Unfortunately the same thing must be said of the two authors who have come closest to a coherent and integrated presentation of the psychoanalytic ego paradigm, Loewald (1951, 1960), a psychoanalyst, and Ricoeur (1970), a philosopher. I have written extended summaries of the latter contributions (Loevinger, 1969), but the summaries are neither substitutes for the originals nor more intellectually accessible. Erikson's (1963, 1969) writings are a more accessible version of the psychoanalytic ego paradigm, but his deceptive simplicity masks some of the problems that Loewald presents in detail.

As time permits, there are many topics one can pursue further, for example, alternative theories of anxiety, aggression, identification, and ego autonomy. I avoid the theory of ego development in terms of countercathexis and neutralization of drives, partly because its terms are so removed from the students' experience that they would memorize it by rote rather than absorb it by insight. Further, I have found no suitably clear, concise, nontechnical statement of it, nor can I produce such a statement myself.

GROWTH OF CONSCIENCE

The final topic of the course is the growth of conscience and of a sense of guilt. This topic is a central one for ego development, and it is both theoretically vexing and practically important. Flugel's (1945) *Man, Morals, and Society* reveals the complexity of the topic and spans the psychoanalytic and other psychological contributions. It is not, however, organized to stress the developmental logic, so it leaves much for the student to work out for himself. A major value of choosing this as the final topic is to give the student an opportunity to draw together insights from many sources. The student cannot be expected, however, to find for himself the connection between Loewald's (1962) conception of the superego, Baldwin's (1897) conception of the ego ideal, and contemporary experimental work on pacers (Dember, 1965).

Baldwin wrote of the child's ideal self as representing originally the standards set up by parents and teachers as a "copy for imitation." With growth, the child incorporates the ideal self into himself, but as he progresses, new patterns are set for him. Thus his "ethical insight must always find its profoundest expression in that yearning which anticipates but does not overtake the ideal" (Baldwin, 1897, p. 166). Now Loewald:

Parental and other authorities, as internalized in the agency of the superego, are related to the child as representatives of a future and of demands, hopes, misgivings or despair, which pertain to an envisaged future of the child. . . . Con-

science, the mouthpiece of the superego, speaks to us, one might say, in the name of the inner future which envisages us as capable or incapable, as willing or unwilling to move toward it and encompass it, just as parents envisaged us in our potentialities and readiness for growth and development (1962, p. 265).

Dember summarizes recent experimental work in cognitive psychology showing that people seek out problems of an appropriate level of difficulty for them, not too hard and not too easy. They tend, moreover, while sampling various levels of difficulty, to concentrate on that level just a little above their current level of functioning. Problems at that level are called "pacers." "It is the pacer, if one is available, that enables the individual to change. . . . As he maintains active contact with the pacer and eventually masters it, his own level of complexity grows, and he is ready for a new pacer" (Dember, 1965, p. 421). Evidently there is here another theoretical contribution to the dynamics of ego development, superego as pacer. Loewald (1960) has applied this schema to the dynamics of psychoanalysis as therapy, showing that the psychoanalyst functions as a pacer in his relation with the patient.

SOME RECURRENT THEMES

Certain themes recur throughout the course. One is that one's view of the world in general and man in particular is itself a sign of one's ego level. Many psychological theories can be aligned with the ideology characteristic of one or another of the several ego stages. These monolithic theories take the characteristic motive of one stage and make it the explanatory principle for all persons and for the transition between stages. This is the ontological fallacy: It asserts that, whatever motives a person may seem to have, at bottom, really and truly, we all have the same motive. The view is called a fallacy not because one can prove it wrong, but because it ignores the transformation of motives, which is one way of looking at what ego development is.

The course is blatantly organized around ideas rather than around data. With luck, a few students will come to appreciate that scientific rigor is conferred neither by dissectionism and reductionism nor by antitheoretical empiricism. Logical analysis is not a second-rate substitute for empirical investigation. On the contrary, a careful logical analysis will often show laborious empirical studies to have been foolish, their results being obtainable more quickly and more surely by forethought (Ossorio and Davis, 1968).

MECHANICS OF THE COURSE

The class meets once a week for an hour and a half. The understanding is that the main substance of the course is reading and writing. The students and I have turned against examinations. Although they are used in psychology departments, true-false and multiple-choice questions neither encourage nor measure preparation for a professional career, much less one's ability to absorb ideas and use them in life. The aim of the course is to introduce the students to a new psychological paradigm. They need not adopt it as their own, but it is hoped that their own approach to all of psychology will be influenced in some way. The students' openness to the ideas of the course is facilitated by dropping the objective-examination set.

Students are required to write four short essays, preferably about five typewritten pages, but allowably shorter and usually longer. Letting students select their own topics has not worked well, nor have oral reports. Four topics are assigned from the following or something like them. The last two topics are always assigned in some form.

What are the applications in contemporary psychology of the ideas in Mill's essay on Bentham?

Show the correspondence between Kohlberg's stages of moral judgment and Loevinger's ego stages. Align the developmental sequences traced in Piaget's The Moral Judgment of the Child *on the same grid.*

Using Loevinger's ego stages as a framework, (1) show where the developmental sequence that Ausubel calls satellization and desatellization fits, and (2) show where Perry's stages fit.

Compare and align Erikson's stages of psychosocial development and Sullivan's stages of the self-system. Contrast their theories of the dynamics of development.

Trace the growth of conscience, bringing together observations and theoretical insights from all available sources.

If students are allowed to substitute topics of their own choosing, one can predict that they will choose topics that do not force them to confront uncomfortable issues. They may write longer or better essays, but they are less likely to change the preconceptions with which they entered the course. Some students report, often resentfully, sitting for hours before beginning to write one of their essays. Surely those are the most productive hours. Some students drop out, but those who survive often pattern their own subsequent teaching on the course. I doubt that one can challenge students in this manner without the risk of losing some of them.

Certain misinterpretations of the assignments occur with disconcerting regularity. Some students believe they are expected to propound their own theory of the growth of conscience, whereas it is both more reasonable and more rewarding for them to review and to integrate the theories of others. Again, some students tend to give evaluations rather than summaries, apparently because they have been told that in college one should write critically. Critical they should be, of course, but in a different meaning.

Many students slip into using Kuhn's conception of paradigm in a vague way to mean theory, notion, or style, a vagueness that Kuhn specifically warns against (1970, p. 208). To apply Kuhn's ideas with any precision there must be a methodological exemplar. In the case of psychoanalysis this is the case history, as Sherwood (1969) has argued. The unit of study in psychoanalysis is the psychoanalytic narrative, that is, the case history, according to Sherwood; moreover, explanation in psychoanalysis is exactly puzzle solving, which is one of Kuhn's distinctive criteria for science.

Some topics that are conveyed in a paragraph of this syllabus are scarcely more extended in the course; other paragraphs summarize several weeks' work. The topics treated extensively are not the same from year to year, nor is the division of topics between lecture and readings constant. The business of the ego is to keep in touch, and one teaches by example as well as by precept. The program for a course in ego theory therefore cannot be final or fixed.

REFERENCES

Adler, A. (1956). *The Individual Psychology of Alfred Adler,* ed. H. L. Ansbacher and R. R. Ansbacher. New York: Basic Books.

Adorno, T. W., Frenkel-Brunswik, E., Levinson, D. J., and Sanford, R. N. (1950). *The Authoritarian Personality.* New York: Harper.

Ausubel, D. P. (1952). *Ego Development and the Personality Disorders.* New York: Grune and Stratton.

Baldwin, J. M. (1897). *Social and Ethical Interpretations in Mental Development.* New York: Macmillan. Excerpts in: *The Self in Social Interaction,* ed. C. Gordon and K. J. Gergen. New York: Wiley, 1968, pp. 161–169.

Block, J. (1971). *Lives through Time.* Berkeley: Bancroft Books.

Chein, I. (1972). *The Science of Behavior and the Image of Man.* New York: Basic Books.

Cooley, C. H. (1902). *Human Nature and the Social Order.* New York: Scribner. Excerpts in: *The Self in Social Interaction,* ed. C. Gordon and K. J. Gergen. New York: Wiley, 1968, pp. 87–91, 137–143.

deCharms, R. (1968). *Personal Causation.* New York: Academic Press.

Dember, W. N. (1965). The New Look in Motivation. *American Scientist,* 53:409–427.

Dewey, J, and Tufts, J. H. (1908). *Ethics.* New York: Holt.

Erikson, E. H. (1946–1959). Identity and the Life Cycle. *Psychological Issues,* Monograph 1. New York: International Universities Press, 1959.

———— (1963). *Childhood and Society,* 2nd ed. New York: Norton.

———— (1969). *Gandhi's Truth.* New York: Norton.

Ferenczi, S. (1909). Introjection and Transference. In: *Sex in Psychoanalysis.* New York: Dover, 1956, pp. 30–79.

———— (1913). Stages in the Development of the Sense of Reality. In: *Sex in Psychoanalysis.* New York: Dover, 1956, pp. 181–203.

Flugel, J. C. (1945). *Man, Morals, and Society.* New York: Viking, 1961.

Frenkel-Brunswik, E. (1949). Intolerance of Ambiguity as an Emotional and Cognitive Personality Variable. *Journal of Personality,* 18:108–143.

Freud, A. (1936). *The Ego and the Mechanisms of Defence.* New York: International Universities Press, 1946.

Freud, S. (1910). Five Lectures on Psycho-Analysis. *Standard Edition,* 11:1–55. London: Hogarth Press, 1957.

———— (1914). On Narcissism: An Introduction. *Standard Edition,* 14:67–102. London: Hogarth Press, 1957.

———— (1917). Mourning and Melancholia. *Standard Edition,* 14:237–260. London: Hogarth Press, 1957.

———— (1920). Beyond the Pleasure Principle. *Standard Edition,* 18:7–64. London: Hogarth Press, 1955.

—— (1923). The Ego and the Id. *Standard Edition,* 19:3–66. London: Hogarth Press, 1961.

—— (1926). Inhibitions, Symptoms and Anxiety. *Standard Edition,* 20:75–174. London: Hogarth Press, 1959.

—— (1930). Civilization and Its Discontents. *Standard Edition,* 21:61–145. London: Hogarth Press, 1961.

Hartmann, H. (1939). *Ego Psychology and the Problem of Adaptation.* New York: International Universities Press, 1958.

——, Kris, E., and Loewenstein, R. M. (1945–1962). Papers on Psychoanalytic Psychology. *Psychological Issues,* Monograph 14. New York: International Universities Press, 1964.

Harvey, O. J., Hunt, D. E., and Schroder, H. M. (1961). *Conceptual Systems and Personality Organization.* New York: Wiley.

Hendrick, I. (1942). Instinct and the Ego during Infancy. *Psychoanalytic Quarterly,* 11:33–58.

Holt, R. R. (1965). Ego Autonomy Re-evaluated. *International Journal of Psycho-Analysis,* 46:151–167.

—— (1967). The Development of the Primary Process: A Structural View. In: Motives and Thought: Psychoanalytic Essays in Honor of David Rapaport, ed. R. R. Holt. *Psychological Issues,* Monograph 18/19:345–383. New York: International Universities Press.

Isaacs, K. S. (1956). Relatability, a Proposed Construct and an Approach to Its Validation. Unpublished doctoral dissertation, University of Chicago.

Jahoda, M. (1958). *Current Concepts of Positive Mental Health.* New York: Basic Books.

Jaspers, K. (1948). The Axial Age of Human History. In: *Identity and Anxiety,* ed. M. R. Stein, A. J. Vidich, and D. M. White. New York: Free Press, 1960, pp. 597–605.

Jones, E. (1953). *The Life and Work of Sigmund Freud,* Vol. 1. New York: Basic Books.

—— (1955). *The Life and Work of Sigmund Freud,* Vol. 2. New York: Basic Books.

Klein, G. S. (1969). Freud's Two Theories of Sexuality. In: *Clinical-Cognitive Psychology,* ed. L. Breger. Englewood Cliffs, N.J.: Prentice-Hall, pp. 136–181.

Kohlberg, L. (1964). Development of Moral Character and Moral Ideology. In: *Review of Child Development Research,* Vol. 1, ed. M. L. Hoffman and L. W. Hoffman. New York: Russell Sage Foundation, pp. 383–431.

—— (1968). Early Education: A Cognitive-Developmental View. *Child Development,* 39:1013–1062.

Kris, E. (1934). The Psychology of Caricature. In: *Psychoanalytic Explorations in Art.* New York: International Universities Press, 1952, pp. 173–188.

Kuhn, T. S. (1970). *The Structure of Scientific Revolutions,* 2nd ed. Chicago: University of Chicago Press.

Lévi-Strauss, C. (1958). *The Savage Mind.* Chicago: University of Chicago Press, 1966.

Lewin, K. (1931). The Conflict between Aristotelian and Galilean Modes of Thought in Contemporary Psychology. *Journal of General Psychology,* 5:141–177.

Loevinger, J. (1963). Conflict of Commitment in Clinical Research. *American Psychologist,* 18:241–251.

—— (1966a). The Meaning and Measurement of Ego Development. *American Psychologist,* 21:195–206.

—— (1966b). Models and Measures of Developmental Variation. In: The Biology of Human Variation, ed. J. Brozek. *Annals of the New York Academy of Sciences,* 134:585–590.

—— (1966c). Three Principles for a Psychoanalytic Psychology. *Journal of Abnormal Psychology,* 71:432–443.

—— (1969). Theories of Ego Development. In: *Clinical-Cognitive Psychology,* ed. L. Breger. Englewood Cliffs, N.J.: Prentice-Hall, pp. 83–135.

——, and Wessler, R. (1970). *Measuring Ego Development I. Construction and Use of a Sentence Completion Test.* San Francisco: Jossey-Bass.

——, ——, and Redmore, C. (1970). *Measuring Ego Development II. Scoring Manual for Women and Girls.* San Francisco: Jossey-Bass.

Loewald, H. W. (1951). Ego and Reality. *International Journal of Psycho-Analysis,* 32:10–18.

—— (1960). On the Therapeutic Action of Psycho-Analysis. *International Journal of Psycho-Analysis,* 41:1–18.

—— (1962). The Superego and the Ego-Ideal. II. Superego and Time. *International Journal of Psycho-Analysis,* 43:264–268.

—— (1971). Some Considerations on Repetition and Repetition Compulsion. *International Journal of Psycho-Analysis,* 52:59–66.

McDougall, W. (1908). *An Introduction to Social Psychology.* London: Methuen.

Mead, G. H. (1934). *Mind, Self, and Society.* Chicago: University of Chicago Press.

Merleau-Ponty, M. (1942). *The Structure of Behavior.* Boston: Beacon Press, 1963.

Mill, J. S. (1838). Bentham. In: *Utilitarianism, On Liberty, Essay on Bentham,* ed. M. Warnock. Cleveland: World, 1962, pp. 78–125.

Ossorio, P. G., and Davis, K. E. (1968). The Self, Intentionality, and Reactions to Evaluations of the Self. In: *The Self in Social Interaction,* ed. C. Gordon and K. J. Gergen. New York: Wiley, pp. 355–369.

Peck, R. F., and Havighurst, R. J. (1960). *The Psychology of Character Development.* New York: Wiley.

Perry, W. G., Jr. (1970). *Forms of Intellectual and Ethical Development in the College Years.* New York: Holt, Rinehart and Winston.

Piaget, J. (1932). *The Moral Judgment of the Child.* Glencoe, Ill.: Free Press, 1960.

Preyer, W. (1881). *Mind of the Child.* Excerpts in: *The Child,* ed. W. Kessen. New York: Wiley, 1965, pp. 134–147.

Rapaport, D. (1958). A Historical Survey of Psychoanalytic Ego Psychology. In: *Collected Papers.* New York: Basic Books, 1967, pp. 745–757.

—— (1959). The Structure of Psychoanalytic Theory. *Psychological Issues,* Monograph 6. New York: International Universities Press, 1960.

—— (1960). Psychoanalysis as a Developmental Psychology. In: *Collected Papers.* New York: Basic Books, 1967, pp. 820–852.

Ricoeur, P. (1970). *Freud and Philosophy.* New Haven: Yale University Press.

Rogers, C. R. (1959). A Theory of Therapy, Personality, and Interpersonal Relationships, as Developed in the Client-Centered Framework. In: *Psychology: A Study of a Science,* Vol. 3. *Formulations of the Person and the Social Context,* ed. S. Koch. New York: McGraw-Hill, pp. 184–256.

Schafer, R. (1968). *Aspects of Internalization.* New York: International Universities Press.

Sherwood, M. (1969). *The Logic of Explanation in Psychoanalysis.* New York: Academic Press.

Sullivan, C., Grant, M. Q., and Grant, J. D. (1957). The Development of Interpersonal Maturity: Applications to Delinquency. *Psychiatry,* 20:373–385.

Sullivan, H. S. (1946–1947). *The Interpersonal Theory of Psychiatry.* New York: Norton, 1953.

Tanner, J. M., and Inhelder, B., eds. (1956). *Discussions on Child Development,* Vol. 1. New York: International Universities Press.

——, ——, eds. (1960). *Discussions on Child Development,* Vol. 4. New York: International Universities Press.

Werner, H. (1940). *Comparative Psychology of Mental Development.* New York: International Universities Press, 1964.

White, R. W. (1960). Competence and the Psychosexual Stages of Development. In: *Nebraska Symposium on Motivation,* Vol. 8, ed. M. Jones. Lincoln: University of Nebraska Press, pp. 97–141.

—— (1963). Ego and Reality in Psychoanalytic Theory. *Psychological Issues,* Monograph 11. New York: International Universities Press.

SOME MUTUAL CONTRIBUTIONS OF PSYCHOANALYSIS AND CHILD DEVELOPMENT [1]

Lois Barclay Murphy, Ph.D.

INTRODUCTION

The gulf, or communication gap, between psychoanalysis and child development from the 1930s to the 1960s is hard to understand, as well as unfortunate for both disciplines. It was a leader in child development—G. Stanley Hall—who invited Freud to the United States for his first lectures in 1909. And it was a psychoanalyst, Siegfried Bernfeld (1925), who in the twenties published a major book on *The Psychology of the Infant*. Around the same time and later, the great child analyst, Susan Isaacs, was receptively reading studies in the field of child development (1933, 1949).

Granted the preoccupation of developmental psychology with normative studies and the careful delineation of maturational sequences, it is hard to understand how observers of infants and children could have paid so little attention to the evidence of pleasure and pain so obvious in reaction to their manipulation of infants—not to mention the dynamic and unconscious influences reflected in the individuality of children's responses to tests long before projective methods focused on these forces. And it is equally hard to understand how a major psychoanalyst like Glover (1947) could have blandly implied, even in the forties, that before the age of six months nothing much happens in the infant except eating and sleeping.

Whatever the nature of the blinders that disrupted the process of mutual communication which had begun so early and with such promise of enriching both disciplines, the situation has been changing for the better in the last decade.

[1] This paper draws on work conducted at The Menninger Foundation under United States Public Health Service Grants No. MH-27, M-680, M-4093, PH-43-65-41, and 5-R12-MH-09236; it also uses observations made at the Children's Hospital of Washington, D.C., from 1967 to 1971. The topic involves such a wide area of functioning that a volume would be required to deal with it adequately. In this paper I can offer only selected illustrations of contributions from each discipline to the other.

Some analysts have been paying special attention to the implications of Piaget's work for understanding ego development, and have welcomed evidence from such psychologists as Escalona (1952) that the infant contributes much to the development of object relationships. On the other side, an increasing number of psychologists—for instance, Brody (1956) and Korner (1971)—have found psychoanalytic training important for a deeper understanding of the interactions between drives or motivation and development, and between early experience and constitutional patterns. The ground is being prepared for a fuller understanding of the plasticity of functions originally regarded in child development as under rigid genetic control. A fuller appreciation of the complexity of integration-achieving processes at different levels from the physiological level to that of psychological functioning and a greater understanding of the individuation of dynamic processes are now resulting from the collaboration of psychoanalysis and child development (Ritvo et al., 1963). Psychodynamic orientations are already bringing greater sensitivity to the personality changes that come with development influenced both by epigenetic changes in drive emphases and by experiences in the environment (Yarrow, 1964; M. C. Jones, 1924; Bayley, 1956).

It is also hard to understand why it has taken so long to integrate individual differences into a dynamic theory of development. Galton's first major work was published in 1869, and during this century extensive work on human genetics has provided material that could contribute to a more differentiated understanding of individuality. Harold Jones (1944) and the Stolzes (1951) at the University of California were demonstrating during the forties the wide range of individual variation in the onset of the puberty growth spurt. They showed that the 20% of boys who develop most slowly have the greatest difficulty in negotiating the transition to adolescence. Bayley (1956) and others have shown that very slowly growing boys tend to continue growing longer than those who grow more rapidly, and that although their whole childhood may be spent struggling with a feeling of inadequacy related to being short and light in weight, they may end up being taller than some of the rapidly growing boys. In other words, we could say that prepubertal misery and maladjustment is normal for this slow-growing subgroup in our competitive culture. Evidently the preoccupation with the normal and the pathological, dictated by the urgency of dealing with practical problems in school and community, contributed to the stranglehold of a normative approach based on averages. Demands based in turn on these norms contribute to difficulties for the slow-growing boys.

In 1956 Roger J. Williams made a frontal attack on such rigid ways of viewing the individual in his brilliant book, *Biochemical Individuality*. He documented the incredible range of individual differences in everything from the sizes and shapes of stomachs to the quantities of specific vitamins required by different persons. Taking the bull by the horns, he stated flatly that everyone is a deviant in one way or another. A totally average person is a figment of the statistician's imagination. Respect for biological models of scientific work, rather than awe of the laws of physics, might have enabled the developmental theoreticians to give due consideration to the constitutional rights of individuality in science. The desire for laws of exceptionless validity led many an investigator to overlook the potentially important implications of the responses of, say, the one third of his subjects who did something different from the two thirds who provided his longed-for generalization. I was startled to find this true even of one of my idols, Kurt Lewin, and his associates (Barker, Dembo, and Lewin, 1943) in their study of regression in response to frustration. Two thirds of the children did regress according to their definition, but others did the opposite, that is, were stimulated by the frustration, treated it as a challenge, and increased their efforts and resourcefulness. Certainly this type of finding suggests that it is extremely important to find, in each individual child, both the point at which frustration will evoke regression or disorganization and the point at which frustration or challenge may stimulate greater mobilization of resources, new integration, or increased ego strength.

This introduction, then, is by way of an indication that I am concerned not only with the mutual contributions of psychoanalysis and child development, especially those concerned with plasticity and integration, but also with the contributions that a serious consideration of individuality could make to both these disciplines and to their influence on each other.

THE NEED FOR NATURALISTIC OBSERVATIONS OF NORMAL SAMPLES OF CHILDREN

Freud's theories and insights were formulated on the basis of close and highly differentiated observations of patients in analysis; illustrations of these are of course given in his early case histories (Breuer and Freud, 1893–1895), and in subsequent writings. The parallel approach to the understanding of normal development is naturalistic observations of children in everyday life situations, which provide for the study of normal adaptational challenges what clinical observations provide for the study of disturbance. Beginning with the nineteenth-century biographies of infants, and continuing with the 24-hour observations made by Charlotte Bühler's team (1930), Susan Isaacs's (1933) observations in nursery school, and Anna Freud's and Dorothy Burlingham's observations of children in a wartime nursery (1943), there have been major examples of the productivity of this kind of material for both psychoanalysis and child development. Although Piaget (1936) is usually thought of as deriving his concepts from experiments, these grew from earlier naturalistic observations in a home situation. Escalona (1963, 1968; Escalona and Heider, 1959), Peter Wolff (1966), Burton White et al. (1964), all working with infants, and Barker and Wright (1951) and Murphy et al. (1956), working for the most part with older children, for example, have made major contributions by developing refined methods of naturalistic observation. But, in view of the productiveness of this approach, it is tragic that it has for the most part been applied only to a homogeneous sample of white, middle-class children. We have little data on a wider variety of samples of children from different subcultural, ethnic, and socioeconomic groups.

While psychoanalysis was concerned with drives and their relation to pleasure and pain, the insights that emerged from this interest never led to a comprehensive naturalistic study of the development of resources for pleasure or susceptibility to pain in childhood. Many errors, even in the last decade, as well as throughout this century, could have been avoided if experimental studies shaped by theory had been based on a solid foundation of naturalistic observation which could provide an adequate context for the experimental work. Over and over again, in both psychoanalysis and child development, theory has proved to be a trap unless constantly confronted with data. The assumption of I.Q. stability is one example. But there are larger assumptions limiting our thinking. One illustration might be Charlotte Bühler's formulation of infant behavior (1930) into "negative" and "positive" categories, which obscured the fundamentally functional understanding reflected in her rich observations. This kind of adultocentric conceptualizing, which regards a baby's spitting out, for instance, as a "negative behavior," probably reflects Judeo-Christian moralistic dichotomizing. At any rate, it overlooks the baby's adaptational dilemmas. What should a two-months-old baby do when he is confronted with too much food too fast, or something that tastes bad? From the baby's point of view, spitting it out is an efficient way of coping with something unpleasant in his mouth. It is only the defeat of the adult that leads to calling this behavior "negative." Such adultocentric blindness to the child's adaptational situation permeates much developmental and psychoanalytic thinking. Piaget (1936), Prechtl (1961), Wolff (1966), and Escalona (1952, 1963, 1968; Escalona and Heider, 1959), however, have not been caught in this trap.

Up to the time of Hartmann's contributions to the understanding of ego development (1939), much clinical thinking was colored by the same adultocentric dye. The concept of symptoms included too much behavior that the grownups did not like because of their own defensive needs. An obvious example is thumb-sucking, which, to an uncomfortable infant, is a useful adaptive resource; it becomes maladaptive only when it interferes with other resources which later become available to the child. Similarly, a tendency to regard "dependency needs" as problems, or resistance and protest as stubbornness or even as expressions of anal character defect, reflects rigid and unproductive categorizing whether it occurs in psychoanalytic or developmental thinking.

Among our Topeka children, those capable of protesting, resisting, or ending unwanted stimulation in infancy were, at preschool age, able to fend off excessive environmental demands and stimulation, and to find ways of restructuring environmental situations (Murphy and Moriarty, in preparation). The child's adaptational effort is directed toward his own task of maintaining sufficient homeostatic comfort. Naturalistic observations are needed for an adequate record of the context of and sequelae of behavior, and thus to provide a basis for inferring motivation.

From the twenties to the forties the major institutes of child development were preoccupied with maturational problems (Olson and Hughes, 1943). The children studied were almost exclusively middle-class white children from adequately stimulating homes, development was generally assumed to proceed under genetic controls, and little or no attention was paid to the contribution of experience to patterns of development considered to be universal. Psychoanalysis, however, emphasizes the contribution of experience even to basic adaptational capacities. An example is Spitz's discussion of "fundamental education" (1970). He offered the hypothesis that active interaction, that is, interplay, between mother and infant is the necessary precursor of later play and the capacity to integrate perceptual, affective, and motor responses, including the capacity to learn.

In the present era we are trying to understand certain differences between poor and most middle-class children. Significant differences exist, for example, in school learning and the capacity to integrate new materials through selection and organization. A number of efforts to provide foundations in infancy for later learning have focused on the contribution of the mother, and some of these have emphasized teaching the mother how to play with her baby (Gordon and Lally, 1967).

Thus we have Spitz's thesis independently illustrated in the educational experiments of current child development. Few of the infant educators, however, have extended their approach to the full dimensions of Spitz's concept. To do so would involve a broad education of the mother to respond to and build on the baby's primitive signals, cues, expressions of liking and dislike, pleasure and discomfort. Such a broadened responsiveness is needed for the most adequate socialization of the child.

In connection with my own observations of ghetto children and babies, I have ruminated about possible precursors of the preschool capacity to organize. Spitz's paper stimulated me to formulate a sequence of levels of organization and integration in this way:

from the increasing organization and differentiation of embryonic structure,

to the intrinsic organization of the input sequence: receiving food—swallowing—digesting—eliminating,

to the integration of the experience of hunger with this sequence, leading to the series: hunger—demand—receive food, etc.,

then, as visual associations with the hunger-satisfying activities of the mother become established, the sequence hunger—demand—promise becomes possible to achieve and, with this, the sequence hunger—demand—perceive—promising—cues—wait can be achieved.

It seems clear that oral gratification (along with pleasant tactile experience) provides a context for sustained visual investment in the mothering person, and through her, the environment. This is not to deny that initially vision, along with every other organic structure, is apparently satisfied by its own functioning; we can see the baby's increasing span of attention even in the first days and weeks of life, as he stares at a bright light or at his mother's eyes as he nurses. But if the perceptual experiences are embedded in orally frustrating experience, the investment may peter out, as Spitz documented a generation ago (1945) in his study of babies suffering from hospitalism.

How important these early gratifications are is indicated by quite different data: I have photographs of a baby at four weeks who had been nursed at the breast up to that time; he was given a bottle and frowned as he began to suck on its nipple. Moreover, oral gratification (and good vegetative functioning) in the first months is positively correlated with perceptual clarity at the age of five years (Murphy and Moriarty, in preparation).

We might call this integration of satisfying oral experience with good perceptual functioning a precursor of later integration, or better, a prerequisite for good later integration; but it is not enough to guarantee later active organizing and integrating capacities. I think we can hypothesize that the gratifying reinforcement of the earliest recognition and anticipation makes it possible for the baby to wait, and to accept the sequence of need—exchange of signals—wait—then-be-gratified. And this sequence is not only a prerequisite for later impulse control, it is also an expression of cognitive integration which can be a foundation for planning ahead at a later stage of development.

It hardly seems necessary to review the basic sequence of psychosexual development as Freud (1905) outlined it, or its confirmation by work in child development. Any mother of a vigorous baby can report the urgency of the oral drive in the fast-growing baby who triples his weight in a year, and later the child's rambunctious resistance to dressing and toileting routines as locomotor drives become urgent. Sexual curiosity is illustrated in every nursery-school group, and many a mother has gently or laughingly turned down a proposal or a promise of marriage from her five-year-old son. Only the child-development expert who is, like Isaacs (1933), psychoanalytically trained, has discussed these developments in detail.

PHYSIOLOGICAL AND EXPERIENCE FACTORS RELATED TO EGO FUNCTIONING

Psychoanalytic thinking about ego functioning has been much influenced by Hartmann's (1939) concepts of ego autonomy, the conflict-free sphere of the ego, ego boundaries, and so forth. The relativity and vulnerability of ego boundaries is documented by developmental studies from different settings, for instance, by Sontag's (1966) data on labile cardiac reactors among normal males and their tendency to be more emotional and to see the emotional aspects of picture stimuli. The affective factors involved in I.Q. have been discussed in both Sontag's studies of children whose I.Q.s change (Sontag, Baker, and Nelson, 1958) and in Moriarty's work on the Topeka children. Moriarty (1966) showed that only a minority of the children maintained a stable I.Q. to puberty. She carefully analyzed the concomitant experiences of children whose I.Q.s accelerated, chil-

dren whose I.Q.s remained stable or who developed slowly in cognitive functioning, and children who showed marked variability in the level of cognitive
functioning, documenting the interaction of complex affective factors with
level of cognitive competence. The point was illustrated long ago by Liss (1937)
in his reports of I.Q. changes following therapy. Sequences of test results in
other longitudinal studies provide evidence that can be similarly understood.

Thus we see that autonomy of cognitive functioning is by no means the
rule. It is an ideal—relative, variable from child to child, and vulnerable to shifts
in affect, motivation, or drive. This is not to say, however, that the children in
our group all tended to respond to stress with decreased cognitive functioning;
on the contrary, the level of functioning in some children remained stable even
under severe stress, whereas in other children it was more easily affected by
what might seem to an adult less severe stress.

Individual differences in cognitive and motor functioning in infancy were
not emphasized in Gesell's (Gesell et al., 1940) and Bühler's (1930) early work.
But Shirley (1931–1933), in her study of 25 babies, carefully reported the ages at
which each quartile of babies in her sample succeeded with each item of perceptual, motor, and social tests. She did not discuss the relation between precocity in any area to interest in that area of functioning on one hand or environmental stimulation on the other; nor the contribution of either precocity or
lag in any area to adaptational problems or difficulties in ego integration; nor
the imbalances that sometimes exist in particular children between precocity in
some areas and lag in others. More recently, Wolf (1952), of the Yale child study
group, and others such as Alpert, Neubauer, and Weil (1956), have traced the
impact of special sensitivities and intensities of drives on the personality development of the child.

The problem of sensitivities brings us to the concept of ego boundaries as
conceptualized by Escalona in her intensive study, The Roots of Individuality
(1968). She formulates differences not only in terms of strong and weak boundaries, but in terms of variations within the same infant in the strength of boundary
in different sensory zones. For instance, some babies are markedly sensitive to
lights, others to sounds, still others to skin contact. Her modification of Lewin's
(1943) approach could also be considered in relation to the work of Voth and
Mayman (1967) on ego-close and ego-distant relations to reality.

Psychoanalysis has offered child development tools for understanding the
inner world of the child, his subjective experience, and relations between this
subjective experience and his overt behavior. Child-development studies, in
turn, especially longitudinal investigations like those of Macfarlane, Allen, and
Honzik (1954) at Berkeley, document the variability in adaptation (as judged by
adults) in the child who outgrows certain fears with increasing mastery and understanding, and whose level of inhibition-versus-spontaneity varies according
to such basic biosocial factors as the interaction between major body changes,
self-image, and changes in environmental demands before, during, and after
puberty. This does not contradict data on differences in disturbance at different

ages, for instance Levy's (1945) observations that more children developed fears after tonsillectomies at the age of two than did children whose operations occurred at the age of five.

Temporary patterns of defense against fear of being overwhelmed in a new situation are sometimes mistaken for enduring traits shaped by the outcome of psychosexual conflicts (Murphy, 1970). The difference between them may be ignored, especially when we overlook the threats evoked by the interaction of complex outer and inner changes at puberty. It seems clear that we need to define normal adaptation in terms of the total pattern of the child's biological equipment at a given time in relation to the realistic adaptational problems presented by his environment and the consequences for the child of his ways of solving these problems.

Two cases in point are (1) what appears to be the increasing number of hyperactive children who cannot be handled by teachers and parents, and (2) quiet children who, in this action-oriented culture, disappoint the expectations of both parents and teachers for motor and verbal participation. Children who do not talk much, or do not move into action easily, are sometimes considered withdrawn. Actually there is an enormous difference between a withdrawn child, who does not invest any interest in the environment, and the nonpathologically quiet child whose response to the environment is primarily looking or listening. Some of these latter children are, later, intellectuals, engineers, or designers.

OBJECT RELATIONS IN PSYCHOANALYSIS AND CHILD DEVELOPMENT

In the psychoanalysis of the thirties and forties the interaction between mother and child was recognized to be basic to the development of object relations, and the emphasis, whether by Melanie Klein (1932) or by Sullivan (1946–1947) or by others, was typically on the behavior of the mother, who was regarded essentially as an independent variable. The child analyst David Levy's work on *Maternal Overprotection* (1943) was an exception: he observed that overprotective mothers tended to be permissive with dominant children and dominating with passive children. Child-development studies in more recent years, particularly since Erikson's (1950) emphasis on the mutual regulations of mother and child, have shown the great complexity of the mother-infant relationship and have made generalizations hazardous (Murphy, 1964). Our data on the Topeka children indicate what should be obvious, that too much attention is just as likely to contribute to difficulty as is too little attention—including the fact that it is overstimulating and may be irritating to an infant. But further, Heider's (1966) analyses have emphasized the importance of the givens in both mother and baby. For instance, when a specific mother and baby seem naturally suited and appropriate to each other, the mother is comfortably able to respond to the level of the infant's demands and vice versa. In contrast, the very gentle mother who has an extremely vigorous, energetic, demanding baby who likes forceful play and very active interaction may, through no fault of her own, find it very difficult to meet his needs. Similarly, a naturally vigorous, energetic, rapidly moving woman may not be a suitable mother for an extremely sensitive, quiet baby who needs to be handled very carefully and protected from overstimulation.

But the adaptational problems that arise when mothers and babies do not fit each other very well are not the sole determinants of the outcome for the child. For the outcome depends upon the resources the baby has for dealing with the discomforts that inevitably arise in a nonfitting mother-baby relationship. A baby who is skillful in handling his body from the earliest weeks, who is flexible in protesting unwanted stimulation, who lets you know what he wants and what he needs, and who evokes appropriate responses from the environment through his capacity to indicate what is too much and what is not enough, may become an adaptable, resourceful, and independent child (Murphy, 1968; Murphy and Moriarty, in preparation). In fact, we have instances of such children turning out to be more successful and independent than children whose needs have been "ideally" met by mothers who understood what they wanted before they made the demand. Brody's (1956) comprehensive review of the mother-infant literature provides a rich mine of hypotheses about relationships between mothers' behavior and infants' functioning.

SEPARATION AND DEPRIVATION

While the child psychologist Shirley (Shirley and Poyntz, 1941) documented the distress of infants separated from their mothers, it was left to the psychoanalysts to probe more deeply into the meaning of such experiences, as Spitz (1946), Bowlby (1969), and others have done (Ainsworth, 1962; Lambo, 1961; A. Freud and Burlingham, 1944). Then it was a psychologist, Yarrow (Yarrow et al., 1971), of the Institute of Child Health and Human Development, who with his colleagues carried out a sensitive long-term study of this subject. The infants studied included (1) babies placed in adoptive homes directly from the hospital within 10 days after birth, (2) babies shifted from foster care to adoptive homes before the age of six months, and (3) babies moved from foster homes into adoptive homes after the age of six months. The tests, interviews, and ratings of behavior at the age of six months were compared with the child's performance on the WISC at 10 years, and his social functioning in the same situation. There were no significant differences in either intellectual or social functioning between those adopted within the first two weeks of life and those adopted from foster homes before six months of age. Children separated from foster mothers after the age of six months, however, were scored significantly lower than those separated earlier on the variable of social discrimination, which reflects the capacity to establish different levels of relationships with people.

As evaluated by Yarrow's group, the quality of maternal care of the six-months-old infant showed many relationships to the child's performance on the WISC at 10 years: appropriateness of stimulation; responsiveness of the mother to the infant's attempts at communication; the degree to which she treated the infant as an individual; the depth of emotional involvement; and the extent to which she expressed positive affect toward the infant. Correlations of these ratings of maternal care of the infant with the child's performance on the WISC at 10 years ranged from .32 to .38 for the whole group, but boys' correlations ranged from .46 to .68. As Yarrow indicates (Yarrow et al., 1971), these findings are highly relevant to recent questions about the kind of infancy experience which might provide an adequate foundation for learning and later cognitive functioning.

We have to suggest that the affective responsiveness of the mother contributes to an enlivening of the child's perception of the environment, which may in turn foster the vividness of his memory. We have only to recall Thorndike's (1933) emphasis on the role of vividness in memory and learning to appreciate how the very early experience of vividness may contribute to cognitive development. Escalona (1963, 1968) has spoken of the mother's "animating" influence on the infant, and in our further studies of her data on Topeka infants and comparison with later functioning, significant correlations between the mother's enjoyment of the child and the child's later coping ability are impressive. In addition to the direct stimulus and reinforcement value of the mother's interested and appropriate responsiveness, outcomes of related interactions with the baby such as the over-all level of oral gratification correlate with such variables as range of sources of gratification at the preschool age (Murphy and Moriarty, in preparation).

We have seen Spitz's (1970) concern with the interrelations of cognitive and affective development. His recent thinking provides the theoretical basis for his findings in the forties: loss of the mother for longer than three months (if it occurs after the age of eight or nine months) may permanently retard the child's development; isolation in the hospital may produce a serious depression which is the more severe the better the "mothering" of the baby has been. Currently he is formulating the process of internalization and structuring from birth on, as it involves the affectively charged sensorimotor as well as need-gratifying interaction with the mother. This theory is congruent with the sophisticated experimental studies of Carpenter and her colleagues (1970) at the Harvard Medical School and Boston University Medical Center, who have provided important evidence that infants can differentiate the mother from other nonhuman, nonalive stimuli even at the age of two weeks. (Others had reported that a stranger's face can be differentiated from the mother's face by the age of four months.) Carpenter's evidence is the meaningful approach-withdrawal behavior of the two-week-old, indicating active regulation of visual input from the targets, and the infant's crying at the sight of the mother's face in a static "port," immobile like the nonliving targets. What a disturbing way for mother to behave! The authors cautiously speculate that even by the age of two weeks the infant has developed expectations of his mother which the conditions of the experiment do not fulfill. And they remind us of the chimps who panicked at the sight of a modeled head of a chimp without the body, and at the sight of an anaesthesized chimpanzee (Hebb, 1946). Seeing the familiar mother in an unfamiliar context is a source of distress to be avoided.

These observations imply that differentiating the familiar from the strange begins much earlier than we had thought. Many others have already documented the preference of the very young baby for complex or moving or meaningful and also varied stimuli over undifferentiated, static, nonsense, and monotonous stimuli (Fantz, 1963; Haith, 1968; B. White, 1971). We can hypothesize a need for Piaget's nutriment—that is, appropriate quality, quantity, and variety of stimulation—for adequate psychological or neuropsychological development. For the meaning of development here, we can refer to Werner's (1940) emphasis on the process of differentiation and integration, which we now see as active from birth; this process contributes to the emergence of perceptual structures and conceptual units and, as Kagan (1967) has emphasized, involves at first "merely" looking and listening. But we cannot leave out the role of affect, as seen in Levy's (1960) observations of infants' differentiation of the inoculation needle.

Kagan also notes that an infant who has become habituated to the repeated presentation of the same, initially novel, stimulus shows a dramatic change in fixation time when presented with a transformation of that standard. His use of the concept of mental representations echoes, shall I say, the language of psychoanalysts such as Hartmann who also assumed the very early formation of cognitive structures.

A more subtle and complex process of differentiation and integration of experiences at different times and places is involved in the emergence of the concept of a stable object, discussed by Piaget in terms of the behavior of an infant in the last quarter of the first year of life. Psychoanalysis is interested in this idea in relation to the development of the infant's concept of the mother as a stable object, enduring even when absent—a concept necessary for trust and the capacity to tolerate the mother's departure from the room, and for the development of stable attachments and differentiated relationships.

Infrahuman studies (Rosenzweig, 1966) are showing the importance of opportunities for differentiation which may contribute not only to cognitive functions such as problem solving, but even to the development of the brain itself.

MUTUAL INFLUENCES OF EGO AND ID

Our discussion of early relationships between affect and cognition brings us to Hartmann's interest in processes of adaptation, which led to his concern with the mutual influences of ego and id (1952). For a full understanding of what goes on here, factors in the earliest development of both need to be taken into account. In our Topeka data, for instance, as well as in other reports, there is evidence that certain babies have sucked their thumbs in utero. In one of our Topeka subjects in whom this was particularly obvious because of her red thumb and early thumb-sucking, it was part of a pattern of versatile mouthing games with which she amused and comforted herself at later stages of infancy. Incidentally, these games seem to have reflected a capacity for elaboration of gratifications which subsequently appeared in her versatility in many areas—currently, as an adult, she is skillful with several different musical instruments, not just concentrating on the piano. In a paper on "Implications of Fetal Behavior and Environment for Adult Personalities," Sontag (1966) reported that the level of fetal activity appears to predict the degree of the infant's activity, restlessness, and sometimes resistance to handling during the first year of life. Richards and Nelson (1938) of his staff found that active fetuses were more advanced at six months after birth on Gesell tests. Sontag also provides many examples of fetuses that vigorously responded to sound with violent kicking and moving. Some mothers among his subjects could not go to symphony concerts because of the intense activity of the responsive fetus—so intense that it was painful. In the laboratory, with carefully controlled experimental procedures, he documented an increased heart rate in reaction to sudden sound. He also had several mothers who had experienced severe trauma, through the death of a husband or other events, to which they reacted with anxiety or grief or fear. When the children who had been in utero during these severe experiences were growing up, they were irritable, hyperactive, and tended to have frequent stools; some of them had marked feeding problems implying difficulties in vegetative integration. I need not spell out the ways in which such restlessness and reactivity would contribute both to drive patterns and to interactions with the impersonal environment which would pattern perceptual and adaptive styles during development. Nor do I need to spell out the challenge to a mother, the frustrations and irritations which efforts to cope with such highly reactive children would arouse, and altogether the combined effects of all of these on object relations.

In an early report, Shirley (1938) described the characteristic patterns of premature babies whom she had an opportunity to study after her famous longitudinal study of normal infants during the first two years. She observed the heightened sensory sensitivity of these premature babies in contrast to their less adequate motor coordination, and commented on the difficulties in social development resulting from this combination. Subsequently Bergman and Escalona (1949) described, on the basis of retrospective data, the unusual sensitivities in infancy of children who were later observed to be emotionally disturbed. Greenacre, in *Trauma, Growth, and Personality* (1952), places major emphasis on the biology of birth, discussing the implications of the contribution of birth difficulties to a predisposition to anxiety, which will obviously shape the baby's and growing child's experiences and both his perceptual and social interactions with his environment.

This formulation by an analyst can be seen in relation to the Laceys' studies (Lacey et al., 1962). They pursued the relationship of individual patterns of autonomic reactivity to differences in cognitive style, ways of thinking and perceiving. Strong reactors tend to attribute emotion or feeling to the human figure and to other pictured situations, and are also much more imaginative. Weak reactors have better emotional control and are less likely to act out their emotions. The Laceys have also studied the relation between autonomic reactivity and motor impulsiveness (Lacey and Lacey, 1958). A child with a highly labile heart rate at the age of six will also have a highly labile heart rate at 16 and 26, and in view of the other data in their studies they feel justified in the inference that the variability in the fetal heart rate will also be characteristic of the adult. In males, they find that the child with a highly labile heart rate has greater conflicts over dependency, is more compulsive, more indecisive, and more introspective as an adult.

So far we have been considering contributions of somatic reactivity to cognitive patterns; the studies we have discussed imply that ego and id have to be seen as aspects of a developing organism whose sensitivity and reactivity are expressed at cognitive, behavioral, affective, and somatic levels.

PRECURSORS OF DEFENSE AND ADAPTATIONAL PATTERNS

Psychoanalysis has long been interested in the question of constitutional factors in, or early precursors of, defense mechanisms and preferred coping methods. Here the longitudinal study at Topeka, with its detailed observations of the babies' ways of dealing with normal frustrations, obstacles, disappointments, or other difficulties, provides relevant data: Statistically significant correlations were found between early infantile tendencies to protest actively, to resist, or to terminate unwanted stimulation on the one hand, and the child's preschool tendency to fend off unwanted stimulation, impose his own structures on the environment, and so on, on the other. In other words, an active coping orientation can be followed in some children from early infancy through the childhood years (Murphy and Moriarty, in preparation).

The great psychoanalyst Bernfeld, author of *The Psychology of the Infant* (1925), might have subsumed such evidence under the concept of the drive toward mastery. Hartmann included these active coping and defense techniques, as well as useful avoidance (withdrawing, hiding) techniques, under the general concept of adaptation.

PLASTICITY OF EARLY EGO FUNCTIONS

A wide range of individual differences is evaluated by Escalona and Heider in *Prediction and Outcome* (1959). The data they provide make it possible to distinguish patterns that are more likely to be persistent and predictable from patterns that are less likely to persist without change. This fact suggests that certain tendencies may be more plastic, more subject to affect and interpersonal influence, than others. Other investigators have demonstrated the plasticity of even such basic patterns as sensorimotor functioning (B. White et al., 1964; B. White, 1971) and smiling (Rheingold, 1956) in early infancy. The relative persistence of patterns of attention and of the quality of motor functioning may indicate that these areas are less plastic than are such social responses as shyness, which Escalona did not find relatively predictable.

Korner (1971), in her review of differences in newborns, seems to assume that major prior shaping of response tendencies has not occurred. We must not forget, however, that Marquis (1931) long ago demonstrated conditioning in the newborn. In other words, whenever we are dealing with patterns that occur in frequently repeated encounters with the environment, conditioning has to be allowed as a possibility even within the first week. I have observed active practice and learning in the neonatal period. For instance, in efforts to get thumb to mouth, one baby required 10 attempts on the fifth day but succeeded on the first attempt by the tenth day—an example of reinforcement of mastery efforts by drive gratification. So we must not be too cavalier about assuming that in the neonatal period we are dealing with individual differences free from conditioning or from learning initiated by the infant.

Korner notes both variations in irritability and differences in how readily babies are soothed and how long they remain comforted, as well as differences in the tendency to evoke a caring response (Moss and Robson, 1968). She also notes important variations in the degree to which newborns make postural adjustments or mold to the person holding them—presumably for greater bodily comfort. She comments that restless, highly aroused, and active babies are the least cuddly, an observation which may help to answer the question about the relation between the restlessness discussed by Sontag and the experience of the baby-mother pair. For satisfactory development, cuddly babies may require more comfort from contact than do uncuddly ones. Korner interprets these data as evidence for quantitative differences in the manifestations of the oral drive and the capacity to deal with this drive—differences which should influence both the kind of homeostatic adjustment the infant makes in the earliest weeks of life and the degree to which the infant requires his mother to be a mediating, tension-reducing agent. These differences in the strength of the oral drive and the capacity for self-comforting may also influence the intensity with which weaning is experienced, quite apart from what the mother's handling of this situation may contribute to this experience. We may add that the efficacy of very early self-comforting efforts may also influence the foundations for a capacity to cope with separation from the mother and thus avoid serious separation anxiety.

Korner also comments on the implications of such differences for the babies' experiences of pleasure and pain, the memory traces they may leave, and what is required for optimal mothering. She also suggests that from the very start there may be differences in the degree to which infants "avail themselves of others for purposes of seeking comfort." These differences, along with differences in the mothers' contribution and reactions, may contribute to differences in the intensity and depth of infants' first attachments. She believes that these are the types of individual tendencies that "become part of larger schemata so they are not necessarily recognizable in their original form at a later time." She also suggests that these types of differences may contribute to vague feelings of helplessness, omnipotence, dependence, separateness, or oneness with the mother, and, together with maternal differences, may feed into the kinds of object relations the child will develop. Some of these same variations are discussed by Heider (1966) in her Topeka study of vulnerability in infants and young children.

INTEGRATIVE CAPACITY

We have already referred to the individual differences in reactivity to sensory stimulation reported by Bergman and Escalona (1949). Both the Topeka studies and Korner focus on the importance of a *balance* between the capacity to take in sensory stimuli and the ability to synthesize them. As Heider (1966) pointed out, an imbalance between the amount of sensory stimulation to which the baby responds and his capacity for synthesizing it may constitute a major source of vulnerability through interference with the integration and cognitive programming of stimulation. Thus alertness to what amount constitutes over-stimulation is just as important as concern with understimulation in guiding the baby's cognitive development. And, as Heider has pointed out, not only the quantity of stimulation is important but the qualities are also important. She describes babies who were more disturbed by strange soft sounds than by loud sounds, and others who were disturbed by sounds of one or another special quality.

The analyst Benjamin (1961) has commented on the maturational spurt in sensory capacities around the end of the first month, before babies have developed an adequate "stimulus barrier." He adds that very sensitive babies tend to become overwhelmed by stimulation unless a mothering person acts as a shield and tension-reducing agent. He believes that the outcome of this early critical phase could have important implications for the predisposition to anxiety, and we could go beyond this to suggest that all babies with special sensitivities, or tendencies to be more than usually reactive to stimulation, have a greater need for shielding from and dosing of stimulation. Korner (1971), like Heider, also notes that babies who are less responsive to sensory stimulation need to have more of it. Korner suggests that soothing the baby and other handling actually contributes to providing the kind of stimulation that he needs, since when a baby is picked up and put to the shoulder he usually stops crying and frequently also becomes bright-eyed and scans his whole visual surrounding. Consequently, in addition to whatever reduction of tension and development of positive affective responses this experience gives him, it also provides him with visual stimulation. Korner further suggests that infants with high sensory thresholds will show the effects of maternal neglect more markedly than infants who are more receptive to environmental stimuli.

Korner also makes the important suggestion that the balance between sensory threshold levels and the integrative functions may critically contribute to how development will proceed. We agree that in this balance we may some day find "the predispositional core" that influences the choice of later cognitive-control and defense structures and persistent styles of managing impulse and affect. She points to the work of Thomas et al. (1963) which showed the strong persistence of children's tendencies to seek out new stimuli or to withdraw from new situations, and to Kagan's (1967) observations of children who respond quickly and impulsively to problem situations, in contrast to others who respond consistently with reflectiveness and caution.

In our work at Sarah Lawrence we found similar differences between chil-

dren who quickly jump into a new situation and those who maintain a receptive stance for a longer period. I reported an extreme example of such a child
who remained quietly observing for the first couple of months of nursery school,
after which she created more complex structures with blocks than children who
had made more immediate active responses (Murphy, 1941). Korner refers to
Pavlov's (1926) distinction between vivacious and exuberant dogs who react
quickly to every stimulus, and dogs who are inhibited by a new and unfamiliar
stimulus. The second type of dog was extremely slow in getting used to new
surroundings but, once familiar with them, became an excellent subject for
conditioning. The first type, on the other hand, could be conditioned only by
continually varying the stimulation.

The first serves to sift, to diminish, or to make manageable incoming stimuli,
Korner formulates two basic regulatory principles for dealing with over-
stimulation, "each of which, if excessively relied upon, favors the adoption of
broad categories of ego characteristics, ego defenses and cognitive styles." One
of these serves to sift, to diminish, or to make manageable incoming stimuli,
and focusing, sharpening, a field-independent and an analytic-reflective approach
are likely to characterize cognitive control patterns. Obsessive-compulsive mechanisms, isolation, intellectualization, and rationalization are frequent defense
mechanisms; and caution or avoidance of novel stimuli and strong excitation are
likely to characterize the coping style of the ego.

The other regulatory principle favors the management of strong stimulation by motor or affective discharge, impulsiveness, action rather than reflection, externalization, field dependence, and/or displacement behavior. Novelty,
change, and strong excitation would be experienced as ego syntonic. Korner
believes that heavy reliance on any one type of coping strategy or defense
mechanism within these two broad categories of reaction is probably rooted
in an experiential and/or maturational matrix. The first type of regulatory principle is suggested by statistically significant correlations between the infants'
tendencies toward motor inhibition and the frequency of visual behavior, and
reliance on small motions. Infants prone to motor discharge, in contrast, were
much less visually exploratory and displayed more diffuse motor activity.

In the meantime, Escalona (1968) made an intensive study of the most
active and least active infants in her sample of 128 infants studied in detail at
one phase during the first six months of life. She delineates the kinds and
quantities of experience that emerge for these two kinds of babies and the
developmental outcomes. Escalona recognizes the double implications for adaptation of certain aspects of functioning. She notes that in the clinical evaluation
of infants it is generally assumed that a thriving and well-adapted baby is one
who eats well, sleeps well, and in general shows bodily well-being. Smooth
integration of bodily functions is thus considered one index of adaptation. "We
might with equal reason have assumed that adequate integration of vegetative
functioning is a precondition for optimal development and functioning," and
the rating of vegetative functioning would become one of the "stable patterns of experience" (SPE) determinants.

In her study, activity level is treated as an important determinant of SPE.

Her rich and detailed summaries of individual babies of high activity level and low activity level at successive ages during the first six months provide colorful evidence of some of the varieties of increasing integration seen in evolving adaptive resources. Highly active babies five to six months old showed more varied and more complex spontaneous behavior, reflecting the expected developmental changes. The most frequent and most prominent "behavior activations" were, first, complex position changes, often to and from a sitting position (probably motivated by the effort to reach for, contact, and manipulate objects), and second, persistent efforts to elicit social responses from an impassive person (by physical approach, squealing, or laughing in a provocative manner), squealing both joyously and impatiently, and multisyllable babbling. In my own observations as well, the latter behavior is characteristic of the outgoing responsiveness and expressiveness of active babies of this part of the world. (Babies in slings on the mother's hip as in India, or wrapped in a wide sash as in Nigeria, or strapped to a cradleboard as in certain American Indian groups, probably do not receive the stimuli which bring about this kind of diffuse motor and expressive activity. Yet in Nigeria, at least, at later ages they become very active.)

Escalona notes that most new patterns reflected the expansion of the effective environment through an increase in the tendency of these babies to behave so as to change their environments. Infants may become active agents of change in a variety of ways; experiences of varying relationships between one's body and the environment presumably contribute to an early awareness of the self or body ego and, I believe, to an awareness of the possibility of making an impact on the environment.

Escalona also comments that during spontaneous activity the behavior of the active babies is more intense; they not only range over space more freely, they make more noise. Their behavior is more complex, as they alternately pivot, scoot, or creep, and frequently try to achieve upright kneeling or standing postures; some of them bounce and jump vigorously. Interestingly enough, because it does not seem to be of a piece with this serially shifting behavior, Escalona reports that the active babies manipulated two objects simultaneously more often than inactive subjects. The fact that Escalona's active babies were persistent in their efforts to provoke a social interaction with initially unresponsive persons implies a strong urge toward interplay as contrasted with solitary play. They also squealed and babbled a great deal during motor or manipulatory activity.

Escalona found that inactive babies, in contrast, generally tended to remain where they had been placed, changing position mildly by rolling from prone to supine (and vice versa) and by alternating horizontal and sitting postures, none of which changes took them to new locations. They cooed and occasionally whimpered in annoyance, but seldom squealed or babbled. Inactive babies spent more time visually exploring the environment, and also directed more attention to parts of their own bodies.

This review of a small part of Escalona's discussion (1968, pp. 188–190) may be enough to hint at the implications of her observations for diverse processes of adaptation, with their different sources of drive gratification and range of opportunities for cognitive mastery as well as early differences in cognitive style.

FRUSTRATION

The role of frustration in development has been discussed in psychoanalysis in several different contexts. It has long been recognized that an important learning process is involved in developing the capacity to delay, an early and basic function of the ego. The child analyst Fries (1946) long ago wrote a helpful article on the importance of dosing frustrations according to the child's level of tolerance, with appropriate but gradual increases, for the ego development of the child. Here again our data on the Topeka infants gives ample evidence of the constructive role of appropriate doses of frustration, obstacles, challenge, and the like, which stimulate the coping efforts of the child as well as contribute to the development of tolerance of frustration, ability to accept substitutes, adaptive flexibility, and other adaptive assets (Murphy and Moriarty, in preparation).

AGGRESSION

The problem of aggression has been of special interest in psychoanalysis since Freud's *Beyond the Pleasure Principle* (1920), in which he suggested that a destructive instinct was needed to account for human aggression but added that the theory of instincts is "our mythology." Longitudinal studies document behavior even in the early weeks of the infant's life which the dismayed mother may experience as aggressive: for instance, consider the baby who blows his unwanted new cereal into his mother's face. If, however, we subsume this behavior under the rubric of active coping, we allow for the possibility that the infant may develop more civilized expressions of his capacity for active protest.

Anna Freud (1971) has said that we do not yet have an adequate theory of aggression. This is another area where detailed naturalistic observations of samples of normal children in different subcultures could provide contextually adequate data for both psychoanalytic and child-development studies. In this area, as in the whole area of motivation, affect, and investment in the environment, further progress needs the collaborative efforts of psychoanalysis and child development. Whiting and Child's (1953) cross-cultural study of aggression is a beginning; but in view of the correlation of .44 found between sympathetic behavior and aggression in a sample of preschool children (Murphy, 1937), we have to carry our study of aggression much further.

That most hostile behavior can be liquidated by opportunities for cooperation has been brilliantly demonstrated by Lewin, Lippitt, and White (1939) and Sherif et al. (1961). We need to reflect on the processes involved here, and their dynamics in relation to the difficult problems of reorienting delinquent "children who hate" (Redl and Wineman, 1951).

Further study is also needed to bring together psychoanalytic concepts of the development of control functions as seen, for instance, by Rapaport (1951), and medical concepts of the physiological precursors of disorganized or problem behavior. Pasamanick and his collaborators (Pasamanick, Rogers, and Lilienfeld, 1956; Knobloch and Pasamanick, 1960), Drillien (1964), Bender (1953), and others have documented connections between early infantile difficulties and later personality disturbances. And Glueck (1966) has offered a formula for prediction of later aggression (including delinquency) on the basis of infancy data. But Kagan and Moss (1962) found that latency-age behavior (when conscience and control habits are being organized) predicts adult aggressiveness better than does infancy behavior. Psychoanalytically oriented longitudinal studies of children who show early infantile difficulties of the sort referred to above could make possible a better understanding of processes leading to outcomes other than aggression. It is possible, for instance, that children with early impulse-control problems have to develop compulsive controls in order to cope with aggressive impulses. One extreme may require the opposite extreme, if socialization is to occur. The point here is that both psychoanalytic and child-development techniques for studying these children are needed.

EXPERIENTIAL SEQUENCES CONTRIBUTING TO EGO DEVELOPMENT

Anthropologists such as Bateson and Mead (1952) have been able to observe age sequences in the behavior of children in relatively homogeneous groups of various types. For instance, they suggested that in Bali tender care of the infant followed by teasing at the toddler stage contributed to a defensive pattern of detachment or "awayness" which they saw as typical of Balinese personal relationships. The ways in which the baby is fed, bathed, put to sleep, and played with can all be assumed to contribute to schemata of expectancies from the environment.

These may be what Erikson (1950, 1963) implies in his broad concept of basic trust-mistrust, which he sees as a major contribution to ego development from the oral phase, that is, infancy. While he emphasizes the climaxing of autonomy in the phase of locomotion and sphincter control, Murphy's (1962) analysis of Escalona and Leitch's (1952) data documents very early infantile expressions of autonomous coping. Erikson recognizes the emergence of pride parallel with the flowering of autonomy in the second year of life. Bühler (1930) had illustrated the expression of "triumph" even before the end of the first year.

In his most recent paper, "On Play," Erikson (1972) elaborates on the rich integration of body image, inner conflict, and life task in play constructions which show both continuity and variation of themes close to the core of a person's development, as documented in the later development of the person.

I cannot review all of Erikson's well-known gifts to the field of child development; I will merely comment that the extraordinary usefulness of his formulations is to a considerable degree the result of his capacity to document, in culturally relevant terms, some of the everyday expressions of the principles he sets forth.

Following Hartmann, Rapaport, and Erikson, Robert W. White (1963) gave us a careful analysis of the developing ego's functioning in dealings with reality, and offered the term "competence" as an integrative concept referring to achieved skill—a concept widely welcomed in child-development research.

NEED FOR FURTHER INTEGRATION OF PSYCHOANALYTIC AND CHILD-DEVELOPMENT CONCEPTS

In both psychoanalysis and child development crucial concepts have been left by the roadside, as it were, when in reality we need to cultivate and develop them. From psychoanalysis I have in mind Hendrick's (1942) "instinct to mastery" and Mittelmann's (1954) concept of the "motor urge," which he placed on a par with oral and libidinal drives. From child development I would mention, first, Karl Bühler's concept of "function pleasure," which implies that satisfaction accrues from a wide range of functioning of the child, and second, Bridges's (1931) conception of the sequences in differentiation of emotion in the infant. All of these, if developed and considered in relation to our need for a comprehensive dynamic understanding of motivation, should be further developed, elaborated, and applied to the gamut of childhood behaviors, including the wide individual differences in the stimuli that provide gratification.

Parallel with this need, and complementary to it, is the need for analysis of such careful documents as One Boy's Day (Barker and Wright, 1951). This detailed record of a seven-year-old child's behavior—from morning awakening to going to bed—begs for a study of the series of motivations implied in his everyday behavior. Burton White's (1971) plea for an adequate descriptive base for the formulation of child-development principles implies the need for just such comprehensive records of the child's spontaneous behavior and experience in the culture.

While the facts of shifting fears and anxieties are documented by child-development studies, and certain psychoanalytic principles offer explanations of the differences in sources of fear at different ages, we do not have adequate documentation of processes of outgrowing fears. Long ago Mary C. Jones (1924) demonstrated experimentally the reconditioning—or should we say deconditioning—of a child's fear by associating the fear stimulus with a more important stimulus for gratification. Is this the only or chief process of outgrowing fear in everyday life? Only long-term records of children's experiences can provide data on the processes and dynamics of "outgrowing" maladaptive behavior. An important record from the Hampstead Nurseries (Hellman, 1962) is an example of what could be done—a record of observations of a child's mastery of traumatic loss.

We are currently struggling for solution of problems in raising children who can enhance, not destroy, civilization. These solutions will require all the insight our disciplines can contribute, not only separately but through a process of mutual deepening.

It is clear that we need not only further collaboration between psycho-analysis and child development for the mutual validation and deepening of both approaches: we need collaborative thinking to *extend the range* of concepts available for understanding the complexity of personality development.

REFERENCES

Ainsworth, M., ed. (1962). *Deprivation of Maternal Care: A Reassessment of Its Effects.* Geneva: World Health Organization.

Alpert, A., Neubauer, P. B., and Weil, A. P. (1956). Unusual Variations in Drive Endowment. *The Psychoanalytic Study of the Child,* 11:125–163. New York: International Universities Press.

Barker, R. G., Dembo, T., and Lewin, K. (1943). Frustration and Regression. In: *Child Behavior and Development,* ed. R. G. Barker, J. Kounin, and H. F. Wright. New York: McGraw-Hill, pp. 441–458.

——, and Wright, H. F. (1951). *One Boy's Day.* New York: Harper.

Bateson, G., and Mead, M. (1952). *Balinese Character: A Photographic Analysis.* New York: New York Academy of Sciences Special Publication.

Bayley, N. (1956). Individual Patterns of Development. *Child Development,* 27:45–74.

Bender, L. (1953). Childhood Schizophrenia. *Psychiatric Quarterly,* 27:663–681.

Benjamin, J. D. (1961). The Innate and the Experiential in Development. In: *Lectures in Experimental Psychiatry,* ed. H. W. Brosin. Pittsburgh: University of Pittsburgh Press, pp. 19–42.

Bergman, P., and Escalona, S. K. (1949). Unusual Sensitivities in Very Young Children. *The Psychoanalytic Study of the Child,* 3/4:333–352. New York: International Universities Press.

Bernfeld, S. (1925). *The Psychology of the Infant.* New York: Brentano, 1929.

Bowlby, J. (1969). *Attachment and Loss,* Vol. 1. New York: Basic Books.

Breuer, J., and Freud, S. (1893–1895). Studies on Hysteria. *Standard Edition,* 2. London: Hogarth Press, 1955.

Bridges, K. B. (1931). *The Social and Emotional Development of the Preschool Child.* London: Kegan Paul, Trench, Trubner.

Brody, S. (1956). *Patterns of Mothering.* New York: International Universities Press.

Bühler, C. (1930). *The First Year of Life.* New York: Day.

Carpenter, G., et al. (1970). Differential Visual Behavior to Human and Humanoid Faces in Early Infancy. *Merrill-Palmer Quarterly,* 16:91–108.

Drillien, C. M. (1964). *The Growth and Development of the Prematurely-Born Infant.* Edinburgh and London: Livingston.

Erikson, E. H. (1950). *Childhood and Society.* New York: Norton.

—— (1963). *Childhood and Society,* 2nd ed. New York: Norton.

—— (1972). On Play. In: *Play and Development,* ed. M. Piers. New York: Norton.

Escalona, S. (1952). Emotional Development in the First Year of Life. In: *Problems of Infancy and Childhood; Transactions of the Sixth Conference,* ed. M. J. E. Senn. New York: Josiah Macy, Jr. Foundation, 1953.

—— (1963). Patterns of Infantile Experience and the Developmental Process. *The Psychoanalytic Study of the Child,* 18:197–244. New York: International Universities Press.

—— (1968). *The Roots of Individuality.* Chicago: Aldine.

————, and Heider, G. M. (1959). *Prediction and Outcome.* New York: Basic Books.

————, and Leitch, M. (1952). Early Phases of Personality Development: A Non-normative Study of Infant Behavior. *Monographs of the Society for Research in Child Development,* 17(1, Whole No. 54).

Fantz, R. L. (1963). Pattern Vision in Newborn Infants. *Science,* 140:296–297.

Frank, L. K. (1966). *On the Importance of Infancy.* New York: Random House.

Freud, A. (1971). Address at the 1971 International Congress of Psychoanalysis, Vienna.

————, and Burlingham, D. (1943). *War and Children.* New York: International Universities Press.

————, ———— (1944). *Infants without Families.* New York: International Universities Press.

Freud, S. (1905). Three Essays on the Theory of Sexuality. *Standard Edition,* 7:130–243. London: Hogarth Press, 1959.

———— (1910). Five Lectures on Psycho-Analysis. *Standard Edition,* 11:3–55. London: Hogarth Press, 1957.

———— (1920). Beyond the Pleasure Principle. *Standard Edition,* 18:7–64. London: Hogarth Press, 1959.

Fries, M. E. (1946). The Child's Ego Development and the Training of Adults in His Environment. *The Psychoanalytic Study of the Child,* 2:85–112. New York: International Universities Press.

Galton, F. (1869). *Hereditary Genius.* New York: Macmillan, 1914.

Gesell, A., et al. (1940). *The First Five Years of Life: A Guide to the Study of the Preschool Child.* New York: Harper.

Glover, E. (1947). *Basic Mental Concepts: Their Clinical and Theoretical Value.* London: Imago.

Glueck, E. T. (1966). Identification of Potential Delinquents at Two to Three Years of Age. *Excerpta Criminologica,* 6:309–314.

Gordon, I. J., and Lally, J. R. (1967). *Intellectual Stimulation for Infants and Toddlers.* Gainesville: University of Florida, Institute for Development of Human Resources.

Greenacre, P. (1952). *Trauma, Growth, and Personality.* New York: Norton.

Haith, M. M. (1968). Visual Scanning in Infants. Paper read at Regional Society for Research in Child Development meetings, Clark University.

Hall, G. S. (1891). The Contents of Children's Minds on Entering School. *Pedagogical Seminary,* 1:139–173.

Hartmann, H. (1939). *Ego Psychology and the Problem of Adaptation.* New York: International Universities Press, 1958.

———— (1952). The Mutual Influences in the Development of Ego and Id. *The Psychoanalytic Study of the Child,* 7:9–30. New York: International Universities Press.

Hebb, D. O. (1946). On the Nature of Fear. *Psychological Review,* 53:259–276.

Heider, G. M. (1966). Vulnerability in Infants and Young Children. *Genetic Psychology Monographs,* 73:1–216.

Hellman, I. (1962). Hampstead Nursery Follow-Up Studies: 1. Sudden Separation and Its Effect Followed over Twenty Years. *The Psychoanalytic Study of the Child,* 17:159–174. New York: International Universities Press.

Hendrick, I. (1942). Instinct and the Ego during Infancy. *Psychoanalytic Quarterly,* 11:33–58.

Isaacs, S. (1933). *Social Development in Young Children: A Study of Beginnings.* New York: Harcourt, Brace.

———— (1949). *Childhood and After.* New York: International Universities Press.

Jones, H. E. (1944). The Development of Physical Abilities in Adolescence. *43rd Yearbook, National Society for the Study of Education,* Part I. Chicago: University of Chicago.

Jones, M. C. (1924). Elimination of Children's Fears. *Journal of Experimental Psychology,* 7:382–390.

Kagan, J. (1967). Biological Aspects of Inhibition Systems. *American Journal of Diseases of Children,* 114:507–522.

————, and Moss, H. A. (1962). *Birth to Maturity: A Study in Psychological Development.* New York: Wiley.

Klein, M. (1932). *The Psychoanalysis of Children.* New York: Norton.

Knobloch, H., and Pasamanick, B. (1960). Environmental Factors Affecting Human Development before and after Birth. *Pediatrics,* 26:210–218.

Korner, A. (1971). Individual Differences at Birth: Implications for Early Experience and Later Development. *American Journal of Orthopsychiatry,* 41:608–619.

Lacey, J. I., Kagan, J., Lacey, B. C., and Moss, H. A. (1962). The Visceral Level: Situational Determinants and Behavioral Correlates of Autonomic Response Patterns. In: *Expression of the Emotions in Man,* ed. P. J. Knapp. New York: International Universities Press, pp. 161–196.

————, and Lacey, B. C. (1958). The Relationship of Resting Autonomic Activity to Motor Impulsivity. In: *The Brain and Human Behavior. Proceedings of the Association for Research in Nervous and Mental Disease,* 36:144–209.

Lambo, T. A. (1961). Growth of African Children (Psychological Aspects). In: *Pan African Psychiatric Conference,* ed. T. A. Lambo. Abeokuta, Nigeria: Ibadan, Government Printer.

Levy, D. M. (1943). *Maternal Overprotection.* New York: Columbia University Press.

———— (1945). Psychic Trauma of Operations in Children. *American Journal of Diseases of Children,* 69:7–15.

———— (1960). The Infant's Earliest Memory of Inoculation. *Journal of Genetic Psychology,* 96:3–46.

Lewin, K. (1943). Defining the 'Field at a Given Time.' *Psychological Review,* 50:292–310.

————, Lippitt, R., and White, R. K. (1939). Patterns of Aggressive Behavior in Experimentally Created "Social Climates." *Journal of Social Psychology,* 10:271–299.

Liss, E. (1937). Emotional and Biological Factors Involved in Learning Processes. *American Journal of Orthopsychiatry,* 7:483–488.

Macfarlane, J. W., Allen, L., and Honzik, M. P. (1954). *A Developmental Study of the Behavior Problems of Normal Children between 21 Months and 14 Years.* Berkeley: University of California Press.

Marquis, D. P. (1931). Can Conditioned Reflexes Be Established in Infancy? *Journal of Genetic Psychology,* 39:479–492.

Mittelmann, B. (1954). Motility in Infants, Children, and Adults: Patterning and Psychodynamics. *The Psychoanalytic Study of the Child,* 9:142–177. New York: International Universities Press.

Moriarty, A. E. (1966). *Constancy and I.Q. Change.* Springfield, Ill.: Charles C Thomas.

Moss, H., and Robson, K. (1968). The Role of Protest Behavior in the Development of the Mother-Infant Attachment. Paper presented at the 76th annual convention of the American Psychological Association, San Francisco.

Murphy, L. B. (1937). *Social Behavior and Child Personality.* New York: Columbia University Press.

———— (1941). Joyce from Two to Five. *Progressive Education,* 18:46–53.

———— (1962). *The Widening World of Childhood.* New York: Basic Books.

———— (1964). Some Aspects of the First Relationship. *International Journal of Psycho-Analysis,* 45:31–43.

———— (1968). The Vulnerability Inventory. In: *Early Child Care: The New Perspectives,* Appendix A, ed. L. Dittmann, C. Chandler, R. Peters, and A. Peters. New York: Atherton.

———— (1970). The Problem of Defense and the Concept of Coping. In: *The Child in His Family,* ed. E. J. Anthony and C. Koupernik. New York: Wiley-Interscience.

————, et al. (1956). *Personality in Young Children,* 2 vols. New York: Basic Books.

————, and Moriarty, A. E. (in preparation). *Development, Vulnerability, and Resilience.*

Olson, W. C., and Hughes, B. O. (1943). Growth of the Child as a Whole. In: *Child Be-*

havior and Development, ed. R. G. Barker et al. New York: McGraw-Hill, pp. 199–208.

Pasamanick, B., Rogers, M. E., and Lilienfeld, A. M. (1956). Pregnancy Experience and the Development of Behavior Disorder in Children. *American Journal of Psychiatry,* 112:613–618.

Pavlov, I. P. (1926). *Conditioned Reflexes.* New York: Dover.

Piaget, J. (1936). *The Origins of Intelligence in Children.* New York: International Universities Press, 1952.

Prechtl, H. F. R. (1961). Neurological Sequelae of Prenatal and Paranatal Complications. In: *Determinants of Infant Behavior.* Proceedings of a Tavistock Study Group, ed. B. M. Foss. New York: Wiley.

Rapaport, D., ed. (1951). *Organization and Pathology of Thought.* New York: Columbia University Press.

Redl, F., and Wineman, D. (1951). *Children Who Hate.* Glencoe, Ill.: Free Press.

Rheingold, H. L. (1956). The Modification of Social Responsiveness in Institutional Babies. *Monographs of the Society for Research in Child Development,* 21(2, Whole No. 63).

Richards, T. W., and Nelson, V. L. (1938). Studies in Mental Development: II. Analysis of Abilities Tested at the Age of Six Months by the Gesell Schedule. *Journal of Genetic Psychology,* 52:327–331.

Ritvo, S., et al. (1963). Some Relations of Constitution, Environment, and Personality as Observed in a Longitudinal Study of Child Development: Case Report. In: *Modern Perspectives in Child Development,* ed. A. J. Solnit and S. A. Provence. New York: International Universities Press, pp. 107–143.

Rosenzweig, M. R. (1966). Environmental Complexity, Cerebral Change, and Behavior. *American Psychologist,* 21:321–332.

Sherif, M., et al. (1961). *Intergroup Conflict and Cooperation: The Robbers Cave Experiment.* Norman: University of Oklahoma, Institute of Group Relations.

Shirley, M. M. (1931–1933). *The First Two Years: A Study of Twenty-Five Babies,* 3 vols. University of Minnesota Institute of Child Welfare Monographs 6–8.

———— (1938). Development of Immature Babies during Their First Two Years. *Child Development,* 9:347–360.

————, and Poyntz, L. (1941). The Influence of Separation from the Mother on Children's Emotional Responses. *Journal of Psychology,* 12:251–282.

Sontag, L. W. (1966). Implications of Fetal Behavior and Environment for Adult Personalities. *Annals of the New York Academy of Sciences,* 134:782–786.

————, Baker, C. T., and Nelson, V. L. (1958). Mental Growth and Personality Development: A Longitudinal Study. *Monographs of the Society for Research in Child Development,* 23(2, Whole No. 68).

Spitz, R. (1945). Hospitalism. *The Psychoanalytic Study of Child,* 1:53–74. New York: International Universities Press.

———— (1946). Anaclitic Depression. *The Psychoanalytic Study of the Child,* 2:313–342. New York: International Universities Press.

———— (1970). Fundamental Education. Paper presented at the annual conference of the Academy of Pediatrics, Washington, D.C.

Stolz, H. R., and Stolz, L. M. (1951). *Somatic Development of Adolescent Boys.* New York: Macmillan.

Sullivan, H. S. (1946–1947). *The Interpersonal Theory of Psychiatry.* New York: Norton, 1953.

Thomas, A., et al. (1963). *Behavioral Individuality in Early Childhood.* New York: New York University Press.

Thorndike, E. (1933). Lectures at Teachers' College, Columbia University. Unpublished.

Voth, H., and Mayman, M. (1967). Diagnostic and Treatment Implications of Ego-Closeness-Ego-Distance: Autokinesis as a Diagnostic Instrument. *Comprehensive Psychiatry,* 8:203–216.

Werner, H. (1940). *Comparative Psychology of Mental Development,* rev. ed. New York: Follett, 1948.

White, B. (1971). *Human Infants; Experience and Psychological Development.* New York: Prentice-Hall.

———, et al. (1964). Observations on the Development of Visually-Directed Reaching. *Child Development,* 35:349–364.

White, R. W. (1963). Ego and Reality in Psychoanalytic Theory. *Psychological Issues,* Monograph 11. New York: International Universities Press.

Whiting, J., and Child, I. L. (1953). *Child Training and Personality: A Comparative Study.* New Haven: Yale University Press.

Williams, R. J. (1956). *Biochemical Individuality.* New York: Wiley.

Wolf, K. M. (1952). Observation of Individual Tendencies in the First Year of Life. In: *Problems of Infancy and Childhood; Transactions of the Sixth Conference,* ed. M. J. E. Senn. New York: Josiah Macy, Jr. Foundation, 1953, pp. 97–137.

Wolff, P. H. (1966). The Causes, Controls, and Organization of Behavior in the Neonate. *Psychological Issues,* Monograph 17. New York: International Universities Press.

Yarrow, L. J. (1956). The Development of Object Relationships during Infancy, and the Effects of a Disruption of Early Mother-Child Relationships. *American Psychologist,* 11:423 (abstract).

——— (1964). Personality Consistency and Change: An Overview of Some Conceptual and Methodological Issues. *Vita Humana,* 7(2):67–72.

———, et al. (1971). Infancy Experiences and Cognitive and Personality Development at Ten Years. Paper presented at the annual meeting of the American Orthopsychiatric Association.

LANGUAGE AND NONVERBAL COMMUNICATION IN COGNITIVE AND AFFECTIVE PROCESSES

McCay Vernon, Ph.D., and William Gene Miller, Ph.D.

The nature of the interaction of language and thought is a profound issue, and its resolution is basic to understanding human psychology. The problem has attracted the leading scholars of many areas and varying disciplines, among whom are Plato, Socrates, Hobbes, Coleridge, Galton, Freud, Croce, Piaget, and Ruesch (VanderWoude, 1970; Vernon, 1967). Recently, the study of persons born deaf has yielded scientific data which have permitted experimentally derived conclusions about the role of language in cognition and inferences about its role in affective functioning.

LANGUAGE AND COGNITION

The congenitally deaf provide a unique opportunity for the study of thought and language. Deaf children go through their early years with no verbal symbol system whatever. When the child born deaf begins his formal education, he does not know the names of the food he eats, the clothes he wears, or even his own name. Nor does he have any concept of the syntactical rules required to join words together. In contrast, normally hearing children by the age of six have almost complete mastery of syntax and a vocabulary estimated at around 25,000 words (Moores, 1970). Cases of congenitally deaf persons who grow to adulthood never having attended school are not uncommon. They obviously represent an even more extreme situation than the deaf child who attends school.

Thus, in the congenitally deaf child we have, in a sense, the setting for the medical model of studying the pathological to understand the normal. That is, if we could describe the effect of the absence of verbal language on thought and affect in the congenitally deaf, we would then know the role played by language in the development of thought and affect in the nondeaf or "normal" population. Stated somewhat differently, congenital deafness offers a "natural"

124

control of the experimental variable of verbal language, the effects of which can be measured, thereby determining the role of language in thought.

LANGUAGE AND PROBLEM SOLVING

Extensive work has been done in language and problem solving by experimental psychologists (Blanton and Nunnally, 1964; Furth, 1966; Kates, Kates, and Michael, 1962; Rosenstein, 1960, 1961; VanderWoude, 1970; Vernon, 1967). Basically, all of these researchers, and those whose work they review, used the same experimental design. They matched nondeaf and deaf subjects on key variables such as age, IQ, sex, and years in school so that the only relevant variable in which the two groups differed was that one had a verbal symbol system and the other did not. The two groups were then given a multitude of problems to solve which involved abstracting, generalizing, memory, reasoning, concept formation, and the other processes which characterize thought.

It has been found that when groups are matched in this way, subjects with no verbal language solve problems in the same way and with the same efficiency as those with high levels of linguistic competence. In other words, when the experimental variable of verbal language is systematically manipulated there is no change in the dependent variable of problem-solving efficiency or in the steps used in solving the problems (Darbyshire and Reeves, 1969; Furth, 1966; Rosenstein, 1961; VanderWoude, 1970; Vernon, 1967).

The study of aphasic patients has yielded similar results. Despite not having verbal language, the aphasic often has exceptional problem-solving skill (Geschwind, 1970).

Furthermore, Rosen's (1964, 1967) studies of mathematical geniuses and of artists demonstrate that their outstanding creative accomplishments are conceptualized nonverbally. In fact, these abstract creative processes frequently are beyond the verbal description of the person who performs them.

The obvious conclusion from all of this research is that verbal language is not a relevant variable in cognition, i.e., the mediating process of thought is not a system of verbal symbols. Piaget himself said that in his own study of thinking he had failed to recognize that the roots of cognitive processes lie deeper than language (1962).

LANGUAGE AND MEMORY

The enigma of how the brain stores and retrieves the billions of bits of information which it takes in during a lifetime is as yet unresolved. In the work directed by Grinker (1969), deaf, i.e., essentially nonverbal, subjects were used as the experimental group for study of the role of language in short- and long-term memory. Just as with problem solving, it was found that subjects with linguistic competence functioned no better and no differently on memory tasks than did those who were without a system of verbal symbols (Koh, Vernon, and Bailey, in press). Memory, like problem solving, seems to be independent of language.

THE VERBAL AND NONVERBAL IN AFFECTIVE
DEVELOPMENT AND COMMUNICATION

A comprehensive psychology must address itself not only to the role of language in cognition but also to its role in the development and communication
of affect. Existing theoretical models of man which have placed great emphasis
on the role of words in the communication of affect do not stand up in the face
of the evidence of relatively normal adjustment in most congenitally deaf persons—persons who grew through early childhood and into adolescence without
significant verbal interaction with parents and others.

According to prominent existing theories of schizophrenia, for example,
such isolation as is created by deafness would impair affective functioning and
object relations seriously enough to cause schizophrenia. Deafness produces
many of the key experiences thought to be conducive to schizophrenia (Vernon
and Rothstein, 1968). In other words, the experience of deaf persons cannot
be accommodated in these theories.

Arieti (1967) has stressed the importance of cognition and concept formation in the genesis of schizophrenia. He has gone so far as to say that what may
prove most pathogenic is not instinctual impulses or instinctual deprivations,
but ideas—the cognitive component of human beings which has been neglected
in psychoanalysis as well as in general psychiatry and psychology. Despite severe
limitations in cognitive achievement (not cognitive capacity) and concept formation in the deaf, the prevalence of schizophrenia among them is no greater than
in the general population, a fact which casts obvious doubt on Arieti's theory
(Rainer et al., 1963). An explanation of why deaf persons are not seriously mentally ill, or even schizophrenic, comes primarily from an understanding of the
relative roles played by verbal and nonverbal communication in affective development. Major aspects of this explanation deserve special attention and are
discussed below.

Body Language

The recent study of body movements, long demeaned as "veterinary psychiatry,"
is now revealing that such movements are perhaps the primary communicators
of human feelings. It was Darwin who initially postulated the presence of universals in the "body language" of animals and men. He found that persons of
widely different cultures had no trouble recognizing the emotions expressed in
the drawings and photographs of persons of other cultures. These observations,
made in *The Expression of the Emotions in Man and Animals,* have gone un-
noticed over the years, while his *Origin of Species* has received almost total acceptance. Even today, Darwin's conclusions about nonverbal behavior, when
discussed at all, are a matter of controversy. Some current scholars, such as
Birdwhistell (1970), contend that there are no universal gestures, body motions,
or facial expressions, but only culturally determined ones. However, Ekman,
Sorenson, and Friesen (1969) conducted studies in Borneo, New Guinea, Brazil,
Japan, and the United States, five widely different cultures, and discovered that

observers recognized some of the same emotions when they were shown a standard set of photographs of faces. This evidence supports Darwin's earlier observations regarding the universality of recognition, and contradicts the assumption of Bruner and Tagiuri (1954) that facial displays of emotion are socially learned.

In other research, Ekman and Friesen (1968, 1969) have found that while some superficial body expressions may vary culturally, the more deep-seated ones are common to people everywhere in the world. For example, when Ekman showed films of surgery to native Japanese and Americans when they were alone in a dark room, both groups registered facial disgust. Yet when interviewed about the movies in filmed conversation afterward, the Japanese smiled, a culturally appropriate response for them, whereas the Americans continued to register disgust, a reaction acceptable in American society.

Ekman and Friesen (1968) developed sophisticated techniques of analysis, involving 52 catalogued facial movements and their combinations, to identify the clues which distinguish between genuine affect and cultural masks.

Interestingly, Ekman has found that the same kind of counterphobic phenomena occurs in body communication as in conventional verbal psychotherapy. For example, persons who themselves have problems with anger tend to misinterpret other people's body communication of anger, just as psychotherapists who have problems with their own feelings are unable to perceive those same feelings in patients.

The work of Rosenthal (1967) indicates that the objectivity of even rigorously designed psychological research is undermined by the power of nonverbal cues. The experimenters were discovered to be forcing the desired results from the experimental subjects through unconscious affective body communication. Hess (1965) demonstrated that the involuntary dilating and constricting of the pupil of the eye manifest many interests, emotions, thought processes, and attitudes far more directly and accurately than does verbalization. Hess found, for example, that while the man looking at a *Playboy* fold-out denied any response to it, his pupillary responses were giving him away.

The relatively healthy psychological adjustment of the congenitally deaf as adults is evidence of the important role played by "body language" in affective development, especially in parent-child interactions, and of the lesser role of conventional verbal communication. Only because basic affect is communicated by the body, i.e., nonverbally, does the deaf child have sufficient affective interaction with his parents to permit normal psychological growth. Through such communication, he is saved from potentially fatal psychological deprivation. If verbal language were the major vehicle for affective interaction, children whose deafness deprives them of this input would experience severe psychopathology. They do not.

In everyday life, the typecasting of theatrical performers is a familiar example of the importance of body language. Liberace's body language would make his casting as Tarzan ludicrous. Mae West would have difficulty playing the Virgin Mary. The "heavy" in Westerns is inevitably an actor whose "facial atlas," posture, and mannerisms communicate deviousness and hostility. Even in roles in which the dialogue clearly establishes a given type of personality, the actor's inherent body language cannot be disguised. The unconscious dynamics of the personality will be conveyed despite the verbal message the lines of the script are intended to communicate. It is always necessary to some extent to typecast the performer in a role that is in keeping with what his body communicates, i.e., a role compatible with his unconscious. If this is true of the professional actor trained to convey many characters, how much more transparent does body language leave the rest of us?

Both the professional's and the lay person's "gut-level" reactions to others involve a response to body communication. Such communication is often unconscious and preconscious, or, in the vernacular of the experimental psychologist, subliminal. For this reason, the "body-language" message is a powerful one. We can all exercise a degree of conscious control over our selection of words, but we rarely have the same control over our body postures, gestures, and facial expressions. Here leakage of unconscious material approaches a condition of continuous flood. For example, the affective message of a conventional greeting is carried not by the verbal symbols "Good morning," but by the over-all motoric behavior (smile, aversive glance, hasty departure, etc.). When a dinner guest compliments the hostess's cooking, the true feeling is not in the cliché of verbal praise, it is in the expressions and gestures which accompany it. A more romantic example of the intensity of nonverbal affective communication is the feeling conveyed by the eyes of a lover when he looks at the loved person.

Ironically, we as therapists pride ourselves on our assiduous attention to the words spoken in the treatment session while largely ignoring the nonverbal signals which often communicate the very content in which we are most interested—unconscious and affective material. Of course, in reality the good therapist, like the good poker player, does not rely solely on the dialogue; he would soon be bluffed out of the game if at some preconscious or unconscious level he were not responding appropriately to the other participant's body language, voice quality, and related nonverbal cues.

Perhaps Freud sensed the role of body language and the leakage of cues of conscious and unconscious affect through body movements and gestures. Possibly this was one reason he structured classical analytic treatment with the patient fully visible to the analyst but the analyst concealed from the view of the patient.

Spatial Language

So important is the study of the deaf in understanding the role of body language in normal human psychology that some additional aspects of it deserve attention. The entire positioning of the body in relation to others is communicative.

Hall (1959) argues that people communicate by the way they arrange themselves spatially. Each person has his own spatial preferences and communicates with others through the physical distance he establishes in relationship to them.

Violent people, for example, require a larger "body-buffer zone," i.e., space around them, than do the normal (Winick and Holt, 1961). Any violation of the human body-buffer zone results in anxiety and in sham or actual violence, just as does violation of the interspecies distance maintained by animals (Kinzel, 1970). A related finding is that the farther from the speaker a participant in a group is, the more likely he is to respond to or to challenge what is said.

In group therapy and other kinds of meetings, people communicate extensively by their choice of chairs, the seating arrangements created, and their posture (Winick and Holt, 1961). For example, the paranoid patient in group therapy will invariably sit in a position where he can see others but is himself relatively inconspicuous. Eminent psychiatrists at the famed Psychosomatic and Psychiatric Institute of Michael Reese Hospital in Chicago would invariably communicate their deference to the Director, Dr. Grinker, by leaving the centrally placed, comfortable chair for him at weekly colloquia.

Studies of psychotherapy have shown that patient and therapist preen, position, and in other postural ways unconsciously go through quasi-courtship body-movement rituals (Scheflen, 1965), not unlike those of birds in mating routines. Many of these complex behaviors have cultural overtones and must be learned. A failure to learn and to send appropriate nonverbal messages is one characteristic of hysterics and of schizophrenics who perseverate in inappropriate courting or quasi-courting posturing and gesturing, or else practice one when the other is appropriate. The research on psychotherapy shows that the more important feelings in therapy are communicated by body language and spatial language, not by words (Shapiro, 1966, 1968; Shapiro, Foster, and Powell, 1968).

The relevance of the deaf population to all of this is that they are totally or in large part denied verbal interaction with others during the crucial preschool years and later. The fact that they still develop into relatively normal adults (Rainer et al., 1963; Grinker, 1969) is overwhelming evidence against assigning a primary role to verbal language in affective development. It is very possible that body language and spatial language are the major sources of affective interaction and nurture for both the deaf and the hearing.

Vocal Communication

Perhaps the most interesting aspect of speech is what it communicates when its verbal content is filtered out. Speech is filtered by eliminating with audiological screens the sounds of higher frequencies, which include sibilants and other phonemes necessary to understand the words and context of the message. What is left is the essential quality of the voice. And whereas words are subject to conscious control, voice quality is not.

Numerous studies of filtered speech have been conducted, a few of which will be described. Milmoe (Milmoe et al., 1967) as a private practitioner had noted that alcoholics were especially sensitive to rejection, particularly in the form of anger or disgust. She therefore taped outpatient-clinic interviews in which the therapist was referring alcoholic patients to another setting where therapy was available for them. The criterion in this study was whether or not the patient showed up for the treatment.

Raters listened to the filtered tapes (minus the content) and made a judgment of whether or not the doctor was angry. Doctors whose filtered speech was judged to be angry had far fewer alcoholics show up for treatment than did those whose speech was judged to be not angry. When raters judged anger from the actual verbal content of the sessions using typed transcripts of the referral sessions, there was no correlation with whether or not the alcoholics showed up for treatment.

The point is that the affect in therapy is not transmitted nearly as well by verbal language as by the unconscious message the therapist conveys through his voice quality.

Milmoe also found that the filtered speech of mothers of small babies, when rated for factors such as anxiety, anger, warmth, and pleasantness, was as good as or better than their nonfiltered speech as a predictor of insecurity and inhibition in the babies (Milmoe et al., 1968). As Walsh (1968) has noted, the auditory aspect of language never loses its close connection with id processes. The obsessive-compulsive person attempts to rid language of this affective cathexis by making it as intellectual as possible, but he fails.

Once again, as with body language and spatial language, the major conclusion to be drawn is that affect is transmitted not through verbal language but by a means less subject to conscious control—in this case the voice quality.

Olfactory Communication

It has been noted by Grinker (personal communication) that in our society natural responsiveness to odors is repressed and disdained. Direct evidence of this repression is the huge amount of money spent on the marketing and purchase of products designed to disguise or eliminate natural odors. At the other end of the continuum, the sale and use of perfumes is acknowledgment of the strong positive affective message communicated by certain pheromones (a chemical signal perceived olfactorily).

In subhuman animal species, olfaction is an essential means of communication. The "get-acquainted" rituals of dogs are an example. Fear, sexuality, aggression, territorial rights, and other basic affects and life-preserving signals are transmitted through olfactory stimuli (Denny and Ratner, 1970, pp. 420–421). Bees, with their elaborate movement patterns and auditory behavior, make an even more extensive use of pheromones (Wenner, Wells, and Johnson, 1969). Such findings from research on olfaction provide still more evidence that significant amounts of affect are communicated through means other than verbal language.

Tactile Communication

Touching another person is a very significant act, but the touch-taboo in our culture has hampered research into the conditions, loci, meanings, and consequences of physical contact. The paucity of information necessitates our looking at observations of "handling" (or neglect of handling) and the importance of "mothering" for relevant data on this topic.

Spitz (1945) observed that infants deprived of handling over a long period are prone to succumb to a disease called marasmus, a listless withering away into death. Harlow's (1958) monkeys preferred physical contact with a terrycloth mother, or even a wire mother, to no contact at all. Levine (1960) has experimentally demonstrated in rats that even the biochemistry of the brain and resistance to leukemia are favorably affected by handling.

Kessen and Mandler (1961) have stated that physical contact between a mother and child is a "specific inhibitor" of the cyclic "fundamental distress" to which children are subject. These studies strongly suggest that tactile communication in some measure mediates physical, mental, and emotional development.

Jourard (1966), in one of the few formal investigations of tactile communication, conducted an exploratory study of body accessibility in college students to answer some questions about the parameters of touching. The male subjects touched fewer areas of their mothers' bodies than were touched by their mothers, and they were not touched by their mothers on as many or the same areas as were females. Females exchanged physical contact on more areas of the body with their fathers than did the male subjects and their closest friends of the opposite sex. Jourard's data generated the hypothesis that parents convey their acceptance of their children's bodies through physical contact and, more specifically, that children may come to like or accept only those areas of their bodies which the parents have touched in a positive way.

The most primitive mode of establishing contact with another human being is to touch him—hug him, hold his hand, or put an arm around him. Words are not needed in this kind of exchange. Indeed, psychotherapists may convey their willingness to remain with a patient, e.g., a catatonic, by holding his hand when he cannot communicate verbally. We need to learn much more about touching and its meaning as an expression of therapeutic intent.

IMPLICATIONS FOR PSYCHOTHERAPY

It is apparent from the data presented thus far that patients communicate much affective, preconscious, and unconscious material by their nonverbal behavior. Similarly, we as therapists are inevitably communicating our feelings and reactions through the same modalities. Although this clearly applies to traditional psychoanalytic techniques, we will consider only developments that psychoanalysts at any rate regard as no longer psychoanalytic in a strict sense.

Historically, it was Ferenczi who first introduced an emphasis on nonverbal techniques to the then embryonic psychoanalytic movement (Jones, 1957, pp. 163–164). His emphasis was on tactile stimulation intended to supply what he felt were missing aspects of a warm relationship with one's mother. Ferenczi's approach involved cuddling, sitting patients in his lap, and even kissing.

Freud questioned the validity of the therapist's offering erotic gratification to the patient. In part, he was concerned that this might discredit psychoanalysis. Moreno's psychodrama technique offers an alternative to direct physical contact between therapist and patient. Moreno's method enables the patient to re-enact conflicts under the direction of a person with the skills of a producer, counselor, and analyst (Moreno, 1953, pp. 39–48). For example, if a patient needs love, the affection of a mother or father, a specially trained professional takes the part of parent and acts it out with the patient, under the supervision of the analyst. With this technique Ferenczi could have avoided accusations of giving or receiving erotic gratification wihle maintaining the positive aspects of his therapeutic approach.

Moreno utilizes nonverbal activities, such as bodily contact, touching, caressing, embracing, sharing in silent activities, eating, and walking as important preliminaries for the psychodramatic situation. The patient is given freedom of expression and the verbal level is transcended, and later included, in the level of action. Psychodrama is concerned with action, encounter, and spontaneity. The patient dramatizes his problem, handles it well, and then begins to understand the dynamics and implications of his behavior. Words alone are often not convincing.

Continuing in the therapeutic tradition of Moreno, Perls, who has labeled his approach "gestalt therapy," has been particularly concerned with nonverbal communication (Perls, Hefferline, and Goodman, 1951). Perls developed a series of 18 mainly nonverbal "experiments" or techniques for making contact with the environment, sharpening the body sense, and integrating awareness. He uses a method known as "exaggeration" to encourage the patient to express abortive, undeveloped, or incomplete movements or gestures. Sometimes the patient is asked to develop the movement into a dance to get more of his self into integrative expression. Perls's dictum to "lose your mind and come to your senses" suggests that awareness of bodily sensations constitutes our most certain knowledge.

The use of the "awareness continuum" (remaining in the here and now) in gestalt therapy is the therapist's best means of leading a patient away from the emphasis on the *why* of behavior and toward the *what* and *how* of behavior. For example:

P.: "I feel afraid."
T.: "How do you experience your fear?"
P.: "My voice is quivering."
T.: "Can you take responsibility for that by saying, I'm quivering?"

The gestalt therapist interprets the nonverbal voice cue and asks the patient to assume responsibility for both his words and actions. Perls considers the nonverbal to be basic material of psychotherapy.

A recent approach to nonverbal therapy which includes a conceptual framework as well as comprehensive techniques is that of Pesso (1969). His systematic psychomotor training involves three stages: sensitization to motoric impulses, sensitization to spatial placement of others with tactile exploration, and handling feelings and emotional events.

Thus, in the work of Ferenczi, Perls, Moreno, and Pesso we see efforts to use nonverbal material in diagnosis and treatment. With the wealth of new information coming from studies of nonverbal behavior there is every reason to expect further advances in relating the nonverbal to the improvement of psychotherapy.

SUMMARY AND CONCLUSIONS

The role of verbal language in problem solving has been examined theoretically and empirically from the perspective of deafness as an experiment of nature. This use of the medical model, i.e., studying the pathological, leads to some fundamental conclusions about the role of verbal language in the areas of cognition and affect.

Cognitively, it is apparent that congenitally deaf persons solve problems with the same efficiency and using the same steps as do hearing persons. The only conclusion which can be derived from this is that verbal language is not a relevant variable in cognition. Furthermore, the mediating process of thought is not a system of verbal symbols. This conception is so foreign to the conventional understanding of the relationship of language and thought that it deserves restatement for clarification.

Using the S → R (stimulus-response) terminology of the experimental psychologist, stimuli, i.e., problems, are presented to two groups whose only relevant difference is that one group has a verbal symbol system (the experimental variable) and the other does not. Their solution (the R or response) to the problems is then measured (the dependent variable). In the mass of research cited it was found that in this S → R paradigm there was no difference between the responses of the two groups. Thus, the hypothesized intervening variable of verbal language is found to be irrelevant to cognitive processes.

In the realm of affect it has been shown that verbal language communicates less effectively than paralinguistic phenomena such as body language and voice quality. Tactile sensitivity and olfaction, although not directly compared with verbal language, have been demonstrated to be major communicants of feelings.

When considering the congenitally deaf who are deprived of both verbal language and the perception of voice quality, the question becomes, Why do they, as a group, develop normally? And why do the blind, deprived of the perception of "body language," not manifest signs of severe psychological deprivation? These questions are fundamental to an understanding of the process of human communication.

Our conclusions are, first, that verbal language is clearly not as necessary or important to the communication of affects as has always been assumed. This has special pertinence to psychotherapy. Man's egotistical assumption that he is "human," i.e., different from all other animal species, is intimately tied to other assumptions regarding the possession and use of verbal language.

Second, there is obviously tremendous redundancy in human affective communication. In general, messages are simultaneously delivered verbally, kinesically, tactually, auditorily, and even olfactorily. The blind or deaf person is therefore able to receive affective messages even when, as in the case of the deaf, certain contents in verbal form are missing. Both society and psychotherapy have been preoccupied with verbal communication and oblivious to nonverbal communication. This may well account for some of the misunderstandings which contribute to man's inhumanity to man, the often less than successful results of conventional psychotherapy, and even for the breakdown of the communication process which threatens our society.

REFERENCES

Arieti, S. (1967). New Views on the Psychodynamics of Schizophrenia. *American Journal of Psychiatry*, 124:453–458.

Birdwhistell, R. L. (1970). *Kinesics and Context: Essays on Body Motion Communication.* Philadelphia: University of Pennsylvania Press.

Blanton, R. L., and Nunnally, J. C. (1964). Semantic Habits and Cognitive Style Processes in the Deaf. *Journal of Abnormal and Social Psychology*, 68:397–402.

Bruner, J. S., and Tagiuri, R. (1954). The Perception of People. In: *Handbook of Social Psychology*, Vol. 2, ed. G. Lindzey. Cambridge, Mass.: Addison-Wesley, pp. 634–654.

Darbyshire, J. O., and Reeves, V. R. (1969). The Use of Adaptations of Some of Piaget's Tests with Groups of Children with Normal and Impaired Hearing. *British Journal of Disorders of Communication*, 4:197–202.

Denny, M. R., and Ratner, S. C. (1970). *Comparative Psychology: Research in Animal Behavior*, rev. ed. Homewood, Ill.: Dorsey.

Ekman, P., and Friesen, W. V. (1968). Nonverbal Behavior in Psychotherapy Research. In: *Research in Psychotherapy*, Vol. 3, ed. J. Shlien. Washington, D.C.: American Psychological Association, pp. 179–216.

———, ——— (1969). Nonverbal Leakage and Clues to Deception. *Psychiatry*, 32:88–106.

———, Sorenson, E. R., and Friesen, W. V. (1969). Pan-Cultural Elements in Facial Displays of Emotion. *Science*, 164:86–88.

Furth, H. G. (1966). *Thinking without Language: Psychological Implications of Deafness.* New York: Free Press.

Geschwind, N. (1970). The Organization of Language and the Brain. *Science*, 170:940–944.

Grinker, R. R., Sr. (1967). Symbolism and General Systems Theory; Discussion of a paper by L. von Bertalanffy. Presented at a meeting of the American Psychiatric Association.

———, ed. (1969). Psychiatric Diagnosis, Therapy, and Research on the Psychotic Deaf. Final report, Grant No. RD-2407-S, Social Rehabilitation Services, Department of H. E. W. (Available from Dr. Grinker, Michael Reese Hospital, 2959 E. Ellis, Chicago, Illinois 60616.)

Hall, E. T. (1959). *The Silent Language.* New York: Doubleday.

Harlow, H. F. (1958). The Nature of Love. *American Psychologist*, 13:673–685.

Hess, E. H. (1965). Attitude and Pupil Size. *Scientific American*, 212(4):46–54.

Jones, E. (1957). *The Life and Work of Sigmund Freud*, Vol. 3. New York: Basic Books.

Jourard, S. M. (1966). An Exploratory Study of Body-Accessibility *British Journal of Social and Clinical Psychology*, 5:221–231.

Kates, S. L., Kates, W. W., and Michael, J. (1962). Cognitive Processes in Deaf and Hearing Adolescents and Adults. *Psychological Monographs*, 76(32, Whole No. 551).

Kessen, W., and Mandler, G. (1961). Anxiety, Pain, and the Inhibition of Distress. *Psychological Review*, 68:396–404.

Kinzel, A. F. (1970). Body-Buffer Zone in Violent Prisoners. *American Journal of Psychiatry,* 127:59–64.

Koh, S. D., Vernon, M., and Bailey, W. (in press). Free Recall of Word Lists by Prelingually Deaf Subjects. *Journal of Verbal Learning and Verbal Behavior.*

Levine, S. (1960). Stimulation in Infancy. *Scientific American,* 202(5):80–86.

Milmoe, S., Novey, M. S., Kagan, J., and Rosenthal, R. (1968). The Mother's Voice: Postdictor of Aspects of Her Baby's Behavior. *Proceedings of the 76th Annual Convention of the American Psychological Association,* 3:463–464.

———, Rosenthal, R., Blane, H. T., Chafetz, M. E., and Wolf, I. (1967). The Doctor's Voice: Postdictor of Successful Referral of Alcoholic Patients. *Journal of Abnormal Psychology,* 72:78–84.

Moores, D. F. (1970). An Investigation of the Psycholinguistic Functioning of Deaf Adolescents. *Exceptional Children,* 36:645–652.

Moreno, J. L. (1953). *Who Shall Survive? Foundations of Sociometry, Group Psychotherapy and Sociodrama,* 2nd ed. Beacon, N. Y.: Beacon House.

Perls, F., Hefferline, R. F., and Goodman, P. (1951). *Gestalt Therapy: Excitement and Growth in Psychotherapy.* New York: Dell.

Pesso, A. (1969). *Movement in Psychotherapy: Psychomotor Techniques and Training.* New York: New York University Press.

Piaget, J. (1962). *Comments on Vygotsky.* Cambridge, Mass.: M. I. T. Press.

Rainer, J. D., Altshuler, K. Z., Kallman, F. J., and Deming, W. E., eds. (1963). *Family and Mental Health Problems in Deaf Populations.* New York: Columbia University Psychiatric Institute.

Rosen, V. H. (1964). Some Effects of Artistic Talent on Character Style. *Psychoanalytic Quarterly,* 33:1–24.

——— (1967). Disorders of Communication in Psychoanalysis. *Journal of the American Psychoanalytic Association,* 15:467–490.

Rosenstein, J. (1960). Cognitive Abilities of Deaf Children. *Journal of Speech and Hearing Research,* 3:108–119.

——— (1961). Perception, Cognition and Language in Deaf Children: A Critical Analysis and Review of the Literature. *Exceptional Children,* 27:276–284.

Rosenthal, R. (1967). Covert Communication in the Psychological Experiment. *Psychological Bulletin,* 67:356–367.

Scheflen, A. E. (1965). Quasi-Courtship Behavior in Psychotherapy. *Psychiatry,* 28:245–257.

Shapiro, J. G. (1966). Agreement between Channels of Communication in Interviews. *Journal of Consulting Psychology,* 30:535–538.

——— (1968). Responsivity to Facial and Linguistic Cues. *Journal of Communication,* 18: 11–17.

———, Foster, C. P., and Powell, T. (1968). Facial and Bodily Cues of Genuineness, Empathy and Warmth. *Journal of Clinical Psychology,* 24:233–236.

Spitz, R. (1945). Hospitalism: An Inquiry into the Genesis of Psychiatric Conditions in Early Childhood. *The Psychoanalytic Study of the Child,* 1:53–74. New York: International Universities Press.

VanderWoude, K. W. (1970). Problem Solving and Language. *Archives of General Psychiatry,* 23:337–342.

Vernon, M. (1967). Relationship of Language to the Thinking Process. *Archives of General Psychiatry.* 16:325–333.

———, and Rothstein, D. A. (1968). Prelingual Deafness: An Experiment of Nature. *Archives of General Psychiatry,* 19:361–369.

Walsh, M. N. (1968). Explosives and Spirants: Primitive Sounds in Cathected Words. *Psychoanalytic Quarterly,* 37:199–211.

Wenner, A. M., Wells, P. H., and Johnson, D. L. (1969). Honey Bee Recruitment to Food Sources: Olfaction or Language? *Science,* 164:84–86.

Winick, C., and Holt, H. (1961). Seating Position as Nonverbal Communication in Group Analysis. *Psychiatry,* 24:171–182.

THE DEVELOPMENTAL SCIENCES
A Bibliographic Analysis of a Trend

Ilse Bry, Ph.D.

WHAT ARE THE DEVELOPMENTAL SCIENCES?

Development in nature and in the condition and affairs of man has never been as intensively studied as it is today. A world-wide effort is now under way to bring this work into focus and to utilize its fruits for the betterment of human life. This process has not been heralded, however, as was the advent of the behavioral sciences. In the mid-1950s that term began to make its way from being a semantic puzzle to becoming a household word, as familiar to the educated public and to policy makers as to the scientific community. A decade later the less artificial, if no less elusive, term "developmental sciences" entered the behavioral-science literature as if it were self-explanatory and without arousing any discussion.

The term "developmental sciences" as currently used provides a unifying name for work in the behavioral sciences that results from, and contributes to, theory and research concerning the growth and development of man and animals. At the core of the developmental sciences is developmental psychology, the first specialty to be so designated. In 1967, a contributor to a symposium on The Neuropsychology of Development characterized this field in words that capture the spirit of the new trend: "Although one could easily form a different impression from the number of texts and articles on the subject, *developmental psychology* represents an approach to problems rather than a distinct subject matter. Almost any psychological problem can be approached developmentally. . . ." He then set forth the advantages that result from asking how a particular phenomenon came about and from considering the nature of the changes that occur in organisms as they interact with the environment (Isaacson, 1968, p. 1). These observations also hold true for the developmental sciences in the broader sense suggested here.

A relationship between the developmental and the behavioral sciences was first implied when the Developmental Sciences Trust, founded in England in 1967 under the chairmanship of Lord Adrian, made known its plan to open a "Centre for Advanced Study in the Developmental Sciences," a name obviously modeled after that of the influential Center for Advanced Study in the Behavioral Sciences at Palo Alto, California. The first two volumes of proceedings of international study groups held under the joint auspices of the projected Centre and the Ciba Foundation, 1967 and 1968, in a program on "The Origins of Human Behaviour," described the Centre's activities as related "to all those sciences and disciplines that can contribute to greater knowledge of the biological, social and psychological principles that govern the development and functioning of human behaviour over the life-cycle." In addition to stimulating and coordinating research and fostering a developmental perspective on human nature, the Centre was "to encourage the application of knowledge from the developmental sciences by those, in all sectors of society, engaged in coping with or preventing human problems" (Ambrose, 1969; Robinson, 1969). Although, according to information obtained from the Ciba Foundation, the project of opening the Centre has since been abandoned, the Developmental Sciences Trust continues to organize international study groups and to pursue the initial scientific aim.

In 1968, the article on "developmental psychology" in the *International Encyclopedia of the Social Sciences* referred to the National Institute of Child Health and Human Development (NICHD) as established "to provide leadership in training of investigators and research in developmental sciences including developmental psychology" (Stevenson, 1968, p. 139). There was no further explanation. Since 1963, when NICHD was founded as one of the National Institutes of Health, the annual reports of the Department of Health, Education, and Welfare have repeatedly referred to "the basic sciences related to processes of human growth and development." Although again these sciences are not specified, the series of reports makes the nature and scope of the NICHD program very clear: it is "focusing not on any one disease or part of the body but on the continuing process of growth and development, biological and behavioral, from reproduction and perinatal development, through infancy and childhood to maturation and aging." The same reports also set forth the broad range of social issues with which the Institute is concerned. These include the need to develop contraceptive methods that are, among other things, suited to the diverse requirements of the world's varied population groups; poor nutrition, and how it affects the childbearing woman and her progeny; the social, economic, and cultural factors that can contribute to mental retardation; the interrelationships of biological, social, and environmental factors in aging; and such questions as how children acquire values and how changes in our culture affect personality structure.

As recently as April, 1971, an editorial in the British journal *Developmental Medicine and Child Neurology* (Bax, 1971), in questioning certain current practices, suggested that they must displease "any true student of the developmental sciences," also without a further comment on this term. In view of the fact that important scientific and social issues have been made the province of the developmental sciences, the question, "What are the developmental sciences?" is certainly legitimate, indeed overdue.

Without trying to fathom the mystery of the sudden emergence of the developmental sciences or to probe into their past progress from mere observation to scientific conceptualization, methodology, research, theory, knowledge, and social application, this essay will suggest new bibliographic approaches to the literature currently evolving in this field. The processes of identifying this literature will be linked with an effort to find answers to the question of what the developmental sciences are. The analysis will be based on a sample drawn from the nearly 1,000 bibliographic entries for books listed in the *Mental Health Book Review Index*, Volumes 14, 15, and 16, 1969–1971 (Bry and Afflerbach, 1956–1971). These books were published during the period that coincides with the recognition of the developmental sciences as lying within the area of, and yet being or becoming separate from, the behavioral sciences—roughly 1965 to 1970.

THE CONCEPT OF DEVELOPMENT

Definitions of development relating to a general theory, apart from concrete applications, are hard to find, with one notable exception. Contributors to a Conference on the Concept of Development, held in 1955 at the University of Minnesota (Harris, 1957), addressed themselves to this question. They pointed out the variety of meanings of the word "development." It can be used to connote a process or the product of a process. If interpreted in the original sense of the word as an unfolding, development means a sequence of continuous changes, leading to an outcome that is potentially present in the earlier stages of the process. In contemporary theory, the older "preformistic" ideas have been replaced by an "epigenetic" view, which acknowledges that organization is created anew in development. Not every sequence of changes is designated as developmental. The changes must be cumulative and irreversible and, in addition, they must lead to a new mode of organization in the developing system, with an increased capacity for self-regulation and independence. The construct of "directiveness" is implied in the definition of organic development in its two major aspects, namely, that the developmental process involves progressive changes from a more simple to a more complex organization, and that development proceeds from the general to the specific. One of the contributors to this 1955 Conference, Heinz Werner, combined these two aspects into one regulative principle of development, "which states that wherever development occurs it proceeds from a state of relative globality and lack of differentiation to a state of increasing differentiation, articulation, and hierarchic integration." He also discussed development not only in the light of specific theories and principles but "as a concept that proposes a certain manner of viewing behavior in its manifold manifestations." He recognized, therefore, the potentially unifying influence on the life sciences of the developmental approach, with its basic assumption "that wherever there is life there is growth and development, that is, formation in terms of systematic, orderly sequence." In analogy to a unified developmental biology, Werner saw developmental psychology as providing a single framework for forms of behavior observed in such varied fields as comparative animal psychology, child psychology, psychopathology, ethnopsychology, and the psychology of man in our own culture (Harris, 1957, pp. 125–126).

THE WORD "DEVELOPMENT" IN RECENT BOOK TITLES

Present bibliographic techniques and systems do not identify work concerned with developmental theory, research, and methodology in a form that would permit observing the progress of the developmental sciences. Publications recording this work remain embedded in the literature of the behavioral sciences and the various parent disciplines, which are as diverse and separately organized as genetics, neurology, ethology, psychology, gerontology, and education, to name a few of the many contributory fields.

Books that use the word development, or a close variant, in the title or subtitle, may provide first clues for identifying developmental studies. The present sample contains more than 50 such books. They vary greatly, however, especially with respect to their scope and the developmental processes specified as the object of study. A number of these books are compendia by one or more authors, or reviews of progress. Notable among these are Baldwin's (1966) *Theories of Child Development,* Hoffman and Hoffman's (1966) *Review of Child Development Research,* Lipsitt and Spiker's (1967) *Advances in Child Development and Behavior,* Brackbill's (1967) *Infancy and Early Childhood: A Handbook and Guide to Human Development,* and Chess and Thomas's (1968) *Annual Progress in Child Psychiatry and Child Development.* The emphasis on child development in these titles is striking. Two other books concerned with developmental theories and concepts are equally limited (Maier, 1965; Neubauer, 1965). One historical treatment is more comprehensive (Grinder, 1967); one presentation of an author's "epigenetic view" is based on his animal studies (Kuo, 1967).

In many of the books the term "development" appears in a specific context, for example, development in learning, cognition, perception (Staats, 1968; Lunzer and Morris, 1968–1969; Fellows, 1968; Kidd and Rivoire, 1966; Warren and Warren, 1968), development of the brain and of sex differences (Völgyesi, 1966; Maccoby, 1966; Stoller, 1968), of role-taking and communication skills and political attitudes (Flavell, 1968; Hess and Torney, 1967), character, conscience, and moral development (Abraham, 1966; Stephenson, 1966; Kay, 1968). Three titles lead to Piaget (Piaget, 1968; Beard, 1969; Elkind and Flavell, 1969), four to the approaches of comparative and psychoanalytic psychology, psychobiology, and neuropsychology (Stevenson, Hess, and Rheingold, 1967; Nagera, 1966; Newton and Levine, 1968; Isaacson, 1968). Other books are concerned with the psychopathology of mental development (Zubin and Jervis, 1967) or, more specifically, with studies of language disability (Wood, 1964; Rawson, 1968) and of mongoloid babies (Cowie, 1970), a few with giving therapeutic help in developing ego and ego-social functions and in other cases of developmental problems (Llorens and Rubin, 1967; D'Amato, 1969; Senn and Solnit, 1968). Personality development appears as a topic by itself and in diverse contexts such as social class and race, marriage, death in the family, and play therapy (Ratcliffe, 1967; Deutsch, Katz, and Jensen, 1968; Blanck and Blanck, 1968; Moriarty, 1967; Axline, 1964). Finally, the term is used in relation to obvious developmental stages: infancy, preadolescence, and the whole life cycle (Bijou and Baer, 1965; Escalona, 1968; Gardner and Moriarty, 1968; Lidz, 1968).

Two of the titles refer to community and political development (Biddle, 1965; Pye, 1968). "Development" as used in economics, sociology, political science, and other social sciences is not, however, now encompassed by developmental research, which is limited to the study of living organisms. The remaining titles in the sample use "development" in the sense of advances in theory or research in a special field. They are mentioned here only as a reminder that "development" as a technical term has to be clearly established. This should not be more difficult, however, than it was in the 1950s to establish the difference between "child behavior" and the good or bad behavior of a child.

DEVELOPMENTAL STAGES AND THE LIFE CYCLE

Further clues to current trends in the developmental sciences may be found in books explicitly concerned with major developmental stages, with what one contributor to the 1955 Conference on the Concept of Development called "the age-bound behavior of the person as it takes on form or shape . . . the person whom we study from birth on to maturity" (Harris, 1957, p. 25). Ideas about the periods encompassed in the life cycle have been changing, especially in recent decades, and this central aspect of the developmental sciences is even now far from crystallized. Not only have the major stages become more closely subdivided, as more and more transitional periods have been recognized and studied, but the concept of the life cycle as a whole has been extended at both ends.

As early as 1911, J. M. Baldwin's *Dictionary of Philosophy and Psychology* defined (biological) "development" as "the entire series of vital changes normal to the individual organism, from its origin from the parent cell or cells until death" (J. M. Baldwin and Poulton, 1911, pp. 273–275). This inclusive meaning was lost sight of during the period of progressing research, which only now, six decades later, has caught up with the earlier formulation. To embryology, one of the oldest and primary disciplines in the province of the developmental sciences, more recent multidisciplinary studies of prenatal and perinatal influences on development have been added. A further extension in this direction may come about if "genetic engineering" and related work aimed at changing the hereditary basis of life, which is as yet only on the horizon, should become a scientific and social reality. At the other end, studies of aging and the aged have been drawn together in the still relatively young, multidisciplinary field of gerontology. A further extension, which makes the study of death and dying germane to the developmental sciences, is becoming manifest right now. This may account in part for the dramatic increase in the recent literature related to death. Lidz (1968, p. 496) has made the point explicit: "It may seem strange for an unconsidered moment to conclude this guide to the life cycle with a chapter on death. But death is part of the life cycle, an inevitable outcome of life that brings closure to a life story; and, because the human from early childhood is aware of his ultimate death, it influences his development and his way of life profoundly."

Even when, as before, only the titles of books are considered, the present limited sample of the literature of the developmental sciences covers all the stages of the life span. Joffe (1969) reviews research "which relates events prior to birth to effects on the postnatal behaviour of organisms." *Childbearing* (Richardson and Guttmacher, 1967), a volume of critical reviews of studies of reproduction with a social-science viewpoint, grew out of the rising concern about the social aspects of developmental stages that had long been approached only from a biomedical point of view. Other trends are illustrated in three books on infancy: interest in data from non-Western cultures (Ainsworth, 1967); a historical interest, shown in a collection of readings going back to 1907 (Brackbill and Thompson, 1967); and the search for an understanding of normal development, the subject of Escalona's (1968) study.

Escalona's research spans the period from the mid-forties to the mid-sixties and thus coincides with the formative period of the developmental sciences in the current sense. Her introductory review of trends in research, which shows the fluctuations of interest in the neonate and the period of earliest infancy, contributes to an understanding of the difference between the vast field of child study and developmental science. Interest in the extensive studies of newborns carried out during the 1920s and 1930s waned because they were purely descriptive and not effectively linked to a developmental theory. In contrast, the researchers of more recent years have been concerned with the implications of their work for the study of human development. They have, for example, focused their interest on factors that codetermine the course of subsequent development, on the processes and mechanisms that constitute developmental change, and on determining what continuity exists between learning processes during the early months of life and learning processes at later ages (Escalona, 1968, pp. 3–6).

Data that potentially lend themselves to longitudinal studies can, therefore, become an important resource for the developmental sciences. Perhaps the most comprehensive longitudinal research yet undertaken resulted from the study of 17,000 babies born during one week in March, 1958, in England, Scotland, and Wales, which had yielded perinatal data said to be unparalleled in the world. Another part of this project, conducted in the mid-sixties, forms the first report of the National Child Development Study, *11,000 Seven-Year-Olds* (Pringle, Butler, and Davie, 1966). More typical of longitudinal developmental research, however, is the intensive study of relatively small samples; for example, in Escalona's (1968) book, 32 infants were selected from the 128 studied in her previous project entitled *Early Phases of Personality Development* (Escalona and Leitch, 1952), and 42 children were selected from the 136 in the longitudinal study begun by Thomas et al. in 1956 (Thomas, Chess, and

Birch, 1968). The importance of such data for developmental research is under-
lined by the interlocking of projects. For instance, the authors of *Personality
Development at Preadolescence* (Gardner and Moriarty, 1968)—in part an outgrowth of the Longitudinal Study Project at the Menninger Foundation—drew
their subjects, 60 boys and girls 9 to 13 years old, from the group of children
from the Topeka, Kansas, area studied in infancy by Escalona.

THE LIFE CYCLE AFTER CHILDHOOD

Some of the studies on adolescence have resulted from projects conducted
over periods of four or five years: the Symptomatic Adolescent Research
Project reported in *The Psychiatric Dilemma of Adolescence* (Masterson, 1967),
and the Modal Adolescent Project, which Offer (1969) reported in his book
subtitled *A Study of Normal Adolescent Boys*. In addition to Offer's study, a
report issued by the Group for the Advancement of Psychiatry (1968), *Normal
Adolescence*, shows that psychiatrists share the psychologists' interest in normal
development. The next phase of the trend relates the study of problems of
adolescence to psychosocial and sociocultural forces. Examples are two volumes
resulting from international congresses, one concerned broadly with psychosocial perspectives (Caplan and Lebovici, 1969), the other specifically with adolescent drug dependence (Wilson, 1968); a British study of *The Sexual Behaviour
of Young People* (Schofield, 1965); and *Minority Group Adolescents in the
United States* (Brody et al., 1968), a collection of papers concerning Negro,
Mexican, Puerto Rican, Oriental, and American Indian adolescents, introduced
with an essay, "Adolescents as a United States Minority Group in an Era of
Social Change."

Two books on postadolescence and the young adult present aspects of
psychotherapy (Wittenberg, 1967, 1968), but one resulting from a Social Psychology Symposium again pursues the social theme, as indicated in the title:
Problems of Youth: Transition to Adulthood in a Changing World (Sherif and
Sherif, 1965).

A beginning toward filling a gap in the literature on the developmental
stages, the study of middle life, was made when the Scientific Committee of
the World Federation for Mental Health initiated a survey of research relating
to the 40–60 age period and then discussed the data (Soddy and Kidson, 1967).
Another effort to bring together the literature on middle age and aging took
the form of a reader in social psychology, based mainly on publications of the
period 1956–1968 (Neugarten, 1968). Research conducted in England in the early
1960s with 90 persons ranging in age from 20 to 79 is reported in *Age and
Function* by Heron and Chown (1967), assisted by the Staff of the Medical
Research Council Unit for Research on Occupational Aspects of Aging.

Some of the books on aging reflect the thinking that has brought gerontology into the mainstream of the developmental sciences. In the preface to
his *The Psychology of Human Ageing*, Bromley (1966) observes: "We spend
about one quarter of our lives growing up and three quarters growing old."
He considers the study of human aging a logical extension of developmental

psychology, and finds it strange "that psychologists and others have devoted most of their efforts to the study of childhood and adolescence." The foreword to this book by B. M. Foss notes, however, "that psychologists have already come to regard the study of old age as part of developmental psychology, with the implication that development never stops." This comment carries special weight in view of the fact that its author is the Executive Chairman of the Developmental Sciences Trust mentioned at the beginning of this essay. The editor of a series of studies representing recent advances in research and theory on human aging relates the notable growth of this research over the past decade to an expanding awareness of the problems presented by a population with a long life expectancy (Talland, 1968). Botwinick (1967) concludes his review of the research literature on *Cognitive Processes in Maturity and Old Age* with a word of caution: ". . . through long life experience, older people may develop a degree of wisdom and sagacity not likely to be found in young people. The elements of wisdom and sagacity are not represented in the scientific data, and therefore, were not given the emphasis in this book they deserve." It will be important, therefore, to include in the developmental literature about the adult personality and the human life cycle works that represent the viewpoint of humanistic psychology and stress the processes of integration (Arasteh, 1965; Bühler and Massarik, 1968).

The convergence of scientific and social concerns is again illustrated in two research reports, the first forming one of the Langley Porter Institute Studies of Aging (Lowenthal et al., 1967), the second resulting from a proposal by the Committee on Older Persons of the Cleveland Welfare Federation (Rosow, 1967). Of the last three books on this subject in the present sample, one is limited to retirement (Geist, 1968), the others are more comprehensive, include theories of aging, and attempt to integrate diverse contributions (Burch, 1968; Busse and Pfeiffer, 1969). One chapter in *Behavior and Adaptation in Late Life* (Busse and Pfeiffer, 1969), entitled "How the Old Face Death," illustrates the recent transition from gerontology to the study of death and dying.

Twenty books in the present sample deal wholly or in significant part with death. Six of the books are concerned with suicide: the most comprehensive is *Suicidal Behaviors* (Resnik, 1968), with contributions by 48 authors, but even the slim monograph of the World Health Organization (1968), *Prevention of Suicide,* shows that many countries share the rising concern about this problem. Several other books deal with anxiety, bereavement, mourning, and other aspects of the problems surrounding death that are experienced by the living (Rheingold, 1967; Gorer, 1965; Kutscher, 1969; Sudnow, 1967; Moriarty, 1967). A book of unusually broad scope is *Man's Concern with Death,* by Toynbee et al. (1968). Closest to the view that death is the final stage of the life cycle are Eissler's (1955) *The Psychiatrist and the Dying Patient,* recently reissued in a paperback edition; *Awareness of Dying* (Glaser and Strauss, 1965) and *Time for Dying* (Glaser and Strauss, 1968), two studies resulting from a long-term research project; *Communication with the Fatally Ill* (Verwoerdt, 1966); and the account of an interdisciplinary academic program, *On Death and Dying* (Kübler-Ross, 1969). A link between childhood and death is offered in a British study (Mitchell,

1966) and in *Psychological Emergencies of Childhood* (Kliman, 1968), based in part on a study of children's reactions to the death of a parent and including a case report of a dying child in analysis at the age of four.

ISSUES AND CONCEPTS IN
DEVELOPMENTAL THEORY AND RESEARCH

The growing interest in early determinants of development has drawn on and has further stimulated the study of animal behavior. The resulting books range in scope from a comprehensive review of research aimed at a synthesis of ethology and comparative psychology (Hinde, 1966) to a review of studies on *Imprinting and Early Learning* (Sluckin, 1964). Increasingly, developmental animal research has been directed to exploring "the biodynamic roots of human behavior" (Masserman, 1968a), but this orientation is seldom as explicitly and succinctly suggested as in the proceedings of the American Academy of Psycho- analysis of 1967, entitled *Animal and Human* (Masserman, 1968b). Indeed, the extent to which animal and human studies tend to be intertwined in books on early behavior and experience is usually not apparent from the titles which spell out the developmental orientation (Stevenson, Hess, and Rheingold, 1967; Isaacson, 1968; Newton and Levine, 1968; Ambrose, 1969; Joffe, 1969; Robinson, 1969). This is also true for books on more specific issues such as the origins and development of aggression, which has been approached from a variety of disciplines and perspectives, including neurology, psychiatry, ethology, psychol- ogy, and anthropology (Clemente and Lindsley, 1968; Lorenz, 1966; Storr, 1968; Frank, 1967; Fried, Harris, and Murphy, 1968).

The problem of applying findings from animal studies to human develop- ment is not easily resolved, however, and some attempts to do so have led to intense controversies. Nevertheless, the trend has been to draw together work on the study of developmental problems despite great diversity in origins and approaches. Harriet L. Rheingold, a coeditor of *Early Behavior: Comparative and Developmental Approaches,* sees in this work the possibility of a common area and a new division of knowledge: the development of behavior in immature organisms, man and animal, leading to "a unified science of development" (Stevenson, Hess, and Rheingold, 1967, p. 292).

The effects of mother-infant relations on development have also been extensively studied. *Attachment,* the first volume of Bowlby's (1969) two-volume work *Attachment and Loss,* is an outgrowth of research begun in the 1960s at the Tavistock Clinic and Tavistock Institute of Human Relations. The 24 reviews of this book cited in Volume 16, 1971, of the *Mental Health Book Review Index* (Bry and Afflerbach, 1956–1971) show that it is of great current interest, with ramifications in many different fields. In another first volume of a two-volume work, Mahler (1968) presents her concepts of human symbiosis and separation- individuation in their pathological aspects—infantile psychosis—although she has also studied "the normal separation-individuation process." *Psychic Trauma* (Furst, 1967) and *The Birth of the Ego* (Glover, 1968) can further illustrate the developmental ramifications of contemporary psychoanalytic thinking. The classical psychoanalytic theory of libido development is represented in the present sample through the coincidence of a recent reissue of papers first published five and six decades ago (Abraham, 1966). In discussing changing and current concepts, Escalona (1968) mentions Erikson's influence on the concept of developmental stages (pp. 15–16). In a broad synthesis that integrates concepts from three schools of thought—psychoanalysis, Heinz Werner, and Piaget— Arieti (1967) offers his own developmental viewpoint as an approach to "the intrapsychic self."

Another concept that can potentially unify developmental studies conducted in diverse fields is "socialization," defined as the social process through which an individual becomes integrated into a social group. Although the term is sometimes limited to processes that occur in childhood, socialization, like development in the broader sense, has come to be seen as a lifelong process. It is one of the concepts that may help to mark the fine line that separates the developmental from the behavioral sciences. Through a developmental approach, studies of attitude formation and change have turned into research on the socialization process and moral development, as conducted in England under the auspices of the Television Research Committee (Halloran, 1967). In this country, some large-scale attitude studies with school children have been concerned with political socialization (Hess and Torney, 1967). Dawson and Prewitt (1968) state that "among the most significant questions about political socialization is: how does it fit into the individual life cycle," and they view "political socialization as a process that continues through the life span" (pp. 41–42). The relevance of this work to current public issues such as the impact of television and the lowering of the voting age is obvious. A study of professional socialization in the field of nursing (Olesen and Whittaker, 1968) is another example of the expanding scope and application of this concept.

Such related topics as social competence, societal expectations, and the social bases of adaptation and failures are treated in a book on human adaptation (L. Phillips, 1968). A British study using the Vineland Social Maturity Scale contains a chapter on the discrepancies between intelligence and social competence (Pringle, 1966). A much broader cross-cultural study with still another perspective has as its major objective "to explore the environmental and other factors which hinder the development of abilities within underdeveloped countries or depressed minority groups" (Vernon, 1969, p. 7).

A "developmental sequence" is illustrated by considering three books together: a comprehensive study of The Development of Sex Differences (Maccoby, 1966), Sex and Gender (Stoller, 1968), which reports research on the development of masculinity and femininity, and Transsexualism and Sex Reassignment (Green and Money, 1969), which is concerned with a deviant development that can usually be traced to cross-gender identification in childhood.

Sometimes the subjects used indicate the developmental orientation of the research, for example, twin studies (Koch, 1966; Scheinfeld, 1967). A study of 106 preschool children, designed to predict reading failure, included 53 prematurely born children and thus provided data that throw light on problems of maturational lag (De Hirsch, Jansky, and Langford, 1966). Extensive case studies, for example, of the development of one child's personality or language (Axline, 1964; Wyatt, 1969), may also provide valuable data and insights.

Child-rearing practices, child care, and child guidance have always been subjects in the borderland between the fields of child study and child development, depending on the emphasis of the research. In *The Children of the Dream,* Bettelheim (1969) has added his observations to those made from time to time in earlier studies of Israeli children reared in a kibbutz. For various specific subjects, including foster care, adoption, and child abuse, the main effort is still directed toward ascertaining the basic facts. Perhaps most promising from the viewpoint of the developmental sciences are long-term follow-up studies (Davis, 1966; Ferguson, 1966; Robins, 1966; McWhinnie, 1967; Newson and Newson, 1968), comprehensive reviews of research (Pringle, 1967), and multidisciplinary explorations (Helfer and Kempe, 1968).

Research that contributes to an understanding of the influences of social and cultural conditions on human development also contributes to the social significance of the developmental sciences. It has had, and continues to have, an impact on national policy and important court decisions. A retrospective assessment of the social impact of the behavioral sciences may show that the research findings that have been translated into new national programs and legislation, such as school desegregation, the Head Start program, and the reform of adoption laws, grew out of work that would now be associated with the developmental sciences. Especially in the past two decades, growing scientific interest in human development has coincided with the growing awareness of the need to improve conditions and opportunities for the poor, the disadvantaged, and the deprived. Among the books that illustrate the merging of these trends are two reviews of the literature, *Low Income Youth in Urban Areas* (Goldstein, 1967) and *Growing Up Poor* (Chilman, 1966); *Children of Crisis* (Coles, 1967), an account of a psychiatrist's eight-year study based on interviews with Negro children in the South; *The Drifters* (Pavenstedt, 1967), a long-term study of children of disorganized lower-class families; and two collections of papers, *The Disadvantaged Child* (Deutsch et al., 1967) and *Social Class, Race, and Psychological Development* (Deutsch, Katz, and Jensen, 1968). A new perspective was opened in 1967 by the international and multidisciplinary conference on Malnutrition, Learning, and Behavior (Scrimshaw and Gordon, 1968), whose organizers, in the words of one reviewer, "directed attention to an urgent and persistent problem that confronts the world" (Kare, 1970).

THE EVOLVING ORGANIZATION
OF THE DEVELOPMENTAL SCIENCES

Finally, it would be timely to observe and study how the developmental sciences are organizing themselves. Although broad programs like those of NICHD and the Developmental Sciences Trust mentioned earlier provide a new focus for these processes, such organization requires a long preparation through small, often barely visible steps, for which the scientific community and concerned citizens and professionals take the initiative. One such sequence of steps, for example, takes the form of progressive recognition of the scientists and scholars who have made significant contributions to knowledge. In the field of developmental theory and research, a listing of those who have received lasting recognition would have to go back at least to Freud, G. Stanley Hall, and other late nineteenth-century pioneers in genetic psychology. Grinder's (1967) history of this field as "the first science of human development" includes Darwin and even Aristotle. The names of several contemporary authors of work that has been recognized as original, important, and influential appear in the present limited sample. To the books cited earlier (e.g., Maier, 1965; Baldwin, 1966; Lorenz, 1966; Bühler and Massarik, 1968; Piaget, 1968; Beard, 1969; Bowlby, 1969; Elkind and Flavell, 1969) can be added further books by or about Piaget (1967; Piaget and Inhelder, 1969; J. L. Phillips, Jr., 1969), Erikson (1958, 1968; Evans, 1967), Sears (Sears, Rau, and Alpert, 1965), Anna Freud (1968), and Kurt Lewin (Marrow, 1969).

A retrospective survey of the gradual organization of the developmental sciences is not within the scope of this essay. A few examples, however, will illustrate the trends that can currently be observed.

The present sample includes fourteen conferences, symposia, and society proceedings,[1] and various volumes of invited papers (e.g., Newton and Levine, 1968; Busse and Pfeiffer, 1969; Elkind and Flavell, 1969). Many of their organizers and contributors have worked at the frontiers of developmental research. That a new monographic series can focus on recently opened perspectives even in an older field is shown, for example, in the British series "Studies in Child Development," sponsored by the National Bureau for Co-operation in Child Care (Gooch and Pringle, 1966; Pringle, Butler, and Davie, 1966; Pringle, 1967; Parfit, 1967; Humphrey, 1969). In the newly emerging field concerned with the scientific study of death, three journals were launched in 1970–1971: *Omega,* published under the auspices of the Center for Psychological Studies of Dying, Death, and Lethal Behavior, Wayne State University; *Life-Threatening Behavior,* the official publication of the American Association of Suicidology; and the *Journal of Thanatology,* sponsored by the Foundation of Thanatology, Columbia-Presbyterian Medical Center.

Institutions have played a vital role in the progress of the developmental sciences, by sponsoring conferences and publications and by providing the settings where the authors gained their pertinent experience or conducted their research. The programs of developmental studies of some institutions are already well-known, for example, those existing at the Tavistock and the Hampstead Child-Therapy Clinics in England (Bowlby, 1969; Nagera, 1966; Freud, 1968), at the Menninger Foundation (Gardner and Moriarty, 1968) and the Langley Porter Neuropsychiatric Institute (Lowenthal et al., 1967) in this country; others, such as the studies carried out at the Pediatric Language Disorder Clinic, Babies Hospital, Columbia-Presbyterian Medical Center (De Hirsch, Jansky, and Langford,

---

[1] Ambrose (1969), Caplan and Lebovici (1969), Clemente and Lindsley (1968), Fried, Harris, and Murphy (1968), Hirsch (1967), Isaacson (1968), Masserman (1968b), Neubauer (1965), Robinson (1969), Scrimshaw and Gordon (1968), Sherif and Sherif (1965), Stevenson, Hess, and Rheingold (1967), Wilson (1968), Zubin and Jervis (1967).

1966) and at the Gender Identity Research Clinic at the University of California, Los Angeles (Stoller, 1968), are made known through the authors' acknowledgments. An institution specifically dedicated to developmental studies may show this fact in its name, for example, the Laboratory of Human Development, Stanford University (Sears, Rau, and Alpert, 1965), the Child Development Center, New York City (Neubauer, 1965), and the Center for the Study of Aging and Human Development, Duke University (Busse and Pfeiffer, 1969).

Organizations and special committees may recommend or initiate the conferences and literature surveys that bring new work on a subject into focus, for example, the Perinatal Research Committee established by the National Institute of Neurological Diseases and Blindness (Richardson and Guttmacher, 1967; see also Stevenson, Hess, and Rheingold, 1967; Soddy and Kidson, 1967). On a smaller scale, individual projects of limited duration can contribute to the emerging identity and organization of the developmental sciences (Masterson, 1967; Offer, 1969). Sometimes the names of such projects provide the main clue to the book's relevance to developmental research, for example, "Parental Influences on Early Ego Development in the Child" (Des Lauriers and Carlson, 1969) and "Child Rearing Practices among Low Income Families in the District of Columbia" (Liebow, 1967).

Innovations in the organization of science often begin outside of universities, but lead later to new centers and institutes in academic settings and ultimately to new disciplines or subdisciplines. Since the mid-sixties the transformation of older disciplines under the influence of the spreading developmental orientation has gathered momentum. So far, the trend has been not to strive from the start for a unified developmental science—an effort that was made for the behavioral sciences in the 1950s—but to recognize, within a field of specialization, a section that further specializes in a developmental approach. In recent years, there has been a marked increase in the use of the word "developmental" in a form suggesting a subdiscipline. An example was set earlier when the name of genetic psychology was changed to "developmental psychology." In titles of recent books and journals, anatomy, biology, cytology, genetics, immunology, medicine, neurobiology, neurology, and psychobiology are each preceded by the word "developmental."

One would be ill-advised, however, to define "the developmental sciences" according to such outward indicators. In addition to old disciplines such as embryology, various new disciplines that are also central to developmental research do not show this relevance in their names. Examples are behavior genetics (Hirsch, 1967) and teratology, which attained extraordinary social significance through the thalidomide crisis in the early 1960s and the intensified study of the causes of congenital malformations. Moreover, the bulk of work on developmental problems is still being done within the domain of one or another of the biomedical, psychological, and social sciences, without any organized differentiation.

In his Aldrich Award Address entitled "Child Development: A Basic Science for Pediatrics," presented in 1966 to the Section of Child Development of the American Academy of Pediatrics, Julius B. Richmond analyzed some of the issues that enter into the developmental reorientation of an established field. Pointing beyond the limits of his own specialty, he urged that "the concept of human development must become a central theme of medical education if it is to meet the changing needs of society." In light of the shift in the fields of human biology and medicine from an emphasis on disease to one on process, he proposed that "processes may be ordered around development as a unifying concept" (Chess and Thomas, 1968, pp. 141–142).

As has been shown earlier in this essay, the same thought underlies most efforts to come to grips with this new course of human affairs which has been equally and simultaneously spurred by three converging trends: scientific advances, the pressures of social needs and cultural crises, and the call on national governments and world bodies for programs designed to alleviate, if not to solve, the ensuing problems. Recognition of the developmental sciences, as here outlined, might help to reveal and to promote progress on each separate, as well as on the common, front.

REFERENCES

Abraham, K. (1966). *On Character and Libido Development: Six Essays.* New York: Basic Books.

Ainsworth, M. D. S. (1967). *Infancy in Uganda: Infant Care and the Growth of Love.* Baltimore: Johns Hopkins Press.

Ambrose, A., ed. (1969). *Stimulation in Early Infancy.* Proceedings of a C.A.S.D.S. [Centre for Advanced Study in the Developmental Sciences] Study Group on "The Functions of Stimulation in Early Postnatal Development" Held Jointly with the Ciba Foundation, London, November 1967 . . . London: Academic Press.

Arasteh, A. R. (1965). *Final Integration in the Adult Personality: A Measure for Health, Social Change, and Leadership.* Leiden: Brill.

Arieti, S. (1967). *The Intrapsychic Self: Feeling, Cognition, and Creativity in Health and Mental Illness.* New York: Basic Books.

Axline, V. M. (1964). *Dibs: In Search of Self: Personality Development in Play Therapy.* Boston: Houghton Mifflin.

Baldwin, A. L. (1966). *Theories of Child Development.* New York: Wiley.

Baldwin, J. M., and Poulton, E. B. (1911). Development (Biological). In: *Dictionary of Philosophy and Psychology,* new edition, ed. J. M. Baldwin. New York: Macmillan.

Bax, M. (1971). 'The Larger Half.' *Developmental Medicine and Child Neurology,* 13:135–136.

Beard, R. M. (1969). *An Outline of Piaget's Developmental Psychology for Students and Teachers.* London: Routledge and Kegan Paul.

Bettelheim, B. (1969). *The Children of the Dream.* New York: Macmillan.

Biddle, W. W. (1965). *The Community Development Process: The Rediscovery of Local Initiative.* New York: Holt, Rinehart and Winston.

Bijou, S. W., and Baer, D. M. (1965). *Child Development,* Vol. 2: *Universal Stage of Infancy.* New York: Appleton-Century-Crofts.

Blanck, R., and Blanck, G. (1968). *Marriage & Personal Development.* New York: Columbia University Press.

Botwinick, J. (1967). *Cognitive Processes in Maturity and Old Age.* New York: Springer.

Bowlby, J. (1969). *Attachment and Loss,* Vol. 1: *Attachment.* London: Hogarth Press.

Brackbill, Y., ed. (1967). *Infancy and Early Childhood: A Handbook and Guide to Human Development.* New York: Free Press.

————, and Thompson, G. G., eds. (1967). *Behavior in Infancy and Early Childhood: A Book of Readings.* New York: Free Press.

Brody, E. B., et al. (1968). *Minority Group Adolescents in the United States.* Baltimore: Williams and Wilkins.

Bromley, D. B. (1966). *The Psychology of Human Ageing.* Harmondsworth, Middlesex: Penguin Books.

Bry, I., and Afflerbach, L., eds. (1956–1971). *Mental Health Book Review Index: An Annual Bibliography of Books and Book Reviews in the Behavioral Sciences,* Vols. 1–16. Flushing, N.Y.: Council on Research in Bibliography.

Bühler, C. M., and Massarik, F., eds. (1968). *The Course of Human Life: A Study of Goals in the Humanistic Perspective.* New York: Springer.

Burch, P. R. J. (1968). *An Inquiry Concerning Growth, Disease and Ageing.* Edinburgh: Oliver and Boyd.

Busse, E. W., and Pfeiffer, E., eds. (1969). *Behavior and Adaptation in Late Life.* Boston: Little, Brown.

Caplan, G., and Lebovici, S., eds. (1969). *Adolescence: Psychosocial Perspectives.* New York: Basic Books.

Chess, S., and Thomas, A., eds. (1968). *Annual Progress in Child Psychiatry and Child Development.* New York: Brunner/Mazel.

Chilman, C. S. (1966). *Growing Up Poor: An Over-View and Analysis of Child-Rearing and Family Life Patterns Associated with Poverty . . .* Washington: U.S. Department of Health, Education, and Welfare, Welfare Administration, Division of Research.

Clemente, C. D., and Lindsley, D. B., eds. (1968). *Aggression and Defense: Neural Mechanisms and Social Patterns. Proceedings of the Fifth Conference on Brain Function, November 1965.* Berkeley: University of California Press.

Coles, R. (1967). *Children of Crisis: A Study of Courage and Fear.* Boston: Little, Brown.

Cowie, V. A. (1970). *A Study of the Early Development of Mongols.* Oxford: Published for the Institute for Research into Mental Retardation by Pergamon Press.

D'Amato, G. (1969). *Residential Treatment for Child Mental Health: Towards Ego-Social Development and a Community-Child Model.* Springfield, Ill.: Charles C Thomas.

Davis, C. (1966). *Room to Grow: A Study of Parent-Child Relationships.* Toronto: University of Toronto Press.

Dawson, R. E., and Prewitt, K. (1968). *Political Socialization: An Analytic Study.* Boston: Little, Brown.

De Hirsch, K., Jansky, J. J., and Langford, W. S. (1966). *Predicting Reading Failure: A Preliminary Study of Reading, Writing, and Spelling Disabilities in Preschool Children.* New York: Harper and Row.

Des Lauriers, A. M., and Carlson, C. F. (1969). *Your Child Is Asleep: Early Infantile Autism: Etiology, Treatment, Parental Influences.* Homewood, Ill.: Dorsey Press.

Deutsch, M., et al. (1967). *The Disadvantaged Child: Selected Papers of Martin Deutsch and Associates.* New York: Basic Books.

————, Katz, I., and Jensen, A. R., eds. (1968). *Social Class, Race, and Psychological Development.* New York: Holt, Rinehart and Winston.

Eissler, K. R. (1955). *The Psychiatrist and the Dying Patient.* New York: International Universities Press. Paperback edition, 1969.

Elkind, D., and Flavell, J. H., eds. (1969). *Studies in Cognitive Development: Essays in Honor of Jean Piaget.* New York: Oxford University Press.

Erikson, E. H. (1958). *Young Man Luther: A Study in Psychoanalysis and History.* New York: Norton.

———— (1968). *Identity: Youth and Crisis.* New York: Norton.

Escalona, S. K. (1968). *The Roots of Individuality: Normal Patterns of Development in Infancy.* Chicago: Aldine.

————, and Leitch, M. (1952). Early Phases of Personality Development: A Non-normative

Study of Infant Behavior. *Monographs of the Society for Research in Child Development,* 17(1, Whole No. 54).

Evans, R. I. (1967). *Dialogue with Erik Erikson.* New York: Harper and Row.

Fellows, B. J. (1968). *The Discrimination Process and Development.* Oxford: Pergamon Press.

Ferguson, T. (1966). *Children in Care—and After.* London: Published for the Nuffield Foundation by Oxford University Press.

Flavell, J. H. (1968). *The Development of Role-Taking and Communication Skills in Children.* New York: Wiley.

Frank, J. D. (1967). *Sanity and Survival: Psychological Aspects of War and Peace.* New York: Random House.

Freud, A. (1968). *The Writings of Anna Freud,* Vol. 4: *Indications for Child Analysis and Other Papers, 1945–1956.* New York: International Universities Press.

Fried, M., Harris, M., and Murphy, R., eds. (1968). *War: The Anthropology of Armed Conflict and Aggression.* Garden City, N. Y.: Published for the American Museum of Natural History by the Natural History Press.

Furst, S. S., ed. (1967). *Psychic Trauma.* New York: Basic Books.

Gardner, R. W., and Moriarty, A. E. (1968). *Personality Development at Preadolescence: Explorations of Structure Formation.* Seattle: University of Washington Press.

Geist, H. (1968). *The Psychological Aspects of Retirement.* Springfield, Ill.: Charles C Thomas.

Glaser, B. G., and Strauss, A. L. (1965). *Awareness of Dying.* Chicago: Aldine.

——, —— (1968). *Time for Dying.* Chicago: Aldine.

Glover, E. (1968). *The Birth of the Ego: A Nuclear Hypothesis.* London: Allen and Unwin.

Goldstein, B. (1967). *Low Income Youth in Urban Areas: A Critical Review of the Literature.* New York: Holt, Rinehart and Winston.

Gooch, S., and Pringle, M. L. K. (1966). *Four Years On: A Follow-Up Study at School Leaving Age of Children Formerly Attending a Traditional and a Progressive Junior School.* London: Longmans.

Gorer, G. (1965). *Death, Grief, and Mourning in Contemporary Britain.* London: Cresset Press.

Green, R., and Money, J., eds. (1969). *Transsexualism and Sex Reassignment.* Baltimore: Johns Hopkins Press.

Grinder, R. E., ed. (1967). *A History of Genetic Psychology, the First Science of Human Development.* New York: Wiley.

Group for the Advancement of Psychiatry. Committee on Adolescence (1968). *Normal Adolescence: Its Dynamics and Impact.* New York: Group for the Advancement of Psychiatry. (Report No. 68.)

Halloran, J. D. (1967). *Attitude Formation and Change.* Leicester: Leicester University Press.

Harris, D. B., ed. (1957). *The Concept of Development: An Issue in the Study of Human Behavior.* Minneapolis: University of Minnesota Press.

Helfer, R. E., and Kempe, C. H., eds. (1968). *The Battered Child.* Chicago: University of Chicago Press.

Heron, A., and Chown, S. M. (1967). *Age and Function.* Boston: Little, Brown.

Hess, R. D., and Torney, J. V. (1967). *The Development of Political Attitudes in Children.* Chicago: Aldine.

Hinde, R. A. (1966). *Animal Behaviour: A Synthesis of Ethology and Comparative Psychology.* New York: McGraw-Hill.

Hirsch, J., ed. (1967). *Behavior-Genetic Analysis.* New York: McGraw-Hill.

Hoffman, L. N. W., and Hoffman, M. L., eds. (1966). *Review of Child Development Research,* Vol. 2. New York: Russell Sage Foundation.

Humphrey, M. (1969). *The Hostage Seekers: A Study of Childless and Adopting Couples.* London: Longmans.

Isaacson, R. L., ed. (1968). *The Neuropsychology of Development: A Symposium.* New York: Wiley.

Joffe, J. M. (1969). *Prenatal Determinants of Behaviour.* Oxford: Pergamon Press.

Kare, M. R. (1970). Review of Scrimshaw, N. S., and Gordon, J. R., eds., *Malnutrition, Learning, and Behavior. Contemporary Psychology,* 15:20–21.

Kay, W. (1968). *Moral Development: A Psychological Study of Moral Growth from Childhood to Adolescence.* London: Allen and Unwin.

Kidd, A. H., and Rivoire, J. L., eds. (1966). *Perceptual Development in Children.* New York: International Universities Press.

Kliman, G. (1968). *Psychological Emergencies of Childhood.* New York: Grune and Stratton.

Koch, H. L. (1966). *Twins and Twin Relations.* Chicago: University of Chicago Press.

Kübler-Ross, E. (1969). *On Death and Dying.* New York: Macmillan.

Kuo, Z.-Y. (1967). *The Dynamics of Behavior Development: An Epigenetic View.* New York: Random House.

Kutscher, A. H., ed. (1969). *Death and Bereavement.* Springfield, Ill.: Charles C Thomas.

Lidz, T. (1968). *The Person: His Development throughout the Life Cycle.* New York: Basic Books.

Liebow, E. (1967). *Tally's Corner: A Study of Negro Streetcorner Men.* Boston: Little, Brown.

Lipsitt, L. P., and Spiker, C. C., eds. (1967). *Advances in Child Development and Behavior,* Vol. 3. New York: Academic Press.

Llorens, L. A., and Rubin, E. Z. (1967). *Developing Ego Functions in Disturbed Children: Occupational Therapy in Milieu.* Detroit: Wayne State University.

Lorenz, K. (1966). *On Aggression.* New York: Harcourt, Brace and World.

Lowenthal, M. F., et al. (1967). *Aging and Mental Disorder in San Francisco: A Social Psychiatric Study.* San Francisco: Jossey-Bass.

Lunzer, E. A., and Morris, J. F., eds. (1968–1969). *Development in Learning: Behaviour: Learning: Education,* Vol. 1: *The Regulation of Behaviour;* Vol. 2: *Development in Human Learning;* Vol. 3: *Contexts of Education.* London: Staples Press.

Maccoby, E. E., ed. (1966). *The Development of Sex Differences.* Stanford: Stanford University Press.

McWhinnie, A. M. (1967). *Adopted Children: How They Grow Up: A Study of Their Adjustment as Adults.* London: Routledge and Kegan Paul.

Mahler, M. S. (1968). *On Human Symbiosis and the Vicissitudes of Individuation,* Vol. 1: *Infantile Psychosis.* New York: International Universities Press.

Maier, H. W. (1965). *Three Theories of Child Development: The Contributions of Erik H. Erikson, Jean Piaget, and Robert R. Sears, and Their Applications.* New York: Harper and Row.

Marrow, A. J. (1969). *The Practical Theorist: The Life and Work of Kurt Lewin.* New York: Basic Books.

Masserman, J. H. (1968a). *The Biodynamic Roots of Human Behavior.* Springfield, Ill.: Charles C Thomas.

———, ed. (1968b). *Science and Psychoanalysis,* Vol. 12: *Animal and Human: Scientific Proceedings of the American Academy of Psychoanalysis, May, 1967.* New York: Grune and Stratton.

Masterson, J. F., Jr. (1967). *The Psychiatric Dilemma of Adolescence.* Boston: Little, Brown.

Mitchell, M. E. (1966). *The Child's Attitude to Death.* London: Barrie and Rockliff.

Moriarty, D. M., ed. (1967). *The Loss of Loved Ones: The Effects of a Death in the Family on Personality Development.* Springfield, Ill.: Charles C Thomas.

Nagera, H. (1966). *Early Childhood Disturbances, the Infantile Neurosis, and the Adulthood Disturbances: Problems of a Developmental Psychoanalytic Psychology.* New York: International Universities Press.

Neubauer, P. B., ed. (1965). *Concepts of Development in Early Childhood Education:*

An Institute Conducted by the Child Development Center, New York City. Springfield, Ill.: Charles C Thomas.

Neugarten, B. L., ed. (1968). Middle Age and Aging: A Reader in Social Psychology. Chicago: University of Chicago Press.

Newson, J., and Newson, E. (1968). Four Years Old in an Urban Community. London: Allen and Unwin.

Newton, G., and Levine, S., eds. (1968). Early Experience and Behavior: The Psychobiology of Development. Springfield, Ill.: Charles C Thomas.

Offer, D. (1969). The Psychological World of the Teen-Ager: A Study of Normal Adolescent Boys. New York: Basic Books.

Olesen, V. L., and Whittaker, E. W. (1968). The Silent Dialogue: A Study in the Social Psychology of Professional Socialization. San Francisco: Jossey-Bass.

Parfit, J., ed. (1967). The Community's Children: Long-Term Substitute Care: A Guide for the Intelligent Layman. London: Longmans.

Pavenstedt, E., ed. (1967). The Drifters: Children of Disorganized Lower-Class Families. Boston: Little, Brown.

Phillips, J. L., Jr. (1969). The Origins of Intellect: Piaget's Theory. San Francisco: Freeman.

Phillips, L. (1968). Human Adaptation and Its Failures. New York: Academic Press.

Piaget, J. (1967). Six Psychological Studies. New York: Random House.

—————— (1968). On the Development of Memory and Identity. Worcester, Mass.: Clark University Press.

——————, and Inhelder, B. (1969). The Psychology of the Child. New York: Basic Books.

Pringle, M. L. K. (1966). Social Learning and Its Measurement. London: Longmans.

—————— (1967). Adoption, Facts and Fallacies: A Review of Research in the United States, Canada and Great Britain between 1948 and 1965. London: Longmans.

——————, Butler, N. R., and Davie, R. (1966). 11,000 Seven-Year-Olds: First Report of the National Child Development Study (1958 Cohort), Submitted to the Central Advisory Council for Education (England), April 1966. London: Longmans.

Pye, L. W. (1968). The Spirit of Chinese Politics: A Psychocultural Study of the Authority Crisis in Political Development. Cambridge, Mass.: M.I.T. Press.

Ratcliffe, T. A. (1967). The Development of Personality. London: Allen and Unwin.

Rawson, M. B. (1968). Developmental Language Disability: Adult Accomplishments of Dyslexic Boys. Baltimore: Johns Hopkins Press.

Resnik, H. L. P., ed. (1968). Suicidal Behaviors: Diagnosis and Management. Boston: Little, Brown.

Rheingold, J. C. (1967). The Mother, Anxiety, and Death: The Catastrophic Death Complex. Boston: Little, Brown.

Richardson, S. A., and Guttmacher, A. F., eds. (1967). Childbearing: Its Social and Psychological Aspects. Baltimore: Williams and Wilkins.

Robins, L. N. (1966). Deviant Children Grown Up: A Sociological and Psychiatric Study of Sociopathic Personality. Baltimore: Williams and Wilkins.

Robinson, R. J., ed. (1969). Brain and Early Behaviour: Development in the Fetus and Infant. Proceedings of a C.A.S.D.S. [Centre for Advanced Study in the Developmental Sciences] Study Group on "Brain Mechanisms of Early Behavioural Development" Held Jointly with the Ciba Foundation, London, February 1968 . . . London: Academic Press.

Rosow, I. (1967). Social Integration of the Aged. New York: Free Press.

Scheinfeld, A. (1967). Twins and Super-Twins. The First Comprehensive Account of the Lives of the Multiple-Born from Conception Through Maturity . . . as Revealed by Scientists, by Parents of Twins, and by Twins Themselves. Philadelphia: Lippincott.

Schofield, M. G. (1965). The Sexual Behaviour of Young People. London: Longmans.

Scrimshaw, N. S., and Gordon, J. E., eds. (1968). Malnutrition, Learning, and Behavior: Proceedings of an International Conference Cosponsored by the Nutrition Foundation, Inc., and the Massachusetts Institute of Technology, Held at Cambridge, Massachusetts, March 1 to 3, 1967. Cambridge, Mass.: M.I.T. Press.

Sears, R. R., Rau, L., and Alpert, R. (1965). *Identification and Child Rearing*. Stanford: Stanford University Press.

Senn, M. J. E., and Solnit, A. J. (1968). *Problems in Child Behavior and Development*. Philadelphia: Lea and Febiger.

Sherif, M., and Sherif, C. W., eds. (1965). *Problems of Youth: Transition to Adulthood in a Changing World*. Chicago: Aldine.

Sluckin, W. (1964). *Imprinting and Early Learning*. London: Methuen.

Soddy, K., and Kidson, M. C., eds. (1967). *Men in Middle Life. Based on the Study Made by the One-Time Scientific Committee of the World Federation for Mental Health*. London: Tavistock.

Staats, A. W. (1968). *Learning, Language, and Cognition: Theory, Research, and Method for the Study of Human Behavior and Its Development*. New York: Holt, Rinehart and Winston.

Stephenson, G. M. (1966). *The Development of Conscience*. London: Routledge and Kegan Paul.

Stevenson, H. W. (1968). Developmental Psychology. I. The Field. In: *International Encyclopedia of the Social Sciences*, Vol. 4, ed. D. L. Sills. New York: Macmillan and Free Press.

————, Hess, E. H., and Rheingold, H. L., eds. (1967). *Early Behavior: Comparative and Developmental Approaches*. New York: Wiley.

Stoller, R. J. (1968). *Sex and Gender: On the Development of Masculinity and Femininity*. New York: Science House.

Storr, A. (1968). *Human Aggression*. London: Allen Lane, The Penguin Press.

Sudnow, D. (1967). *Passing On: The Social Organization of Dying*. Englewood Cliffs, N.J.: Prentice-Hall.

Talland, G. A., ed. (1968). *Human Aging and Behavior: Recent Advances in Research and Theory*. New York: Academic Press.

Thomas, A., Chess, S., and Birch, H. G. (1968). *Temperament and Behavior Disorders in Children*. New York: New York University Press.

Toynbee, A., et al. (1968). *Man's Concern with Death*. London: Hodder and Stoughton.

Vernon, P. E. (1969). *Intelligence and Cultural Environment*. London: Methuen.

Verwoerdt, A. (1966). *Communication with the Fatally Ill*. Springfield, Ill.: Charles C Thomas.

Völgyesi, F. A. (1966). *Hypnosis of Man and Animals, with Special Reference to the Development of the Brain in the Species and the Individual*, 2nd ed. London: Baillière, Tindall and Cassell.

Warren, R. M., and Warren, R. P. (1968). *Helmholtz on Perception: Its Physiology and Development*. New York: Wiley.

Wilson, C. W. M., ed. (1968). *The Pharmacological and Epidemiological Aspects of Adolescent Drug Dependence: Proceedings of the Society for the Study of Addiction, London, 1 and 2 September 1966*. Oxford: Pergamon Press.

Wittenberg, R. M. (1967). *The Troubled Generation: Toward Understanding and Helping the Young Adult*. New York: Association Press.

———— (1968). *Postadolescence: Theoretical and Clinical Aspects of Psychoanalytic Therapy*. New York: Grune and Stratton.

Wood, N. E. (1964). *Delayed Speech and Language Development*. Englewood Cliffs, N.J.: Prentice-Hall.

World Health Organization (1968). *Prevention of Suicide*. Geneva: World Health Organization.

Wyatt, G. L. (1969). *Language Learning and Communication Disorders in Children*. New York: Free Press.

Zubin, J., and Jervis, G. A., eds. (1967). *Psychopathology of Mental Development: The Proceedings of the Fifty-Sixth Annual Meeting of the American Psychopathological Association, Held in New York City, February, 1966*. New York: Grune and Stratton.

4

CLINICAL-EXPERIMENTAL STUDIES

THE EFFECTS OF AGGRESSIVE STIMULATION ON SUICIDAL PATIENTS
An Experimental Study of the Psychoanalytic Theory of Suicide [1]

Eleanor H. Rutstein, Ph.D., and Leo Goldberger, Ph.D.

Of the psychological theories that have been formulated to account for suicidal behavior, Freud's psychoanalytic theory is outstanding, not only because of the economy and power of its explanatory constructs but also because of its influence on subsequent theories, many of which differ only in qualifications and specifications (Williams, 1936; Zilborg, 1937; Menninger, 1938; Palmer, 1941; Teicher, 1947).

Freud's classical statement of the dynamics of suicide (1917) focused on the vicissitudes of the aggressive impulse. First, he assumed a narcissistic choice of a love object, followed by a relationship which became undermined either by the loss of the object or by hurt, neglect, or disappointment at the hands of the object. This situation either imparted ambivalent feelings of love and hate toward the object or reinforced pre-existing ambivalent feelings. Normally, under these conditions of object loss or disappointment, the libido is withdrawn from the object and transferred to a new one. In cases of depression, however, the libido becomes withdrawn into the self rather than transferred to another object. A narcissistic identification with the abandoned object is established, allowing the self to become the target of the aggression originally leveled at the love object. In depression and in the extreme case, suicide, it is the unconscious sadism and hatred of the original love object which become turned back upon the self. Thus, according to Freud, the turning inward of aggression toward the original, ambivalently cathected love object is a necessary (but not sufficient)

[1] This paper is based on a study conducted by the senior author as part of her Ph.D. dissertation at New York University, October, 1970. She is grateful for the co-operation received at the Bronx State Hospital where the experiments were carried out; special thanks go to Drs. Irwin Greenberg, Saul Grossman, and Morris Klein. Miss Myrna Sameth and Mr. Joseph Wanderling provided valuable help with the statistical analysis of the data under National Institute of Mental Health Research Grant No. MH-14934. We are grateful to Dr. Lloyd Silverman, who was closely associated with all phases of the study.

condition for the precipitation of a suicidal act. One would, therefore, expect people who have attempted suicide to have difficulty in directing their hostility outward, turning it inward instead. It is this segment of Freud's theory of suicide that this study was designed to test empirically.

A look at the pertinent empirical research literature reveals that, of the very small number of experimental studies of suicidal persons, few have touched on the role of aggression in suicide, and none has employed an experimental manipulation to study suicidal persons. Studies which do not employ an experimental manipulation may suggest, but cannot in a strict sense establish, causal relationships between the hypothesized motivating factors and the suicidal act.

Previous attempts to study the role of aggression in suicide have all followed one basic experimental design: tests are given to psychiatric patients after their attempts at self-destruction and the results are compared with those of other groups of subjects—"normals," nonsuicidal psychiatric patients, psychiatric patients threatening suicide, or, in one study, automobile accident victims who were presumed to be accident prone (Eisenthal, 1967; Farberow, 1950; Lester, 1967; McEvoy, 1963; Shneidman and Farberow, 1957; Winfield and Sparer, 1953). These studies have merely demonstrated the abreactive effects of suicidal attempts on self-directed aggression; because they did not use an experimental manipulation of aggression they were unable to shed light on psychoanalytic propositions concerning the direction in which aggression is expressed in suicidal persons.

How can one experimentally trigger aggression without causing undue anguish and harmful effects in patients? L. H. Silverman's technique for studying the effects of unconscious processes on psychopathology seemed suited to the purpose of stirring the impulses that, theoretically, lead to the suicidal act. By presenting drive-related stimuli at a subliminal level, Silverman and his associates have presumably triggered aggressive or sexual drive derivatives and have studied the ensuing psychopathology postulated by psychoanalytic theory (L. H. Silverman, 1965, 1966; L. H. Silverman and Candell, in press; L. H. Silverman and Goldweber, 1966; L. H. Silverman and D. K. Silverman, 1964; L. H. Silverman and S. E. Silverman, 1967; L. H. Silverman and Spiro, 1967, 1968; L. H. Silverman, Spiro, Weisberg, and Candell, 1969; S. E. Silverman, 1969; Spiro and Silverman, 1969).

The present study was designed primarily to test the hypothesis that suicidal persons will show increased inward aggression and depression (presumably a manifestation of aggression turned inward) on presentation of an aggressive stimulus compared (1) with themselves under conditions when an aggressive stimulus is not presented and (2) with nonsuicidal (control) subjects; that the effect will be evoked to a greater extent by subliminal than by supraliminal presentation of the same aggressive stimulus; and that the effect will not be elicited by a libidinal stimulus.

One assumption underlying this study is that aggressive and libidinal stimuli tend to activate, respectively, aggressive and libidinal impulses. Another assumption is that subliminal stimuli will activate mainly unconscious impulses.

A third assumption is that the effect will depend on the ability of the stimuli selectively to involve an early introjected love object (presumably the mother) in its arousal of impulses. The stimuli were chosen on the basis of this asssumption.

METHOD

Subjects

The subjects for this study were 64 female patients at the Bronx State Hospital. Thirty-two had made serious attempts at suicide before or during hospitalization; 32 had never made a suicidal attempt or gesture and had not received a primary diagnosis of depression. The control and suicidal subjects did not differ significantly in age, race, education, or severity of illness. Severely psychotic persons, that is, patients known by their ward psychiatrists to be actively hallucinating, were excluded from the study.

The following methods of attempting suicide were used by members of the suicidal group: fifteen took overdoses of pills, eight slit their wrists, three jumped from high places, two attempted to drown, two jumped in front of trains, one attempted to hang herself, and one took gas.

Stimuli and Tachistoscope

The stimuli used in this study contained both pictures and verbal messages.

The content of the aggressive stimulus was chosen on the assumption that its effectiveness in stimulating unconscious aggressive impulses depended on its ability to involve selectively an early introjected love object (presumably the mother). The stimulus depicted a young, menacing-looking woman with a large dagger about to stab an older woman; below the picture was the caption, DESTROY MOTHER.

The stimulus intended to gratify the subjects' libidinal impulses toward the early introjected love object depicted a little girl embracing and being embraced by a young woman; below the picture was the caption, MOMMY LOVES ME.

A control stimulus depicted two women walking and was captioned PEOPLE WALKING.

In addition, four other neutral stimuli were used in order to tap the subjects' baseline functioning (see below). In Session I, the neutral stimulus depicted two women and was captioned PEOPLE TALKING. In Session II, the neutral stimulus depicted two women and was captioned GIRLS LOOKING. In Session III, the neutral stimulus depicted two women and was captioned DISCUSSION. In Session IV, the neutral stimulus depicted two women and was captioned WOMEN SMILING.

Efforts were made to select pictures which were equivalent in terms of the shapes depicted and the amount of space occupied by the figures and captions.

The stimuli were shown through an electronically controlled mirror tachistoscope. The subject looked through an eyepiece at a blank field and the stimuli were exposed from a second field. The viewing distance was 49 in. and the surface brightness of a white card for the intensity setting used was 32 footlamberts.

Response Measures

The following instruments were used to measure the concepts relevant to aggression and its various manifestations.

THE MULTIPLE AFFECT ADJECTIVE CHECK LIST—TODAY FORM   The Zuckerman-Lubin (1965) "Multiple Affect Adjective Check List" (MAACL) consists of 132 adjectives related to feelings or moods. The subject is asked to check the words which describe his feelings "now" or "today." The MAACL has three empirically derived scales for the measurement of hostility, depression, and anxiety.

For the purposes of this study, the MAACL was somewhat modified. Zuckerman's check list was replaced by a five-point scale on which subjects indicated whether they experienced each listed feeling "very much," "a good deal," "moderately," "slightly," or "not at all." This modification was intended to minimize the possibility of any subject reaching the ceiling of a particular score during baseline measurements.

The MAACL was administered twice during each testing session, and scores were obtained on the Hostility, Depression, and Anxiety scales. The Hostility scale was interpreted as reflecting outward aggression, Depression as reflecting at least in part the process of turning aggression inward; the Anxiety scale was used to determine the specificity of the effects.

THE RORSCHACH TEST   L. H. Silverman and his associates have used the Rorschach test and alternate sets of inkblots devised by Harrower (1945) and Zulliger (1941) to measure the effects of drive-related subliminal stimuli. Because of the need for many inkblot stimuli, in this study too the Harrower and Zulliger sets, as well as the Rorschach, were used.

Rorschach Scoring Categories. The "Manual for the Scoring of Primary Process Manifestations in Rorschach Responses" developed by Holt (1968) provides scoring categories which are classifiable as "aggression turned inward" and "aggression turned outward." Holt's category "subject aggression" refers to responses in which the person, animal, or object of the responses is the subject initiating or carrying out the actual or potential aggressive action; this is here classed as "aggression turned outward." The category "object aggression" refers to responses in which the person, animal, or object of the response is the object against which the aggression may be or is being directed, and "results of aggression" refers to responses in which the results of destructive action or processes are seen; it was assumed that these latter two categories were classifiable as "aggression turned inward."

While this study was undertaken primarily to assess the effects of the experimental conditions on aggression, another variable tapped by the Holt manual was also of interest—"libidinal content," i.e., content with oral-receptive, oral-aggressive, anal, sexual, homosexual, or exhibitionistic-voyeuristic implications. Within this category, special attention was paid to oral-aggressive responses.

Scores for both aggressive and libidinal content were further categorized, as specified in the Holt manual, according to the level of the expression of the given drive: responses that reflected crude, direct, and primitive drive expression were scored Level 1, those that reflected indirect, controlled, socialized drive expression were scored Level 2.

A score for "total aggression" was obtained by adding together the "subject aggression," "object aggression," "results of aggression," and "oral-aggression" scores.

Scoring of the Rorschachs. The experimenter scored the Rorschach responses for the above categories without knowing which subliminal stimuli preceded each Rorschach administration. In addition, in order to provide data on interrater reliability, half of the protocols, selected at random, were scored by one of two other psychologists,[2] both of whom were highly experienced with the Holt scoring system. These raters did not know the nature of the stimuli, the hypotheses being tested, or the tachistoscopic conditions preceding each Rorschach administration.

In the final tabulation of the Rorschach categories, Level 1 responses received twice the weight of Level 2 responses. The sums yielded were then divided by the total number of responses for that particular series.

Experimental Procedure

The experiment followed the procedure devised by Silverman for studying psychodynamic relationships.

Each subject served as her own control and was seen in four experimental sessions whose order was counterbalanced. A fifth session was conducted in order to test for the "subliminality" of the tachistoscopic exposures. Each session was conducted on a separate day.

The experimental sessions were designated as (1) "subliminal aggressive"; (2) "subliminal libidinal"; (3) "subliminal control"; (4) "supraliminal aggressive." Comparisons among these four conditions allowed for a determination of the effects of the content of the stimulus (aggressive versus neutral, aggressive versus libidinal) and the type of exposure (subliminal versus supraliminal).

Each session included a baseline and a "critical" assessment of the subject's functioning. The changes in the subject's response from the former to the latter reflected the effects of the stimulation used in that session.

Each subject was introduced to the experiment as follows: [3]

---

[2] Miss Reeva Safrin and Dr. Tupper Pettit.
[3] Instructions taken from Silverman (1966, pp. 104–105).

I am a research psychologist here at the hospital and am trying to learn as much as possible about the patients who are here. Your name was given to me by the doctor on your ward as one of the patients who is highly cooperative and willing to help. Thus, I am going to ask you to engage in some tasks that will give me some of the information that I am looking for. Are you willing? (The subject indicates her willingness to participate.) Fine! You will engage in a few different kinds of tasks. One of them involves looking at inkblots and describing what you see in them. Another involves indicating how much you feel the moods and feelings listed on this paper. Another involves looking into the eyepiece of the machine next to you through which you will see flashes of light.

The subject was then given a brief warm-up period to introduce her to the tachistoscope and the Rorschach. She was shown two inkblots, one achromatic and one chromatic (different from those used in the experiment proper) and was asked to describe what she could see in them. When this task was completed, subjects about to receive subliminal stimuli were told:

Fine! Bear in mind when I show you more cards that there are no right or wrong answers to these. Different people see different things and what I am interested in is what they look like to you. Now I would like you to swing your chair around and put your eyes against the eyepiece of the machine. I will say, "Ready, get set," and then press a button. Then you will tell me what you have seen, such as "flash of light," or anything else you might see.

Subjects about to receive supraliminal stimuli were told:

I will say "Ready, get set" and a picture should appear. Say, "I see it," if you see it and look it over carefully, but do not describe it.

The subject was then given four exposures of the neutral baseline stimulus at 15-sec. intervals. In the three subliminal conditions the exposure time was four msecs; this exposure time has been found by Silverman and his associates to be one at which subjects are not only unable to recognize an aggressive stimulus, but also cannot consciously discriminate between an aggressive stimulus and its control. In the supraliminal condition, the stimulus was exposed for 10 secs. Each exposure of the stimulus was introduced by the words, "Ready, get set." The subject was then told:

Now I'm going to show you some more cards with inkblots on them. To each card I want you to describe everything that you can find that looks like something.

The subject was then shown four inkblots ("Baseline Rorschach 1"); after the first two, she received four refresher flashes of the neutral baseline stimulus. After she finished responding to each card or had produced five responses, an inquiry was held. The location of the image was ascertained, elaborations were sought, and ambiguities were clarified. The experimenter attempted to take down verbatim everything the subject said and did in responding to the inkblots; it was possible to do so in most cases.

When Baseline Rorschach 1 was concluded, the subject was shown four more flashes of the same neutral baseline stimulus, followed by the administration of the MAACL ("Baseline MAACL 1").

After the baseline performance had been measured, the same procedure was repeated except that a different stimulus was now shown to the subject. Eight subjects were given the subliminal aggressive condition, eight the subliminal libidinal condition, eight the subliminal control condition, and eight the supraliminal aggressive condition. The experimenter then administered four new inkblots ("Critical Rorschach 1") with four refresher flashes of the stimulus after the first two cards. The subject then received four more flashes of the stimulus and was told,

I am interested in slight changes in mood that people experience over brief periods of time. Therefore, please indicate how much of these moods and feelings you experience now.

This instruction was intended to provide the subject with a comprehensible rationale for being asked to repeat the same task within such a brief period of time ("Critical MAACL 1"). The procedure for Session I is summarized in Table 1.

Table 1   SUMMARY OF EXPERIMENTAL PROCEDURE

Session I

1. "Warm-up" period (Cards H5, Z8)
2. Four exposures of neutral stimulus (subliminal for three quarters of subjects, supraliminal for one quarter)
3. Baseline Rorschach (Cards R^a5, H^b3; four refresher flashes; H6, R8)
4. Four refresher flashes of same neutral stimulus under same condition as in Step 2
5. Baseline MAACL 1
6. Four exposures of critical stimulus (subliminal control for one quarter of subjects, subliminal aggressive for one quarter, subliminal gratification for one quarter, and supraliminal aggressive for one quarter)
7. Critical Rorschach 1 (Cards Z^c1, R2; four refresher flashes; R7, H9)
8. Four refresher flashes of same critical stimulus under same condition as in Step 6
9. Critical MAACL 1

   [a] From the Rorschach series
   [b] From the Harrower (1945) series
   [c] From the Zulliger (1941) series

It should be noted that following the critical measurement during the supraliminal condition, the subject was asked to describe the aggressive stimulus, and the experimenter continued to inquire until the subject's awareness of the aggressive content of either the picture or the verbal message seemed to be sufficient. This was done in the light of an interesting finding (L. H. Silverman and Goldweber, 1966; L. H. Silverman and Spiro, 1968) that subjects who defended themselves against supraliminal aggressive content by not being aware of it evidenced the same psychopathology on dependent measures as when they had been exposed to a subliminal aggressive stimulus.

Sessions II, III, and IV followed on subsequent days. The procedure was the same as that of Session I, except that a different neutral baseline stimulus was used for each session. The baseline and critical series of tasks was the same throughout, except that different inkblots were used. The order of the conditions was counterbalanced for each subject.

For the sessions in which the stimuli were exposed subliminally, the experimenter did not know whether the sessions were experimental or control. This was arranged by having an assistant insert the stimuli into the tachistoscope before each session, according to a prearranged order of which only she had knowledge.[4]

In the fifth session, the subject was given a discrimination task to determine whether the differential effects of the subliminal aggressive and control stimuli were a function of differences of which the subject was aware. The subject received the following instructions:[5]

I have two cards here, each having a different picture on it. Let us call one picture A, and the other picture B. I am going to flash each of these pictures at a very rapid rate of speed so that you probably won't see much more than a flash of light or perhaps some coloring. Your task will be to discriminate between the two pictures. First, let me show you what picture A looks like at this rapid speed. I'll show it to you four times. (Four flashes of the aggressive stimulus shown during the subliminal experimental session were then given.) Now I will show you picture B. (Four flashes of the control stimulus shown during the subliminal control session were then given.) Now your task is to try to tell them apart. I am going to now give you ten groups of four flashes and after each group of four flashes I want you to tell me if you think it was picture A or picture B that was shown. If you think you know which picture it was before the four flashes, wait for all four flashes anyway to make sure you really know. The four flashes in any one group always will be of the same picture. Try as hard as you can in this task because the person who does best will win a $5.00 prize. If you're not sure, take a guess.

The subject was then given the opportunity to ask questions, and clarifications were offered. During the discrimination task, the exposure time, illumination, and time interval between flashes were identical to the conditions used during the experiment proper, and each flash was preceded by the words, "Ready, get set."

[4] Miss Susan Levenstein and Miss Christine Huff assisted in the tachistoscopic procedures.

[5] Instructions taken from Silverman (1966, p. 107).

Reliability of Rorschach Scoring Categories

Reliability of ratings was determined on the Rorschachs obtained from 32 randomly selected subjects—128 Rorschachs in all. Product-moment correlations between the raters' scores were obtained and were found to be satisfactory for all variables (ranging from an r of .83 to .94).

Discrimination Task for Subliminality

Regarding the results of the discrimination task for subliminality, if one considers either eight or more correct responses or eight or more incorrect responses out of the 10 trials as a nonchance performance ($p < .10$, two-tailed test), only three subjects out of 64 were able to make this discrimination (two guessed wrong eight out of 10 times and one guessed right). However, these subjects reported that the only difference they could discriminate was that one flash seemed brighter than the other. One would expect that, by chance, one out of 20 subjects would be able to make this discrimination. It can therefore be concluded that the presentation of the stimuli during the three "subliminal" conditions was below the subjects' limen of awareness.

Results [6]

In line with the main hypothesis, the suicidal group showed a significant increase in Depression as measured on the MAACL following the subliminal aggressive stimulus ($t = 2.17$; $p < .05$, two-tailed test) (see Table 2). However, the other critical measure, Inward Aggression as measured on the Rorschach, did not change significantly, either within each condition or between conditions. The control group showed no significant differences following the subliminal aggressive stimulus, nor when the critical measures were compared between conditions.

The results of the control conditions were also negative.

In the subliminal condition, the suicidal group, as expected, showed no significant changes in Inward Aggression and Depression, nor were any other significant differences obtained. The control group, however, showed significant *decreases* in Rorschach measures of Inward Aggression ($t = 2.34$; $p < .05$) and Total Aggression ($t = 3.01$; $p < .01$) (see Table 3).

It was hypothesized that the supraliminal presentation of an aggressive stimulus would *not* lead to or would lead to less Inward Aggression or Depres-

---

[6] Tests for the significance of the difference between paired observations were performed on the baseline and critical means obtained on the dependent measures. In addition, a split-plot factorial analysis of covariance was used to analyze the effects of the stimuli on all dependent measures. This technique statistically equates the groups with respect to the independent variables, thereby making it possible to study the performance of the groups as though they were equal before the experimental manipulations. Although the analysis of covariance showed insignificant Fs, tests of significance (planned in advance) were performed on the data using the error term derived from the analysis of covariance (Winer, 1962).

Table 2 COMPARISONS OF BASELINE AND CRITICAL MEAN SCORES DURING SUBLIMINAL AGGRESSIVE CONDITION

Variable	Suicidal Group (N = 32)				Control Group (N = 32)			
	Baseline Mean	Critical Mean	Standard Error of Difference	t	Baseline Mean	Critical Mean	Standard Error of Difference	t
Depression (MAACL)	68.50	75.09	3.22	2.17*	59.78	62.38	2.44	.80
Hostility (MAACL)	40.78	40.66	2.31	.01	30.00	29.66	1.62	.21
Anxiety (MAACL)	41.81	41.69	2.38	.05	35.06	34.75	1.73	.18
Inward Aggression (Rorschach)	2.52	2.37	.39	.40	1.57	1.75	.55	.33
Outward Aggression (Rorschach)	1.81	1.59	.34	.61	2.03	1.55	.42	1.15
Oral Aggression (Rorschach)	.75	.88	.45	.29	.59	.35	.25	1.03
Total Aggression (Rorschach)	4.93	4.69	.66	.31	4.20	3.65	.74	.74
Libidinal (Rorschach)	3.03	3.57	.80	.36	3.28	4.20	.64	1.43

*p < .05 (two-tailed test)

Table 3 COMPARISONS OF BASELINE AND CRITICAL MEAN SCORES DURING SUBLIMINAL LIBIDINAL CONDITION

Variable	Suicidal Group (N = 32)				Control Group (N = 32)			
	Baseline Mean	Critical Mean	Standard Error of Difference	t	Baseline Mean	Critical Mean	Standard Error of Difference	t
Depression (MAACL)	80.56	81.00	2.35	.19	59.84	60.00	3.47	.05
Hostility (MAACL)	41.56	44.41	1.91	1.49	30.31	29.63	1.48	.46
Anxiety (MAACL)	43.44	44.47	1.39	.74	34.34	34.28	3.17	.02
Inward Aggression (Rorschach)	1.84	2.26	.33	1.26	2.56	1.63	.39	2.34*
Outward Aggression (Rorschach)	1.96	1.59	.43	.86	1.38	1.31	.25	.28
Oral Aggression (Rorschach)	.47	.68	.27	.78	.58	.25	.19	1.74
Total Aggression (Rorschach)	4.28	4.53	.62	.41	4.52	3.12	.46	3.01**
Libidinal (Rorschach)	3.28	3.58	.57	.54	3.90	4.57	.87	.77

*p < .05 (two-tailed test)
**p < .01 (two-tailed test)

sion in suicidal subjects.[7] The results were in line with expectation (see Table 4); the suicidal group showed no significant effects on the measures of Inward Aggression and Depression following the supraliminal aggressive stimulus. They did, however, show a significant increase in Outward Aggression as measured on the Rorschach $(t = 2.43; p < .05)$.

The only significant difference obtained for the control group following this experimental manipulation was a decrease in Anxiety measured on the MAACL $(t = 2.18; p < .05)$.

When comparisons were made between the conditions it was found that, in addition to Depression on the MAACL (already mentioned above), the only other measures to differ significantly were Outward Aggression during the supraliminal aggressive condition compared to the subliminal aggressive condition $(t = 2.33; p < .05)$, the subliminal control condition $(t = 2.22; p < .05)$, and the subliminal libidinal condition $(t = 2.46; p < .05)$. The control group also scored significantly higher on Outward Aggression during the supraliminal aggressive condition compared to the subliminal aggressive condition $(t = 2.23; p < .05)$. The same tendency was shown in the control group's Total Aggression score; it was significantly higher during the supraliminal aggressive condition than during the subliminal libidinal condition $(t = 2.52; p < .05)$. These results are presented in Table 5.

The hypothesis that suicidal subjects, compared with control subjects, would show increased Inward Aggression and Depression following the presentation of a subliminal aggressive stimulus was not supported. Comparisons between the adjusted means [8] of the suicidal and control groups during the subliminal aggressive conditions revealed no significant differences between the two groups on the response measures.

The results of comparisons between the adjusted means of the suicidal group and the control group during the subliminal control condition were also negative.

When the adjusted means of the suicidal group and the control group were compared during the subliminal libidinal condition, the only measures that discriminated between the two groups were Inward Aggression $(t = 2.20; p < .05)$ and Total Aggression $(t = 2.21; p < .05)$ as measured on the Rorschach; the suicidal group scored significantly higher than the control group on both measures. These differences reflect the decreases within the control group in Inward Aggression and Total Aggression mentioned above.

Finally, comparisons were made between the adjusted means of the suicidal group and the control group during the supraliminal aggressive condition. Though there were no significant differences between the groups on the Rorschach

[7] Following the supraliminal presentation of the aggressive stimulus, a check on the subject's awareness of the aggressive content of the stimulus was made; only one subject (a member of the suicidal group) was unaware of its aggressive content.

[8] In the analysis of covariance the means are adjusted to compensate for differences between the groups on the independent variables. Thus, the adjusted means indicate how each group would have performed on the dependent measures if the groups had been equivalent at the outset with respect to these measures.

Table 4 COMPARISONS OF BASELINE AND CRITICAL MEAN SCORES DURING SUPRALIMINAL AGGRESSIVE CONDITION

Variable	Suicidal Group (N = 32)				Control Group (N = 32)			
	Baseline Mean	Critical Mean	Standard Error of Difference	t	Baseline Mean	Critical Mean	Standard Error of Difference	t
Depression (MAACL)	82.43	80.25	2.89	.76	63.90	63.56	1.29	.27
Hostility (MAACL)	42.44	44.84	2.03	1.18	35.69	32.56	1.92	1.63
Anxiety (MAACL)	42.34	43.78	2.35	.61	35.19	32.89	1.06	2.18*
Inward Aggression (Rorschach)	2.30	2.19	.44	.23	1.64	1.67	.46	.06
Outward Aggression (Rorschach)	1.67	2.79	.46	2.43*	1.59	2.42	.47	1.77
Oral Aggression (Rorschach)	.67	.67	.23	.02	.62	.64	.25	.10
Total Aggression (Rorschach)	4.65	5.56	.77	1.18	3.87	4.73	.73	1.18
Libidinal (Rorschach)	2.73	2.95	.62	.36	4.46	3.86	.94	.64

*$p < .05$ (two-tailed test)

Table 5 DEPRESSION (MAACL) COMPARISONS BETWEEN CONDITIONS

Conditions	Suicidal Group (N = 32)			Control Group (N = 32)		
	Adjusted Means	Standard Error of Difference	t	Adjusted Means	Standard Error of Difference	t
Sub. Control	74.22			66.35		
vs.		3.90	2.30*		3.88	.32
Sub. Ag.	83.19			67.58		
Sub. Control	74.22			66.35		
vs.		3.89	.86		3.88	.31
Gratification	77.56			65.16		
Sub. Control	74.22			66.35		
vs.		3.89	.21		3.88	.36
Supra. Ag.	75.02			64.94		
Sub. Ag.	83.19			67.58		
vs.		3.91	1.44		3.88	.63
Gratification	77.56			65.16		
Sub. Ag.	83.19			67.58		
vs.		3.92	2.08*		3.88	.68
Supra. Ag.	75.02			64.94		
Gratification	77.56			65.16		
vs.		3.89	.65		3.88	.05
Supra. Ag.	75.02			64.94		

* $p < .05$ (two-tailed test)

measures of Inward Aggression and Depression, the suicidal group scored significantly higher than the control group on Hostility as measured by the MAACL ($t = 2.20$; $p < .05$).

DISCUSSION

The major aim of this study was to test empirically a core notion of the psychoanalytic theory of suicide. On the basis of the theory, it was expected that people who had made suicidal attempts would turn their aggression inward in response to a subliminal aggressive stimulus. This expectation derived from the assumption that the subliminal stimulus would arouse unconscious aggressive impulses and from the further assumption that, because of the nature of the stimulus (a menacing young woman with a dagger), these impulses would be directed toward an ambivalently loved introjected object. The results partially supported our expectation; suicidal subjects showed significantly more depression (conceived of as a manifestation of inward aggression) following a subliminal aggressive stimulus than following both the control and supraliminal aggressive stimuli. While it is true that the experiment was not designed to test the relative efficacy of different forms of aggressive stimuli, some effects of the particular stimulus used are compatible with relevant aspects of the theory. The specificity of the effect is striking; Depression was the only one among all the measures to change significantly during the subliminal aggressive condition and, in addition, the subliminal aggressive condition was the only experimental condition which significantly affected Depression in the suicidal subjects. When, however, the suicidal group was compared to the control group following the subliminal aggressive stimulus, the expected differences in inward aggression or depression were not found. This may be because the control group, although nonsuicidal, also represents a psychiatric population, predominantly schizophrenic, whose problems with the experiencing and expression of aggression are probably also severe (Bak, 1954). Perhaps, because of this, more sensitive measures may be required to differentiate between subjects who have problems with aggression in general and those who deal with aggression in a specific way —i.e., turning it inward. Had we used a control group of normal subjects, we might well have succeeded in demonstrating our initial hypotheses, which specified that differences would occur not only when a subject was used as his own control but also when compared to a control subject (i.e., a nonsuicidal person). The results as they stand do, however, support the existence of the relationship between aggression and depression postulated by psychoanalytic theory—a relationship which is certainly compatible with the psychoanalytic theory of suicide.

It was also hypothesized that the subliminal presentation of a libidinal stimulus to suicidal subjects would not differentially affect their scores on Inward Aggression and Depression. The results supported this hypothesis: The suicidal subjects showed no significant changes in Inward Aggression and Depression during the subliminal libidinal condition.

Finally, it was hypothesized that the subliminal presentation of an aggressive stimulus would be more effective in increasing Inward Aggression and Depression in suicidal subjects than the supraliminal presentation of the aggressive stimulus. The results supported this hypothesis. Not only was the suicidal group's depression significantly higher during the subliminal aggressive condition than during the supraliminal aggressive condition, but the group showed higher Outward Aggression following the supraliminal aggressive stimulus than during any other condition.

To explain this last finding we begin with the assumption that a nonpathological reaction to an aggressive stimulus would be the development of an aggressive idea or affect, while a pathological reaction to such a stimulus would be a depressive reaction, in which the aggression is presumably directed inward. The latter reaction, according to psychoanalytic theory, is characteristic of the suicidal person, the suicidal act representing the extreme form of this behavior. And indeed, when an aggressive stimulus was presented subliminally to suicidal subjects in this study, they became more depressed. Yet when the same stimulus was presented within the subjects' awareness, there was a significant decrease in Depression (see Table 5), and an increase in Outward Aggression (see Table 4).

Thus, one condition for the development of suicidal subjects' characteristic adaptational reactions to an aggressive stimulus is that they be unaware of it. Silverman and Spiro (1968) have postulated that only when aggressive content registers without awareness will triggering of drive derivatives occur. Conversely, they maintain, "awareness of a potentially noxious external stimulus serves a prophylactic function as far as the developing of pathological reactions is concerned" (p. 60). This is the case, they maintain, because awareness of the aggressive stimulus may prevent it from reaching drive derivatives. In the present study, we also see the prophylactic function that awareness of the aggressive stimulus serves. However, we cannot assume, as do Silverman and Spiro, that it prevents drive derivatives from being triggered, since outward aggression increased. Rather, it seems to trigger drive derivatives appropriate to the stimulus, so that pathological reactions no longer occur, and more appropriate ones take their place.[9]

A word about the control group's decreased anxiety in response to the supraliminal presentation of the aggressive stimulus. Apparently, the socially sanctioned conscious stimulation of aggression is prophylactic to nonsuicidal subjects, and perhaps even pleasurable, since it seems to promote an organization of the aggressive affect that counteracts anxiety.

It is a curious finding that the subliminal presentation of an aggressive stimulus affected the suicidal subjects' Depression on the MAACL, whereas the Rorschach measures were unaffected. There may be a number of reasons for this finding. It may be that the equation of Holt's categories "subject" and "object" aggression with "inward" and "outward" aggression is faulty. It may indeed be difficult to equate in a simple fashion the kind of ideation and preoccupation that is reflected on the Rorschach with such specific dispositional tendencies as the directional nature of aggressive expression. The fact that depressive affect tends to have a constricting effect on Rorschach ideation is a further complication in the present study. Nevertheless, the Rorschach did produce some interesting and seemingly consistent results. During the supraliminal presentation of the aggressive stimulus, however, the suicidal subjects responded with increased Outward Aggression on the Rorschach, whereas the MAACL measures remained unaffected. Thus, in the case of suicidal patients, while a subliminal aggressive stimulus elicits only a depressive response and only on the MAACL, the same stimulus presented supraliminally alerts the patients to perceive and/or describe things on the Rorschach categorized by the scorer as expressions of outwardly directed hostility, which, however, do not unequivocally correspond to what the patient feels as indicated by the MAACL. It is assumed that the Rorschach and the MAACL tap different levels of a person's functioning; the MAACL, a self-report inventory, deal with affects of which the subject is aware, whereas the Rorschach taps areas of functioning of which the person may be unaware.[10]

The results support one of the cornerstones of psychoanalytic thought concerning the important role that unconscious processes play in psychopathology

[9] Dr. Silverman's most recent position (1972) is in accord with the views of the present authors.
[10] Two recent studies have also found an increase in psychopathology following the subliminal presentation of drive-related stimuli when measured directly, but not when measured indirectly; e.g., by projective tests (Krawar, 1970; Silverman, Klinger, Lustbader, and Farrell, in press).

and, conversely, the prophylactic effect that awareness has in serving a conflict's link to psychopathology. For we have seen that when suicidal subjects were made aware of a drive-related stimulus of which they had been previously unaware, their reactions changed from pathological to nonpathological; that is, whereas they responded to an aggressive stimulus of which they were not aware with depression, when they became aware of the stimulus, they reacted with aggressive ideas and images. This finding provides experimental support for the therapeutic technique of bringing the suicidal patient's unconscious aggression into awareness, thereby severing the link to depression and, ultimately, self-destruction.

The present study supports Silverman's contention that the subliminal presentation of drive-related stimuli can be used to test empirically various aspects of the psychoanalytic theory of psychopathology. Most of Silverman's work has dealt with the relationship between aggresssive stimuli and psychopathological thinking. The present study, however, extends Silverman's technique to the study of the relationship between aggressive stimuli and depressive affect.

REFERENCES

Bak, R. C. (1954). The Schizophrenic Defense against Aggression. *International Journal of Psycho-Analysis*, 35:129–134.

Eisenthal, S. (1967). Suicide and Aggression. *Psychological Reports*, 21:745–751.

Farberow, N. L. (1950). Personality Patterns of Suicidal Mental Hospital Patients. *Genetic Psychology Monographs*, 42:3–79.

Freud, S. (1917). Mourning and Melancholia. *Standard Edition*, 14:243–258. London: Hogarth Press, 1957.

Harrower, M. R. (1945). *Psychodiagnostic Inkblots*. New York: Grune and Stratton.

Holt, R. R. (1968). *Manual for the Scoring of Primary Process Manifestations in Rorschach Responses*, Draft 10. New York University, Research Center for Mental Health (mimeograph).

Krawar, J. (1970). The Effects of Subliminal Psychodynamic Activation upon Homosexual Manifestations in Males. Unpublished doctoral dissertation, New York University.

Lester, D. (1967). Suicide as an Aggressive Act. *Journal of Psychology*, 66:47–50.

McEvoy, T. L. (1963). A Comparison of Suicidal and Nonsuicidal Patients by Means of the Thematic Apperception Test. Unpublished doctoral dissertation, University of California, Los Angeles.

Menninger, K. A. (1938). *Man against Himself*. New York: Harcourt, Brace.

Palmer, D. M. (1941). Factors in Suicidal Attempts: A Review of 25 Consecutive Cases. *Journal of Nervous and Mental Disease*, 93:421–442.

Shneidman, E. S., and Farberow, N. L. (1957). Clues to Suicide. In: *Clues to Suicide*, ed. N. S. Shneidman and N. L. Farberow. New York: McGraw-Hill.

Silverman, L. H. (1965). A Study of the Effects of Subliminally Presented Aggressive Stimuli on the Production of Pathologic Thinking in a Nonpsychiatric Population. *Journal of Nervous and Mental Disease*, 141:443–455.

———— (1966). A Technique for the Study of Psychodynamic Relationships: The Effects of Subliminally Presented Aggressive Stimuli on the Production of Pathological Thinking in a Schizophrenic Population. *Journal of Consulting Psychology*, 30:103–111.

———— (1972). Drive Stimulation and Psychopathology. *Psychoanalysis and Contemporary Science*, 1:306–326. New York: Macmillan.

————, and Candell, P. (in press). The Effects of Subliminal Drive Stimulation on Schizo-phrenic Functioning: A Further Report.

————, and Goldweber, A. M. (1966). A Further Study of the Effects of Subliminal Agres-sive Stimulation on Thinking. *Journal of Nervous and Mental Disease,* 143:463–472.

————, Klinger, H., Lustbader, L., and Farrell, J. (in press). The Effects of Subliminal Drive Stimulation on the Speech of Stutterers. *Journal of Nervous and Mental Disease.*

————, and Silverman, D. K. (1964). A Clinical-Experimental Approach to the Study of Subliminal Stimulation: The Effects of a Drive-Related Stimulus upon Rorschach Responses. *Journal of Abnormal and Social Psychology,* 69:158–172.

————, and Silverman, S. E. (1967). The Effects of Subliminally Presented Drive Stimuli on the Cognitive Functioning of Schizophrenics. *Journal of Projective Techniques,* 31:78–85.

————, and Spiro, R. H. (1967). Further Investigation of the Effects of Subliminal Aggres-sive Stimulation on the Ego Functioning of Schizophrenics. *Journal of Consulting Psychology,* 31:225–232.

————, ———— (1968). The Effects of Subliminal, Supraliminal, and Vocalized Aggression on the Ego Functioning of Schizophrenics. *Journal of Nervous and Mental Disease,* 146:50–61.

————, ————, Weisberg, J. S., and Candell, P. (1969). The Effects of Aggressive Activation and the Need to Merge on Pathological Thinking in Schizophrenics. *Journal of Nervous and Mental Disease,* 148:39–51.

Silverman, S. E. (1969). The Effects of Subliminally Induced Drive Derivatives on Ego Functioning in Schizophrenics. Unpublished doctoral dissertation, New York Uni-versity.

Spiro, R. H., and Silverman, L. H. (1969). Effects of Body Awareness and Aggressive Activa-tion on Ego Functioning of Schizophrenics. *Perceptual and Motor Skills,* 28:575–585.

Teicher, J. D. (1947). A Study on Attempted Suicide. *Journal of Nervous and Mental Dis-ease,* 105:283–298.

Williams, E. Y. (1936). Some Observations on the Psychiatric Aspects of Suicide. *Journal of Abnormal and Social Psychology,* 31:260–265.

Winer, B. J. (1962). *Statistical Principles in Experimental Design.* New York: McGraw-Hill.

Winfield, D. L., and Sparer, P. J. (1953). Preliminary Report of the Rosenzweig Picture-Frustration Study in Attempted Suicide. *Journal of Clinical Psychology,* 9:379–383.

Zilborg, C. (1937). Considerations in Suicide with Particular Reference to That of the Young. *American Journal of Orthopsychiatry,* 7:15–31.

Zuckerman, M., and Lubin, B. (1965). *Manual for the Multiple Affect Adjective Check List.* San Diego, Cal.: Educational and Industrial Testing Service.

Zulliger, H. (1941). *Behn-Rorschach-Versuch.* New York: Grune and Stratton.

LANGUAGE DEVELOPMENT IN YOUNG SCHIZOPHRENIC CHILDREN
Direct Observation as a Constraint on Constructions in Analysis [1]

Theodore Shapiro, M.D.

Psychoanalytic treatment began as and remains a retrospective, reconstructive method of inquiry. Although always highly dependent on verbalization as the important datum for analysis, psychoanalysts early recognized that nonverbal behavior was also a carrier of meaning. With the discovery that the play of children roughly approximates free association, behavioral analysis revealed wish and defense and organized themes. However, this methodological advance has not enabled analysts to rescue the preverbal period from designation as a mental ice age. It can be approached or approximated only by inference from direct observations or retrospective reconstructions.

The schizophrenic child, with his sometimes minimal speech and his developmental lag in language organization, presents a problem for analysis which resembles the problem of the preverbal period. Only as the psychotic child develops language and begins to organize his behavior does interpretation become possible as in the case of the neurotic child. However, the interpretations and constructions used in treatment and in theory should be consonant with the child's cognitive and integrative structures at the stage of development to which they refer (Hartmann, 1948; Frankl, 1961). Ignorance of this caution has encumbered psychoanalysis with the historical errors of Rank's overinterpretation of the psychic responses to birth trauma and Melanie Klein's notions about what infants think.

Although it would have pleased Freud greatly to find that his reconstructions of early childhood seduction indicated a universal environmental precursor to psychoneurosis, it is also a fact that verification of that idea would have precluded Freud's most interesting discovery of psychic reality. From his earliest writings (Freud, 1899) to one of his last papers (1937), Freud reaffirmed

[1] This investigation was supported by United States Public Health Service Research Grant No. MH-04665 from the National Institute of Mental Health, and by a grant from the Harriet Ames Charitable Trust.

the idea that memory organization is not simply a replay of environmental occurrence but is intrapsychically formed and structured. The interpretations and constructions offered in the analysis of adults were meant to serve as stepping stones to further work which helped to solidify their impact rather than uniformly verifiable past events. In "Constructions in Analysis," he wrote: "The path that starts from the analyst's construction ought to end in the patient's recollection; but it does not always lead so far" (1937, p. 265). Kris (1956) also emphasized that experience is not a simple recording of actuality: "the present selects, colors, and modifies" (p. 65). Thus, they both clarify the notion that we are dealing with *constructions* rather than *reconstructions*.

Mahler (1952, 1961) has identified the developmental level at which ego disruption of children with early childhood schizophrenia takes place by retrospective inference drawn from psychoanalytic treatment. She has expanded her studies by directly observing normal children and their mothers, studying the vicissitudes of emergence from the "somatopsychic dual unity" (Mahler, 1963, 1968). Her work implicitly rests upon the idea that developmentally the body ego precedes ego and that identification with the object runs *pari passu* to separation.

Our own work began from the vantage point of direct observation in a clinical setting. We have been studying the relevant descriptive variables which determine which schizophrenic children will develop into socially adequate persons (Fish, Shapiro, Campbell, and Wile, 1968). There are ample data to suggest that, if a child does not develop communicative speech by the age of five, his prognosis is poor (Eisenberg, 1956; Bender, 1964). In the light of this finding, we began an investigation of the language of children diagnosed as suffering from early childhood schizophrenia (Fish, Shapiro, Campbell, and Wile, 1968; Shapiro and Fish, 1969; Shapiro, Roberts, and Fish, 1970). Our hope was that an intensive study of a restricted area of behavior which is referable to complex psychological organization would serve as a window to more global ego organization. We believe that language is particularly suited to this purpose because it holds a unique position among the higher psychological capacities. Its integrity depends upon the construction of mental schemata, the utilization of auditory input, motor control, affective responses, and modification of drive representations. Moreover, it is clear that the emerging capacity to speak and understand a mother tongue involves not only an imitation of the mother as a conveyor of her culture, but also an intrinsic capacity within the child to synthesize what the mother has said. The child uses the mother's words to create new formulations which correspond to the ideas which he constructs according to his maturing ability to structure ideas grammatically.

While not identical, normally developing language and speech share a close kinship to constructions in analysis. The child incorporates the phonetic shape of the words he hears in a particular language community but he also synthesizes, integrates, and puts the words together into unique formulations according to innate species-specific syntactic forms. This re-creation of words into new structures to express relationships parallels his own growing unique identity.

At a higher level the analyst audits and observes his patient, using the day-to-day data to synthesize new constructions which he posits as an organizer of the patient's behavior.

One other influence on our work, from academic psychology, must be mentioned. Werner and Kaplan (1963) view language from a developmental standpoint. They suggest that three dimensions of change, in *time*, in *context*, and in *structure*, can be used as indices of alteration in psychic structure. That is, a child's growing ability to represent the *not here and now in a form different from the original* must reflect a progressive change in his representational reality. If he can represent percepts or relationships in a medium other than the one initially presented, he can qualify as a *symbolizer*.

From an analysis of the speech of young schizophrenic children I will attempt to show (1) that they are deviant in the development of flexible *context* and *structure*, (2) that these inflexibilities in turn reveal the rigid identifications and ego structures so often alluded to by clinicians, and (3) that the analyst must take the rigidity of identifications and structures into account and restrict his range of *reconstructions* accordingly, if he is to reflect the minimal cognitive schemata available to the children he treats.

POPULATION AND PROCEDURES

The subjects of this study were children between the ages of two and seven at an inpatient and day-care nursery at the Bellevue Psychiatric Hospital. Most had been admitted because they were severely withdrawn from social relations, and speech was retarded more than 70% according to standards established by Gesell (Gesell and Amatruda, 1941). The nursery program included milieu therapy, drug therapy, and individual play psychotherapy by the resident physician, under supervision where indicated. Diagnoses were independently arrived at by three psychiatrists.

For the purposes of our study of language development, the examiner saw each child at regular intervals in a playroom. The child played quietly for 10 minutes without interruption and then was stimulated to speech for 10 minutes. The structure of the session was open. The interviewer followed the child's lead and/or introduced material (toys, books) to elicit speech. The child's utterances were taped, and a second observer recorded his activities and the context in which they took place.

The tape from each session was transcribed, and all utterances were counted and coded along two dimensions:

(1) *Speech morphology.* Utterances were divided into two major categories, prespeech and speech. Vowel sounds through babbling and jargon were classified as prespeech, single words through five-word phrases as speech (see Table 1).

(2) *Speech function.* Utterances were divided into two major categories, noncommunicative and communicative. The former consisted of isolated expressive speech, imitative echoing, and speech which was completely or partially "out of context"—that is, inappropriate rigid remarks for which the

Table 1   MORPHOLOGY

PRESPEECH
    Vowels and Vowel-Consonant Combinations
    Babbles and Jargon
SPEECH
    Conventional Sequences
    Single Words
    Two- to Five-Word Combinations
    Disjunctive Syntax

examiner could find no referent in the room or in common experience. The communicative range consisted of appeals and referential speech of varying quality, including naming, questioning, and simple sharing of events (see Table 2). (For a detailed description of the method, see Shapiro and Fish [1969]).

Table 2   FUNCTION

NONCOMMUNICATIVE
    A. Isolated Expressive Speech (6 items)
    B. Context Disturbance (complete) (1 item)
    C. Imitative Speech (3 items)
    D. Context Disturbance (partial) (2 items)
COMMUNICATVE
    E. Appeal Speech (wish oriented) (5 items)
    F. Signal/Symbol Speech (propositional) (7 items)

CONTEXT PROBLEMS

Data drawn from the observation of two children and analyzed both for morphology and function will demonstrate the differences between a schizophrenic child and a child with a developmental speech lag.

    Figures 1 and 2 present the speech morphology records over six months of Dale (developmental speech lag) and Gloria (schizophrenic child). By this criterion, Dale's speech improved: He learned to speak more and the length of his sentences increased. The number of Gloria's utterances did not increase, but the length of each did (see Figure 2). Thus, according to traditional measures of speech morphology, both children changed for the better.

    Turning to the speech function analysis of the two children, Figure 3 shows that the communicative quality of what Dale said increased, although his echoing also increased during this developmental burst.

    The communicative quality of Gloria's speech also increased (Figure 4). However, the amount of her speech which was *out of context* continued to be sizable.

    She would spontaneously make remarks which the observer could not easily tie to the immediate environment. They seemed to emerge from nowhere or were only partially referential. In less severe form they were tangential or overelaborated, with a ring of the bizarre. For example, while playing with a doll she might repeat the words of a television commercial, or make a remark about

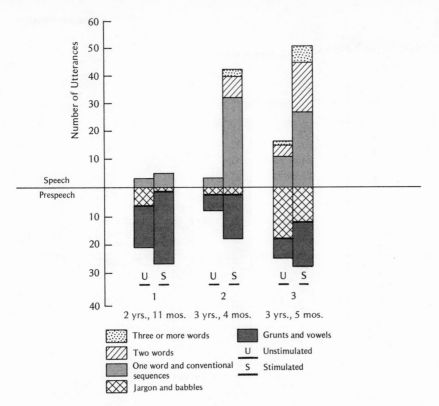

Figure 1. Speech morphology (Dale).

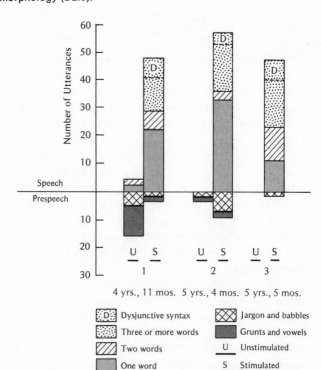

Figure 2. Speech morphology (Gloria).

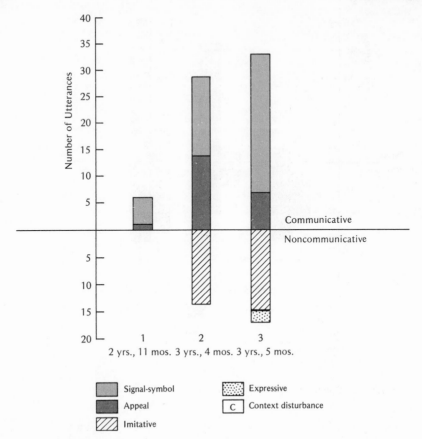

Figure 3. Speech function: utterances of one or more words (Dale).

a car ride, with no "bridge" for the examiner. It is true that if the examiner had had a more intimate knowledge of the child's life experience he might have been able to infer the connections, but the majority of a child's contacts lack this knowledge.

At other times she, and other children like her, would pick up something from the immediate context and respond with vocalizations which showed a relation to the stimulus, but the responses would become distorted in elaboration. For example, she once named a nose on a doll appropriately, only to go on talking of "a nose, a nosery boy." Such neologistic clang associations are familiar to psychiatrists. At other times, not content with counting the three items present, she insisted on counting to 100 and singing a counting song as an extra embellishment.

Thus, simply distinguishing and counting the functional characteristics of utterances revealed the lack of flexible response to changed context which clinicians often describe. This is a disturbance which seems to disappear as we become increasingly familiar with the child; because we know his world more intimately, we can pick out his referent even if it is remote. It is this familiarity which sometimes causes the therapeutic optimism of professional personnel

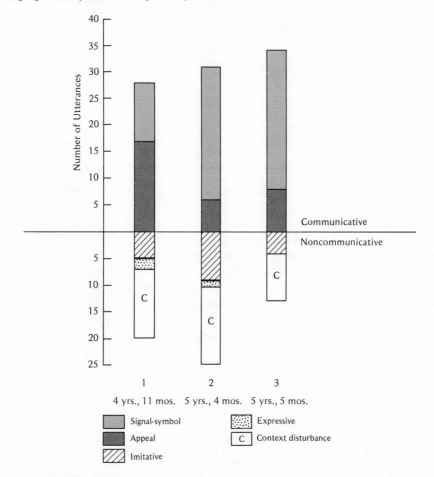

Figure 4. Speech function: utterances of one or more words (Gloria).

close to the child. However, to those unfamiliar with him his utterances are strange, because they seem to refer to nothing in the immediate field or are very tangential to it.

RESTRUCTURING PROBLEMS

The echoing of both children led us to seek a method by which we could differentiate normal from pathological imitation. This seemed a dimension through which we could gather information about the degree of integrative function which the child has at his disposal. If he merely echoes exactly what is said to him, one need postulate only an apparatus adapted to recording and repeating. Selection according to relevance and meaning on the other hand, as in telegraphic selection or restructuring into new sentences, would indicate functions fitted for symbolic use.

We defined a spectrum of imitative responses ranging from echoing to restructured sentences (see Table 3). This structural measure was then applied to

Table 3 SPECTRUM OF IMITATION

Model:	"Bobby, should we play with the car?"
RIGIDLY CONGRUENT ECHOES:	". . . car" ". . . play with the car?" "Bobby, should we play . . ."
NONGRAMMATICAL FRAGMENTS:	"Car, car we"
JARGON ADDITIONS; COMPLETIONS:	*"play ga bo ca"*
TELEGRAPHIC; INFLECTIONS:	"play(ing) car(s)"
GRAMMATICAL RESTRUCTURING:	"(play with the car) no, *we should play with the boats."*

the speech of our clinical population and to controls. (For a detailed description of the method, see Shapiro, Roberts, and Fish [1970]).

Because we expect normal children to construct original sentences by their fourth birthday, we selected samples of speech uttered as near as possible to that time. Of the 14 children in our population, three did not utter recognizable speech and were excluded. Three others were nonschizophrenic children, one with a clearly organic mental syndrome, one with a developmental lag, and one with a severe behavior disorder. The other eight were schizophrenic children, and their imitative utterances were compared to control groups of six normally developing four-year-olds, six three-year-olds, and six two-year-olds.

The schizophrenic children averaged as many utterances as the controls, but their utterances were shorter. The mean sentence length (MSL) (McCarthy, 1954) of normal four-year-olds is between 4.2 and 4.9 words. Only one schizophrenic child had a MSL of even 3.1; the MSLs of the others ranged from 1.0 to

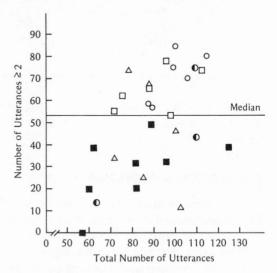

Figure 5. Proportion of utterances ≥ 2 in schizophrenic, nonschizophrenic, and control children.

■ Four-year-old schizophrenics
◑ Hospitalized nonschizophrenics
△ Two-year-old controls
○ Three-year-old controls
□ Four-year-old controls

2.3, which is at the 30-month level. In the number of utterances that were two or more words long, the schizophrenic children clustered with the two-year-olds (see Figure 5).

However, it would be incorrect to say that the schizophrenic children were simply retarded, i.e., like normal two-year-olds. When the structure of their imitations is analyzed we can see that, in addition to the contextual problems described above, they have another developmental defect: they restructure what they hear only to a minimal degree.

The schizophrenic children uttered significantly more imitations than the three- or four-year-old controls, and significantly more rigid *congruent* imitations than the four-, three-, and even two-year-old controls. Conversely, the normally developing four- and three-year-old children uttered significantly more structurally creative imitations than the schizophrenic children. The hospitalized non-schizophrenic children are too small a group to allow generalizations from our results; however, their percentages of imitation fall between the normal two-year-old and the schizophrenic populations, never attaining the magnitude of the schizophrenic group's. Moreover, if we group together the percentages of

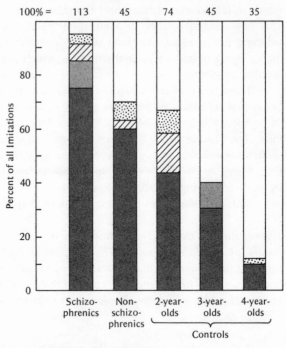

Figure 6. Proportion of types of imitation (mean percentages of imitative utterances).

all restructured and telegraphic utterances, which are the best evidence of movement toward an integrative capacity for language, their 4.11% is considerable
compared to the schizophrenic group's 1.42% (see Figure 6).

DISCUSSION

Our data indicate that schizophrenic children are deviant as well as defective
on two of the three indices of psychic differentiation described by Werner and
Kaplan (1963). Although they retain some image of reality over time, analysis of
their speech behavior reveals that changed context does not lead to appropriately changed speech in a large and consistent portion of their utterances. Moreover, their rigidly congruent imitation and the lack of structural differentiation
of their speech from that of the examiner reveals their deficiency in the integrative functions necessary to reformulate what they hear into new combinations
for communicative speech. Even normally developing two-year-olds are more
flexible and creative in their imitative speech: They seem to select phrases from
here and there and restructure them by inflecting verbs, selecting contentive
words in telegraphic phrases, and transforming given structures into new ones.
This linguistic integration is viewed as paralleling ego integration: The developing ego draws from many partial identifications and integrates the fragments into a unique individual structure, which is the beginning of a new personality or identity.

   The rigidity of the schizophrenic child's speech is viewed as merely one
behavioral reflection of the more global rigidity of his inner world. An analysis
of his speech behavior yields quantitative data that corroborate our clinical surmise. The "brittle ego," "fragmented ego," "incorporated introjects" so often
spoken of in clinical theory are given some substantiation by such direct observation. Moreover, we believe that such observation should be taken into account
by analysts treating schizophrenic children.

   Mahler (1968) states in the concluding chapter of her book:

*The situation of the psychotic child does not involve a regression to any known
normal phase of development. The concepts of a normal autistic, normal symbiotic, and subsequent normal separation-individuation phase of development were
derived in part from genetic reconstructions that had been made during the
course of study of symptom pictures presented by children with psychoses
. . . (p. 232).*

*. . . in the psychotic syndrome the mother's ministrations are not perceived as
a "mothering principle . . ." that is, as coming from the outside to relieve the
child's inner tension; much less is she perceived as an increasingly differentiated
object that can supply the needed external ego. Instead, in that condition the
mother is delusionally drawn into the internal milieu. Hence, the psychotic child
more or less lacks the faculties for differentiation and for individuation from the
object (from the "external ego"—Spitz) (p. 233).*

These ideas are consistent with the evidence we have gathered from the direct observation of language function. While in examining the product of the child, his speech, our vantage point does not stress interactional factors, it is abundantly clear that the words of a specific language are learned at the mother's knee. This "nutriment" from the actual world must be reorganized for the final output to be called language. The reorganization necessary for the comprehension and flexible use of language is dependent upon the highly complex, largely unknown processes that in psychoanalytic theory are referred to collectively as the ego's synthesizing and integrating functions. Our data suggest that the defect of these children consists in the fact that their egos, as inferred from their behavior, are capable only of stereotyped replays of former experiences without regard for context and without signs of structural change.

What are the implications of our findings for reconstructions?

In reconstructing the experiences of psychotic children it is tempting to assume that they resemble the experiences of neurotic children, about whom we have wider knowledge. However, our data warn us to proceed with caution. Similar behavior does not necessarily reflect similar inner structure. A parrot's mimicry is not a child's imitation, and a child repeating his mother's words verbatim in her presence is a far cry from a child playing in a "mommylike" manner in her absence.

It is a general maxim of child analysis that we interpret at the level of the child. If interpretations are to be made to the children whom I have described, they would have to be made at the simplest phonetic and syntactic levels: statements of dynamic tension might have to be short phrases describing the conflicting wants, e.g., "You want to go and you want to stay"; even gestural imitation with a doll or demonstration might be better understood. In these children distinctions between past, present, and future are uncertain, so that use of those tenses may not be understood in genetic interpretations, if they were possible. Words for emotions which are not visible or tangible as simple referents have to be taught, and even then we cannot be certain a shared understanding exists. To be absorbed, phrases must be short and repeated frequently and slowly, as though one were feeding the phonetic form first which, when accommodated as a new and permanent structure, may then be associated meaningfully to things, and ultimately to processes and relationships which are symbolically represented in syntactic structures.

Constructions made for academic understanding and case formulation should take into account the inner deviance of schizophrenic children and their inability to select, decipher, and code their experiences according to any but the most primitive mental organizations. Postulations of defense and structural differentiation as activators of their behavior must await signs of greater maturation than we observed in the children we studied. I believe that Mahler (1968) uses such terms as "maintenance mechanisms" rather than more familiar terms for similar reasons.

Our data further suggest that the schizophrenic child's warding off of the human environment, on which we place such emphasis in clinical therapeutic work, might best be construed as an outgrowth of inadequate central integrative capacities. That is, the child's incapacity to organize may lead to his selecting less varied stimuli. If this is so, it will be necessary to re-evaluate explanations based on receptor problems, such as the imbalance around the stimulus barrier postulated by Bergman and Escalona (1949), and those theories which suggest simple environmental etiologies.

To be sure, there are wide developmental differences among the children studied by different observers. Some psychotic children are quite precocious in their language development, and demonstrate structural defenses similar to those of neurotics. However, as we watch such children develop and emerge from their restricting psychoses, there are indications that the earlier developmental behaviors do not disappear but remain side by side with their new adaptive abilities. They are both differentiated and not differentiated; the picture they present suggests a pattern disturbance (Fish, 1961; Bender, 1947). Only at times in therapy can we plot the defensive use of the more deviant behaviors. At other times we may have to be content to describe them. To reach too far beyond observation in attempting to attribute structural significance to an inner organization which does not permit such inference stretches belief beyond necessity. Our constructions describe our surmises about the inner organization of experience. In the children described, "inner experience" is limited by defects in the ego's integrating capacities, and verification by recall as demanded by Freud and Kris is difficult to come by.

REFERENCES

Bender, L. (1947). Childhood Schizophrenia; Clinical Study of One Hundred Schizophrenic Children. *American Journal of Orthopsychiatry,* 17:40–56.
——— (1964). A Twenty-Five-Year View of Therapeutic Results. In: *The Evaluation of Psychiatric Treatment,* ed. P. H. Hoch and J. Zubin. New York: Grune and Stratton, pp. 129–142.
Bergman, P., and Escalona, S. (1949). Unusual Sensitivities in Very Young Children. *The Psychoanalytic Study of the Child,* 3/4:333–352. New York: International Universities Press.
Eisenberg, L. (1956). The Autistic Child in Adolescence. *American Journal of Psychiatry,* 112:607–613.
Fish, B. (1961). The Study of Motor Development in Infancy and Its Relationship to Psychological Functioning. *American Journal of Psychiatry,* 117:1113–1118.
———, Shapiro, T., Campbell, M., and Wile, R. (1968). A Classification of Schizophrenic Children under Five Years. *American Journal of Psychiatry,* 124:109–117.
Frankl, L. (1961). Some Observations on the Development and Disturbance of Integration in Childhood. *The Psychoanalytic Study of the Child,* 16:146–163. New York: International Universities Press.
Freud, S. (1899). Screen Memories. *Standard Edition,* 3:303–322. London: Hogarth Press, 1962.
——— (1937). Constructions in Analysis. *Standard Edition,* 23:257–269. London: Hogarth Press, 1964.
Gesell, A., and Amatruda, C. S. (1941). *Developmental Diagnosis.* New York: Hoeber.
Hartmann, H. (1948). Comments on the Psychoanalytic Theory of Instinctual Drives. *Psychoanalytic Quarterly,* 17:368–388.

Kris, E. (1956). The Recovery of Childhood Memories in Psychoanalysis. *The Psychoanalytic Study of the Child,* 11:54–88. New York: International Universities Press.

Mahler, M. (1952). On Child Psychosis and Schizophrenia: Autistic and Symbiotic Infantile Psychoses. *The Psychoanalytic Study of the Child,* 7:286–305. New York: International Universities Press.

———— (1961). Sadness and Grief in Childhood. *The Psychoanalytic Study of the Child,* 16:332–351. New York: International Universities Press.

———— (1963). Thoughts about Development and Individuation. *The Psychoanalytic Study of the Child,* 18:307–324. New York: International Universities Press.

———— (1968). *On Human Symbiosis and the Vicissitudes of Individuation.* New York: International Universities Press.

McCarthy, D. A. (1954). Language Development in Children. In: *Manual of Child Psychology,* ed. L. Carmichael. New York: Wiley, pp. 492–630.

Shapiro, T., and Fish, B. (1969). A Method to Study Language Deviation as an Aspect of Ego Organization in Young Schizophrenic Children. *Journal of the American Academy of Child Psychiatry,* 8:36–56.

————, Roberts, A., and Fish, B. (1970). Imitation and Echoing in Young Schizophrenic Children. *Journal of the American Academy of Child Psychiatry,* 9:548–567.

Werner, H., and Kaplan, B. (1963). *Symbol Formation.* New York: Wiley.

TRACING A THOUGHT STREAM BY COMPUTER [1]

Donald P. Spence, Ph.D.

We were strolling one night down a long dirty street in the vicinity of the Palais Royale. Being both, apparently, occupied with thought, neither of us had spoken a syllable for fifteen minutes at least. All at once Dupin broke forth with these words:

"He is a very little fellow, that's true, and would do better for the Théâtre des Variétes."

"There can be no doubt of that," I replied, unwittingly, and not at first observing (so much that I have been absorbed in reflection) the extraordinary manner in which the speaker had chimed in with my meditations. In an instant afterwards I recollected myself, and my astonishment was profound.

"Dupin," said I, gravely, "this is beyond my comprehension. I do not hesitate to say that I am amazed, and can scarcely credit my senses. How was it possible you should know I was thinking of—?" Here I paused, to ascertain beyond a doubt whether he really knew of whom I thought.

"—of Chantilly," said he, "why do you pause? You were remarking to yourself that his diminutive figure unfitted him for tragedy" (Poe, The Murders in the Rue Morgue).

After more amazed exclamations by the narrator, Dupin finally agrees to explain how he followed his line of thought.

We had been talking of horses, if I remember aright, just before leaving the Rue C. This was the last subject we discussed. As we crossed into this street, a fruiterer, with a large basket upon his head, brushing quickly past us, thrust you upon a pile of paving-stones collected on the spot where the causeway was un-

[1] This study was prepared with the support of United States Public Health Service Research Scientist Award No. KO5-MH-14120 from the National Institute of Mental Health.

*dergoing repair. You stepped upon one of the loose fragments, slipped, slightly
strained your ankle, appeared vexed or sulky, muttered a few words, turned to
look at the pile, and then proceeded in silence. I was not particularly attentive
to what you did; but observation has become with me, of late, a species of
necessity.*

*You kept your eyes upon the ground—glancing, with a petulant expression,
at the holes and ruts in the pavement (so that I saw you were still thinking of the
stones), until we reached the little alley called Lamartine, which has been paved,
by way of experiment, with the overlapping and riveted blocks. Here your
countenance brightened up, and, perceiving your lips move, I could not doubt
that you remembered the word "stereotomy," a name very affectedly applied
to this species of pavement. I knew that you could not say to yourself "stereotomy" without being brought to think of atomies and . . .*

Dupin then proceeded from one association to another until he saw the narrator draw himself up to his full height; then, sure that he was thinking about
the diminutive figure of Chantilly, he interrupted his meditations to say, "Yes,
as a matter of fact he was a very little fellow, and would do better in the Théâtre
des Variétes."

Writing in the spirit of the later emerging associationists, Poe has described
a chain of reasoning in which each premise is tightly locked to its conclusion.
Because his model is entirely deterministic, Dupin can follow the narrator every
step of the way, given only the first piece of information. Although the episode
is slightly fanciful, the model is a familiar one. Freud spoke frequently of trains
of thought and argued that they might even be set in motion outside of awareness if their contents, for some dynamic reason, could not be allowed into consciousness. Klein has elaborated on this view in his discussion of peremptory
ideation (1967).

Freud's theory of day residues in particular took advantage of the associa-
tionist model. "The daytime thought," he wrote, ". . . was obliged to find a
connection in some way or other with an infantile wish which was now unconscious and suppressed, and which would enable it" to emerge in the dream
(1900, p. 556). The time that was assumed to elapse between the occurrence of
the daytime thought and its later emergence in the dream was rather long—a
much longer period than that described by Poe in the Dupin incident—and
many of the associative linkages were supposed to take place outside of awareness. Yet the two conceptions are similar in many ways. A single initial incident
—the day residue or the collision with the fruiterer—sets in motion a chain of
associations that leads to a final conclusion—a dream or the recognition that
Chantilly, because of his small size, was best suited for the Théâtre des Variétes.

Recently an incident came to my attention which seemed to have many of
the same characteristics as these examples, and which offered a good testing
ground for the train-of-thought model. A patient began treatment with an
analyst who was five months pregnant. The patient did not raise the subject of

pregnancy until five sessions later, when she finally asked the analyst if a child was coming. The initial meeting could be compared to the encounter with the fruiterer in Poe's story, and the question "Are you pregnant?" to the thought that Chantilly was a small man. We are in the position of Dupin. Can we follow the chain of associations that intervened between the moment when the patient first saw the analyst and the moment when she asked about pregnancy? To do so, we must assume that a systematic train of thoughts led from the first encounter with the analyst to the question "Are you pregnant?" This paper is devoted to a study of this train of thought and to an examination of the forms it might take.[2]

The tool used was a computer, programmed to count words in preselected categories. A tally was made of the frequency of every word spoken by the patient in the first five sessions which might be related to the theme of pregnancy. The shape of the frequency curves would tell us something about the form of the associative train in the patient's awareness. The form of the thought stream could take many shapes, an issue that will be discussed in more detail at a later point.

The clinical situation was, briefly, as follows. The patient was a woman in her early thirties who had been accepted by an experienced male analyst as a research patient (all sessions were tape-recorded). After eight months the analyst became ill and the treatment was suddenly broken off. During the following months, the patient was told at weekly intervals that treatment would be resumed as soon as possible. It finally began again some five months later, still as a research case but with another analyst, the first one being more seriously ill than had been realized at first, and in no position to continue. The second analyst was a woman who was five months pregnant. In the fifth hour with the second analyst the patient began by asking if she were pregnant. In the present study an attempt was made to document the history of this remark, to establish the necessary and sufficient conditions for its occurrence, and more specifically, to trace the ups and downs of pregnancy-related associates in the period up to the question about pregnancy.

Separation was a critical theme in this patient's life even before the first analyst suddenly abandoned her. Her father had a heart condition that made the patient fear that any argument with him might result in his death (and permanent departure). She remembered quite clearly being abandoned at the age of three by her parents on the night her sister was born. Early in the analysis the patient had repeated fantasies that she would be found too banal a subject for research and therefore would be prematurely dropped. She also feared that she might be found too crazy to be a research case and dropped for that reason. Thus she was afraid that the analyst would drop her if she was found wanting in any way. Therefore, when the analyst actually did leave her—with no warning —the patient felt partly responsible. The fact that she had nothing to do with it was never really clarified because the analyst's reason for leaving her and his

    [2] I am indebted to Drs. Geraldine Fink and Justin Simon for giving me access to the five hours of transcribed material.

subsequent condition were never explained to her. She received only terse and quite ambiguous messages from his office and, given this ambiguity, her fantasies were given full opportunity to flourish and develop further.

When a second analyst finally did appear, the patient was fully sensitized to the trauma of separation, and was presumably on the alert for any signs that her second analyst might also leave her. Her alertness was probably one of the factors which contributed to her question about pregnancy (considering that her mother had left her for the hospital when she was pregnant and that therefore pregnancy and separation were probably closely associated in her mind). But why did she wait until the fifth hour to ask the question? Why did she not ask it as soon as she saw that the analyst was pregnant?

One might assume, to begin with, that the patient was afraid that the analyst was indeed pregnant but did not want to risk finding out for certain. In that case the question might have entered her mind immediately but was not asked until a later time—when separation anxiety was lower or anger at the analyst was higher. This line of reasoning suggests an *avoidance* model, in which the pregnancy question loomed large at the beginning, receded as an issue until a new equilibrium had been established, and then came forward again to be acted upon when conditions were right. The patient might have been preoccupied with it as an issue on the first and fifth days, but less so, because of the contingent anxiety, during the intervening period. The critical associations would start high, drop gradually, and then begin to reappear as the fifth hour approached, describing a large U.

A second model, which might be called the *continuous-increase* model, would suggest that the pregnancy issue gradually became important as the days went by, finally emerging as an explicit question. According to this model, time was needed for the patient to become aware of an anxiety-arousing piece of reality (that the analyst might leave) and the time was probably used to build defenses against this anxiety.

Both these models assume continuity: there is a gradual development over time in critical factors which eventuate in the crucial question being asked. In the first, the function takes the form of a large U, and in the second, it takes the form of a monotonic increase. But it is also possible that the change was not continuous over time but rather episodic and broken by the intervals between sessions. The sessions under consideration, after all, occurred at the beginning of treatment. Little transference involvement had really been established, and there is probably no basis for assuming that very much analytic work went on outside of the hour. Therefore we might expect change to be taking place *within* an hour but probably not between hours. A third model, then, would assume that whatever changes occurred during a session were so closely tied to the analyst that they were dissipated before the beginning of the next, and we would expect a stepwise function something like the one shown in Figure 1. In this case the readiness to ask the critical question would rise within each hour only to drop again before the beginning of the next hour. This will be called the *working-through* model, because it focuses on the fact that change occurs primarily within the hour, not between hours.

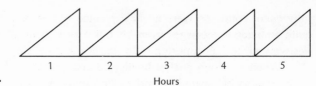

Figure 1.

1   2   3   4   5
Hours

All three models rest on the assumption that the amount of concern about a theme will be reflected in the number of direct and indirect associations to it.

METHOD

The recorded protocols of the initial five hours with the second analyst were transcribed and keypunched on standard IBM cards. A list of denotative categories was then compiled by looking through the five hours and selecting words which belonged to the themes of separation and togetherness, broken down into the three subcategories of Family–Sharing–Marriage; Anger; and Psychiatric Terms (one of the patient's primary defenses was intellectualization). Then a list of connotative categories was assembled, derived from free associations to pregnancy and including the subcategories of Suspicion, Hospital, Pregnancy Associations, Pregnancy Terms, and Appearance. Some words were placed in more than one category because they have alternate meanings.

The grouping of words into the categories of Family–Sharing–Marriage, Anger, and Psychiatric Terms was done by a doctoral candidate who was not aware of the models proposed above, and therefore could not have chosen words that would support one or another of them. The free associations were generated by two experienced female psychologists [3] who were asked to write down, as "freely" as possible, all the words they could think of that seemed related to pregnancy—from either the mother's or the child's point of view. It was assumed that a fair number of these associations would correspond to pregnancy associations used spontaneously by the patient. The subcategory of Pregnancy Associates, for example, includes such words as "fat," "food," "illness," "milk," "new," "nipple," "rabbit," "tumor," etc. The subcategory of Appearance includes such words as "balloon," "puffy," "cabbage," "hidden" etc. The subcategory of Hospital includes such words as "birth," "blind," "cry," "deaf," "deformity," "dumb," "formula," "nausea," etc. It can be seen that the subcategories are not clearly separated.

Finally, we added three formal categories which deal less with content and more with the way the words were used. The first of these, type-token ratio (TTR), is an index of redundancy or repetitiousness. If no one word is used more than once in a given segment, the TTR has the maximum value of 1.00. As redundancy increases, TTR declines. A TTR of .50, for example, would indicate that each word, on the average, was used twice. The second and third formal indices

[3] I am indebted to Michael Varga for making up the categories of Separation, Togetherness, Anger, and Psychiatric Terms; and to Dr. Mary Collins and Adela de Duarte for free-associating to pregnancy.

stem from a previous analysis of this particular patient's verbal style. In sessions from somewhat later in treatment, we found that certain words or phrases (Reflectors) such as "I wonder," "it seems to me," "maybe," etc., occurred more often during sessions classified as productive (i.e., good hours—the patient was working well) than in sessions rated as nonproductive (see Spence, 1969a). The measure used was the ratio of Reflectors to total words. Further work on the same data (unpublished) showed that the number of *different* Reflectors was also correlated with ratings of productivity. Brief descriptions of all indices are presented in Table 1.

Table 1 CONTENT AND FORMAL INDICES USED IN COMPUTER ANALYSIS

CONTENT		*Number*
Denotative:		*of Words*
Anger	(rage, storm, rave, pant, fume, stew, boil, etc.)	27
Family	(brother, sister, father, mother, etc.)	30
Marriage	(paired, matched, wedded, partner, etc.)	34
Psychiatric		
Terms	(orgasm, symbol, dream, fantasy, phallus, etc.)	39
Sharing	(chum, colleague, ally, playmate, etc.)	16
Connotative:		
Appearance	(balloon, cabbage, puffy, hidden, etc.)	36
Hospital	(birth, blind, cry, deaf, deformity, dumb, formula, etc.)	27
Pregnancy		
Associations	(fat, food, illness, milk, new, nipple, rabbit, etc.)	42
Pregnancy		
Terms	(term, diaphragm, illegitimate, fifth month, etc.)	69
Suspicion	(detect, spy, discover, peeping, search, etc.)	36
FORMAL		
Type-Token Ratio (TTR)	(No. of different words/No. of total words)	
Reflector Ratio	(No. of Reflectors/No. of total words)	
Different Reflectors	(No. of different Reflectors)	

Scoring was done as follows: All the therapist's remarks were removed from the protocols. All words in each dictionary category were counted (by a computer program developed by the author [see Spence, 1969b]) and then grouped by category. Each hour was roughly divided into four quarters, and category counts were tallied for each quarter of each of the five hours—20 data points in all. In this way we could plot each category over time. Finally, the three formal indices were computed for each quarter by a separate program.

RESULTS

When all categories are plotted across the 20 points in time, there is clearly no monotonic increase in any single category. More characteristic is an oscillation that sometimes—but not always—coincides with the beginning and end of each hour. To determine which of the models described above best characterized the data, idealized forms of all models were entered in a multiple-regression analysis.[4] The model which had the highest correlation with the majority of the variables would be the best predictor; the associated correlation could show which categories best conformed to that particular model.

The findings are shown in Table 2. Of the three models proposed above, only one—working through—accounts for a significant amount of the variance, and only one variable—Different Reflectors—is crucial to this model. The patient shows a regular increase in the number of different reflectors within each hour.

Table 2 CORRELATIONS OF BEST SEVEN PREDICTORS WITH EACH MODEL

		MODEL					
Continuous Increase		Avoidance		Working Through		Actual Change	
Category	R	Category	R	Category	R	Category	R
Preg. Terms	.30	−TTR	.38	Diff. Ref.	68***	−Appearance	.46*
−Suspicion	.37	−Preg. Terms	.48	Family	.73	−Family	.57
Anger	.44	Marriage	.58	−Preg. Asso.	.77	−Diff. Ref.	.73**
Diff. Ref.	.47	Appearance	.66	Appearance	.79	−Suspicion	.79*
−Psych. Terms	.49	−Diff. Ref.	.68	Hospital	.82	−Psych. Terms	.83
−Family	.51	−Family	.71	Ref. Ratio	.82	−TTR	.85
Preg. Asso.	.51	−Suspicion	.73	−Sharing	.83	−Marriage	.87
						−Anger	.92*

* p < .05
** p < .01
*** p < .001
Note: − Categories preceded by a minus sign should be interpreted in the direction opposite from the model shown; thus Suspicion in the first column *decreases* over time, etc.

As already noted, the number of different reflectors was highly correlated with ratings of analytic productivity in a different sample of material from the same patient. If the same relationship holds here, it would appear that productivity follows the sawtooth function pictured in Figure 1: i.e., it increases within the hour but tends to fall off between hours; the level of productivity at the start of a new hour is lower than that at the end of the previous hour. We might assume that increase in productivity is partly a function of the therapeutic relationship which increases within each session but—because the relationship is relatively new—is not maintained between sessions. More speculatively, we might assume that there is, as yet, no internalized transference figure and that analytic work

---

[4] Each model was tested by using the number series most appropriate to it. Thus for model 1, continuous increase, the series of numbers from 1 to 20 was used. For model 2, a parabolic function, which dipped at the third hour, was used. For model 3, the series 12341234 . . . 1234 was used. For model 4, the series 18, 16, 17, 9, 14, 12, 13, 4, 1, 10, 8, 6, 7, 19, 15, 3, 20, 5, 2, 11 was used.

can occur only in the presence of the therapist and not in her absence. Sessions taken from periods later in treatment might show a more consistently high level of productivity.

Except for this one finding, all the results are nonsignificant. None of the content variables proved to be an important predictor, which means that if there is a trend in the associations, it is more complex than we had originally assumed. These disappointing results suggest that the Dupin anecdote from Poe is misleadingly simple and that the critical question about pregnancy was not preceded by either a gradual, a stepwise, or a U-shaped increase in associates.

But we have an alternative. Instead of specifying the function first and taking the chance that we may guess wrong, we can let the data determine which function is most appropriate. We do this by letting the 20 data points group themselves naturally to see what clusters emerge, and from the clusters we can form a new function.

Systematic Grouping Analysis

The five therapy hours, each divided into quarters, represent 20 points over time. Each of these points has a profile across the 13 categories described above —high on some, low on others, and in between on the rest. The critical point for our study is the first quarter of the fifth hour (5–1) because it was then that the patient asked the critical question. Now we can ask: Which of the other points in time has the same profile as the critical segment? If others share the critical profile, they would presumably also share many of the same dynamic features.

The 20 profiles were grouped by a hierarchical grouping procedure developed by Ward (1963) and programmed by Veldman (1967). Profiles are grouped according to similarity; therefore the first two to be grouped together are the more similar in terms of an over-all D^2 formula. The grouping considers both the pattern and the level of each profile.

The first two profiles to be grouped were 1–1 (the first quarter of the first hour) and 4–2 (the second quarter of the fourth hour): Of the 20 profiles, these two are the most similar to one another. Next to be added was the critical profile 5–1. These three profiles form a group. The next group to be formed consisted of 1–2—the quarter following the initial segment—and 5–2—the quarter following the critical segment. The second group was not combined with the first until well along in the grouping, an indication that the two groups are quite distinct.

This analysis makes clear that the three most similar profiles of the 20 are the critical segment, the first quarter of the first hour, and the second quarter of the fourth hour, as shown by the fact that they were grouped first. It also suggests that key elements of the critical segment were present in the very first quarter (because the profiles are similar) and that they dropped out of sight until the second quarter of the fourth hour, and then emerged once more in the critical segment when the question was asked. We also see that the quarters that followed the critical segment and the first segment had something in common because they formed the second group. It is as if the pregnancy issue, whether manifest or latent, produced a similar defensive reaction.

We next looked at quarters 1–1 and 4–2 in more detail to see in what respects they resemble the critical segment (5–1) which contained the question. In 1–1, the patient is told quite bluntly that the first analyst will be unable to continue. She asks what is wrong and is told that she cannot be told for reasons of privacy. She replies that although she wants to continue, her feelings are mixed, and then she begins to cry. When queried about the crying, she enlarges on her reaction to the separation and her increased concern when she found that the analyst was too sick to write directly but had to communicate through a third person.

In 4–2, the patient is describing a dream about a little girl whose dress was too short. This reminds her of the thought that she had noticed that her first hour was too short. Then she describes the father of the little girl who has ambivalent feelings toward her in the dream, and this reminds her of her ambivalent feelings toward the therapist which were discussed in 4–1. She was reminded then of her mother and of the man's wife in the dream who resembles the analyst "not in manner or face but in *body type*" (my italics). The she describes a fantasy that the analyst would not come for the fourth hour and that she (the patient) would quit, leaving an outraged note. "I can see before I'm barely in the analysis that I'm reacting as I have in any relationship that ever meant anything to me. I'm quick to feel injured. . . ."

Segment 4–2, one might say, looks both ways. On the one hand, the patient is reminded of the first hour and of her thought that it was over too quickly. On the other hand the dream about the girl with too short a dress is a striking anticipation of segment 5–1, the critical segment, which begins as follows:

"As we were coming down the stairs I looked at you and thought that you were wearing a maternity dress. If that were the case, I just don't know how I would feel. I think it would upset me a good deal."

It is tempting to argue that the patient was aware of the pregnancy in the first hour but that the knowledge was too upsetting for her to accept. The awareness emerges a second time in the dream of a little girl in too short a skirt (representing a maternity dress), and a third time—explicitly—in her question to the analyst in the fifth hour. The point to keep in mind is that sorting according to profile similarity pulls together segments which seem to have clinical themes in common. We also see, as we have seen before, that the ideas associated with pregnancy do not emerge gradually but in a more cyclical fashion.

The second group of segments—1–2 and 5–2—suggests one reason why the question was so slow in coming. In 1–2, the patient is speaking of being deserted by the first analyst and assumes that she had similar feelings when her mother went to the hospital to give birth to her sister. In 5–2, she is reminded of a cartoon of a room with three beds in it, two larger beds (triple beds) on either side of a smaller bed; three boys are in one of the beds. The threesome of beds reminds her of the male genitals and the three boys together in one bed remind her of the child-labor laws (a pun on pregnancy which could be interpreted as a continuation of the question asked earlier about the analyst). The patient then thinks of another dream in which an old man was about to leave her and she felt great grief.

Both segments in this second group contain references to desertion and to the strong feelings that come in its wake. In the first hour, the memory of being left by her mother when her sister was born may have been triggered by the latent thought that the analyst was pregnant. The anxiety aroused by the earlier separations was probably too strong to be experienced immediately—consequently the question was not raised. When the question finally did come (aided and abetted by the dream about the girl with a short skirt), it was followed by a similar thought of desertion, but this time the critical figure was an old man whose relationship to the patient was less intense. Once again the grouping according to similar profiles reveals the underlying similarity of the clinical material.

The grouping procedure also gives us information on the extent to which each segment is different from the critical segment. This information enables us to plot the course of the question over time if we make the assumption that it is closest to awareness in the segments that are most similar to the critical segment, and farthest from awareness in the most dissimilar segments. This function is shown in Figure 2 in which we have plotted each segment to show its

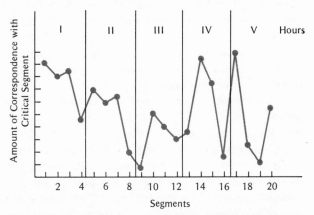

Figure 2. Assumed course of critical theme over 20 segments. The higher the point, the greater the correspondence with the critical segment.

similarity to the critical segment; the higher it is on the vertical axis, the greater the similarity. The three peaks are the segments previously studied: 1–1, 4–2, and 5–1. The function reaches a low point at 3–1 and the over-all function resembles an inverted U which starts high in the first hour and rises again in the fourth (the dream).

What variables are the best predictors of this refined function? The results of another regression analysis, using the refined function as the criterion, are shown in the last column of Table 2. The best predictors of the criterion are listed in order of importance. The first variable listed—Appearance—contributes a significant amount of the variance and is composed of such words as "cabbage," "balloon," "hidden," "puffy," "dissembling," etc.—words which *might* refer to the appearance of pregnancy. This category correlates *negatively* with the refined function, which means that these words appear most often during segments that are quite unlike the critical segment. That is, words which describe a pregnant appearance occur in the patient's associations when she is *least* likely to ask the analyst whether she is pregnant.

Two other content variables contributed significantly to the prediction of the criterion function: Suspicion (which includes such words as "detect," "spy," "discover," "peeping," "search," etc.) and Anger ("rage," "storm," "rave," "fume," etc.). These variables too correlate negatively with the assumed course of the critical theme (as shown in Figure 2). Since all three content variables correlate negatively with the theme, we can say that associations related to pregnancy are most likely to emerge when the patient is *least* likely to ask the question directly, and conversely, when the question is closest to being asked, related associations are few and far between.

The number of different reflectors is negatively related to the criterion function. Applying the earlier findings with this patient to the present data would suggest that she is most productive—that is, reflective, associates freely, observes and explores her own defenses, etc.—during periods when she is *least* likely to ask about the pregnancy issue. On the other hand, during the critical segment (5–1) and during other segments which are similar, the number of different reflectors decreases, which suggests that the patient is in a state of high resistance, is not affectively involved, is not free-associating or reflecting on the material she has produced.

Now we also know, from the content categories, that derivatives of the pregnancy theme tend to appear at times when the patient is not confronting the question directly. Since these are also the times when she is associating freely, we may speculate that such derivatives as "balloon," "puffy," "peeping," "search," "rage," and "pant" have so little direct reference to the threatening theme of the analyst's pregnancy and possible departure that the patient is not "aware" of what she is saying. The content is so well disguised that it does not disrupt her stream of associations; furthermore, it is so far from awareness that it does not force the question. But at certain times during the process of association the theme becomes more explicit; at these points, the process begins to break down and the patient is less inclined to reflect on what she is saying.

Directly or indirectly, the theme of the analyst's pregnancy seems to dominate the first five hours of the analysis. Either it is raised explicitly (as in segment 5–1), is close to consciousness (as in segments 1–1 and 4–2), or is not mentioned directly but appears as a cluster of derivatives that pertain to the themes of bulging appearances, suspiciousness, and anger. When the theme is closest to awareness the analytic process is operating poorly, presumably because the patient is not able to control the emerging anxiety; when the theme is well disguised and only hinted at in the material, her anxiety is under control and her associations are flowing freely.[5] This formulation is in keeping with what is known about the patient: Free associations were frequently in the service of resistance, and material which appeared to be obeying all the rules of good therapy turned out later to be quite uninformative.

DISCUSSION

To what extent can we assume that a continuous stream of associations connects the opening contact with the therapist to the question "Are you pregnant?" The evidence here is much more fragmentary than that mustered by Poe, and the function shown in Figure 2 which links the segments is much more complex than we had originally speculated. Can we make sense of this function in the light of what we know about the patient?

The fact that it is more complex than the model suggested by the Dupin fragment should not be surprising. Aside from the fact that one is truth and the other fiction, we are dealing with two quite different sets of themes. Poe's narrator was pursuing a question that we can assume involved little if any conflict, and therefore there is no theoretical reason to postulate complexity in the stream of associations. Because there is no conflict, there is no defensive process to confuse the train of associations: as a result, Dupin is able to follow easily from one association to the next and surprise the narrator at the end of the episode by "reading" his thoughts. The patient, on the other hand, is following a theme about which she has strong conflicts, and we would not assume that her associations would lead to the question directly. Instead, several types of defensive processes intervene.

The first defensive maneuver is a kind of linguistic disguise. At several points during the five hours, the patient uses words which can be placed in such categories as Anger, Suspicion, and Appearance; they can be seen as derivatives of the underlying pregnancy question, and one might expect either that the associations would lead, more or less directly, to the critical question, or that an interpretation based on these derivatives would bring the question closer to awareness. But these are also periods when the patient uses such expressions as "I wonder," "it seems to me," "that reminds me"—the words and phrases we have categorized as Reflectors. These expressions tend to be associated with high productivity ratings; that is, they give judges the impression that good analytic work is being done. We are faced with the possibility that during the times when the derivatives were most frequent, the analyst, perhaps sensitive to the high number of Reflectors, may have assumed that the patient was associating freely and did not feel called upon to interpret. Thus the patient, by the accident of using many "good" expressions, is able to disarm the analyst and minimize interpretations when they might have been most timely.

Another mechanism worth mentioning is a type of isolation. The derivatives of Anger, Suspicion, and Appearance were spread over the five hours, tend-

[5] I am indebted to Dr. Justin Simon for this formulation.

ing to occur most often at the low points of the function shown in Figure 2. To become aware of these themes, the analyst would have had to keep careful track of word distribution over a relatively long time span. By spreading the significant derivatives over a long period the patient was able (not necessarily by design) to reduce their cumulative significance. Their central theme cannot be detected until a computer (at some later date) brings them all together.

Finally, it is worth noting that the derivatives which were identified were all rather distantly associated to the pregnancy question. We might call this a disguise by displacement; the patient never talks about the main issue but about themes which are several steps removed from it. Removed in meaning and distributed in time, the derivatives can be used freely with little risk of their significance being appreciated.

Comparable disguises have been noted in other therapy material (see Spence, 1970) where key words appear, for example, in idioms or in constructions where they are secondary to the main theme. A computer can pick them out because it is word sensitive, but they slip by the human observer who is listening for meaning and not necessarily for word usage.

What seems to trigger the defenses in the present situation? Inspection of Figure 2 shows that the segments which are most similar to the critical segment come early in the hour—1–1, 2–1, 3–2, and 4–2. We also know that the use of different Reflectors tends to be low at the beginning of each hour and to increase within the hour. The critical question itself was asked early in the fifth hour. Putting these facts together suggests that the patient has two views of the analyst—an "outside" and an "inside" view. Away from the treatment situation or at the beginning of the hour when the relationship is not yet established, therapeutic factors may play a smaller role and the patient is free to observe such things as the pregnant appearance of the analyst. Her appearance is particularly noticeable, of course, in the initial minutes of the session when patient and therapist greet one another. But awareness of pregnancy also implies the threat of loss, and as the relationship becomes solidified during the treatment session, the danger of loss becomes increasingly hard to tolerate. The "inside" view of the therapist as a helping figure tends to conflict with the "outside" view of her as a pregnant woman; therefore as the relationship becomes more intense, the patient tried to deal with the conflict by the mechanisms of displacement and isolation outlined above. She also tells the analyst, by using a wider variety of Reflectors, that she will be a "good" patient. The defensive shift seems to occur at the point when the awareness of pregnancy and the threat of separation it embodies are confronted by the need to maintain the relationship.

Finally, a few words are in order about the prospects of tracing associations by computer. Perhaps a study of five continuous hours is not productive until the treatment is fairly well advanced and much better continuity from session to session can be assumed. Later material should also be associatively freer, another advantage. Better continuity within and between hours would generate smoother functions which might better lend themselves to the method described. Further studies from successful analytic cases are clearly in order.

REFERENCES

Freud, S. (1900). The Interpretation of Dreams. *Standard Edition,* 4 & 5. London: Hogarth Press, 1953.

Klein, G. S. (1967). Peremptory Ideation: Structure and Force in Motivated Ideas. In: Motives and Thought: Psychoanalytic Essays in Honor of David Rapaport, ed. R. R. Holt. *Psychological Issues,* Monograph 18/19:80–128. New York: International Universities Press.

Spence, D. P. (1969a). Computer Measurement of Process and Content in Psychoanalysis. *Transactions of the New York Academy of Sciences,* 31:828–841.

——— (1969b). PL/1 Programs for Content Analysis. *Behavioral Science,* 14:432–433.

——— (1970). Human and Computer Attempts to Decode Symptom Language. *Psychosomatic Medicine,* 32:615–625.

Veldman, D. J. (1967). *Fortran Programming for the Behavioral Sciences.* New York: Holt, Rinehart and Winston.

Ward, J. H., Jr. (1963). Hierarchical Grouping to Optimize an Objective Function. *American Statistical Association Journal,* 58:236–244.

5

MODELS DERIVED FROM INFORMATION-PROCESSING THEORY

THE ASSOCIATIVE MEMORY TREE

Stanley R. Palombo, M.D.

In one of his last technical papers, "Constructions in Analysis," Freud reiterated his view that the patient "must be brought to recollect certain experiences and the affective impulses called up by them which he has for the time being forgotten" (1937, pp. 257–258). In this paper I shall examine some ways of thinking about the process through which the patient is enabled to achieve this recollection.

Freud went on to say:

We know that his present symptoms and inhibitions are the consequences of repressions of this kind: thus that they are a substitute for these things that he has forgotten. What sort of material does he put at our disposal which we can make use of to put him on the way to recovering the lost memories? All kinds of things. He gives us fragments of these memories in his dreams, invaluable in themselves but seriously distorted as a rule by all the factors concerned in the formation of dreams. Again, he produces ideas, if he gives himself up to "free association," in which we can discover allusions to the repressed experiences and derivatives of the suppressed affective impulses as well as of the reactions against them. And, finally, there are hints of repetitions of the affects belonging to the repressed material to be found in actions performed by the patient, some fairly important, some trivial, both inside and outside the analytic situation. Our experience has shown that the relation of transference, which becomes established towards the analyst, is particularly calculated to favour the return of these emotional connections. It is out of such raw material—if we may so describe it— that we have to put together what we are in search of (p. 258).

In what follows Freud described not so much a process of searching as the process of reconstruction by the analyst of a coherent understanding of the patient's life experience from these raw materials. He compared the role of the analyst with that of the archaeologist, taking some pains to point out that the patient differs from the archaeological site in that he is able to produce new materials which correct, confirm, and enlarge the analyst's tentative formulations. He said little about the way in which the actual course of the patient's self-revelation influences the analyst in the building of his constructions, except insofar as the patient's response to a given construction provides new materials upon which further constructions may be raised.

My aim is to look a bit further into the structure of the interaction between the patient and the analyst, keeping in mind, as Freud (p. 258) put it, "that the work of analysis consists of two quite different portions, that it is carried on in two separate localities, that it involves two people, to each of whom a distinct task is assigned." [1] In pursuit of this aim I shall take as my point of departure the analyst and the patient engaged together in a search for something which troubles the patient deeply but remains obscure to him.

In concentrating on the collaborative aspect of psychoanalytic treatment, I am departing from the notion that the analyst merely reflects back to the patient what was in his mind all along and therefore plays no direct part in the patient's problem-solving activity. The view of the analyst as a catalyst of, rather than a participant in, the analytic process is at times very useful. It helps us to avoid the pitfalls inherent in one of the major components of the transference situation, i.e., the patient's attempt to elevate the analyst to a position of magical potency by depreciating himself and his own contribution to the analysis. Nevertheless, the cumulative effect of analytic treatment arises out of a process in which the analyst works by adding something to the patient's problem-solving capabilities, as well as by removing obstacles to the patient's self-expression. He helps the patient to see himself differently, to incorporate new and more inclusive data into his evaluation of the important events of his life. Our need to emphasize what we do *not* do for the patient often distracts us from examining in detail what actually happens in the day-to-day proceedings of the analytic process.

To do so one need not underestimate the importance of the human relationship within which the process develops. If there is no mutual respect between patient and analyst, there will be no working alliance and no joint psy-

---

[1] "It may for a moment seem strange that such a fundamental fact should not have been pointed out long ago; but it will immediately be perceived that there was nothing being kept back in this, that it is a fact which is universally known and, as it were, self-evident and is merely being brought into relief here and separately examined for a particular purpose. We all know that the person who is being analysed has to be induced to remember something that has been experienced by him and repressed; and the dynamic determinants of this process are so interesting that the other portion of the work, the task performed by the analyst, has been pushed into the background. The analyst has neither experienced nor repressed any of the material under consideration; his task cannot be to remember anything. What then *is* his task? His task is to make out what has been forgotten from the traces which it has left behind or, more correctly, to *construct* it. The time and manner in which he conveys his constructions to the person who is being analysed, as well as the explanations with which he accompanies them, constitute the link between the two portions of the work of analysis, between his own part and that of the patient" (Freud, 1937, pp. 258–259).

chotherapeutic effort. In the early stages of analysis much of the activity of both the patient and analyst may be an exploration, a testing, of their respective assumptions about the possibilities for trust and respect, and the way in which these assumptions mesh or fail to mesh. Not all of this activity will be directly related to or a part of the process of self-revelation.

Furthermore, while it may be of value to the patient for the analyst to describe the therapeutic session as a refuge from the ordinary pretenses of daily living, the work of analysis only begins here. It is in many ways akin to the process of mourning, which Freud (1915, pp. 244–245) reminded us is lengthy and painful:

Normally, respect for reality gains the day. Nevertheless its orders cannot be obeyed at once. They are carried out bit by bit, at great expense of time and cathectic energy, and in the meantime the existence of the lost object is psychically prolonged. Each single one of the memories and expectations in which the libido is bound to the object is brought up and hypercathected, and detachment of the libido is accomplished in respect of it. Why this compromise by which the command of reality is carried out piecemeal should be so extraordinarily painful is not at all easy to explain in terms of economics. It is remarkable that this painful unpleasure is taken as a matter of course by us. The fact is, however, that when the work of mourning is completed the ego becomes free and uninhibited again.

In psychoanalysis we are trying to recover aspects of the patient's self-image buried along with the memories of lost objects. Following common psychoanalytic usage we may say that for this reason the functioning cognitive ego of the analyst is a necessary partner in the process, as it is not in the case of healthy mourning. The patient will suffer anxiety and pain. The analyst must learn to deal with these unpleasant affects without compromising his or the patient's cognitive functioning.

THE PROCESS

The patient approaches the analyst aware of unpleasant feelings and generally with a sense that there is something he doesn't know or can't figure out about himself. In its most primitive form his expectation is that the analyst will simply tell him whatever it is he doesn't know and that the unpleasant feelings will then disappear. From the analyst's responses and his own reflections he soon comes to realize that his picture of the situation that disturbs him is incomplete.

What is missing? To the patient that is an impossible question. The analyst encourages him to report whatever comes into his mind, in the belief that sooner or later all will become clear. We know that the patient does not share the analyst's belief, except as the most abstract expression of faith in the analyst's expertise.

For the patient there must be some model of what is to happen next, for he is quite incapable of literally following the analyst's instruction to free associate. According to psychoanalytic theory, unconscious fantasies may cause the patient to react as if he were being attacked in any of a variety of ways. Unconsciously he may believe that the analyst is threatening to cut him open, rip him apart, blast out the hateful impulses within him, and so on. To deal with these fantasies he adopts a strategy which will permit him some control over the rate and direction of his productions during the many hours to follow.

From what we take to be the patient's unconscious fantasies and his strategy to minimize the damaging effect of the fantasies will develop a pattern of alternating discovery and obscuration.

Let us examine a simple model of this process as it is seen by the patient. He is searching for something hidden from him. The analyst is above all an expert in finding what is hidden. The patient scans the analyst's words and other expressive acts for information that will improve his own half-serious, half-evasive searching. After some hints from the analyst about where he thinks it would be best to look, the patient will become fairly adept at arriving at what he thinks is the analyst's preferred destination. Alas, when the anticipated moment is announced by an interpretation, there is often great disappointment for both. The patient will say that the interpretation makes sense but "doesn't lead me anywhere," or that it arouses no feeling in him, or that he can't quite grasp it, or some such. At worst, the patient will break off the chain of associations and try to begin again somewhere else. At best, he will accept the interpretation as a clue, and try to incorporate it into the increasingly complex task of tracking the analyst through realms of difficult theorizing.

This treasure-hunt model is unpopular with analysts because it lends itself so easily to the patient's wish to believe that the lost object is in the analyst's mind rather than in his own. Since it is compounded of the analyst's intention to draw out the latent meaning in the patient's utterances and the patient's intention to proceed without revealing himself, the treasure hunt might be taken as a model of the unfolding of the patient's resistance to the analysis, a caricature of the analytic process rather than the thing itself.

Another simple model of the searching process appears to be much more satisfactory to the analyst, giving as it does a reasonable picture of how the searching in the analysis ought to go. This is the familiar view of the analytic process as the solving of a jigsaw puzzle. Here the associations produced by the patient are the pieces of the puzzle. The patient produces them one by one and the analyst functions by helping the patient fit them together. Momentarily unusable pieces can be set aside and later integrated into the larger pattern. The fitting together acts as a stimulus to the production of new items, so that eventually all the pieces are laid out and the puzzle is solved. In this model the achievement of the goal, the solution of the puzzle, is determined by the fitting-together process itself.

The jigsaw-puzzle model represents an ideal expectation for psychoanalysis rather than the process as it is. In working with our patients we do, in fact, often go in circles, reach impasses, lose our way, lose sight of our goal. We are seldom fully certain just when the therapeutic process has been completed, as the jigsaw-puzzle model would lead us to expect.

A fully adequate model for the searching process in psychoanalysis must accommodate aspects of both the treasure hunt and the jigsaw puzzle. It must make allowances for redundancy, meanderings, detours, obscurity of goals, and the vulnerability to misunderstanding of the guiding role of the analyst. It must also account for the fact that the process is cumulative, that is, that materials which are disconnected when they first appear eventually converge toward a goal which can be defined with some degree of agreement and satisfaction. As this unfolding takes place the analyst will often have the experience of seeing new areas of the patient's personality suddenly come into view. At the same time new obstacles will appear which temporarily block his looking any further.

THE ASSOCIATIVE MEMORY TREE

In order to improve our understanding of the searching process we would like to know as much as we can about the actual location of particular memories in the human memory store and the ways in which these locations are connected. What we know about this most elaborate network is as yet quite meager. There is much evidence, of course, that there are functional associative links which bind a given item in the memory store to other items related to it by formal similarity, simultaneity of input, and symbolic value. Because of the size and complexity of the system and the motivational factors involved in the input-output process, it is difficult to go very far beyond this simple statement. However, in recent years it has been possible to program the memory store of the electronic computer in such a way that it functions very much as the human memory does in such varied activities as problem solving (Newell and Simon, 1961), decision making (Feldman, 1962), memorizing and forgetting (Feigenbaum and Simon, 1961), and even the production of neurotic resistances in psychotherapy (Colby, 1963, 1964). Compared with a human being, the computer is drastically restricted in its contact with the outside world, but the similarities between the symbolic transformations performed on available information by the computer and by the human mind are striking and suggestive. The programming device which enables a computer to simulate the functioning of the human memory is appropriately called an associative memory organization.

The computer memory initially consists of a fixed number of locations, numbered consecutively so that each location has its own fixed address. For the computer to operate on data stored in these locations, the programmer ordinarily must decide in advance the address at which each of the items required by the program will be stored. This imposes severe limitations on the flexibility of the computer. It cannot make new connections between items in the memory store while the program is running and it cannot extend the number of items in the memory as intermediate results accumulate. For ordinary mathematical operations these limitations are not a handicap. For the computer to simulate more complex symbolic operations, however, a new set of linkages must be introduced by the program. This is accomplished in the following way (Newell and Shaw, 1959).

Items are entered in the memory in a sequence called a list. As each item is entered in the memory, there is entered with it, as part of the data, the address number of the location at which the next item of the list is to be placed. When the first item of the list is recovered from the memory the address of the next item comes with it. In this way the whole list can be recovered if the address of only the first item, the head of the list, is known. Branches can be introduced at any point in the list simply by including the address of the first item on the new branch along with that of the next item on the old list. Hierarchies of qualifying information can therefore be recovered at once. New lists can be generated at any time from the intermediate results produced by the actual computational part of the machine. These branching list structures have the form known mathematically as the semilattice or, more simply, the tree (see Figure 1).

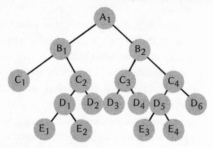

Figure 1.   A semilattice.

The tree form is familiar as the genealogical tree and as the organizational chart of a business or social structure. An item on the tree is connected to a superordinate item and any number of subordinate items. (In Figure 1 only two subordinate branches are shown with each node.) Among the subordinate items connected with a given item may be the address of the head of some other list which is relevant to the item in question. In this way the entire memory can be linked in a single hierarchial structure.

My proposed model for the searching process in psychoanalysis is this: The patient's associations follow a pathway which progresses from superordinate to subordinate nodes along a particular branch of the associative memory tree (e.g., A_1–B_2–C_3–D_4). I assume that the items on the memory tree have stored with them an indication of their affective value, positive or negative, strong or weak. The patient tests the affective value of the next item on each branch which leads away from a nodal point. He follows the branch which offers the greatest affective reward and/or the least pain. From the point of view of his own comfort, the path he chooses is therefore the path of least resistance. From the point of view of the therapeutic purpose, however, it is the path of greatest resistance.

The patient's decision about which path he will take from a given nodal point is, of course, determined by the nature of his psychopathology. For example, the rejected pathways might have brought to mind the derivatives of forbidden bodily impulses; the path of least resistance is then the one least contaminated by such dangers. We may assume that the person of the therapist has become both the object of these impulses and the imagined source of retribution for them. The chosen path will therefore be calculated to keep the therapist in a state of friendly attention, potentially gratifying but not close enough for the underlying conflict to be exposed. At a given moment the safest course may seem to the patient to be to drive the therapist further away.

The chosen path will sooner or later reach what appears to be a dead end (e.g., D_4). The patient can signal this fact to the therapist in many ways: For example, by becoming silent, asking a question, announcing that he can think of nothing else to say, complaining that the therapy is not working, reporting that he feels worthless. His memory-searching apparatus may do one of several things at this point. It may momentarily stop functioning. It may find the address of another major branch of the associative tree and move over to this branch. Or it may start back along the pathway which it has already traversed to the previous nodal point (e.g., C_3). The patient may indicate that he is backing up in this way by asking himself where he was before he reached the apparent end point, or he may simply appear to be doing something repetitious and rather laborious compared with his previous associations.

From the point of view of the analysis, the most useful of these alternatives is for the patient to try to retrace his steps to the previous nodal point and to face the affect to be uncovered in searching through the unexplored branches leading away from this point. One major implication of this model of memory and searching is that the return to a passed-over nodal point will be difficult for the patient, for reasons quite apart from unconscious resistances, but rather similar to those which prolong the process of mourning. As we noted in describing the associative tree in the computer, no information is stored at a given nodal point about the locations of points preceding it in the structure. Each unit of memory contains the address of the next item after it, but nothing about the address of the previous node. The model therefore requires an auxiliary mnemonic device for the location of passed-over nodes.

The device used in the computer program is a listing, separate from the memory structure, of the nodes which are being traversed, constructed according to the last-in-first-out principle. Each new item is entered at the head of the list of previously explored nodal points (e.g., C_3–B_2–A_1). A list of this type is sometimes called a push-down list, because the older items become increasingly remote from the point of access to the list, which is always the newest item. If the address of each node which has been searched is entered in sequence at the head of the mnemonic push-down list, then it is possible to search back along the list by repeatedly calling for the head item (e.g., C_3). The equivalent of this push-down list in the human memory is most likely not a part of its original neurological equipment, but rather a structural component of the executive apparatus which develops through experience with similar structures in other people.

It would follow that the analyst must function as a monitor of the pathways the patient has traversed in his associations, identifying, ordering, and recording the nodal points as they emerge.

It goes without saying that the items on the associative memory tree need not be complete memories of actual experiences. They are, rather, the fragments, allusions, and hints of which Freud speaks. The sensory record of an experience may be isolated from the impulses evoked by it, the visual aspects from the auditory, the verbal from the kinesthetic, and so on. These fragments will be reassembled as the search continues.

A second major implication of the semilattice model is that a nodal memory may have to be recovered many times in the course of an analysis, depending on the number of branches leading away from it and the intensity of the affect associated with each branch. The content of such a memory may be of relatively minor importance compared with the significance of its position and connections in the memory structure. An example would be the taste of the "petite madeleine," which brought back a flood of childhood memories in Proust's *Remembrance of Things Past.*

In recovering for the first time what analysts usually refer to as a dynamically repressed memory, we often do not experience a flood of new material so much as a sliding away along the path of least resistance. We must return again and again to the nodal memory, tracing each of its ramifications, before we can understand its full meaning (e.g., $D_4-C_3-D_3-C_3-B_2-C_4-D_6-C_4-B_2$, etc.). This is, of course, the work of the working-through phase of an analysis.

A screen memory is one which occupies a node whose subordinate branches contrast sharply in their affective values. It may be an easy matter to bring the memory itself to consciousness but very difficult to explore its affect-laden associations.

The identification of the nodal points in the patient's associative tree may, in a given instance, be a fairly routine operation. A sudden loss of momentum, an unexpected silence, a gratuitous change of subject, an out-of-context reference to the analyst, and many other familiar alterations in the pace and direction of associations will serve to call attention to them. As long as the patient follows a relatively tension-free pathway, the nodes will be inconspicuous.

When the patient arrives at a nodal point from which there is no comfortable exit, he usually makes an appeal to the analyst for help in moving ahead. Depending on his understanding of the patient's current location in the associative tree, the analyst may choose one of many possible responses. The simplest and often most effective is simply to wait. This may serve as a signal to the patient that he overestimates the danger of following out the branches now open to him. Repeating or paraphrasing the critical portion of the patient's last statement may achieve the same purpose. What we are dealing with here is the everyday texture of the associative process, about which little need be said.

A greater degree of skill may be required when the flow of associations fails despite the analyst's facilitating efforts. It will sooner or later become apparent that what must happen next is a return to something left far behind, to another fragment of the dissociated experience now at issue (e.g., that which follows from node B_1). At this point the participation of the analyst will go beyond mere facilitation, for he will be in a position to offer the patient information not available to his own executive apparatus. This is the information encoded in the analyst's monitoring and mapping of the patient's associative pathway, of which the patient cannot be directly conscious.

Can we estimate at any given point how far back the patient must go in order to recover the significant but passed-over fragment? In practice we assume that a trial return to the just-preceding identifiable node would be reasonable, and that we can proceed in single steps from there. Conceivably a successful analysis could be accomplished in this way purely on a trial-and-error basis. However, experience with computer simulation of complex processes demonstrates quite conclusively that a trial-and-error search would be many magnitudes beyond the capacity of even the most sophisticated mechanism. To achieve any probability of success, even the most powerful computer must have programmed into it a strategy based on theoretical considerations. It is only when we ask the computer to decide among already highly elaborated searching strategies that we enter the realm of achievable research goals. In the case at hand, where enormous quantities of data about human emotion and behavior must be sorted and condensed by the analyst, we are justified in speaking of psychoanalysis as an art.

The analyst's technique for shortening the searching process is what we customarily call interpretation. Experience confirms Freud's advice to interpret what is nearest the surface, i.e., the immediately preceding nodal points, but we are aware that issues arise in every analysis which require interpretation in depth. In this context, our concept of "depth" refers largely to the inaccessibility to the patient's consciousness of memories associated with the nuclear conflicts of childhood.[2]

Our model of the associative memory tree permits us to give greater precision to the notion of depth embodied in this tradition of clinical observation. The number and order of the nodal points provide a measure of distance from the current allowable state of consciousness to the inaccessible material. The pathway will involve repeated returns to a number of critical nodal points in order to explore the increasingly affect-laden branches which depart from these points. An especially important function of the analyst is to recognize which of the previously passed-over nodal points have such affect-laden unexplored branches. ("Depth" in this definition refers not simply to location in the memory tree, but to the dynamically determined pathway through it.)

---

[2] In his important paper on the recovery of childhood memories, Ernst Kris (1956) speaks of the process through which these critical memories become buried: ". . . even the single dramatic experience is built into the sequence of time, and merges into the course of the life history out of which, by reconstructive work, some episodes can be regained; it will be those episodes which have become dynamically operative, because they became, when they occurred, or later in life, at one of its crucial crossroads, invested with greatest 'meaning.' The memories of such events seem then to become nodal points" (p. 77).

Moreover, it is not necessarily the childhood memory itself which is being withheld from consciousness but the connection between the areas of experience which intersect in the nodal point containing the memory. The unidirectional flow of association through the tree accounts for the patient's difficulty in recovering these connections by himself, and for the analyst's usefulness in expanding the patient's self-awareness by renewing the search from points superordinate to the repressed memory. The analyst turns the natural gradient of associative flow away from its defensive function of evasion, putting it to work instead in a segment of the memory tree where further self-discovery is most likely.

Of course, the analyst's success in directing the patient's attention to these critical nodal points depends not only on the analyst's ability to recognize them, but equally on the patient's readiness to accept the analyst's help. This readiness is, in turn, a function of the state of development of the patient's relationship with the analyst, as illustrated by the following clinical example.

The patient, E.D., a philologist in his late thirties, came to analysis because of obsessive character problems and difficulties associated with an extreme polarization of feelings toward the important people in his life. In the first hours of the analysis it became fairly clear that the central conflict arose from a strongly negative Oedipus complex fixated by his father's accidental death during his early latency. His idealized memories of his father contrasted with a violent antipathy toward his mother.

The transference neurosis seemed to crystallize around the fantasy that had his father lived he would have guided the patient through all the hazards of life, especially those connected with women, his mother in particular. The analyst was now expected to fill this role, and the associative material presented by the patient was meant to demonstrate his helpless victimization by his mother's controlling and rejecting tendencies.

Whenever his thoughts drifted in the direction of the Oedipal triangle, as they often did, he would come to an abrupt stop. After some minutes of silence, he would complain that his mind had become blank, or that he "couldn't do anything" with a statement made by the analyst. He became very fidgety at these moments, and often mentioned feelings of bodily discomfort or fear of illness. He felt tired, hungry, in need of a cigarette, hurting in one or another part of his body. Reminders by the analyst of the thoughts which had preceded these blank moments evoked no response.

It was not until much later in the analysis, after the analyst had survived wave after wave of disappointment and anger, that the meaning of these episodes emerged. It became apparent that when the patient's thinking stopped it was because unconsciously he imagined that his father had returned. It was not the idealized teacher-father he had expected, but rather a withholding, defensive father who had quite willingly allowed the patient to think that only he could or would ever love the patient or take him seriously as a person.

A new segment of the memory tree was exposed when the patient reached the point in his relationship with the analyst at which he could express his disappointment without fear. The memories which now came to light no longer excluded the submissiveness and self-depreciation on the part of the patient which had been the condition for his father's allegiance to him. As the analysis proceeded, the father emerged as a more believable person and the patient felt less and less dependent on the idealized father projected onto the analyst.

In the phenomenon of the screen memory we often see a deep nodal point of the memory tree exposed early in the analysis. Only after a great many unproductive journeys from this point do we find ourselves suddenly facing in a new direction, toward a segment of the tree previously concealed.

Patient J.S., a thirty-year-old lawyer, presented himself for analysis because of anxiety attacks brought on by any effort he made to advance himself in his career. He dated his difficulties from the age of nine when he and a friend asked his two-and-a-half-years younger sister to decide which of them had the larger penis. Despite her carefully equivocal and extremely judicious response, the patient came away from the incident believing that his penis was unusually small and that he had committed an unforgivable sin by showing it to her. Associations to this memory concerned the feelings of impotence and badness which he thought explained an endlessly repetitious list of failures throughout his life. At this time he described his mother as an idealized caretaking person and his father as passive almost to the point of nonexistence.

After some months of work on the transference relationship, the patient's deference to the analyst was revealed to be an elaborate cover-up for messianic feelings connected with his positive relationship with his mother. Recall of the incident with his sister now carried him into memories of a series of ritualistic denials of his developing masculinity. Further associations to the original screen memory included images of his father in a monstrous and terrifying form and murderous impulses toward his sister. From there on the dominant theme of the analysis was his lifelong neurotic effort to deny the nature and intensity of his incestuous feelings toward his mother.

In focusing on a single turning point in each of these cases I am, of course, oversimplifying. In every analysis there are many such points, some of much greater depth and significance than others. The relationships among these points may be most easily understood if we picture them as embedded in the hierarchical structure of the memory tree.

As an example of the searching process at work in a particular analytic session we might look at the second analytic hour described in Freud's "Notes upon a Case of Obsessional Neurosis" (1909, pp. 165–170).

The patient's associations come to an abrupt halt when he reaches the first critical nodal point of the analysis, the memory of the cruel Captain's story about the "horrible punishment used in the East." He breaks off, gets up from the sofa, and begs Freud to spare him the recital of the details.

Freud's response is based on an analysis of the immediately preceding material, which indicates that the patient felt himself to be submitting to the cruel Captain. At the time he had just suffered a symbolic self-mutilation following a forbidden wish to demonstrate his manliness to his comrades. Freud writes, "I assured him that I myself had no taste whatever for cruelty, and certainly had no desire to torment him, but that naturally I could not grant him something which was beyond my power" (p. 166). Freud assures him that he is not the cruel Captain and that free association is not a submission to the person of the analyst.

Freud continues in a supportive way to reinforce the distinction between analytic situation and transference experience. Apparently the patient does not respond and Freud continues:

I went on to say that I would do all I could, nevertheless, to guess the full meaning of any hints he gave me. Was he perhaps thinking of impalement?—"No, not that; . . . the criminal was tied up . . ."—he expressed himself so indistinctly that I could not immediately guess in what position—". . . a pot was turned upside down on his buttocks . . . some rats were put into it . . . and they . . ."—he had again got up, and was showing every sign of horror and resistance—". . . bored their way in . . ."—into his anus, I helped him out (p. 166).

Freud has made a deeper interpretation which activates superordinate nodal points in the associative tree. The first of these, mentioned at the end of the previous hour, is the patient's fear that his wish to see girls naked would cause his father to die. Second, there is his preoccupation with the female anatomy, connected with obvious castration fears. Third, there is the first communication of the analysis, a story about an older male friend who used the patient only to gain access to his older sister.

From these Freud has inferred that the patient fears a retaliatory homosexual attack by his father. The patient then reveals his pleasurable fantasies of carrying out the "punishment" first on his fiancée and then on his father. Next we have the first long and confused description of the obsessive rituals, involving the pince-nez and Lt. A., which were to have warded off the forbidden wishes.

Freud describes his way of dealing with the latter material as follows:

It was only when he told the story for the third time that I could get him to realize its obscurities and could lay bare the errors of memory and the displacements in which he had become involved. I shall spare myself the trouble of reproducing these details, the essentials of which we shall easily be able to pick up later on, and I will only add that at the end of this second session the patient behaved as though he were dazed and bewildered. He repeatedly addressed me as "Captain," probably because at the beginning of the hour I had told him that I myself was not fond of cruelty like Captain N., and that I had no intention of tormenting him unnecessarily (p. 169).

In this very rich hour we see Freud demonstrating many of our now standard techniques for restoring the associative flow by the recovery of a preceding nodal point. These include: a transference interpretation/clarification referring to the immediately preceding nodal point; a highly condensed dynamic interpretation using material from several nodal points but ultimately leading back to the first communication; paraphrases, anticipations, requests for clarification, all clustering around the immediately preceding nodal point; and, finally, repeated returns to the important nodal point which forms the link between forbidden wishes and obsessive defenses against them.

A problem of scale arises when we try to relate the macrostructure formed by the critical nodal points of a complete analysis with the microstructure of a single hour or even a single interchange. Can we use the same structural terms to describe both? In the mind of the human observer this difference of scale is accentuated by the differences in capacity and structure between the short-term memory which operates in the course of a single hour and the permanent memory which orders the experiences of many years.[3] Viewed as larger and smaller substructures of the associative memory tree, the complete analysis and the single hour fit together without difficulty. The tree is simply the structure formed by the repeated embedding of smaller units within larger ones. For this reason it seems to me to be an extremely valuable tool for research into the psychoanalytic process, where the subjective discontinuity between single hour and complete analysis causes so many difficulties.

CONCLUSION

The reconstruction of the patient's memory tree from his associations during analysis, a linear sequence of expressive acts, is typical of what may be called the fundamental problem of cognitive functioning. For every information-storing system which is in contact with its environment, the *sine qua non* of adaptive functioning is the ability to interconvert the hierarchical structures which establish order within the system and the linear strings of symbols which form the basis of communication with the outside world (Chomsky, 1957; Yngve, 1961; Simon, 1969). The involuted syntax of every natural language owes its complexity and individuality to the difficulties inherent in solving this problem of interconversion.

We may think of a series of cognitive levels of ever-increasing complexity and coherence, beginning with universal symbolic systems much less structured than language (e.g., the various sublevels of primary-process thinking) and extending to the highest levels of integration of the individual human personality. Each higher level presupposes the intact functioning of those below it. On all levels the relationship between internal structure and the outside world is the same. Inner hierarchies must be reversibly translated into linear sequences of shared symbols. The success of psychoanalytic treatment depends on the solution of this interconversion problem at the highest level. Nevertheless, our ability

---

[3] The short-term memory takes in a relatively high proportion of items which impinge upon it, but gives them little structure. The permanent memory takes in very few of the items offered to it, but orders all of them in the semilattice form. In the process of dreaming, items collected by the short-term memory (day residues) are matched with significant items in the permanent memory (latent content) as a test of their desirability for entry into permanent storage.

to reach the highest level with a given patient at a given moment requires us to understand symbolic processes in both their hierarchical and sequential forms at all levels.

Psychoanalysis has made extraordinary technical and theoretical progress, in spite of the handicap imposed by the primitive state of the basic psychological sciences throughout the early part of this century. Many of our old theoretical assumptions were based on educated guessing about the nature of mental processes. The model I have suggested for the process through which significant memories are recovered during psychoanalytic treatment may not at first glance seem to be anything more than a slightly different way of describing what we already know very well. I have, in fact, tried here to emphasize the considerable degree to which it overlaps our traditional ways of thinking about the recovery of memories in analysis.

What I hope it will do, beyond this, is to open to view the possibility that in the not very distant future we will evolve a conceptual framework within which we may be able to understand both the intrapsychic activity of the patient and the interpersonal process through which the therapeutic achievements of psychoanalysis are effected. In order to reach this goal we will have to adopt a language in which it is possible to specify with equal precision the fine structure of the psychic apparatus, the nature of the information transmitted between patient and analyst, and finally the process through which structure is translated into communication and vice versa. I believe that the beginnings of such a framework and such a language already exist in the information-processing sciences.

SUMMARY

Significant memories are usually recovered in the course of psychoanalysis through a gradual process of unfolding. This process is often conceptualized in terms suggested by a variety of activities such as the archaeological dig, the treasure hunt, and the jigsaw puzzle. Each of these simple models may help to focus our attention on a particular aspect of the psychoanalytic process. A more complex model of human psychological processes, derived from digital computer simulation, is offered here. This new model is based on the supposition that the cognitive operations necessary for the efficient searching of an associative memory tree play an important but hitherto poorly described role in the functioning of the analyst. The model may be helpful in clarifying this part of the analyst's function. In addition, it suggests the possibility of a unified theoretical approach to the intrapsychic and interpersonal aspects of psychoanalytic treatment.

REFERENCES

Chomsky, N. (1957). *Syntactic Structures*. The Hague: Mouton.
Colby, K. M. (1963). Computer Simulation of a Neurotic Process. In: *Computer Simulation of Personality*, ed. S. S. Tomkins and S. Messick. New York: Wiley, pp. 165–179.

—— (1964). Experimental Treatment of Neurotic Computer Programs. *Archives of General Psychiatry,* 10:220–227.

Feigenbaum, E., and Simon, H. A. (1961). Forgetting in an Associative Memory. *Proceedings of the Association for Computing Machinery National Conference,* 16:2C2–2C5.

Feldman, J. (1962). Computer Simulation of Cognitive Processes. In: *Computer Applications in the Behavioral Sciences,* ed. H. Borko. Englewood Cliffs, N. J.: Prentice-Hall, Chapter 15.

Freud, S. (1909). Notes upon a Case of Obsessional Neurosis. *Standard Edition,* 10:155–318. London: Hogarth Press, 1955.

—— (1915). Mourning and Melancholia. *Standard Edition,* 14:243–258. London: Hogarth Press, 1957.

—— (1937). Constructions in Analysis. *Standard Edition,* 23:257–269. London: Hogarth Press, 1964.

Kris, E. (1956). The Recovery of Childhood Memories in Psychoanalysis. *The Psychoanalytic Study of the Child,* 11:54–88. New York: International Universities Press.

Newell, A., and Shaw, J. C. (1959). Programming the Logic Theory Machine. *Proceedings of the Western Joint Computer Conference, 1957,* pp. 230–240.

——, and Simon, H. A. (1961). Computer Simulation of Human Thinking. *Science,* 134:2011–2017.

Simon, H. A. (1969). *The Sciences of the Artificial.* Boston: M.I.T. Press.

Yngve, V. H. (1961). The Depth Hypothesis. In: *Structure of Language and Its Mathematical Aspects. Proceedings of Symposia in Applied Mathematics,* 12:130–138.

ON INFORMATION, MOTIVATION, AND MEANING

Emanuel Peterfreund, M.D., and Edi Franceschini

A. INTRODUCTION

The concepts of motivation and meaning are fundamental in clinical psycho-analysis and probably in all of psychology. Indeed, one can reasonably define the psychoanalytic process as an attempt to discover the unique, personal, unconscious motivations and meanings of individual experiential phenomena—thoughts, fantasies, feelings, and behavior. This paper will focus primarily on the problem of motivation, and will deal with only a few aspects of the problem of meaning. We are interested in attempting to delineate information-processing models—albeit very crude and elementary ones—which may begin to explain some of the clinical phenomena referred to as "motivation." We hope to begin to explain such vital aspects of motivational phenomena as repetitiveness, strength, peremptoriness, changes in motivation, the overriding aspects of some motivational phenomena, priorities, hierarchical arrangements of motivation, complex conditional relationships among motivations, and so on. We will use brief clinical vignettes to illustrate and develop our themes. It is our firm conviction that more is accomplished in the long run by attempting to explain simple, clear, clinical phenomena—elementary though these explanations may be—than by attempting global explanations of vague and poorly delineated clinical phenomena. It can therefore be expected that in this paper we will begin to answer only a few questions.[1]

[1] This paper is a supplement to a recent discussion of motivation and meaning by Peterfreund (1971). We will not attempt a survey of the literature on motivation. Many authors take an approach that is consistent with the one presented here, and we are especially indebted to Taylor (1960) and Simon (1967) for many stimulating ideas. Taylor seems to have been one of the first to take an information-processing approach to the problem of motivation. Interestingly enough, his article is not even mentioned in Cofer and Appley's (1964) important and highly regarded survey of motivation. Nor will we discuss important psychoanalytic approaches to motivation such as those of Rapaport (1960) and Klein (1967). Rapaport worked within the frame of reference of current psychoanalytic metapsychology (using such concepts as that of psychic energy), a theoretical frame of reference which, in many ways, we have abandoned. Klein's article is more sophisticated than Rapaport's, and he recognized many of the difficulties presented by the concept of psychic energy. But Klein never recognized the power and significance of information-processing concepts.

When used by psychologists in reference to activity or behavior, the term "motivation" generally connotes "energizing," "arousing," "invigorating," "regulating," "purposiveness," "goal direction," and also persistent "patterning, aims, and direction." When, for example, someone goes to a store to buy a newspaper, we can say that a certain form of behavior has been aroused; there is a patterning and direction to the behavior, an obvious purpose or goal. A specific selection has been made from the enormous ensemble of things that could have happened—a highly ordered selection based on a great deal of prior learning.

When psychoanalytic clinicians speak about motivation in connection with some activity or behavior they generally have in mind many if not all of the above mentioned connotations. But in addition they are interested in the problem of meaning.[2] Indeed, for the psychoanalytic clinician, motivation and meaning—both conscious and unconscious—are inseparable. For example, in the course of analysis four different patients have asked one of the authors (E.P.) if he was a Jew. These behaviors were motivated; they were highly selected; they had directions, aims, and goals. Superficially, they were very similar, but in each case analytic work revealed that the term "Jew" had different, unique, personal meaning—individual unconscious meaning. One patient, a young woman, asked the analyst if he was a Jew because to her the term "Jew" at that time meant someone who can engage in perverse sexual activity, unlike her image of the well-spoken, Ivy League WASP. If he was a Jew, in the sense that she meant it, he would not condemn her interest in "perverse" sexual activity. Another patient asked the analyst if he was a Jew at a time when she felt quite guilty about her sexual activities. If he was a Jew, a "member of the tribe," he would tend not to condemn her; a gentile might have. A third patient asked the analyst if he was a Jew because he did not wish to associate with Jews. For this patient, a Jew was someone who rots, unlike gentile Englishmen. When he was quite young he saw his dead grandmother "thrown" into a grave without a coffin, according to the customs of orthodox Jews, to be "eaten by the worms and to rot." In his mind, Jews rot; elegant Englishmen live in airtight mausoleums after death, and do not rot, nor are they eaten by the worms. A fourth patient asked the analyst if he was Jewish because he felt rootless, uncontrollable, and without a conscience. He wanted a Jewish analyst because he felt that someone brought up with the Jewish ethic might bring something to the analytic situation which would enable him to control himself and would counteract his feeling

---

[2] We will not attempt to define the term "meaning," which Cherry (1966, p. 114) discouragingly calls a "harlot among words." We suspect that too great a preoccupation with rigorous definition may hinder one's efforts to conceptualize the phenomena referred to. In the history of science, often more has been accomplished in the long run by beginning with loose and inexact terminology and focusing on conceptualizations of the phenomena referred to than by beginning with efforts to find exact definitions. More rigorous definitions may emerge from good explanatory ideas. For example, Staddon (1971) writes: ". . . it would have been senseless for Newton to have been exact in his use of the term 'force' before he discovered the laws of motion; afterwards the proper definition was obvious. The point is that the laws come first, definitions afterwards." A related point of view was expressed by Freud in "Instincts and Their Vicissitudes" (1915, p. 117).

that he had no ethics, no conscience, and that he could do socially irresponsible things.

None of the above patients was psychotic. In other words, the common denotative and connotative meanings of the term "Jew" were available to all of them, and could be used appropriately. They all knew the "reality," so to speak. For each of them, however, the term "Jew" had a unique, personal, "emotional," unconscious meaning at the moment when the question was asked. Their motivations for asking the analyst "Are you a Jew?" were inseparably related to specific meanings at the given moment, and these personal meanings can change over time. Indeed, a term such as "Jew" can have very different, even seemingly contradictory personal meanings for a patient at any given time.[3]

When psychoanalytic clinicians speak about a subjective personal experience—thoughts, fantasies, feelings—in contrast to overt activity or behavior, they tend not to use the term "motivation," but they are generally interested in many aspects of such experiences which represent connotations of the term "motivation." For example, they are interested in the specific patterning of the experience; why it was selected (generally unaccompanied by awareness); what are its purposes or goals, and so on. Frequently, the purposes or goals may be defensive ones, to protect the person from experiencing something more painful or distressing. For example, a woman patient in her late thirties persistently maintained the feeling and fantasy that she was young, that a great romance lay ahead of her, and that in a sense life had barely begun. This persistent patterning of experience represented a specific unconscious selection from the enormous number of possible experiences that could have been selected, and served defensive purposes. These attitudes protected the patient from anxieties about death, aging, and the impoverishment of her marriage. And here too the clinician is interested in meaning. For example, he is interested in knowing what death and aging meant to this patient, the various layers or levels of meaning based on her entire past history. In the above case, "death," at one level, meant a state of complete helplessness and aloneness.

In general, one important approach to motivation will dominate this paper: the idea of patterning and selection. We view the organism as always being motivated in some way, in the sense that it always reveals some patterning of activity, behavior, or subjective psychological experience—some feeling or thought. We believe that one can most profitably come to grips with motivational phenomena by inquiring why, at a particular moment, one specific pattern of behavior, activity, or subjective psychological experience was selected from all possible behaviors, activities, or experiences. And when we speak of "selection,"

---

[3] To anticipate some of the general ideas to be presented later on, it is reasonable to suggest that, from the standpoint of memory organization, in each of the above cases the term "Jew" was classified in memory in different ways: as one of the class of people who engages in perverse sexual activity; as one of the class of noncondemning people; as one of the class of things that rot; and as one of the class of people with an ethic and a conscience. These different classifications correspond to the different meanings, and retrieval of information from these different memory organizations determines how "unconscious" meanings enter into motivational phenomena.

which we will discuss extensively later on, we by no means imply any necessary awareness of the selections, nor any idea of "free will," nor any idea of a conscious selection process.

Before going on to clinical examples, we believe it is necessary to make some general comments about the nature of scientific theory, about the concepts of information and information processing, and about the general conceptual frame of reference we are using.

B. A FUNDAMENTAL DISTINCTION

If our effort is not to be misunderstood, we must emphasize a fundamental distinction. We believe that it is most useful to begin with the idea that distinctions exist between the phenomena of observation and levels of theory about these phenomena. Granted that these distinctions are not always simple or clear and that the scientific and philosophical issues involved here are enormous; nevertheless, we believe that it is useful to begin with the idea that practical, useful distinctions can be made.

To be specific, patients have experiences—sensations, feelings, images, fantasies, thoughts, and so on. These can be thought of as the raw data of psychoanalysis, the phenomena of observation. Patients communicate these experiences both verbally and nonverbally. Verbal communication includes both the lexical aspects of language and the paralinguistic aspects (intonation, rate, amplitude of speech, and so on). Nonverbal communication includes posture, gestures, facial expressions, and so on. The words used by the patient to describe his experiences may be thought of as the language of persons, the language of ordinary discourse.[4] The psychoanalyst uses the language of persons as one level of clinical language. Indeed, when he communicates with a patient he tries to use the patient's own personal images, metaphors, and analogies. Other levels of clinical language include the language used to express clinical inferences. For example, a patient is using the language of persons if he says, "I hate my boss; I am furious; I would love to annihilate him; he makes me feel like a screaming, helpless, frustrated child." If the analyst says that this patient was quite tense and agitated, he is using clinical language to express his inferences about the patient's inner state.

There is a level of conceptualization in psychoanalysis which may be called the level of clinical empirical generalization, or the level of clinical theory. This level is still fairly close to empirical observations. The term "defense" is a good

---

[4] We emphasize that words are *not* the *fundamental* raw data of psychoanalysis. Even the language of persons is quite removed from personal experiences and can only refer to them. Language is successfully used by patients in psychoanalytic communication if it enables the analyst to empathize with the patient and to experience to some extent whatever the patient experiences. These processes are crucial in making it possible for the analyst to arrive at correct inferences about the patient's inner life. In brief, language is not a substitute for experience, it is merely the vehicle for communicating the nature of inner experience. Language is the vehicle of exchange that allows analytic "trade" to take place, but the "real stuff," so to speak, is experience.

example of a clinical theoretical term. When we say that a patient is defending himself, we are implicitly saying that he does not allow himself to experience something that is painful. If we say that all children tend to have sexual thoughts and feelings, we have suggested a clinical empirical generalization.

In all sciences there are high-level theories which use terms that are quite abstract and remote from the observable phenomena. For example, everyone can observe the phenomenon described as a "thunderstorm," but high-level theories about this phenomenon are expressed in a language appropriate for physical systems and use terms that are abstract and remote from the observable phenomenon—electrical and mathematical terms, for example. Psychoanalysis, as a science, has also attempted to develop a body of high-level, abstract theory. It has been given the name of "metapsychology," and it uses such terms as "ego" and "psychic energies."

We have abandoned much of current psychoanalytic metapsychology. We have discarded such hallmarks of the theory as the ego, psychic energies, primary and secondary processes, and so on, as well as many of the implicit assumptions of this theory—the fundamental anthropocentric and anthropomorphic points of view, for example, and the implicit mind-body dualism.[5] And we have been attempting to develop an information model to replace it. But note that we are attempting to replace only the existing metapsychology. Psychoanalysis as a science must be empirically based. The valid clinical observations of psychoanalysis and the valid empirical generalizations or clinical theory—the very essence of psychoanalysis—cannot be replaced, as Freud so well understood when he wrote: "For these ideas [high-level, abstract theories] are not the foundation of science, upon which everything rests; that foundation is observation alone. They are not the bottom but the top of the whole structure and they can be replaced and discarded without damaging it" (1914, p. 77).

For example, sexuality as an experiential phenomenon can be described in the language of persons. One can proceed further in the development of a scientific system to valid clinical generalizations about the phenomenon, such as that all children tend to have sexual feelings and fantasies. One can proceed still further, developing higher levels of theory to explain the phenomenon, as psychoanalysis has attempted to develop higher-level theories for the phenomenon in terms of psychic energies. We believe that the phenomenon of sexuality can be more meaningfully and accurately explained in information terms that are consistent with modern neurophysiology. Replacing the higher levels of theory does not replace the phenomenon to be explained or the valid clinical generalizations about the phenomenon. However, a better higher-level theory allows one to observe clinical phenomena more carefully, widens the scope of understanding and prediction, and links the phenomena to the wider world of biology and evolutionary time.

---

[5] An extensive critique of current psychoanalytic metapsychology appears elsewhere (Peterfreund, 1971).

C. THE BASIC FRAME OF REFERENCE

In this section we will present a brief statement of our frame of reference and some of its implications for psychoanalysis. A more complete statement appears elsewhere (Peterfreund, 1971).

We view the central nervous system as a highly complex, hierarchically arranged, feedback-regulated information-processing system consisting of innumerable subroutines or subprograms, and probably capable of extensive time-sharing and parallel operations. It is a total functioning system, all parts of which are in some way interconnected and interrelated. It can be thought of as a system that learns and that evolves and readapts over time. It processes information from the genetic code; from short- and long-term memory; from internal sources (such as the autonomic system, proprioceptive receptors); and from external sources (external sensory input, for example).[6] Only a very small part of the functioning of this vast system is accompanied by corresponding awareness. The psychological phenomena that we refer to as emotion or cognition correspond to different aspects of the functioning of this system. And every psychological phenomenon or experience will reflect the complex and multidetermined nature of the corresponding information processing. The ultimate aim of those who think in information-processing terms is the delineation—point for point, so to speak—of the nature of the information processes to which various psychological phenomena correspond. Such delineations should be completely consistent with other approaches to the CNS, chemical or electrical models, for example.

An information-processing model has several very significant advantages over psychic-energy and ego-psychological theories. First, such a model offers a unified language and enough variables (the innumerable sources of information including a vast memory and highly varied programming possibilities) to begin to conceptualize the specificity, complexity, and interrelatedness of the observed clinical phenomena. This is in distinct contrast to the possibilities offered by current psychoanalytic theory, which has very few meaningful variables and which forces one to think in discontinuities or dichotomies (ego versus id, for example) which are poorly related to the clinical phenomena to be explained. Second, information-processing models appear to be completely consistent with the findings of modern biology and neurophysiology—the genetic code, for example—in contrast to current psychoanalytic theory, in which many of the fundamental theoretical concepts cannot be meaningfully related to contemporary scientific thought.

Several points should be emphasized about our frame of reference. We

---

[6] Interestingly enough, even some sophisticated colleagues have objected to the idea that genetic information is processed throughout life. They take the position, for example, that the genetic code is like the blueprint of a house: it determines only the nature of the initial structure. This approach, however, completely misses the dynamic nature of the genetic code. How can we explain predictable pubertal development, for example, if we view the genetic code as a static blueprint which is not active in some way throughout life?

view the phenomenon called mind as a manifestation of biological processes. We view consciousness, for example, as a transient manifestation of the activity of the central nervous system, activity expressible in chemical, electrical, or information terms. And the psychological phenomena referred to as "I" or the "self" correspond to or are manifestations of innumerable relatively stable processes in the central nervous system, also eventually expressible in chemical, electrical, or information terms.[7]

Furthermore, we view the phenomenon of consciousness as an exceptional state; the overwhelming number of processes in the central nervous system are not accompanied by corresponding awareness. We view all of the processes in the central nervous system, both those that are and those that are not accompanied by awareness, in information-processing terms, ultimately reducible to basic elements: carriers of information and processing units—the fundamental so-called "logical" elements. Behavior, activity, or psychological phenomena may appear to be irrational, unrealistic, or illogical depending on the kind and amount of information processed and on the nature of the programming.

Our approach in no way degrades, neglects, or minimizes emotions. True, we may use the "cold" and "mechanical" terms of an information-processing frame of reference to speak about emotions, and in such an approach human qualities may appear to be lost. But it must be remembered that the term "emotions," or "feelings," refers to human experiences, and we are discussing a *theory* about these experiences. Clinical language and the language of a particular theory about clinical phenomena must always be separated. A chemical theory of moods, tension, depression, and so on, for example, will also use terms that appear to be "cold" and "mechanical," but such chemical terms are appropriate for the particular theoretical frame of reference.

Furthermore, it is most important to point out that the experiences called "emotions" are hardly random or chaotic. On the contrary, they are often quite specific and predictable in individual cases. For example, one can often predict that a given event will evoke sadness in a certain patient. Certainly such specificity speaks for selections, for ordered sequential events in the central nervous system, exactly the kind of phenomena which information and information-processing concepts can model. Similarly, drives and the phenomenon of sexuality in general can hardly be considered as random, wild, or chaotic, to be

---

[7] The general approach which we have adopted to the phenomenon of consciousness is, we believe, quite consistent with that of Langer (1967), whose approach was recently adopted by Bowlby (1969). Langer writes: ". . . the phenomenon usually described as 'a feeling' is really that an organism feels something, i.e., something is felt. What is felt is a process, perhaps a large complex of processes, within the organism. Some vital activities of great complexity and high intensity, usually (perhaps always) involving nervous tissue, are felt; being felt is a phase of the process itself. A phase is a mode of appearance, and not an added factor. Ordinarily we know things in different phases as 'the same'—ice, water and steam, for instance—but sometimes a very distinctive phase seems like a product. When iron is heated to a critical degree it becomes red; yet its redness is not a new entity which must have gone somewhere else when it is no longer in the iron. It was a phase of the iron itself, at high temperature" (p. 21). The discussions of these issues by Langer and by Wooldridge (1968) are recommended.

described in terms of vague "psychic energies" or "forces." On the contrary, sexuality, for example, has a reasonably predictable developmental history, as psychoanalytic clinicians have long emphasized. This too speaks for a conceptual approach capable of explaining selection, order, and specificity, as well as the effects of phylogenetic history.

D. SOME COMMENTS ON INFORMATION AND INFORMATION PROCESSING

The aim of this section is to point out a few aspects of the concepts of information and information processing that are of significance to psychoanalysis and especially relevant to the topic at hand.[8]

We use the term "information" in a strictly physical sense, with no psychological implications—no implications concerning meaning, for example. True, many have used the concept of information with psychological or semantic implications. But the approach presented here seems to us to be almost a necessity for psychoanalysis. After all, the psychoanalyst attempts to understand, for example, what a given event in the outer world may mean to a man, a child, and an infant. And meanings change over time and multiple meanings can exist simultaneously. To arrive at a parsimonious theory one must, we believe, begin with a concept free of psychological implications and then conceptualize how the various meanings may emerge. If one were to attribute psychological implications to the concept of information, what meaning would one select, the man's, the child's, or the infant's? And the given event will have different "meanings" to lower animal forms. Thus, if we free the concept of information of psychological implications, we can hope to work toward a unified theory which roots the human mind in the general world of biology and evolutionary time.

Information has to do with patterns of physical events or the relationship between patterns of physical events. A pattern of one physical form can be transduced into a pattern of another physical form and the latter, in turn, can be transduced into a pattern of still another physical form. What remains the same is the information; it is the common factor in the sequence of changing patterns. In ordinary teletype communication, for example, the receiving apparatus can duplicate the original printed message. The original information is carried by patterns of electromagnetic waves, and by the patterned movements of keys on a keyboard.

In general, information can be transferred by any pattern, any measurable change in a system—marks on a paper, arrangements of atoms in a molecule as in

[8] Additional discussion can be found in Peterfreund (1971). There is no substitute for actual experience with computer programming to get a feeling for the nature of information processing and for the actual complexity of events which are often described in the current psychoanalytic literature in rather simplistic terms. Many useful, elementary, readable books on computers and information processing are available to the interested reader with no experience with computers. Those by Adler (1962), Davidson and Koenig (1967), Fink (1966), and Murphy (1970) are suggested.

the genetic code, electrical impulses, hormonal secretions, and so on. Information is not a thing; it is an abstraction about things. It represents a hypothetical factor common to changing patterns of things, just as energy is a hypothetical entity that is conserved in a series of physical transformations. Information can be processed, arranged, and rearranged in complex ways, and the rules for this processing remain the same regardless of the way the information is carried or represented. The term "programming" refers to the instructions for these operations. Situations like this are familiar to all of us. We all speak about "number." But "number" is not a thing; it is an abstraction about things. One can add, subtract, and multiply numbers regardless of the physical entities to which they are applied or which they represent.

The usefulness to biology of the concept of information lies in the fact that one can think of the central nervous system as fundamentally a processor of information—a general point of view that has gained wide acceptance in recent years. And it processes information from multiple sources: current stimuli—from the inner and outer world; the genetic code; ontogenetic sources—memory or residue of the person's past history; and feedback from ongoing operations.

Modern digital computers are one of the class of information-processing devices, the best-understood member of this class. We believe that existing knowledge of computers can help one understand how other members of this class—the central nervous system, for example—may operate.

Modern computer programming is based on the idea that highly complex events can eventually be broken down into a series of relatively simple sequential steps which the computer can handle. Astonishingly enough, these ultimate specific processes—the ultimate building blocks of even the most complicated program—are very few. They consist of circuits which express only a few simple relationships, such as AND or OR. Although this basic, elemental, "molecular" level is of little immediate interest to the psychiatrist or psychoanalyst (or even to the practical programmer), it is of enormous theoretical interest because the hypothesis that the central nervous system can be viewed as an elaborate processor of information becomes reasonable when one recognizes how simple are the basic building blocks and how readily they can be implemented by electronic or mechanical devices, and presumably also by electrical or chemical "machine" processes in biological systems. In fact, the discovery that highly complex processes can be broken down into simple sequential steps, and, ultimately, into simple relationships which can be expressed by simple circuits or combinations of such circuits, may be among the most significant discoveries of the century.

Figures 1 and 2 represent what computer scientists call "logical circuits." Figure 1 illustrates an AND circuit in the form of a simple switching circuit. In this circuit, information from A closes a switch, thus allowing I to affect O. Information from A is said to control the "gate." In other words, information from I *and* from A are necessary for the circuit to be active and for information to pass to O. An OR circuit is illustrated in Figure 2. Here I affects O if either C *or* D is active. This type of circuit is said to form an OR "gate."

Figure 1. An "and" circuit.

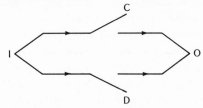

Figure 2. An "or" circuit.

The importance of such circuits lies in the fact that they can be used to express or implement logical or causal relationships. From the standpoint of logical relationships, Figure 1 can be interpreted as expressing the following: *If I is true and if A is true, then O is true.* And Figure 2 can represent: *If I is true and if C or D is true, then O is true.* From the causal standpoint, Figure 1 can be interpreted as expressing or implementing the following: *If I takes place and if A takes place, then O takes place; or, alternatively: O takes place because I and A take place.* Figure 2 can be interpreted as follows: *If I takes place and if C or D takes place, then O takes place; or, alternatively: O takes place because I and (C or D) take place.* Notice the common contingent relationship in causal and in logical systems, a common "If . . . , then . . ." form.

Because of the analogous relationships between elements of causal systems, elements of logical systems, and the elements of switching circuits, one can use switching circuits either to simulate causal systems or to deal with logical problems.[9]

From another important point of view one can speak of such basic or elemental building blocks and their elaborations and combinations as "decision" circuits: They result in specific selections. In Figure 1, for example, when I and A are both active an automatic "decision" is made and O is affected. One can also say that an automatic "choice" is made by such circuits. In Figure 3, for

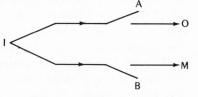

Figure 3. Diagram illustrating decision or selection depending on ancillary information (A and B represent ancillary information input).

example, with I active, the input from A will lead to the choice of O; the input from B will lead to the choice of M. The selection of either O or M is contingent on input at I and on input at either A or B. If one views the central nervous sys-

---

[9] Actually, these analogous relationships can be expressed by a common Boolean algebra. Our discussion has been an oversimplified one. More complete yet elementary and readable discussions of some of these issues can be found in Adler (1962) and Fink (1966).

tem as fundamentally an information processor, with only a very limited amount of its activity being accompanied by corresponding awareness, one must recognize that an enormous number of "decisions," "choices," and "selections" are constantly being made, unaccompanied by awareness.

The above points cannot be emphasized too strongly. When we speak of "decisions" and "selections" we are in no way implying the existence of an anthropomorphic "decider" or "selector." It is of crucial importance to recognize that we are speaking of automatic processes, countless "decisions" and "selections" that do take place in existing computers and that may take place in the central nervous system unaccompanied by awareness.[10] It is crucial to our thesis that the ideas of "decision," "choice," and "selection" have no implications of "free will" accompanied by awareness. True, if one consciously decides to move an arm, one has an experience of "free will" associated with awareness, but a high-level decision such as this must be implemented by innumerable lower-level automatic decisions in the central nervous system that are unaccompanied by awareness. For example, innumerable decisions must be made automatically to control the rate, degree, amplitude, and sequence of the many muscles involved in moving an arm.

Furthermore, if one examines circuits such as those we have shown in Figures 1–3, it becomes very difficult to say exactly where control lies. For example, in Figure 1, does the input at I control what happens at O? Only in part, because the activation of O depends on conditions at A. One can easily see that in any program which involves many levels of what computer scientists call "logical" organization, many subroutines, and countless building blocks such as the above (and any central nervous system program undoubtedly does so), it is virtually impossible to say exactly where control lies and exactly what is the determinant of the final output. One can say only that every element in the active "logical" organization plays some role. To state this idea in a somewhat different way, in any complex program the ultimate choices or selections are determined by the information input, the active ancillary information (the context), and the nature of the programming.

The above idea, we believe, is basic to understanding the nature of motivation. It is a central theme of this paper that, in any clinical phenomenon, whatever is "energized," "aroused," "invigorated," and the nature of the "aims," "patterning," "direction," and "selection"—all of the connotations of what we think of as motivation—are the attributes of a total program, all of the active sources of information and the nature of the programming logic. Indeed, we find it very helpful to think of information-processing circuits as "tracking" through an ensemble of possibilities as a result of repeated decisions or choices. They therefore determine the ultimate direction and selection from the vast ensemble of possibilities, and the ultimate patterning of clinical phenomena.

An important implication of the above ideas for psychoanalytic theory may be mentioned here. Psychoanalysis has attempted to use a concept of psychic

---

[10] In the central nervous system the synapse may be the basic site for such "decisions" and "selections."

energy to explain motivation (see Rapaport, 1960) and it has attributed aim, direction, and so on, to the activity of various psychic energies. The confused nature of this concept has been discussed elsewhere (Peterfreund, 1971). Here we wish only to point out that the concepts of information and information processing offer psychoanalysis a meaningful replacement for this concept. Indeed, we believe that in many ways psychoanalytic theoreticians have used the concept of psychic energy more like a rudimentary informational idea than as a true energy concept.

Finally, we wish to emphasize that the nature of information processing has another important implication for psychoanalytic theory in general and especially for the problem of motivation. Although active inhibiting or "interrupt" mechanisms are well-known in information-processing systems, it is not necessary to postulate an active inhibiting mechanism to explain why something is not active at any given moment. This idea is in distinct contrast to the approach of psychoanalytic theory, which is constantly invoking the idea of an active "force" to explain why something is inhibited or seems not to be active. Repression, for example, is conceptualized in this manner. Information processing leads to selections or choices, and this fact automatically implies the notion of inhibition: What is not selected is automatically inhibited. For example, in Figure 3, when information is put in at I and A, O will be active. Under these conditions M is not active. Its activity appears to be inhibited. But this inhibition is not the result of an active, constantly applied "force" acting counter (countercathexis, to use the terminology of current psychoanalytic theory) to the "force" or "energy" of M. M appears to be inhibited because it is not selected to be active by the circuit arrangement; it has not been "energized" or "aroused."

It is most instructive to examine some of the capabilities of modern information-processing systems to understand their general relevance to psychoanalysis and, more specifically, to the problem of motivation. For example, the basic circuits mentioned above, plus others, arranged in complex and elaborate ways, permit a computer to deal with intricate contingent relationships, both logical and causal. For example, a computer can deal with the following situation: A is true if (B is true) or if (C and D are true and also E is not true). Similarly, it can deal with the following analogous causal situation: A is greater than v if (B is greater than w) or if (C is greater than x, D is greater than y, and E is less than z). The significance of these ideas for psychoanalysis can be exemplified as follows:

Let A represent the ability of a child to play and explore with pleasure and let v represent some relevant threshold value (or range of threshold values).[11]

Let B represent the availability of the mother (as experienced by the child) and w a relevant threshold value.

---

[11] We introduce the idea of threshold values here without further elaboration. In general, in regard to biological organizations the idea of threshold values is of great significance, and it is one of the special merits of an information-processing frame of reference that it can begin to conceptualize thresholds and their variations. By changing the existing biological thresholds the organism is able to change its priorities. Here we have one of the biological or "hardware" implementations of the idea of "priorities" discussed in this paper.

Let C represent the familiarity of the surroundings to the child; and x a relevant threshold value.

Let D represent the availability of a familiar mother substitute; and y a relevant threshold value.

Let E represent the anxiety level of the child; and z a relevant threshold value.

In a given situation, a child may be able to play and explore with obvious pleasure (A is greater than v) if he experiences the mother as being available (if B is greater than w); or if the surroundings are experienced as familiar, a familiar mother substitute is available, and if he is not overwhelmed with anxiety (or if C is greater than x, D is greater than y, and E is less than z). In brief, the clinical situation has exactly the general causally contingent relationships mentioned above. One can represent the situation in flow-chart form as in Figure 4.

If we examine the above clinical situation, what can we say about the child playing and exploring with obvious pleasure? Certainly he reveals motivated

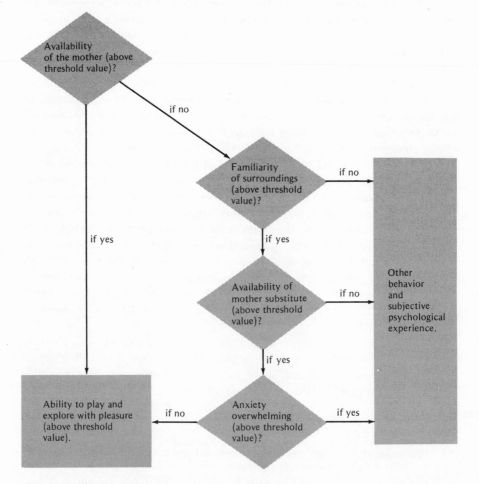

Figure 4. Causal relationships involving a child at play.

behavior; it has direction, aim, purpose; it represents specific selections from a very large number of possibilities. But it is contingent in specific ways. It is contingent on the availability of the mother above some threshold value, on the degree of familiarity of the surroundings, and so on. Indeed, the motive to maintain contact with the mother or with a mother substitute and familiar surroundings has overriding priority. Play will be interrupted if the latter conditions are not fulfilled; or, to state the matter in another way, if the latter motives are not fulfilled or satisfied. In brief, in this simple example we can already recognize the existence of levels of motivation which have contingent and priority relationships.

The following point, however, must be emphasized. The above clinical statements and the relationships between them represent ways in which an adult observer can describe the causal "anatomy" of the events. This observer is in effect saying that a given event (which he calls "the child's ability to play with obvious pleasure") is contingently related to other events: (a) an event which the observer would refer to as "the availability of the mother," or (b) a set of events which he would refer to as "the surroundings being familiar to the child," and "a mother substitute being available."

We are certainly not suggesting that the child himself goes through a process in which he thinks and perhaps verbalizes: "My mother is available; therefore I can explore with pleasure. And if my mother is gone I can explore with pleasure if a mother substitute is available," and so on. Such a suggestion would implicitly adultomorphize the situation in an absurd way. In fact, it is extremely difficult to empathize with the child's experiences, and even more difficult to find appropriate words to describe them. In the above situation, the words "the mother is available" are useful to the adult for the purpose of describing and communicating the child's experience. But for the child, the experience may be one of a vague but familiar presence associated with a feeling of comfort. The words "mother is available" per se may have little meaning for him.

The previously mentioned statements and associated flow chart merely represent an attempt to describe the underlying basic causal relationships in the situation, fundamental relationships which can be described in a high-level language and which can be implemented or expressed in information processes and associated circuits. The child experiences the events without recognizing the causal connections. An adult too, of course, may experience many phenomena without recognizing their causal connections. Indeed, one of the fundamental tasks of the analytic process is to discover and make the patient aware of the causal relationships between experiential phenomena. And we believe that it is reasonable to suggest that making such relationships explicit is uniquely associated with high levels of awareness and attention. For example, an analyst is suggesting a causal relationship to a patient if he says, "You apparently tend to get depressed, guilt-ridden, and self-depreciatory whenever you masturbate." [12]

[12] This interpretation is not only an expression of a causal relationship, it is also an expression of a generalization about the patient. Generalization is an important aspect of psychoanalytic interpretations.

It is of great interest that for some years now computer programming has reached such a level of sophistication that a programmer can use an artificial language, such as Fortran, which allows him to think in terms that closely resemble those of a natural language such as English. For example, with some modifications to conform to the specific rules of the particular artificial language being used, a programmer can write out explicitly such statements as the one previously mentioned: A is true if (B is true) or if (C and D are true and E is not true); A is greater than v if (B is greater than w) or if (C is greater than x, D is greater than y, and E is less than z). Programs written in such artificial languages generate a vast amount of machine code which is unique to the particular computer being used, and the computer, in turn, activates an enormous number of basic hardware circuits of the type previously discussed.

Some of the ideas mentioned above may be puzzling to many analysts, especially to those not familiar with information-processing concepts. Perhaps an example from the inanimate world may clarify matters (leaving out threshold considerations in order to simplify the illustration). In many modern cars a buzzer sounds if the door is opened and if the key is in the ignition; and a buzzer will sound and a warning light will flash if the door is opened and if the headlights are on. One can express these causal relationships as in Figure 5 and as follows:

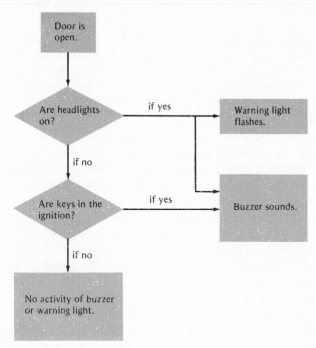

Figure 5. Flow chart of causal relationships between elements of a car.

If the door is open and if the key is in the ignition, then the buzzer sounds: if the door is open and if the headlights are on, then the buzzer sounds and the warning light flashes. Note that either condition "key in the ignition" or "headlights are on" can "gate" the activity of the buzzer under the specific condition that the door is also open. In other words, the buzzer sounds if the door is open, and the key is in the ignition and/or the headlights are on.

All of the above verbal or diagrammatic descriptions of the phenomena in the car attempt to delineate the causal relationships or the causal "anatomy" of the circuits. This causal anatomy will hold true if a bell rings instead of a buzzer sounding; and it will hold true regardless of the nature of the specific hardware—the specific kinds of wires or switches, for example. The car certainly does not "know" and is not able to verbalize the nature of the causal relationships between buzzer, key, headlights, and warning light. Similarly, the child may not be aware of nor be able to verbalize the explicit nature of the causal relationship between the mother's not being available and a feeling of discomfort and anxiety. And an adult analytic patient may not be aware of the causal relationship between a feeling of depression and the analyst's sudden, unexplained cancellation of a session until the analyst verbalizes the relationship in the form of an interpretation.

To go on with the illustrative example, the causal relationships between door, buzzer, headlight, warning light, and key were arranged by the designer of the car and built into the wiring arrangements. Imagine now that a computer is connected to various parts of the car and can control them. A programmer might then be able to arrange the causal relationships between the parts via explicit instructions, using a high-level programming language. For example, he could instruct the computer as follows: *If* the door is open *and* the headlights are on, *then* flash the warning light and sound the buzzer. On the other hand, he could instruct: *If* the door is open *and* the key is in the ignition, *then* flash the warning light. If the computer had access to the motor, it could conceivably be programmed to slow down the car if the door is opened or if the oil pressure drops below a specified value while the car is in motion. In other words: *If* the door is open *or* the oil pressure drops below a specified value, *and* the car is in motion, *then* deaccelerate the engine. Notice in all of the above statements the repeated use of contingent relationships: "If . . . , then . . ." and "and," "or."

E. CLINICAL EXAMPLES [13]

(a) We will begin with an example of a "simple" motivated behavior, one that can be characterized as simple reflexive behavior. A man is walking down a street, preoccupied with his own everyday thoughts. Suddenly an object appears

[13] Some of the examples to be presented may illustrate so-called "peremptory phenomena." Experientially, such phenomena are usually described as "demanding," "imperious," "allowing no denial or refusal." They seem to take over, often seemingly against one's will. Such phenomena have been of great interest to psychoanalytic theoreticans. Rapaport (1960), for example, seemed to believe that such phenomena were explainable only with the aid of psychic energy concepts. It seems to us, however, that "peremptory" is a catchall term for the group of phenomena referred to. Apparently included are obsessive preoccupations, obsessive thoughts, hypochondriasis, even short schizophrenic manifestations. It is our opinion that psychic energy concepts are not needed to explain these phenomena, and moreover that the so-called peremptory phenomena cannot all be encompassed under any simple explanatory model.

in his field of vision, moving at high speed toward his head. Automatically, uncontrollably, his thoughts and behavior are interrupted against his will: He steps
aside, ducks his head, and closes his eyes. The causal relationships in this "simple" activity can be diagramed as in Figure 6. Note that the input information

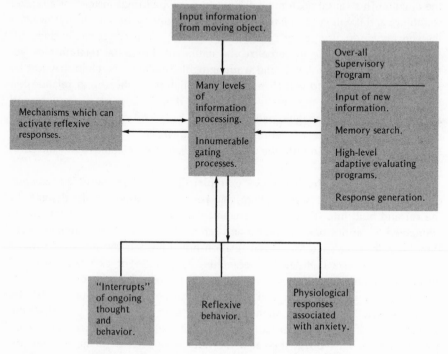

Figure 6.   Diagram of a simple reflex phenomenon.

activates the reflexive behavior unconditionally; in its absence the reflex would
not occur. In phenomena such as these it seems reasonable to suggest that there
is no prior scanning or monitoring. In other words, normally the man is not
constantly looking out for objects that may be flying toward his head.

Actually, the situation presented in this example is much more complicated
than we have thus far indicated; some of these complications are suggested in
the figure, but we will not dwell on these issues here. For instance, the man's
thought processes will undoubtedly be interrupted; anxiety will be experienced;
information relevant to the flying object will be sought, selected, and evaluated
on the basis of past experience (memory and stored programs). Experientially,
attention will turn to the event in question, one that has high priority. In brief,
many processes take place which an external observer would recognize as having
evolved over the course of evolutionary time and which serve to insure the
survival of the organism.

It must be emphasized that in the above-mentioned figure no attempt has
been made to represent neurophysiological events. It represents only some of
the broad causal relationships involved in these events. Complex chemical or
electrical neurophysiological mechanisms can implement these relationships. In

general, all of the flow charts to be presented are crude. They are at the level of beginning systems analysis, and delineate only a few important relationships.[14]

(b) In general, it seems likely that information input into the central nervous system is not handled in simple linear fashion. In other words, information does not simply go from input point A to processing point B, then to processing point C, then on to output center D, like stops on a railroad line. Information from various sources is undoubtedly organized and reorganized at many points from input to output. Input from various sources is probably tested for relevance, pertinence, danger, and so on, and on the basis of these tests further input is either allowed or interrupted. These processes are probably basic mechanisms in attention (Norman, 1968, 1969) and repression (Peterfreund, 1971). For example, when we cross a street we process information and attend to relevant input with the basic goal of getting across the street safely. In such a case we attend to input from the traffic lights and from oncoming cars; we do not attend to or extensively process input from sources which on other occasions would command our attention.

In all probability, in just about every area of life we are testing input at every moment—measuring, comparing, contrasting, and so on—in very complex ways, using goals or norms established on the basis of learning and experience. Most of this activity is not accompanied by full awareness. If tests fail, the first indication may be alertness, alarm, stress; attention then automatically turns to the specific situation at hand, thought and activity are interrupted, relevant information is actively sought, selected and evaluated, and appropriate action taken.[15]

Here is a specific example to illustrate the above ideas: One day one of the authors of this paper was driving on a familiar country road at a moderate speed. He was quite comfortable; all of the input passed the test for "normal" and "familiar." The road, the feel of the car, and so on, all indicated that "it is safe." He was able to carry on a conversation with only minimal awareness that he was driving. Suddenly he felt uneasy, alarmed; something was wrong. He immediately became alert, and all of his attention turned to the car; his conversation was automatically interrupted. He quickly checked many things to see exactly what was bothering him, to find out what had made him acutely uncomfortable. He realized finally that he had lost some control of the car. The familiar feeling that "I can stop the car at any time with minimal effort of my foot" was no longer present. Something was wrong with the brakes. He checked repeatedly (using familiar standards, the familiar feeling of how the brakes normally work) and realized that although the brakes were not gone, he had to work much harder than usual to stop the car. His initial diagnosis of the situation, which subsequently proved to be correct, was that the power braking mechanism had failed. While he was evaluating the situation he recalled that his brakes had once failed completely on a major highway, a situation that

---

[14] The idea of a supervisory program, as suggested in the figure, will be discussed later.

[15] Some aspects of this type of situation have been conceptualized by psychoanalytic theorists in terms of "signal anxiety."

could have been extremely dangerous. When he bought his present car, his first one with power brakes, he inquired about the braking mechanism and was told that if it failed he would still be able to stop the car, although more effort would be required. Information from these past experiences played a major role in allaying his anxiety, helped him arrive at a quick diagnosis of what was wrong, and enabled him to take appropriate action. Notice, incidentally, that an emotional response—alertness, alarm, unease—seemed to precede the more elaborate cognitive processes accompanied by full awareness. The emotional responses seemed to provide the first fully conscious clues about the reality of the situation.

When one learns to drive a car one has to pay full attention; full awareness accompanies the establishment of relevant programs. When learning is adequate the established programs are capable of dealing with a range of conditions. Indeed, when learning is optimal the activity can proceed with minimal awareness as long as conditions remain within the appropriate range, and it then seems as though the activity is being handled by a well-adapted subroutine capable of operating while one is simultaneously carrying out other activity, even high-level cognitive activity, unrelated to the learned task. Good drivers, for example, report that they can drive safely over a familiar route, carry on a conversation, and even work on important intellectual problems, and that after they reach their destination they cannot recall having stopped for a familiar red light, slowing down at a particular intersection, or making a particular turn— conditions that were in the range of the normal learned programs.[16]

It does seem, though, that in such situations there is a constant active scanning or monitoring process that checks for normal conditions. Much of this activity seems to take place with minimal awareness. As one enters a car one goes into "drive-a-car mode," relevant programs based on past learning and experience are activated, appropriate priorities are used, and input is checked against learned and familiar standards. In the above case the brakes did not feel right when used to slow the car on a familiar turn; they did not check against a learned norm; and a host of motivated, peremptory phenomena took place.

Figure 7 represents a simplified sketch of the above example. Note an important difference between the last two examples. In example (a) we suggested that the input information automatically and unconditionally activated interrupt mechanisms and a host of motivated phenomena, without a parallel or time-shared active scanning and monitoring process. In example (b) we suggest an active parallel or time-shared scanning or monitoring mechanism. Of course, it may be artificial to separate these two mechanisms; there is certainly no reason to make them mutually exclusive. It is probably most reasonable to suggest that

---

[16] It is not the aim of this paper to focus on the problem of consciousness or awareness. In general we take the position (Peterfreund, 1971) that full awareness seems to accompany learning: the establishment of new programs and the reprogramming, modification, or updating of old programs. It accompanies situations of danger, alertness, and the input of new information which requires elaborate calculations and the extensive use of central processing circuitry. In the above example, for instance, when the brakes failed the test for normal, the driver became fully aware of the situation. It had to be fully evaluated, and relevant new information had to be actively sought and processed.

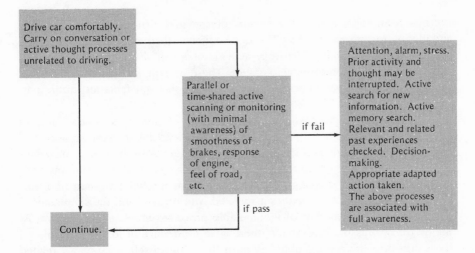

Figure 7. Scanning and monitoring processes while driving a car.

as a result of phylogenetic evolutionary history and ontogenetic learning, both mechanisms develop and both may be operative in any given complex phenomenon.[17]

(c) Sexuality must be considered in any discussion of motivation and in any discussion of peremptory phenomena. In psychopathological states sexual urges can be overwhelmingly peremptory, as, for example, in an adolescent who cannot attend to intellectual tasks because he is so preoccupied with sexual fantasies and urges. In the normal person, sexual urges can assume varying degrees of peremptoriness, and can at times be difficult to postpone. Certainly, at the height of sexual excitement, the need for consummation has the highest priority.

One can begin an information-processing approach to the phenomena of sexuality by postulating a sexual control system which operates incrementally until a threshold is reached, at which point a full activation takes place.[18] The subjective feeling of sexual excitement accompanies the incremental activation of this system. The activity of the control system is stepped up by various information input which, as a result of learning and experience, is actively sought by

[17] We have spoken of parallel and time-shared processes. In parallel operations, different sources of information are processed simultaneously by different central processing arrangements. In time-shared operations, different sources of information are processed sequentially by the same central processing unit. In the latter arrangement, the central processing unit may begin to process one input, and, depending on priorities, interrupt this processing, "turn its attention" to another source of information, and subsequently return to the first input. In modern time-sharing computer installations, because of the rapidity of computer processes, a user at a remote terminal may be totally unaware that he is sharing a central processing unit with many other users.

[18] Again we emphasize that our primary focus is not neurophysiology. We are speaking about the informational "physiology" or causal "anatomy" of the phenomenon of sexuality, however these may be implemented by actual neurophysiological processes—chemical, electrical, or hormonal "hardware." From the standpoint of the central nervous system, the sexual control system postulated may actually include many interrelated structures and processes.

the organism. For example, the normal person may first detect a vague urge and desire for sexual activity. Those who know their sexual needs and are neither fearful nor guilt-ridden may actively seek stimuli that lead to maximal excitement and accompanying pleasure. These stimuli include the gamut of foreplay stimuli—visual, olfactory, tactile, and so on—and fantasies, both "perverse" and "infantile." [19]

In general, we suggest that the activation of processes which interrupt everyday thought and activity—and such interruptions are an essential aspect of the idea of peremptoriness—depends roughly on how close the increasing values of the control system are to the threshold of discharge. And in an information-processing approach, discharge is conceptualized as the full activation of a host of autonomic and motor activities associated with orgasm, and the simultaneous deactivation or interruption of innumerable processes unrelated to orgasm. At the height of orgasm, for example, there is an experience of loss of control and there may be a momentary obliteration of the sense of self, presumably related to the massive interruption or deactivation of innumerable programs associated with normal, everyday experience. Feedback from consummatory activity is probably involved in inhibiting or interrupting the original excitatory mechanisms and is associated with the experience of satiation and satisfaction.

Figure 8 is a highly oversimplified flow chart of normal sexual activity.

(d) Everyone monitors his body, his appearance, his feelings, moods, and accomplishments. We glance at a mirror as we dress in the morning; we have an awareness of how we feel during a particular day—sad, happy, well; as we walk we may be dimly aware of moving freely, without pain or effort. We take note of aches, pains, things that do not feel right. We constantly monitor the flow of experience, using standards or norms based on past learning. Such extensive monitoring may occur in parallel or in time-sharing relationships with normal everyday thought and activity. If standards are reasonable, this monitoring serves its normal adaptive function. For instance, one may not like to observe a blemish on one's face which one evaluates to be benign, but this observation generally does not lead to alarm and distress, or to frantic, panic-ridden activity and obsessive preoccupation. If on the basis of learning and experience one evaluates a skin blemish as possibly malignant, one can then proceed to take appropriate action. Figure 9 presents a crude flow chart of the normal kind of monitoring that is ever-present.

Here is an example of a patient whose standards of monitoring were neither reasonable nor normal. The patient, a young man who started treatment because of a potency disturbance, was obsessed with his body and general appearance.

---

[19] There are many phenomena in the human organism which suggest the existence of a group of processes that closely resemble the activities of supervisory systems in complex computer systems. These activities include time-sharing control, priority setting, the selection of general operating modes, the allocation of information-processing capacity, and so on. In the above example, the search for information input that leads to the increased level of activity of the sexual control system (and a corresponding increase of the psychological experience of sexual excitement) may be under the aegis of such a postulated over-all supervisory program.

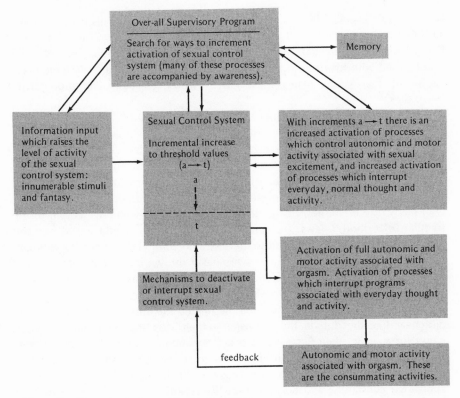

Figure 8. Flow chart of normal sexual activity.

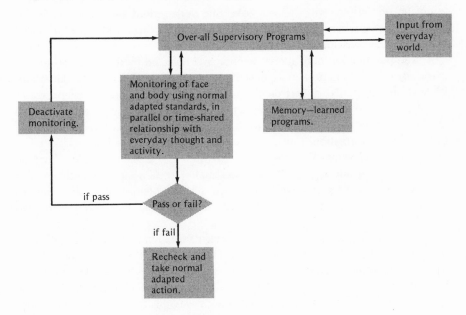

Figure 9. Flow chart of normal monitoring processes.

He constantly checked his face for any sign of a skin blemish; his penis to make sure that it was neither small nor rotting; and his general appearance to see if he looked like an elegant Englishman and not like an orthodox Jew. He was preoccupied with his professional success. He had to be brilliant, dashing, ever-successful, the "young man on the move" whose creativity and productivity never dies.

His standards for evaluating his body, appearance, and skin blemishes were hardly reasonable or realistic. His criteria for "pass" or "fail" were hardly ordinary ones. When he checked his face, every skin blemish he observed, even those that were obviously benign, meant that something was very wrong: he might be ill, perhaps dying and rotting. For him Jews were people who rot. He often recalled the vivid childhood memory of seeing his dead grandmother, shriveled and with many skin blemishes, being "thrown" into a grave without a coffin, in the tradition of orthodox Jews. He fantasied that the worms could get at her and that she would certainly rot because there was no coffin. Englishmen, he thought, were not dirty, orthodox Jews; they were never thrown into the ground without coffins; they "lived" on after death in airtight mausoleums; worms could never get at them and they therefore never rotted.

One of his greatest fears was that he might fade into oblivion, be lost, and disappear like the dot on the television screen after the set is turned off; it glows for a while, then fades out. He did not monitor his professional success by ordinary standards, although he was quite successful by such standards; he did not use reasonable standards for "pass" or "fail." He had to be lauded and applauded constantly, and be ever more successful; he was not going to glow for only a short time and then fade into oblivion. His early history was a very traumatic one. There was, for example, one very serious febrile illness in his early childhood when apparently he did "fade out"; there was either a partial or total loss of consciousness.

The peremptory motivational phenomena revealed by this patient were inextricably related to important aspects of meaning. Information from a skin blemish was only in part classified on the basis of information-processing programs based on normal learning and experience. The patient knew at one cognitive level that in reality his skin lesions were benign. But at another level of cognitive organization, information from the skin blemish was processed and classified in highly abnormal ways. As a result, the blemish meant to this patient that he might be rotting and dying. To state the matter somewhat differently, in this pathological level of cognitive organization, all skin blemishes on the patient's face were classified as members of the class of grossly abnormal structures related to death and rotting.

Similarly, this patient knew the normal denotative and connotative meanings of the term "Jew," and at one level of organization he enjoyed being Jewish and had many fond memories of past experiences related to Jewish things. But the term "Jew" was also classified in his memory in a unique pathological way, as one of the class of things that rots. It was this latter "emotional," connotative meaning that was involved in his symptoms and that had to be uncovered in treatment.

Incidentally, this patient was not psychotic. As already noted, the normal denotative and connotative meanings of the term "Jew" were available to him, and he was aware that his personal meanings were abnormal. He could therefore complain about the fact that he was conflicted; he was attracted to Jewish things on one hand, but repelled by them on the other. A psychotic patient may act only on the basis of his personal connotative meanings, and not recognize the reality of the generally accepted denotative and connotative meanings. Such patients may therefore appear to be unconflicted and without awareness of being ill.

Figure 10 is a crude flow chart of the above pathological situation. We believe that the flow chart suggests how a pathological formation can begin to consume a patient's psyche, seem to take over completely, until, in extreme

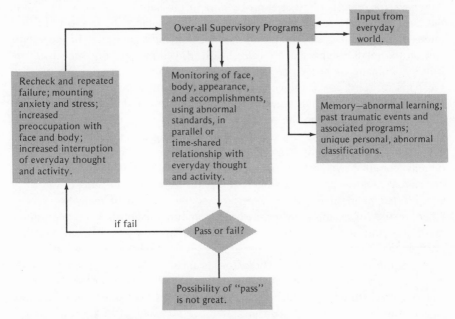

Figure 10. Flow chart of abnormal monitoring processes.

cases, a patient can become virtually paralyzed in everyday life as he becomes increasingly obsessed with his morbid symptoms. Note that there is little possibility for "pass" when this patient checks the blemishes on his face because he is using totally abnormal standards, the full nature of which is not within his realm of awareness. Actually, a vicious circle is built into the situation: Standards for "pass" are so unrealistic that monitoring and checking can usually lead only to "fail," with mounting anxiety and repeated frantic checking and rechecking of the blemishes in a vain effort to "pass," to reassure himself and to quiet himself down. And very often, as panic mounts, the standards become even more unreasonable then they were before.[20]

[20] Although, as noted earlier, this paper is not focused primarily on the idea of meaning (discussed more fully in Peterfreund, 1971), it is pertinent to point out here

(e)   Monitoring is characteristic of mental functioning, as previously discussed, and another very significant characteristic is planning, including anticipation or looking ahead. Monitoring and planning are closely related, and both are
basic aspects of motivated phenomena.

It is astonishing, when one thinks of it, how much planning we all do. We
think ahead and make plans on a large scale; we plan schooling, careers, family;
we save, invest, purchase insurance—all with consideration for future possibilities and contingencies, hopefully realistically evaluated. We plan on a small
scale—how to spend the day, when to eat, when to run errands, how to attain
special pleasures, how to take care of uncomfortable situations, and so on. We
plan and look ahead whenever we verbally express our thoughts. And we monitor
the results of our plans. We check the length and the accomplishments of an
interview, for example, how it is proceeding in the light of our plans, including
the aims and goals of the interview. We may cut a lunch hour short and not
interrupt an interview, depending on the meaning and significance of the events
and on the relationships and priorities involved. We monitor our speech to see
if it is grammatically correct and if it expresses our intent. In brief, we plan on
the basis of aims, goals, values, and meanings, using a host of strategies and
innumerable priorities. We alter or readapt our plans and reallocate time and
effort, depending both on the results of monitoring and on everchanging aims,
goals, values, strategies, and priorities—ever-changing throughout life.

The above comments are only a cursory summary of a few of the extraordinarily complex events that are involved in some important motivated phenomena. When we speak of strategies and priorities we are speaking of a host of
complicated phenomena which have aroused the interest of many workers in
recent years. For example, in recent years computer scientists have been interested in artificial intelligence and the simulation of many human cognitive
phenomena. They have become increasingly aware of the importance of strategies and priorities. In a game of chess, for instance, neither human nor computer
can look ahead and evaluate every conceivable move and countermove. Heu-
ristics (special strategies or rules of thumb) are used to cut down on blind, rote
calculations concerning every conceivable move. Actually, in all kinds of circumstances we employ similar methods to guide our efforts and to save time, as al-

---

that, as used psychoanalytically, there appear to be two important general ways whereby
meaning emerges from information. First, input information acquires meaning depending on how it is processed, and processing includes how the information is classified
by a receiver. In the above case, information from the observed skin blemishes was
processed in different ways and thereby acquired corresponding meaning. In addition,
there is a class of meaning that refers to the meaning of a phenomenon to the person
whose organism manifested it. Included here are such things as the meaning of an
utterance to a speaker. For example, when the patient discussed above used the term
"Jew" he may have meant any one of several different things depending on the nature
of the information processing that corresponded to the utterance. Included in this
processing is the particular memory classification that was used. In the above case, we
suggest that the term "Jew" was classified in many ways corresponding to common
denotative and connotative meanings, and also in a way that corresponded to his
unique connotative meaning: one of the class of things that rot.

ready indicated. Indeed, the establishment of efficient strategies is basic in learning and adaptation. For example, no one reads every book that is published, nor even every book or paper published concerning one's own profession. We all use many different strategies or rules of thumb to guide our selections.[21]

Normally, planning for contingencies depends on a realistic evaluation of the situation, the probable dangers, for example. In recent flights to the moon, for instance, the most minute plans had to be made. Fuel and oxygen use had to be planned in the most detailed way. But in a simple trip between two cities in the United States one does not generally have to make very extensive or detailed plans. One does not, for example, plan every stop for fuel replenishment. If one did get involved in planning such minute details, it would be recognized as overplanning, and would be a definite clue to the clinician that some psychopathological phenomena existed, and certainly that anxiety was very great.

Just like overplanning (an evaluation based on an idea of a norm), underplanning too may indicate psychopathology. For example, we speak of psychopathology when a drug addict lives only for the pleasures of the moment and the relief of anxiety obtainable from drugs, oblivious of the long-term consequences of his behavior. One of the authors had occasion to ask a young addict what he expected was going to become of him in a few years if he continued his uncontrolled consumption of drugs. He replied, "I never think of that; I never think ahead for more than a half hour." Obviously, he was a very ill young man.

In pathological states, normal adapted planning is frequently interrupted and the programming may be "hung up." The normal flow of experience may be seriously disrupted and all attention seems to be focused on morbid, anxiety-ridden preoccupations. For example, for most people eating is enjoyable, and most of us plan our meals and coffee breaks or snacks with pleasurable anticipation. We look forward to eating and to the temporary relief from many everyday cares that eating also affords. Such relatively unconflicted interruptions of everyday thought and activity are generally brief, although perhaps frequent, and are accompanied by pleasure. They do not interfere with everyday thought and activity or with the normal flow of experience—indeed, they are intrinsic parts of the normal flow of experience. But this is not true of patients who have serious problems centered on food. For such patients food and eating have a host of pathological meanings, and thoughts about food, plans for eating, even the merest mention of food, may activate innumerable problems and conflicts. As a result, normal, adapted programming may get "hung up," and the normal flow of affective and cognitive experience is interrupted. Time and attention are pre-empted by a morbid preoccupation with food.

For example, a male anorexia nervosa patient was repelled by food and could not tolerate the thought of eating, although he was quite aware that he had to eat to stay alive. Among other things, eating was associated with becom-

---

[21] See Peterfreund (1971) for an approach to the psychoanalytic process in terms of an optimal strategy.

ing fat, feminine, and helpless, and becoming a prey to the destructiveness of his mother. One can say that for him eating had a special meaning, and was classified in memory as one of the class of things associated with helplessness and femininity. Any thought about food, any plan for meals, activated overwhelming anxiety and fear. If he attempted normal looking ahead and planning about meals he would become preoccupied with a host of issues which are of little significance for the nomal person. For example, he would begin to debate whether he should eat or not. He would become preoccupied with what to eat; how he would be able to eat in front of others; what kind of excuses he could make when others saw that he could not eat; fear of getting fat; losing control, eating too much, and looking like a pig or like a woman; fear of becoming ill if he did not eat, and so on. In brief, whereas in a normal person thoughts and plans about food are associated with pleasure and are intrinsic aspects of normal experience, in this patient such thoughts and plans were associated with extreme anxiety and innumerable conflicts which at times preoccupied him almost completely and which seriously interfered with the normal flow of pleasurable, adapted experience.

(f) This example illustrates some aspects of the immensely complicated nature of motivation in the analytic process, the innumerable sources of information and complex programming, and the close relationship of motivation and meaning.

One day a patient quite correctly identified a sound that came from in back of the couch as that of a ruler accidentally hitting the rings of a loose-leaf notebook. Subsequently, with an embarrassed laugh, he told the analyst of having the odd thought that the analyst had picked up a ruler to hit him. No psychoanalyst will be surprised to learn that at the very moment when the patient heard the sound, he was speaking of some "perverse" sexual activity.

Certainly this patient was motivated in many ways. For example, of all the possible activities or behaviors only certain ones were selected, actually a group of processes identifiable as an analytic process. The patient was in the analytic "mode." Thus he spoke of his "perverse" sexual interests, something that he would never do outside of the analytic context. He attended to and observed his inner emotional responses and reported them. He also evaluated his responses on the basis of normal everyday standards and laughed with embarrassment at his "odd" thought. Multiple levels of meaning emerged in response to the input from the ruler, and it is reasonable to suggest that several programs were active, either simultaneously or sequentially. One program allowed him to identify correctly the nature of the sound and to come to the reasonable conclusion that the analyst was either doodling or taking notes. But another program was active, one that led to the interpretation that the ruler was an object that the analyst was going to use punitively. Within the context of guilt, embarrassment, and fear of punishment, the sound of the ruler was categorized in a unique way, and took on special, personal, "emotional" meaning. Here again we see the significance of context, an idea already mentioned in our discussion of the elemental, so-called logical circuits. At all levels of programming, choices or selections are dependent, in great part, on ancillary information—the general information context.[22] Thus, in the above case one can reasonably suggest that information related to the general sexual context served, in great part, to determine the selection of the classification in memory that corresponded to the unique personal meaning of the ruler. Such personal meanings can, of course, change over time, depending in part on the changing contexts.

Note too that information corresponding to the meaning of the ruler was, in itself, motivational. It in part determined his recognition that he had an "odd" thought. Information corresponding to his personal meaning served as input to programs which monitor and evaluate experience on the basis of learned standards or norms.

Figure 11 (page 248) illustrates some of the above processes.

(g) For the final example we will again turn to the psychoanalytic process. A female patient came in one day rather upset and depressed and reported that her husband had had a coronary on the weekend. She handled all of the reality problems in an intelligent, considerate, and thoughtful manner. She called the doctor, arranged for hospitalization and special nurses, and took care of the business and financial matters that required immediate attention. But in the analytic hour she spoke of what the event meant to her, all of the personal meaning and implications. She spoke of what her husband's illness meant in terms of the difficulties that already existed in the marriage, what it would mean in terms of their future sex life, and so on. Since the hour took place only shortly after the coronary, and since her husband was still in danger and under intensive care, she spoke of the possibility of his dying and what that would mean to her. For our present purposes there is no need to go into all of the details. We will add only that while she had not been able to cry during the hectic hours of the acute situation, and came to the hour depressed, by the end of the hour she was able to cry freely and talk about the ever-present illnesses and difficulties that seemed to plague her life, of which the current problem was but one.

In the above situation we see motivated phenomena, distinct patterns of activity with aims and goals. This patient functioned quite well in many areas of life, and when her husband became ill she did not fall apart and cry helplessly; she handled the situation realistically, appropriately, in an adapted manner. She acted in the reality "mode"; his care and survival had the highest priority. One can reasonably suggest that the processing of information related to personal meanings was incomplete; it had to be suspended because of the demands of reality and survival, though some undoubtedly took place, as evidenced by the depression which she experienced when she started the hour.

---

[22] This idea probably deserves greater elaboration. For any given input, and for any given set of information-processing instructions, the program will branch in ways that are determined by ancillary information input (other sources of information, or the general, active information context). For example, in modern computers, for a given set of instructions, input A may be processed differently as follows: If information C and D are present and active, with the input of A the program branches to subroutine 1; if information C is present and D is not, with the input of A the program branches to subroutine 2. One can extend this example in an almost infinite number of ways. Preceding every branching there is a decision point.

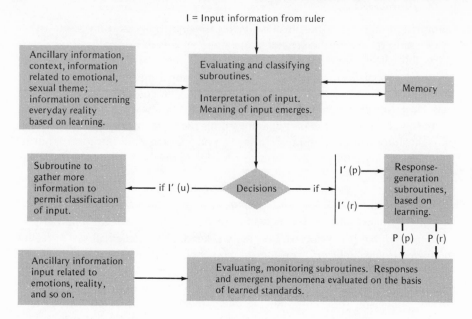

I   Information from ruler

I' (p)   Classification of input using emotional context; personal meaning of ruler emerges

I' (r)   Classification of input using context of everyday world of reality; "real" meaning emerges

I' (u)   Unclassifiable category

P (p)   Emergent phenomena based on I' (p)

P (r)   Emergent phenomena based on I' (r)

Figure 11. Flow chart of the responses to the sound of a ruler during the psycho-analytic process.

During the analytic hour she entered into the analytic "mode," and proc-essed the information concerning her husband's illness so that the personal meanings came to the fore and a full expression of her feelings took place. In other words, personal meanings and implications now had priority instead of the demands of the reality situation. Indeed, had this patient merely recited factual details about her husband's illness, the analyst would rightfully have wondered if some important "resistance" was active. He would have wondered why the patient was not talking about the emotional meaning of the events.

In general, in a good analytic process a patient acts as though under the implicit instructions to change priorities from those of ordinary life, abandon everyday norms, allow apparently random and odd experiences to emerge, even those that appear to be grossly illogical. Indeed, when there are alternative paths during free association, a good strategy for patients is to follow the emotional line; follow those paths which lead to maximal emotional expression. Actually, a certain amount of testing must be done to detect which paths may lead to such expression. Obviously, the information processing involved here is extremely intricate. A similar strategy is also useful for the analyst when there are alternative possibilities for interpretation.

In brief, in the above example we see different motivated phenomena and their relationship to aspects of meaning. And we can see some of the relationships of these phenomena to different goals, different "modes" of processing, priorities, and strategies.

F. CHANGES IN MOTIVATION—
SATISFYING CONDITIONS

In regard to motivated phenomena one can begin to think of the conditions that alter motivations, conditions that change the patterning, direction, aims, and goals.

When a sexual urge is fulfilled, "interrupt" signals at consummation deactivate the original source of excitation. This is typical of the operation of negative feedback loops. We can say here that the original aim was fully satisfied. But not all motivated phenomena terminate in this way. A sexual pursuit may end in failure and substitute activity may be used to satisfy the original aim. For example, one may masturbate if full sexual aims cannot be achieved. A motivated behavior may change if the priorities change, or if there are "interrupts" from systems with higher priority. To take an extreme example, sexual aims cannot be normally fulfilled in the face of extreme danger to life which demands immediate attention. Finally, repeated failure to fulfill some aim can lead to an abandonment of the aim. There is discouragement, a complicated phenomenon dependent on a host of factors.[23]

Important as these issues are, we must set them aside in order to deal with a phenomenon of central interest to clinical psychoanalysis. The clinician constantly meets situations in which neither logic, nor reassurances, nor "reality" can satisfy the apparent aim of a motivated phenomenon. There appear to be no terminating or satisfying conditions. For example, in the illustration previously discussed, no amount of reassurances, logic, or "reality" testing could talk the patient out of his preoccupation with not looking like a Jew; no amount of rational medical knowledge could eliminate his fear that a blemish on his face meant that he was dying and rotting. This man's personal beliefs in regard to Jews and skin blemishes were untouched by logic or science. These levels of belief were even untouched by the higher cognitive understanding that he could himself bring to the situation. Every experienced analyst works constantly with patients who tell him, "I know it isn't rational; I think it is really crazy, but nevertheless I still feel that . . ." That was the case with this patient.

The above situation represents nothing new in clinical psychoanalysis, but our explanatory theoretical approach to it is rather different and, we hope, more accurate than the one offered by classical psychoanalytic theory. Nothing in

---

[23] Some of the ideas mentioned in this paragraph may be useful in conceptualizing clinical phenomena generally subsumed under "sublimation." We will not, however, deal with this very complicated issue here.

"reality," no logic or reasonableness, can satisfy, terminate, or turn off this man's obsessive preoccupations because the preoccupations emerged from unique connotative meanings; they emerged from personal beliefs which were not based on outer-world information input and outer-world reasonable criteria. To state the matter somewhat differently, a medical jury of reasonable man may decide that this patient's skin blemishes are benign. They are working with full medical knowledge based on a very wide range of information from the outer world. The patient's personal beliefs about his blemishes and his criteria for evaluating them are based on a very restricted and unique range of information related to personal experiences—early emotional traumata—the overwhelming majority of which is not accompanied by awareness. In his context of personal, unique meanings, viewing the skin blemishes not only does not terminate his preoccupations, it may actually enhance his preoccupations, as already discussed. We have here the potential for a kind of positive feedback situation. In general, the task of the psychoanalytic process is to bring to awareness these personal unconscious meanings, and the early traumata and associated experiences which were their prime determinants. As a result, modification, updating, and reprogramming may possibly take place.

Similar considerations apply to the anorexia nervosa patient. A medical jury of reasonable men can tell this patient that eating and even becoming fat have nothing to do with femininity and helplessness, and the patient can even tell himself these things. Such realistic knowledge is based on a wide range of information from the outer world, but at one important level the patient was operating on the basis of a restricted range of information related to personal experiences, and unique connotative meanings based on profound early traumata.

But we have said little to explain *why* such psychopathological situations have overriding priority. To state that these psychopathological motivations and meanings exist and perhaps even to present circuit diagrams to show *how* such psychopathological formations can have overriding priority and can pre-empt much of normal experience does not tell us *why* this patient is unable to choose freely the more realistic rational paths, *why* he cannot circumvent personal meanings. We would like to begin to answer these important questions by placing the issues in a larger perspective.

Let us return to our first example. The intelligent adult might be interested in knowing *how* circuits can be arranged so that whenever an object approaches one's head at high speed, ongoing thought and activity are interrupted and one automatically gets out of the way. He would probably accept the suggestion that as a result of evolutionary processes the central nervous system is programmed to respond on a high-priority basis to those stimuli which involve survival. And he would find reasonable the suggestion that the genetic code acts as though it transmits the instructions: Duck your head unconditionally whenever an unknown object approaches your head at a rapid rate. He might be interested in the nature of the genetic code, *how* it transmits such instructions, *how* the circuits are formed, and so on—all profound and complex issues for which there are few answers—but he would not be likely to ask *why* all of this happened because the resultant activity seems so reasonable and rational. It is reasonable and rational to the intelligent adult mind that evolutionary processes have evolved specific mechanisms to insure one's survival.

Similarly, if an adult automatically interrupts his thoughts and activity when he smells smoke and sees an uncontrolled fire in his home, one tends not to ask *why* these phenomena developed. And one would accept as reasonable the suggestion that as a result of ontogenetic learning the central nervous system acts as though under the instruction: If ever there is input related to un-explained smoke and fire in the home, interrupt all thought and activity uncon-ditionally. Here too the resultant activity seems so reasonable and rational that it is easy to accept the general idea that one important function of ontogenetic learning is to insure survival. And here too, although the intelligent adult tends not to ask *why*, he may ask *how:* for example, *how* does learning take place, *how* does the central nervous system apparently program itself, and so on.

But the intelligent adult *does* tend to ask *why* in regard to the activities of the patient preoccupied with not being a Jew and the patient with anorexia nervosa. He asks *why* because their psychopathological activities seem crazy and irrational and he cannot understand why rational activity does not prevail or have priority. He may accept reasonable suggestions about *how* it happens that rational phenomena do not have priority, but this does not answer *why* it came to be that way.

It is our suggestion, however, that the activities of these patients are neither obviously crazy nor irrational if one evaluates them from the standpoint of their unique world of assumptions and meanings. Indeed, we suggest that their morbid preoccupations cannot be overridden by what the normal person calls "rational," "realistic," and "adapted" behavior because for them survival is just as much involved as it is for the normal person who ducks when an object flies toward his head and for the man who interrupts all activity to attend to the fire in his home. In other words, we suggest that learning mechanisms grant these psychopathological formations high priority just as phylogenetic evolutionary and ontogenetic learning mechanisms grant priority to those mechanisms related to "real" survival. The patient who avoided looking like a Jew and who was pre-occupied with his skin blemishes was struggling with survival, with death and rotting, in a most primitive but powerful way. Similarly, for the anorexia patient not eating was a form of survival in an archaic and deeply primitive way. This anorexia patient was not psychotic; he knew the "reality," and did attempt to eat in order to insure his physical survival. If he had been sicker (and many anorexia nervosa patients are) he might not have eaten anything and might actu-ally have died, paradoxically in order to "survive." His not eating was maladapted in a reality sense, in the sense of biological evolutionary time, and in the sense that a jury of reasonable men would evaluate the situation. He was, however, not unadapted from the standpoint of his own inner world of private meanings.

The above general state of affairs is well known to clinicians. Suicidal pa-tients often seek not real, biological death but mainly relief from pain and suffering; often they hope to enter a fantasied Nirvana of bliss. Often they seek relief from profound loneliness and emptiness—an inner psychological death. Paradoxically, they turn to real biological death to find something that for them is life.

G. SOME GENERAL THEORETICAL REMARKS

We have viewed motivation in terms of patterning, direction, aims, and goals, in terms of the specific selections from the vast ensemble of possibilities. We view ultimate patterning as an attribute of the total organism and we have attempted to demonstrate that information and information-processing concepts are extremely useful to explain the nature of such patterning.

In general, we hold the view that all aspects of the active program, all of the active sources of information and the nature of the programming, can be motivational insofar as they determine the nature of the resultant specific patterns. Of course, this does not mean that all aspects of any program are equally important or crucial. And certainly there is a profound difference between existing computers and the central nervous system. It may well be, for example, that, because of redundant functions, the inactivity or defectiveness of certain information processes only minimally affects over-all patterning in the central nervous system. And certainly, too, there is nothing in the point of view presented that is inconsistent with the idea that relatively stable information-processing subprograms may exist which will determine characteristic persistent or repetitive motivations. In this sense, the frequently used term "motivational structure" has a referent in an information-processing frame of reference.

The advantage of an information-processing approach, as we see it, is that it offers a dynamic language consistent with modern neurophysiology to explain the observed phenomena. One is not forced to think in terms of dichotomies (ego versus id, for example, as in current psychoanalytic theory) which actually do not fit the realities of the observed phenomena. Nor is one forced to make any artificial distinctions between emotions and cognition. Some information processes correspond to the psychological phenomena that we call emotion; others to the phenomena called cognition. And both types of processes determine the nature of motivated phenomena.

It seems to us rather difficult to think in terms of simplistic dichotomies or in terms of artificial distinctions between emotions and cognition when we recognize, as some of the clinical examples illustrated, that (a) in actuality human phenomena are multidetermined and are based on complex contingencies; some reactions take place only when certain processes occur and not others; and (b) the output of information processing becomes input that is then processed in turn. Thus we react cognitively to emotions, and emotionally to cognitions. Indeed, we react emotionally and cognitively seemingly simultaneously to the same input. It is a serious question whether, practically speaking, any true clinical distinction can be made between emotional and cognitive phenomena—a state of affairs that one might well predict on the basis of information-processing models.

For example, when one works on a high-level mathematical problem, one is certainly engaged in a cognitive activity, but such activities are hardly divorced from emotions—pleasurable anticipations, excitement, and so on. And during the height of orgasm one can be said to be having an emotional experience, but such experiences are often contingent on a host of fantasies—cognitive phenomena—and during the experience there may be profound changes in body representations, changes in the cognitive "map" of oneself. Indeed, many patients fear the orgastic experience because they fear losing control. They fear not only the mounting excitement but also the changing body representations.

We have tried to delineate some aspects of the complex nature of motivated phenomena and the relationship of such phenomena to some aspects of meaning. The attempt to devise information-processing models forces one to focus on the details of such phenomena, crucial details which get lost in the ego-function and psychic-energy approach of current psychoanalytic theory. Thus we have emphasized the innumerable sources of information, context, differences in programming, modes of operation, the importance of priorities, strategies, and feedback. And this is but a bare beginning. It is a major programming task to simulate a cognitive process such as the game of chess, in which the sources of information are known and the rules and aims defined. Imagine how much more difficult it will be to specify in exact detail complex emotional and psychological phenomena in which many of the major active sources of information (current, genetic, and ontogenetic) are unknown, and in which there are no generally agreed-upon fixed aims or rules. Thus it can be expected that full-scale models or simulations of such phenomena will not be forthcoming in the foreseeable future.[24] But such difficulties in no way detract from the value of information-processing models as explanatory models and as sources of useful ideas.

Furthermore, an information-processing approach may cast new light on seeming puzzlers about motivation. For example, what would we say about behavior resulting from toxicity, from alcoholism, for example (an issue discussed by Rapaport, 1960)? Alcohol unquestionably affects the "hardware" of the central nervous system; in some way it affects chemical or electrical events. But hardware changes invariably change the nature of the information processing to the extent that information storage, "logical" circuits, and so on, are embodied in chemical or electrical events. Our general thesis in regard to motivation can, therefore, encompass such situations.

Finally, we wish to say something about the problem of conflict. Many theoreticians have pointed out that current psychoanalytic theory is useful because it helps in conceptualizing the basic clinical ideas of conflict, explainable presumably in terms of ego, id, and superego concepts. We have always had many questions about this point of view. We do not see how conflict can be adequately explained in these terms. These issues are important not only for clinical psychoanalysis in general, but also for the specific topics at hand: motivation and meaning.

[24] For a related and relevant point of view, see Neisser (1967, p. 9). The first chapter of Neisser's work is relevant for an understanding of the general frame of reference of this paper.

Clinically, conflict is often a complex contingent situation, involving "if . . . , then . . ." relationships. For example, a patient was able to have intercourse with her boyfriend if her parents were not in the house, but was too conflicted to allow herself to have intercourse with him if her parents were asleep in a nearby room. On other occasions conflict may involve a complex branching tree of contingencies and decisions.[25] For example, a patient was considering divorcing her husband. Then he became ill, and this fact created additional problems for her. Her conflicts could be described approximately as follows: If she divorced him she would have to face her guilt about abandoning an ill man; she would have to face problems concerning money and supporting a child, problems concerning marriage, sex, and so on—each of which areas involved a host of specific conflicts and problems. If she did not divorce her husband she would have to deal with her anger toward him, her frustrated sexual desires, and so on, and here too each area involved specific conflicts and problems. One can begin to conceptualize such complex contingent situations within an information-processing frame of reference. We fail to see how such situations can be conceptualized in any sort of parsimonious way in terms of ego-psychological concepts.

H. THE PROBLEM OF REPRESSED MOTIVATIONS

We believe that it is most important to approach the idea of repressed motivations from an information-processing point of view. Unfortunately, the issues here are extraordinarily complicated, and our remarks must be tentative and limited. Inseparably linked with the idea of repressed motivations are the problems of consciousness, defenses, and so on—all difficult issues. Moreover, we believe that one of the difficulties involved in the idea of repressed motivations is the catchall nature of the concept of repression. Subsumed under the term are a host of phenomena which, we believe, cannot be conceptualized in any simple or uniform way. Finally, the term "repression" has longstanding connotations in psychoanalysis and these connotations—actually an implicit theory—color any discussion of the issues. For example, as used in psychoanalysis the term connotes an active process, an expulsion from consciousness, a holding down, a "force" versus a "counterforce."

Certainly it is not difficult to conceptualize an active dynamic repressive process in information-processing terms. For example, programs associated both with the psychological experiences of pain, guilt, or embarrassment, and with awareness may be deactivated after quick tests for acceptability. Such tests may take place with minimal awareness. For example, programs corresponding to overt sexual curiosity may be activated by some source of excitation, but be deactivated after quick tests for acceptability. Related substitute programs may be activated instead—curiosity of a different nature, for example—which may serve to "satisfy" the original source of excitation, satisfy in an information-

[25] This issue is discussed more fully elsewhere (Peterfreund, 1971, pp. 172–174).

processing sense as already mentioned. One can say here that the original program related to sexual curiosity represented a repressed motivation.[26] But we
wish to focus on certain phenomena of great interest to psychoanalysis which
may require rather different explanatory approaches and which we believe may
have important general theoretical implications.

Specifically, we are interested in explaining the well-known clinical idea
that "somethings" associated with ideas or feelings may have very powerful influences on behavior or subjective psychological experiences, yet in themselves
not be within the realm of awareness nor easily available to awareness. For example, in the cases of the patient who did not wish to look like a Jew and the
patient with anorexia nervosa, there were "somethings" that determined the
nature of their bizarre behavior and subjective psychological experiences, but
these "somethings" were not completely available to awareness. We suggest
an approach to this problem in the general context of learning. As background
for this approach we must discuss briefly some general ideas about learning
which are discussed more fully elsewhere (Peterfreund, 1971).

Learning is a constant selecting, abstracting, generalizing, or classifying
experience. When a child is learning to walk, for example, he carries out innumerable trial-and-error efforts, as a result of which specific useful movements
are selected from the vast ensemble of possibilities, movements useful for
achieving the desired goal. Good walking movements consist of an optimum
arrangement of basic, elemental, more general body movements. A child classi-
fies an object in multiple ways and differentiates the objects on the basis of
these classifications. Two objects, for example, may be considered to be similar
insofar as they have been classified as members of the general class of round
and suckable objects, but different insofar as one may be a member of the class
of movable objects whereas the other is a member of the class of nonmovable
objects. The concept "apple" emerges from a learning experience as a result
of which it is classified as referring to one of the class of objects that are fruit,
and that are round, red, good-tasting, and so on. In brief, the term "apple" is
"filed" and "cross-filed" in innumerable ways in memory and becomes differentiated from other objects on the basis of such multiple classifications. Indeed,
it is just such "filings" and "cross-filings," the multiplicity of classifications, that
give "apple" specific meanings.

Interestingly enough, modern computer technology, we believe, can offer
some ideas about how such "filings" and "cross-filings" might be conceptualized
in information terms, although the nature of the hardware implementations is
almost totally unknown. Complex multilinked memory structures, consisting of
nodes to which linked branches are attached, are well-known.[27] If one imagines
that the information associated with a word such as apple is at such a node, the
linked branches may possibly store information of different general categories,

[26] Again we are dealing here with the problem of changes in motivation—an
issue previously mentioned. And again, the ideas mentioned here may be useful in
conceptualizing clinical phenomena subsumed under the general term of "sublimation."
[27] See the article by Palombo in this volume for some related ideas.

and thereby serve to file and cross-file the information at the node. Thus in this simple model the node representing the word apple would be linked to branches representing fruit, redness, roundness, and so on. In general, we are suggesting that the activation of different cross-linked branches may give different meanings to the word or concept represented at any node. One group of branches may give a word its generally accepted denotative meaning, another its generally accepted connotative meaning, and a third the personal connotative meanings.

Before going on, a few important ideas must be mentioned in connection with these ideas about learning. Any given learned program at any given moment can be said to have been patterned during all of the previous learning experiences. The program can be said to contain selected information about all of these previous experiences, the input that stimulated learning, the context, and so on. If a person uses the concept apple correctly—i.e., with the generally accepted denotative and connotative meanings—we can be fairly sure that he has gone through experiences which allowed him to learn that "apple" is a fruit, that it is round, red, and so on. We are therefore able to make a rudimentary reconstruction about the person's past history. When we observe normal walking movements we can be quite sure that the person grew up in our world of gravity because his movements contain information about the effects of gravity. The force of gravity was basic in determining the nature of the patterning. Here too we have made a rudimentary reconstruction about the person's past life based, in part, on the observed information. If a person's walking movements are pathological, a competent neurologist or orthopedist could perhaps interpret the observed information on the basis of his general knowledge and experience, and reconstruct the nature of the illness, its possible course, and so on. Similar reconstructions are made in other branches of science. A botanist, for example, may be able to reconstruct some important facts about the weather conditions during the early life of a tree on the basis of a study of tree rings.

A crucial point is that, in the concept of apple, the past history of experiences associated with apples "lives on" in the form of highly *selected* information about these experiences. But *detailed* memories or information concerning the actual experiences are probably erased. Indeed, it would seem grossly inefficient if the central nervous system were to have evolved so that detailed information concerning such experiences tended to persist and take up valuable storage space. We suggest that what remains is essentially only the useful selections from experiences. Similarly, in walking, selected information of the entire learning effort "lives on" in the form of the final walking pattern, but for the most part one is unable to recall the tedious trial and error necessary to achieve the final program, and we suggest that in all likelihood the detailed information concerning these experiences is erased.

Infantile amnesia may in great part be due to the fact that, since so much basic learning takes place in the first years of life, storage capacity would be unnecessarily burdened if we stored detailed information about all of the tedious trial and error involved in such things as learning motor control, speech, sphincter control, and so on. All one needs for normal adapted life is essentially the final learned program which is capable of being modified throughout life; one does not need the detailed steps by which this program was acquired.

There may be one important exception to the above considerations, however. If some important pathological event took place during the learning experiences, detailed information about it may persist, unerased and activatable, because of the multiple links that are established in memory. For instance, details of a traumatic surgical experience which interfered with normal learning and development may persist unerased in part because of the meaningfulness of the event, its association with pain, anxiety, multiple fantasies, and so on.

To return to the examples of normal walking and the concept of apple, here we can see how past "somethings" influence present behavior or ideation without necessarily being in the realm of awareness or available to awareness. And these are the very conditions clinically associated with the idea of "repressed motivations."

In general, we are suggesting that *selected* information from the past, in both normal and pathological learning, will be present in any program at any given moment and will in great part determine the nature of the corresponding behavior or subjective psychological experience. One can make reconstructions about the actual detailed past learning experiences on the basis of this information, just as an orthopedist may reconstruct the past disease process from a diseased limb currently under observation. This selected information can be said to represent "repressed motivation" in the clinical sense.

Detailed information about the past learning experiences—normal and pathological—may or may not be present and retrievable for processes associated with awareness. Detailed information about such events which is not directly retrievable for processes associated with awareness (and one can suggest many reasons for this—the association with extreme pain and anxiety, for instance) can also be part of the "repressed motivations" if it enters into the programming associated with current experience. As we all know, such detailed information is often present and retrievable for processes associated with awareness, and when this occurs one has a very important source of information for use in reconstructing the past. Here there are no true analogies in other realms of biology. A very fanciful analogous situation would be if an orthopedist were able to turn back the clock and "replay" in some form the record of a diseased limb, viewing the normal limb as it goes through the disease experience which determined its subsequent pathology. And even this analogy is far from satisfactory.

Returning now to the specific example of the patient who did not wish to look like a Jew, Figure 12 outlines in skeletal fashion the memory structure that gives the nodal term "Jew" its meanings. As already mentioned, for this patient the term "Jew" had unique personal connotative meanings. It meant someone who dies, rots, and is eaten by worms. These classifications emerged from a host of experiences; they represent highly selected information, selected in part from experiences involving his dead grandmother and in part from earlier traumatic experiences. The developmental line here is also discernible. In general,

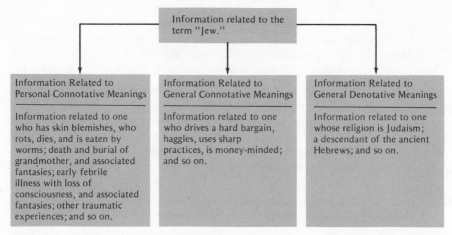

Figure 12. Schematic memory organization related to meaning of term "Jew."

every event is interpreted or takes on meaning in terms of the existing information-processing programs and existing memory, and these, in turn, are based on
selected information from the past. The death of the grandmother therefore took
on meaning or was interpreted in terms of what had been selected from previous
traumatic episodes—the loss of consciousness (his "death"), the vomiting, the
loss of bowel control, and so on.[28] When the patient learned the term "Jew" it
too was interpreted and took on meaning in terms of information selected from
all previous experiences—the death of the grandmother and the earlier traumatic
events, including fantasy elaborations of them.

In brief, in any ongoing life process, in any learning experience, new information is "assimilated to existing schemas," to use the language of Piaget;
new information is processed in terms of existing programs and classifications
which represent selected information from the past. And the current learning
experience is, in turn, subject to selections, resulting in some modification of
existing programs and classifications. As a result of this evolving process, pro-
gressively more complex memory organizations and programming capabilities
emerge. More complex motivations and new levels of meaning are now discernible in any given phenomenon.

In the case of the patient who did not wish to look like a Jew, we are suggesting that selected information from the past existed, determined the meaning of the idea "Jew," and was involved in many motivational phenomena. This
selected information can be said to represent "repressed motivations." Also in
this case, detailed information about the past pathogenic experiences existed in
two forms. First, the patient could easily recall many details about the burial of
his grandmother and his reactions to that event. And second, interestingly
enough, some details of the early febrile illness emerged in direct bodily form
during the analytic experience. For example, while on the couch the patient at

[28] Clinicians will recognize this case report as oversimplified. The reconstruction
of the early febrile illness was confirmed on inquiry of the parents. But it was strongly
suspected that there were other, multiple early traumata which for the most part were
not understood or worked out.

times experienced the urge to vomit uncontrollably and to curl up in the manner of a very ill child.

In this case a reconstruction was made in part in the manner of an ortho-pedist looking at an existing diseased limb—the end product of a disease process; and in part in a manner that is unique to psychoanalysis. Thus, the patient's anxiety about dying, his ever-present fear of "fading out like a dot on a tele-vision screen," and other such phenomena, suggested to the analyst that the patient might once have experienced some traumatic event or events involving a loss of consciousness. Here the analyst was attempting to reconstruct the past using information from the current existing pathological picture, the selected end product of a disease process, and information from his general knowledge and experience, in the manner of an orthopedist who reconstructs the past when viewing a diseased limb. But the information provided by his apparent reliving of some of the details of the early febrile illness was also used in the reconstruction. Here the analyst had a unique opportunity to observe what ap-peared to be a direct "replay" of parts of an early trauma.[29]

I. ARE INFORMATION-PROCESSING MODELS DEHUMANIZING?

In recent years, in our attempt to bring information-processing models to the attention of psychoanalysts, we have found that all too often they are rejected almost automatically. Some colleagues consider them to be "reductionistic," "mechanistic," "dehumanizing," "nothing but analogies." "Information models," these colleagues say, "lose the very qualities that we associate with being human." Such automatic objections generally greet efforts to conceptualize emotional phenomena in information terms; there is less automatic objection to attempts to conceptualize cognitive processes in information terms although, here too, a comparison of thought processes to the activities of a cold machine seems to

---

[29] Again, we have oversimplified to make our points. The two forms of detailed memory are different, and one may ask many questions about them. For example, when the patient recounts the details of his grandmother's death and burial and his reactions to these events, are we truly getting details of the events at the time as experienced by the child, or are we getting some subsequent reinterpretation of those events, perhaps "reworked" many times over? We tend to believe the latter (Peterfreund, 1971, p. 214). Memories of old events are probably "reworked" many times over and thereby acquire new meanings depending on the then-operating information-processing programs. In general, we tend to agree with Freud when he wrote (1899, p. 322): "It may indeed be questioned whether we have any memories at all *from* our childhood: memories *re-lating* to our childhood may be all that we possess."

In regard to this patient, it seems reasonable to suggest that what he tells us about his grandmother's death and burial represents aspects of the *detailed* record of this experience only as this *detailed record now exists*. The early detailed memory has probably been "revised" and reinterpreted in many ways. In contrast, the personal connotative meanings of the term "Jew" represent only specially *selected* information from the early pathogenic events. One gets no detailed picture of any sort, "reworked" or not "reworked," "revised" or not "revised," directly from this information alone. To use this selected information to reconstruct a detailed picture, a great deal of addi-tional information and processing would be necessary. The memories that emerged in bodily form, seen in this patient and at times in other patients with early traumatic his-tories, appear to be relatively undistorted, unreworked, direct "replays" of some part of the past febrile illness.

violate something that we all hold dear. It may be helpful to close this paper with a few general remarks which may help place some of the issues in perspective.

Scientific explanations attempt to make useful generalizations concerning the phenomena of observation. And, as already discussed, it is absolutely essential to distinguish between (1) observable clinical phenomena and the clinical language (including the language of persons) used to describe them; (2) empirical generalizations about these phenomena; (3) more abstract levels of explanation. Each level may have its own vocabulary; each level has its place in scientific thinking. Higher levels of theory (e.g., statements concerning abstract information models of memory or of the genetic code) tend to move away from the specific data of observation and therefore tend to seem dehumanized; they are generally expressed in language that differs from the language used to describe human experience. This apparent dehumanizing is of necessity the case; it is inherent in theory building because higher-level generalizations encompass a much wider world than the immediate data of observation. But even the most abstract theory, if it is a meaningful one, can be linked to the specific phenomena that we observe. Appreciating the glories of a sunset is not inconsistent with an electromagnetic theory about this phenomenon. Similarly, to feel and sense a patient's anguish, joy, depression, or sadness is not at all inconsistent with information-processing explanations of such phenomena.

About the problem of artificial information-processing systems and their relationship to psychological phenomena, a few remarks may be helpful.

Certainly no artificial information-processing system has an "experience" of thinking or feeling in any way similar to that of human beings. Artificial information-processing systems (computers, for example) are not alive. But it is our point of view that an understanding of such systems may provide elementary models or theories or a frame of reference to begin to explain psychological experience, just as at one time the very simple mechanical pump provided an elementary model of the heart, an organ once as mysterious and as unfathomable as the brain appears to be at the present time. Artificial information-processing systems will not have experiences of thinking, or feeling, or of being motivated in the manner of human beings until life itself is synthesized and until the information of eons of evolutionary time is built into such systems. And then such systems will be "artificial" in only a very limited sense.

Those who advance information-processing models are not saying that the brain is nothing but a simple computer comparable to existing computers. Such a statement is a patent absurdity. Nor are they saying that a human being is nothing but an information-processing system. This statement would be ridiculous "reductionism," because a human being is many things. Those who propose information-processing models are suggesting that it is extremely useful, scientifically, to approach the central nervous system as a member of the class of information-processing systems, a class of which the computer and other systems are members. Knowledge about one system of the class may help to explain the function of other members of the class. The central nervous system, as one of the class of information-processing systems, is not necessarily the same as other members of the class. It is obviously infinitely more complex than any existing artificial information-processing system and may well operate on some basically different principles.

The above general theoretical approach has been successfully used in many other branches of science, in cardiology, for example, as we have already mentioned. Physiologists do not take a "reductionistic" attitude toward the heart and say that it is nothing but a simple pump. They do not even say that it is the same as any existing pump. The heart is thought of as one of the class of pumps. But it is also one of the class of living systems, electrical systems, chemical systems.

And, we wish to add, it is meaningless to dismiss a theory on the ground that it is "merely an anology." All theories are "merely" analogies. All models or mathematical equations for natural phenomena are "merely" analogies. The question is not: Is a theory an analogy or not an analogy? The true scientific question is: How accurate is the analogy; does it help us understand, predict, and explain? Does it have heuristic value and open up new avenues for exploration? Does it link and relate the observed phenomena to other phenomena?

Information-processing models are models or theories, nothing else. And all of us accept this general approach in innumerable branches of science. None of us automatically object to the idea that fatigue may be explained in terms of thyroid function values. The physiologists who propose such ideas are not saying that there are no other explanations for fatigue, or that one can use a thyroid function value as a substitute for the feeling of fatigue, or as a substitute for a clinical description of this experience. Not at all! People feel fatigue; theoretical concepts do not. The term "fatigue" is a clinical term that refers to human experience. A mathematical value for thyroid function is only a mathematical expression for one theoretical idea concerning the psychological experience of fatigue. Similarly, an information-processing program is only one quasi-mathematical expression of one theoretical approach to human psychological experience.

In general, we have learned to use all of the attributes of artificial systems —electrical, chemical, mathematical—and all of the known natural physical laws to help us understand the biology of the human organism. Vitalism (the thesis that life cannot be understood in terms of natural law and which invokes mysterious "vital forces" to explain natural phenomena) has done nothing throughout history but obstruct the progress of science.[30] Those who propose information-processing models to explain motivation, emotion, and cognition may perhaps not be proposing accurate theories, but certainly they are working in the tradition that has led to the major advances in biology and medicine in the past several centuries.

It may comfort those who are disturbed by information-processing models for human psychological processes to recognize that in the ultimate sense there is only one world. It is rather questionable whether an easy distinction can be

---

[30] Vitalism is a basic characteristic of current psychoanalytic theory. The concept of psychic energy, for example, is essentially a vitalistic one (Holt, 1967; Peterfreund, 1971).

made between animate and inanimate, artificial and natural, human and sub-human. After all, the concepts which we use to understand the world—electrical, chemical, mathematical—are human creations. They reflect the way human beings view the world. A mouse does not recognize the word "mouse," cannot describe the members of his class, and cannot understand his place in evolutionary history. To attempt to conceptualize the mind in terms of concepts created by human beings is hardly dehumanizing. For us, it seems dehumanizing not to use the most advanced creations of the human mind to attempt to explain the mind itself.

REFERENCES

Adler, I. (1962). *Thinking Machines.* New York: New American Library.
Bowlby, J. (1969). *Attachment and Loss,* Vol. 1: *Attachment.* New York: Basic Books.
Cherry, C. (1966). *On Human Communication,* 2nd ed. Cambridge, Mass.: M.I.T. Press.
Cofer, C. N., and Appley, M. H. (1964). *Motivation.* New York: Wiley.
Davidson, C. H., and Koenig, E. C. (1967). *Computers.* New York: Wiley.
Fink, D. G. (1966). *Computers and the Human Mind.* Garden City: Anchor Books.
Freud, S. (1899). Screen Memories. *Standard Edition,* 3:303–322. London: Hogarth Press, 1962.
———— (1914). On Narcissism: An Introduction. *Standard Edition,* 14:73–102. London: Hogarth Press, 1957.
———— (1915). Instincts and Their Vicissitudes. *Standard Edition,* 14:109–140. London: Hogarth Press, 1957.
Holt, R. R. (1967). Beyond Vitalism and Mechanism: Freud's Concept of Psychic Energy. In: *Science and Psychoanalysis,* ed. J. H. Masserman, 11:1–41. New York: Grune and Stratton.
Klein, G. S. (1967). Peremptory Ideation: Structure and Force in Motivated Ideas: In: Motives and Thought: Psychoanalytic Essays in Honor of David Rapaport, ed. R. R. Holt. *Psychological Issues,* Monograph 18/19:80–128. New York: International Univerties Press.
Langer, S. K. (1967). *Mind: An Essay on Human Feeling,* Vol. 1. Baltimore: Johns Hopkins Press.
Murphy, J. S. (1970). *Basics of Digital Computers,* 2nd ed. New York: Hayden Book.
Neisser, U. (1967). *Cognitive Psychology.* New York: Appleton-Century-Crofts.
Norman, D. A. (1968). Toward a Theory of Memory and Attention. *Psychological Review,* 75:522–536.
———— (1969). *Memory and Attention.* New York: Wiley.
Peterfreund, E. (1971). *Information, Systems, and Psychoanalysis.* New York: International Universities Press.
Rapaport, D. (1960). On the Psychoanalytic Theory of Motivation. In: *Nebraska Symposium on Motivation, 1960,* ed. M. R. Jones. Lincoln: University of Nebraska Press, pp. 173–247.
Simon, H. A. (1967). Motivational and Emotional Controls of Cognition. *Psychological Review,* 74:29–39.
Staddon, J. E. R. (1971). Darwin Explained: An Object Lesson in Theory Construction; Review of *The Triumph of the Darwinian Method,* by M. T. Ghiselin. *Contemporary Psychology,* 16:689–691.
Taylor, D. W. (1960). Toward an Information Processing Theory of Motivation. In: *Nebraska Symposium on Motivation, 1960,* ed. M. R. Jones. Lincoln: University of Nebraska Press, pp. 51–79.
Wooldridge, D. E. (1968). *Mechanical Man.* New York: McGraw-Hill.

6

ISSUES IN THE PHILOSOPHY OF PSYCHOANALYSIS

VALIDATION OF MOTIVATIONAL FORMULATIONS
Acknowledgment as a Criterion

Morris Eagle, Ph.D.

This paper deals with certain conceptual problems inhering in motivational formulations and explanations. It is particularly concerned with problems of validation (or falsification) of motivational formulations and attributions and the nature of the terms and concepts employed in such formulations.

Questions such as "Why did he do that?," "Why did he experience that?," and "Why did he show such and such a symptom?," and answers in terms of motives, purposes, and wants play an important role both in ordinary discourse and in psychoanalytic explanations. How does one validate or falsify such motivational accounts and attributions? This is a particularly important question for psychoanalytic theory and psychoanalytically influenced "dynamic" psychologies, for without some reliable and systematic means of validation, it is difficult to see on what formal basis motivational accounts in psychoanalytic theory can be distinguished from ordinary discourse—that is, can claim scientific status. Certainly the claim cannot rest on the distinction that psychoanalytic explanations are concerned with unconscious motivation, whereas ordinary discourse deals with conscious motives. In either case, one is still left with the question of how the motivational explanation is validated or falsified.

Recently, a number of philosophers and psychoanalysts have attempted to deal with the problem of the nature of motivational accounts in psychoanalytic formulations and the criteria employed in evaluating these accounts (e.g., Sherwood, 1969; Home, 1966; Farrell, 1964; Mischel, 1963, 1966). Different criteria have been suggested by the different authors. In this paper I will describe and evaluate critically the proposal offered by Mischel.

In some recent papers, Mischel (1963, 1966) has proposed that for explanations in terms of an agent's intentions and motives the agent's own acknowledgment or avowal of the motive attributed to him is an essential criterion for establishing the validity of the explanation. The following quotations show that Mischel believes avowal to be a critical criterion in ordinary situations as well as in psychoanalytic interpretations dealing with unconscious intentions and unconscious motives:

> The analyst's explanations (interpretations of behavior in terms of his patient's "unconscious intentions") can, I think, be regarded as extensions of our ordinary explanations. . . . They explain the neurotic's actions by attributing "repressed desires" and "unconscious intentions" to him. . . . In such cases, though the agent sincerely denies that he was committed to a certain rule of conduct, or that what he did (or desired) can be described as X, the clinician . . . claims that he is deceiving himself. Such explanations are still in terms of the agent's intentions (in a widened sense), because it is essential to their correctness that the agent, without being conscious of it, really followed this rule, really intended (or desired) X. If the clinician is right, then the agent must, at least ideally and in the long run, come to acknowledge that, though he did not know it at the time, he really was committed to this rule, this really was the description which the action (or desire) had for him. The neurotic's irrational actions are thus explained by showing that he really did intend them—from his distorted "point of view" they were the "thing to do" (1966, p. 55).

> And when the analyst proceeds to ascribe an "unconscious motive" to the patient, though the latter's denial of this motive does not overthrow the analyst's interpretation, if the interpretation is correct it is expected that the patient will, at least ideally, come to agree with it in the end . . . (1963, p. 590).

I will try to show that neither in ordinary social life nor in psychoanalytic theory or practice is the agent's acknowledgment an indispensable criterion for establishing or evaluating a motivational explanation; and, further, that the nature of the concept of motive (as well as the nature of motivational explanations and attributions) does not require that the agent's acknowledgment be given a privileged status. Rather, it is only one of a number of possible criteria. I will also try to show that Mischel's insistence on acknowledgment as an essential criterion for the correctness of a motivational explanation is based on a misapprehension about the concept of motive as well as a misapprehension about the logic of how motivational explanations and attributions are used and verified in psychoanalysis.

Outside the psychoanalytic context, there are many instances in ordinary social life in which the agent's acknowledgment is not a critical criterion for judging the correctness of a motivational explanation. Consider the case of someone who is accused of a murder, denies the accusation, and avows the more acceptable motive of self-defense. Certainly avowal is not given any privileged status in such an instance. We recognize that the person has too much to lose by acknowledging the attributed motive and too much to gain by avowing the self-defense motive. We would make a judgment about his motives by taking into account knowledge of the action, of the circumstances in which the action took place, and of the person's character and history. His failure to acknowledge the attributed motive would play little part in our judgment of the motive for the crime. We recognize not only that the person may be lying to others, but that he may come to deceive himself about his motives. And, considering the stakes involved, it is entirely possible that under no circumstances—that is, neither "ideally" nor "in the long run"—will the accused come to acknowledge the motive attributed to him.

We also recognize, in less extreme circumstances, that in general people may disown unflattering motives and avow flattering ones. Precisely such observations—that one can deceive oneself about one's own motives—form the basis for the more radical idea of unconscious motives, as Flew (1956) points out. And, of course, when one is speaking of unconscious motives, the very definition of the concept would lead one to *expect* denial of attributed motives. (The whole question of defense and resistance enters here.) Contrary to Mischel's claim, in actual practice therapists do not necessarily interpret disavowal as evidence of the incorrectness of their interpretation or attribution, nor do they necessarily accept avowal as evidence of correctness. In fact, the opposite is often the case. A therapist may take passionate disavowal as evidence for the truth of his interpretation, and give bland, intellectualized avowal little importance. Thus acknowledgment is not necessarily used as an indispensable criterion for interpretive validity. It is only one of a number of criteria, and the weight assigned to it will depend upon a variety of other factors including the circumstances and nature of the acknowledgment and its congruence with other criteria.

The issue of insight is relevant here. Certain kinds of acknowledgment, in certain circumstances, may be taken as evidence of the patient's insight, that is, as evidence that the patient has understood some important things about himself and is willing and able to confront certain aspects of himself.

The ability to experience such self-confrontation is taken as a sign of increasing growth and strength. But if this description of the meaning of insightful avowal in psychoanalysis is accurate, it is clear that avowal *cannot* be a criterion of interpretive validity. For, if insightful avowal is a sign of such self-confrontation ability, and if increasing ability to experience self-confrontation is evidence of therapeutic improvement, it is clearly, although tacitly, assumed that the truth about the patient has been independently determined by the analyst, and that the patient's avowal is merely a clinical sign of his ability to accept this independently determined truth. Here we see sharply a logical difficulty with avowal as a criterion. How can it serve both as a sign of ability to face the truth about oneself and as a criterion of that truth?

The fact is that psychoanalysis, correctly or mistakenly, does *not* stress avowal as a criterion of validity, neither in theory (i.e., the role assigned to unconscious motives) nor in practice. The kernel of truth in Mischel's notion of "ideal" acknowledgment lies in the fact that probably every therapist would like his patient, at some time before he finishes his therapy, to be able to avow about himself what he could not avow when he entered therapy. But, as I have already noted, this consideration does not make avowal a criterion of validity. For insofar as the therapist makes judgments about the validity of his interpretations at least somewhat independently of the patient's acknowledgment, he is clearly relying on evidence other than the patient's acknowledgment. And it is, indeed, important to rely on other kinds of evidence. For, as Wittgenstein (1967) pointed out (with regard to dream interpretation, but it is applicable here too), even sincere avowal may entitle us to speak, not of the truth or validity of an interpretation, but only of its persuasiveness or "believableness." The particular problem of suggestibility inherent in the therapeutic and many other situations further highlights the issue of persuasiveness.

It seems clear, then, that we need criteria for judging the adequacy of the very criterion of acknowledgment itself. It does not help to say, as Mischel (1966) does, that in a clinical situation (and, presumably, also in other situations) the patient's avowal "ideally" or "in the long run" is the main criterion for the validity of an interpretation. What are the criteria for "ideal" circumstances and what is the time limit for the "long run"?

The point is not that acknowledgment cannot serve at all as a criterion, but that it has no privileged logical status. It is one of many possible criteria and, as noted earlier, its usefulness depends upon a variety of factors including its agreement with other kinds of evidence.

Mischel's position involves another difficulty, which is that acknowledgment can have a variety of meanings. If it means that the interpretation was intelligible—a kind of "Yes, that makes sense" response [1]—it is not clear why it would serve any special role as a criterion of validity. For why should the agent's acknowledgment that an interpretation was intelligible or made sense be more critical for the validity of the interpretation than anyone else's judgment? The interpretation may be more important to the agent in a broad *therapeutic* way— that is, it may (or may not) help him see things in a new way or make connections between events of his life that he could not make before. But the judgment that a given interpretive formulation makes sense or is intelligible can be made by anyone presented with certain evidence. Implicit in the position Mischel gives to acknowledgment is the idea that it means, not simply any kind of agreement, but something of the order of "Yes, that is what I was (or am) really intending, wanting, experiencing." In other words, acknowledgment could conceivably constitute a privileged criterion only if it meant that the agent was acknowledging his own *experiences*—that is, was experiencing such contents as intentions, impulses, wishes, urgings, memories, etc., which were hitherto unavailable because they were kept from awareness by repression and other defenses. Mischel is relying on the psychoanalytic formulation that when repressions are lifted and the unconscious is made conscious, impulses, wishes, early memories, etc., that were out of awareness are now consciously experienced.

Even if, however, one accepts the above psychoanalytic formulation, it does not follow that the agent's acknowledgment is necessary before one can consider an interpretation valid. First, because of the status of his defenses, the agent

---

[1] Although I am not aware of any empirical research on the matter, my impression is that quite frequently in psychotherapy this is precisely what the patient's acknowledgment of an interpretation means.

may never experience the unconscious contents attributed to him. Second, interpretive inferences about unconscious motives, wishes, etc., can (and should) be evaluated on the basis of other criteria (e.g., prediction of subsequent behavior, symptoms, associations) which have little to do with acknowledgment defined either as agreement or as conscious experience of attributed unconscious contents. If one makes inferences about certain unconscious motives on the basis of a person's verbalizations, behavior, symptoms, and developmental history, the validity of the inferences certainly does not depend ultimately on the person's avowal or acknowledgment. Further, one can attempt to determine the degree of consensus from others who have access to the same evidence. Let us assume that the inference elicits wide intersubjective agreement and permits prediction of other behavior and symptoms. Would one still want to say, as Mischel is saying, that without the agent's acknowledgment of the attribution, one could not consider the inference valid?

To take a concrete case, let us suppose that Freud's interpretation that Dora was unconsciously in love with Frau K. elicited wide consensus and permitted prediction of Dora's subsequent dreams, behavior, symptoms, etc. Would Dora's acknowledgment (which was not forthcoming) be necessary before one could evaluate the validity of the interpretation? It should also be noted that outside the therapeutic situation there are instances when one cannot possibly obtain the agent's acknowledgment because the agent is not available either to deny or to avow the attributions and interpretations. A classic example is Freud's analysis of the Schreber case. Again, if there is consensus that the formulation fits the data and if it permits testable empirical assertions, would one nevertheless insist that the agent's acknowledgment is indispensable in evaluating the formulation?

It seems to me that even the clear report by the agent of conscious experience of attributed unconscious contents has the same status as other data (behavior, symptoms). That is, the ability to predict the occasions and kinds of previously unconscious contents that will be consciously experienced is one indicator, among many, that one's inferences about unconscious motives are correct. Conscious experience of previously unconscious contents may be an especially important *therapeutic* indicator, but I do not believe that it should have any special status as a criterion of validity.[2] Successful prediction of symp-

---

[2] A particular problem mentioned by Wittgenstein (1967) must be considered in evaluating reports of conscious experience of presumably hitherto repressed impulses, wishes, etc. As noted earlier, if a patient finds an interpretation sufficiently persuasive or believable, he may, indeed, experience the wishes and impulses attributed to him in that interpretation. But it would be difficult to say whether we are dealing with conscious experience of previously repressed material or simply suggestibility. Empirical studies need to be carried out in which the nature of repressed contents is inferred on the basis of certain kinds of observable evidence (e.g., symptoms, behavior patterns, associations, dreams) and predictions are made about the specific conditions under which these repressed contents will be consciously experienced. Within the context of psychoanalytic theory, the variable that is likely to be most relevant to such predictions is the status of the person's defenses. Such studies would, of course, be circular unless defense was successfully measured independently of whether or not the presumably repressed contents were in awareness. One could attempt to guard against the methodo-

toms, associations, behavior patterns, etc., would be as important in assessing the validity of inferences about unconscious motives as successful prediction of acknowledgment or experience.[3]

Although Mischel does not explicitly say so, it seems clear that the philosophical basis for the importance he gives to acknowledgment is his understanding of motive and intention as essentially *experiential* concepts. Implicit in his argument is the idea that when one makes an inference about X's unconscious motives, one is saying something only or mainly about X's potential ("in the long run") experiences—that is, what X would experience (know, be aware of) were it not for resistance, defense, and other barriers to experience. The fact is, however, that a statement about unconscious motives is also saying something about what X will do, what he will say and dream, what symptoms he will show, and a variety of other things. It may well be that a critical *therapeutic aim*, as well as the main process by which other changes are effected in psychoanalysis, has to do with experiencing, being aware of, knowing (making the unconscious conscious). But, of course, it does not therefore follow that only what X experiences or acknowledges is relevant to evaluating inferences or interpretations about unconscious motives.

For if terms like intention and motive always referred to experience (in the way that pain, for example, does), the agent would indeed have—to borrow a term from Ryle (1949)—"privileged access" to his intentions and motives. And, in turn, Mischel's insistence that the agent must acknowledge a motivational attribution before it is considered correct would seem quite reasonable. But if one's motives, strivings, and desires were always conscious experiences and one therefore always had "privileged access" to them, self-knowledge would be a "natural" and inevitable condition which could be taken for granted, instead of the goal of a lifelong quest, which is, at best, only partly achieved.

It is clear that statements about motives and intentions are not like statements about being in pain or having an itch. The former do not necessarily refer to sensations directly given in phenomenal experience. If they did, it would make little sense to talk about self-deception in connection with one's motives, or about unconscious motives—as little sense as it generally makes to talk about self-deception or the unconscious in regard to pains and itches. That we do use such terms as "self-deception" and "unconscious" in regard to motives, in-

---

logical problem of suggestibility or "persuasiveness" by a number of expedients. One example is keeping the interpretation "silent"—that is, not imparting to the subject one's inferences or interpretations about his unconscious motives, wishes, etc.—and nevertheless predicting the conditions under which this material will (and will not) be consciously experienced by the subject. What such studies would imply is that one has made a successful effort to define and measure defense and resistance and to predict the conditions under which defense will and will not block conscious experience and other expressions of presumably unconscious material.

[3] It should be noted that an open-ended prediction of acknowledgment "ideally" or "in the long run" is not very useful in evaluating interpretations and inferences. It would be more meaningful to predict acknowledgment and other behavior in the specific context of the relationship between defense on the one hand and impulses and wishes on the other.

tentions, and desires clearly implies that the latter have a broader reference than conscious experience. It is the peculiar character of terms like want, desire, and particularly motive that they are used in more than one way.

Terms like want and desire are of course used to refer to direct experiences like consciously felt urgings and impulses, and in such cases one probably is entitled to talk about "privileged access." And it is true that insofar as one has one's own experiences and knows what one is doing, one has the advantage of greater familiarity with the relevant data for knowing one's own motives and wants. But this advantage is often more than offset by the blindness that results from the vested interest one has in maintaining a particular self-image and in warding off the anxiety that would follow from certain awarenesses. It is in such situations that we speak of the agent's not knowing what he wants and of self-deception. And these terms clearly imply the *absence* of direct experience, "privileged access," and the primacy of acknowledgment and avowal. For, particularly in the context of self-deception, we accept the likelihood that, if you are wise and experienced and a good observer and know me well, you may be in a better position than I am to know what I unconsciously want and what my motives are. This likelihood was accepted long before the introduction of Freudian concepts like unconscious wish or motive.

Mischel is obviously aware of the problem presented by the fact that, by definition, unconscious motives and motives about which one deceives oneself are neither consciously experienced nor available in awareness. But because "such explanations are still in terms of the agent's intentions (in a widened sense)," he insists on the agent's acknowledgment, even if only "ideally" or "in the long run." The words "ideally" and "in the long run" reflect Mischel's approach to the problem: that is, although the agent cannot experience his unconscious motives and intentions *now* (in fact, as Mischel recognizes, the agent may vehemently deny the attributed motives), because we are still talking about motives and intentions, even if in "a widened sense," the agent must at some point or other come to acknowledge the attributions and explanations if they are to be considered correct. What Mischel neglects is the conceptual nature of the "widened sense" in which motives and intentions are used when they are prefixed by the term "unconscious." As Flew (1956) points out, this is the critical philosophical problem presented by the psychoanalytic extention of ordinary concepts and is the problem that requires critical examination. An analysis of the "widened sense" may indicate that some properties of (some) ordinary motives and intentions—"privileged access" and the necessity of acknowledgment, for example—are not properties of unconscious motives and intentions or motives and intentions about which one deceives oneself. One cannot simply assume, as Mischel appears to do, that everything which applies to ordinary motives and intentions applies to unconscious motives and intentions, albeit in a delayed or "long-run" way.

Such an assumption involves a curious paradox. That is, the importance of the agent's acknowledgment is based on the assumption that one's own motives and intentions are the kinds of things one is in the best position to know and experience. But if one's *unconscious* motives and intentions, are, by definition, the kinds of things one is *not* in the best position to know and experience, then why insist on acknowledgment when the very basis for this insistence—namely, that one is in the best position to know and experience one's own motives and intentions—has been removed and does not apply? The argument that unconscious motives and intentions, when brought to awareness, function in essentially the same way as conscious motives and intentions does not resolve the paradox. For, as noted earlier, even if one accepts this argument, it does not logically require the agent's acknowledgment as a necessary criterion for the validity of interpretations regarding the "presence" of unconscious motives.

Mischel's treatment of the problem involves still another difficulty. He states that while the agent's acknowledgment is necessary for an interpretation to be considered correct, the agent's denial (that is, nonacknowledgment) "does not overthrow the analyst's interpretation" (ascribing an unconscious motive to the patient). What is being proposed here is that the agent's acknowledgment is a criterion for the validity of an attribution of unconscious motives, but that the agent's denial is *not* a criterion for the *invalidity* of the attribution. As proposed by Mischel, this proposition is of the "Heads I win, tails you lose" kind, and is of the kind that justifies Popper's (1963) criticism that psychoanalytic interpretations are nonempirical because they cannot be refuted. Mischel's formulation comes dangerously close to implying that certain psychoanalytic interpretations can only be confirmed, never disconfirmed or falsified. In Mischel's formulation, the weakest status an interpretation could logically have is that of being in a "suspended" state—that is, neither confirmed nor disconfirmed. That would be the situation when an interpretation is not acknowledged by the agent. Since, for Mischel, acknowledgment is necessary for validation "ideally" or "in the long run," the interpretation would be "not yet" validated. But since the interpretation is not "overthrown" by nonacknowledgment or denial, neither would it be falsified. Hence, it would be in what I have called a "suspended" state—awaiting validation through acknowledgment. But—and this is a critical point—if one accepted Mischel's formulation, the interpretation could only await validation, not falsification.[4]

These difficulties arise because Mischel insists on acknowledgment as a critical criterion for validating an interpretation and does not indicate the kind of evidence that would invalidate an interpretation. They would not arise if one accepted, for psychoanalytic inferences, the same means that are employed in evaluating any hypothesis or inference—that is, a determination of the degree to which what is, according to the inference, supposed to happen empirically does happen.

It seems to me that the only way one could escape Popper's (1963) criti-

[4] I am aware that the issue of falsification is a complex one and that there is much debate about the general question of evaluation of hypotheses and theories. But I think that, without getting involved in the complexity of that debate, one can recognize the inadequacy of an approach to interpretations that makes provision only for acceptance or "delayed" acceptance and not for rejection, even if the acceptance or rejection is made, as indeed it must be, on a probabilistic basis.

cism would be by attempting to define the conditions under which psychoanalytic interpretations would be rejected or would be assigned a low probability. Denial and nonacknowledgment do not, according to Mischel, constitute such a condition. But he offers no suggestions about what would falsify or "overthrow" an interpretation.

In the last few paragraphs I have been discussing the difficulties involved in Mischel's criterion for validating interpretations. But I would stress again that the basic difficulty in Mischel's formulation is his implicit treatment of motivational terms in general as referring to contents of conscious experience to which we therefore have "privileged access." And, as I have argued, even without taking into consideration the psychoanalytic concepts of repression and the unconscious, the possibility of talking about someone's not knowing what he wants and about self-deception indicates that motivational terms are "broad spectrum" concepts that refer to more than conscious experience.

There are, of course, many occasions when I experience what I want directly and immediately, and there are occasions when only I may know what my motives are (I may be withholding or lying, for example). In these instances, one can, with good sense, speak of privileged access. But there are also many occasions when, because I do not know what I want or because I am deceiving myself, others may be in a better position than I am to judge my wants and motives. Are we, therefore, to speak of the observer's "privileged access"?

If the quality and circumstances of A's action and knowledge of A's character and history lead an observer to conclude that A has deceived himself about his motives, intentions, wishes, is A's asknowledgment necessary for that judgment to be valid? If self-interest (including self-esteem) is sufficiently involved and if A's capacity and willingness for self-confrontation are limited, A may never be able to acknowledge the motive attributed to him—even when his attention is called to the same things that led the outside observer to make his judgment.[5] In view of these considerations, what sense is there is saying that the validity of the motivational judgment depends ultimately or "in the long run" upon A's acknowledgment?

To put it somewhat differently, it is possible to act (or to reveal by quasi acts such as symptoms) as if one wanted Y and yet sincerely deny that one wants Y (that is, experiences wanting Y). But if one is observed to be behaving as if one wanted or intended Y or, to use Mischel's rule terminology, as if one were following rule Y, then one is behaving in that way. It does not require the

---

[5] I have not used the term "defense" in the above discussion because broader and more general processes than defense may be involved in self-deception and failure to acknowledge motives. There are instances that one would describe as self-deception which simply do not fit the psychoanalytic model of defense. Technically, defense refers to inner impulses. One can, however, deceive oneself about the meaning of certain events, about one's behavior patterns, one's character traits, intentions, etc. What is so difficult (and interesting) about a concept like self-deception is that it cannot be described either simply in terms of the operation of unconscious defense (although defense may be involved) or in terms of conscious withholding or lying. A fuller treatment of this issue is beyond the scope of this paper. Fingarette (1969) has discussed this issue.

agent's acknowledgment to make that observation. His acknowledgment or denial will not change the judgment that he was behaving in that way or following a particular rule.[6] That is, insofar as behavior is purposive, motives and wants are immanent in one's acts, whether or not these motives and wants are consciously experienced or in awareness. Motives, intentions, and wants are broad constructs which can be at least as legitimately inferred from behavior as from the agent's acknowledgment and reports of his experiences. Essentially, this is so because behavior is striving and purposive and has intentionality even without (and often despite) conscious purposes, plans, wants, and motives.[7]

As Allston (1967) suggests, it makes more sense to treat such terms as wants and motives as constructs which are manifested in and inferred from experience, behavior, thought (and, I would add, physiological indices). If it were not so cumbersome, it would be more accurate to attach subscripts to terms like motive, want, and intention: i.e., $want_E$ would refer to a want that is consciously experienced (and reported), and $want_A$ would refer to a want that is revealed in action without necessarily being consciously experienced as an urging or feeling.

In summary, then, I have tried to show that the agent's acknowledgment is not a logically privileged or indispensable criterion for validating a motivational formulation. Indeed, the very basis for stressing the primacy of the agent's acknowledgment involves confusion about the nature and role of motivational concepts. The agent's acknowledgment is, rather, only one of many possible criteria available for evaluating such formulations.

[6] I have tried to argue in this paper against the most convincing form of Mischel's position, that is, acknowledgment defined as acceptance or experience of one's motives, intentions, wishes, etc. But when one talks about formulations of what rules one is following, it is especially difficult to see why acknowledgment is essential as a criterion of validity—why "If the clinician is right, then the agent must . . . come to acknowledge that, though he did not know it at the time, he really was committed to this rule . . ." It is clear that in learning and using a language, for example, we follow extraordinarily complex rules which we do not and, if Chomsky is correct, cannot know or acknowledge. But we nevertheless formulate the kinds of rules an agent is following in using a language and evaluate these formulations independent of whether or not the agent can acknowledge them.

Again, Mischel seems to confuse therapeutic considerations with those involved in evaluating formulations and inferences. Thus, in a clinical situation, it may be important *therapeutically* for the agent to acknowledge that his behavior could be described as following such and such a rule. But, as noted above, it does not follow that acknowledgment is necessary to validate or legitimize the description. Whether or not the rule-following description is an accurate one and whether or not it has heuristic value can be judged quite independently of the agent's acknowledgment.

[7] It is this kind of consideration that makes the Freudian idea of the unconscious seem less radical and arbitrary and more continuous with earlier commonsensical ideas and observations. (Or, to put it conversely, it is this kind of consideration that makes motivational formulations susceptible to Freudian formulations.) For insofar as we can be ignorant of and self-deceptive about our motives, wants, and desires, they cannot be equated with conscious mental life. Some concept similar to Freud's unconscious is one logical possibility that suggests itself. And, it should be noted, the Freudian unconscious is more intimately linked with *motivational* aspects of mental life than with any other aspect—the cognitive or the perceptual, for example.

REFERENCES

Allston, W. P. (1967). Motives and Motivation. *The Encyclopedia of Philosophy*, 5:399–409.

Farrell, B. A. (1964). The Criteria for a Psychoanalytic Interpretation. In: *Essays in Philosophical Psychology*, ed. D. Gustafson. New York: Doubleday, pp. 299–323.

Fingarette, H. (1969). *Self-Deception*. London: Routledge and Kegan Paul.

Flew, A. (1956). Motives and the Unconscious. In: *Minnesota Studies in the Philosophy of Science*, 1:155–174, ed. H. Feigl et al. Minneapolis: University of Minnesota Press.

Home, H. J. (1966). The Concept of Mind. *International Journal of Psycho-Analysis*, 47:42–49.

Mischel, T. (1963). Psychology and Explanations of Human Behavior. *Philosophy and Phenomenological Research*, 23:578–594.

———— (1966). Pragmatic Aspects of Explanation. *Philosophy of Science*, 33:40–60.

Popper, K. (1963). *Conjectures and Refutations*. New York: Basic Books.

Ryle, G. (1949). *The Concept of Mind*. New York: Barnes and Noble.

Sherwood, M. (1969). *The Logic of Explanation in Psychoanalysis*. New York: Academic Press.

Wittgenstein, L. (1967). *Lectures and Conversations on Aesthetics, Psychology and Religious Belief*, ed. C. Barrett. Berkeley: University of California Press.

FREUD'S CONCEPTS OF MEANING

Robert K. Shope, Ph.D.

Thus in the Interpretation of Dreams *every page deals with what we are calling the letter of the discourse. . . . The first sentence of the opening chapter announces what for the sake of the exposition could not be postponed: that the dream is a rebus. . . . This derives from the persistence in the dream of that same literal (or phonematic) structure through which the signifier in ordinary discourse is articulated and analyzed. . . . The structure of language which enables us to read dreams is the very principle of the "meaning of dreams," the* Traumdeutung.

—*Jacques Lacan (1966, p. 128)*

But the interpretation of symptoms always remains for Freud the establishment of the causal mental nexus. . . . If, therefore, a symptom is, in Freud's terminology, considered to be "meaningful," this simply refers to the possibility of assigning it a place in the (causal) relationships of the mind. When Freud shows that dreams are "meaningful," he intends to say that they have their foundation in unconscious (though analogous to conscious) and often meaningful thought-connections on the basis of which the apparently absurd manifest content can be explained with the aid of our knowledge of dream mechanisms.

—*Heinz Hartmann (1927, p. 400)*

Freud's account of the meaning or the sense of a mental phenomenon is central to his explanations of the human condition. Certain psychoanalysts and philosophers have recently championed the view that when Freud employs the term "meaning" (*Sinn, Bedeutung*), he is essentially concerned with the symbolizing and signifying functions which have been studied, for example, by Cassirer and de Saussure, and with the presence in mental phenomena of what phenomenologists call intentionality.

I believe, however, that a close reading of Freud's texts will reveal several concepts of meaning or sense which are much closer to the type of concept that Hartmann attributes to Freud. Hartmann does not cite any specific passages from Freud concerning this point, and his account is extremely simplified. The task I shall undertake in the present discussion is to articulate and relate the three or four major senses of the term "meaning" which Freud used, and to defend my interpretations by an extensive consideration of Freud's actual statements.[1]

In *The Interpretation of Dreams,* Freud (1900) first explicitly introduces a concept of meaning by connecting it with the concept of interpretation in the following passage:

My presumption that dreams can be interpreted at once puts me in opposition to the ruling theory of dreams and in fact to every theory of dreams with the single exception of Scherner's; for "interpreting" a dream implies assigning a "meaning" [Sinn] to it—that is, replacing it by something which fits into the chain of our mental acts as a link having a validity and importance equal to the rest. As we have seen, the scientific theories of dreams leave no room for any problem of interpreting them, since in their view a dream is not a mental act at all, but a somatic process signalizing its occurrence by indications registered in the mental apparatus. Lay opinion has taken a different attitude throughout the ages. It has exercised its indefeasible right to behave inconsistently; and, though admitting that dreams are unintelligible and absurd, it cannot bring itself to declare that they have no significance [Bedeutung] at all. Led by some obscure feeling, it seems to assume that, in spite of everything, every dream has a meaning [Sinn], though a hidden one, that dreams are designed to take the place of some other process of thought, and that we have only to undo the substitution correctly in order to arrive at this hidden meaning [Bedeutung] (p. 96).

If we are to clarify this passage, a number of topics must be considered: the respect in which the dream is a *substitute;* the locus of *validity;* the fact that the dream is *designed* to be a substitute; *Scherner's* views on dreams; and the *mental acts* involved.

THE DREAM AS A SUBSTITUTE

In the passage quoted above, Freud tells us that the hidden meaning of a dream is the process of thought for which the dream is a substitute. Such a hypothesis, taken in isolation, seems to allow the possibility that the process of thought which constitutes this meaning did not actually exist in the dreamer's mind, and that the dream filled in as a substitute for that process of thought. It seems to allow that the absent thought process would have been "valid" and "important" in its connections with other actual mental processes of the dreamer, if only it had been allowed to occur.

Such an interpretation would explain how Freud could immediately give

[1] I shall directly respond only to the alternative account given by Ricoeur (1970) and in passing take note of Brenner's views (1955). Space does not permit a consideration of Rosen's (1969) interesting treatment of Freud's famous "Signorelli" example, but Rosen's own conception of meaning is not defended by discussion of other passages in which Freud more explicitly defined the term "meaning." In view of the density and *preciosité* of Lacan's writings, any brief discussion of his views is out of the question; for an exposition see Wilden (1968), and for criticism see Ricoeur.

as an example of "symbolic dream interpretation" Joseph's explanation of Pharaoh's dream. Joseph's substituted account is not implied in the Biblical story to have existed in Pharaoh's mind before Joseph's formulation of it.

Again, the interpretation in question makes sense of the following passage in which Freud discusses uncovering the meaning for which the dream substitutes:

The true meaning [Sinn] of the dream, which has now taken the place of its manifest content, is always clearly intelligible; it has its starting-point in experiences of the previous day, and proves to be a fulfilment of unsatisfied wishes. The manifest dream, which you know from your memory when you wake up, can therefore only be described as a disguised fulfilment of repressed wishes (1910, pp. 35–36).

If this passage were read as speaking of a nonexistent thought process for which the dream substitutes, it could be said that in dreaming, no "fulfillment of a desire" in an unqualified sense occurs, but instead the dream substitutes as a mere "disguised fulfillment." For complete fulfillment, in the ordinary sense, would require conscious action on the desire.

Such an interpretation of Freud's statements might suggest that what constitutes the valid but missing thought process for which the dream substitutes is conscious awareness of or action upon desires and memories which were kept in a state of unconsciousness during sleep.

However, a more careful reading of Freud's works shows that he did postulate an existing wish fulfillment kept in the unconscious parts of the mind while the manifest dream substitutes for it in consciousness, and that this is what he meant when he said that "the meaning [Sinn] of every dream is the fulfilment of a wish" (1900, p. 134). This existing mental element is what he explicitly labels the preconscious dream wish in "A Metapsychological Supplement to the Theory of Dreams":

. . . the preconscious dream-wish is formed, which gives expression to the unconscious impulse in the material of the preconscious day's residues. This dream-wish must be sharply distinguished from the day's residues . . . and . . . must not be confused with the wishful impulses which may have been present . . . amongst the preconscious (latent) dream-thoughts. . . .

We have now to consider the further vicissitudes undergone by this wishful impulse, which in its essence represents an unconscious instinctual demand and which has been formed in the Pcs. as a dream-wish (a wish-fulfilling phantasy) (1917a, p. 226).

In his earlier work, The Interpretation of Dreams, Freud made no explicit mention of the wish-fulfilling aspect of the preconscious dream wish, but he did say that the dream wish arises "like a mushroom out of its mycelium" from the dream thoughts, and that the "true wish" behind the dream "transfers" some of its "quantity" of energy, and "wishful force," onto the "transferred dream-wish" (1900, pp. 311, 525, 561–564, 594, 604). In that work, Freud allowed that the dream wish either may be one that arises only in sleep, or may be a preconscious wish left over from the previous day reinforced by the true dream wish in the unconscious (1900, pp. 551, 573). After the dream wish arises, it "seeks to force its way along the normal path taken by thought-processes, through the *Pcs.* (to which, indeed, it in part belongs) to consciousness. But it comes up against the censorship . . ." (p. 573).

The wish-fulfilling aspect of this preconscious derivative is at least implied in *The Interpretation of Dreams* when Freud says that in dreaming the preconscious system both "binds" the unconscious excitation and "discharges" it, that is, that dreaming

. . . serves it as a safety valve and at the same time preserves the sleep of the preconscious in return for a small expenditure of waking activity. Thus, like all the other psychical structures in the series of which it is a member, it constitutes a compromise; it is in the service of both of the two systems, since it fulfils the two wishes [the true, repressed wish and the preconscious wish to sleep] in so far as they are compatible with each other (1900, p. 579).

Here, wish fulfillment is clearly conceived in terms of energy processes, in terms of the fate of an "excitation," although Freud may also be implying that the manifest dream itself partly discharges or binds this excitation. The connection with energy concepts is worth emphasizing, since we shall later have to consider an alternative account of what Freud meant by "wish fulfillment." [2]

Freud's (1917a) discussion of the metapsychology of dreams actually conflates the preconscious dream *wish* with a preconscious, wish-fulfilling dream *fantasy.* Freud does not suppose that repressed wishes associate with preconscious day's residues and then give rise to a conscious visual hallucination which itself is a wish fulfillment. Instead, he hypothesizes an intermediate step consisting in the formation of a preconscious fantasy, and he calls this a wish fulfillment. He notes that this fantasy achieves undisguised, conscious hallucinatory status in some dreams, in acute hallucinatory confusion, and in the hallucinatory phase of schizophrenia (1917a, pp. 229–230). But to suppose that no intermediate dream wish or fantasy intervenes and that the manifest dream is itself the wish fulfill-

---

[2] We may note a passage in the *Introductory Lectures* in which wish fulfillment is conceived at least partly in terms of energy processes. Freud admits that in some anxiety dreams "it may be that the dream-work has not completely succeeded in creating a wish-fulfilment; so that a portion of the distressing affect in the dream-thoughts has been left over in the manifest dream. In that case analysis would have to show that these dream-thoughts were far more distressing than the dream constructed out of them" (1916–1917, pp. 214–215). Freud says later in the same work that, strictly speaking, there are no unconscious affects but only quantities of energy which have the potential for being released in conscious affects. Thus, the above passage implies that anxiety dreams partly succeed as wish fulfillments since they bind or discharge at least part of the energy of the wish behind the dream. That is why Freud says that those dreams in which anxiety actually corresponds to the repressed libidinal energy "come near the limit at which the wish-fulfilling purpose of dreams breaks down" (1900, p. 236). He is not concerned in this statement with the ideational content of the manifest dream, but with the fact that it does not succeed to any useful extent in binding or discharging the psychic energy of the repressed wish, which instead manifests itself through anxiety.

ment seems to yield a simpler theory of dreams which are distorted wish fulfillments and even of some which are undistorted. Freud gives no reasons to reject
this as a general account. Of course, if a schizophrenic or a patient suffering from
amentia frequently has the same hallucinations, or if we frequently dream the
same dream, then it may be a simpler hypothesis to admit that in those special
cases there is continued existence of the same organized unit in the unconscious.

Nonetheless, we must notice Freud's claim that for many dreams the preconscious fantasy is freshly constructed out of new day's residues, and his
qualification in *The Interpretation of Dreams* that these fantasies belong only in
part to the *Pcs*. He says in "The Unconscious" that because these fantasies are
not easily accessible to introspection, they belong to that class of fantasies which
"qualitatively . . . belong to the system *Pcs.*, but *factually* to the *Ucs*." He
continues:

Of such a nature are those phantasies of normal people as well as of neurotics
which we have recognized as preliminary stages in the formation both of dreams
and of symptoms and which, in spite of their high degree of organization, re-
main repressed and therefore cannot become conscious (1915b, p. 191).

The fact that Freud relegates such fantasies and wishes to the *Ucs*. may
help explain why the wish-fantasy stage or dream-wish stage in dream construction is almost entirely ignored in the *Introductory Lectures*. There Freud merely
says that the latent dream thoughts give rise to the manifest dream. When he
does nod toward the more complicated theory, he speaks inconsistently of the
"dream proper, which has been completed in the unconscious and is the fulfilment of an unconscious wishful phantasy" involving "the unconscious libidinal
wish-fulfilment" (1916–1917, p. 360). But this confusedly abandons the account
which he upholds almost everywhere else, namely, that it is only outside the
unconscious that binding, discharge, substitute gratification, and wish fulfillment
can be found. Perhaps this momentary aberration is due to a failure to free his
thoughts of the unnecessary postulate that the preconscious fantasy or dream
wish partially binds the energy of the repressed wishes, and of the unnecessary
interpolation of such derivatives between the latent dream thoughts and the
manifest dream.[3]

Once we are willing to regard the dream as a substitute for unconscious
thought processes, we need not suppose that it substitutes for a wish fulfillment.
We can admit that if the unconscious wishes entered consciousness they might
actually be condemned or suppressed, as is often the case at the end of analysis.
Thus, the dream on this view seems best described as a substitute for the
presence of active but repressed *wishes* and associated *thoughts* in consciousness. From there is but a short step to the redefinition of "meaning" in terms
of such unconscious contents which Freud offers in the *Introductory Lectures*:

[3] By 1933, in the *New Introductory Lectures*, Freud's outline of the formation of
a dream no longer made any mention of the preconscious dream wish or fantasy.
Nonetheless, Freud did claim that the meaning (significance?) of all dreaming (*Sinn*
alles Träumens) is the satisfaction obtained from using the psychic energy of an unconscious wish to display that wish as fulfilled (1933, pp. 18–19).

*Let us once more reach an agreement upon what is to be understood by the
"sense" [Sinn] of a psychical process. We mean nothing other by it than the intention [Absicht] it serves and its position in a psychical continuity. In most of
our researches we can replace "sense" by "intention" or "purpose" [Tendenz]
(1916–1917, p. 40).*

I shall later discuss this definition of "meaning." Let us refer to it as concerning the concept of meaning₂, and to the earlier passages as concerning the
concept of meaning₁: that for which a mental phenomenon substitutes.

Before taking up at greater length this useful shift from one sense of the
term "meaning" to the other, it is necessary to consider other issues involved in
the passage from *The Interpretation of Dreams* in which Freud's original definition of "meaning" was offered.

THE LOCUS OF VALIDITY

If the dream is viewed as a substitute for the presence of wishes or fantasies in
consciousness which remain repressed or preconscious, then one may say that
all these items have validity in that they are genuine mental contents, coherent
in their "inner structure." They lack validity only in the sense that they "may already display the irrational character possessed by everything that is unconscious
when we translate it into the conscious" (1917a, p. 226).

What must be realized in order to avoid confusion is that Freud sometimes speaks of the manifest dream *itself* as a valid mental act:

*Dreams . . . are not meaningless [sinnlos], they are not absurd; they do not
imply that one portion of our store of ideas is asleep while another portion is
beginning to wake. On the contrary, they are psychical phenomena of complete
validity—fulfilments of wishes; they can be inserted into the chain of intelligible
waking mental acts; they are constructed by a highly complicated activity of the
mind (1900, p. 122; see pp. 227, 533, 580).*

Waking mental acts are not necessarily conscious ones, but ones which are
active, perhaps unconsciously active. The manifest dream arises in response to
active thoughts continuing unconsciously, and is constructed by the highly complicated dream work, thus having a place in a sequence of mental acts. But the
manifest dream is valid, not in the sense of being internally coherent and well-
organized, but in the sense of having a "value" which consists in a "useful
achievement" or "function." Its function is to be a safety valve for conflicting
forces, and to that extent it is "intelligible" (see Freud, 1900, pp. 79, 580; 1933,
pp. 9, 12, 16).

Suppose that a phenomenon is intelligible in relation to a given theory or
type of explanation, insofar as it has a certain place in relation to the rest of the
subject matter of that theory or explanatory context. It is then common in ordinary speech to use the term "meaning" to label the significance of that item,
and to speak of it as meaningful or making sense. In this manner, a doctor might
speak of the significance or meaning of a certain organic symptom in diagnosing

an organic disease or might say the symptom makes sense in the light of the disease. Freud sometimes seems to have included the intelligibility of a mental phenomenon as part of what he wished to convey by speaking of the meaning or sense of that mental phenomenon. For example, he suggested in the above passage that dreams are not absurd but have validity, and he says in the *Introductory Lectures* that "By 'sense' [*Sinn*] we understand 'meaning' [*Bedeutung*], 'intention' [*Absicht*], 'purpose' [*Tendenz*] and 'position in a continuous psychical context' " (1916–1917, p. 61).

It is not at all clear, however, that Freud does use *Bedeutung* in the latter passage in that sense of "significance" which I have just been considering. Freud may simply be repeating the definition of *meaning₂* mentioned earlier. Thus, it is with some diffidence that I label this *meaning₃*, which is simply *meaning₂* plus the idea of the "significance" of the mental phenomenon.[4]

DREAMS DESIGNED AS SUBSTITUTES

Once we notice that Freud speaks of a dream as having a function, we might suppose that all he means by saying that a dream is "designed" to substitute for its meaning is that it *functions* as a substitute, much as one might say the gall bladder is designed to store bile. Thus, Freud might be saying that when neither open release of accumulating psychic energy nor consciousness of conflicting forces is able to occur, the dream substitutes for those phenomena and thereby fulfills its function, its useful purpose, as a safety valve and as a protector of sleep.

However, the fact that Freud connects the meaning of a dream with the "motive for" it suggests another possible interpretation. He writes of the Irma dream that "in the meantime the 'meaning' [*Sinn*] of the dream was borne in upon me. I became aware of an intention [*Absicht*] which was carried into effect by the dream and which must have been my motive for dreaming it [*Motiv des Träumens*]" (1900, p. 118). This might lead us to suppose that to say a dream occurs by design is to assert that there is a motive for it, that dreaming is a motivated act. Should this prove to be Freud's view, we must decide just what he means by speaking of the motive for something or by saying that something has a motive.

Some psychoanalysts seem to think that Freud is actually prepared to define "meaning" in terms of "motive." For example, Brenner (1955) says of a slip of the tongue that sometimes only chance allows one "to guess more or less accurately at the 'meaning' of the slip, that is, at the unconscious motives which produced it," and that an analyst may discover, for example, a "motive for forgetting" (pp. 143–144). If there is a fourth concept of meaning in Freud, *meaning₄*, that is, if he sometimes uses the phrase "the meaning of" as synonymous with

---

[4] Even in the passage cited at the start of our discussion from which we extracted the definition of *meaning₁*, Freud stresses the validity, significance, and place in a chain of mental acts which a meaningful mental phenomenon has. Thus, Freud's definition of *meaning₁* at the end of that passage may actually just abbreviate another definition in the same passage which includes mention of those additional characteristics.

"the motives behind" or "the unconscious motives behind," then we have another reason for investigating Freud's concept of motivation.

THE MEANING OF "MEANING" VERSUS
WHAT CONSTITUTES THE MEANING

Before continuing, it is best to prevent misunderstanding of the way in which I have been speaking of the differences among various concepts of meaning, that is, the differences among $meaning_1$, $meaning_2$, etc.

I shall employ the common distinction between the meaning or sense of a linguistic expression and the referent of the expression, the actual things to which the expression is correctly applied. The expression "the topic of conversation" may apply, for instance, to the Eiffel Tower, assuming that the conversation at a given time concerns the Eiffel Tower. The Eiffel Tower is a referent of the expression relative to that conversation. But if a person were to state the linguistic meaning, the sense, of the expression "the topic of conversation," he would not need to mention the Eiffel Tower—any more than he would need to mention Freud in explaining the sense of the expression "those with medical training."

We may say, for example, that at a particular moment the topic of conversation *consists in* the Eiffel Tower, or that the topic of conversation *is* the Eiffel Tower. But we do not thereby imply that we are defining the sense of the expression "the topic of conversation" by mentioning the Eiffel Tower. If we utter the sentence "The topic of conversation is the Eiffel Tower," then we are not using the "is" of definition but the "is" of identity; here the referents of the expressions "the Eiffel Tower" and "the topic of conversation" are identical.

In my previous discussion, I have indicated at least three different senses which Freud gave to the expression "the meaning." I regard these as different senses because I take seriously his claims in various works to be defining the expression. One statement in *The Interpretation of Dreams* suggests the possibility of yet a fourth sense. Correspondingly, I speak of three or four concepts of meaning expressed by the term "meaning." When Freud says that the meaning of a dream consists in a wish fulfillment, or that it is a wish fulfillment, I take him to be employing the "is" of identity and not the "is" of definition. Freud never explicitly defines the sense of "meaning," the meaning of "meaning," by mention of wish fulfillment. As some philosophers might put it, the property of being the meaning of a mental phenomenon is not the same as the property of being a wish fulfillment, but this would still permit the properties to belong to the same things.

Freud's empirical hypotheses account for his occasional identification of the referent of "wish fulfillment" with the referent of "meaning." Likewise, for many phenomena the referent of "meaning" in the sense of $meaning_1$, that for which the phenomenon substitutes, is eventually viewed by Freud as at least partly identical with the referent of the term in the sense of $meaning_2$, the intention or purpose (tendency) which the phenomenon serves and the place it has in a psychical continuity. For Freud finally advanced the putatively empirical hypothesis that a manifest dream, for example, substitutes in consciousness for unconscious intentions and purposes, and he stopped claiming that it substitutes for a fantasy which is a wish fulfillment. Likewise, the referent of "meaning" in the sense of meaning$_2$ (and also in the sense of meaning$_1$) is obviously at least partly identical with the referent of "meaning" in the sense of meaning$_3$, the significance of the phenomenon plus the intention or purpose (tendency) which it serves and its place in a psychical continuity. For the definition of the former sense forms part of the definition of the latter.

Once we consider Freud's own use of the term "motive for," we shall see that if he did use the term "meaning" in the sense of meaning$_4$, the motives for the phenomenon or the motives behind the phenomenon, then the referent of the term used in this sense also overlaps that of the other senses. For the motives turn out to be the relevant intentions and purposes.

Because of the overlap between the applications of "meaning" in these senses, and in view of the great ambiguity of the term in ordinary speech, it is understandable that Freud should have shifted as he did from one concept of meaning to another.

Let us now continue our analysis of Freud's discussion in *The Interpretation of Dreams* in order to develop an account of his concept of motivation.

SCHERNER'S VIEWS ON DREAMS

Of all the previous theories of dreams which Freud discusses at the beginning of *The Interpretation of Dreams,* only those based upon Scherner's views are said to allow that dreams have meaning. Yet it is most important that we take note of certain respects in which Freud admits that his account differs from Scherner's.

According to Freud, Scherner held that in sleep the mental activities of cognition, ideation, feeling, and willing are modified so as to lose their "truly mental character" and become nothing but "mechanisms"; in contrast, the mental activity of "imagination" is heightened, so that "liberated from the domination of reason and from any moderating control, [it] leaps into a position of unlimited sovereignty . . . possessing not merely reproductive but *productive* powers" (1900, p. 84). But it is without the power of conceptual "speech" and its speech is in images (p. 84), so that "the symbolizing activity of the imagination remains the central force in every dream" (p. 86).

Freud criticizes the speculative nature of Scherner's elucidation of exact dream symbols, and his assumption that dream images always represent the same underlying thoughts (1900, pp. 225–226). But what is most important for our present discussion is to decide whether he rejects Scherner's description of dreams as *speech* and Scherner's description of the processes behind the manifest dream as an exercise of *imagination*. For this is relevant to the central problem of whether Freud thought that mental phenomena such as dreams have meaning in the manner in which a language or speech signifies something. It is also relevant to the problem of whether Freud regarded dream images as having intentionality, as philosophers put it, directed upon those other thoughts which are (disguisedly) represented or portrayed in the manifest dream. The latter question is whether the manifest, conscious dream content "points toward" the hidden content in the sense of somehow "designating" it and thus "referring to" it. I shall eventually argue that Freud regards the manifest content as pointing toward the hidden content only in the sense in which a *clue* points toward something.

Scherner is said to have thought that in dreams the imagination "seeks" to give "symbolic representation" to factors such as a somatic stimulus impinging on the mind (1900, p. 225). Freud does agree that "the imagination's pre-occupation" with the subject's own body occurs both in dreams and in neurosis (1900, p. 346; see also p. 227). But Freud actually displaces the locus of what is here called "imagination" into the unconscious itself, contrasting it with the dream-work activities which connect the unconscious with the manifest dream:

We have fully appreciated the importance of the part ascribed by Scherner to "dream-imagination," as well as Scherner's own interpretations, but we have been obliged to transport them, as it were, to a different position in the problem. The point is not that dreams create the imagination, but rather that the unconscious activity of the imagination has a large share in the construction of the dream-thoughts. We remain in Scherner's debt for having indicated the source of the dream-thoughts; but nearly everything that he ascribes to the dream-work is really attributable to the activity of the unconscious during daytime, which is the instigating agent of dreams no less than of neurotic symptoms (1900, pp. 591–592; see also p. 349).

That is to say, the original occurrence in the person's mind of associative links between symbols and the related thoughts is in the unconscious, and is not created afresh by the dream work, which "is doing nothing original in making substitutions of this kind" (1900, pp. 345–346).

A person may use very common symbols because "the way has been well prepared by linguistic usage" (1900, p. 346). However, the dream is not an example of the clever use of linguistic skills, of intellectual subterfuge. For the ambiguity and symbolism connected with linguistic usage are themselves "the precipitate [*Niederschlag*] of imaginative similes reaching back to remote antiquity" (1900, p. 346). What must be emphasized is that Freud does not claim that the dreamer himself does more than respond to the *residue*, the precipitate, of past *conscious* imaginative similes such as "the Lord's vineyard, the seed, and the maiden's garden in the *Song of Solomon*" (p. 346). More generally, he suggests that the basic symbolic associations in the unconscious of today's man are "paths along which all humanity passed in the earliest periods of civilization" (p. 347). The moot question is whether Freud literally means that "imagination" acts in our unconscious as it did in ancient conscious thinking or whether the "paths" in our unconscious are to be described in more mechanistic terms as mere associations of ideas.

Several passages help to indicate Freud's opinion on this question. The first is his suggestion that there were ancient languages in which a word had one sexual meaning and another meaning which is now the conscious content of the dream symbol for that sexual idea. He says that such a hypothesis would "give us a possibility of understanding dream-symbolism. . . . The symbolic relation would be the residue of an ancient verbal identity; things which were once called by the same name as the genitals could now serve as symbols for them in dreams" (1916–1917, p. 167). He states that "the ultimate meaning of the symbolic relation . . . is of a genetic character" (1900, p. 352). Freud's view seems to be that the ancient language established a common association between the ideas which the ancient word expressed by its double meaning, and that we today have inherited that type of association (perhaps one should say a disposition to it), a "relic and mark of former identity" (1900, p. 352). I can see no other way to interpret him, for he does not say that today the one idea expresses the other or that an image of the one content expresses the other or that we have unconscious knowledge of the ancient word.[5] In the *Introductory Lectures*, he presents this explanation of symbolism as a substitute for understanding it instead as the product of "unconscious pieces of knowledge, of connections of thought, of comparisons between different objects which result in its being possible for one of them to be regularly put in place of the other," which he indicates would be a doctrine that "is not easy to account for . . . by the help of our psychological views" (1916–1917, p. 165). For "It is strange . . . that if a symbol is a comparison it should not be brought to light by an association, and that the dreamer should not be acquainted with it but should make use of it without knowing about it" (p. 152).

Another relevant passage occurs in the discussion of symbolism in the 1917 paper "On Transformations of Instinct as Exemplified in Anal Erotism":

. . . it appears as if in the products of the unconscious—spontaneous ideas, phantasies and symptoms—the concepts faeces (money, gift), baby and penis are ill-distinguished from one another and are easily interchangeable. We realize, of course, that to express oneself in this way is incorrectly to apply to the sphere of the unconscious terms which belong properly to other regions of mental life, and that we have been led astray by the advantages offered by an analogy. To put the matter in a form less open to objection, these elements in the unconscious are often treated as if they were equivalent and could replace one another freely (1917b, p. 128).

Here, Freud restricts himself to the minimal assumption necessary to trace a symbolic content of a symptom or dream back to its unconscious sexual idea or wish. He supposes that in the unconscious the two ideas are interchangeable

[5] In *The Interpretation of Dreams*, Freud does make the claim that there was in ancient times both a linguistic *and* a conceptual identity (1900, p. 352). However, this astonishing claim is dropped in the *Introductory Lectures*, and is mitigated by the passage discussed below from Freud's (1917b) paper on anal erotism. Indeed, a 1925 footnote to the surprising remark in *The Interpretation of Dreams* relates it to Sperber's theory, according to which ancient words shifted meanings because nonsexual things were "compared with" sexual ones. There, only comparison and not conceptual identity is claimed. Obviously, in any usual sense of the term "concept," an ambiguous term even in ancient times must have linguistically expressed two or more concepts which were not identical; otherwise, it was a univocal term. Nonetheless, the one concept may have been of things comparable or analogous in some way to those things to which the other concept applied.

in the following sense: A train of thought in which the one idea (or its registration) is unconsciously active may causally activate a train of thought in which that idea is replaced by the associated one, which then enters consciousness, more or less directly or after further substitutions. Freud shows that he does not need to speak of conceptual identity in the unconscious or of the unconscious as using imagination. The term "imagination" seldom, if ever, reappears in such a context after Freud's initial acknowledgment of Scherner as his precursor. Freud needs only to insist that the unconscious gives ideas and thought contents a new form. That is, one idea substitutes for another, arises in place of another, or receives its activation from the other (or, if you will, what Freud sometimes calls the registrations of ideas have these connections). In this very essay, Freud speaks interchangeably of a wish's being *changed into* another wish and of its being *replaced by* the other wish (1917b, pp. 129, 132).[6]

We can now comprehend Freud's reasons for admitting in *The Interpretation of Dreams* that the processes relating to dream thoughts and extending into the dream work are "abnormal" and for claiming that they "depart so widely from what we recognize as rational thought-processes that the most severe strictures passed by earlier writers on the low level of psychical functioning in dreams must appear fully justified" (1900, p. 592). Freud does not think of the unconscious as making allusions through its associations in the sense in which the writer of the *Song of Solomon* made allusions. The dreamer is not literally an unconscious poet. I shall argue in the next section that the processes connecting dream thoughts are not what Freud calls the "mental acts" connected with dreams. We must take quite seriously Freud's admonition that the dream work, which may avail itself of symbolic "allusions," nonetheless is also

. . . not simply more careless, more irrational, more forgetful and more incomplete than waking thought; it is completely different from it qualitatively and for that reason not immediately comparable with it. It does not think, calculate or judge in any way at all; it restricts itself to giving things a new form (1900, p. 507).

MENTAL ACTS

In the passage from *The Interpretation of Dreams* that began our discussion, Freud said that what constitutes the meaning of the manifest dream, that which it replaces, is something which fits into the chain of our mental acts and which consists in processes of thought. Dream thoughts, considered in themselves and apart from the processes that connect them, are "rational" and "normal." They are wishes and the day's residues, the latter consisting largely in memories but also, for example, in leftover worries (1900, pp. 506, 550, 560, 592). When Freud

[6] This is the sense in which we must construe Nunberg's remarks concerning neurotics who express fear of castration by withholding feces, if we are to interpret Nunberg as explaining Freud's views. Nunberg claims that "the fear of the loss of the penis is, to their unconscious, identical with the fear of the loss of feces. Unconsciously they believe that they save the genital from castration by retaining their feces, that they *keep* it in this way. In intercourse, the semen symbolically represents the feces, to them . . . the ejaculation . . . is treated as if it were feces, it is retained" (1955, p. 290).

has in mind these *latent* dream thoughts, he can intelligibly say that dreams (i.e., latent dream thoughts) are psychical acts which we have difficulty in recognizing as *wishes* (versus as wish fulfillments) because of the censorship (1900, p. 80). And it must be in regard to the processes connecting the latent dream thoughts that he rejects Robert's theory that "dreams are not psychical processes, they have no place among the psychical processes of waking life . . ." (p. 80). For the processes of waking life which Freud connects with dreams are the unconscious processes in the latent dream thoughts which are already associating along the paths later to be followed in sleep, and already in waking life constructing the dream wish:

The view that dreams carry on the occupations and interests of waking life has been entirely confirmed by the discovery of the concealed dream-thoughts. These are only concerned with what seems important to us and interests us greatly (1900, p. 589).

. . . what is suppressed continues to exist in normal people as well as abnormal, and remains capable of psychical functioning. . . . *In waking life the suppressed material in the mind is prevented from finding expression and is cut off from internal perception . . . but during the night . . . this suppressed material finds methods and means of forcing its way into consciousness. . . .*
     The interpretation of dreams is the royal road to a knowledge of the unconscious activities of the mind (*1900, p. 608; see also pp. 576, 592*).

Freud speaks of the manifest dream as capable of being "inserted at an assignable point in the mental activities of waking life" not in the sense that the manifest dream existed during waking life or is exactly the same kind of process which did, but in the sense that it has "its true, psychically significant source in waking life" (1900, pp. 1, 177).
     However, the fact that this source is itself something mental leads Freud to call the manifest dream itself a mental process and to say that it is constructed by a mental activity. He introduces the contrast between somatic and mental processes by saying that "The application to dreams of the term 'somatic' . . . has more than one bearing. . . . For theories of this kind involve a tendency to limit the instigation of dreams so far as possible to somatic causes" (1900, p. 77). Secondly, it implies that "dreams are unworthy to rank as psychical processes" (p. 78). This second implication is partially explained in terms of Strümpell's comparison of dreaming with the fingers of a man ignorant of music wandering over a keyboard, and Freud adds that this implies that dreams cannot be interpreted (p. 78). This second criterion is clarified later when Freud again refers to Strümpell's simile, saying that "a dream is not, on this view, a mental phenomenon based on psychical motives, but the outcome of a physiological stimulus which is expressed in psychical symptoms because the apparatus upon which the stimulus impinges is capable of no other form of expression" (1900, pp. 222–223). Thus the first criterion of being a mental process is that of having something mental as a cause, and the second criterion is that of being based on a specific type of psychical cause, namely, a "psychical motive or motives."

At this point, it is helpful to consider Freud's discussion of mental acts in the *Introductory Lectures:*

Let us pause a moment longer over the assertion that parapraxes are "psychical acts." Does this imply more than what we have said already—that they have a sense [Sinn]? I think not. I think, rather, that the former assertion [that they are psychical acts] is more indefinite and more easily misunderstood. Anything that is observable in mental life may occasionally be described as a mental phenomenon. The question will then be whether the particular mental phenomenon has arisen immediately from somatic, organic and material influences—in which case its investigation will not be part of psychology—or whether it is derived in the first instance from other mental processes, somewhere behind which the series of organic influences begins. It is this latter situation that we have in view when we describe a phenomenon as a mental process, and for that reason it is more expedient to clothe our assertion in the form: "the phenomenon has a sense." By "sense" we understand "meaning" [Bedeutung], "intention" [Absicht], "purpose" [Tendenz] and "position in a continuous psychical context" (1916– 1917, pp. 60–61).

Here, Freud separates the sense of the term "mental act" from the second criterion mentioned in *The Interpretation of Dreams.* Something which is in itself admittedly a mental "phenomenon" will now be a mental "act" or "process" in addition only if it has something mental as one of its immediate causes.[7] That makes it subject to psychological investigation. Since this definition of "mental act" does not require that the psychical causes themselves be *psychical motives,* the expression "being a mental act" now has a broader sense than that given in the above passage to "having a meaning" in the sense of *meaning₃.* For the latter expression as used here requires that the phenomenon not only occupy a position in a causal sequence of mental phenomena, but also "have intention" and "purpose (tendency)."

We must now consider what Freud means by speaking of a dream, for example, as having psychical motives. We have already noted that this hypothesis might form a bridge for a transition from use of the concept of *meaning₁,* the concept of that for which a mental phenomenon is designed to substitute, to use of the concept of *meaning₄,* the concept of the motives or unconscious motives behind the phenomenon. Since a psychical motive is regarded by Freud as an intention or purpose (tendency), it also becomes easy to use the concept of *meaning₄* in place of the concept of *meaning₂,* the concept of the intention or purpose (tendency) of the phenomenon and its place in a psychical continuity. (Similarly for *meaning₃.*) This type of transition is made appropriate, moreover, by the fact, which I have indicated elsewhere (Shope, 1970), that Freud uses the term "intention" in the *Introductory Lectures* to cover what at other times even in the same work he calls wishes or desires. In addition, in the

[7] It is possible that Freud, a student of John Stuart Mill's writings, drew this distinction from Mill's *Logic* (cf. 1872, pp. 33–34, p. 560). Certainly, Freud's remarks about the need for a study of the mind to remain at least for the present on psychological rather than physiological ground appear to mirror Mill's similar claims (cf. p. 556).

third introductory lecture Freud uses the term "purpose (tendency)" (*Tendenz*) to label these "intentions," speaking of them as forces which may compete by striving in opposing directions and saying that his project is to conceive phenomena "as signs of an interplay of forces in the mind, as a manifestation of purposeful intentions [*von ziel strebungen Tendenzen*] working concurrently or in mutual opposition. We are concerned with a *dynamic view* of mental phenomena" (1916–1917, p. 67).[8]

PSYCHICAL MOTIVES FOR A MENTAL PHENOMENON

It can be shown that Freud does not regard dreams, errors, symptoms, and related phenomena as *intentional* actions, even though their causes are "intentions" and they are meaningful.[9] The question that must be decided here, however, is whether he speaks of the "motives for" them or speaks of them as "having a motive" in a certain everyday sense of the term, an ordinary sense which prima facie Freud might be using since it does not require all motivated actions also to be intentional.

In ordinary language, we sometimes speak of an intentional hostile act and even an unintentional hostile remark as "motivated" by anger or by a hostile wish, but we do not commonly describe stumbling as "motivated" by such mental states. However, in this sense what may be, broadly speaking, an "action" or something we "do," such as stumbling or running off the edge of the road because of anger or inattention, is ordinarily spoken of as *caused* by but not *motivated* by the anger or inattention. In certain examples, some philosophers would point out this *conceptual* contrast (the facts are not at issue here) by use of the related contrast between "my reason" and "the reason," e.g., the reason I stumbled was my anger but anger was not my reason for stumbling in the sense that my hostility toward someone is my reason for intentionally or uninten-

---

[8] Indeed, at one point in the *Introductory Lectures*, Freud defines "meaning" or "sense" without explicitly mentioning purpose (tendency): "We have comprised two things as the 'sense' [*Sinn*] of a symptom: its 'whence' and its 'whither' or 'what for'— that is, the impressions and experiences from which it arose and the intentions [*Absichten*] which it serves" (1916–1917, p. 284). But he immediately goes on to speak of the "whither" as being the *Tendenz*, the purpose or tendency, of the symptom, and calls it an endopsychic process. (In view of the fact that this definition explicitly mentions experiences and impressions rather than merely psychical continuity, strictly speaking we would have to count it as defining yet a fifth sense of the term "meaning," whose overlap in application with the other senses is obvious.)

In the same work, Freud at one point offers a shortened definition of *meaning₂* or perhaps *meaning₃* when he speaks of the "purely psychological investigations into the sense [*Sinn*]—that is, the meaning [*Bedeutung*] or purpose [*Absicht*]—of parapraxes" (p. 36). This is reminiscent of the fact that after his original definition of *meaning₂* Freud suggested an abbreviated definition: "In most of our researches we can replace 'sense' by 'intention' or 'purpose' " (p. 40).

[9] I have elsewhere contended that, although Freud speaks of intentions as being carried out in the slip, or speaks anthropomorphically of intentions as themselves making use of parapraxes for their own ends, he usually refuses to say that the *person* intended the act to accomplish the suppressed or repressed intention or that accomplishing it was an *intended* act (Shope, 1970). The *Standard Edition* translation obscures this point in rendering "*der Absicht . . . in deren Dienst sie die Zwangshandlung ausführte*" as "the intention with which she was performing the obsessional action" (Freud, 1916–1917, p. 277). She acts here in the service of a power unknown to her.

tionally acting hostilely toward him. We would commonly say that there was nothing that was *my* reason for stumbling or for running off the edge of the road. Again, we sometimes say that something "expresses" anger, e.g., trembling or reddening, even though anger is not thereby implied to be a motive for it in this ordinary sense.

Contrary to the opinions of a number of philosophers and psychoanalysts, Freud does not maintain that dreams, errors, or symptoms are motivated or express motives in an everyday sense. (I have not attempted explicitly to define but only to call attention to a certain everyday sense of "motive.") Freud speaks of motives in his own, technical sense.

This is clearly indicated, for example, in "Five Lectures on Psycho-Analysis," in which Freud speaks interchangeably of men's craving to find *causes* and the psychoanalyst's search for *motives:*

As you already see, psycho-analysts are marked by a particularly strict belief in the determination of mental life. For them there is nothing trivial, nothing arbitrary or haphazard. They expect in every case to find sufficient motives where, as a rule, no such expectation is raised. Indeed, they are prepared to find several motives for one and the same mental occurrence, whereas what seems to be our innate craving for causality declares itself satisfied with a single psychical cause (1910, p. 38).

Even in *The Interpretation of Dreams,* it is clear that Freud uses the phrase "motive for" in a special sense. He considers theories which trace the dream to a merely somatic exciting cause, such as the ringing of an alarm clock or kinesthetic sensations from the positions of our limbs during sleep, that is, to an "objective sensory stimulus." He argues that different dreams may be related to the same objective stimulus, and that such theories cannot explain how these differences arise. Therefore, we may ask "whether there may not be other determinants governing the interpretation put by the dreamer upon the illusion called up by the sense-impression," other factors "generating his dream" (1900, p. 29). After mentioning an example of a peculiar interpretation placed upon this illusion by one dreamer in response to his memories, Freud asks, "Is it not probable, then, that the choice of such an unusual group of memories as these was facilitated by motives other than the objective stimulus alone?" (p. 30). Later in the work, he again affirms the view that "the motive for dreaming lay *elsewhere than in somatic sources of stimulation*" (p. 224). If Freud were using the ordinary concept of motivation mentioned above, then these claims would be true by definition and not be a matter of probability or require special discussion. For motives would logically have to be mental states and not merely somatic stimuli. Moreover, Freud characterizes the empirical theory that he rejects as a theory concerning the "choice" made by the "external stimuli" in the course of their productive activity, and these external factors are said merely not to constitute a *sufficient* motive for such choice rather than to be no motive (p. 223). That Freud employs the concept of motivation in a special way is also apparent from his remark that in sleep the absence of the "progressive current" in the mind flowing from the sensory end of the psychic apparatus may be one of the "motives for regression" (*Regressionsmotive*) (pp. 547–548).

The sense which Freud gives to the expression "motive for" is indicated by his willingness to speak of the "motive force" behind the dream as the "dream-instigator" (1900, pp. 541–542, 560–561, 81–82). He is concerned with the sense in which an engine may be said to be the motive for the motion of an automobile, which now verges on an archaic use of the term in English,[10] or, as we still express ourselves, with the sense in which the motor supplies the motive power and force behind the motion. Freud thus finds it natural to speak of wishes as the only things which can "set the apparatus in motion" or "at work" (pp. 567, 598). This reference to forces as exciting causes is built into the very meaning of the term "motive" as Freud uses it. Even when he introduces the more complex idea of a *psychical* motive, he presents it as a substantive, empirical issue whether nonconative factors such as judgments, inferences, or denials are the "psychical acts" which have the "power to instigate" dreams (p. 550). Freud does not settle such questions merely by appeal to an everyday sense of the sort we considered as belonging to the expressions "motive for" or "motivated by." [11]

[10] Compare John Dewey's use of the term in the following passage: "History must be presented, not as an accumulation of results or effects, a mere statement of what happened, but as a forceful acting thing. The motives—that is, the motors—must stand out. To study history is not to amass information, but to use information in constructing a vivid picture of how and why men did thus and so, achieved their success and came to their failures" (1899, p. 151).

[11] Orthodox psychoanalysts themselves do not always interpret Freud in the manner I have suggested. For example, Brenner (1955) explains the meaning of a mental phenomenon as the "unconscious motives which produced it," thus neglecting conscious intentions that may form part of the meaning of a parapraxis or memories from the previous day which may form part of the meaning of a dream (p. 144).

Brenner also illustrates his account of meaning by speaking of a man who was struck by lightning upon sitting under a chain dangling from a tree as "deliberately, though unconsciously, trying to get it to strike him," and Brenner views all parapraxes as "the result of a purposeful and intentional action of the individual involved, although the intent is unknown to the actor himself" (pp. 142, 150). Brenner argues that the man well knew the danger involved in such a situation. However, this knowledge can be regarded as knowledge which was caused to lie dormant rather than influence behavior on account of the presence of unconscious motives. Again, when Brenner offers an example of a patient who hit an elderly man with his car, he argues that this patient was later "able to recall that he was not surprised when he felt his car hit something. In other words, he was dimly aware of his unconscious intent to strike the man with his fender at the moment of the 'accident.' On the basis of his associations to the various circumstances of what had happened," Brenner continues, "it was possible to discover that the chief, unconscious motive for the mishap was the patient's wish to destroy his father . . . displaced onto an unknown, elderly man" (pp. 152–153). But, once again, it is not necessary to assume intentional or voluntary action against this elderly man, but only to suppose that, because of the associations which it had, the perception of the propinquity of the man to the car, registered unconsciously, was causally prevented from triggering the normal, habitual change of direction in driving. No momentary wish to harm that man need be postulated. Surely this is the simpler explanation. Moreover, Brenner confuses awareness of the presence of the man with awareness of an intention to strike him.

It is extremely difficult, in fact, to find an analyst who reports that a patient *recalls* not just the presence of an unconscious wish or intention but an intentional or voluntary *connection* it had with a symptom or error. For example, a patient who Freud

DREAMS, ERRORS, SYMPTOMS
AS EXPRESSIONS OF MEANING

When Freud tells us that a dream is "a form of expression of impulses," his use of the term "expression" is open to a number of interpretations (1900, p. 614). I have argued elsewhere that it is not being used in a certain ordinary sense in which we commonly speak of a threatening gesture as an expression of anger, or of an attempt to obtain something as an expression of a desire for it (Shope, 1967). To be sure, dreams, errors, and symptoms are conceived by Freud as having something in common with such phenomena. First, they are the manifestations or effects in consciousness or overt behavior of mental states. Further, they certainly are expressions of those mental states in one sense, insofar as they offer some evidence that the states are present, i.e., they are expressions of them in the sense of being clues to them, just as the presence of an organic disease entity such as a virus may express itself in certain physical symptoms, or a rise in prices be the expression of a change in some other economic variable.

However, I wish in the remainder of my discussion to argue that in saying that a phenomenon is meaningful Freud is not implying that it is a certain type of "symbolic expression" of the underlying mental states. I wish to oppose the reading of Freud which has been argued at great length and with considerable skill by the philosopher Paul Ricoeur. I have not the space to appraise all of Ricoeur's own arguments for viewing mental phenomena as symbolic expressions, but I shall consider those passages which he cites from Freud's texts to support his view (where I have not already considered them) and shall argue for an alternative exegesis of Freud's own account.

Ricoeur's use of the term "symbol" is actually narrower than the one I wish to consider, but it is a species of the latter use. The interpretation of Freud's remarks which I shall defend renders Ricoeur's use of "symbol" as well as the more general one quite distinct from Freud's own concepts of meaning.

Ricoeur explains that he wishes to restrict the term "symbol" to only part of the area covered by what Cassirer called the symbolic function or what Ricoeur prefers to call the signifying function. In everything which carries a sig-

---

said was "correcting" and "putting right" a past traumatic scene in her obsessional acts, and who discovered "the interpretation of the symptom herself at a single blow, without any prompting or intervention on the analyst's part" is nonetheless later described as not having been able to grasp and admit without much labor on Freud's part that such a motive was the driving force behind her actions. What she had spontaneously *recalled* was only the traumatic experience and she spontaneously *noticed* its similarity to the contents of her symptom. This connection is the content of the interpretation, which unravels the factors constituting the particular meaning of the dream (1916–1917, pp. 261–263, 276–277). Again, in discussing another patient's obsessional ritual of keeping the pillow from touching the bedstead, Freud reports the patient as having found out the central meaning of her ritual when she said that the pillow had always been a woman to her and the upright wooden back a man (p. 267). But he does not report that she recalled having *tried* to keep her *parents* apart through this symptom, only that she recalled the general fantasied similarity.

It certainly would not do to claim that such recall of an intentional act is always theoretically possible because all unconscious motives were at one time conscious. We saw that the preconscious dream wish, for example, is not viewed by Freud as ever having been conscious.

nifying function, every "sign," Ricoeur distinguishes its sensory content, the signification or sense which it carries, and the object designated (which may be
nonexistent, as in the case of the linguistic sign "unicorn").[12] What must be pre-
supposed in order for us to be able to say we have a genuine sign is the signification, something that "refers to," "intends," or "designates" something else,
and in that respect "stands for" it (1970, pp. 9–13).

A symbol, for Ricoeur, is a species of sign, one in which the overt signification "designates another meaning attainable only in and through the first intentionality," so that, thanks to their overt sense, symbols have a second, hidden
meaning (p. 16). Ricoeur contends that finding this hidden meaning is what Freud
rightly views as interpretation, which is thus concerned with "hermeneutics."

I shall argue that the passages Ricoeur cites from Freud do not even show
that Freud regarded dreams, symptoms, or parapraxes as signs in Ricoeur's sense,
i.e., symbolic expressions in Cassirer's broad sense, let alone as what Ricoeur
calls symbols. Freud views the relation between these mental phenomena and
their meaning as similar to the relation between the symptoms of measles and its
cause. They *express* the underlying states as effects manifest a cause. They are
signs only in the sense that organic symptoms are signs of a disease organism, or
dark clouds signs of rain to come. Symptoms are signs to the investigator, and
may arouse his expectations about finding their source, as dark clouds may arouse
expectations of rain. If the investigator chooses, he may make these phenomena
or representations of them into signs, in Ricoeur's sense, in the investigator's sign
language. But *to the patient* symptoms do not yet designate or intend their underlying sources, any more than the darkness of a cloud designates or intends
rain to the cloud or to any person before an observer devises a sign language.
Rather, the symptoms of neurosis *stand for* their psychic sources in the sense of
being *stand-ins,* that is, they appear in consciousness in place of the appearance
of their hidden $meaning_1$; they are substitutes for it.

When Ricoeur cites that passage from *The Interpretation of Dreams* which
we have been considering from the beginning of the present paper, he does so
in order to persuade us that when Freud says that dreams have a meaning, he intends to imply that "one can always substitute for the dream account another account, with a semantics and a syntax, and that these two accounts are comparable
to one another as two texts" (1970, p. 89; see also p. 25). Yet Freud speaks of
replacing the manifest dream *itself* by the mental acts that constitute its meaning, and not of replacing the waking *account* of the dream by the meaning. One
wonders whether Ricoeur is careful to distinguish the account of the manifest
dream from the dream images themselves.[13] However, he does go on to ac-

___

[12] This is somewhat like the distinction between an expression, its sense, and its
referent, except that when there is no referent Ricoeur still speaks of an object designated. Similarly, Brentano spoke of the intentional inexistence of the object in such a
context.

[13] For example, when Ricoeur interprets Benveniste's claim that the analyst's substituted text "refers back to underlying structures of the psychism" as saying that the
relations of motivations belonging to the unconscious of the patient themselves constitute another discourse, or when Ricoeur says that "the unconscious is another discourse" and that symptoms and dreams are the "meaningful effects" of "another
language" (1970, pp. 92, 366–367, 396).

knowledge that the processes in the unconscious do not literally constitute a language, and he does describe dreams, symptoms, ideas, and affects themselves as signs or symbols (1970, pp. 26, 313, 370, 396ff.). He admits that although "the dream as a nocturnal spectacle is unknown to us" in the obvious sense that "it is accessible only through the account of the waking hours," nonetheless "dreams in themselves border on language, since they can be told, analyzed, interpreted" (p. 15).

Clearly, the claim that dreams need to be *told* in order to be known is an overstatement, for a person might have memory knowledge of at least some of his own dream without having uttered even to himself any description of the dream. It would be a *non sequitur* to argue (as Ricoeur, indeed, does not) that merely because the dream must be verbalized in order to be known by persons other than the dreamer, the dream has in itself, even before being verbalized, a signifying function. Nor does the mere fact that a person has what philosophers call a type of "private access" to some of his mental phencmena make them signifying phenomena.

DERIVATIVES

Ricoeur notes that when Freud considers the intersystemic relations between the *Ucs.* and the *Pcs.* at the end of "The Unconscious" (1915b), he emphasizes that fantasies and derivatives of the repressed impulses are important as intermediaries between the systems. They provide a way for therapy to influence the *Ucs.* Ricoeur rightly concludes that this shows that the economic point of view does not "free itself entirely" from the interpretation of meaning. However, Ricoeur takes this to be a meaning that designates and is intentionally connected with another, hidden meaning (1970, pp. 15–16, 150–151) and appears to speak interchangeably of meaning and signification (p. 12). He later defends this view by arguing that fantasies "have a relationship of substitution with respect to the lost objects of desire; but they would not be derivatives, nor would those derivatives be remote or distorted, if they did not first of all have a relationship of meaning to something that presents itself as lost" (p. 368).

Freud is not claiming, however, that derivatives refer to or signify either their underlying impulses, or the objects of those impulses, or significations of those impulses or objects. When he discusses derivatives in "The Unconscious," he does say, as Ricoeur points out, that "the *Ucs.* is continued into what are known as derivatives" (1915b, p. 190). But Freud explains this in terms of the economic point of view, saying that the "unconscious libidinal cathexis" is discharged as anxiety by "a substitutive idea," which in that sense "acts . . . as a point at which there is a passage across from the system *Ucs.* to the system *Cs.*" Because of "the instinctual cathexis from the system *Ucs.* which is condensed in the symptom," a symptom becomes a "source for the release of anxiety." Thereupon, a second censorship between the *Pcs.* and *Cs.* is needed for "inhibiting the development of the anxiety which arises from the substitute" (1915b, pp. 182, 185, 183). This anxiety arises because of the nature of the energy possessed by the substitute. It is only when the substitute becomes "cathected with special intensity" that defensive measures are aroused against the substitute and its associated thoughts. These derivatives and fantasies may reach a certain degree of cathexis and remain in the *Pcs.;* "When, however, this intensity is exceeded and they try to force themselves into consciousness, they are recognized as derivatives of the *Ucs.* and are repressed afresh . . ." (1915b, p. 193). Thus, when Freud says in his companion paper, "Repression," that "It is as though the resistance of the conscious against them was a function of their distance from what was originally repressed," he does not mean except as a metaphor that the censorship is sometimes fooled by disguise, but means merely that the tendency toward arousing anxiety does not always overtake such derivatives (1915a, p. 149).

What Freud calls the "distortion" and "remoteness" of a derivative can be understood as concerning (1) the fact that the ideational content of the derivative is different in varying respects and degrees from what would be the ideational content of the conscious mental state for which it substitutes, and (2) the fact that these related states are linked by shorter or longer chains of associations. In this sense, a horse phobia is *about* horses, not about the patient's father. It merely serves, in spite of its literal ideational content but because of its energic nature, as a counterforce against the entrance into consciousness of the hostile wish *about* the patient's father.[14] This is not to say that the ideational content of the phobia is irrelevant to its arising as a link in the chain of associations produced by the wish.[15] But Freud's only putative explanation for why at a given point in time the chain stops at one link, which becomes a counterforce, rather than proceeding further or extending into consciousness, is to cite the energy state of the phobic ideas and their relation to anxiety. He does not mention any intentional direction of their content back down the associative paths.

THE NATURE OF REPRÄSENTANZ

Ricoeur also points out that Freud coined the term *Repräsentanz* to speak of ideas and affects as representatives of instincts separate from them, and to speak of instincts themselves as representatives of bodily sources separate, in turn, from those instincts. Since instincts are not viewed as internally ideational, the meaning of *Repräsentanz*, Ricoeur suggests, is not representation or presentation in the sense of being an idea of something, a *Vorstellung*. Ricoeur claims

---

[14] I cannot here assess the plausibility of Freud's account, but it is worth noting that even without the concept of energy (which Freud and many analysts do not intend as a mere metaphor [Shope, 1971]), he can speak of a derivative as something causally activated by its repressed source and which itself may be repressed because of that causal history and its resulting tendency toward producing anxiety.

A thorough discussion of Freud's concept of causality is needed to supplement the present paper. (For a beginning, see Sherwood [1969], and Shope [1970].) It would show that Freud utilizes a very scientific concept of causation modeled on medical concepts. He does not use the Spinozistic concept which Althusser attributes to him when, speaking of derivatives as effects of the Oedipal complex, Althusser adds: "If this term 'effect' is examined in the context of a classical theory of causality, it reveals a conception of the continuing presence of the cause in its effects (cf. Spinoza)" (1969, p. 63n.).

[15] For an outline and some discussion of the "loose" ways in which Freud thinks that one content may be associated with another (and thus be able to form the basis for a counterforce against the other), see Gill (1967).

that the only way to understand why Freud chooses the single term *Repräsentanz* to cover all these phenomena is to suppose that he saw them all as involving signifying functions, as involving intentional connections (1970, pp. 134–135, 150, 398).

But it is entirely possible, and indeed makes Freud's theory simpler, if we suppose that he is concerned with the way in which something *causally* mediates between the beginning and end of a causal chain. That is, activation of the physical source in the body causes an accumulation of the instinctual energy. This accounts for its increased causal activity toward inciting the increased activity, in turn, or origination of certain ideas and quotas of affect in the unconscious. Freud seems to think of this second step in the mediation as involving the transfer of some instinctual energy from the instincts to the ideas. (This energy is the quota of affect, as distinct from the conscious affect itself.) Such an interpretation does not require us to regard any intentionality as being involved in the very notion of a *Repräsentanz* and invokes only causal concepts of the general type Freud wishes to employ elsewhere in his theory.

Indeed, in common speech, we sometimes speak of causal mediation among variables by saying that changes in one variable *represent* changes in another, and in that sense express them. For example, an increase in demand may be represented by a rise in prices, and changes in prices express changes in demand. Again, the increased pressure of a gas may be represented by increased stress on the walls of the container and changes in that stress express changes in the pressure. The fact that Freud is considering what he calls excitations and accumulations of forces and energies means he is thinking of the occurrence and alteration of ideas and quotas of affect as being due to changes in the level of instinctual excitation. The latter changes, in turn, are causally due to changes in the level of physical excitation in the bodily sources. So it is natural to employ the common notion of representation. In the absence of more decisive textual evidence, I believe that for these reasons it is preferable to interpret Freud's notion of *Repräsentanz* in such a fashion.[16]

WISH FULFILLMENT

As we have seen, Freud sometimes says that the meaning of a dream is a wish fulfillment, and that dreams are valid and significant as wish fulfillments. Ricoeur,

---

[16] Ricoeur argues that there is an "intentional connection" between affects and ideas insofar as "affects are the charge of ideas" (1970, p. 150). However, the charge of an idea, the quota of affect, is for Freud a quantity of psychic energy dischargeable through conscious, felt affects but not identical with them before discharge. Ricoeur appears to confuse the two. To treat quota of affect as intentionally connected with ideas would imply that even *physical* energy intentionally belongs to something, be it a particle or a field, and would even make the concept of color intentional insofar as we cannot conceive of the presence of color without the presence of size. Assuming that Freud did not intend such implications, we cannot agree with Ricoeur that "this intentional connection . . . is why affects [i.e., quotas of affect] look for another ideational support to force their way into consciousness" (1970, p. 150). Ricoeur's insistence on an intentional connection might be more plausible regarding conscious, felt affect. if it could be shown, for example, that anxiety must always be anxiety about something, directed onto something.

who does not distinguish the concepts of validity and meaning in this context, argues in support of his account of meaning by claiming that Freud's concept of wish fulfillment is a hermeneutic one rather than an energic or dynamic concept.

Ricoeur reminds us that both Freud and Husserl were students of Brentano (1970, p. 379). He claims that Freud's use of the term *Erfüllung* is in Husserl's sense:

> . . . *accounting for the mechanisms of the dream-work . . . requires combining two universes of discourse, the discourse of meaning and the discourse of force. To say that a dream is the* fulfillment *of a repressed wish is to put together two notions which belong to different orders: fulfillment* (Erfüllung), *which belongs to the discourse of meaning (as attested by Husserl's use of the term), and repression* (Verdrängung), *which belongs to the discourse of force. The notion of Verstellung* [transposition or distortion] *. . . combines the two universes of discourse. . . . The concept of "censorship," correlative to the concept of distortion, belongs to this same mixed discourse (1970, p. 92).*

Here Ricoeur claims that some terms, such as "distortion" and "censorship," must have their sense defined both in terms of meaning and in terms of energy. He insists, however, that the term "fulfillment" belongs neither to this mixed discourse nor to the discourse of force and energy, but solely to the discourse of meaning. Ricoeur thus claims that this type of fulfillment is involved when the content of the manifest dream represents the ideational content of the repressed wish. Likewise, another type of fulfillment, namely, "verification," occurs for a person's conscious beliefs about scientific objects, there being "several ways of fulfilling various intentions of meaning according to various regions of objects" (p. 30). Obviously, this type of fulfillment is not at all defined in terms of energy processes.

Not only does Ricoeur fail to show that Freud knew anything of Husserl's views, but he ignores those passages I have previously discussed which present wish fulfillment as an essentially dynamic and energic concept. Indeed, even in the passage Ricoeur does emphasize (pp. 108, 266–267) from *The Interpretation of Dreams,* which harks back to the earlier discussion of hallucinatory response to wishes given in the "Project for a Scientific Psychology," the dynamic and energic aspect is part of the meaning of "fulfillment." Freud calls the infant's hallucination of a previous perception which originally accompanied the satisfaction of a need a wish fulfillment. But he speaks of such a hallucination as a "complete cathexis" of the perception, and says that in that case wishing "ended" in hallucinating (1900, pp. 565–566). He adds that this internal cathexis would have the same value as an external one if only it could be maintained indefinitely —apparently because it would continue to discharge the energy accumulating in the wish owing to the continuously unsatisfied organic need, and not because the hallucination has or is caused by exercising a signifying function (1900, pp. 565– 566, 598). When Freud says that "the reappearance of the perception is the fulfillment of the wish" he is employing the "is" of identity and not the "is" of definition. He is not stating the sense which he gives to the expression "wish fulfillment," not defining the expression, but claiming that the reappearance of the perception is identical with a phenomenon constituting a wish fulfillment.[17] It is because the reperception is an "internal cathexis" which is an "expenditure of psychical force" that it counts by definition as a wish fulfillment when that force is a wish.

It is also important to notice that Freud does not speak of the value of the hallucination as lying in the infant's *belief* that the wish is fulfilled and thus being temporarily contented. Indeed, when he discusses the hallucinations in dreaming, he associates our belief in the contents of a manifest dream *not* with wish fulfillment but with the different function of representation by means of sensory images and with the reduction of reality testing in dreams.[18] Moreover, belief in a hallucinated reality is not mentioned in connection with many symptoms or psychopathological phenomena of everyday life, yet Freud counts these errors and symptoms as wish fulfillments and expressions of wishes. Thus he requires no belief at an unconscious level to the effect that a wish is being fulfilled in any ordinary sense. His concept of wish fulfillment is not a concept of deceiving oneself by use of the signifying function. It is a technical concept of certain psychic energy processes which mental entities undergo.

MNEMIC SYMBOLS AND SYMBOLIZATION
IN *STUDIES ON HYSTERIA*

Ricoeur seeks confirmation for his reading even in the early publications of Breuer and Freud. He claims that what they call "mnemic symbols" are symbols which, as Ricoeur puts it, "take on the value of recollection of pain." Ricoeur adds:

If it is true, as was already said in the "Preliminary Communication," that "hysterics suffer mainly from reminiscences" [Breuer and Freud, 1893–1895, p. 7], mnemic symbols are the means by which the trauma continues to exist in the form of symptoms. Mnemic symbols, unlike the (chronic) "mnemic residues," are deformed or converted, in the sense that one speaks of hysterical conversion. Symbolization therefore is coextensive with the whole field of distortion connected with repression (the latter being identified at this period with defense) (1970, p. 97n.).

There are several mistakes in this interpretation. First, memory symbols of a trauma, for example, the hallucinated odor of burnt pudding in the case of

---

[17] To say that "psychoanalysis never confronts one with bare forces, but always with forces in search of meaning" (Ricoeur, 1970, p. 151) may be allowed if it is just to claim that any *referent* to which the discourse of force and energy applies is one identical with a referent to which the discourse of meaning applies, or to which a mixed discourse applies (in the senses of "meaning" I have presented). But that does not deny that some psychoanalytic *terms*, e.g., "wish fulfillment," belong solely to the discourse of force and energy so far as their linguistic *sense* is concerned.

[18] Freud says that "if we eliminate the wish-fulfilment" then the only feature left to distinguish waking awareness of a dream thought from the manifest dream is that the latter involves a thought which in most, but not all, dreams is "objectified . . . , is represented as a scene, or, as it seems to us, is experienced" (1900, p. 534).

Miss Lucy R., are sometimes literal and not distorted reproductions of a portion
of a traumatic experience (Breuer and Freud, 1893–1895, pp. 115–119). Second,
symbolization is a *process* existing only in *some* formations of symptoms which
are mnemic symbols (pp. 5, 152–153, 174–175). It is frequently described in
terms of the patient's *conscious* thought about part of the traumatic experience
(either when it happened or during the rise of the symptom) in terms of linguistic expressions forming a bridge between the trauma and the symptom (pp.
152–153, 178).[19] Third, Breuer and Freud offer no explanation of what they mean
by "symbol," not even to the extent of saying that a symbol stands for a trauma.[20]
Freud does say that the symptoms "join in the conversation" in the sense that
as the content of the discussion draws close to the reminiscences behind the
formation of a symptom, the latter becomes more intense and is, "we might say,
on the agenda all the time." Freud says that this symptom "takes the place of a
psychical act (in this instance, the act of utterance)" but does not say it is an act
of speaking or of signifying (p. 297). Finally, the content of an unconscious
memory trace is what is said to be the reminiscence producing symptoms "as a
directly releasing cause," and its effect is eliminated or lessened when it becomes a "reminiscence which emerges [that is, enters consciousness] during an
analysis" (pp. 7, 295).

It is interesting to notice Freud's description of cases in which the patient's
mental pain and discomfort was described during a trauma or is now consciously
thought of by the patient as feeling like a "slap in the face" or "a stab in the
heart." Freud says that hysteria may not have taken speech as a model for the
creation of such symptomatic sensations. It may only have followed a pre-existing disposition for the traumatic emotion to produce such pains, and this disposition may be the common source for both those sensations and the related
figures of speech. He alludes to Darwin's theory that sensations and innervations
which express emotion are weak accompaniments of those emotions which make
the figures of speech literally applicable (p. 181). Here we see an example of
Freud's tendency to view "symbols," in his restricted sense of the term, as occurring in neurosis and in the psychopathology of everyday life because of an
inherited residue which is not itself intrinsically linguistic or signifying in
Ricoeur's or Cassirer's sense.[21] In his reference to Darwin, Freud does not even
consider the residue as that of an old identity in words. This possibility of seeing

---

[19] However, the authors do refer without further comment to the existence of "a
'symbolic' relation between the precipitating cause and the pathological phenomenon—
a relation such as healthy people form in dreams" (Breuer and Freud, 1893–1895, p. 5).

[20] Freud speaks of an "uninterrupted series" of conscious mental phenomena,
running from conscious memory pictures through reproduced thoughts to hysterical
symptoms, the latter of which he calls "memory symbols." He labels only the first
two "mnemic residues" because they are evoked through the "pressure of the hand
technique" which Freud used in therapy at that time (Breuer and Freud, 1893–1895, p.
296; see also p. 110, passim). They are called mnemic residues because they are the
patient's attempts to respond to Freud's suggestion to try to remember past traumas or
related materials upon pressure of his hand on the forehead. These residues are thus
contrasted with the spontaneous eruption of a symptom.

[21] In his contribution Freud does add, without explanation, that in some symptoms "we clearly also find a symbolic version in concrete images and sensations of
more artificial turns of speech" (p. 181n.).

both neurotic associations and linguistic, signifying associations as emerging from
a single, primitive level of mental functioning suggests the further possibility that
Freud regards secondary-process associations in actual signifying functions as developments of the nonsignifying, primitive, primary-process functioning of the id,
and as more restricted, sometimes rule-governed, analogues of them.

One last point of interest in *Studies on Hysteria* is that considerations of
intentionality are, indeed, injected when Freud says that he could not help thinking that Miss Elizabeth v. R. had "done nothing more nor less than look for a
symbolic expression of her painful thoughts and that she had found it in the in-
tensification of her sufferings" (p. 152). Nonetheless, Freud later warns us that
this way of putting it is misleading when he says of her conversion:

I cannot, I must confess, give any hint of how a conversion of this kind is brought
about. It is obviously not carried out in the same way as an intentional and vol-
untary action. It is a process which occurs under the pressure of the motive of
defence in someone whose organization—or a temporary modification of it—
has a proclivity in that direction (p. 166).

He also warns that there is no secondary intelligence outside of consciousness
controlling unconscious material and arranging when it will return to consciousness (p. 272). The implication of these statements is that we must be careful to
emphasize the presence of the phrase "as though" in the following statement
concerning symbolization, which Ricoeur cites (1970, p. 97n.), from a lecture
Freud gave shortly before the appearance of *Studies on Hysteria:* "It is as
though there were an intention to express the mental state by means of a physical one; and linguistic usage affords a bridge by which this can be effected"
(1893, p. 34).[22]

THE DREAM AS REBUS AND
DREAM WORK AS TRANSLATION

After the extensive consideration we have already given to Freud's views on
meaning, we are finally in a position to assess judiciously the comparisons referred to by Ricoeur (1970, p. 89n.) which appear in Freud's brief introductory
remarks to the chapter on dream work in *The Interpretation of Dreams.*

There Freud begins by saying that the dream is "like" a picture puzzle, a
rebus, and that the relation between manifest dream and the dream thoughts is
"as it were" a translation of the latter into another language, a pictographic
script. But by the end of the paragraph, Freud is stating bluntly that the dream
"is" a rebus (1900, pp. 277–278).

The same transition from merely affirming an analogy to speaking of a
common characteristic occurs in "The Claims of Psycho-Analysis to Scientific
Interest" (1913). There, Freud first says that interpreting dreams is "completely

---

[22] In that lecture Freud also said that hysterics suffer not from reminiscences but
from *"incompletely abreacted psychical traumas"* (1893, p. 38).

analogous" to translating Egyptian hieroglyphs, and then says that in each case there are certain elements not "intended" to be interpreted or read but "designed" to establish the meaning of other elements (p. 177).

But we have seen that there is good textual evidence that Freud has again been led astray by the advantages offered by an analogy, and has overstated his considered views. He is momentarily ignoring his admission in *The Interpretation of Dreams* that the most severe strictures of earlier writers regarding the low level of mental functioning in dreams were justified, as well as his later admission that "a dream does not want to say anything to anyone. It is not a vehicle for communication . . ." (1916–1917, p. 231).

In the *New Introductory Lectures* (1933), Freud does suggest taking as communication the dreams of persons actually in therapy. But since he speaks anthropomorphically of *motives* as "saying" something in a disguised way, he is apparently using a figure of speech, and is regarding those dreams as communications merely in the sense of a transmission of information to the analyst from clues (pp. 8–9, 15). In this sense, rock strata communicate the past to the geologist by serving as clues to the past, but not through any intentionality. Of course, the "communications" of the patient are *causally* influenced by his desire to get well and by the transference.

THE SIGNIFYING FUNCTION AND THE UNCONSCIOUS

In a psychology in which desires and the mental registrations of experiences are conceived as causally activating one another and causally interfering with one another, a potential is already present for explaining symptoms, dreams, or parapraxes as effects of these interacting causes without adding the hypothesis that a signifying function is involved (whose actual use as opposed to its putative products is never *recalled* by patients). A developmental psychology may see this type of mental functioning as a precursor of or regression from a higher type of functioning which includes the signifying function. But in the absence of special reasons to the contrary, it seems a simpler hypothesis to view any residues in the unconscious of this higher functioning as merely associative links between ideas or registrations of ideas that at a higher level were connected by signification. It is simpler to view these residues as associative links such that the activation of one idea in a chain of mental events leads that chain off into a new direction through the activation of the associated idea, which is in this sense treated as though it were an equivalent idea.[23] There may be reasons for complicating this type of explanation and for extending the signifying function into the very activities of that "seething cauldron" which is the unconscious and into the links it has with other psychical systems. But Freud does not consider such reasons. What he offers as explanations is nonetheless concerned with the uniquely

---

[23] Even if some symbols are *initially culturally instilled* and initially have various preconscious signifying functions, their *residues* in the unconscious may be of this simpler nature. Obviously, such a concept of residues deserves more thorough discussion and investigation.

human effects of uniquely human causes, hidden from open view, and it is this causal nexus that Freud included in his account of meaning.

REFERENCES

Althusser, L. (1969). Freud and Lacan. *New Left Review*, No. 55:48–65.

Brenner, C. (1955). *An Elementary Textbook of Psychoanalysis.* New York: International Universities Press.

Breuer, J., and Freud, S. (1893–1895). Studies on Hysteria. *Standard Edition,* 2. London: Hogarth Press, 1955.

Cassirer, E. (1923–1929). *The Philosophy of Symbolic Forms,* Vols. 1–3. New Haven: Yale University Press, 1953–1957.

Dewey, J. (1899). *The School and Society.* Chicago: University of Chicago Press, 1923.

Freud, S. (1893). On the Psychical Mechanism of Hysterical Phenomena: A Lecture. *Standard Edition,* 3:27–39. London: Hogarth Press, 1962.

———— (1900). The Interpretation of Dreams. *Standard Edition,* 4 & 5. London: Hogarth Press, 1953.

———— (1910). Five Lectures on Psycho-Analysis. *Standard Edition,* 11:9–55. London: Hogarth Press, 1957.

———— (1913). The Claims of Psycho-Analysis to Scientific Interest. *Standard Edition,* 13:165–190. London: Hogarth Press, 1955.

———— (1915a). Repression. *Standard Edition,* 14:146–158. London: Hogarth Press, 1957.

———— (1915b). The Unconscious. *Standard Edition,* 14:166–215. London: Hogarth Press, 1957.

———— (1916–1917). Introductory Lectures on Psycho-Analysis. *Standard Edition,* 15 & 16. London: Hogarth Press, 1963.

———— (1917a). A Metapsychological Supplement to the Theory of Dreams. *Standard Edition,* 14:222–235. London: Hogarth Press, 1957.

———— (1917b). On Transformations of Instinct as Exemplified in Anal Erotism. *Standard Edition,* 17:127–133. London: Hogarth Press, 1955.

———— (1933). New Introductory Lectures on Psycho-Analysis. *Standard Edition,* 22:5–182. London: Hogarth Press, 1964.

Gill, M. M. (1967). The Primary Process. In: Motives and Thought: Psychoanalytic Essays in Honor of David Rapaport, ed. R. R. Holt. *Psychological Issues,* Monograph 18/19:260–298. New York: International Universities Press.

Hartmann, H. (1927). Understanding and Explanation. In: *Essays on Ego Psychology.* New York: International Universities Press, 1964, pp. 369–403.

Lacan, J. (1966). The Insistence of the Letter in the Unconscious. *Yale French Studies,* No. 36:112–147.

Mill, J. S. (1872). *A System of Logic,* 8th ed. London: Longmans, Green, 1941.

Nunberg, H. (1955). *Principles of Psychoanalysis: Their Application to the Neuroses.* New York: International Universities Press.

Ricoeur, P. (1970). *Freud and Philosophy: An Essay on Interpretation.* New Haven: Yale University Press.

Rosen, V. (1969). Sign Phenomena and Their Relationship to Unconscious Meaning. *International Journal of Psycho-Analysis,* 50:197–207.

Sherwood, M. (1969). *The Logic of Explanation in Psychoanalysis.* New York: Academic Press.

Shope, R. (1967). The Psychoanalytic Theories of Wish-Fulfilment and Meaning. *Inquiry,* 10:421–438.

———— (1970). Freud on Conscious and Unconscious Intentions. *Inquiry,* 13:149–159.

———— (1971). Physical and Psychic Energy. *Philosophy of Science,* 38:1–12.

Wilden, A. (1968). *The Language of the Self.* Baltimore: Johns Hopkins Press.

THE STRUCTURAL HYPOTHESIS AND PSYCHOANALYTIC METATHEORY [1]
An Essay on Psychoanalysis and Contemporary Philosophy of Science

Emmett Wilson, Jr., M.D., Ph.D.

I. THE FUNCTIONAL ANALYSIS OF PSYCHIC STRUCTURE

In *The Ego and the Id* (1923) Freud introduced into his theory the claim that there are three divisions of the mind, the id, the ego, and the superego. These divisions of the mental apparatus are called psychic structures, and this aspect of the theory has been designated the structural hypothesis. Freud attempted to specify the functions performed by each of these divisions of the mind. More recently, the claim has sometimes been made that psychic structure is "defined by its functions." This view is frequently found in the psychoanalytic literature, and is associated with Heinz Hartmann and his collaborators. It is a view that has had great influence on the teaching of psychoanalytic theory. In the literature this thesis has appeared as the standard by which other theoretical discussions are judged and criticized. Moreover, some theorists, notably David Beres (1958, 1965), have developed Hartmann's view into a functional theory of mind, replete with widespread implications for the relationship of mental to physical phenomena, the nature of the mental apparatus, and the nature of theorizing in psychology. However, the meaning, implications, and possible difficulties of this emphasis on function have remained comparatively unexamined.[2]

---

[1] I wish to acknowledge in this paper special indebtedness to the work of Jerry A. Fodor, whose views on psychological theory are particularly important for psychoanalysis.

[2] A few examples may be in order to illustrate how widespread this functional analysis of structure has become. Moore and Fine (1967, p. 31) write: "The ego should not be thought of as an anthropomorphic executor or as an actual part of the brain, but as a useful way of thinking about the basic aspects of human behavior. It is best defined as a group of functions." In a major work on the structural theory, Arlow and Brenner (1964, p. 32) say: "The structural theory . . . divides the mind into three groups of functions called the id, the ego, and the superego. . . . Each group of functions is often called a mental structure, whence the name, the structural theory." The influence of Beres's paper is shown by Hayman (1969). Dr. Hayman suggests that the substantival use of the term "id" is misleading, and that we should understand the term as adjectival, i.e., as more correctly spelled with an adjectival ending, such as "idic." Nagera (1967, 1968) also seems to endorse Beres's interpretation. Some criticism has also appeared in the literature: see Holt (1967, p. 350); Apfelbaum (1966); Schafer (1968, pp. 11f.); Eissler (1962).

My purpose in this paper is twofold. First, I wish to show that many problems arise with the functional view of structure, and many misunderstandings have characterized the discussions of this view, hampering the recognition of an important element of truth that may be contained in it. Second, I shall take this consideration of the structural hypothesis as an occasion to show how a familiarity with issues in the philosophy of science might have lessened the temptation to fall into a narrow empiricistic formulation of the relation between structure and function. An understanding of certain issues in contemporary philosophy of science might have prevented a hasty and simplistic methodological approach to the difficult problem of theoretical entities in psychoanalysis. I shall try to show the origins of the methodological hesitancy concerning the concept of psychic structure, and how this hesitancy gives rise to the functionalist interpretation. I then propose briefly a more tolerant view of the nature of psychic structure, a view that will, I believe, place fewer a priori restrictions on the phenomena that psychoanalysis is trying to study.

It is my hope that this discussion will prompt psychoanalytic theoreticians to take into account these advances in the contemporary philosophy of science. Unfortunately, analysts have remained isolated from these developments, and have continued to voice a radical empiricism many decades after its abandonment by philosophers of science. The result has been detrimental for the formulation of an adequate metatheory for psychoanalysis.

My remarks should not be construed as a defense of the structural hypothesis per se. We may come to abandon it or the particular theoretical entities introduced by it into the theory. I wish, however, to focus attention on the nature of theoretical entities in psychoanalysis, independent of any particular hypothesis about them. Although I do believe that the structural hypothesis has an assured place in the theory, what I suggest here will be applicable even if the structural hypothesis is abandoned and some other theoretical move substituted for it.

II. HARTMANN AND THE STRUCTURAL HYPOTHESIS

Perhaps no one since Freud has done so much to plead the cause of theoretical sophistication in psychoanalysis as Heinz Hartmann. It is therefore particularly important that we attend to his efforts at a conceptual analysis of the structural hypothesis. Hartmann elaborates his views on psychic structure in many passages. For example, in a paper written with Ernst Kris and Rudolph Loewenstein,[3] we find the following statement:

These three psychic substructures or systems are conceived of not as independent parts of personality that invariably oppose each other, but as three centers of psychic function that can be characterized according to their developmental

---

[3] Collaborative authorship by these three writers will hereafter be designated as HKL. Hartmann has discussed his views on psychic structure in several papers (see Hartmann, 1950, 1951, 1952, 1956, 1958, 1959).

level, the amount of energy invested in them, and their demarcation and interdependence at a given time. . . . [We] have indicated the criteria used in defining the three substructures: the psychic systems are defined by the functions attributed to them (1946, p. 14).

The authors apparently sense a need to explain this concept of "definition by function," for they immediately append a defense of this conceptual move. They continue:

A word need be said here as to how these definitions were arrived at. Definitions are matters of "convenience," and convenience in science consists of an adequate relation to observed facts. Freud established his definitions of the psychic systems after careful and repeated scrutiny of his clinical material. The material suggested that in a typical psychic conflict one set of functions is more frequently on "the one side" than on "the other side" of the conflict. Functions that we find "together on one side" have common characteristics or properties. The relatedness is one of frequency (pp. 14–15).

It seems, however, that still more words are in order concerning what sort of process the authors thought was involved in this "definition by function." I can deal here only briefly with the complex roles of definition in science. It will be sufficient to point out some of the difficulties that arise directly from this passage, and to show how these difficulties encroach on larger issues in the philosophy of science.

It is unclear what the authors mean by "convenience." Probably what has occurred here is the conflation of two ideas. The first is the idea that definitions are established by *convention*. The second seems to be some idea concerning the purpose of establishing these definitions, i.e., to serve as a convenient aid in our pursuit of the science in question. Be that as it may, the important issue here is the manner in which new terms are introduced into a theory. Probably Hartmann and his colleagues meant that a new concept in a theory is introduced by definitions that stipulate the meaning in terms of the antecedently available vocabulary, in this case, the "clinical material." On this view, we establish a convention to hold as true certain sentences that give the meaning of the new term.

We might rephrase this claim in a fashion more in keeping with the terminology employed in the philosophy of science. The theoretical terms of the structural hypothesis are given empirical content by a set of rules that define these theoretical terms by correlating them with the observational data. These rules have been given a number of different names, all roughly equivalent. I shall, in this paper, refer to them as "correspondence rules." [4] By means of these rules, an "adequate relation to observed facts," that is, empirical content, is assigned to the theoretical concepts.

[4] Other terms that have been employed are: operational definitions, semantical rules, epistemic correlations, and rules of interpretation.

Two questions arise immediately. First, can *all* the theoretical terms in a theory be so defined? Second, what is the nature of these correspondence rules that give empirical content to the theoretical concepts? I shall take up the second question directly; discussion of the first issue must be postponed until later when we come to a consideration of the nature of theoretical terms.

Hartmann does not, to my knowledge, give us a clear indication of what would constitute an "adequate relation to observed facts." It is quite possible that these definitions would have ideally, for Hartmann, the character of explicit definitions. An explicit definition provides for the complete eliminability of the defined term from any context in which it occurs, by replacing it with the defining expression, without loss of cognitive meaning. An example might be "an oculist is an eye doctor." The defined term, "oculist," is completely eliminable in any of its occurrences merely by replacing it with the defining term "eye doctor." For a number of reasons it is quite clear that this cannot be the type of definition that HKL are offering us here.

First, if a structure, the ego, were equivalent definitionally to a certain group of functions, say, a, b, c, d, and e, then we must be puzzled by the claim that sometimes some members of this set of functions may appear "on the other side of a conflict," that is, say, in the group of id functions, g, h, and i. If at one time the ego consists only of functions a, d, e, and, at another time, of functions a, b, d, then it is difficult to see how the ego could be defined as the group of functions a, b, c, d, and e. For if these were the defining characteristics of the ego, then, invariably, when the ego is on one side of a conflict this set of functions will be on that side of the conflict. For such is the meaning of the term 'ego,' by definition. The geometer would find it difficult to accept the definition of a triangle as "a closed plane figure bounded more often than not by three straight lines." Yet HKL emphasize the statistical character of the association of the functions together when they tell us that a set of functions is "more frequently" on one side of a conflict than on the other.

Such considerations make it difficult to maintain that explicit definition is involved in the concept of definition by function. Hence, the definition is much looser than first appears. What, then, is the "adequate relation to observed facts" which HKL want for their theoretical concepts?

The rules relating the theoretical term 'ego' with clinical situations are quite imprecise and loosely stated. Such looseness is a general characteristic of correspondence rules (E. Nagel, 1961; Hempel, 1970). The imprecision is quite clearly illustrated in the present context by the haziness concerning the concept of function itself. 'Function' is a complex theoretical term that refers not to specific behavior, or to bits of behavior, but to a complex set of activities which would be difficult to spell out exactly. That is, perception, memory, motility, conscience, etc., are hardly first-order behavioral or observational concepts, but are rather complex and unclear notions in themselves. The theoretical term 'function' is certainly more closely linked to the empirical data than the term 'ego,' but it is not a simple matter to give an account of the empirical data that would lead us to talk of functions. Even Hartmann has shown some hesitancy about whether to include the physiological apparatus necessary for perception as a part of the ego (Nagera, 1967).

This lack of unique correspondence between the term 'ego' and the clinical material is also shown by the frequent appeal to other criteria for the definition of the ego. We are told that the frequently associated functions have "common characteristics or properties." Thus there would seem to be other characteristics, besides being together on one side of a conflict, that might also be used to define the ego. For example, Hartmann (1956) discusses the ego as "characterized by its functions *and* its relations to the external world *and* to other mental processes" (p. 427; italics added). Arlow and Brenner (1964) similarly offer us a choice of definitions:

. . . *the ego may be characterized in either of two ways. (1) It may be defined as a group of functions of the mind which are usually associated with one another in situations of mental conflict; or (2) it may be defined as the group of mental functions which in one way or another have to do with mediating between the demands of the id and those of the outer world (p. 41).*

We can see, then, that even those authors who are inclined toward a functional analysis of structural terms give us many indications of the looseness and systematic vagueness of the defining rules that they invoke for the structural concepts. These writers make no pretense to logical rigor in their presentations, and would probably accept the suggestion that what is at issue are rules which correlate statements about the ego with statements about observed facts. They probably would also acknowledge that these rules must be looser than they seem to suppose. What is of utmost importance to these theorists is that there be some way of giving empirical content as directly as possible to the terms introduced by the structural hypothesis. They want some means by which the meaning of these theoretical terms can be specified by an appeal to the clinical material. But this apparently commendable program is, as we shall see, misguided in a number of ways.

It should be noted, before leaving the discussion of Hartmann, that he and his co-workers are misleading on one point. Ostensibly, they are not introducing a new term into the theory, and thus would seem to be offering a descriptive account either of the manner in which the term 'ego' is used in present psychoanalytic discourse or of its use historically by Freud. Yet their account is clearly neither. The actual use of the term by the analytic community, or in the Freudian texts, is at variance with the definition they propose. HKL's injunctions against anthropomorphism, if nothing else, show that this divergence of actual usage exists. The definition that they introduce is in fact a stipulative redefinition of the term. They are attempting to tell us how the term *should be* used henceforth, if their views are accepted. They are reformers, trying to clarify and redefine a term already in use in the theory. There is, of course, nothing objectionable in concept improvement in science. Philosophers (Quine, 1966; Hempel, 1970) have noted that conventionality characterizes scientific concepts only at their introduction into the theory; later on these concepts become vulnerable to revision just as does any other scientific concept, when empirical considerations or theoretical developments make modification necessary. In the case of this conceptual revision, however, it is urgent to spell out the presuppositions that led to the recommended modifications. Are there theoretical problems, or new empirical observations, which necessitate a revision in the structural concepts? I suggest that the actual impetus toward revision stems from certain a priori assumptions about the nature of theories and about the nature of psychology. These presuppositions must be clearly articulated before the proposed conceptual revision can be fully evaluated. We shall find that these presuppositions derive from an outmoded empiricism. David Beres's interpretation of the structural hypothesis is the logical extension of Hartmann's position. A consideration of his view will, I think, make more explicit the difficulties involved in the functional view of structure.

III. BERES'S FUNCTIONAL THEORY OF THE EGO

David Beres (1965) proposes a strongly reductionist interpretation of the structural hypothesis. He even suggests that "the functional theory of psychoanalysis" would have been a more fortunate choice of term than "the structural hypothesis." In his paper he interprets the concept of definition by function to mean that the ego is, or is composed of, its functions.

The genesis of many of Beres's concerns is the fact that the distinction between structure and function seems to be clear when "as in the biological sciences, structure refers to morphology and function refers to physiological activity, both of which can be *directly observed*" (p. 53; italics added). It is, apparently, the demand to produce a purely psychological theory that causes the difficulty for Beres, for he is worried by the fact that observational correlates for psychological terms are not readily available. He writes, "With psychological phenomena the inter-relationship between structure and function is not as easily demonstrable" (p. 53).

Beres claims that the structure-function relationship was clear in Freud's monograph *On Aphasia* (1891), as well as in the "Project" (1895), since both these works refer to a neurological structure as the morphology. He claims, however, that "In Freud's later writings structure is not considered in morphological terms but in terms relating to function" (p. 54). According to Beres, many theorists unfortunately have failed to see this functional characterization of structure in the later writings, and have been wont to misuse or misconceive the structural hypothesis because of the lack of a "morphological substrate."

What are the abuses that may befall the structural theory? Beres fears that the introduction of structural terms carries with it the danger of what he calls "reification." By this he seems to mean that while there is no "morphological substratum" to which the functions of the ego may be attributed, nonetheless a theorist may be tempted to suppose that the terms do refer to some thing. Curiously, Beres also seems to assume that this thing must be a physical entity:

". . . it must be remembered that the psychological structures are not physical entities and should not be treated as such" (p. 54). Reification seems to mean, to Beres, the supposition that the structural terms refer to some physical, presumably neurophysiological, structure.

In other passages, however, Beres seems to understand reification as the use of anthropomorphic metaphor, as in the statement he quotes from Freud (1926, p. 126): ". . . what the ego regards as the danger and responds to with an anxiety signal is that the super-ego should be angry with it or punish it or cease to love it (p. 56)." Thus far, Beres's concerns about the structural hypothesis seem to parallel Hartmann's.

Beres attempts further to specify the danger of reification, and here he seems to pursue a different line of thought. He equates reification with what Whitehead (1926) called the "fallacy of misplaced concreteness," and with Reichenbach's (1951) "substantialization of abstracts." Beres claims that reification involves the mistake of taking abstractions for "concrete reality." By this he seems to mean that the theoretical terms of psychoanalysis are "abstractive" (see E. Nagel, 1961, and p. 321 below) and do not refer to any actually existing thing. Theoretical terms are, for Beres, something like 'shorthand' summations or abstractions from a large body of clinical observations. In the case of the structural hypothesis, these observations would be about those sets of behavior that we call functions, e.g., perception, memory, motility, etc. Beres's remarks can only lead us to suppose that on his view the theoretical terms of psychoanalysis are devoid of any content except that empirical content assigned to them in definitional postulates. In particular, Beres apparently believes that statements about theoretical entities are devoid of any ontological commitment, that is, of any implication that there are entities of such nature and characteristics as described in the structural hypothesis. No claim is to be made for the existence of egos and superegos when we use these terms in theoretical discourse. Rather, the term 'ego' is simply an abstractive term used in a shorthand fashion to summarize a large amount of clinical data concerning psychic functions. We saw earlier that he rejected any reduction of the entities of psychoanalytic theory to physical or neurological structures. Now, in effect, he has introduced another sort of reduction. He has taken Hartmann's claim that the ego is defined by its functions and interpreted this to mean that the ego is composed of its functions.

Those who are familiar with the history of philosophy will have by this time a slightly uneasy feeling of déjà vu, an impression that they have seen all this before. It is exactly parallel to some familiar moves in philosophical discussions. These developments will be reviewed here briefly, since Beres's claim so strikingly recapitulates the history of philosophy.

Consider the problem of our knowledge of material objects. We can illustrate this by starting with John Locke, who tried to justify claims to knowledge of material objects by grounding those claims in sense perception. He argued that all our concepts of material objects are abstracted out of sense experience, and, if we want to know whether a particular claim about a material object is true, we should merely have to check to see whether certain experiences occur.

Thus he thought he could show that our knowledge of the external world is firmly based on sense observation.

But there are problems which develop with such an attempted analysis. These can be seen in Locke's well-known discussion of the concept of a substance:

> The mind . . . takes notice . . . that a certain number of these simple ideas [sense perceptions] go constantly together; . . . not imagining how these simple ideas can subsist by themselves, we accustom ourselves to suppose some substratum wherein they do subsist, and from which they do result; which therefore we call substance. . . . If anyone will examine himself concerning his notion of pure substance in general, he will find he had no other idea of it at all, but only a supposition of he knows not what support of such qualities which are capable of producing simple ideas in us (Locke, An Essay concerning Human Understanding, Book II, Ch. xxiii, sec. i).

In this passage Locke indicates that he is unable to analyze the concept of a substance (substratum) entirely in terms of sense perception. There remains a residuum, an indeterminate something that causes the sense perceptions, but which is essentially unknowable by means of sense experience itself. The next empiricist move at this point, as exemplified by George Berkeley, was to point out the skepticism into which Locke's position should have led him. Berkeley held that on Locke's view we could never know that we were perceiving a material object. The sense experiences might be the same and yet there might not be any substratum, hence no material object was present, and our experience becomes purely illusory. To avoid falling into skepticism concerning our knowledge of material objects, Berkeley *identified* the material object with the sense perceptions. That is, the material object became, for Berkeley, just a bundle of sense perceptions. Berkeley and philosophers of this persuasion held that a material object was a collection of actual or potential sense perceptions.

We can speak of this thesis in two ways. We might speak of equating physical objects with sense data, in which case we would claim that a table is a collection of actual and possible sense perceptions. Or we can, as some later philosophers preferred to do, analyze the *statements* about material objects in terms of *statements* about sense impressions. In the latter case our claim would be that all statements about material objects can be translated without remainder into statements about sense impressions. This shift is sometimes known philosophically as the shift from the material mode to the formal mode. Beres thus might have expressed his view as "the ego *is* a group of functions" (material mode); or he might have claimed that "statements about the ego can be translated without remainder into statements about functions" (formal mode). Thus we see that Beres's attempt to reduce structure to function is reminiscent of the sort of manoeuvre developed by certain empiricist philosophers to account for knowledge of material objects. The psychoanalytic theorist who makes a comparable move about psychic structure asks us to believe that when we talk about egos, superegos, and ids, what we are actually talking about are functions. On this view, statements about egos could be replaced by statements about functions, just as many empiricist philosophers wished to analyze statements about tables and chairs into statements about sense experience.

It is not possible to review here all the reasons why this attempted analysis has in general been rejected. Questions have been raised about the present unavailability of any such translation for material-object statements. Many have doubted whether any such translation would ever be possible. The artificial character of such a translation is a serious obstacle when compared to the material-object language. We clearly must question why this approach should be any more appropriate in the philosophy of psychoanalysis when it has generally been rejected in epistemology. Further, we must question the wisdom of replacing structural terminology by statements about functions when we are not asked at the same time to replace statements about unconscious ideation— or for that matter, about mental items in general—by some sort of reference to overt manifestations or behavior. Certainly we need some arguments to show us why we should accept reductionism for structure and not for any other mental states or events.

What has become apparent now is that the theorists whose view we have examined are struggling with a reluctance to countenance the admission into the theory of certain terms which do not have immediate and direct empirical content. They are willing to go along with the ordinary psychological talk about ideas, and with the well-confirmed scientific statements about unconscious mental contents. But, curiously, the credentials for any higher-level theoretical concepts are being checked for a guaranteed grounding in empirical observations. The reason for this naïve reiteration of empiricist dogma seems to be a reluctance to accept theoretical entities in psychology. At this point it should be recognized that the problem is larger than psychoanalytic theory, and is a part of the general concern shown in the philosophy of science about the status of theoretical entities.

IV. FREUD AND THE STRUCTURAL HYPOTHESIS

Beres suggests that his view of the structural hypothesis is that which Freud had in mind. He cites translation problems and Freud's use of anthropomorphic metaphors as factors that might have led one to suppose otherwise. It will be well to examine Freud's view of the structural hypothesis, to determine whether Beres is correct in relying on Freud's authority for a functional view of structure.

A cursory examination of those passages in which Freud is trying to clarify his use of the new theoretical term 'ego,' etc., shows that he frequently does refer to functions to characterize these theoretical concepts. He says, for example, that "we have allotted to [the superego] the function of self-observation, of conscience, and of the ego-ideal" (1933, p. 58). Of the ego he says, "It is entrusted with important functions," among which he includes reality testing, motility, and perception (1923, p. 55). There are many similar passages in which Freud invokes the concept of function in this manner.

But is this to define the psychic systems by their functions? There does not seem to be any textual warrant for the supposition that Freud endorsed the sweeping generalization that structure is defined by function, or that structures are groups of functions, even though it is clear that he was using evidence about the performance of certain functions as the clinical material that warranted his introduction of the structural terminology. To understand more clearly the theoretical move involved it will perhaps be helpful to examine in greater detail Freud's views on the structural hypothesis.

Freud's use of the term 'structure' (in the sense with which we are concerned in this paper) is not extensive. References to a 'structural theory' are not found at all, and it has been suggested that the latter term was coined by Ernst Kris (Nagera, 1967). However, what we refer to as the structural hypothesis actually developed over the course of many years in Freud's work, and did not suddenly appear on the scene in 1923. In *The Ego and the Id* Freud merely specifies and modifies the concepts of psychic or mental structures which had been implicit in the concepts of "regions of the mind," or the "systems" or "agencies" of earlier discussions. There are anticipations of the hypothesis in the Fliess letters and in the so-called prepsychoanalytic papers, and one version of it appears in the "Project." This point has sometimes been missed, even by able theoreticians. Gill (1963) acknowledges that he and Rapaport erred in their joint paper on metapsychology (Rapaport and Gill, 1959) in claiming that Freud gave no definition of the structural hypothesis, for the requisite definition had been given in his discussions of the topographic point of view. The concept of psychic structure has, therefore, a long history in Freud's writings. Gill has shown in his monograph on the topographic point of view (1963) that the topographic systems in 1900 were characterized by (1) relation to consciousness, (2) mode of organization (primary or secondary process), (3) energic condition (free versus bound energy), and (4) the degree of neutralization of the energy involved. Whether or not we agree with these specific extractions from *The Interpretation of Dreams* (1900), it is quite clear that Freud characterized the systems by multiple means. Hence Hartmann, and Arlow and Brenner, were correct to modify the functional characterizations that they propose for the structural entities. Functions, indeed, do not seem to be the main modality for the characterization of the systems. Gill's considerable documentation suggests that Freud regarded the structural and topographic points of view as essentially the same. In *The Ego and the Id* the later modifications of the theory are formally presented and described, with those revisions that were made necessary by the abandonment of the first of Gill's criteria, i.e., the relation of contents to consciousness. If Gill is correct, the other defining criteria listed above are implicit in the discussion in *The Ego and the Id,* and the main textual emphasis in the work is on the rearrangement of functions necessitated by this theoretical modification.

So far I have cited evidence that Freud did not single out functions as the sole or main criterion for the definition of the structural terms. But there is also considerable evidence that Freud took a realist position concerning the structural entities, in contrast to the view that Beres would have us adopt. Hartmann (1959, p. 29) seems to suggest that Freud's view was realist. Even when we discount the many obviously metaphorical or anthropomorphizing passages, we still find that Freud was not inclined to take a reductionist view of the theoretical entities he was introducing. For example, he says in *The Ego and the Id:*

I propose to take [Groddeck's work] into account by calling the entity [Wesen] which starts out from the system Pcpt. and begins by being Pcs. the "ego," and by following Groddeck in calling the other part of the mind, into which this entity extends and which behaves as though it were Ucs., the "id" (1923, p. 23).

And in a passage in the *New Introductory Lectures* we find an even clearer statement of an existential assumption. Beres cites this passage, but curiously fails to notice the existential claim that it involves:

But it is more prudent to keep the agency [the superego] as something independent and to suppose that conscience is one of its functions and that self-observation . . . is another of them. And since when we recognize that something has a separate existence [Existenz] we give it a name of its own, from this time forward I will describe this agency in the ego as the "super-ego" (1933, p. 60).

We may recall, too, Freud's contemptuous dismissal of Janet precisely on the question of the existence of the unconscious:

. . . [Janet] has expressed himself with exaggerated reserve, as if he wanted to admit that the unconscious had been nothing more to him than a form of words, a makeshift, une façon de parler—that he meant nothing real [nichts Reales] by it. Since then I have ceased to understand Janet's writings . . . (1916–1917, p. 257).

Thus we have an array of passages in which Freud's interpretation of the structural entities is an expressly realist one. There does not, on the other hand, seem to be any passage that forbids such an interpretation, or which proposes a view such as Janet and Beres suggest.

Freud certainly does warn against misunderstanding his anthropomorphic metaphors. He recognized, too, that conceptual revision of his theory might become necessary, and so stressed the provisional character of the propositions he was introducing concerning structure. There is an apparently antirealist comment by Breuer in *Studies on Hysteria* (Breuer and Freud, 1893–1895, pp. 227–228). There Breuer warns against reification in the sense of supposing that every substantive term has a substance behind it. But in the examples he gives Breuer refers to spatial analogies, anthropomorphization, or the specification of neurological correlates. His caveat seems to be similar to that of more recent writers whose work we have been considering. Breuer, then, does not seem to have considered the problem in the form in which we are framing it, that is, the ontological status of entities introduced into theoretical discourse.

In view of all this, it is interesting to return to and examine in greater detail the passage from Freud's *New Introductory Lectures* (1933) that Beres cites as corroborating his own view of the structural hypothesis, when correctly translated.[5]

Beres suggests that sometimes the translation may mislead us in the interpretation of Freud's meaning. He (1965, p. 55) contrasts the Sprott translation of a sentence in the *New Introductory Lectures*:

I hope you will by now feel that in postulating the existence of a superego I have been describing a genuine structural entity, and have not been merely personifying an abstraction, such as conscience,

with Strachey's revision:

I hope you have already formed an impression that the hypothesis of the superego really describes a structural relation and is not merely a personification of some such abstraction as that of conscience.[6]

Beres cites these passages because he feels that the changes are significant modifications. I would acknowledge that Sprott perhaps to a degree overtranslated the German by giving "structural entity" for "structural relation" (*Strukturverhältnis*). However, Strachey's change to "hypothesis" rather than "entity" does not help matters as much as Beres seems to think. If Beres feels more comfortable with the word "hypothesis" it is apparently because he takes it to mean something weak like "supposition" or "conjecture" and opposed perhaps to some such category as "established fact." But to take "hypothesis" here to mean "supposition" is to beg the question concerning the nature of scientific hypotheses. This is a philosophical problem, rather than a linguistic problem

[5] A methodological point is in order here. Beres is curiously disdainful of the importance of detailed attention to the Freudian texts. He states: "I see little advantage in the formalistic concern with Freud's use of terms which admittedly was often not precise" (1965, pp. 54–55). We must question this abrupt dismissal of the importance of exegesis of Freud's texts. Much is to be gained if we try to understand the apparent imprecisions and seeming inconsistencies. There may well be a way of reconciling the difficulties which, if discovered, will enable us to understand more fully this extraordinarily rich theory. The "imprecisions" of the text may reflect conceptual difficulties of which Freud was aware but which he did not fully articulate. The theory is complex, and Freud's apparent asides and casual footnotes furnish important leads into the nuances and intricacies of the theory. These "imprecisions" may amply reward further consideration and exploration. There is much to be said for developing the fine art of attention to the Freudian texts. To ascribe the difficulties to carelessness, as Beres does, is to take the easy way out.

[6] The original German is as follows: "*Ich hoffe, Sie haben bereits den Eindruck empfangen, dass die Aufstellung des Über-Ichs wirklich ein Strukturverhältnis beschreibt und nicht einfach eine Abstraktion wie die des Gewissens personifiziert.*" One of the main differences in the two translations is in the rendering of the German word *Aufstellung*: Strachey translates "hypothesis," whereas Sprott gives "postulating the existence." But the usual word for hypothesis in German is *Annahme*; the derivative from the Greek is also used, i.e., *Hypothese*. The question arises whether *Aufstellung* is a stronger word, and, if so, it is not incorrect for Sprott to have reflected that fact.

about the best translation. Whether Freud did or did not spell out existential postulates for his structural hypothesis is not the main issue. The philosophical problem is whether the introduction of a hypothesis concerning the superego requires us at the same time to "postulate the existence" of the superego. And this concern is a reflection of the more general issue concerning scientific hypotheses; that is, whether theoretical entities introduced into any scientific discourse must be regarded as existing in some sense. Thus it is a question for the philosophy of science, and not a question limited to psychoanalysis only.

There is, moreover, a passage in Freud (1916–1917) that indicates very clearly his recognition of the issue that we have been discussing. He states: ". . . the possibility of giving a sense to neurotic symptoms is an unshakeable proof of the existence [*Existenz*]—or, if you prefer it, of the necessity for the hypothesis [*Annahme*]—of unconscious processes (p. 279)." And Freud, *pace* Beres, seems very often to have preferred an interpretation of the structural hypothesis in which the terms of the hypothesis referred to actual entities.

V. MODELS AND THE STRUCTURAL THEORY

One of the purposes of this paper is to show how the philosophy of science might be of help in formulating and clarifying problems that arise concerning psychoanalytic theory. We may begin this task by pointing out the role of models in psychoanalytic theory. The question of the theoretical model is intricately involved in the misunderstandings that have led some theorists to regard the theoretical terms of the structural hypothesis as abstractions. It will help to trace the role of models in Freud's theorizing. Although Freud's use of models gradually became clearer during the development of his theory, he did not fully articulate the difficulties involved, and may not have been completely aware of them.

Many philosophers of science have argued that a theory has, as one of its constituents, a model or analogy.[7] The model specifies the basic ideas of the theory in concepts with which we are already familiar. The model then permits the theory to become intuitively understandable, and thus serves a heuristic role as an aid to imagination. While some models may represent the actual structure of the phenomena that the theory studies, many models are clearly not intended to do so. The latter type of model has been characterized as carrying with it an obvious "as if" quality that limits its function simply to the heuristic one of making the theory understood more easily, in readily available and usually visualizable materials. Such, for example, would be the model that Freud found in the "mystic writing-pad" (Freud, 1924). Freud saw in this "contrivance" a superb model of some of the most important aspects of the mental apparatus, for it illustrated in a simple, clear, and obvious fashion the principle of the incom-

---

[7] The parts of a theory are sometimes held to be (1) the theoretical statements, (2) the correspondence rules linking certain levels of the theoretical statements with observation statements, and (3) the model or analogy that illustrates the theory. See E. Nagel (1961).

patibility of perception and mnemic registration. The pad offered, according to Freud, "a concrete representation of the way in which I tried to picture the functioning apparatus of the mind" (p. 232). This was in 1924, however, when Freud's sophistication about metatheoretical issues permitted him to be comparatively at ease in his use of models.

It was not always so. Earlier the physicalistic thesis Freud inherited from his teachers had led him to confuse the model with the theory. He supposed at the time of the "Project" (1895) that his theory was actually about the central nervous system and its mode of functioning. In a sense, the model for the mental apparatus was thought to be available in neurology, but the model was devoid of any "as if" quality. It was assumed that the neurological model was the actual object of study. Because of this assumption that the mental apparatus was the brain, the representational quality of the model dropped out, and the theory and the model virtually coalesced.

Only gradually did Freud come to realize that he could specify the theoretical characteristics of the mental apparatus in isolation from the specification of the neurological correlates with which the mental apparatus appears to be intimately associated. As he abandoned the neurological postulate of the "Project" his theory moved on to what he called "purely psychological ground." But this move left a number of unresolved questions and problems.

One problem was, of course, the need to work out some other model for the theory when it was seen that the neurological model was for the moment unsatisfactory. We cannot here trace the intricate and involved problems associated with the use of the so-called "telescopic" or "picket fence" model in *The Interpretation of Dreams*. There, however, it is clear that Freud was able only by a slow process to deal with the specification of a model, for the discussions in Chapter VII of that work involve many confusions arising from the use of the model, and sometimes the model may have adversely affected the theory. Many of the difficulties associated with the topographic point of view may indeed stem from a confusion between model and theory. There are difficulties about models for psychoanalytic theory that continue to the present day, as reflected in some recent attempts to impose revisions on the theory deriving from a tempting contemporary source of models for the mental apparatus, i.e., computers. Here again we may find that the model adversely influences the theory rather than illustrates it. The comparative lack of readily available models to illustrate a psychological theory accounts in part, too, for the marked tendency to express structural relations in anthropomorphic metaphor. Our commonsense knowledge of relationships between people serves as a vivid way to express the processes that take place intrapsychically between systems.[8]

However, the more interesting conceptual problem left in the aftermath of the retreat from the neurological theory of the "Project" concerns the nature of the purely psychological theory that evolved. What are the phenomena that a purely psychological theory describes? What are the entities to which the theo-

[8] A confusion between theoretical models and theoretical statements mars an otherwise interesting exploration of anthropomorphism by Grossman and Simon (1969).

retical statements of a purely psychological theory refer? These are the questions that Hartmann and Beres have attempted to deal with in their functional analysis of structure. We must turn to this issue next, and to the philosophical issues that are intricately involved in these metatheoretical questions.

VI. THEORETICAL ENTITIES IN PSYCHOANALYSIS

It is at this point that some theorists take a reductionist approach. Many analysts develop a certain uneasiness before a purely psychological theory that has no "morphological substratum" to which the terms of the theory refer. Consequently they make vigorous attempts to construe the theoretical terms as mere abstractions from the clinical material. The result is the reductionist account exemplified by Beres. 'Ego,' as a theoretical term, is to be analyzed as having no referent, but merely as summarizing a large amount of empirical information at a lower level in the theory. Since these summarized clinical data are eventually specified in observational terms, we seem thus to have avoided any introduction into the theory of strange mental things like egos. But this approach, as we shall see, is severely restrictive for the development of an adequate psychological theory.

The impetus to achieve some sort of reductionist analysis stems from the belief that a denial of reductionism commits us to what Holt (1967) has termed the "twin hobgoblins" of empirically-minded theorists: mentalism and reification. If we take the theoretical statements literally, they seem to refer to peculiar sorts of mental things. We then seem on the one hand to be committed to a view that there is mind-stuff, that is, to be committed to a dualism of mind and body, with all the attendant dissatisfactions and difficulties involved in this view. On the other hand, we seem to be referring to things that cannot be directly observed. Hence we seem to have posited the existence of unobservable entities, and thus to have reified, or taken as real, the items named in the theoretical statements. The psychoanalytic theorist has frequently recoiled both from dualism and from the reification of unobservables. Hence, he opts for a reductionist account, and claims that the thingish character of theoretical entities is only a *façon de parler*.

We shall take up the issues of mentalism and reification in turn. These questions are philosophical ones, and some awareness of the current way of meeting these difficulties in the philosophy of science might allay the methodological skittishness of the analytic theoretician, and diminish the eagerness with which he accepts a reductionist view.

(a) Mentalism

One point that must be made here, parenthetically, is that the question of a dualistic metaphysics is not so moribund as analytic theoreticians seem to suppose. The relationship of mind and body, or of mental and physical predicates, is one of the perennial problems of philosophy, and should not be dismissed so lightly as it is sometimes in analytic discussions. It is curious to find that many analytic theorists regard the question of dualism as solved, or as an issue to be dismissed with contempt. For it is often assumed that to propose a dualistic view is to be in some sense patently fallacious, unscientific, outmoded, and obviously wrong. The philosophical problem of the mind-body relationship is thus dismissed as an anachronism.[9]

Yet is should be realized that if the mind-body problem were not a very difficult one philosophically it would not continue to be of such paramount philosophical concern. The concern is reflected in the intense interest in recent philosophical studies of a theory of mind-body identity that was proposed by U. T. Place (1956) and J. J. C. Smart (1959). An enormous literature has grown in recent years around the possibility that some tenable form of the identity thesis may be developed.[10] The urgency and interest in this pursuit of a satisfactory theory for identification of mental and bodily states is perhaps in itself evidence that the Cartesian program continues to be compelling and difficult to refute. It is true that the dualist or Cartesian position is less often propounded now than in the past. One may have an intuitive response that dualism is in error, yet the arguments for dualism are not laid to rest simply because of a visceral response that their conclusion is untenable. Especially in view of the enormous difficulties that have been encountered so far in working out any satisfactory materialistic ontology, we must recognize that dualism is not to be immediately dismissed.

In any event, we need not be committed to a dualistic position when we allow mental terms to enter our theory. Recently a philosophical attempt to work out an alternative to dualism has been made. I shall sketch this alternative view briefly because it may be helpful to psychological theorists in that it permits an escape from behaviorist analyses while at the same time affording, if one wishes, a degree of neutrality on matters that are philosophical rather than scientific.[11]

We may summarize the view as follows. The rejection of mental entities seems to derive from the assumption that mentalism is the same as dualism. The theoretician fears that if his theoretical terms do not refer to observable behavior

---

[9] One example of this is Beres's failure even to mention dualism as a possible view. He immediately assumes that reification means taking the theoretical entities as *physical* entities. To show just how highhanded the dismissal of dualism may be, I quote from the American Psychoanalytic Association's 1965 Panel discussion on instinctual drives. There Robert Holt, according to the panel reporter, disagreed with Freud's 1915 definition of instinctual drives. Holt stated that this view assumed "a mental realm and a physical realm . . . a very clear position of classical interactional dualism. . . . According to Holt, "This passage is better simply forgotten than really dwelt upon" (Dahl, 1968, p. 636).

[10] For a review of the issues and the literature see Schaffer (1965). An excellent anthology is O'Connor's (1969). See also Hampshire (1966) and T. Nagel (1965).

[11] This theory is found in the writings of Putnam (1965, 1966) and Fodor (1965, 1968). The Fodor-Putnam theory has received some of its impetus from the recent intense activity in the philosophy of language, which led to the reintroduction into linguistic theory of references to mental events and structures, in contrast to earlier behavioristic accounts of language. It is a view that is associated with several philosophical writers who have been influential or instrumental in the development of contemporary philosophy of language. It is a view that also shows the influence of recent work on the so-called identity thesis. See Katz (1964); Chomsky (1959, 1966, 1968); Dennett (1969). For a critique of this approach see Rorty (1972) and Kalke (1969).

or to neurological entities, he is committed to a two-substance metaphysics. It can be argued, however, that there is a distinction between mentalism and dualism.

On this view, the category opposing mentalism is not materialism but behaviorism. A theory that introduces terms which do not refer to behavior, or to classes of bits of behavior, is a mentalistic theory. The mental terms introduced in the theory are not defined in a way that makes reference to behavior, and cannot be eliminated in favor of behavioral terms. The mental terms are therefore logically distinct from behaviorist descriptions, and cannot be eliminated from theoretical discourse. But in this theory mentalism is still compatible with materialism, for we may still hold that in the broad sense human beings are to be regarded as physical systems obeying the laws of physics. Thus, it is maintained, mental terms and behavioral terms *may* apply to the same material thing, i.e., the person.

Mental terms could, of course, apply to mind substance on this theory, too, and a dualist (who holds a two-substance metaphysical position) is quite likely to be a mentalist in this sense. But the theorist who wishes to opt for a materialist view could still claim that the mental terms, as a matter of fact, apply to the same material substance that behavioral terms apply to.

We specify the internal mental or psychological states of the person by attributing to them just those characteristics which would cause the behavior in which we find him engaged. No attempt is made, however, to specify what these internal states are states of. The mechanisms which correspond to the mental states are left open, and the internal state is functionally compatible with any number of mechanisms which might be devised. It may be realized in structures of many different physically possible (or, if we are so inclined, metaphysically possible) constitutions. The brain may be one such model that functions in the way that we have described the mental apparatus. The theory that correlates the various aspects of the mental apparatus with neurophysiological events could then be compared to the specification of the particular material instantiation of a pattern of functioning. The theory which describes how a particular system functions can be independent of the particular physical (or metaphysical) instantiation of that system. The theoretical principles, in other words, might be the same regardless of the material chosen for the manufacture of the mechanism. To allow a moment of science fantasy, we could conceivably have various functionally equivalent, and theoretically equivalent, "devices"; for example, an earthman, a Martian, or robots made by competitive firms. All these "devices" might operate on vastly different physical principles and yet, conceivably, be programmed according to the same functional pattern (Putnam, 1965, 1966).

These internal states are indeed characterized purely functionally. The mental events or states are assigned just those properties required to produce the observed behavior. We attribute to the individual just those internal states that function in a manner to produce the behavior we wish to explain (Fodor, 1965). Thus we come to see that there is an important element of truth in the claim that the mental structures in psychoanalysis are functionally defined. But the functional characterization of the mental apparatus has been obscured in psychoanalytic discussions by the methodological worries about dualism and reification, until, as we saw in Beres's paper, the structural entities become nothing but groups of functions. There is an important difference, however, in this Fodor-Putnam view of functional definition. At the moment of the introduction into the theory of a mental term, we indeed do know the event or entity it specifies only by its functioning to produce certain aspects of behavior. This does not mean, however, that we henceforward limit the meaning of that theoretical term to the functions that led us to introduce the term. We leave open the possibility that we may discover interrelationships between other mental items, further character-istics we were not aware of at first, and other phenomena which might be ex-plained by this mental state or event. We shall see that this is an important differ-ence when we examine the question of theoretical entities in science. Whether or not we accept the Fodor-Putnam philosophical notion of functionalism, it is interesting to consider for its possible implications for psychoanalytical theory, and for any illumination it might provide for the problem of mental structures as theoretical entities.

(b) The Status of the Theoretical Entities of Psychoanalysis

The second problem that seems to cause skittishness about the structural hypothesis concerns the question whether theoretical entities are being "reified." Taken literally, the theory seems to refer to things, or quasi things, which are removed from empirical observation. Accordingly we are in a dilemma: Either we construe these things as mere *façons de parler,* or we countenance into the catalogue of things that exist some very queer things which we know about only through the occurrence of terms designating them in the higher-level theoretical discourse of psychoanalysis.

One element involved here is the distinction between what E. Nagel (1961), following Rankine (1855), has called "abstractive" theories and "hypothetical" theories. "Abstractive" theories do not introduce anything hypothetical or conjectural, but merely establish the relations which hold between observable objects, events, or phenomena. An abstractive theory is then a sort of convenient shorthand for the observational statements, and all theoretical statements of an abstractive theory could be translated without remainder, at least in principle, into the language of observation. Thus the theory is logically equivalent to a class of observational statements. The theoretical concepts of an abstractive theory have no "surplus meaning" since they refer to nothing over and above the empirical data which they summarize. "Hypothetical" theories, on the other hand, do introduce hypothetical entities, and formulate relationships which hold between these unobservable entities and the observational data. The empirical validity of the statements concerning these hypothetical entities can be established only indirectly, via the consistency of the implications of these statements with the observational statements. Various terms have been introduced to characterize the distinction between the theoretical terms of the two types of theories. The theoretical entities of hypothetical theories have been termed "transcendent" or "inferred" entities, and in psychological discussions they have often been called "hypothetical constructs" (see MacCorquodale and Meehl, 1948).

In the earlier decades of this century the preference among many empiricist philosophers of science was for abstractive theories, which were held to be advantageous because of their lack of "occult" entities, and their supposed greater degree of certainty which resulted from their more direct relation to observed fact. Beres apparently wishes to place himself within this empiricist tradition, in his attempt to restrict the structural hypothesis to abstractive theoretical terms which merely summarize the data of clinical experience. Theorists such as Beres apparently prefer that the psychic structure be thought of merely as abstractions from the data, rather than as inferred entities. Such theorists seem to hold that Freud introduced many psychoanalytic terms, including those of the structural hypothesis, as abstractive terms, but in the course of discussion there has developed a tendency for these abstractive terms to take on the role of inferred entities with certain properties assigned to them which were not directly correlated with observation. Such theorists fear that if the relation between psychic structure and observable behavior becomes indirect, the behavior then serves merely as inductive evidence for the existence of entities which we cannot immediately observe.

The difficulty with this approach is that it clings to a concept of empiricism that has long been abandoned by contemporary philosophers of science. It is an approach that neglects some of the more interesting features of current work on the problem of theoretical entities. Philosophers have moved on from the narrow empiricist interpretation of the meaning of theoretical terms, and have ceased to claim that such terms must be construed as completely definable in the observational vocabulary. If such definition is possible at all, it is so only for the low-level empirical concepts.

I shall try to sketch briefly the main reasons why reductionism is an unsatisfactory approach to the problem of theoretical entities. The meaning of theoretical concepts of such a degree of complexity as those of the structural hypothesis is generally now regarded as specifiable only by taking into account their role within the entire theoretical scheme, including other theoretical statements, the postulates of the theory, correspondence rules, and the observational data. This means that the terms are given a meaning within the theory, rather than merely by means of observational statements. Thus the meaning of a theoretical term is quite complex. It is now recognized that these higher-level theoretical terms are "open-textured." Their meaning is never completely exhausted or completely specified. This openness of meaning has been regarded as a distinct advantage, for several reasons: It increases the potential explanatory power of the theory, it is heuristically advantageous in permitting discoveries of a wider range of interrelationships among the constituents of the theory, and it increases the range of phenomena which may eventually be brought under the theory. The advantage of this view of theoretical terms over the narrow reductionist interpretation is that it permits the development of theoretical concepts which are of adequate complexity and scope to permit the science to advance.

Although several programs for the elimination of theoretical terms in favor of the observational vocabulary have been developed, these have in general been regarded as feasible only at the price of stultification of the further development of the theory.[12]

Yet, someone may ask, do egos and ids exist? I have so far attempted to show that the present view of theoretical terms makes them much more complex than some empiricists believed. Does this complexity require us to acknowledge the existence of the entities to which the terms seem to refer? There is no simple answer to this question. Whether egos and ids exist is a special case of a general question for the philosophy of science: Are theoretical entities really entities? What is important to recognize here is that the structures of psychoanalytic theory are bona fide theoretical entities, and an answer to the question whether they exist or not must take into account the treatment of the epistemological and ontological status of theoretical entities in the philosophy of science. We cannot hope to evaluate the status of theoretical entities in psychoanalysis in isolation from more general philosophical concerns about the status of such terms in any theory. There are many possibilities to be considered. We might claim that theoretical entities are entities which exist in a special way, that is, by their appearance in the statements of a well-confirmed theory. Or we might claim that theoretical entities do exist, for they are what the theory is about. Or we might find reasons for withholding existence postulates from the theoretical entities of any science. We should then have to acknowledge that no theoretical entities exist, and that all apparent references to supposed entities are merely figurative and convenient ways of expressing the data. Or we might even find that there are reasons for supposing that electrons exist but ids do not. The point is that this is not a question for psychoanalysis to solve, even for its own entities. When the analytic theoretician considers the question he is no longer engaged in psychoanalytic theorizing, and he should realize that he is speaking as a philosopher of science, and that his arguments should reflect what generally have been regarded as advances in this field, rather than appear as quaint antiques on the philosophical scene.

VII. PSYCHOANALYSIS AND THE CONTEMPORARY PHILOSOPHY OF SCIENCE

I have attempted to summarize, if only briefly, something of the vast amount of work that is being done in the contemporary philosophy of science. In doing so I hope to call the attention of psychoanalytic theorists to this work, and to make them aware of what Fodor has called the conceptual lag that characterizes psychological metatheory (Fodor, 1968). This conceptual lag is nowhere more acute than in psychoanalysis. Much of what I have to say is obvious to the philosopher of science, and I do no more than repeat the criticisms that some

[12] The literature on this topic is vast. For a general idea of the problems involved, see Achinstein (1968); Achinstein and Barker (1969); Carnap (1956); Feigl (1970); Hempel (1958, 1959, 1965); Sellars (1965).

philosophers of science have voiced about psychology for some time. Yet apparently no apology for repetition is needed, since analytic theoreticians have in general ignored these developments. Like Beres, they seem unaware of their isolation from the contemporary philosophy of science. The metatheory of psychoanalysis has been dominated by a view of empiricism which has been used to justify very restrictive accounts of the theoretical propositions of psychoanalysis. These theoreticians have apparently supposed that, in adhering to their "empiricism," they are adopting the best principles of scientific theorizing. As we have seen in Beres's view of structure, the effect has been to place crippling restraints of one kind or another on psychoanalysis. Under the banner of "empiricism," or "operationalism," or some other such catchword, the theory has been subjected to restrictions that in point of fact actually serve to hamper the development of psychoanalytic metatheory, and possibly hinder psychoanalysis itself. Further, since many of the tenets were abandoned by philosophers of science some time ago, the unfortunate result is that psychoanalytic metatheory is cut off from the mainstream of thought in the contemporary philosophy of science.

Psychoanalysis has thus failed to participate in what are some of the most important aspects of the contemporary philosophy of science, which has begun almost systematically to explore the possibilities opened by the rejection of various aspects of the empiricist thesis (Fodor, 1968). In particular, those hallowed shibboleths of the empiricists in their earlier and more unguarded pronouncements have been questioned and the consequences of their rejection investigated. These include some of the more conspicuous of Beres's presuppositions: verification as an account of meaning; the view that theoretical constructs are conventionally defined; the claim that a sharp dichotomy exists between the observational language and the theoretical language. All of these have, at one time or another, come up for intense scrutiny in recent philosophical literature. Though no consensus has been reached from these explorations, it has become clear that these supposed fundamental tenets of empiricism are not indispensable requirements for scientific theorizing. Yet, in the psychoanalytic literature, there has been almost no reflection of all this intensive exploration of these so-called empiricist dogmas. Indeed, it is precisely these dogmatic assertions of empiricism that most psychoanalytic theoreticians invoke when they come to discuss analytic metatheory.[13]

In the interest of fairness it should be recognized that these theorists have probably opted for their views in the hope of maintaining a relative neutrality while theorizing, by avoiding any imposition on the theory of a metaphysical point of view. Unfortunately the neutrality is illusory. Far from being neutral or nonmetaphysical, the adoption of stringent empiricist restrictions is actually to pronounce certain strong a priori assumptions, not only about the theory but about the nature of the phenomena which the science is attempting to investi-

[13] One glaring example of this conceptual lag concerns operationalism. Although this view is in general disrepute, in psychoanalysis we still find apologies for not being ready to be operational (Pumpian-Mindlin, 1959). See Martin (1969).

gate. Beres is in effect speculating or legislating about the phenomena we are to explore. He has decided in advance that abstractive theoretical terms, and the limited methodology associated with them, are adequate to explain whatever phenomena psychoanalysis is to account for. The phenomena may be far more complex than this. Certainly we should not legislate in advance about them.

Finally, another important reason for permitting psychoanalytic theory to develop as it will, rather than as empiricist theoreticians say it must, may be seen in the following considerations. One of the problems that has been in the background of all this discussion is the failure of the reduction that was envisaged in the "Project," in which psychological terms are linked to neurological theory. The correlation between mental and physical predicates has not yet been achieved, although there still remains a hope that we shall someday be able to effect a closure with neurology in some systematic and complete fashion. But at the moment attempts to correlate psychological structures with specific areas of the brain, or with neurophysiological processes, seem ill-advised and bound to fail. We do not know as yet whether a correlation will become possible even in principle. If such a reduction eventually becomes possible it will depend on many factors. One of these factors may be that advances will have to take place in *both* psychological theory and neurological theory before the closure is effected.

Some theorists advise us to restrict psychoanalytic theory to concepts that are already consistent with contemporary neurology (Applegarth, 1971). But it was pointed out some years ago by Adrian (1946) that neurological influences on psychoanalysis, so prevalent at the beginning of the formulation of psychoanalytic theory, are now in a sense being matched by influences flowing in the opposite direction, from psychoanalytic theorizing toward neurology. It is probable, then, that the independent development of psychoanalytic concepts may lead to advances in neurological theory. It may well be that neurophysiological researches are stimulated by developments in psychoanalytic theory. This may lead to theories of the complexity requisite for a correlation to occur.

Psychological theory must therefore be permitted to advance freely, and independent of our knowledge of the exact form that such a reduction will take, and, for the present, psychological theory must maintain a relative independence from contemporary neurological theory. Both sciences should continue to pursue their subject matter independently, and develop that theoretical superstructure, and those theoretical entities, which seem most appropriate for the explanation of the phenomena they study. For if an eventual reduction takes place it is quite possible that it will occur between the theories at stages more advanced than either has yet reached. The reduction will probably occur not in terms of the present psychoanalytic theoretical structures and present neurological states, but more likely in the concepts of a considerably more advanced psychological theory and a considerably more advanced neurological theory (T. Nagel, 1970). Probably the terms in which an eventual reduction will occur are not to be found either in the present neurological vocabulary or in the descriptions of the mental apparatus available at present in psychoanalysis. Development of this future vocabulary may well depend upon the separate and independent development of the two sciences. Narrow empiricist restrictions on the conceptual apparatus of psychoanalysis, limiting theoretical terms to abstractive accounts of clinical data, may in effect hamper the development of psychoanalytic theory, and delay the eventual closure with neurology. A freedom to credit theoretical concepts with those attributes which we come to discover in them may be the best policy in the long run.

REFERENCES

Achinstein, P. (1968). *Concepts of Science.* Baltimore: Johns Hopkins Press.

———, and Barker, S. F., eds. (1969). *The Legacy of Logical Positivism.* Baltimore: Johns Hopkins Press.

Adrian, E. D. (1946). The Mental and Physical Origins of Behavior. *International Journal of Psycho-Analysis,* 27:1–6.

Apfelbaum, B. (1966). On Ego Psychology: A Critique of the Structural Approach to Psycho-Analytic Theory. *International Journal of Psycho-Analysis,* 47:451–475.

Applegarth, A. (1971). Comments on Aspects of the Theory of Psychic Energy. *Journal of the American Psychoanalytic Association,* 19:379–416.

Arlow, J., and Brenner, C. (1964). *Psychoanalytic Concepts and the Structural Theory.* New York: International Universities Press.

Beres, D. (1958). Vicissitudes of Superego Function and Superego Precursors in Childhood. *The Psychoanalytic Study of the Child,* 13:324–351. New York: International Universities Press.

——— (1965). Structure and Function in Psycho-Analytic Theory. *International Journal of Psycho-Analysis,* 46:53–63.

Breuer, J., and Freud, S. (1893–1895). Studies on Hysteria. *Standard Edition,* 2. London: Hogarth Press, 1955.

Carnap, R. (1956). The Methodological Character of Theoretical Concepts. In: *Minnesota Studies in the Philosophy of Science,* Vol. 1, ed. H. Feigl and M. Scriven. Minneapolis: University of Minnesota Press.

Chomsky, N. (1959). Review of *Verbal Behavior,* by B. F. Skinner. *Language,* 35:26–58.

——— (1966). *Cartesian Linguistics.* New York: Harper and Row.

——— (1968). *Language and Mind.* New York: Harcourt, Brace, and World.

Dahl, H. (1968). Panel Report: Psychoanalytic Theory of the Instinctual Drives in Relation to Recent Developments. *Journal of the American Psychoanalytic Association,* 16:613–637.

Dennett, D. C. (1969). *Content and Consciousness.* New York: Humanities Press.

Eissler, K. R. (1962). On the Metapsychology of the Preconscious. *The Psychoanalytic Study of the Child,* 17:9–41. New York: International Universities Press.

Feigl, H. (1970). The "Orthodox" View of Theories: Remarks in Defense as Well as Critique. In: *Minnesota Studies in the Philosophy of Science,* Vol. 4: *Analysis of Theories and Methods of Physics and Psychology,* ed. M. Radner and S. Winokur. Minneapolis: University of Minnesota Press.

Fodor, J. A. (1965). Explanations in Psychology. In: *Philosophy in America,* ed. M. Black. Ithaca: Cornell University Press.

——— (1968). *Psychological Explanation: An Introduction to the Philosophy of Psychology.* New York: Random House.

Freud, S. (1891). *On Aphasia.* New York: International Universities Press, 1953.

——— (1895). Project for a Scientific Psychology. *Standard Edition,* 1:283–397. London: Hogarth Press, 1966.

——— (1900). The Interpretation of Dreams. *Standard Edition,* 4 & 5. London: Hogarth Press, 1953.

―――― (1915). The Unconscious. *Standard Edition,* 14:159–215. London: Hogarth Press, 1957.

―――― (1916–1917). Introductory Lectures on Psycho-Analysis. *Standard Edition,* 15 & 16. London: Hogarth Press, 1963.

―――― (1923). The Ego and the Id. *Standard Edition,* 19:3–66. London: Hogarth Press, 1961.

―――― (1924). A Note upon the 'Mystic Writing-Pad.' *Standard Edition,* 19:227–232. London: Hogarth Press, 1961.

―――― (1926). Inhibitions, Symptoms and Anxiety. *Standard Edition,* 20:75–175. London: Hogarth Press, 1959.

―――― (1933). New Introductory Lectures on Psycho-Analysis. *Standard Edition,* 22:5–182. London: Hogarth Press, 1964.

Gill, M. M. (1963). Topography and Systems in Psychoanalytic Theory. *Psychological Issues,* Monograph 10. New York: International Universities Press.

Grossman, W. I., and Simon, B. (1969). Anthropomorphism. Motive, Meaning and Causality in Psychoanalytic Theory. *The Psychoanalytic Study of the Child,* 24:78–111. New York: International Universities Press.

Hampshire, S., ed. (1966). *Philosophy of Mind.* New York: Harper and Row.

Hartmann, H. (1950). Comments on the Psychoanalytic Theory of the Ego. *The Psychoanalytic Study of the Child,* 5:74–96. New York: International Universities Press.

―――― (1951). Technical Implications of Ego Psychology. *Psychoanalytic Quarterly,* 20:31–43.

―――― (1952). The Mutual Influences in the Development of Ego and Id. *The Psychoanalytic Study of the Child,* 7:9–30. New York: International Universities Press.

―――― (1956). The Development of the Ego Concept in Freud's Work. *International Journal of Psycho-Analysis,* 37:425–438.

―――― (1958). Comments on the Scientific Aspects of Psychoanalysis. *The Psychoanalytic Study of the Child,* 13:127–146. New York: International Universities Press.

―――― (1959). Psychoanalysis as a Scientific Theory. In: *Psychoanalysis, Scientific Methodology and Philosophy,* ed. S. Hook. New York: New York University Press, pp. 3–37.

――――, Kris, E., and Loewenstein, R. M. (1946). Comments on the Formation of Psychic Structure. *The Psychoanalytic Study of the Child,* 2:11–38. New York: International Universities Press.

Hayman, A. (1969). What Do We Mean by "Id"? *Journal of the American Psychoanalytic Association,* 17:353–380.

Hempel, C. G. (1958). The Theoretician's Dilemma. A Study of the Logic of Theory Construction. In: *Minnesota Studies in the Philosophy of Science,* Vol. 2, ed. H. Feigl, M. Scriven, and G. Maxwell. Minneapolis: University of Minnesota Press.

―――― (1959). The Logic of Functional Analysis. In: *Symposium on Sociological Theory,* ed. L. Gross. New York: Harper and Row.

―――― (1965). *Aspects of Scientific Explanation.* New York: Free Press.

―――― (1970). On the "Standard Conception" of Scientific Theories. In: *Minnesota Studies in the Philosophy of Science,* Vol. 4: *Analysis of Theories and Methods of Physics and Psychology,* ed. M. Radner and S. Winokur. Minneapolis: University of Minnesota Press.

Holt, R. R. (1967). The Development of the Primary Process: A Structural View. In: Motives and Thought: Psychoanalytic Essays in Honor of David Rapaport, ed. R. R. Holt. *Psychological Issues,* Monograph 18/19:345–383. New York: International Universities Press.

Kalke, W. (1969). What Is Wrong with Fodor and Putnam's Functionalism. *Nous,* 3:83–94.

Katz, J. J. (1964). Mentalism in Linguistics. *Language,* 40:124–137.

MacCorquodale, K., and Meehl, P. (1948). On a Distinction between Hypothetical Constructs and Intervening Variables. *Psychological Review,* 55:95–107. Also in: *Read-*

ings in the Philosophy of Science, ed. H. Feigl and M. Brodbeck. New York: Appleton-Century-Crofts, 1953.

Martin, M. (1969). An Examination of the Operationists' Critique of Psychoanalysis. *Social Science Information,* 8:65–85.

Moore, B. E., and Fine, B. D. (1967). *A Glossary of Psychoanalytic Terms and Concepts.* New York: American Psychoanalytic Association.

Nagel, E. (1961). *The Structure of Science.* New York: Harcourt, Brace, and World.

Nagel, T. (1965). Physicalism. *Philosophical Review,* 74:339–356. Also in: *Modern Materialism: Readings in Mind-Body Identity,* ed. J. O'Connor. New York: Harcourt, Brace, and World, 1969.

——— (1970). Armstrong on the Mind. *Philosophical Review,* 79:394–403.

Nagera, H. (1967). The Concepts of Structure and Structuralization. *The Psychoanalytic Study of the Child,* 22:77–102. New York: International Universities Press.

——— (1968). The Concept of Ego Apparatus in Psychoanalysis. *The Psychoanalytic Study of the Child,* 23:224–242. New York: International Universities Press.

O'Connor, J., ed. (1969). *Modern Materialism: Readings in Mind-Body Identity.* New York: Harcourt, Brace, and World.

Place, U. T. (1956). Is Consciousness a Brain Process? *British Journal of Psychology,* 47:44–50. Also in: *Modern Materialism: Readings in Mind-Body Identity,* ed. J. O'Connor. New York: Harcourt, Brace, and World, 1969.

Pumpian-Mindlin, E. (1959). Propositions concerning Energetic-Economic Aspects of the Libido Theory. Conceptual Models of Psychic Energy and Structure in Psychoanalysis. *Annals of the New York Academy of Sciences,* 76:1038–1052.

Putnam, H. (1965). Brains and Behavior. In: *Analytical Philosophy,* ed. R. J. Butler. Oxford: Basil Blackwell.

——— (1966). The Mental Life of Some Machines. In: *Intentionality, Minds, and Perception,* ed. H.-N. Casteneda. Detroit: Wayne State University Press. Also in: *Modern Materialism: Readings in Mind-Body Identity,* ed. J. O'Connor. New York: Harcourt, Brace, and World, 1969.

Quine, W. O. (1966). *The Ways of Paradox and Other Essays.* New York: Random House.

Rankine, W. J. M. (1855). Outlines of the Science of Energetics. *Miscellaneous Scientific Papers.* London, 1881, pp. 209–228.

Rapaport, D., and Gill, M. (1959). The Points of View and Assumptions of Metapsychology. *International Journal of Psycho-Analysis,* 40:153–162.

Reichenbach, H. (1951). *The Rise of Scientific Philosophy.* Berkeley: University of California Press.

Rorty, R. (1972). Functionalism, Machines, and Incorrigibility. *Journal of Philosophy,* 69:203–220.

Schafer, R. (1968). *Aspects of Internalization.* New York: International Universities Press.

Schaffer, J. A. (1965). Recent Work on the Philosophy of Mind. *American Philosophical Quarterly,* 2:81–104.

Sellars, W. (1965). Scientific Realism or Irenic Instrumentalism. In: *Boston Studies in the Philosophy of Science,* Vol. 3, ed. R. S. Cohen and M. Wartofsky. New York: Humanities Press, pp. 171–204.

Smart, J. J. C. (1959). Sensations and Brain Processes. *Philosophical Review,* 68:141–156.

Whitehead, A. N. (1926). *Science and the Modern World.* New York: New American Library, 1962.

7

DISCUSSION OF MICHAEL SHERWOOD'S "THE LOGIC OF EXPLANATION IN PSYCHOANALYSIS"

SHERWOOD ON THE LOGIC OF EXPLANATION IN PSYCHOANALYSIS

Morris Eagle, Ph.D.

In *The Logic of Explanation in Psychoanalysis,* Michael Sherwood (1969), a psychiatrist with a background in the philosophy of science, makes a valiant effort to confront the problem of establishing standards and criteria by which psychoanalytic explanations (or, as he calls them, "narratives") can be evaluated. Sherwood discusses other matters, such as the legitimacy of the distinction between reasons and causes and the qeustion whether psychoanalytic explanations are necessarily based on empirical generalizations. But the issue to which I shall mainly address myself is that of standards and criteria for psychoanalytic explanations. For, to quote Sherwood's final statement in the book, "We must be able to agree on . . . what is to count as a good explanation. If we cannot do this, we must forsake any claim to a scientific status and rest content in the solitude of our incontestable, because incommunicable, musings" (p. 260).

The book is an important one, I believe, because it raises certain critical issues that need to be faced by anyone interested in the status of psychoanalytic explanations. I agree with one of Sherwood's main conclusions—namely, that if psychoanalysis and psychoanalytic explanations are to have any legitimate claim to scientific status, they cannot at the same time claim to be a "private domain" with private rules of procedure, but rather must be evaluated by the same criteria that are applied to all scientific explanations. In fact, my main criticism of the book is that Sherwood tends to introduce implicitly a "separate domain" view into some of his characterizations of psychoanalytic explanations and "narratives" and into his discussion of the criteria to be employed in evaluating such narratives.

Sherwood proposes three criteria for evaluating psychoanalytic (and other) explanations. One, the criterion of appropriateness, is essentially concerned with whether the explanation is placed in the proper frame of reference, whether it addresses itself to the specific questions raised, and whether it is formulated at the proper level of complexity. The second criterion is adequacy, which includes self-consistency, coherence, and comprehensiveness. The third criterion, accuracy, constitutes a "truth claim"; the explanation is evaluated for its ability to yield an accurate "prediction of a particular behavior, past or present."

It seems to me that of the three criteria proposed by Sherwood—appropriateness, adequacy (which, in turn, is judged by self-consistency, coherence, and comprehensiveness), and accuracy—only accuracy is critical for evaluating a scientific explanation. This becomes apparent from the following considerations: An explanation may be appropriate, that is, may properly address itself to the question raised. It may be, according to Sherwood's definition, adequate, that is, self-consistent, coherent, and comprehensive. And yet, if the explanation is not empirically evaluated for accuracy—that is, if one does not determine, to use Sherwood's terms, the degree to which there is correspondence between what is supposed to happen empirically and what does happen—the explanation has not been *tested*. And if the explanation cannot be evaluated with regard to such correspondence, it is not an empirical explanation, however appropriate and adequate it may seem and however much puzzlement it may appear to resolve. For, however complex the issue of what constitutes scientific explanation, surely there would be little dispute that empirical test of a "truth claim" is one of its indispensable criteria.

Thus, appropriateness and adequacy become relevant criteria for evaluating a scientific explanation only after it is clear that the explanation is making a "truth claim" and is capable in some way, directly or indirectly, of being evaluated with regard to that claim. In this sense, then, appropriateness and adequacy are luxuries and do not have the same status as accuracy.

Appropriateness is a peculiar criterion in that it is something one normally takes for granted. Further, an explanation may be inappropriate in that it does not address itself to a specific question raised. But if it is, indeed, an explanation, it will be appropriate to *some* question (that is or could be raised). And one will still need to consider how accurately it answers *that* question. If the explanation is inappropriate to *any* question that is or could be raised, it is likely to be nonsensical or reflect tangential thinking. Appropriateness, then, seems more properly a property one assumes an explanation to possess before one considers the explanation any further rather than a criterion for evaluating an explanation. If an explanation is inappropriate to any question, one would not bother with further evaluation of adequacy or accuracy.

With regard to self-consistency, even when an explanation is internally inconsistent, one may, nevertheless, find it useful and powerful insofar as particular *parts* of it are highly accurate. As for comprehensiveness, it becomes relevant only when two explanatory accounts or theories are equally accurate. One may then want to invoke comprehensiveness as a basis for preferring one account to the other. But it is difficult to imagine the reverse, that is, preferring an account that is more comprehensive but less accurate. Again, the point is that, for evaluating scientific explanations, accuracy is the bedrock criterion, and appropriateness and adequacy are not, in any general sense, either necessary or sufficient criteria.

Sherwood himself implicitly demonstrates the dispensability of adequacy as a criterion for the empirical evaluation of scientific explanations when he discusses adequacy in a therapeutic context and notes the possibility that "truth is not even *necessary* for therapeutic efficacy" and the possibility that "therapeutic efficacy, while not correlated with the truth or accuracy of the narrative, *is* related to its adequacy as we have defined this term" (p. 250).

If adequacy and truth or accuracy are so readily separable and, as Sherwood suggests, even uncorrelated in certain contexts, it seems clear that adequacy would have to be considered dispensable if one were discussing its empirical status as a scientific explanation. For if an explanatory account is untrue and inaccurate, of what value is it to point to its adequacy—its consistency, coherence, and comprehensiveness—if we are interested, not in its therapeutic efficacy, but in its scientific status?

Elsewhere, too, Sherwood's discussion implies that accuracy and adequacy may not be congruent criteria. He notes that psychoanalytic narratives, because they are so complex, may be neither totally true nor totally false, but may be correct in certain respects and erroneous in others. This means that the criterion of accuracy or "truth claims" can be applied to specific parts of a narrative, even single statements or propositions. But it makes no sense to apply the criteria of adequacy—self-consistency, coherence, and comprehensiveness—to single statements within a narrative. These latter criteria are applicable only to the whole narrative or major sections of it. Thus, in this context accuracy and adequacy do not properly belong on the same level of discourse.

With regard to the issue of therapeutic efficacy and adequacy, it should be noted that while truth value and therapeutic efficacy (of narrative) can, indeed, be separated, the latter also involves truth claims, although at a different level. That is, the proposition that self-consistent, coherent, and comprehensive sets of statements are therapeutic is an entirely testable assertion:[1] It involves empirical assertions and truth claims about the kinds of statements that are therapeutic, even if it is not concerned with the truth or falsity of the statements themselves. The situation is somewhat analogous to the administration of a drug. One would not speak of a drug as being true or false, one would speak of its effectiveness in bringing about the state—let us say, relief of pain—it was intended to bring about. That is the work the drug was meant to do and its "validity," so to speak, is determined by whether or not it does its work successfully. And one would say that, while it would be absurd to speak of a drug as being true or false, its effectiveness (or lack of effectiveness) does have implications for the truth or falsity of a theory or hypothesis about its chemical action. That is perfectly true, and its proper counterpart in the case of therapeutic interpretations is as follows: If my therapeutic interpretation is effective (according to specific criteria), it will support the truth (or falsity) of some theory about the kinds of interpretive statements that are effective. But here we are

[1] Assuming that one can obtain reliable measures of self-consistency, coherence, and comprehensiveness and that one has some reliable criteria for therapeutic efficacy.

dealing with the truth or falsity of a theory about the *effects* of interpretive statements. The truth or falsity of interpretive statements themselves is a separate matter, which has to be determined independently. And it may turn out that some true statements—determined to be true by criteria which are independent of therapeutic effect—are ineffective, while some false statements—independently determined to be false—are effective. In any case, if the relationship between the truth and the therapeutic effectiveness of a statement is to be tested, we need to have two independent sets of criteria, one for therapeutic effectiveness and one for the empirical truth of a statement.

It is both in Sherwood's elucidation of the adequacy criterion and in his discussion of the role of prediction and generalization in psychoanalytic narratives that the implicit reintroduction of the "private domain" view is particularly apparent. With regard to the first, in discussing the fact that the context-dependent nature of explanation makes completeness impossible, Sherwood states that context dependence

. . . likewise allows for several explanations being equally adequate. As long as we stick to the criteria of consistency, coherence, and comprehensiveness, it seems that several different narratives might rank equally. The comparison with historical narratives is instructive here. Just as different explanations in history offer new perspectives and viewpoints, so too do the various sorts of psychoanalytic explanations. We speak of Marxist historians and capitalist historians in much the same way as Jungian analysts and Freudian analysts. Each group may produce evocative and perceptive, but radically different, views of the same subject matter that are each self-consistent, coherent, and comprehensive. It might even be said that psychoanalysis, particularly in its clinical and therapeutic setting, functions essentially in this way, by presenting new and varied perspectives to patients of their own behavior, rather than by telling them the true causes of their behavior (p. 249).

Later Sherwood again notes that "It is true that more than one psychoanalytic narrative may be equally adequate in a particular case, according to the criteria we have outlined." He adds, however, that "this is only part of the story, for the close examination of an actual narrative makes clear that something more than either adequacy or therapeutic efficacy is at stake, namely, that some sort of truth claim is being made" (p. 251).

If it is, indeed, true that different narratives may rank equally according to the criteria of consistency, coherence, and comprehensiveness, that is, it seems to me, an indication that these criteria are not critical for the evaluation of scientific explanations. If we speak of Freudian and Jungian analysts in much the same way that we speak of Marxist and capitalist historians, recognizing that "Each group may produce evocative and perceptive, but radically different, views of the same subject matter that are each self-consistent, coherent, and comprehensive," then perhaps we should question whether these criteria are especially relevant for the evaluation of scientific explanations and theories, one essential aspect of which I take to be the fact that they permit empirical test and enable one to choose between them.[2] It would, for instance, make little sense to talk about choosing among different literary works according to the criteria of self-consistency, coherence, and comprehensiveness; all could rank equally. Nor would there be any need to choose among them. But it is the essence of scientific theories (about presumably the same kinds of phenomena) that one needs to and ultimately can choose among them and that one is committed to developing criteria and procedures which will enable one to choose among them. And these criteria and procedures all rest squarely on questions of accuracy, "truth claim," and empirical test.

With regard to the issue of the role of prediction and generalization in psychoanalytic narratives, I find, as noted earlier, that Sherwood's discussion involves a subtle and unwitting reintroduction of the "private domain" view. Sherwood argues that an emphasis on the narrative aspect of psychoanalytic explanations has the following implications:

In the first place we would argue that the simple either–or criterion of logical validity is inadequate. The concept of logical validity seems appropriate only to deductive schemas. It does make sense to say that a prediction necessarily follows from certain general statements, and also that certain sets of statements are logically sufficient to make a prediction. Predictions, then, can be valid or invalid, that is, properly deduced or not. On the other hand, when we turn to explanations we find additional parameters of appraisal. We speak of explanations that are more or less adequate, incomplete, partial, shallow, deep, and a variety of other terms besides. Yet none of these terms seems applicable to deductions. What, for instance, would a partial or shallow deduction look like? One of the useful features of a contextual account of explanations is that it allows for the ranking of explanations along a whole spectrum of adequacy. Because there is an unavoidable contextual aspect to explanations that is absent from predictions based upon the H-D model, we must substitute for the simple

[2] That Marxist and capitalist accounts or Freudian and Jungian narratives may rank equally with regard to the criterion of adequacy reflects some essential properties of this criterion which Sherwood tends to overlook. That is that ultimately the issue of whether an account or narrative is self-consistent, coherent, and comprehensive is a question of *judgment*. Sherwood could argue that theoretically one could obtain intersubjective agreement among judges. But the fact is that Freudian judges would judge their own narratives to be more coherent, self-consistent, and comprehensive, while Jungian judges would judge their own narratives to be more coherent, self-consistent, and comprehensive (in fact, by virtue of their theoretical affiliations, they have already made these judgments), just as Marxist and capitalist historians would manifest their respective affiliations in their judgments. By contrast, in determining accuracy, that is, in determining whether what is supposed to happen empirically does or does not happen, one's biases, affiliations, and values do not rule one's decisions so easily. It is easy to intuit, but not as easy to formulate, the reasons for this being the case. Suffice it to say for the present purposes that perception is less subject to bias, possible distortion, and individual differences than judgment. It is easier, generally, to get agreement about what happened (or did not happen) than to obtain agreement about the consistency, coherence, and comprehensiveness of an account.

two-valued standard of logical validity a more flexible set of criteria. For this reason, then, we speak of evaluation, rather than verification or proof (pp. 244–245).

If Sherwood is speaking only of evaluation and not of verification or proof (and let us assume that a prediction could be confirmed or disconfirmed only probabilistically), then what does his inclusion of the criterion of accuracy mean? Sherwood is certainly correct in noting that prediction is not explanation. Nevertheless, it seems quite clear that successful prediction is the most critical criterion for determining the validity or accuracy of most scientific explanations. And, as far as I can see, to speak of accuracy is, indeed, to speak of verification and confirmation.

In my view, it is Sherwood's emphasis on the narrative as the basic unit of explanation that is mainly responsible for the difficulties in his position that I have described thus far. An important further example of this fact is the relationship between his emphasis on the narrative as the basic explanatory unit and his view of the role of generalization in explanation. Sherwood states that "If, as we have argued, the narrative is independent of the general psychoanalytic theory of human behavior in the sense of not being dependent on the truth of it, then the particular individual himself must remain the final touchstone for determining the narrative's accuracy" (p. 255). He adds that the truths gained from general theory and past experience play a directive role in evaluating the narrative and, in fact, form a second criterion of accuracy for a psychoanalytic narrative. But these considerations do not change the fact that "ultimately, the accuracy of the narrative depends upon the accuracy of . . . assertions" about the particular individual concerned.

Sherwood may be correct in believing that the accuracy of the narrative is independent of the general psychoanalytic theory of human behavior. But if this is so, it seems to me to indicate that the choice of the narrative as the basic unit of explanation is an unwise one if one is interested in building a general scientific theory of human behavior: because however important the narrative is to the individual patient and analyst, and however much the narrative may be a *source* of generalizations about human behavior, it is the establishment and testing of empirical generalizations and theories that are the main jobs of a science rather than the formulation of accurate narratives about single individuals. And, in order to do these jobs, the procedures and criteria that are employed by all sciences should be applicable to psychoanalysis insofar as its claim to scientific status is a legitimate one.

The situation is somewhat analogous to a physician's trying to formulate a diagnosis of a patient's physical illness. In making his diagnosis, which of course he wants to be as accurate, coherent, consistent, and comprehensive as possible, he is drawing upon a variety of general empirical findings, hypotheses, and theories regarding physiological and biochemical processes. And the accuracy, adequacy, and value of his diagnosis or "narrative" will, in the long run, depend upon the validity of these general findings, hypotheses, and theories—

which are verified or refuted, supported or not supported in the same empirical way that any hypothesis or theory is tested.

It is my judgment that in claiming that the narrative is a special form of explanation requiring special criteria, Sherwood has reintroduced in a new guise the relatively spurious issue of idiographic versus nomothetic explanation (see Holt, 1967). This issue has been sufficiently debated. I want to add merely that the presentation of as full and consistent a picture of a single individual as possible (in the form of a narrative, for example) does not necessarily entail new forms of explanation for which special criteria are appropriate. The most coherent, consistent, comprehensive, and accurate picture of an individual one could possibly present would involve the individual patterning of structures and processes that are not unique to that particular person but are, rather, generally found in the experiences and behavior of all persons.

Although I do not believe that Sherwood has made a successful case for his conception of the nature of psychoanalytic narratives and the criteria by which they are to be evaluated, he has addressed himself to critical problems. Others interested in the status of psychoanalytic explanations must deal with these problems. I agree entirely with Sherwood that if we cannot deal with the question of what is to be considered a good explanation, "we must forsake any claim to a scientific status." Which is not to say that psychoanalytic theory and practice may not be justifiable on other grounds. But to claim scientific status, it must confront the issues of criteria, standards, and evaluation.

REFERENCES

Holt, R. R. (1967). Individuality and Generalization in the Psychology of Personality. In: *Personality: Selected Readings,* ed. R. S. Lazarus and E. M. Opton. Harmondsworth, England: Penguin, pp. 38–65.

Sherwood, M. (1969). *The Logic of Explanation in Psychoanalysis.* New York: Academic Press.

ON THE LOGIC OF EXPLANATION IN PSYCHOANALYSIS

Benjamin B. Rubinstein, M.D.

I.

Certain serious reservations notwithstanding, in the opinion of this reviewer *The Logic of Explanation in Psychoanalysis* by Michael Sherwood (1969) is a remarkable book. It literally has no rivals. The science that most philosophers of science are concerned with is physics. Some have considered chemistry or even biology. At various times the attention of a few philosophers of science has been attracted by psychology. Often the practitioners of a science have also contributed to its philosophy. But whoever thought seriously about psychoanalysis from a philosophical point of view? A number of philosophers have approached the subject, somewhat cautiously perhaps, but not without initial respect or at least curiosity. But they found it too confusing, shot through with too many inconsistencies and contradictions, to give it much further attention; or they simply relinquished the attempt without explanation. Foremost among these philosophers are Carnap (1956), Hempel (1965), and Nagel (1959). But Wittgenstein too felt uneasy about psychoanalysis (1967, pp. 41, 52), as did Murdoch (1964, p. 364) and Scriven (1962a). According to Malcolm (1958), Wittgenstein in a letter acknowledged Freud's "extraordinary scientific achievement" (p. 45) but nonetheless regarded his work as "full of fishy thinking" (p. 44).

It is at this point that Sherwood enters the story. One might almost say that he does so with a trick. He simply ignores Freud's most questionable formulations, such as those involving the concepts of psychic energy, ego, id, and superego, thus successfully circumventing at least some of the difficulties that presumably bogged down the above-mentioned philosophers. Indirectly he says as much himself (p. 76). This is not a criticism. Sherwood is not trying to duck the issue. The procedure he follows is largely a consequence of his assumption that in the main the *logical features* of explanation in psychoanalysis have remained untouched by the almost incessant changes and developments of psychoanalytic theory (p. 76). And it is these features, as the title of the book indicates, that he is primarily interested in. As far as I can see, his assumption is most probably correct.

II.

I mentioned that the professional philosophers who tried to approach the subject did not penetrate very far into the philosophy of psychoanalysis. But what about the psychoanalysts themselves? There is not very much to be said about this question. Psychoanalysts seem by and large to lack the requisite understanding of philosophical points of view, let alone their at least potential significance for the development of psychoanalysis as a science. In a general way Waelder (1960) shows some grasp of the difficulties involved, but not enough to encourage further inquiry. He is no doubt right in saying that by and large psychoanalysis succumbs neither to the avowedly antiscientific German philosophy of *Verstehen* nor to the mindlessness of early American behaviorism. But in trying to characterize what psychoanalysis is, by contrast to what it is not, he becomes so vague that he succeeds in covering up the problems rather than in materially contributing to their solution (pp. 3–31). For one thing, his differentiation between psychoanalytic observation and inference is quite confused (1962, pp. 619f.). This lack of proper understanding of the niceties of philosophical distinctions is also revealed in his blunt remarks about Nagel's (1959) admittedly unfair criticism of psychoanalysis in Hook's (1959) symposium on *Psychoanalysis, Scientific Method and Philosophy* (Waelder, 1962, pp. 635f.). Were it not for the fact that a great many analysts still have not freed themselves from the parochialism of this attitude, it would hardly have been worthwhile to mention Grotjahn's declaration (1959, pp. 536f.) (a) that the philosophical discussion recorded in this symposium is without interest to practicing psychoanalysts, and (b) that the criticism of psychoanalysis by some nonanalysts is due exclusively to their "misunderstanding," "ignorance," "unnecessary defensiveness," and "dogmatic insistence." Sherwood, who deplores the indifference shown by most philosophers, is even more disheartened by the complacent lack of understanding of crucial philosophical questions on the part of psychoanalysts generally (pp. 1f.).

Of the questions a philosopher of psychoanalysis, like a philosopher of any science (whether he be a philosopher by profession or not), immediately comes up against, the most vital concerns what is and what is not to count as knowledge or as reasonable rather than as unreasonable surmise. It is obvious that every competent scientist from time to time asks himself this question—usually, however, without pursuing it in all its ramifications. Simple though the question may seem, the answers to it are often highly complicated; and not every aspect of it has an answer, at any rather not an unequivocal answer. One thing is certain, however; as Sherwood, at least by implication, observes (p. 2), we cannot forever hide behind the often-heard claim that only psychoanalysts are competent judges of the scientific merits of their own method. By his way of writing, Sherwood, who by training is both a psychiatrist and a philosopher of science, in effect refutes this claim, at any rate in its usual categorical formulation. Hence the refreshing philosophical openness of his book.

To put the issue quite simply: Given a set of psychoanalytic data and a set of rules connecting some data with other data, one need not be an analyst to determine whether the rules function as they are supposed to, and if they do, why they do, and if not, why not. Neither does one need to be an analyst to determine whether the rules are consistent with what we believe the world is like and, regardless of whether or not they are consistent with our beliefs, whether the statements they generate are confirmable in some agreed-upon sense of "confirmable," and if they are, whether and to what degree they are in fact confirmed. The time is long since past when the majority of nonanalysts high-handedly tried to rule psychoanalytic data out of existence.

III.

It would not be fair either to the book or to the attitude it represents were I merely to applaud the effort and unquestionable achievement of the author and then pass on. The book is admirable in many ways: in its often sharp distinctions, in its penetrating, sometimes highly complex analyses, in the clarity of thought that enlivens many of its sections. In spite of these qualities, however, there is room for disagreement on a number of points, even on some major ones. Disagreement does not in all instances imply criticism. The subject matter is too complicated, too vague, beset with too many uncertainties, not to spark divergent opinions on several of the issues it comprises. I think I owe it to the author (as well as to our common concern about psychoanalysis) to set forth these disagreements as best I can. It is possible that at least some of them can be reconciled. I am not sure, however—disagreements sometimes have a way of being recalcitrant. But let me first touch on some of the points on which I agree with the author. Obviously I cannot mention every one of these points. But neither does space permit me to indicate every single point on which, at least as of this writing, I disagree with him.

I may as well start with the most incisive criticism Sherwood directs at psychoanalysis as a science. He emphasizes that in psychoanalysis the "basic problems of establishing procedures for the observation of phenomena and validation of hypotheses, so essential for the orderly growth of any discipline, were only partially recognized and never adequately dealt with" (1969, p. 70; see also pp. 1f.). And he adds that "in perhaps no other field has so great a body of theory been built upon such a small public record of raw data" (p. 70). It is a fair guess that at least in part this peculiar lack of proportion, this luxuriance of theoretical speculation, on which Scriven (1962a) also comments, is a consequence of the shortcomings Sherwood points up in the just-cited passage. When validation limps, speculation is apt to take over and soar into the unknown and perhaps beyond. One can hardly disagree either with the criticisms or the implication that we have here problems psychoanalysis must deal with if it is ever to leave behind its "early pioneering stage" and grow into a mature—or at least a maturing—science. In part Sherwood deals with them himself. To get his sample of "raw data" he summarizes Freud's analysis of the so-called Rat Man, the patient referred to as Paul Lorenz (pp. 76–92; Freud, 1909). On this basis Sherwood then tries to elucidate the nature of psychoanalytic explanation.

I need hardly emphasize that this variety of explanation is full of complexities. One question is: Do we explain *causally* or do we rather explain by pointing to the (obvious or presumptive) *reasons* why people act, feel, dream, etc., as they do? Lately this has become a much-debated question. Reasons and causes are seen by some as essentially *alternative* modes of understanding and description, while others—perhaps unwittingly flirting with a dualistic interpretation of the mind-brain relationship—regard the two sets of determiners as separated from one another by an unbridgeable gap. At first Sherwood seems to leave us in no doubt about where he stands on this issue. Characterizing the second of the indicated views as the "thesis of the separate domain" (pp. 37, 125), he proceeds to demolish it with often surgical directness and precision. But then all of a sudden he becomes ambiguous.

The problem has many facets and Sherwood deals with each of them in turn. I will try to summarize his argument without, however, always following his order of presentation. Let me start with his claim that the distinction made by some authors between movements and actions is in many ways confused. According to Peters (as quoted by Sherwood), actions cannot be fully described in terms of movements because, while in themselves movements obviously are not intelligent, efficient, and correct, actions may be (p. 135). This no doubt is true. As Sherwood points out, however, it does not follow that actions cannot therefore comprise movements (p. 144) nor that they, unlike movements, cannot be causally determined. In his view, which to me seems unassailable, an action may be said to be intelligent, efficient, or correct only in reference to its observable consequences. The obvious corollary is that, since these are observable, they do not preclude scientific investigation and hence—together with the action itself—causal explanation (p. 139).

This contention is not affected by the fact that the problem is in reality much more complex. An action thus is defined not only in terms of its consequences but also in terms of the situation in which it occurs and often enough in terms of the interests of the observer. In this sense actions, by contrast to movements, may be said to be "context-dependent" (p. 143). As Sherwood observes, the conscious and unconscious intentions of the acting person, to the extent that these can be established, are also relevant for the definition of particular actions as well as for the distinction between action and movement (pp. 143ff.). Nothing of this, however, is likely to invalidate the statement that actions are causally determined. Motives are readily described as causes, and so are intentions and situational factors. In essence, the interest of the observer merely singles out for attention one or the other of these items, say, the consequences of an action rather than its motive(s).

One of Sherwood's most subtle arguments is directed against another claim of Peters's to the effect that actions cannot be causally determined because if they were we should be able to specify both the necessary and the sufficient conditions for their occurrence, and that we are not able to do. Sherwood's point is in essence that our inability to specify the necessary and sufficient conditions for the occurrence of an event by no means precludes its causal explanation. In the case of a flat tire, for example, to say that a nail puncture caused the tire to blow out may be correct even though a nail puncture is certainly not a necessary nor always a sufficient condition for the blowout of tires (pp. 128–131). For example, if in a given case the nail is thin enough and the tire of a certain type, a nail puncture may be immediately sealed so that nothing happens. And a tire may of course blow out for a number of reasons other than a nail puncture (p. 183).

According to Sherwood, it is becoming increasingly clear that, at least in many cases, the sufficient conditions for the occurrence of an event may not be known or even knowable with certainty (p. 132). This state of affairs has far-reaching consequences. To overcome the difficulty it creates, Sherwood distinguishes between *logically sufficient conditions* and *sufficient explanations*. This is an important distinction. An explanation may be sufficient, as in the case of the blowout of the tire, even though reference to the nail puncture may not exhaustively describe the logically sufficient conditions for its occurrence (p. 131). It follows, or so it appears, that the occurrence of an action *can* be sufficiently explained causally without full knowledge of its logically sufficient conditions, among which, obviously, is what Sherwood in a different connection refers to as a "chain of neurological occurrences" (p. 146). Even though (unless I have missed the point) he does not say so directly, there is little doubt that this is what Sherwood has in mind.

I will try to clarify with a psychoanalytic example. Consider the following statement: "He married the girl *because* she was almost a carbon copy of his mother, whom he loved dearly." This statement, it seems, does not describe either a necessary or a logically sufficient condition for the young man's marrying the girl. To claim that the indicated cause was a necessary condition implies that had he not found a girl who was to this extent like his mother the young man would never have married; and to claim that it was a sufficient condition implies that he may have married the girl for no other reason than her likeness to his mother. Without additional data neither of these statements carries much conviction. In many instances we are nevertheless ready, even without such additional data, to accept the statement as a sufficient explanation.

Up to this point I am in full agreement with the author. I have doubts, however, about part of his criticism of the claim, also advanced by Peters, that action describable as a person's "suffering" something (such as action prompted by an overwhelming desire) may be explained causally, whereas action describable as his "doing" something has to be explained in terms of reasons. According to Sherwood, this claim must be rejected for the reason that "only if we first know that a causal explanation is appropriate can we assert that the event was a 'suffering' " (p. 138). But is this really so? Are we not sometimes able to recognize that a person is overwhelmed by an emotion before he acts on that emotion, i.e., since the action has not yet occurred, before we have reason to ask whether the occurrence of it can be explained causally or not? I do not, in other words, find Sherwood's point convincing. But neither do I agree with Peters—even though one might say that his argument has the advantage of opening up a possibility to regard unconscious determiners of action as causes while some conscious ones may still be described as reasons.

That is Peters's own contention. Sherwood objects, rightly I think, that this view contradicts his (i.e., Peters's) basic assumption, according to which movements but not actions can be causally determined (p. 141). In fact, according to Peters, only action describable as "doing" is "genuine action" (p. 137). I agree with Sherwood that this is not a tenable position. As Sherwood points out, when Peters considers unconscious determiners he in effect "is forced to obliterate the movement-action distinction" (p. 142).

IV.

Part of the trouble, it seems to me, can easily be cleared up. Suppose I go out because I want to buy oranges. Unless my desire for oranges is absolutely overwhelming, this is clearly an instance not of "suffering" but of "doing" something. Hence, according to Peters's claim (as quoted by Sherwood), it should not be explainable causally. It is obviously correct to say "My intention to buy oranges was the *reason* I went out." It seems, however, to be just as correct, although perhaps less common, to say "My intention to buy oranges *caused* me to go out." The same dichotomy is reflected in the following sentences: "His *reason* for doing A was that he very badly wanted to achieve B, which normally is achievable through doing A," and "His strong wish to achieve B *caused* him to do A, which normally leads to the achievement of B." I should add that what we refer to in these sentences, respectively, as the reason and the causative wish may be conscious or unconscious.

Thus, at least in a number of cases, an action can apparently be described *either* as a "doing" and hence in terms of reasons, *or* as a "suffering" and hence in terms of causes. In the first instance the person in question is portrayed as playing an active role, in the second a passive role, and appears, correspondingly, as either having a reason for doing whatever he is doing or as in some sense being "made" to do it. It seems that Peters is mistaken not in pairing "doings" with reasons and "sufferings" with causes, but in believing that these pairs represent two distinctly separate classes of psychological events, while in many instances they merely represent two ways of describing the same event or of describing it from different viewpoints.

Along somewhat different lines Sherwood argues effectively in favor of not making an absolute distinction between reasons and causes (pp. 153–159). But then he suddenly turns around and claims that, although in many cases the words "reason" and "cause" are used interchangeably, "There is . . . another use of the term 'reason' in which it is not synonymous with 'cause' " (p. 160). In part I agree with this contention, but in part only. It seems to me that there are flaws in the argument which seriously distort the issue.

To make my point I must consider Sherwood's position in some detail. He first distinguishes between causes and what, following Hart and Honoré, he calls *causally relevant factors* (pp. 147ff.). There are many different types of such factors, causes and necessary but not sufficient conditions, among others. In the case of a necessary but not sufficient condition, one is often present before the introduction of a factor together with which it forms a set of sufficient conditions. The newly introduced factor is then usually designated *the* cause. According to one of the examples cited by Sherwood, a causally relevant factor that in ordinary parlance is not a cause is the presence of air (i.e., oxygen) in a room that is set on fire by a lighted cigarette somebody has dropped. It is of interest that, although a necessary condition, this causally relevant factor as a rule is not even mentioned and the explanation of the fire by the dropped lighted cigarette is still commonly regarded as a sufficient explanation (pp. 147–153).

It is quite consistent with this usage of the terms that what under one set of conditions is merely a causally relevant factor may under another set of conditions be *the* cause. If material that is highly combustible at a certain temperature is kept at that temperature in an oxygen-free container, and if oxygen is now piped into the container whereupon the material immediately starts to burn, then the introduction of oxygen (particularly if it was introduced by mistake) is more or less automatically designated as *the* cause of the fire.

As we have observed, in Sherwood's view the word "reason" may be interchangeable with the word "cause." It may, however, also be used in the sense of a causally relevant factor. In fact, Sherwood believes that a reason is either a cause or a causally relevant factor. There seems to be no third possibility. Thus one *reason* why in the first example the dropped lighted cigarette set the room on fire was the presence in it of a sufficient supply of oxygen. But what about the cases in which, according to Sherwood, the words "cause" and "reason" are not used interchangeably? It seems that, in his view, in these cases too reasons are causally relevant factors, but of a different type than those considered so far. For one thing, apparently in no circumstances can they be causes. The crucial distinction, however, is *in the way* in which a reason *becomes* causally relevant. As Sherwood sees it, reasons of the type he has in mind "are those causally relevant factors which become causally relevant by virtue of the fact that they are *taken account of consciously or unconsciously* and acted upon by the individual in question" (p. 162; italics mine). It follows that reasons of this type can be ascribed only to human beings (p. 160).

I do not think that Sherwood's view on this point is tenable. To begin with, it is not the words "reason" and "cause" that may or may not be interchangeable but the sentences—and the corresponding statements—in which these words occur. In reference to statements about reasons and causal statements that, according to Sherwood, are not interchangeable I will for the sake of simplicity continue to speak about reasons that in no circumstances can be causes. One of Sherwood's examples of a reason of this sort is embodied in the following (slightly modified) statement: "His being offered a bribe of five dollars for doing it was the *reason* he stole the bread" (pp. 156, 160). Sherwood is obviously right in emphasizing that being offered the bribe can hardly have been a sufficient condition for the person's stealing the bread. And, by contrast to the statements that a nail puncture caused the blowout and a dropped lighted cigarette the fire, neither does the statement that this person was offered a bribe for stealing the bread constitute a sufficient explanation of the act. It is decidedly odd to say, "His being offered a bribe of five dollars for doing it *caused* him to steal the bread." I do not see, however, why we could not say "His being offered a bribe of five dollars for doing it was among the factors that *caused* him to steal the bread." This formulation takes account of the fact, which Sherwood clearly recognizes (p. 157), that the bribe, together with some such additional factors as poverty and hunger and/or desire to show off his daring and/or his disdain for bourgeois values, etc., may indeed have formed a set of sufficient conditions for the person's stealing the bread.

It seems to me that *up to a point* there is a parallel between these factors and the presence of air referred to in the previously quoted example and between being offered a bribe and the dropping of a lighted cigarette. Assume that the person we are talking about was hungry and without money at t_1. Given the character traits and attitudes just mentioned and the reality situation at t_1 of this person (and given reliable knowledge on our part of these and other relevant factors), his being offered a bribe at t_1 for doing it may well be described as the cause (i.e., the triggering factor) for his stealing the bread at t_2.

There are presumably a number of reasons why Sherwood avoids a formulation of this kind. One may be that we could not have known in advance *all* the relevant factors operating at t_1 and hence could not with any certainty have predicted the effect of the bribe. It seems to me, however, that Sherwood's main reason for ruling out the possibility of a causal explanation derives from his failure to realize that the expression "taking account of," as he uses it, can be understood as having two meanings. It may refer to an act performed by a person. In the same way as other psychological phenomena, however, it may also refer to a process occurring in a human organism. While "taking account of" in the first meaning of this expression is clearly a "doing" and thus compatible with the notion of a reason that cannot in any circumstances be a cause, the particular process that "taking account of" in its second meaning refers to can, like any process, become a link in a series of causal relationships. It is fairly clear that in its second meaning "taking account of" is not describable as a "doing." Something happens; but there is no subject—and nothing comparable to a subject—that "makes" it happen.

It is evident from the tenor of his argument that Sherwood's positing a class of reasons that in no circumstances can be causes is contingent on his interpretation of the expression "taking account of" as referring *exclusively* to an act performed by a person. Although this interpretation is compatible with—and hence justifiable by—a dualistic view of the mind-brain relationship, Sherwood, as judged by certain passages (pp. 146, 153), unequivocally (albeit merely by implication) abjures any such view. He does not, however, offer an alternative justification for his interpretation of "taking account of." To say, or imply, that psychoanalysis after all concerns persons no doubt is true. But without further specification it is not enough.

That it is not enough is suggested by the lack of consistency in Sherwood's treatment of the indicated class of reasons. Thus a little later in the book, in reference to the Lorenz case, he reiterates that there is no "radical difference" between causes and reasons (p. 179; see also pp. 171, 174, 177). And in trying to clarify the concept of an *unconscious reason* in relation to this case, he speaks interchangeably about reasons and causes (pp. 177f.).

It seems to me that one way out of Sherwood's difficulties is to make a clear distinction between two modes of thinking and speaking, two languages, *ordinary language* and *the language of science*. To the extent that we regard psychoanalysis as a science, its language is a scientific language. One difference between the two types of language is precisely that, while in ordinary language we may speak about persons, their activities, and the *reasons* for these activities, in the language of science we at least implicitly, i.e., *regardless of the words we use*, speak about organisms, organism-environment interactions, and processes inside the organism that are *causally* related to one another and/or to these interactions. Psychoanalysis, obviously, has not yet developed a scientific language of this sort. Accordingly, as the need arises it *borrows words and expressions* from ordinary language and mixes them with the few genuinely scientific expressions it has available.

It is my contention that this fact gives rise to much of the confusion, not only in Sherwood's book but in psychoanalytic discussions generally, about this problem. The question is complex and cannot be discussed here. I will mention only that, as they occur in ordinary language, statements about reasons may be taken at face value, whereas in a scientific language they are strictly stand-ins for causal statements. I may also mention that, since in ordinary language we speak about persons, the expression "taking account of" is in this language readily interpreted as referring to an act performed by a person. If, on the other hand, it occurs in a scientific language, the expression *must* be interpreted as referring to processes of a particular sort. We cannot let ourselves be deterred by the fact that these processes have to be listed as "at present unknown." It is of interest that, as generally understood, ordinary language, in spite of certain suggestive phrases, does not involve a commitment to a dualistic view of the mind-brain relationship nor, for that matter, to any other view of this relationship.

As I see it, this way out of Sherwood's dilemma is compatible with his main points as outlined above; or the latter can, without changing their essential meaning, be made to fit it. It is also compatible with his emphatic repudiation of the "thesis of the separate domain," his conviction that psychoanalysis is not "a radically different discipline from all other sciences" (p. 184). Sherwood's mistake is occasionally to have taken seriously his (necessary) lapses into ordinary language, i.e., to believe that the usual ordinary-language meaning of "reason" may at times have currency in a scientific language.

So far I have not sufficiently specified the ordinary-language meaning of this word. It has a number of meanings, but two are particularly important. According to Toulmin (1970), when we ask about a person's *reason* for an action we may have in mind, among other things, his *justification* for it or the *purpose* he intends it to serve. We should note, however, that Toulmin is careful to point out that the acknowledgment of such reasons does not preclude their causal explanation.

I may mention that clinical statements (whether data statements or statements expressing clinical interpretations) are normally expressed in ordinary language. Although these statements as a rule have reference to persons, the statements about reasons among them are readily understood as substituting for ordinary-language causal statements. The examples I have used above illustrate this point.

V.

I mentioned that in Sherwood's example the statement that the person in question was offered a bribe of five dollars for stealing the bread does not constitute a sufficient explanation of his doing so. We may wonder why that is so. According to Sherwood, as we have seen, an explanation may be sufficient even without full knowledge of the logically sufficient conditions. Let us again consider the blowout of a tire. A blowout has often enough been shown to be temporally connected with a nail puncture to make a causal relationship seem probable; hence, in the case of a particular blowout, if a nail puncture is demonstrated, it is reasonably safe to conclude that the nail puncture caused the blowout. Similar arguments apply to the explanations of a fire by reference to a dropped lighted cigarette and of the young man's marrying a girl who resembles his mother. On the other hand, people do not ordinarily steal bread if offered a bribe of five dollars to do so, nor are such bribes very often, if ever, offered for doing so. It seems that a particular statement can be a sufficient explanation only if it is related in a specific manner to a more general statement.

Throughout much of the rest of the book Sherwood is concerned with the relationship between particular and more general statements. Initially he denies the relevance of general statements for explanation. But then he becomes ambiguous, and finally decides that they may be relevant after all but of only minor significance. Because of the importance to my mind of the issue I will consider these positions in turn. The first Sherwood introduces with two examples. One in essence concerns the relationship between lung cancer and cigarette smoking. Sherwood maintains that, although a high correlation between the two sets of events has been established, we cannot claim that cigarette smoking is *the* cause of lung cancer (pp. 165ff.). That is correct. It is obviously not a necessary and in many instances not even a sufficient condition. It does not follow, however, as Sherwood seems to think, that the correlation therefore can be minimized as comparatively unimportant for the establishment of a causal connection. Nor can we minimize the (clinically plausible) correlation between the looks and/or other attributes of mothers and the similar looks and/or other attributes of the girls their sons marry. Sherwood by and large disregards one of the fundamental assumptions of modern science, namely, the assumption of the validity of probabilistic reasoning. The above discussion of sufficient explanation is obviously based on this assumption. I will have occasion to return to this question.

The second example involves a reason statement. It happens that a certain man shuts the door whenever his mantle clock stops. Sherwood rightly emphasizes that this is incongruous behavior and that therefore, as he has spelled out earlier in the book (pp. 10ff.), it requires an explanation. Why? It seems to me that an incongruity of this sort arises whenever a piece of behavior does not fit any commonly accepted general statement. Even if the man himself asserts that the stopping of the clock is his reason for shutting the door, in my view we cannot accept the reason given. Sherwood disagrees. He does not think that identification of the reason involves reference to general statements. According to him, no matter why the behavior appears incongruous the reason given for it is unacceptable "because we cannot see a connection between this reason and the action" (p. 167). This is true enough. It is also true that we will be satisfied if the man explains further that he has to shut the door to get at the key with which to wind the clock. "His answer," Sherwood claims, "now seems adequate . . . because it has supplied a narrative framework, a model into which we can now accommodate both the antecedent and the action" (p. 168).

The "narrative framework" which, according to Sherwood, provides the missing connection is clearly the account of a series of activities that *together* are instrumental in bringing about a desired end state, namely, the man's being able to wind his clock. That being so, it seems that the account represents an adequate explanation because it fits a means-end generalization that states that if people want to achieve something, and if it is at all possible to do so, they usually act in a way that will enable them to achieve it.

Sherwood denies that a generalization of this or any other sort is involved —at least in a decisive manner. He could hardly do that, however, without having an alternative in mind. To him, these and similar examples are best understood if we assume that "The designation of causes and reasons . . . involves a logical commitment to a theoretical structure or framework or narrative in which the phenomena in question are no longer considered independent entities but interrelated parts of a single unified process or sequence of events" (p. 169).

The reference to a "single unified process" is rather mysterious. And it is not rendered less so by Sherwood's example of the relationship between certain rearrangements of water molecules and ice formation (p. 170). This relationship is most simply described as a correlation. To a physicist, however, it may be said to be analytic in the sense that statements about the molecular rearrangements form part of the physical definition of the formation of ice. Even though, as Sherwood indicates, a layman may here (somewhat sloppily) speak about cause and effect, in the first case a causal relationship is not necessarily implied and in the second the question is not even being touched. Hence, contrary to Sherwood's contention, the example does not illustrate the concept of cause and effect as parts of a single unified process and certainly does not justify it.

It appears that in part at least this concept is made to serve *instead of* the generalizations that, although commonly thought to be related to statements about causal connections, Sherwood at this point outlaws. The issue is by no means clear. Neither is it clear what he means by a "logical commitment to a theoretical structure," etc., and just how such a commitment is supposed to affect a particular causal connection or our recognition of it. He does not return to these conceptions. They seem, however, to be involved in his view of the psychoanalytic narrative which he considers in greater detail later in the book. I will have more to say about them in that connection.

VI.

Before discussing this view I will consider Sherwood's criticism of the hypothet-ico-deductive model, commonly referred to as the H-D model. Although, as we will see presently, certain things may be held against this model, I find his criticism quite unacceptable. Sherwood contends that, while the model is ade-quate for prediction and what he calls description (pp. 218, 224), it "cannot provide an adequate analysis of explanation" (p. 218). But even for prediction the model is, he says, inadequate unless conditional probabilistic statements are admitted (p. 209). The point is well taken. It has, however, by no means been ignored by other philosophers. Hempel, for instance, one of the principal architects of the H-D model, has extensively studied the question of probabil-istic statements (1965, pp. 380–393), and so has Nagel (1961). The irony is that, as we have seen, Sherwood himself tends to disregard statements of this kind.

Sherwood ushers in his attack on the adequacy of the H-D model as an analysis of explanation with the statement that one should be "suspicious of any thesis which insists that prediction . . . could be equivalent to explanation" (p. 215). The H-D model, however, merely implies that prediction and explana-tion are *symmetrical* in a particular sense, not that they are equivalent. And it is the claim of symmetry that has been criticized, among others by Scriven (1959, 1962b, 1963). The following schema represents Sherwood's elaboration and formalization of one of the latter's examples of a nonexplanatory H-D syllogism (see Scriven, 1963, pp. 149, 163):

(a) In July, in England, whenever cows in a field are lying down, it rains within two hours.

(b) It is July, we are in England, and the cows are lying down.
Therefore:

(c) It will rain within two hours.

It is undoubtedly correct that this syllogism, although it yields a prediction, would not, even if statement (a) were true, yield a valid explanation (p. 215). Nothing we know supports the contention that the cows' lying down causes it to rain. But, contrary to what Sherwood seems to believe, that is not a sufficient reason for discarding the H-D model as an analysis of explanation.

Let us disregard the fact that to some people statement (a), at least as formulated here, is somewhat questionable. That is not what makes the explana-tion derived from the argument invalid. Assuming for the sake of argument that statement (a) is true, we must recognize that *primarily* it merely expresses a cor-relation between the occurrence of two events. Let us call these events A and B, respectively. Because B occurs later than A it is possible (1) to predict the occur-rence of B on the basis of the occurrence of A, and (2) to express the correlation in the form of a statement like "If A at t_1, then B at t_2." This statement may or may not be interpretable causally. If it is not, it obviously cannot yield an explanation. A mere correlation does not explain anything. As Sherwood realizes (pp. 216, 219), since both have the form of an "If . . . , then . . ." statement, we cannot *logically* distinguish between an explanatory and a nonexplanatory statement of this type. Partly for this reason some philosophers have given up on the attempt to distinguish between such statements, while others feel that for the sake of clarity they *must* be distinguished from one another. White, in his study of the philosophy of history (1965, pp. 73ff.), takes the latter position.

Most scientists, it seems to me, know that they are in deep trouble if they do not distinguish between *post hoc* and *propter hoc*. This is clearly what the difficulty is all about. The distinction, however, requires empirical investigation, not formal analysis. In the case we are discussing the actual state of affairs, assuming that it exists, might be expressed in the statement "If M at t_0, then A at t_1 *and* B at t_2," where M stands for specific meteorological conditions occurring in July and in England.

This point, I think, is decisive. On the assumption that psychoanalysis is an empirical science, the above-mentioned asymmetry between explanation and prediction is an insufficient reason for us to deny validity for an H-D analysis of psychoanalytic explanation.

I cannot refrain from mentioning in this connection that the asymmetry between explanation and prediction is more complex than the example chosen by Sherwood indicates. In addition to cases in which prediction but not explanation is possible, we have cases where explanation but not prediction is possible. Scriven (1959, 1962b) cites a number of examples of the latter type, the most important perhaps being the theory of evolution. In all of them general statements, mostly of a probabilistic type, are involved. We should not forget, however, that in a number of cases to which the H-D model applies, explanation and prediction are strictly symmetrical in the sense that both are possible.

VII.

Having objected to Sherwood's critique of the H-D model I find myself in the embarrassing position of having to criticize this model myself. But I do not criticize it for the same reasons as Sherwood. The classical H-D model requires its major premise to be a statement of universal validity. Very few, if any, psychoanalytic statements have this characteristic. For the most part, although formulated as universal statements, they are probabilistic (see Hempel, 1965, p. 175).

This fact obviously does not do away with the relevance of general statements for psychoanalytic explanation. According to Nagel (1961, pp. 558ff.), in history we may speak about *probabilistic explanation*. I do not see why we cannot do the same in psychoanalysis. More or less in opposition to this view, it is sometimes maintained that singular historical statements are inferred from other singular historical statements. As Nagel shows, however, this mode of inference is merely apparent. What in fact happens is that the inference here proceeds *in accordance with* a "leading principle (or rule of inference)" which usually is derived from a probabilistic general statement (p. 562). It is fairly clear, I think, that this is the case in psychoanalysis also.

Inference of this type is logically more complex than inference in accordance with the H-D model. For the most part it is inductive, not deductive. Although for this reason it is also more problematical, as I have indicated, it is nevertheless resorted to more or less as a matter of course in most sciences. At any rate, in history the issue is still being debated. For example, according to White (1965, p. 95f.), historical explanation, although often apparently probabilistic, can be interpreted in terms of a specifically modified H-D schema.

The following point is important. Most models of scientific explanation that today are taken seriously have at least one feature in common, namely, their reliance on general statements, whether universal or merely probabilistic. This reliance seems inescapable. How else could we know, say, that an observed sequence of events is not a freak of nature, a chance occurrence that will perhaps never be repeated? Because of this common feature I will collectively refer to the models in question as *scientific explanation schemata,* or S-E schemata or models. Obviously, whereas the strictly deductive S-E schema, i.e., the H-D model, yields *certain* knowledge (if applied in a particular way), the knowledge yielded by an inductive S-E schema is always *probabilistic*.

Let me give an example. To bring out its probabilistic nature I will slightly expand Sherwood's version of Freud's explanation of Lorenz's miserliness. If we reconstruct the reasoning that went into this explanation we can recognize a number of steps. We begin with the observation that Lorenz was a miser and the further observation that his father was a spendthrift. We now adduce the probabilistic clinical hypothesis that if a son hates his father he as a rule wants to be as unlike him as possible. Since being a miser is being in the highest degree a nonspendthrift, we can explain Lorenz's being a miser by positing that he (a) (unconsciously) hated his father and, therefore, (b) (unconsciously) wanted to be as unlike him as possible, for example, since the father was a spendthrift, by being a nonspendthrift.

To complete the explanation of Lorenz's miserliness we must adduce the further probabilistic clinical hypothesis that if a son *wants to be* unlike his father he often enough *will be* unlike him. This last hypothesis is clearly constructed by analogy with the more general clinical hypothesis that people tend to avoid what they for one reason or another detest.

To confirm our particular clinical hypothesis, i.e., the explanation of Lorenz's miserliness, we obviously must show that he indeed (whether consciously or unconsciously) was likely to have hated his father and to have wanted to be as unlike him as possible.

VIII.

Sherwood presumably had some inkling of this state of affairs when, as we have noted, he called for admission of probabilistic statements into the H-D model. In spite of his repeated renunciation of general statements it therefore does not really come as a surprise to read in his discussion of Freud's account of the Lorenz analysis that "Many items seemed inconsistent with what we know about human behavior *generally*" (p. 187; italics mine). This and similar statements (see, e.g., pp. 188, 231) indicate that Sherwood does see the significance of generalizations in the over-all process of psychoanalytic explanation. His point seems rather to be "that the narrative itself does not involve generalizations about human nature" (p. 241).

That may be so. The ambiguity of Sherwood's position remains, however. And it is not removed by his contention that whatever role general statements may play in the formulation and organization of the narrative, "all such statements are no more than *platitudes*" (p. 242; italics mine). Sherwood, who has apparently borrowed this term from Hart and Honoré (as quoted on p. 147), thinks that "they form a part of the *presumption of knowledge* that enters into the explanatory context itself" (p. 242; italics mine). He does admit, on the other hand, that "it is only because some such platitudes are a part of our knowledge in the first place that the patient's behavior appears incongruous and in need of special explanation" (p. 242). He believes notwithstanding that "in themselves these platitudes add nothing to the explanatory strength of the psychoanalytic narrative" and that "it is not the case that the explanation as it stands would be any less explanatory without them" (p. 242).

These are extraordinary statements. We should note that Sherwood includes means-end generalizations in the category of platitudes (p. 242) and even ridicules an attempt to adduce such generalizations for the analysis of explanation of human action (p. 216). By characterizing psychoanalytically relevant generalizations in this way Sherwood evidently plays down their significance and thus relieves himself of the necessity to examine their functions in sufficient detail. Although, in referring to the "platitudes" as "presumptions of knowledge," he indirectly admits their relevance, he immediately retracts this admission when he insists that they do not add to the explanatory power of the narrative. He apparently thinks that, while the general statements he calls platitudes may play a role in the detection of incongruities (see p. 10), they have no function in the process of explanation. I need hardly point out that this attitude is completely at odds with the views of Hempel, Nagel, and White indicated above. Of course, Sherwood is free to differ with these views. But he should at least have given them a fair hearing.

Part of the difficulty no doubt stems from Sherwood's peculiar conception of causal relationships and his overemphasis on the significance of the narrative for psychoanalytic explanation; but part is also due to his not seeing that what he refers to as platitudes are probabilistic hypotheses of various sorts. Even though he does not regard them as hypotheses and apparently does not recognize the relationship, Sherwood has expressed views on the matter that might be reconciled, at least in part, with a functional classification of the hypotheses I would like to propose as an alternative to his conception. According to this classification we have: (a) a set of commonsense generalizations about human behavior, sufficiently gross deviations from which will make the behavior in question seem incongruous, (b) a set of mainly situational and motivational, predominantly causal, hypotheses the operation of which removes the incongruity, (c) a set of noncausal correlations, (d) a set of hypotheses about patient behavior in the psychoanalytic situation, including the hypothesis that sequential items in the patient's verbal productions, although seemingly unrelated, may nonetheless be intrinsically related to one another, and (e) a set of generalizations of particular applications of, mainly, type (b) hypotheses. The hypotheses of type (e) represent the empirical generalizations of psychoanalytic theory, such as the hypothesis of penis envy in women and the hypothesis, cited above, that if a son hates his father he as a rule wants to be an unlike him as possible. I agree with Sherwood that the explanatory function of these hypotheses is limited (see pp. 189, 242ff.), not, however, because they are generalizations but because their scope of application for the most part is poorly defined.

It seems to me rather clear that the hypotheses of type (b) operate in accordance with a probabilistic S-E schema. Apart from means-end generalizations, they include hypotheses about wish fulfillments and substitute fulfillments, about repression and other forms of resolution of inner conflict, about motive arousal situations and situations, particularly in childhood, that are likely to have led to the establishment of particular motives as more or less permanent dispositions, etc. These various hypotheses correspond to the different types of explanation that Sherwood distinguishes (pp. 22–36, 196–202). But, in rejecting the idea that an S-E model may be involved in the analyst's explanatory activities, he cuts off from view the otherwise rather obvious connection between psychoanalytic explanations and some of the "platitudes" he refers to.

We may regard the indicated hypotheses simply as generalizations of experience, everyday as well as psychoanalytic. It is important to note, however, that most of them also point to (and/or presuppose) hypotheses of a different kind, namely hypotheses concerning the specific processes involved in mental functioning. These hypotheses are commonly referred to as metapsychological. From a psychological point of view they may at most be said to "work." For their ultimate confirmation they depend on neurophysiology.

I should add that in psychoanalysis we explain not only in instances of detected incongruities but also in instances when an observation, which is *not* incongruous, suggests an explanation that fits the theory. Thus even ostensibly normal behavior comes under the scrutiny of the psychoanalyst.

IX.

We have come to what Sherwood regards as the core of the matter. According to him, the explanations he lists form an essential part of the psychoanalytic narrative. It is around the latter, or, rather, around a particular aspect of it, that the whole argument revolves. But I, at least, did not discover what that aspect was until fairly late in the book. Sherwood introduces the most important part of his discussion with a series of statements which at first sight seem quite baffling, to say the least. He claims that "the argument . . . is from the over-all explanation of the whole life history to the explanation of particular incidents" (p. 189f.), that "psychoanalysis supplies a context, a narrative about an individual patient within which isolated pieces of behavior come to be understood, fitted together, and organized into a comprehensive whole," that "within that narrative . . . one can isolate various types of explanations accounting in different ways for particular bits of behavior," but that "it would be a grave distortion to see the narrative as simply the summation of separate explanations, for this would be to reverse the order of procedure" (p. 190). He adds, however, that Freud's narrative does not offer "deductive certainty" (p. 236). This is the only point with which I fully agree. We obviously cannot expect "deductive certainty" for explanations derived from probabilistic hypotheses.

Let us first consider the statement that the narrative is not a "summation" of explanations of particular bits of behavior. If Sherwood means merely that the latter are not simply *listed* but organized in respect to the logical and/or factual relationships obtaining between them and that some explanations may be modified in the light of other explanations, I can only agree. This interpretation would also fit the other statements cited. Apparently, however, he means more than that. It seems that, according to Sherwood, in some sense the narrative comes *before* the particular explanations constituting it. To think anything else would be, as he says, "to reverse the order of procedure."

Viewed in this light statements like the ones just quoted can make sense only if we assume that what Sherwood has in mind is not *the process of psychoanalytic explanation in an actual analysis* but the process of deriving particular explanations from a case history *that has already been written up*. Sherwood advances a slightly different view. To him "the real job of explanation" occurs in the process of writing up the case history (p. 231). This, obviously, is still not the same as the explanations or interpretations of particular bits of behavior the analyst formulates in the course of an analysis. It seems that the most accurate description of Sherwood's concept of psychoanalytic explanation is a combination of his view, as just reported, and mine.

If this is correct, then Sherwood's repudiation of the H-D model—and implicitly of other S-E schemata as well—becomes perhaps a little more understandable but also rather irrelevant: it does not apply at the very point, namely, the explanation in an ongoing analysis of particular bits of behavior, at which an S-E schema presumably is most directly involved. This does not mean, however, that Sherwood and I are somehow talking past one another. If, as he claims, a psychoanalytic narrative is indeed a scientific construction, then the way in which its constituent particular explanations are arrived at is at least as important as the way in which they are pieced together. And if generalizations, as I believe, play a prominent part in the aspect of explanation first mentioned, then they play a prominent part in the over-all process of explanation, even if it should be true (which I doubt) that in some aspects they play hardly any role at all.

In his effort to denigrate generalizations in almost every way he can think of, Sherwood writes in reference to the Lorenz case that "the explanatory power of Freud's discussion resides in the narrative itself or else is nonexistent" (p. 240). This statement, curiously enough, suggests that Sherwood somehow sees a parallel between the psychoanalytic narrative of an individual case and a scientific theory. This impression is strengthened by the statement already quoted that in psychoanalysis we move "from the over-all explanation of the whole life history to the explanation of particular incidents." It is at least possible that, contrasting the singularity of a psychoanalytic narrative with the generality of a scientific theory, Sherwood concluded that, in the narrative, generalizations at most play a minor role. This conclusion, however, does not withstand scrutiny. A single individual is only one of a *class* of in many ways similar persons whose behaviors are explained in accordance with related, if not identical, principles. A psychoanalytic narrative, in fact, may be more aptly compared to a description of the functioning of a machine, in which the underlying physical principles are not mentioned, than to a full-fledged theory.

The notion of cause and effect as interrelated parts of a single unified process and the concept of the narrative are tied together in many ways, among others by the fact that both involve a renunciation of generalizations. It is not an exaggeration to claim that if the one crumbles and dissolves, so does the other. Let us therefore take a last look from this point of view at the indicated notion. As I have mentioned, if generalizations are outlawed, then the existence of causal relationships must be substantiated in some other way. In my view, the alternative substantiation proposed by Sherwood is based on a confusion of a particular sort. I suspect that he does not clearly distinguish between an *empirical* statement like "A causes B" and the *analytic* statement that if something is a cause it must have an effect. Thus he writes: "Various experiments may well direct us toward a conceptual framework; in positing that causal framework, however, we commit ourselves to certain logical relationships, not to the truth of any experiential generalization" (p. 169). I confess that I do not understand this statement. Since, however, it occurs in the very connection in which the notion of cause and effect as interrelated parts of a single unified process is advanced, I venture the guess that in its own peculiar manner it is meant to intimate that the indicated notion somehow follows from the logical relationship between the concepts of cause and effect. If so, the inference is illegitimate. *Logically,* we cannot split apart the concepts of cause and effect for the simple reason that nothing can be a cause that does not have an effect and nothing an effect that does not have a cause. This fact, however, does not allow us to infer that the events these concepts stand for are also *factually* inseparable, that they form a "single unified process" in the sense that if one of them occurs then, by necessity, the other must occur as well.

It is odd that if this is indeed part of Sherwood's confusion it may have its root in an astute observation on his part, namely, that (a) perceptions, attitudes, beliefs, and other phenomena he refers to as "primary" are not *in themselves* explanatory (p. 163), and (b) they become explanatory only when they are *interpreted* as causes or reasons, this step clearly being logical, not empirical (p. 164). From the fact, however, that the step, say, from wish to cause is logical, it does not follow that the step from a particular cause to the demonstration not just that it has an effect, but that it has a *particular* effect, is logical also.

X.

It is instructive to consider two further points about generalizations that Sherwood tries to drive home. The first is that a generalization may be used "as a shorthand for some general narrative about the subject in question" (p. 225). It seems to me that it is rather the narrative that may be regarded as a shorthand in the sense of being a *summary description* of highly complex processes comprising observation, the adduction of more or less general hypotheses, and inference in accordance with these. The objection that for the most part we are not aware of processes of these sorts is easily countered. When we speak we are not aware of the syntactical rules that linguistic analysis shows we follow. From the summary that a psychoanalytic narrative can thus be taken to represent, most general statements have been culled. Hence, as we have noted, Sherwood can claim that "the narrative itself does not involve generalizations about human nature but instead makes certain empirical assertions about the particular individual in question" (p. 241). I may mention that the stand I am trying to outline is in essential agreement with the relevant aspects of White's view of historical narration (1965, pp. 219–270).

The second point refers to what Sherwood calls "dispositional generalizations," i.e., statements like "Paul Lorenz has a deep hatred of his father of which he is not aware" (p. 220). Statements of this type express inductive inferences based on a number of observations of a *single* person, not of people generally. Such generalizations may be characterized as summaries of a narrative of the observations in question. Sherwood presumably has generalizations of this or some similar type in mind when he writes, apparently contradicting a number of other assertions, that a "psychoanalytic narrative does contain straightforward empirical generalizations" (p. 205). I should mention that, even though these contradictions may be merely apparent, they are still likely to confuse the reader.

XI.

If we disregard a few points to which I take exception, Sherwood's section on the evaluation of psychoanalytic narratives is for the most part admirable in its clarity, its conciseness, and its emphasis on the need for confirmation of psychoanalytic statements. Sherwood judges a narrative according to its appropriateness, adequacy, and accuracy (p. 246). All of these he has defined early in the book (p. 20). The appropriateness of a narrative he does not discuss further. Among the criteria of adequacy he lists self-consistency (which obviously does not rule out conceptions such as that of ambivalence), coherence, and comprehensiveness (pp. 246–249). The main criterion of accuracy is "correspondence of empirical assertions with what is actually found to be the case" (p. 252).

Space does not permit me even to mention the many excellent and highly important points he makes in discussing these criteria. Let me say only that, whereas his (explicit or implicit) repudiation of S-E models and his emphasis on the explanatory function of the narrative as such seemed to infuse new life into the "thesis of the separate domain" (which, as we have seen, he had already rejected on different grounds), his stress in this section on the need for evidence and even more for a clear definition of what is to count as evidence (p. 253) does a thorough job of discrediting this "thesis." I should add that the criteria of accuracy and in part those of adequacy apply in the same measure to particular explanations as, in Sherwood's view, they do to the narrative as a whole. These remarks are made especially with their application to particular explanations in mind.

All the points to which I take exception in one way or other involve Sherwood's view of the psychoanalytic narrative, his rejection of the H-D model and his at least implicit rejection of other S-E schemata as well. For example, he asserts, but without trying to substantiate the assertion, that the predictions and retrodictions that form an important part of the process of confirmation in psychoanalysis can be derived from a "narrative explanation of behavior" (p. 252). I wonder. He also takes a stab at deductive inference which makes it appear that in science generally the only thing that counts is logical validity, not the empirical checking of inferences (pp. 244f.). It is a commonly accepted idea that either scientific hypotheses are directly testable empirically or they are not. If a hypothesis is not directly testable, we may test it *indirectly* by deducing from it a hypothesis that is directly testable and then proceed to test the latter hypothesis empirically. I am sure that Sherwood is aware of this point but, because of his attitude to the H-D and related models, he chooses to ignore it.

XII.

To sum up: I disagree with Sherwood on four major points: (1) his positing a class of reasons that cannot be viewed as causes, (2) his concept of causal relationships as involving cause and effect in a single unified process, (3) his rejection of the H-D and other S-E models as analyses of explanation, and (4) his attribution of an explanatory function exclusively to the psychoanalytic narrative.

In regard to the last point Sherwood might have made things easier for the reader had he declared from the start that he is at most tangentially concerned with what I for one, until near the end of the book, expected him to be mainly concerned with, namely, an examination of the observations, presuppositions, and *particular* inferences on which Freud based his "narrative," the analytic case history of Paul Lorenz, and, more specifically, an analysis of the logic by which these particular inferences were reached. Since Sherwood was not faced with an ongoing analysis but with the record of one long since terminated, he took this record not just as a report and a summary, but essentially as embodying *in its entirety* the form and substance of psychoanalytic understanding— much as a novel is judged primarily as a whole, not in terms of the research, the observations, the thinking, and perhaps the personal suffering that went into its making. Maybe I should mention that Sherwood does not stick with unswerving consistency to the indicated views. But that does not, I think, invalidate my characterization of them.

In spite of these reservations, as I observed in the first sentence of this review, I find the book remarkable. First, because it was written at all. Few, if any, specialists in psychiatry, psychoanalysis, or even psychology have the philosophical sophistication the task requires. Second, as I have indicated, Sherwood has presented a number of subtle and penetrating, highly knowledgeable, analyses. It is not an overstatement to say that many passages are brilliant. Even the points with which I heartily disagree are for the most part carefully, although to my mind mistakenly, reasoned. It is to be hoped that Sherwood's book will open up a discussion that, as he himself emphasizes, is sorely needed in our discipline. Maybe at least some of my points are less well taken than I myself think. Time will tell, I suppose. Meanwhile I recommend this book, not just for reading but for thorough study, to every person who is seriously concerned about psychoanalysis, its past, its present, and particularly its future.

REFERENCES

Carnap, R. (1956). The Methodological Character of Theoretical Concepts. In: *Minnesota Studies in the Philosophy of Science*, 1:38–76, ed. H. Feigl et al. Minneapolis: University of Minnesota Press.

Freud, S. (1909). Notes upon a Case of Obsessional Neurosis. *Standard Edition*, 10:155–249. London: Hogarth Press, 1955.

Grotjahn, M. (1959). Review of *Psychoanalysis, Scientific Method and Philosophy*, by S. Hook. *Psychoanalytic Quarterly*, 28:536–537.

Hempel, C. G. (1965). *Aspects of Scientific Explanation*. New York: Free Press.

Hook, S., ed. (1959). *Psychoanalysis, Scientific Method and Philosophy*. New York: New York University Press.

Malcolm, N. (1958). *Ludwig Wittgenstein: A Memoir*. London: Oxford University Press.

Murdoch, I. (1964). The Idea of Perfection. *Yale Review*, 53:342–380.

Nagel, E. (1959). Methodological Issues in Psychoanalytic Theory. In: *Psychoanalysis, Scientific Method and Philosophy*, ed. E. Hook. New York: New York University Press, pp. 38–56.

—— (1961). *The Structure of Science*. New York: Harcourt, Brace, and World.

Scriven, M. (1959). Explanation and Prediction in Evolutionary Theory. *Science*, 139:477–482.

—— (1962a). The Frontiers of Psychology: Psychoanalysis and Parapsychology. In: *Frontiers of Science and Philosophy*, ed. R. G. Colodny. Pittsburgh: University of Pittsburgh Press, pp. 79–129.

—— (1962b). Explanations, Predictions and Laws. In: *Minnesota Studies in the Philosophy of Science*, 3:170–230, ed. H. Feigl et al. Minneapolis: University of Minnesota Press.

—— (1963). Discussion. In: *Induction: Some Current Issues*, ed. H. E. Kyburg, Jr., and E. Nagel. Middletown, Conn.: Wesleyan University Press.

Sherwood, M. (1969). *The Logic of Explanation in Psychoanalysis*. New York: Academic Press.

Toulmin, S. (1970). Reasons and Causes. In: *Explanation in the Behavioural Sciences*, ed. R. Berger and F. Cioffi. Cambridge: Cambridge University Press, pp. 1–26.

Waelder, R. (1960). *Basic Theory of Psychoanalysis*. New York: International Universities Press.

—— (1962). Psychoanalysis, Scientific Method and Philosophy. *Journal of the American Psychoanalytic Association*, 10:617–637.

White, M. (1965). *Foundations of Historical Knowledge*. New York: Harper and Row.

Wittgenstein, L. (1967). *Lectures and Conversations on Aesthetics, Psychology, and Religious Belief*, ed. C. Barrett. Berkeley: University of California Press.

ANOTHER LOOK AT THE LOGIC OF EXPLANATION IN PSYCHOANALYSIS

Michael Sherwood, M.D.

I am grateful indeed for the opportunity to respond to the foregoing reviews and thereby to contribute to what in my book I called the continuing dialogue between psychoanalysis and the natural sciences. The wide range of topics in the present volume is itself testimony to the vitality and complexity of that dialogue. My own book, too, touched on many different issues, sometimes I am afraid far too simplistically, as Drs. Eagle and Rubinstein suggest. It is significant in this regard that the two critics focus on entirely different issues; and in both cases, important points are made.

Neither Dr. Eagle nor Dr. Rubinstein argues for the "separate domain" view of psychoanalysis; thus we all share what I take to be one of the most important of the book's conclusions, that psychoanalysis must be made to stand or fall according to the same criteria by which all other sciences are judged, and that it not be accorded a private domain with its own private rules of procedure. Dr. Eagle's two major criticisms are, in fact, that in certain ways I implicitly reintroduce just such a view, at least in the section entitled "The Evaluation of Psychoanalytic Narratives." In that section I refer to the three-tiered system for evaluating explanations which I tried to develop throughout the book, a system which is outlined and diagramed on page 20. The first tier is governed by criteria of appropriateness and is discussed at length in Chapter 2. In that discussion I point out that explanations may be rejected as "inappropriate" because they (1) are not placed in the proper frame of reference, (2) do not address the proper "puzzle" or "incongruity" within that frame of reference, or (3) are not formulated at the proper level of complexity. Examples of each of these types of inappropriateness are presented. The second and third tiers of this system, criteria of adequacy and criteria of accuracy, are discussed in the section to which Eagle addresses himself.

Eagle's first point is that of these three sets of criteria, "only accuracy is critical for evaluating a scientific explanation." The other two share the inter-

esting characteristic of "relative dispensability" for four different reasons, according to Eagle. First, appropriateness and adequacy may apply to explanatory
accounts which are not empirical at all. Second, these criteria are used only *after*
one has ascertained that an explanation is accurate or true. Third, these criteria
apply only to the explanation as a whole, whereas the criterion of accuracy applies to particular propositional statements within that explanatory account or
narrative. Finally, these criteria, and especially the criterion of adequacy, which
I further describe in terms of "self-consistency, coherence, and comprehensiveness," in fact may really apply to an explanation's therapeutic efficacy and not to
its accuracy or truth claim.

   With regard to Eagle's first three arguments, I find myself in basic agreement with the observations, but not the conclusions. The difference, however, is
one of viewpoint, and less fundamental than it might seem. Throughout the book
I am attempting to develop what I call a contextual analysis of explanation, an
account which tries to place scientific explanation within the framework of
everyday, experiential explanations of events. In that context, criteria of appropriateness and adequacy are at least as important, albeit for different reasons, as
criteria of accuracy. Eagle's three points simply underscore that observation. He
concludes, therefore, that scientific explanation is something different, at least
in some respects, and that we should perhaps treat it differently. In the book I
was concluding just the opposite, that we should try to apply to scientific explanations just those criteria which do in fact function so importantly in everyday experience. In retrospect, I think my conclusion less useful, though I am still
not sure. But by no means do we disagree on the above observations, and therefore I do not believe that my discussion surreptitiously or unwittingly reintro-
duces the concept of a "separate domain" within which behavioral explanations
must exist.

   With regard to the fourth observation made above, that criteria of "self-
consistency, coherence, and comprehensiveness" may well apply to an explanation's therapeutic efficacy, there is even less disagreement, on either the facts or
the conclusion; namely, that an explanatory narrative's therapeutic efficacy is
entirely unrelated to its truth. Moreover, as Eagle states, the three criteria above
may well be correlated with therapeutic efficacy, and this is indeed a testable
hypothesis. However, I discuss these criteria in an entirely separate context, to
elaborate my concept of the *adequacy as a scientific explanation* of explanatory
narratives. That these same criteria may in fact also be correlated with therapeutic
efficacy is a true, but independent, point. Admittedly, however, the text is unclear. The truth is that the issue of the role of the psychoanalytic explanation or
narrative in the process of therapy is one that has fascinated me for a long while.
Having broached it I could not resist the temptation to deviate from the main
line of argument and touch, however slightly, on this area. The result is the two-
page digression which Eagle found both confusing and damaging to the general
argument. The single bona fide disagreement would be with Eagle's contention
that "ultimately the issue of whether an account or narrative is self-consistent,
coherent, and comprehensive is a question of *judgment*." I certainly would want

to contend that at least in principle such an evaluation can be just as factual as an evaluation of a narrative's truth or accuracy. To defend this view, however, would be inappropriate at this point.

Eagle's second main criticism is that an unscientific "private domain" view is unwittingly reintroduced by virtue of my emphasis on the narrative as the basic unit of explanation. On this issue, Eagle is raising very much the same point which Rubinstein develops in more detail, and both critics are, I think, indicating a very definite weakness in the original argument. I shall explore the issue in detail when it arises in my discussion of Rubinstein's whole critique, to which I now turn.

Rubinstein's first disagreement concerns my discussion of R. S. Peters's distinction between "doing" something—an action presumably to be explained by a reason; and "suffering" something—an occurrence presumably to be explained by a cause. According to Rubinstein, I reject such a distinction, saying, "only if we first know that a causal explanation is appropriate can we assert that the event was a 'suffering.' " Rubinstein, however, finds such a distinction valid, asking, "Are we not sometimes able to recognize that a person is overwhelmed by an emotion before he acts on that emotion . . . ?" In fact, my sentence begins with the words, "It turns out, however, that . . ." I am actually paraphrasing Peters, and perhaps to have been explicit I should have said "It turns out, according to Peters's argument, that . . ." My point is not whether or not the distinction is valid, but rather that in the context of Peters's full argument his contention involves him in circular reasoning. It was my elliptical paraphrasing that allowed Rubinstein to mistake the view for my own. It is true, however, that I describe this distinction as "misleading and dubious." The important point, which I believe Rubinstein accepts, is that even if we adopt these pairings—"doing-reason" and "suffering-cause"—it is not implied that we are dealing with "two distinctly separate classes of psychological events"—or two distinctly separate sorts of explanation.

The second major criticism concerns what Rubinstein takes to be my insistence upon a class of cases where there are "reasons" which can "under no circumstances" be considered "causes." Rubinstein discusses the first of the two following statements which I present to clarify the situation in which the terms reason and cause are not used synonymously:

A. *His offering me $5 if I would do it was the reason I stole the bread.*
B. *His blow with his fist was the cause of the bruise on my arm.*

I argue in that discussion that these two statements are similar in that both assert that the particular events in question, the bribe and the blow, were causally relevant factors. Nevertheless, I believe that in statement A, by designating "his offering me $5" as a reason, we are saying something *in addition to* the assertion that the bribe was a causally relevant factor. In the B situation the blow on the arm is a causally relevant factor in the bruise's appearance *whether or not* I was aware of the blow at the time. In contrast, in the A situation the $5 bill held in front of me is a causally relevant factor in the occurrence of my stealing the bread (or, instead, my hitting the tempter) *only if* I perceive it, correctly or incorrectly, take some account of it, and act upon that perception. In my book I argue that this is at least an important part of what we intend to differentiate in those circumstances where we distinguish between causes and reasons. Thus, I define reasons as "those causally relevant factors which become causally relevant precisely because they are taken into consideration, or responded to, by the individual." Under this argument, reasons are a subcategory of causally relevant factors, but they are not, as Rubinstein claims I say, causally relevant factors "of a different type . . . [and which] can apparently in no circumstances . . . be causes." Rubinstein is quite right, however, in suggesting that my argument gains plausibility from trading on two different meanings of the phrase "taking account of." In the sense of referring to a process occurring in a human organism, it seems that the distinction I had proposed collapses; one might say that the blow on the arm causes the bruise because my body "takes account of" it. For this and other reasons, it seems to me that the distinction I drew is less persuasive now than I thought it was when I made it. Moreover, insofar as such a distinction might be used to support a mind-body dualism, it must be unequivocally rejected. In this regard, Rubinstein's point concerning ordinary language versus the language of science is well taken; when we use reasons in scientific discussions, then we must be referring to "organisms, organism-environment interactions, and processes inside the organism that are *causally* related to one another."

If the distinction that I drew between causes and reasons seems dubious now, it simply underlines the more important point I made, which still appears to be both valid and interesting; namely, that the fundamental distinction is not between causes and reasons at all, but between our use of these terms and our use of all those other terms which fall into the category of causally relevant factors. Human behavior results from the interaction of sensations, perceptions, beliefs, attitudes, habits, desires, etc.; these are observable and amenable to study and modification. In contrast, causes, reasons, and motives are not elements of the same logical type. These terms occur legitimately *only* in a context that is explicitly or implicitly explanatory. To put it crudely, we do not experience reasons in the way we experience feelings; I do not perceive a reason in the way I perceive a threat, although the threat may *be* the reason for some behavior. We look for causes of behavior among the antecedent conditions and factors acting upon the person, but the cause is not another sort of antecedent condition. We do not discover both antecedent events and antecedent causes. Likewise, we search out a person's beliefs, desires, feelings, but not his reasons. The heart, we should say, has its feelings, needs, and pains, but *not* its reasons. It is rather that once we raise the question of explanation we designate, using various criteria, certain of these antecedent phenomena as either causes or reasons. Thus, the move from a descriptive context, involving antecedent states and events, to an explanatory context, involving causes and reasons, is a logical move, not an empirical one; a decision is made, not a discovery.

The logical ("narrative") and evidential ("explanatory") commitments undertaken when such a designation is made are extremely complex, and they are discussed at length in a section which Rubinstein finds especially puzzling. He suggests that a logical confusion exists there: the failure to distinguish between empirical statements like "A causes B" and analytic statements like "If A is a cause, it must have an effect B." Certainly, this is a valid distinction, but I am not sure that my argument fails on this score. The issue rests primarily upon certain presuppositions or points of view from which one begins. The whole discussion of "narratives" and the "single unified process" which connects events labeled "causes" and "effects" derives from what is sometimes called a "process metaphysic," as opposed to either a "thing" or a "fact" metaphysic. This is a philosophically out-of-vogue position, but one by which I was strongly influenced when I wrote the book. It is a position the elaboration and defense of which, should I even wish to enter it, would lead us into the deepest and murkiest waters of philosophy. As such, it would be out of place in the present discussion.

Rubinstein correctly sums up the basic intuition behind this discussion of causes and reasons as the view that so-called "primary" phenomena such as beliefs, desires, attitudes, etc., are not *in themselves* explanatory, but become so only when *interpreted* as causes or reasons. After praising this as "an astute observation," he then suggests that from this correct beginning I went on to develop the attack on the hypothetical-deductive model and the concept of the psychoanalytic narrative, both of which he criticizes. This insight into the genesis of my thought is by and large correct, especially if one were also to credit Hanson's (1958) *Patterns of Discovery* and a variety of expositions of the nature of historical explanation, all of which, it seems to me, are based on what I called above a form of "process" metaphysic. One such account, namely Morton White's, Rubinstein explicitly develops and adapts to the issues of psychoanalytic explanation. Thus it is no coincidence that in many areas, including some basic premises, we are in fact or can be brought into full agreement. In acknowledging the relevance of historical inquiry to psychoanalysis, we are not suggesting that the latter is merely an "evocative mythology." The whole point of my arguing for the concept of the "narrative" is in fact to emphasize that we are indeed dealing with theories that are meant *not* as literature but as science— just as is historical argument—yet that these theories cannot be evaluated solely on deductive grounds.

Stated bluntly, of course, the issue is, if not quite a dead horse, one which is sorely injured and finds few riders today. Perhaps it was not quite so clear some six years ago when the book was being written. No matter, however, for there are related issues which are still debated. Rubinstein remarks that "either scientific hypotheses are directly testable empirically or they are not." To my mind this either-or dichotomy does not do justice to the complexity of the psychoanalytic narrative explanation, the logically different types of statements employed, or the multiple ways in which such statements are used. One of my goals in giving such a lengthy exposition of the Lorenz case was to dramatize just these issues. Nor does this contention—and this is the key point—do justice to the complexity of even simple explanations in the physical sciences.

This, then, explains the relationship between the two major philosophical sections in my book. In the first, I argue from the "gut" feeling that any lasting defense of the scientific respectability of psychoanalysis must unequivocally reject any form of "separate domain" thesis, any view that we may use special, privileged rules of argument and a unique logic of our own. When, however, this view is combined with my perhaps undue respect for the complexity of the narrative (and perhaps an infatuation with the concept of process), a problem emerges. For if we reject a special form of logic of our own, and if we feel compelled to do justice to the narrative aspects of psychoanalytic explanation, only one solution remains. We must reject the primarily deductive models of explanation posited for the physical sciences and instead attempt to analyze such explanations with the same models as those used for the behavioral sciences; we must move the physical-science mountain to the behavioral Mohammed. Thus, in arguing against the radical difference between causes and reasons, I do not deny that reasons have an "intentional" or "interpersonal" connotation. Instead, I try to show that both causes and reasons share this same contextual aspect. In a parallel fashion, in arguing against a separate domain, I do not deny that there is a contextual complexity to psychoanalytic narratives; instead I attempt to show that this same complexity is present in explanations in the physical sciences. Hence, I am forced to some rather strident and extreme statements against the H-D model which, besides being dubious, also make more ambiguous the "hard-nosed" rigorous scientific stance which is elsewhere assumed.

With the mitigating and clarifying influence of six years' hindsight I really no longer have the ego investment to defend strenuously certain of the statements singled out for particular attack by Rubinstein. I am even less inclined to do so when, as Rubinstein notes at several points, much of the basic position can be reconciled with a more expanded analysis of scientific explanation, along the lines of the S-E model he suggests. For certainly it is true that though the writing is at points obscure, the general position is not obscurantist; I do believe and mean to demonstrate that psychoanalytic narratives can be verified and analyzed along the same lines as physical-science explanations. By the same token I do obviously accept, whatever certain other remarks might imply, the propriety and indeed ubiquity of probabilistic statements in scientific explanations. On pages 58–68, and again on pages 207–214, such probabilistic generalizations are explicitly discussed. And I certainly do agree that many of the hypotheses of "metapsychology" that we currently use in psychoanalytic theory must ultimately depend upon neurology for their confirmation. Of course, this was also Freud's contention.

Areas of uneasiness do remain, however, which make me loath to give up all the arguments put forth in my critique of the H-D model. One important area concerns the concept of "platitude." Rubinstein quotes several so-called "probabilistic clinical hypotheses" in the course of his discussion. Among them is: ". . . if a son *wants to be* unlike his father he often enough *will be* unlike him." Another is: ". . . people tend to avoid what they for one reason or another detest." We might add another, perhaps the archetypal one with regard to purposive explanation: "When people desire certain ends, they will often act in ways believed to be realistic means of achieving those ends." In fact, this latter is really a more general "hypothesis" of which the two previously quoted ones were specific examples. The problem is that I am not at all sure such statements really are empirical hypotheses in the usual sense. I develop the same criticism at length in my discussion of David Rapaport's famous "projective hypothesis": "All behavior is integral to, and characteristic of, the behaving personality," and Carl Rogers' universal generalization, "The organism has one basic tendency and striving—to actualize, maintain, and enhance the experiencing organism." I will not pursue this complex issue here, but only repeat the conclusion I drew then: that such statements appear to me to be neither classically analytic nor synthetic, but rather to fall into one (I am not at all sure which) of those categories delineated by Hanson:

A. *True because it is psychologically inconceivable that it be false; the mind cannot picture circumstances in which this relation would not hold.*
B. *Empirically true, yet not falsifiable, in the usual sense, since it is embedded in theory to such an extent that one would often choose to modify the theory to allow for otherwise inconsistent findings, rather than throw out the law.*

Not only do such descriptions fit many of the so-called laws of human behavior, but the further observation can also be made; namely, that some statements have a life history, passing from simple empirical observation, back through type B, then type A above, and finally becoming "analytic" in the classical sense.

I have no doubt that such statements are vitally important to scientific explanation in at least two ways. First, without such commonly shared beliefs, whatever we may choose to call them, the very demand for explanation, when confronted with seemingly incongruous events, would never arise. Thus I develop the concept of "the context of explanation," and the view that such beliefs form a part of "the presumptions of explanation." This argument is elaborated in Chapter 2 of my book. Second, such statements play an essential role in constructing a logically valid, syllogistic, or H-D model of scientific explanations. In Chapter 7 I give some painfully dull examples of such logical exercises. This dullness is precisely my point. I designate the general statements in these syllogisms "platitudes" both to call attention to their logical ambiguity and, more important, to suggest that while they may be formally necessary to make the models work, they possess precious little explanatory power. Thus, my real quarrel with the H-D model is not that it is false so much as that it is misleading in that it focuses attention on such, by themselves, trivial statements, rather than on the narrative from which they arise; and second, that it thereby mistakes the source of whatever explanatory power such narratives may display. Such misgivings as these, though attenuated, still persist.

Certainly I am wrong to cast into the logical limbo mentioned above all or even most of the hypotheses forming the basis of the behavioral sciences. In this regard Rubinstein's classification of generalizations into five types seems a definite improvement. Once such distinctions are drawn, one can resist the more extreme position I forced myself into, and one can rest comfortably with the obvious, shall I say platitudinous, fact that all of us believe, use, occasionally attempt to verify, and—rarely—even to discard various empirical generalizations concerning human behavior.

All things considered, the above reviews are positive ones, the more valued because they come from theoreticians who have, by and large, read perceptively and interpreted correctly a difficult and at points confusing text. We share, certainly, what I take to be the most important conclusion of the book—namely, that psychoanalysis is a proper subject for philosophic inquiry, that it can withstand the rigors of methodological analysis. And, to paraphrase Houseman, "If it can, it must." It behooves those of us who attempt to use and elaborate psychoanalytic theories to be at the forefront of such philosophic inquiry, to understand the often valid criticisms made by philosophers of science, and to respond to them. The time for haughty disregard of such criticisms on the grounds that they are made by uninitiated, unanalyzed "outsiders" is long since past. My book was meant to make a start at opening the dialogue between psychoanalysis and philosophy on the one hand and the physical sciences on the other. As such, it provided at best only the first words, by no means the last, in an area that Rubinstein rightly characterizes as "too complicated, too vague, beset with too many uncertainties, not to spark divergent opinions." That dialogue evolves significantly in the discussions of Eagle and Rubinstein.

REFERENCE

Hanson, N. R. (1958). *Patterns of Discovery*. London: Cambridge University Press.

8

CRITICISM OF THEORY

MAN, MORALITY, AND MADNESS
Critical Perspectives on the Work of R. D. Laing [1]

Elliot G. Mishler, Ph.D.

This essay is a record of ambivalence only partially resolved. My differences with Laing are too deep to dismiss or gloss over, and yet I regret that this is so. Laing began as a psychiatrist and psychoanalyst, but he has come to address himself to much broader issues than are encompassed within the traditional boundaries of those disciplines. There are precedents, of course. Many of the great figures of twentieth-century psychiatry—Freud, Jung, Reich, Sullivan, among others—have tried to extrapolate their understandings gained in clinical work to the human condition, the great problems of man-in-the-world. Each of these writers captured some part of the spirit of their times, and their works in turn came to affect in a significant way how we define and formulate certain deep and pervasive moral and political issues.

In these respects, Laing might be considered the psychiatrist-philosopher of the sixties. There is a resonance between his work and prominent themes of the counterculture—alienation, estrangement, mysticism; antirationality, antiestablishment, antifamily. Many young radicals, both within and outside psychiatry proper, have found his work a declaration of war against man's inhumanity to man and therefore a resource for their own personal, professional, and po-

[1] This paper is a commentary on major themes in Laing's work and their implications. It is not an introduction to the work and assumes some knowledge of his writings on the part of the reader. Neither is it a comprehensive review, since only his books are used as sources; his articles and lectures are not discussed.

In innumerable ways, the paper reflects a continuing exchange of views and ideas with Anita L. Mishler. The argument developed here was sharpened and clarified in a conference on Laing with the Service I staff of the Massachusetts Mental Health Center, and particularly by discussions with Jon Lomberg. Among colleagues and investigators familiar with Laing's work who responded to various drafts of the paper, I would like to acknowledge the criticisms and suggestions, and particularly the seriousness of their interest in the issues raised, expressed by Louise Carter, Jack Ewalt, Henry Grunebaum, Leston Havens, Merton Kahne, Loren Mosher, and Lyman Wynne.

litical struggles. My own ambivalence stems from the fact that I would like to have found myself allied with them, sharing their enthusiastic response to Laing, since I share their distress and anger about the evils and injustices of psychiatry and society. But, although we begin together on these points, I diverge from Laing in important ways with respect to his analysis of these problems and his proposed solutions. This review is directed to spelling out these differences in some detail.

It is also useful to view Laing as one of the "survivor poets," a psychiatrist-antipsychiatrist among the poet-antipoets, who see themselves as survivors of an already-destroyed civilization, expressing and representing "consciousness in a Last Ditch situation." (See Spender [1971] for a discussion of several of these poets.) When (in an aphorism of Heidegger that Laing quotes in affirmation) "The worst has already happened," the task of the poet—even if he begins as a psychiatrist—is to sharpen our awareness and understanding of the terrors that confront us and try to teach us how to survive. This is the tenor of Laing's later works. Even if a critic does not agree with this vision, he is required to take it into account since, as Spender notes in commenting on the survivor poets, it expresses "that contemporary consciousness of the surrounding destructive reality."[2]

This "contemporary consciousness" is, however, only one of several contexts within which to consider Laing's work. There is also that particular stream of existentialist philosophy on which he draws, both implicitly and explicitly, that flows out of Dostoevski, Kierkegaard, and Nietzsche to Heidegger and Sartre. These broader social and historical contexts may help us to understand the depth and intensity of the response evoked by Laing. At the same time, Laing remains throughout a psychiatrist concerned with specifically psychiatric problems—the nature of schizophrenia and its etiology, the value and disvalue of therapy, the limits of certain types of research methods and the advantages of others. His work, therefore, also needs to be placed in perspective by reference to related developments and studies in psychiatry, psychoanalysis, and the social sciences. Finally, we must attend to the chronology of the work itself, its internal progression and the relation of later to earlier positions and modes of presentation.

Some use will be made of each of these contexts in the following discussion. I will begin with Laing's views of schizophrenia and their development over time, since they are central to his work. He has been particularly concerned with relationships of others to the self, especially those others within the family, and with fantasy as a mode of experience; these will be treated in separate sections. Some observations on research methodology and on therapy will be

---

[2] The resemblance of Laing to this group of writers and poets is strikingly evident in Ted Hughes's (1971) volume, Crow. These poems partake so closely of the same vision that it sometimes seems that Hughes is engaged in a poetic exegesis of Laing's work. Similarly, Doris Lessing's last two novels, The Four-Gated City (1969) and Briefing for a Descent into Hell (1971), work explicitly with his models of madness and normality. I do not mean to suggest that these writers are merely borrowing or reworking Laing's ideas in another form, but that each in his own way is reflecting and formulating the "contemporary consciousness."

incorporated in the discussions of each of these topics and in the concluding section.[3]

SCHIZOPHRENIA: FROM DEATH IN LIFE
TO TRANSCENDENT ECSTASY

Laing's first book, *The Divided Self*, appeared in 1960; in a later prefatory note, he states that it was written when he was 28, which would be about five years before its publication. A sensitive and probing account of the schizoid personality and schizophrenia, using an approach he labeled "existential phenomenology," the book has continued to be praised and admired, particularly by philosophically inclined and psychodynamically oriented psychologists and psychiatrists. Four other books followed over the next half-dozen years. Schizophrenia remained a central concern but each new book reflected another facet of Laing's interests and each in its own way moved beyond the limited boundaries of the traditional clinical situation. Respectively, they focused on fantasy and interpersonal relations in *The Self and Others* (1961), existential philosophy and Marxism in *Reason and Violence* (1964), family processes and schizophrenia in *Sanity, Madness, and the Family* (1964), and methodology in *Interpersonal Perception* (1966). The last three were written with collaborators.

In 1967 came *The Politics of Experience*, a collection of essays most of which were written between 1962 and 1965; with this book, Laing became a public figure and a controversial one. Becoming both public and controversial simultaneously was no accident. In *The Politics of Experience*, traditional psychiatry and traditional society are both subjected to a scathing attack. In *Knots*, published in 1970, we find Laing completely outside the domain of traditional psychiatry; his negation of psychiatry is now so complete that he no longer has to refer to it even for the purpose of rejecting it.

Laing's progression through these books has not been linear, with later works deepening and extending what has gone before; nor is it simply a matter of his addressing discrete and separable problems over time, since important underlying issues recur. Rather, the progression is discontinuous, with the later Laing taking different positions than the earlier one, and having his own reservations about his earlier self.

The course of the work is marked clearly in his own statements of the aims of these investigations. In the Preface to the first edition of *The Divided Self* (1960), we find:

The present book is a study of schizoid and schizophrenic persons; its basic purpose is to make madness, and the process of going mad, comprehensible.

---

[3] Holbrook's (1969) thoughtful and sensitive review of Laing did not come to my attention until I had almost completed the final revision of this paper. In examining Laing's work he draws heavily upon the work of contemporary British psychoanalysts of the object-relations school and on his own studies of two "suicidal" poets, Sylvia Plath and Dylan Thomas. His criticisms and my own parallel and complement each other, and I regret that my late discovery of his paper precluded giving more explicit attention to his views.

. . . *A further purpose is to give in plain English an account, in existential terms, of some forms of madness (p. 9).*

Although *The Divided Self* proposes a new approach to the description and interpretation of psychological states, it retains the "fiction" that there is a phenomenon that can be called "madness" and that there is a difference between being sane and being psychotic. As Laing writes:

. . . *I shall try to show that there is a comprehensible transition from the sane schizoid way of being-in-the-world to a psychotic way of being-in-the-world (p. 17).*

This is the position from which Laing has gradually withdrawn. In a second Preface, prepared for the paperback edition published five years later, Laing refers self-critically to the book:

. . . *I was already partially falling into the trap I was seeking to avoid. . . . Our civilization represses not only the "instincts," not only sexuality, but any form of transcendence. . . . Thus I would wish to emphasize that our "normal" "adjusted" state is too often the abdication of ecstasy, the betrayal of our true potentialities, that many of us are only too successful in acquiring a false self to adapt to false realities (pp. 11–12).*

In *Sanity, Madness, and the Family,* written between the first and second Prefaces to *The Divided Self,* Laing and Esterson (1964) state that they are concerned with persons who have begun "careers" as "diagnosed 'schizophrenic' " patients:

. . *by a schizophrenic we mean here a person who has come to be diagnosed as such and has come to be treated accordingly. . . . We reiterate that we ourselves are not using the term "schizophrenia" to denote any identifiable condition that we believe exists "in" one person (p. 5).*

In the Preface to the second edition (1970) they protest against the "misinterpretation" that the book is about mental illness and the family; they state emphatically:

We do not accept "schizophrenia" as being a biochemical, neurophysiological, psychological fact, and we regard it as a palpable error, in the present state of the evidence, to take it to be a fact. Nor do we assume its existence nor do we adopt it as a hypothesis. We propose no model of it (p. 12).

In *The Politics of Experience* (1967), written between the two editions of the family book, we are offered a more positive definition of schizophrenia and a reversal of traditional categories—normality has become madness.

What we call "normal" is a product of repression, denial, splitting, projection, introjection and other forms of destructive action on experience. . . . It is radically estranged from the structure of being (p. 27).

Very well, let us call schizophrenia a successful attempt not to adapt to pseudosocial realities (p. 67).

Further, schizophrenia is viewed as potentially liberating and as one variant of transcendental experience. Future investigators, looking back on our "age of darkness," will see

. . . that what we call "schizophrenia" was one of the forms in which, often through quite ordinary people, the light began to break through the cracks in our all-too-closed minds (p. 129).

Psychotic experience goes beyond the horizons of our common, that is, our communal sense (p. 132).

Madness need not be all breakdown. It may also be breakthrough. It is potentially liberation and renewal as well as enslavement and death (p. 133).

True sanity entails in one way or another the dissolution of the normal ego, that false self competently adjusted to our alienated social reality; the emergence of the "inner" archetypal mediators of divine power, and through this death a rebirth, and the eventual re-establishment of a new kind of ego-functioning, the ego now being the servant of the divine, no longer its betrayer (pp. 144–145).

I shall return below to the substance of Laing's changing views on schizophrenia, but I think that it is important to take note of a change in tone and style which is barely suggested by these quotations. From *The Divided Self* to *The Politics of Experience* there is a shift from description to rhetoric; the early work is linear and the later postlinear. *The Divided Self* is rich in concrete detail and linguistically elaborated; *The Politics of Experience* is schematic, sloganlike, and linguistically restricted.

To illustrate the nature and degree of these changes in Laing's style, I applied several simple measures of syntactic complexity to the various texts. Five pages were selected at random from *The Divided Self*, *The Self and Others*, *Sanity, Madness, and the Family*, and *The Politics of Experience*. Quotations from other authors and verbatim interview material was excluded from the corpus of sentences, as was the "Bird of Paradise" section from the last book. The results were as follows: The mean length of sentences drops from 25 to 19 words from *The Divided Self* to *The Politics of Experience*, a decline of roughly 25%; the number of words in the longest sentence drops from 50 to 35, a 30% change; the difference between the shortest and longest sentences on a page, an index of style flexibility, decreases from 42 to 26 words, which is a decline of almost

40%; finally, the proportion of simple sentences—sentences that are neither compound or complex nor include embedded clauses—shows an increase from 6% to 21% of the total number of sentences on a page. The texts of the two intervening books are similar to each other and fall between the two books at the beginning and end of the series, except for the sentence-complexity index on which they are similar to *The Politics of Experience;* on this last measure, *The Divided Self* is clearly different from all that follows.

This exercise is not intended to disparage simplicity of sentence structure. Rather, my intention is to underline a change in meaning that is carried by form. Laing is self-conscious about style, as is further evidenced in *Knots,* and the rhetorical style of *The Politics of Experience* is consistent with the political and religious message of the book. The book is a series of slogans and ritual in-cantations. In McLuhan's terms, it is a "cool" medium, to be "filled in" by the reader, as compared to the "hot" medium of *The Divided Self,* which is dense with information. When I first read *Politics,* I thought it was more appropriate for reading aloud in a group than for silent reading to oneself, and that it might serve as part of a dramatic or religious ritual. I discovered afterward that the text of the "Bird of Paradise" has been used in exactly this way by the Living Theater for their ritual drama, *Paradise Now.*

I believe that the popular appeal of *Politics* to the counterculture is in part related to its style as well as to its content; it is a style that corresponds to messages in other media to which the counterculture is responsive. It is also the source of some of the rejection of Laing by "professionals."

The Divided Self is not a traditional psychiatric text, but it is concerned with a traditional and central psychiatric issue, namely the distinction between and the characteristics of sanity and madness. Discarding standard methods of clinical psychiatry and psychopathology, Laing approaches the problem through the route of "existential phenomenology." The essential focus is on the sub-jective experience of certain types of persons—those who do not have a basic sense of "ontological security," that is, a sense of their "presence in the world as real, alive, whole and, in a temporal sense, a continuous person" (p. 39).

Laing argues that such persons "come to experience themselves as pri-marily split into mind and body. Usually, they feel most closely identified with the 'mind' " (p. 65). The book focuses on ". . . anxieties and dangers that I shall suggest arise only in terms of primary ontological insecurity; and with the consequent attempts to deal with such anxieties and dangers" (p. 39).

He describes three types of anxiety experienced by those who are onto-logically insecure: engulfment, implosion, and petrification or depersonalization. The schizoid character, from an existential point of view, represents an attempt to live in the world in the face of these particular anxieties. To be schizoid, however, is not to be psychotic. There are a variety of ways in which the primary schizoid defenses may fail, resulting in the psychotic defense.

The basic defense, so far as I have been able to see, in every form of psy-chosis . . . can be stated in its most general form as: the denial of being, as a means of preserving being. The schizophrenic feels he has killed his "self," and this appears to be in order to avoid being killed. He is dead in order to remain alive (p. 150).[4]

Compare this to an earlier "psychological exposition":

So to be sick unto death is not to be able to die—yet not as though there were hope of life; no, the hopelessness in this case is that even the last hope, death, is not available. . . . When the danger is so great that death has become one's hope, despair is the disconsolateness of not being able to die. It is in this last sense that despair is the sickness unto death, this agonizing contradiction, this sickness in the self, everlastingly to die, to die and yet not to die, to die the death. For dying means that it is all over, but dying the death means to live to experience death; and if for a single instant this experience is possible, it is tantamount to experiencing it forever (Kierkegaard, 1849, pp. 150–151).

Thus Kierkegaard, one of the seminal sources of existentialism, writing in *The Sickness unto Death* more than a century before Laing. Kierkegaard is not discussing schizophrenia but the state of man in the absence of true Christian faith. *The Divided Self* bears a close affinity to this early existentialist analysis; much of its power derives from the sense it conveys that the schizophrenic is in a state of despair. There are other affinities between the later Laing and Kierkegaard in the qualities of alienation and estrangement that they focus upon as characteristics of men "adjusted" to their alienating societies. Further, Laing's comment in *The Politics of Experience*, quoted earlier, that "true sanity" requires a rebirth in which the ego becomes "the servant of the divine, no longer its betrayer," bears a close resemblance to Kierkegaard's prescription:

. . . at least the precise formula for health, that is, for the condition of the self when the sickness is completely eradicated; that the self "be relating itself to its own self and by willing to be itself is grounded transparently in the Power which constituted it." And "this," he says emphatically, "is the definition of faith" (Kierkegaard, 1849, Translator's Introduction, p. 139).

The Divided Self includes two detailed case histories, one of a patient of Laing's and one reported by other investigators. Emphasis is placed throughout on the difficulties experienced by such persons in maintaining a sense of personal identity, of an awareness of one's true self, in the face of splits between parts of the self and in the context of a state of alienation from other persons. Some precursors may be found here of Laing's later stress on the "intelligibility" of schizophrenia; he asserts that the "thesis" of the study is ". . . that schizo-

---

[4] Compare Holbrook's (1969) discussion of schizoid suicide in which, following Guntrip, he notes that the suicidal impulse seems to mean "I want to stop living but not to die," and Guntrip's further observation that it is not really a wish for death but a "secret wish that death should prove a pathway to rebirth."

phrenia is a possible outcome of a more than usual difficulty in being a whole person with the other, and with not sharing the common-sense (i.e., the community sense) way of experiencing oneself in the world" (1960, p. 189).

He approvingly quotes Jung's statement that the schizophrenic ceases to be schizophrenic when he meets someone by whom he feels understood, and notes further:

I must confess here to a certain personal difficulty I have in being a psychiatrist, which lies behind a great deal of this book. This is that except in the case of chronic schizophrenics I have difficulty discovering the "signs and symptoms" of psychosis in persons I am myself interviewing (pp. 27–28).

Sanity, Madness, and the Family marks the next stage in Laing's interpretation of schizophrenia. It consists of the case histories of 11 women diagnosed as schizophrenic in which the case descriptions are discussions and analyses of family processes and relationships rather than accounts of patients' symptoms and their etiology. The aim of the book is to determine ". . . to what extent is the experience and behavior of that person, who has already begun a career as a diagnosed "schizophrenic" patient, intelligible in the light of the praxis and process of his or her family nexus?" (Laing and Esterson, 1964, p. 13).

We noted earlier Laing and Esterson's position that schizophrenia is not a condition that exists "in" one person and their complaint about the misinterpretation of the book as being about mental illness and the family. Reviewers might be faulted for misunderstanding the authors' intentions, but they were helped toward such a view by the hope expressed in the book that it would "constitute a bridge between past and future efforts in the understanding of madness." Advertisements of the second edition continue to refer to it as a study of "schizophrenia seen as a sane reaction to an insane society."

An approach to schizophrenia that treats it as a social category or as a social role, with no further assumptions about its psychological correlates or antecedents, is not unique to Laing. It is, of course, one of the modal paradigms used by sociologists who have studied social deviance, including that form defined as mental illness. This formulation is sufficiently specific and widespread for its adherents to have earned the distinction of being called a school, namely, the "labeling" or "societal reaction" school. Further, the approach has generated a large enough body of work to have recently earned the additional distinction of being subjected to critical empirical attack. (See Gove [1970a, 1970b]; these articles include good sets of references to the work of this school.)

Somewhat more recently, and out of a quite different theoretical and empirical tradition, a similar view has come into some prominence in psychology. Carson's review and analysis of the problem of schizophrenia is a good example:

. . . so-called mental symptoms, unlike physical symptoms, are inextricably tied to the social context in which they occur; the reality of their status as symptoms is a social reality, dependent in the final analysis on judgments as to whether or

not the behavior in question is proper or appropriate for the situation in which it occurs . . . "Mental illness" . . . is a mere habit of speech, a metaphor, a fictional abstraction that we apply to certain kinds of deviant behavior— specifically to behavior that violates in a persistent and/or spectacular way norma- tive expectations concerning what everybody in a particular culture "knows" to be reality and decency . . . a term introduced to account in a pseudo-rational way for behavior thought to be otherwise inexplicable. To make of this metaphor a cause is of course to indulge in fallacious logic . . . (1970, p. 3; see also Carson, 1969).

I have quoted Carson at some length because his work is likely to be more accessible to psychiatrists and psychologists than that of the labeling school of sociologists, since he relies extensively on diagnostic and experimental studies of schizophrenia to develop and support this position. Another instructive feature of Carson's paper is that he makes no reference to any of Laing's work. On the other hand, he refers to a variety of studies by investigators that Laing would be likely to attack on "humanistic" and existential grounds—operant condi- tioners and behavior therapists who treat their subjects and patients as "objects" —to make the same essential point as Laing's, namely, that the symptoms of schizophrenia, as well as the diagnosis and treatment, reflect and are responsive to and under the control of the social and interpersonal environment.

Showing that Laing does not stand alone in his views, and that there are parallel studies and theories which do not derive from nor seem to require his existentialist view of man, does not imply that this social view has supplanted the traditional medical-psychiatric model of schizophrenia. However, even those holding to the latter view are not necessarily restricted to an antihuman approach to schizophrenia as an unmodifiable disease process; an assumption that Laing makes in his critique of traditional psychiatry. Wing and Brown's recent mono- graph is a fine example of this more flexible medical-psychiatric model. They studied the effects on the behavior and symptoms of long-stay schizophrenic patients of changes in the social environment and milieu treatment programs of mental hospitals. They conclude:

The various stages of this study point towards a conclusion which is very dif- ficult to resist—that a substantial proportion, though by no means all, of the morbidity shown by long-stay schizophrenic patients in mental hospitals is a product of their environment (1970, p. 177).

Again, it is instructive to note that although this is a British study, under- taken by the major social psychiatry research unit in England, there is no reference to Laing. This omission is all the more noteworthy in view of the authors' explicit references to a number of literary, journalistic, and reform- oriented accounts to which they contrast their own work.

This lack of reference to Laing's work, particularly by British investigators, tells us more about the "political" climate of psychiatry than it does about the work itself. Wing and Brown are undoubtedly aware of him and his influence; certainly, given the wide circulation of his books, his lectures to lay and professional groups, and the extensive attention he has received in the mass media, no clinician or researcher in psychiatry could fail to be aware of him. The omission is evidently purposeful, and I would guess that its purpose is to deny legitimacy and respectability to Laing and to what he has to say. However, here as in other matters, denial is a risky defense and a poor substitute for direct confrontation and critical analysis. Laing simply refuses to disappear even though ignored by the Establishment.

It should also be noted that this process is reciprocal; Laing refers less and less over time to other investigators, either to critics or to those whose work is congenial to his. Some existentialist philosophers, dramatists, and writers receive due mention, particularly in the first two books, but many theorists whose ideas parallel and in many cases antedate Laing's (and with whose works he is undoubtedly familiar) either receive no mention or only passing reference. The list of such omissions would start with, most notably, H. S. Sullivan and Searles in this country, and would include major figures of the various British psychoanalytic traditions, namely, Bion, Fairbairn, Guntrip, Klein, and Winnicott; other psychoanalysts who have drawn on existentialism in various ways, from Binswanger to Rollo May, are similarly neglected. Like other theorists and social philosophers who have found their own vision, Laing may believe that his major task is to develop and state that vision; others can busy themselves with tracing connections, parallels, and sources. The drawback of this division of intellectual labor is that naïve readers—and these include young nonprofessionals and professionals as well as the proverbial educated laymen—are deprived of an adequate context within which to understand and evaluate Laing's contribution and the implications of his work.

The 11 case studies of schizophrenic women that compose *Sanity, Madness, and the Family* are intended to document in detail the essential idea that schizophrenia is "intelligible." The material is based on interviews with various members of the families either alone or together. In substance, much attention is given to the ways in which members of these families tend to disconfirm each others' experiences, and in particular deny the validity of the patient's experience. Laing argues that the presumed "incomprehensibility" of schizophrenic symptoms reflects the biases of traditional psychiatry that blind the psychiatrist to the "meaning" of a patient's experience and symptoms in the context of her family. The book tries to rectify this omission.

Laing and Esterson propose that patients' reports are "valid" inferences from real relationships within the family. A patient, for example, may say that her mother and father lie to her. Laing produces evidence from family interviews to show that her mother "does" lie to her, and simultaneously denies it; her father tries to restrict the patient to her home but denies this, saying that he always wanted her to have friends. Parents affirm that their child has always been "good," by which they mean she conformed to their wishes, but simultaneously assert that they had always wanted her to be independent.

Laing's work of this period is related to other studies of schizophrenia and the family that both antedated it and have continued since that time. His work drew upon that of other investigators and has in turn served as a resource for them. (Some of the early theories and a group of representative experimental studies are included in Mishler and Waxler [1968b]; a recent article by Reiss and Elstein [1971] contains a useful and extensive bibliography of this work.) As I have indicated earlier, the *Family* book, while critical of traditional psychiatric conceptions, is still concerned with traditional clinical questions. It derives from a perspective on schizophrenia that was also being developed by other investigators of family processes, some of them having quite different points of departure from Laing's.

Sanity, Madness, and the Family is Laing's most empirical book; it includes verbatim quotations from interviews as well as a detailed listing of all interviews conducted. In an earlier review I referred to the book as a "lawyer's brief," with material selected and organized to make a "case" (Mishler, 1966). In his critique of scientific method as applied to human behavior, Laing seems to assume that its essential requirement is that human beings be treated as objects or things. He means to negate this "objective" bias of science by describing subjective experiences. He ignores what most scientists would view as the essential and critical mark of scientific theory and method, namely, that questions be formulated in a testable way. Laing writes interesting stories about families, but he has neither validated his hypotheses nor stated them in such a way that they could be tested by other investigators. Furthermore, these deficiencies in how he formulates and validates his ideas have nothing to do with the issue of subjective experiences versus objective behavior since his data consist of language samples which are as "objective" as any other behavior. Laing's basic hypothesis, that certain family processes are responsible for the development of schizophrenia, cannot be tested with information collected after the patient has already begun her "career" as a diagnosed patient. Alternative hypotheses, for example, that family patterns reflect the members' responses to someone who behaves like a schizophrenic or to someone diagnosed as schizophrenic, are equally plausible and more consistent with other data. (This point is elaborated in Mishler and Waxler [1968a].)

Given Laing's interest in phenomenology and in the social sources of "meaning," it is disconcerting to discover that he does not take into account his own role as an investigator and theorizer. Every young clinical researcher learns that he must be aware of "transference" phenomena when he begins to see his research subjects frequently and focuses on events that are of psychological significance to them. Laing shows no awareness of this and reports interview material as if he had not been present and as if, after 15 or 20 interviews, family members might not be motivated to present themselves to him in special ways and for their own purposes.

Laing's notion of "intelligibility" is naïve and marks yet another instance in which the role of the investigator is ignored. He does not seem aware of the evidence that people will "make sense" out of any set of events, including random ones. It is this apparently limitless human capacity to construct "rational" and intelligible theories that lies behind and gives power to the testability criterion of science. Intelligibility is in the theorist's head and not in the phenomena; in itself it is a poor criterion for truth.

The Politics of Experience (1967) marks a critical change; the Family book seems to have been completed about 1962 and the essays in Politics date from after that. Here Laing "depasses" his earlier views, to use a term he borrows from Sartre's studies of dialectical method and denoting that an original view has been changed by being negated, transformed, and transcended all in one.

The spirit and direction of Laing's new view of schizophrenia are conveyed in the passages quoted earlier. Among the more central propositions in his argument are the following. First, the world is insane or mad and therefore normal adjustment cannot be taken as sanity. Second, some schizophrenics may have mystical or transcendental experiences which are of intrinsic value and give them insights not available to "normal" people. Third, the schizophrenic process has a natural and self-healing course and interfering with it by "treating" the patient will prevent full recovery, although it may sometimes restore him to some state of "adjustment" to the world.

It is not surprising that these views have been greeted with antipathy by the psychiatric profession and with enthusiasm by the counterculture. Laing is widely quoted in radical and "underground" newspapers and his work is reviewed in periodicals addressed to an educated but not professional audience. Although not entirely ignored in the professional literature, he does not figure prominently here even in discussions of schizophrenia, as we indicated in earlier references to Carson and Wing and Brown. Professionals may be prepared to modify their views of schizophrenia in all sorts of ways but not to the view that the schizophrenic is a sacred figure, a prophet engaged in a search from which he will return with new "truths."

A trio of self-styled "square" reviewers label the views presented in Politics a "psychedelic" model of schizophrenia. They chastise Laing for apparently "urging" the benefits of schizophrenia and point out that he casually ignores its personal and social costs. They note further that some persons with chronic or terminal illnesses, such as tuberculosis and cancer, have reported profound personal and mystical experiences, but that this is hardly grounds for suggesting that people should contract these illnesses in order to have such experiences (Siegler, Osmond, and Mann, 1969).

Laing has not bothered to relate his earlier to his later views. It is clear that the suffering of the schizophrenic depicted in The Divided Self, in despair at his death-in-life existence, has been transformed in The Politics of Experience into the suffering of a Christian martyr. His symptoms are now stigmata. His despair, in Kierkegaard's sense, is at a higher level than the "unconscious" despair of the normal adjusted man who is not even aware of his lack of faith. There is a related shift, though a less explicit one, from the earlier view that schizophrenia may result from the oppression of others to the later position that oppression consists in others' trying to "cure" the "illness."

None of this commentary is intended as an argument against the potential value of mystical experiences. But it is an argument against the notion that schizophrenia is a prototype of such experiences. Laing is proposing that the schizophrenic is the archetype of modern man—estranged from self, alienated from others, and in search of his soul. This is the use of schizophrenia as a metaphor.

The value of such a metaphor as an interpretive guide for general problems of man and society, even man in an alienating society, depends on the degree to which the existential situation of people diagnosed and treated as schizophrenic is homologous to that of nonschizophrenic others in society. Schizophrenics may be particularly sensitive to certain persistent and pervasive strains in human relationships, such as the problems of distance and closeness in intimate relationships, or to discrepancies between what people "really" mean as compared to what they say. But their sensitivities are as selective as those of any other social-character "type." From the response to Laing, and from the extensive literature on alienation, the issues he has extrapolated from his studies of schizophrenia appear to be particularly central to the adolescent experience in contemporary Western society. These experiences themselves are, of course, partly shaped by the formulas that Laing among others has been providing. For an earlier generation, for example, Erikson's well-known dilemmas of adolescence—identity versus identity diffusion and intimacy versus isolation— both reflected and entered into how individuals experienced this stage of their lives. I find Laing less relevant to later stages of the life cycle, the dilemmas Erikson refers to as generativity versus self-absorption and integrity versus despair. But, given the complex ways in which experience and formulation reflect and refract upon each other, Laing's metaphor may turn out to have significance for the next cohort passing through these later stages. After all, who would have thought that the writings of a mid-nineteenth-century melancholy and misanthropic Dane would resonate with the experiences of twentieth-century youth?

I still find much to learn in The Divided Self about schizophrenia in particular and about psychological processes in general, but, for me, there are diminishing returns from each succeeding book. Laing began as a defense counsel for an oppressed group, people diagnosed, labeled, and treated as schizophrenic. There is richness, clarity, and power in his descriptions of their subjective experiences, of their existential difficulties, and in his analysis of the coerciveness of a traditional psychiatry allied with and defending the status quo of "normality." Although Laing's views were not unique to him, particularly with regard to the "social reality" of schizophrenia, he was a particularly articulate and eloquent spokesman. If more serious attention were directed to these problems and their implications, psychiatry might become both more humane and more scientific.

But as Laing has come to identify more and more with his "clients" he has become an ideologist of schizophrenia. He is now proposing that schizophrenia is a state of grace to which we should all aspire (although not all of us may have the "calling"). Rather than schizophrenia resulting from oppressive interpersonal environments, he is now suggesting that schizophrenia may elicit oppression from "normal" members of the community who are envious, fearful, and intolerant of such experiences. It is clear from my earlier discussion that I do not share this view, nor do I find it of value as the basis for a radical reconstruction of psychiatry and society. I will return to some of these questions in discussing Laing's views of "others" and of fantasy.

THE SELF, ALONE AND VERSUS OTHERS

In *The Divided Self*, we find: "The self can be 'real' only in relation to real people and things" (1960, p. 142), and an argument that madness involves

. . . an attempt to create relationships to persons and things within the individual without recourse to the outer world of persons and things at all. . . . This autistic, private, intra-individual "world" is not a feasible substitute for the only world there really is, the shared world. If this were a feasible project then there would be no need for psychosis. . . . Moreover, this shut-up self, being isolated, is unable to be enriched by outer experience, and so the whole inner world comes to be more and more impoverished, until the individual may come to feel he is merely a vacuum (pp. 74–75).

In *The Politics of Experience*, however, the possibility of a shared world and of "authentic" personal relationships is made problematic. "Can human beings be persons today? Can a man be his actual self with another man or woman?" (1967, p. 213). Much of *Politics* is devoted to detailing the various forms of violence people perpetrate on each other through "love" and through the basic social norms of reciprocity and loyalty. Could we, Laing asks, strip away all the social forms, the "masks," and "reveal to each other our naked presence?" (p. 39). To each of these questions, Laing's answer appears to be "No!" Or, at least not unless and until we are willing to give up the "false security" of our normal everyday lives as members of families, groups, cultures, and institutions —each of which prescribes values and behaviors that prevent us from becoming and expressing our "true" selves.

Politics concentrates so intensely on the virtues of turning inward to find oneself, on the importance of fantasy, and on the value of an internal voyage away from the external, secular world of others, that Laing appears to have transmuted the impoverished "vacuum" he earlier described as the schizoid experience into Aladdin's cave filled with wonders and riches. This progression from the view that the self depends critically for full development on relations with others to the view that the self can develop only by turning away from others tends to parallel changes in his ideas about schizophrenia. However, the conception of the individual self and others as opposed and exclusive categories is present in earlier works as well.

Reading through the series, I was reminded of Linus's aphorism, in the popular *Peanuts* cartoon strip: "I love mankind, it's just people I can't stand."

Abstractly, Laing professes love for mankind. But concretely, he passionately details our innumerable ways of doing violence to each other, of destroying our chances of authenticity as persons, of denying our opportunities for ecstasy. It is almost impossible to find—in the entire corpus—any description or discussion of the positive aspects of relationships with other persons. Warmth, intimacy, friendship, comradeship, comfort, help, love, nurturance, responsiveness, support, mutuality—all these potentialities and actualities of human relationships are notable by their absence. Some are mentioned in passing as abstract ideals, but in a way that suggests that they do not and presumably cannot exist in the world as it is now constituted.

Love is defined as the opposite of violence, and since for Laing all relationships involve violence directed by others against the "self," it is not surprising to find the explicit definition, "Love lets the other be, but with affection and concern" (1967, p. 58). This is a rather idiosyncratic definition not only from the point of view of ordinary commonsense usage but even within the psychoanalytic tradition. One example may suffice to mark the difference. Melanie Klein describes an adult stable love relationship as implying "a deep attachment, a capacity for mutual sacrifice, a sharing—in grief as well as in pleasure, in interests as well as in sexual enjoyment" (Klein and Riviere, 1937, p. 69). It is this emphasis on sharing, on the essentially collective and social condition of man in the world, that is lacking in Laing. He restates in a contemporary idiom that thread of existentialist thinking that links Kierkegaard's proposal for his own epitaph, "The Individual," to Nietzsche's "superman," to Sartre's proclamation of the "sovereignty" of the self.

Even Freud at his most pessimistic, in *Civilization and its Discontents*, recognizing the "costs" of civilization, notes Laing's alternative but places it in a different context.

Against the suffering which may come upon one from human relationships the readiest safeguard is voluntary isolation, keeping oneself aloof from other people. The happiness which can be achieved along this path is, as we see, the happiness of quietness. Against the dreaded external world one can only defend oneself by some kind of turning away from it. . . . There is, indeed, another and better path: that of becoming a member of the human community, and, with the help of a technique guided by science, going over to the attack against nature and subjecting her to the human will (Freud, 1930, p. 77).

A critic of Sartre's philosophy of "existential subjectivism" is worth quoting at this point since his remarks seem to me to apply directly to Laing.

If, for Sartre, what counts is the self, it appears that for him, more than for many others, it takes the shape of negation. . . . No wonder that the exclusive emphasis upon the subject as the supreme value . . . excludes any philosophy of love. Philosophical subjectivity, which starts with the Self, and measures everything from the viewpoint of the Self, is a form of speculative egotism. . . . We find neither charity nor benevolence. What Sartre wants to make clear . . . is that the Individual is "sovereign" and that the Other is completely incidental. . . . Man is a god in the depths of his dreams only. . . . A lonely Cogito on a bare planet would forever hang between dream and reality. Only the acceptance of the Other can make that which is between us something real. . . . the subject is not the I but the We. . . . For a world in which the solitary adventure gathers meaning only within a collective enterprise, Sartre's philosophy is not prepared. . . . The irony of Sartre's situation is that . . . [he] has in fact created an entity too isolated in a hostile world to be even successfully committed to a group or to anything (Desan, 1966, pp. 260–288).

If others are so dangerous that the best that may be hoped for is an "armed truce," a contract where each agrees not to harm the other and preferably simply lets the other be, then it follows that those from whom we have most to fear are those who are closest to us and are powerful, namely, our parents. Neither the psychiatric literature nor the literature of alienation could be characterized as showing a sympathetic view of parents. Nevertheless, Laing sets a standard in this regard that would be difficult to match. His families are almost totally devoid of positive human qualities. There is no love, no joy, no generosity, no sharing of each other's pleasure, no concern for each other's suffering. It is important to recognize that Laing does not restrict his critique to "pathogenic" families such as those described in *Sanity, Madness, and the Family;* his target is the family as a social unit. In his autobiography, Sartre says:

There is no good father, that's the rule. Don't lay the blame on men but on the bond of paternity, which is rotten. To beget children, nothing better; to have them, what iniquity. Had my father lived, he would have lain on me at full length and would have crushed me. As luck had it, he died young (1964, p. 11).

Sartre's sentiment is shared by Laing, who would see no reason to exclude maternity from the indictment:

The family's function is to repress Eros; to induce a false consciousness of security; to deny death by avoiding life; to cut off transcendence; to believe in God, not to experience the Void; to create, in short, one-dimensional man; to promote respect, conformity, obedience; to con children out of play; to induce a fear of failure; to promote a respect for work; to promote a respect for "respectability" (1967, p. 65).

And, further on, discussing the family as a type of group, i.e., a "nexus," whose unity is achieved through "the reciprocal interiorization by each of each other" (where there is much ambiguity in the text about whether he is referring to pathological families or to inherent features of all families), Laing asserts:

The stability of the nexus is the product of terror generated in its members by the work (violence) done by the members of the group on each other. . . . A family can act as gangsters, offering each other mutual protection against each other's violence. It is a reciprocal terrorism, with the offer of protection-security against the violence that each threatens the other with, and is threatened by, if anyone steps out of line (pp. 88–89).

For contrast, this might be compared to Winnicott's observation (quoted in Holbrook, 1969) based on his experience as a pediatrician-psychoanalyst with 20,000 case histories that the "ordinary good home" is the basis of individual sanity and is "usual."

Nor is Laing's polemic restricted to that one socializing institution, the family: "Our own cities are our own animal factories; families, schools, churches are the slaughter-houses of our children; colleges and other places are the kitchens. As adults in marriages and business, we eat the product" (1969, p. 31).

Given the concentrated force of this attack on the family, it is interesting to discover that although Laing himself has been both husband and father, that is not true of several major existentialist thinkers upon whose works he draws and with whose works his own resonate so deeply. This list of nonfamily men includes Kierkegaard, Nietzsche, and Sartre, as well as Kafka and Beckett whose plays are quoted extensively in *The Self and Others* (1961). I find it somewhat remarkable that these writers who are otherwise so different, for example, in nationality—respectively Danish, German, French, Czechoslovakian, and Irish—should resemble each other in such an essential way. I am not suggesting some common pathology of personality. Rather, it seems to me more important to take note of the consistency between their social position—*sans famille*—and their philosophical position vis-à-vis the family. They speak from an existential situation that matches that of adolescents and youth, trying to chart their own way through the space between the before-them and the after-them, and this seems to be one of the sources of their collective appeal to the young.

I have already noted that Laing and Esterson did not intend their book as a study of mental illness and the family. What they mean is that they reject the category of mental illness. However, the family processes they describe are similar to those reported in other studies of families of schizophrenic patients. Their work has been used to support the general theoretical view that certain characteristic ways of relating to each other within these families are schizophrenogenic. Laing asserts this strongly himself:

In all these places, to the best of my knowledge, no schizophrenic has been studied whose disturbed pattern of communication has not been shown to be a reflection of, and reaction to, the disturbed and disturbing pattern characterizing his or her family of origin. This is matched in our own researches (1967, p. 114).

As an assertion of fact, this statement is simply false. As a hypothesis, first stated systematically about 15 years ago by several investigators, it has remained interesting and productive of research, but it has not been validated in any way that could be considered definitive. Not all families of schizophrenics have been found to have these specific characteristics. Even studies that report significant

differences between patient families and control families also show wide variability within the former group. Further, studies that include control groups within
their research designs often do not find the differences that have been hypothesized by clinical investigators whose samples, like Laing's, have been restricted to
families of patients. Reports of more controlled studies tend to be more qualified
and more complex than Laing's simple paradigms allow for. Two examples may
suffice. First, in Goldfarb's (1961) studies of childhood schizophrenia, pathogenic
features were found only in families of children who showed no soft neurological
signs. Among children with soft neurological signs who became schizophrenic,
families were not distinguishable from normal controls. Although the relations
between childhood and adult schizophrenias are still obscure, the point is that
schizophrenia can be found in families that do not differ significantly from
families in which schizophrenia is not present. Second, in our own studies,
differences in the patterns of interaction between patient families and control
families are evident only when parents are with their patient child: differences
tend to disappear when the same parents are with their well children (Mishler
and Waxler, 1968a). Thus, even in "pathogenic" families, there are circumstances
in which parents behave "normally." A more complex model of the family than
Laing has offered is necessary to account for these findings.

Finally, as we argued in reporting our work, finding differences between
families of schizophrenics and other families does not in itself mean that the
former are pathogenic in the sense of having etiological significance for the development of schizophrenia. There are other plausible interpretations for findings
from what are essentially ex post facto studies. Most prominent among these
are responsive and transactional theories, both of which propose that there is a
reaction of parents to a child who is behaving in some ways differently from
other children. (For a good example of such a model see Reiss and Elstein [1971],
who hypothesize that rigidities in family modes of handling information interact
with atypical behaviors and experiences of the children.)

The etiological disease model is so ingrained in psychiatry that even Laing
seems unable to escape from it. For this reason, I thought it would be useful to
note briefly a few studies that in different ways suggest how the presence of
"pathological" family processes may be made "intelligible" without recourse to
an etiological framework. Using data from a longitudinal study of 23 families of
schizophrenic patients, Scott and Ashworth (1967) report a phenomenon they
call "closure," in which there is a severance in the pre-illness family relations,
which often included positive feelings and satisfactions, at the onset of the
patient's illness. The subsequent illness relationships are characterized by a
"ritual of concern for the patient," a view of the patient as "a condition instead
of a person relating to another," "a rigid unrelated view of the patient's illness,"
"an arrest of the patient's life . . . a standstill and paralysis of substantial areas
of the family life too." All these changed attitudes reflect "a defence mechanism
against the fear of suffering a mortal emotional wound from another person
with whom there is a longing for closeness which is also deeply feared," and
the severance of relations is "clearly an act, involving collusion by both sides."

There is an obvious similarity between these descriptions and those of Laing and other family investigators, but, as Scott and Ashworth state, "By the time the psychiatrist sees the patient, closure has already happened."

Studies of families where children have congenital handicaps are also instructive in helping us to determine whether "pathological" relationships develop in response to the problems of living with a child who is "strange" or different and may require special care. In one experimental study, for example, adults who were not the children's parents were found to change their ways of talking when they interacted with mentally retarded children with high as compared to low verbal ability (Siegel and Harkins, 1963). In another study, the families of children with cerebral palsy are described as "too cohesive." Their high degree of "togetherness" is associated with a marked reduction in levels of community participation and relationships with others outside the family. All this reflected an "intense preoccupation with the handicapped child" and a pattern of overindulgence and passivity in socialization practices with a concomitant repression of hostile feelings and punishment that made the parents' behavior "almost a caricature of what a *good* parent should do" (Schaffer, 1964). These, and other similar studies, suggest that behavior patterns described as "pathogenic" in research with families of schizophrenics can develop in families where the child's illness is clearly not a result of these types of interaction.[5]

In the later Laing, as I have already pointed out, these hypothetically pathogenic processes are taken merely as exemplars of normal family relationships. It is the family as a social unit, rather than certain types of pathological families, that comes under attack. Although Laing has practiced family therapy (all the cases in *Sanity, Madness, and the Family* appear to have been drawn from his and Esterson's own work), there is no reference in the books under review to this general approach or to his own experience with it. Given his views on the inherently destructive nature of families qua families, it is difficult to see what form of this mode of intervention he would advocate or what its objectives might be. He might not agree with his one-time collaborator's proposal for the "death of the family" (Cooper, 1971), although this would not be inconsistent with the substance and tenor of his writings. On the other hand, Laing might be content to help family members separate from each other so that the family unit would simply dissolve as each "let the other be." This is only speculation on my part, but such a solution to the "pathology" of the family would fit with his solution to the "pathology of normality" which involves the dissolution of the ego.

The political and moral implications of Laing's views of the self and others warrant some final comment. First, I believe that a political position based on the idea that other people are our worst enemies is not radical but reactionary.

[5] Nancy Waxler (1968) is currently engaged in a study designed to throw some light on the complex question of etiology. Using the experimental paradigm of "assembled families," she has "normal" and "schizophrenic" parents interacting with both "normal" and "schizophrenic" children. This design makes it possible to separate the degree to which, and the ways in which, parents affect children and children affect parents.

It deflects attention from issues of power, oppression, and violence in the larger society. The basic problems become problems between people and not problems of or between institutions. Laing stated his own position in a recent interview as being not "an activist in the ordinary sense of the word" but as being concerned with "microrevolutions" in individuals, families, and other small institutions; the hope being that changes here would spread through personal contact (Gordon, 1971).

But these microrevolutions, in turn, are made to depend upon individual transformations, primarily through symbolic death and rebirth via the routes of drugs or madness. All this is of a piece with Laing's anti- or at least nonsocial view of man. Although Laing and his adherents loudly proclaim their humanism, while at the same time assaulting the inhumanity of enemies all around them, in rejecting the essentially collective nature of human life they end in an antihumanist position. As Holbrook (1969) points out, the consequence of these contradictory ideas, "yoked together only by violence," is the "reversal of moral values" and an ethic in which "We are offered our freedom at the expense of others, in endless hostility." While this updated romantic anarchism is merely irrelevant to the major issues and problems of society and community, if taken seriously it may be destructive of personal relationships that depend upon trust, mutuality, and love. It seems to me that this strand of Laing's thought may account for his lack of attention to another major current in the counterculture, that is, the effort to establish new communal forms of life as alternatives to traditional family, educational, and work institutions. This last observation must be qualified by Laing's work in developing Kingsley Hall. This was surely a collective enterprise and an effort at a new form of community (although even here the norm appears to have been that of the typical chronic psychiatric ward patient, namely, "You leave me alone and I'll leave you alone"). However, there is no reference to this work in the books under review, and an analysis of Kingsley Hall would require much more information than is available to me.

In the end, Laing's isolated selves, achieving ecstasy on their individual inward voyages, remain alone and powerless. The really powerful and destructive institutions and forces in the society have nothing to fear from them.

FANTASY AND OTHER MODES OF EXPERIENCE

Throughout his work, particularly in *The Self and Others* and in sections of *The Politics of Experience,* Laing emphasizes the significance of fantasy as a mode of experience and argues that this mode is at best ignored and at worst suppressed by society. Fantasies are preverbal and presocial, our primitive feelings and responses uncontaminated by and uninterpretable by rational thought. Fantasy is important both because it enters into our relationships with others and because our response to it affects our own possibilities for authentic growth.

> . . . it appears that our habitual sense of being linked with others, of being ourselves "connected," compounded of common-sense, flesh-and-blood "real-

ity," requires the support of a fantasy modality of which we are unaware (1961, p. 64).

One's self definition is the precipitate of the original effort to make sense out of the world. How desperately, and how precociously, it has been arrived at in the first place seems to be a function of need to discount the reality of fantasy, and this continuing need may determine how tenaciously it is clung to subsequently. I have come to see a person's need to pivot his or her life around complementary self-definitions (i.e., I am my father's son, husband's wife, etc.) as an expression of both a profound fear of "fantasy" and distrust and/or hatred of reality (p. 83).

Fantasy is not a neglected topic in the psychoanalytic literature, but Laing writes with particular power and insight. In The Politics of Experience there is a new element that reflects a view of fantasy which, if not unique to Laing, is radically different from traditional views. Essentially, fantasy is now given preferred status with respect to other modes of experience. When others have written about the value and significance of fantasy, for example, in examining the creative process in art or science, it is usually within the explicit context of reality. "Regression in the service of the ego" is the famous phrase that captures the sense of this work, whether reference is to the collective unconscious or to primary-process modes of experience or to biographically linked repressions. Laing's new slogan is more like "regression in the service of regression." Most simply, fantasy is no longer instrumental to more optimal reality functioning, it is not a means to an end but has become an end in itself.

When Laing's people come back from their voyages they do not return enriched and free, able to enter into more meaningful and deeper relationships with others; they return with messages about how "indescribably" beautiful it is beyond the veil, on the dark side of the moon. Laing cries out, "If I could turn you on, if I could drive you out of your wretched mind, if I could tell you, I would let you know" (1967, pp. 185–186).

It seems to me that this particular "heresy" is another source of Laing's appeal. He is not simply saying that the world of fantasy is both good and necessary; he is saying that it is better. This fits, of course, with views he holds of relationships with other people and of schizophrenia as a sacred and archetypal experience. For the schizophrenic is the one who has made the commitment to fantasy and has turned with finality away from the "real" world of others.

Many writers have been concerned about the suppression of fantasy and mysticism in the modern, secular world and about the negative concomitants of this, such as the constriction and impoverishment of the self and the impersonality of human relationships. I have no quarrel with this view. I believe we are each of us in peril if we repress and ignore these levels of experience, and would agree that our ways of life tend to make us anxious and uncomfortable with them rather than easy and open to them. Here again, however, as Laing has changed from descriptive phenomenology to political rhetoric he has less and less to say that is meaningful and vital. The host of problems that are involved, theoretically as well as existentially, in understanding the relationships of fantasy to other modes of experience and behavior have all been bypassed by the simple assertion that fantasy is good, and the deeper and more pervasive the fantasy, the better it is.

Further, the terrors of such experiences, while occasionally noted, are treated as secondary phenomena, arising from our socially conditioned fear of such experiences and easily transcended with the help of a "guide" who has been "there" himself. Laing casually remarks that some voyagers may be "lost" but apparently that is of little concern to him. While the responsibility that we have for each others' lives is too often corrupted into coercive control, this is another instance in which Laing's solution to inherently difficult and persistent problems of human relationships is to avoid confronting them by opting for irresponsibility.

SOME CONCLUDING OBSERVATIONS

This examination of some major themes in Laing's work has been relatively detailed, but it remains selective. A number of topics have been neglected, among them Laing's notation system and proposed method for studying the "spiral of interpersonal perceptions." *Interpersonal Perception* (Laing, Phillipson, and Lee, 1966) describes a questionnaire designed to explore the degree to which two members of a dyad agree in their perceptions of themselves and each other, recognize or understand each other's point of view, and realize that they are themselves understood or misunderstood. The monograph includes findings from an exploratory study of marital partners in "disturbed" and "nondisturbed" marriages, and a case discussion that relates questionnaire responses to material from therapeutic interviews. The method is aimed at elucidating types of reciprocal perception—variants of the "I think that you feel that I don't understand you" pattern that Laing illustrates in the fragmentary sketches of human "tangles" that compose his most recent volume, *Knots* (1970). Although the method derives from Laing's general ideas about interpersonal relations, it could be used by investigators with quite different theoretical orientations much as can any attitude or value inventory. For the purposes of studying interpersonal behavior, questionnaire methods have, I believe, inherent limitations compared to direct observation of interaction and the analysis of language. Laing's method, despite his approach to "levels" of perception, does not seem to me to overcome these limitations and I have not found this part of his work of much interest. Other investigators, however, with different biases, may find it more instructive.

In addition, there are some topics that would be of interest to psychiatrists, and others concerned with human relationships, that have not been mentioned in this review because they are either ignored or receive scant attention from Laing. Paradoxically, despite his emphasis on despair and on the violence we do unto each other, there is, for example, hardly any reference to death and its consequences, grief, depression, and mourning. Laing seems so immersed in fantasy deaths—in the death-in-life experience of schizophrenics and the "living death" of contemporary man—that death as a reality is simply of little concern to him. And to propose, as Laing does, that an individual's fantasy is his "reality" without further analysis of the difference between this and experience of that other "reality"—hard, obdurate, palpable, mundane, and intersubjective—is simply playing with words, and solipsistic play at that.

Another missing reality is the world of work. One could read all of Laing and never know that most people have to work in order to eat, a necessity that might interfere with their opportunity to experience ecstasy; that they spend most of their waking lives in jobs that may gratify and often frustrate them; that their life chances and their life experiences are affected primarily by what they work at, and its costs and rewards. Society seems to be suspended in thin air; there is no recognition of the "work" we do as members—symbolic as well as productive—in bringing the social world into existence each day, and in sustaining it.

Another neglected area is language, a surprising neglect in view of Laing's interest in existentialism and phenomenology. It is now evident that one of the most important developments in the social sciences over the past 15 years has been the application of concepts and methods from modern linguistics, particularly the work on generative or transformational grammars of Chomsky and his students, and the associated emergence of several new hyphenated disciplines such as ethno-, psycho-, and sociolinguistics. Laing does not explore the complex relationships between language, experience, and thought, nor does he pay any methodical attention to the normative and regulative functions of language in shaping and structuring human relationships. I believe that this neglect, even more than his heresies and his attack on the psychiatric establishment, makes it unlikely that Laing's work will have any significant impact on theory in psychiatry and the related social sciences.

In closing, I want to come back to the note of ambivalence with which I began. My comments on Laing's work have been highly critical and it may appear that I have managed to resolve my ambivalence through this process of negation, but some issues remain unresolved. An experience I had while preparing this review helped to clarify some of the issues involved, issues that I suspect may be present for others who also find themselves simultaneously attracted by and resistant to his work. I was discussing my views on Laing at a psychiatric teaching conference and commented that I thought his development, from *The Divided Self* to *The Politics of Experience* and *Knots*, was "tragic." A young artist, a conscientious objector doing alternate service as an attendant, interjected: "Tragic for you, but perhaps not for Laing." True. What I was expressing, in too pompous a way, was my own regret at discovering how little there was for me in Laing's later, as compared to his earlier, works. After the conference, the artist told me that he had felt a great gulf widen between us when I criticized Laing, and that this saddened him because he had felt previously that there was some communion between us. In his view, I was "nit-picking" and had missed Laing's important role in legitimating mystical experiences and in supporting the search of young people for authentic and meaningful lives outside the boundaries of established roles and institutions. He suddenly saw me on the "other" side, the side of the Establishment and of "respectability," and I too felt saddened by our separation.

Therein lies the problem. The power of Laing's work comes in part from the success with which he has projected his own polarities upon the world so that we feel impelled to deal with the world in his terms. But, although his polarities articulate with and feed into certain fantasies about the world and experience—divine and mystical versus secular and rational, authentic versus adjusted, love versus violence, the self versus others—they do not correspond to my own experience of my realities. Nor are these concepts adequate or helpful for understanding the problems and struggles for selfhood, development, and relatedness of others in my world.

These polarities, however, shape Laing's world view and his rhetoric. Notwithstanding his professed adherence to dialectics and phenomenology, he works within a framework of absolute and mutually exclusive categories, and tends to reify his concepts rather than to use them as analytic tools. But rhetoric turns out to be an uncongenial syntax for critical doubt and the reflective attitude of the phenomenological method. And, notwithstanding his appeal to young radicals, in and out of psychiatry, I believe that to take his distinctions seriously is to interfere with and undermine possibilities of meaningful collective action, which remains the only way to effect real change in the society. We have to learn that "others" are not our worst enemies, even if they are our sons or fathers; that averting our eyes from evils and terrors in the external world does not eliminate them. We must, in the end, find ways to strengthen ourselves as communities, ways of being and working together; it is too late to settle for a strategy of surviving alone.

REFERENCES

Carson, R. (1969). *Interaction Concepts of Personality.* Chicago: Aldine.

———— (1970). Disordered Interpersonal Behavior. Presented at a Symposium on Human Behavior and Its Control, American Association for the Advancement of Science.

Cooper, D. (1971). *The Death of the Family.* New York: Vintage Books.

Desan, W. (1966). *The Marxism of Jean-Paul Sartre.* New York: Anchor Books.

Freud, S. (1930). Civilization and Its Discontents. *Standard Edition,* 21:64–145. London: Hogarth Press, 1961.

Goldfarb, W. (1961). *Childhood Schizophrenia.* Cambridge, Mass.: Harvard University Press.

Gordon, J. S. (1971). Who Is Mad? Who Is Sane? The Radical Psychiatry of R. D. Laing. *Atlantic,* January, pp. 50–66.

Gove, W. R. (1970a). Social Reaction as an Explanation of Mental Illness: An Evaluation. *American Sociological Review,* 35:873–884.

———— (1970b). Who Is Hospitalized: A Critical Review of Some Sociological Studies of Mental Illness. *Journal of Health and Human Behavior,* 11:294–303.

Holbrook, D. (1969). R. D. Laing and the Death Circuit. *Psychiatry and Social Science Review,* 3(4):13–25.

Hughes, T. (1971). *Crow*. New York: Harper and Row.

Kierkegaard, S. (1843, 1849). *Fear and Trembling, and The Sickness unto Death*. Princeton, N. J.: Princeton University Press, 1968.

Klein, M., and Riviere, J. (1937). *Love, Hate, and Reparation*. New York: Norton, 1964.

Laing, R. D. (1960). *The Divided Self*. London: Tavistock. (Pelican paperback edition, 1965.)

———— (1961). *The Self and Others*. London: Tavistock.

———— (1967). *The Politics of Experience*. New York: Ballantine.

———— (1969). *The Politics of the Family*. (1968 Massey Lectures.) Canadian Broadcasting Company.

———— (1970). *Knots*. New York: Pantheon.

————, and Cooper, D. G. (1964). *Reason and Violence*. London: Tavistock.

————, and Esterson, A. (1964). *Sanity, Madness, and the Family*. London: Tavistock. (Penguin paperback edition, 1970.)

————, Phillipson, H., and Lee, A. R. (1966). *Interpersonal Perception*. London and New York: Tavistock and Springer.

Lessing, D. (1969). *The Four-Gated City*. New York: Knopf.

———— (1971). *Briefing for a Descent into Hell*. New York: Knopf.

Mishler, E. G. (1966). Review of *Sanity, Madness, and the Family*, by R. D. Laing. *Community Mental Health Journal*, 2:355–356.

————, and Waxler, N. E. (1968a). *Interaction in Families*. New York: Wiley.

————, ———— (1968b). *Family Processes and Schizophrenia*. New York: Science House.

Reiss, D., and Elstein, A. S. (1971). Perceptual and Cognitive Resources of Family Members. *Archives of General Psychiatry*, 24:121–134.

Sartre, J. P. (1964). *The Words*. New York: Fawcett, 1966.

Schaffer, H. R. (1964). The Too-Cohesive Family: A Form of Group Pathology. *International Journal of Social Psychiatry*, 10:266–275.

Scott, R. D., and Ashworth, P. L. (1967). "Closure" at the First Schizophrenic Break-Down: A Family Study. *British Journal of Medical Psychology*, 40:109–145.

Siegel, G. M., and Harkins, J. P. (1963). Verbal Behavior of Adults in Two Conditions with Institutionalized Retarded Children. *Journal of Speech and Hearing Disorders Monograph Supplements*, No. 10.

Siegler, M., Osmond, H., and Mann, H. (1969). Laing's Models of Madness. *British Journal of Psychiatry*, 115:947–958.

Spender, S. (1971). The Last Ditch. *New York Review of Books*, 17(1):3–4.

Waxler, N. E. (1968). Families and Schizophrenia: Studies in Deviance. Unpublished.

Wing, J. K., and Brown, G. W. (1970). *Institutionalism and Schizophrenia*. Cambridge: Cambridge University Press.

NAME INDEX